THE
MINISTER'S MANUAL

EIGHTIETH ANNUAL ISSUE

THE MINISTER'S MANUAL
2005

Edited by
JAMES W. COX

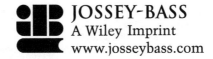
JOSSEY-BASS
A Wiley Imprint
www.josseybass.com

Editors of THE MINISTER'S MANUAL
G. B. F. Hallock, D.D., 1926–1958
M. K. W. Heicher, Ph.D., 1943–1968
Charles L. Wallis, M.A., M.Div., 1969–1983
James W. Cox, M.Div., Ph.D.

Translations of the Bible referred to and quoted from in this book may be indicated by their standard abbreviations, such as NRSV (New Revised Standard Version) and NIV (New International Version). In addition, some contributors have made their own translations and others have used a mixed text.

THE MINISTER'S MANUAL FOR 2005. Copyright © 2004 by James W. Cox.

Published by Jossey-Bass
A Wiley Imprint
989 Market Street, San Francisco, CA 94103-1741   www.josseybass.com

Jossey-Bass books and products are available through most bookstores. To contact Jossey-Bass directly call our Customer Care Department within the U.S. at 800-956-7739, outside the U.S. at 317-572-3986, or fax 317-572-4002.

Jossey-Bass also publishes its books in a variety of electronic formats. Some content that appears in print may not be available in electronic books.

Library of Congress Cataloging Card Number

25-21658
ISSN 0738-5323
ISBN 0-7879-7366-1

Printed in the United States of America
FIRST EDITION
HB Printing
10 9 8 7 6 5 4 3 2 1

CONTENTS

PREFACE

As I have indicated in previous volumes, *The Minister's Manual 2005* presents sermonic contributions from a wide range of preachers, teachers, and writers. They come from many geographical, denominational, and theological backgrounds. Although they do not always agree on every issue, they speak responsibly and their thoughts merit careful consideration. They share our common faith and enrich our personal understanding and devotion. Nevertheless, the contributors speak for themselves, and their views do not necessarily represent those of the publisher, the editor, or the Southern Baptist Theological Seminary.

I am grateful to the seminary, where I have taught since 1959, for providing valuable secretarial assistance in producing the manuscript. Again, I wish to thank Linda Durkin for her faithful and efficient assistance and Katie Law for her aid in preparing this volume. I also wish to thank the authors and publishers from whose works I have quoted. It is hoped that the rights and wishes of no one have been overlooked. Again, I am deeply grateful.

James W. Cox
The Southern Baptist Theological Seminary

SECTION I

GENERAL AIDS AND RESOURCES

CIVIL YEAR CALENDARS FOR 2005 AND 2006

2005

January	February	March	April
S M T W T F S	S M T W T F S	S M T W T F S	S M T W T F S
1	1 2 3 4 5	1 2 3 4 5	1 2
2 3 4 5 6 7 8	6 7 8 9 10 11 12	6 7 8 9 10 11 12	3 4 5 6 7 8 9
9 10 11 12 13 14 15	13 14 15 16 17 18 19	13 14 15 16 17 18 19	10 11 12 13 14 15 16
16 17 18 19 20 21 22	20 21 22 23 24 25 26	20 21 22 23 24 25 26	17 18 19 20 21 22 23
23 24 25 26 27 28 29	27 28	27 28 29 30 31	24 25 26 27 28 29 30
30 31			

May	June	July	August
S M T W T F S	S M T W T F S	S M T W T F S	S M T W T F S
1 2 3 4 5 6 7	1 2 3 4	1 2	1 2 3 4 5 6
8 9 10 11 12 13 14	5 6 7 8 9 10 11	3 4 5 6 7 8 9	7 8 9 10 11 12 13
15 16 17 18 19 20 21	12 13 14 15 16 17 18	10 11 12 13 14 15 16	14 15 16 17 18 19 20
22 23 24 25 26 27 28	19 20 21 22 23 24 25	17 18 19 20 21 22 23	21 22 23 24 25 26 27
29 30 31	26 27 28 29 30	24 25 26 27 28 29 30	28 29 30 31
		31	

September	October	November	December
S M T W T F S	S M T W T F S	S M T W T F S	S M T W T F S
1 2 3	1	1 2 3 4 5	1 2 3
4 5 6 7 8 9 10	2 3 4 5 6 7 8	6 7 8 9 10 11 12	4 5 6 7 8 9 10
11 12 13 14 15 16 17	9 10 11 12 13 14 15	13 14 15 16 17 18 19	11 12 13 14 15 16 17
18 19 20 21 22 23 24	16 17 18 19 20 21 22	20 21 22 23 24 25 26	18 19 20 21 22 23 24
25 26 27 28 29 30	23 24 25 26 27 28 29	27 28 29 30	25 26 27 28 29 30 31
	30 31		

2006

January	February	March	April
S M T W T F S	S M T W T F S	S M T W T F S	S M T W T F S
1 2 3 4 5 6 7	1 2 3 4	1 2 3 4	1
8 9 10 11 12 13 14	5 6 7 8 9 10 11	5 6 7 8 9 10 11	2 3 4 5 6 7 8
15 16 17 18 19 20 21	12 13 14 15 16 17 18	12 13 14 15 16 17 18	9 10 11 12 13 14 15
22 23 24 25 26 27 28	19 20 21 22 23 24 25	19 20 21 22 23 24 25	16 17 18 19 20 21 22
29 30 31	26 27 28	26 27 28 29 30 31	23 24 25 26 27 28 29
			30

May	June	July	August
S M T W T F S	S M T W T F S	S M T W T F S	S M T W T F S
1 2 3 4 5 6	1 2 3	1	1 2 3 4 5
7 8 9 10 11 12 13	4 5 6 7 8 9 10	2 3 4 5 6 7 8	6 7 8 9 10 11 12
14 15 16 17 18 19 20	11 12 13 14 15 16 17	9 10 11 12 13 14 15	13 14 15 16 17 18 19
21 22 23 24 25 26 27	18 19 20 21 22 23 24	16 17 18 19 20 21 22	20 21 22 23 24 25 26
28 29 30 31	25 26 27 28 29 30	23 24 25 26 27 28 29	27 28 29 30 31
		30 31	

September	October	November	December
S M T W T F S	S M T W T F S	S M T W T F S	S M T W T F S
1 2	1 2 3 4 5 6 7	1 2 3 4	1 2
3 4 5 6 7 8 9	8 9 10 11 12 13 14	5 6 7 8 9 10 11	3 4 5 6 7 8 9
10 11 12 13 14 15 16	15 16 17 18 19 20 21	12 13 14 15 16 17 18	10 11 12 13 14 15 16
17 18 19 20 21 22 23	22 23 24 25 26 27 28	19 20 21 22 23 24 25	17 18 19 20 21 22 23
24 25 26 27 28 29 30	29 30 31	26 27 28 29 30	24 25 26 27 28 29 30
			31

Church and Civic Calendar for 2005

January

1	New Year's Day
5	Twelfth Night
6	Epiphany
9	Baptism of the Lord
17	Martin Luther King Jr.'s Birthday, observed
	St. Anthony's Day
18	Confession of St. Peter
25	Conversion of St. Paul

February

1	National Freedom Day
2	Presentation of Jesus in the Temple
6–8	Shrove Tuesday
9	Ash Wednesday
12	Lincoln's Birthday
13	Race Relations Day
	First Sunday in Lent
14	St. Valentine's Day
20	Second Sunday in Lent
21	Presidents' Day
22	Washington's Birthday
24	St. Matthias
27	Third Sunday in Lent

March

6	Fourth Sunday in Lent
13	Fifth Sunday in Lent
17	St. Patrick's Day
19	St. Joseph
20	Passion/Palm Sunday
20–26	Holy Week
24	Maundy Thursday
	Feast of Esther
25	Good Friday
	Purim
	The Annunciation
27	Easter

April

3	Low Sunday
24	Passover
25	St. Mark, Evangelist

May

1	May Day
	St. Philip and St. James
	Loyalty Day
	Law Day
1–5	Cinco de Mayo Celebration
1–7	National Family Week
5	Ascension Day
8	Mother's Day
15	Pentecost
22	Trinity Sunday
29	Corpus Christi (United States)
30	Memorial Day
31	The Visitation

June

11	St. Barnabas
12	Children's Sunday
13	Shavuot
19	Father's Day
24	St. John the Baptist
29	St. Peter and St. Paul

July

1	Canada Day
4	Independence Day
22	St. Mary Magdalene
25	St. James the Elder, Apostle

August

1	Civic Holiday (Canada)
6	The Transfiguration
14	Atlantic Charter Day
15	Mary, Mother of Jesus
24	St. Bartholomew
26	Women's Equality Day

September

5	Labor Day
14	Holy Cross Day
21	St. Matthew, Evangelist and Apostle
29	St. Michael and all Angels

October

2	World Communion Sunday
4	Ramadan
	Rosh Hashanah
10	Columbus Day
13	Yom Kippur
18	Sukkot
	St. Luke, Evangelist
22	St. James, Brother of Jesus
24	St. Simon and St. Jude
31	Reformation Day
	National UNICEF Day

November

1	All Saints Day
2	All Souls Day

11	Veterans Day
	Armistice Day
	Remembrance Day (Canada)
13	Stewardship Day
20	Bible Sunday
24	Thanksgiving Day
27	First Sunday of Advent
30	St. Andrew

December

4	Second Sunday of Advent
11	Third Sunday of Advent
15	Bill of Rights Day
18	Fourth Sunday of Advent
21	St. Thomas
25	Christmas Day
26	Hanukkah
	Boxing Day (Canada)
	St. Stephen, Deacon and Martyr
27	St. John, Evangelist and Apostle
28	Holy Innocents
31	New Year's Eve
	Watch Night

The Revised Common Lectionary for 2005

The following Scriptures are commended for use by various Protestant churches and the Roman Catholic Church and include first, second, and Gospel readings, and Psalms, according to Cycle A from January 2 to November 20 and according to Cycle B from November 27 to December 25.[1]

Jan. 2: Jer. 31:7–14; Ps. 147:12–20; Eph. 1:3–14; John 1:(1–9) 10–18

Epiphany Season

Jan. 6 (Epiphany): Isa. 60:1–6; Ps. 72:1–7, 10–14; Eph. 3:1–12; Matt. 2:1–12
Jan. 9: Isa. 42:1–9; Ps. 29; Acts 10:34–43; Matt. 3:13–17
Jan. 16: Isa. 49:1–7; Ps. 40:1–11; 1 Cor. 1:1–9; John 1:29–42
Jan. 23: Isa. 9:1–4; Ps. 27:1, 4–9; 1 Cor. 1:10–18; Matt. 4:12–23
Jan. 30: Mic. 6:1–8; Ps. 15; 1 Cor. 1:18–31; Matt. 5:1–12
Feb. 6: Isa. 58:1–9a (9b–12); Ps. 112:1–9 (10); 1 Cor. 2:1–12 (13–16); Matt. 5:13–20 or (Transfiguration): Exod. 24:12–18; Ps. 2; 2 Pet. 1:16–21; Matt. 17:1–9

---

[1]Copyright 1992, *Consultation on Common Texts.*

Lenten Season

Feb. 9 (Ash Wednesday): Joel 2:1–2, 12–17; Ps. 51:1–17; 2 Cor. 5:20b–6:10; Matt. 6:1–6, 16–21

Feb. 13: Gen. 2:15–17, 3:1–7; Ps. 32; Rom. 5:12–19; Matt. 4:1–11

Feb. 20: Gen. 12:1–4a; Ps. 121; Rom. 4:1–5, 13–17; John 3:1–17

Feb. 27: Exod. 17:1–7; Ps. 95; Rom. 5:1–11; John 4:5–42

Mar. 6: 1 Sam. 16:1–13; Ps. 23; Eph. 5:8–14; John 9:1–41

Mar. 13: Ezek. 37:1–14; Ps. 130; Rom. 8:6–11; John 11:1–45

Holy Week and Easter Season

Mar. 20 (Palm/Passion Sunday): Liturgy of the Palms—Matt. 21:1–11; Ps. 118:1–2, 19–29; Liturgy of the Passion—Isa. 50:4–9a; Ps. 31:9–16; Phil. 2:5–11; Matt. 26:14–27:66

Mar. 21 (Monday): Isa. 42:1–9; Ps. 36:5–11; Heb. 9:11–15; John 12:1–11

Mar. 22 (Tuesday): Isa. 49:1–7; Ps. 71:1–14; 1 Cor. 1:18–31; John 12:20–36

Mar. 23 (Wednesday): Isa. 50:4–9a; Ps. 70; Heb. 12:1–3; John 13:21–32

Mar. 24 (Thursday): Exod. 12:1–4 (5–10), 11–14; Ps. 116:1–2, 12–19; 1 Cor. 11:23–26; John 13:1–7, 31b–35

Mar. 25 (Good Friday): Isa. 52:13–53:12; Ps. 22; Heb. 10:16–25; John 18:1–19

Mar. 26 (Holy Saturday): Job 14:1–14; Ps. 31:1–4, 15–16; 1 Pet. 4:1–8; Matt. 27:57–66

Mar. 27 (Easter Vigil): Gen. 1:1–2:4a; Ps. 136:1–9, 23–26; Gen. 7:1–5, 11–18, 8:6–18, 9:8–13; Ps. 46; Gen. 22:1–18; Ps. 16; Exod. 14:10–31, 15:20–21; Exod. 15:1b–13, 17–18; Isa. 55:1–11; Isa. 12:2–6; Prov. 8:1–8, 19–21, 9:4b–6; Ps. 19; Ezek. 36:24–28; Ps. 42–43; Ezek. 37:1–14; Ps. 143; Zeph. 3:14–20; Ps. 98; Rom. 6:3–11; Ps. 114; Matt. 28:1–10

Mar. 27 (Easter): Acts 10:34–43; Ps. 118:1–2, 14–24; Col. 3:1–4; John 20:1–18; (Easter Evening): Isa. 25:6–9; Ps. 114; 1 Cor. 5:6b–8; Luke 24:13–49

Apr. 3: Acts 2:14a, 22–32; Ps. 16; 1 Pet. 1:3–9; John 20:19–31

Apr. 10: Acts 2:14a, 36–41; Ps. 116:1–4, 12–19; 1 Pet. 1:17–23; Luke 24:13–35

Apr. 17: Acts 2:42–47; Ps. 23; 1 Pet. 2:19–25; John 10:1–10

Apr. 24: Acts 7:55–60; Ps. 31:1–5, 15–16; 1 Pet. 2:2–10; John 14:1–14

May 1: Acts 17:22–31; Ps. 66:8–20; 1 Pet. 3:13–22; John 14:15–21

May 5 (Ascension of the Lord): Acts 1:1–11; Ps. 47; Eph. 1:15–23; Luke 24:44–53

May 8: Acts 1:6–14; Ps. 68:1–10, 32–35; 1 Pet. 4:12–14, 5:6–11; John 17:1–11

Season of Pentecost

May 15 (Pentecost): Num. 11:24–30; Ps. 104:24–34, 35b; (the Second Lesson): Acts 2:1–21 or 1 Cor. 12:3b–13; John 20:19–23 or John 7:37–39

May 22 (Trinity): Gen. 1:1–2:4a; Ps. 8; 2 Cor. 13:11–13; Matt. 28:16–20

May 29: Gen. 6:9–22, 7:24, 8:14–19; Ps. 46; Rom. 1:16–17, 3:22b–28 (29–31); Matt. 7:21–29

June 5: Gen. 12:1–9; Ps. 33:1–12; Rom. 4:13–25; Matt. 9:9–13, 18–26

June 12: Gen. 18:1–15 (21:1–7); Ps. 116:1–2, 12–19; Rom. 5:1–8; Matt. 9:35–10:8 (9–23)

June 19: Gen. 21:8–21; Ps. 86:1–10, 16–17; Rom. 6:1b–11; Matt. 10:24–39

June 26: Gen. 22:1–14; Ps. 13; Rom. 6:12–23; Matt. 10:40–42

July 3: Gen. 24:34–38, 42–49, 58–67; Ps. 45:10–17; Rom. 7:15–25a; Matt. 11:16–19, 25–30

July 10: Gen. 25:19–34; Ps. 119:105–112; Rom. 8:1–11; Matt. 13:1–9, 18–23

July 17: Gen. 28:10–19a; Ps. 139:1–12, 23–24; Rom. 8:12–25; Matt. 13:24–30, 36–43
July 24: Gen. 29:15–28; Ps. 105:1–11, 45b; Rom. 8:26–39; Matt. 13:31–33, 44–52
July 31: Gen. 32:22–31; Ps. 17:1–7, 15; Rom. 9:1–5; Matt. 14:13–21
Aug. 7: Gen. 37:1–4, 12–28; Ps. 105:1–6, 16–22, 45b; Rom. 10:5–15; Matt. 14:22–33
Aug. 14: Gen. 45:1–15; Ps. 133; Rom. 11:1–2a, 29–32; Matt. 15:(10–20) 21–28
Aug. 21: Exod. 1:8–2:10; Ps. 124; Rom. 12:1–8; Matt. 16:13–20
Aug. 28: Exod. 3:1–15; Ps. 105:1–6, 23–26, 45c; Rom. 12:9–21; Matt. 16:21–28
Sept. 4: Exod. 12:1–14; Ps. 149; Rom. 13:8–14; Matt. 18:15–20
Sept. 11: Exod. 14:19–31; Ps. 114; Rom. 14:1–12; Matt. 18:21–35
Sept. 18: Exod. 16:2–15; Ps. 105:1–6, 37–45; Phil. 1:21–30; Matt. 20:1–16
Sept. 25: Exod. 17:1–7; Ps. 78:1–4, 12–16; Phil. 2:1–13; Matt. 21:23–32
Oct. 2: Exod. 20:1–4, 7–9, 12–20; Ps. 19; Phil. 3:4b–14; Matt. 21:33–46
Oct. 9: Exod. 32:1–14; Ps. 106:1–6, 19–23; Phil. 4:1–9; Matt. 22:1–14
Oct. 16: Exod. 33:12–23; Ps. 99; 1 Thess. 1:1–10; Matt. 22:15–22
Oct. 23: Deut. 34:1–12; Ps. 90:1–6, 13–17; 1 Thess. 2:1–8; Matt. 22:34–46
Oct. 30: Josh. 3:7–17; Ps. 107:1–7, 33–37; 1 Thess. 2:9–13; Matt. 23:1–12
Nov. 6: Josh. 24:1–3a, 14–25; Ps. 78:1–7; 1 Thess. 4:13–18; Matt. 25:1–13
Nov. 13: Judg. 4:1–7; Ps. 123; 1 Thess. 5:1–11; Matt. 25:14–30
Nov. 20 (Christ the King): Ezek. 34:11–16, 20–24; Ps. 100; Eph. 1:15–23; Matt. 25:31–46

Advent and Christmas Season

Nov. 27: Isa. 64:1–9; Ps. 80:1–7, 17–19; 1 Cor. 1:3–9; Mark 13:24–37
Dec. 4: Isa. 40:1–11; Ps. 85:1–2, 8–13; 2 Pet. 3:8–15a; Mark 1:1–8
Dec. 11: Isa. 61:1–4, 8–11; Ps. 126; 1 Thess. 5:16–24; John 1:6–8, 19–28
Dec. 18: 2 Sam. 7:1–11, 16; Luke 1:47–55; Rom. 16:25–27; Luke 1:26–38
Dec. 25 (Christmas, Proper I): Isa. 9:2–7; Ps. 96; Titus 2:11–14; Luke 2:1–14 (15–20);
(Proper II): Isa. 62:6–12; Ps. 97; Titus 3:4–7; Luke 2:(1–7) 8–20; (Proper III): Isa.
52:7–10; Ps. 98; Heb. 1:1–4 (5–12); John 1:1–14

Four-Year Church Calendar

	2005	2006	2007	2008
Ash Wednesday	February 9	March 1	February 21	February 6
Palm Sunday	March 20	April 9	April 1	March 16
Good Friday	March 25	April 14	April 6	March 21
Easter	March 27	April 16	April 8	March 23
Ascension Day	May 5	May 25	May 17	May 1
Pentecost	May 15	June 4	May 27	May 11
Trinity Sunday	May 22	June 11	June 3	May 18
Thanksgiving	November 24	November 23	November 22	November 27
Advent Sunday	November 27	December 3	December 2	November 30

Forty-Year Easter Calendar

2005 March 27	2009 April 12	2013 March 31	2017 April 16
2006 April 16	2010 April 4	2014 April 20	2018 April 1
2007 April 8	2011 April 24	2015 April 5	2019 April 21
2008 March 23	2012 April 8	2016 March 27	2020 April 12

2021 April 4	2027 March 28	2033 April 17	2039 April 10
2022 April 17	2028 April 16	2034 April 9	2040 April 1
2023 April 9	2029 April 1	2035 March 25	2041 April 2
2024 March 31	2030 April 21	2036 April 13	2042 April 6
2025 April 20	2031 April 13	2037 April 5	2043 March 29
2026 April 5	2032 March 28	2038 April 25	2044 April 17

Traditional Wedding Anniversary Identifications

1 Paper	7 Wool	13 Lace	35 Coral
2 Cotton	8 Bronze	14 Ivory	40 Ruby
3 Leather	9 Pottery	15 Crystal	45 Sapphire
4 Linen	10 Tin	20 China	50 Gold
5 Wood	11 Steel	25 Silver	55 Emerald
6 Iron	12 Silk	30 Pearl	60 Diamond

Colors Appropriate for Days and Seasons

White. Symbolizes purity, perfection, and joy and identifies festivals marking events in the life of Jesus, except Good Friday: Christmas, Epiphany, Easter, Eastertide, Ascension Day; also Trinity Sunday, All Saints' Day, weddings, funerals. Gold may also be used.

Red. Symbolizes the Holy Spirit, martyrdom, and the love of God: Good Friday, Pentecost, and Sundays following.

Violet. Symbolizes penitence: Advent, Lent.

Green. Symbolizes mission to the world, hope, regeneration, nurture, and growth: Epiphany season, Kingdomtide, Rural Life Sunday, Labor Sunday, Thanksgiving Sunday.

Blue. Advent, in some churches.

Flowers in Season Appropriate for Church Use

January: carnation or snowdrop	July: larkspur or water lily
February: violet or primrose	August: gladiolus or poppy
March: jonquil or daffodil	September: aster or morning star
April: lily, sweet pea, or daisy	October: calendula or cosmos
May: lily of the valley or hawthorn	November: chrysanthemum
June: rose or honeysuckle	December: narcissus, holly, or poinsettia

Quotable Quotations

1. Without even meaning to, and sometimes even trying very hard not to, [our fathers] would have wounded us, their children, by the way they were fathers, just as we wound our children, and so, without intending to, our fathers pass on a wounded image of God's fatherhood as well.—Roberta C. Bondi, *Memories of God*

2. Come, Lord Jesus is the way the Bible ends, and it is as The One Who Comes that we know him most truly.—Frederick Buechner, *The Longing for Home*

3. Our days are full of nonsense, and yet not, because it is precisely into the nonsense of our days that God speaks to us words of great significance.—Frederick Buechner, *Listening to Your Life*

4. The *full* Gospel is the Good News of redemption from sin *and* suffering, and the salvation of persons *and* powers. We cannot do without either Martin Luther or Martin Luther King.—Dorothy and Gabriel Fackre, *Christian Basics*

5. Too much praise makes you feel you must be doing something terribly wrong.—Dorothy Day, quoted in *Dorothy Day: Selected Writings*, Robert Ellsberg, ed.

6. Our need is for more than we have, and to those whose lives have the dimension of eternity, who know God's purpose and affection, the need is met.—Frederick M. Meek

7. I wouldn't touch a leper for a thousand pounds; yet I willingly cure him for the love of God.—Mother Teresa, *A Gift for God*

8. What matters is to listen attentively to the Spirit and to go obediently where we are being led, whether to a joyful or a painful place.—Henri J. M. Nouwen, *Show Me the Way*

9. The Head and the Heart at last inseparable; they are lost in wonder in the One. —Howard Thurman, *With Head and Heart* (Howard Thurman dedicated his autobiography, published in 1979, "To the stranger in the railroad station in Daytona Beach who restored my broken dream sixty-five years ago." A black man paid his travel expense to school in Jacksonville.)

10. No cross in the world can refute the offer of meaning that was made on the cross of him who was raised to life.—Hans Küng, *Does God Exist?*

11. No name, no office, no authority, and no specialty of any one Church should be permitted to divide the Church.—Hans Küng, *Why I Am Still a Christian*

12. The biblical witness is far less interested in speculation on the origin of evil than on resistance to it in confidence of the superiority and ultimate victory of God's love.—Daniel Migliori, *Faith Seeking Understanding*

13. Perhaps travel cannot prevent bigotry, but by demonstrating that all peoples cry, laugh, eat, worry, and die, it can introduce the idea that if we try to understand each other, we may even become friends.—Maya Angelou, *Wouldn't Take Nothing for My Journey Now*

14. The centuries have shown the wisdom of preaching Christ crucified rather than Christ the successful teacher.—Ralph W. Sockman, *The Meaning of Suffering*

15. Love is the most durable power in the world. This creative force, so beautifully exemplified in the life of our Christ, is the most potent instrument available in mankind's quest for peace and security.—Martin Luther King Jr., *The Words of Martin Luther King Jr.*, selected by Coretta Scott King

16. We are severely impoverished if we do not encounter people of other faiths with reverence and respect for their belief and integrity.—Desmond Tutu, *The Words of Desmond Tutu*, selected by Naomi Tutu

17. We are servants of the God who reigns and cares. He wants us to be the alternative society; where there is harshness and insensitivity, we must be compassionate and caring; where people are statistics, we must show they count as being of immense value to God; where there is grasping and selfishness, we must be a sharing community now.—Desmond Tutu, *Crying in the Wilderness*

18. Let your life be a life affirmative of the sovereignty of the heavenly vision, spent in the pursuit of it and in the service of it. There lies the splendor, there lies the peace, there lies the hope of our human world.—George A. Gordon, *Unto Victory*

19. Religion at its highest conceives God as the God of hope.—George A. Gordon, *And Let Us Reason Together*

20. To feed the poor a nourishing breakfast does not deal with the fact that they will be hungry again by suppertime.—Robert McAfee Brown, *Spirituality and Liberation*

21. Whenever an angel says "Be not afraid!" you'd better start worrying. A big assignment is on the way.—Elie Wiesel, in Robert McAfee Brown, *Spirituality and Liberation*

22. Some are guilty, all are responsible.—Abraham Joshua Heschel, quoted in Robert McAfee Brown, *Saying Yes and Saying No*

23. Compassion is the chief law of human existence.—Fyodor Dostoyevsky

24. Let us be servants in order to be leaders.—Fyodor Dostoyevsky

25. The sensitive individual has purer and broader ideals of brotherhood than any which are realized in any actual community.—Reinhold Niebuhr, *The Children of Light and the Children of Darkness*

26. Life was meant to be lived. . . . One must never, for whatever reason, turn his back on life.—Eleanor Roosevelt, *Autobiography*

27. I am persuaded that nothing but an all-out effort to demand integrity of our political leaders—and of their bosses, by which I mean *us*—will preserve democracy as we have come to know it in the century to come.—Stephen L. Carter, *Integrity*

28. The morning after I won Wimbledon in 1975 I should have asked "Why Me?" and doubted that I deserved the victory. If I don't ask "Why me?" after my victories, I cannot ask "Why me?" after my setbacks and disasters.—Arthur Ashe, *Days of Grace*

29. Stumbling along we suddenly catch our stride, or running confidently we suddenly fall down—and maybe sometimes the "reason" is not in ourselves but in the stars, God's stars: His grace.—Robert Coles, *Harvard Diary*

30. The deep truth is that our human suffering need not be an obstacle to the joy and peace we so desire, but can become, instead, the means *to* it.—Henri J. M. Nouwen, *Life of the Beloved*

31. The ages are progressive, and I look for a far higher manhood and womanhood than we have now.—Susan B. Anthony, 1883, in Lynn Sharr, *Failure Is Impossible*

32. Without the sense that life makes sense, all other motives for virtuous behavior lose their force. If life is "a tale told by an idiot . . . signifying nothing," then it doesn't really matter how one behaves.—William Kilpatrick, *Why Johnny Can't Tell Right from Wrong*

33. All man's miseries derive from not being able to sit quietly in a room alone.—Blaise Pascal (1623–1662)

34. Men are disturbed not by things that happen, but by their opinions of the things that happen.—Epictetus (ca. A.D. 55–135)

35. There is a law in psychology that if you form a picture in your mind of what you would like to be, and you keep and hold that picture there long enough, you will soon become exactly as you have been thinking.—William James (1842–1910)

36. We can control our choices, but we can't control the consequences of those choices. When we pick up one end of the stick, we pick up the other.—Stephen R. Covey et al., *First Things First*

37. I know that He has a time that will be right for me to leave my body the way a butterfly leaves its cocoon.—Elisabeth Kübler-Ross, M.D.

38. I think modern medicine has become like a prophet offering a life free of pain. It's nonsense. The only thing I know that truly heals people is unconditional love. —Elisabeth Kübler-Ross, M.D.

39. My mother's love for me was so great that I have worked hard to justify it. —Marc Chagall, at ninety

40. Love without grace is like a hook without bait.—Anne de Lenclos

41. Live water heals memories. I look up the creek and here it comes, the future, being borne aloft as a winding succession of laden trays.—Annie Dillard, *Pilgrim at Tinker Creek*

42. At school I never minded the lessons. I just resented having to work terribly hard at playing.—John Mortimer

43. I don't want to achieve immortality through my work. . . . I want to achieve it through not dying.—Woody Allen

44. To me old age is always fifteen years older than I am.—Bernard Baruch (1870–1965)

45. Vote for the man who promises the least; he'll be the least disappointing. —Bernard Baruch

46. The great act of faith is when a man decides he is not God.—Oliver Wendell Holmes Jr.

47. History may have consigned to blacks race as an unending negative which will support failure and oppression. That does not have to be the case. Blacks can reject history's negatives and call upon the strengths endemic to us and make America work for us.—Barbara Jordan, to the Urban League, 1981

48. We express our religious interests, dreams, fears, hopes, and desires through popular culture.—Tom Beaudoin

49. Modern life can grow dull and predictable. . . . Still, there's one magic talisman left that has the power to bring freshness, novelty, and surprise into your life: someone else's enthusiasm.—Linda Weltner

50. Faith-based charity provides crumbs from the table; faith-based justice offers a place at the table.—Bill Moyers, in Foreword, *Faith Works,* by Jim Wallis

51. In Washington, D.C., most of our elected officials suffer a common affliction. I call it the "wet-finger politician syndrome." You get it by constantly licking your finger and putting it up in the air to see which way the wind is blowing.—Jim Wallis, *Faith Works*

Questions of Life and Religion

1. How can God help us handle failure?
2. What strengthens and what weakens faith?
3. Can we always count on God?
4. Are there readily available ways to strengthen family ties?

5. When is fasting appropriate?
6. Are the events in our lives fated and beyond our control?
7. Is fault finding a curable habit?
8. What can we do to avoid being overwhelmed by fear?
9. How far should fellowship reach?
10. Is stupidity a major factor in sin?
11. Are some wrongs impossible to forgive?
12. How is our freedom in Christ to be enjoyed?
13. In what ways is generosity a virtue?
14. Is gentleness a powerful motivator?
15. What does the Kingdom of God include?
16. How does God get through to us?
17. How can we know God's will for us?
18. What is the Gospel?
19. Can we reconcile grace and works in the experience of "salvation"?
20. What is true greatness?
21. How can we resolve our feelings of guilt?
22. Can we know joy in spite of unhappy circumstances?
23. Do prayer and faith contribute to physical healing?
24. Why do we share our faith with people of different faiths?
25. Is it possible in this life to know what heaven is like?
26. What is holiness?
27. What are the works of the Holy Spirit?
28. Is hope more than wishful thinking?
29. Of what does a home consist?
30. How do hymns contribute to religious experience and practice?
31. What makes a hypocrite?
32. Where do we get life-changing ideals?
33. Is idolatry ever a threat to churchgoing Christians?
34. How can justice be experienced in our societies?
35. What is the meaning of justification by faith?
36. How much does one have to know in order to experience salvation?
37. Is laughter a desirable human experience?
38. In view of justification by faith, how important is law?
39. Why is marriage important?
40. Is martyrdom a virtue to seek?
41. What are the marks of spiritual maturity?
42. How can meditation contribute to personal spiritual growth and service?
43. What is a miracle?
44. What can money do?
45. How can morality be learned?
46. What are some of the fascinating mysteries of your religion?
47. Discuss the special contribution that old age can make to our life together.
48. What are the problems and joys of parenthood?
49. How can we reconcile patriotism and service to God?

50. Who is a prophet?
51. How should we define and describe the providence of God?
52. What is the motivating role of purpose in achieving the will of God?

Biblical Benedictions and Blessings

The Lord watch between me and thee when we are absent from one another.—Gen. 31:49

The Lord our God be with us, as he was with our fathers; let him not leave us nor forsake us; that he may incline our hearts unto him, to walk in all his ways and to keep his commandments and his statutes and his judgments, which he commanded our fathers.—1 Kings 8:57–58

Let the words of my mouth and the meditation of my heart be acceptable in thy sight, O Lord, my strength and my redeemer.—Ps. 19:14

Now the God of patience and consolation grant you to be like-minded one toward another according to Christ Jesus; that ye may with one mind and one mouth glorify God, even the Father of our Lord Jesus Christ. Now the God of hope fill you with all joy and peace in believing, that ye may abound in hope, through the power of the Holy Ghost. Now the God of peace be with you.—Rom. 15:5–6, 13, 33

Now to him that is of power to establish you according to my Gospel and the teaching of Jesus Christ, according to the revelation of the mystery, which was kept secret since the world began but now is manifest, and by the Scriptures of the prophets, according to the commandments of the everlasting God, made known to all nations for the glory through Jesus Christ forever.—Rom. 16:25–27

Grace be unto you, and peace, from God our Father, and from the Lord Jesus Christ.—1 Cor. 1:3

The grace of the Lord Jesus Christ and the love of God and the communion of the Holy Ghost be with you all.—2 Cor. 13:14

Peace be to the brethren, and love with faith, from God the Father and the Lord Jesus Christ. Grace be with all them that love our Lord Jesus Christ in sincerity.—Eph. 6:23–24

And the peace of God, which passeth all understanding, shall keep your hearts and minds through Christ Jesus. Finally, brethren, whatsoever things are true, whatsoever things are honest, whatsoever things are just, whatsoever things are pure, whatsoever things are lovely, whatsoever things are of good report; if there be any virtue, and if there be any praise, think on these things. Those things which ye have both learned and received, and heard and seen in me, do; and the God of peace shall be with you.—Phil. 4:7–9

Wherefore also we pray always for you, that our God would count you worthy of this calling and fulfill all the good pleasure of this goodness, and the work of faith with power; that the name of our Lord Jesus Christ may be glorified in you, and ye in him, according to the grace of our God and the Lord Jesus Christ.—2 Thess. 1:11–12

Now the Lord of peace himself give you peace always by all means. The Lord be with you all. The grace of our Lord Jesus Christ be with you all.—2 Thess. 3:16–18

Grace, mercy, and peace, from God our Father and Jesus Christ our Lord.—1 Tim. 1:2

Now the God of peace, that brought again from the dead our Lord Jesus, that great shepherd of the sheep, through the blood of the everlasting covenant, make you perfect in every good work to do his will, working in you that which is well-pleasing in his sight, through Jesus Christ, to whom be glory for ever and ever.—Heb. 13:20–21

The God of all grace, who hath called us unto his eternal glory by Christ Jesus, after that ye have suffered a while, make you perfect, establish, strengthen, settle you. To him be glory and dominion for ever and ever. Greet ye one another with a kiss of charity. Peace be with you all that are in Christ Jesus.—1 Pet. 3:10–14

Grace be with you, mercy, and peace from God the Father, and from the Lord Jesus Christ, the Son of the Father, in truth and love.—2 John 3

Now unto him that is able to keep you from falling, and to present you faultless before the presence of his glory with exceeding joy, to the only wise God our Savior, be glory and majesty, dominion and power, both now and ever.—Jude 24:25

Grace be unto you, and peace, from him which was, and which is to come; and from the seven Spirits which are before his throne; and from Jesus Christ, who is the faithful witness, and the first begotten of the dead, and the prince of the kings of the earth. Unto him that loved us, and washed us from our sins in his own blood, and hath made us kings and priests unto God and his Father, to him be glory and dominion for ever and ever.—Rev. 1:4–6

SECTION II

SERMONS AND HOMILETIC AND WORSHIP AIDS FOR FIFTY-TWO SUNDAYS

SUNDAY, JANUARY 2, 2005
Lectionary Message

Topic: Is That *All*?
TEXT: John 1:(1–9) 10–18
Other Readings: Jer. 31:7–14; Ps. 147:12–20; Eph. 1:3–14

I. Christmas is over. All the excitement, all the anticipation is finished for another year. Many families have already packed up their decorations. Years ago Hank Ketchum caught much of our typical post-Christmas response in his Dennis the Menace cartoon. Dennis sits on the floor in front of the Christmas tree on Christmas morning. He is surrounded by mountains of toys and equal mountains of spent wrapping paper and ribbons and asks, "Is that *all*?" We chuckle at his childish response to our overly commercialized and overly materialistic Christmas celebration. But such a question and response isn't merely a child's question. It's also a postmodern question and response to the church, and often by the church. After all the Christmas pageants, cantatas, and special worship services, we ask, "Is that *all*?" We have that let-down feeling that there should be something more—but we aren't exactly sure what. For many people, Christmas is a depressing time, a time when grief over lost loved ones and loneliness overwhelms the anticipated joy of the season. These too ask, "Is that *all*?"

The Apostle John tells us the situation was no different after that first Christmas day: "He was in the world, and the world was made through him, yet the world knew him not. He came to his own home and his own people received him not." Christ was not the kind of messiah most of his people expected. Their expectation was of a royal messiah, a new king like David who would restore Israel to its former glory, who would overthrow the yoke of Rome and assert Israel's independence afresh. A baby born to an unwed mother and her poor carpenter fiancé, and placed in an animal feeding trough? No way! Their response mimics the question, "Is that *all*?"

II. John quickly reminds us that it is *not* all. Christ's own people were looking for the wrong kind of messiah, just as we look for the wrong fulfillment in the Christmas season. If Christ's people had read all their prophets and writings, they would have seen different traditions concerning the messiah, a suffering servant-model alongside the royal model. If we would look beyond the commercialization and secularization of Christmas, we too might find more.

In answer to Dennis's question, let's look again at our text. For John tells us our models are not all there is to Christmas. There are two "*all*'s" in our focal passage. These "*all*'s" are John's answer to our opening question, "Is that *all*?" The answer to Dennis's question and ours is a resounding "No!" No, the material aspects of Christmas are not *all*. No, the expectations Jesus' contemporaries had for the Messiah are not *all*. But now we come with John to say, "This *is all!*"

(a) "But to *all* who received him, who believed in his name, he gave power to become children of God" (v. 12).

This is the "whosoever" of the gospel. "Anyone who believes in him." "Everyone who believes in him." The gospel has no limits, no bounds. Christ's sacrifice was for all: Jew and Gentile, male and female, slave and free, *all*. There is no limit except for human response or its lack. The text defines the *all*. They are "All who received him, that is, *all* who believed in his name." Today maybe we would use as our opposites black and white; Christian and Jew and Muslim; "us" who are good, moral, upright people and "them," the sinners—murderers, drug addicts, prostitutes, and so on. Christ dies for *all* and *all* who receive him, to them he gave power to become children of God. Again note John's emphasis. It *isn't* that "to *some* who received him he gave power to become children of God." How often our limited view of the gospel presents a *some* theology and understanding. John says "to *everyone*, to *all*, who receive him he gave power to become children of God."

(b) "From his fullness we have *all* received, grace upon grace" (v. 16).

John's second *all* builds on the first. First, *all* who receive, who believe in him, become children of God. Then *all* who *received* him as Savior in turn *receive* from him. Note also the double use of the two words *all* and *received*: all who received him—from his fullness we have all received. The first occurrence is near the beginning of our focal passage (v. 12); the second is near the end (v. 16). The two serve to summarize and focus our thoughts on the central message of the text. All who receive him receive from him. And the gift all receive is grace upon grace, grace heaped up with more grace.

Back to the Christmas scene and Dennis the Menace for a moment. We still too often maintain the accounting view of Christmas. "What did I spend?" "What did I get?" "Is that all?" John focuses on what we *all* have the opportunity to receive: "But to *all* who received him, who believed in his name, he gave power to become children of God." And "From his fullness we have *all* received, grace upon grace." Once we see from John's perspective, we have to answer the postmodern question with a resounding "No!" No, the commercialized, materialistic Christmas is *not* all. But thanks be to God for His Christmas gift for *all.*—Joel F. Drinkard Jr.

ILLUSTRATIONS

WHAT IS AHEAD.   Have you ever been in a dark cave in the blackest of night when there was no light, not a glimmer of light at all? Has the darkness that surrounded you pulled in every direction, silently waiting to drop you from the narrow rim into a bottomless pit of despair in which you would never stop falling? And were you afraid to move, but unable to keep still? But at last you must walk. Slowly now. Slowly. And then—and then—in a moment your heart is flooded with something very great. You walk surely now and with steady pace. And you are not afraid anymore. Yonder! Yonder ahead you see a light. At times it is very near to give you heart. Again it is far away to lead you on through the darkness. Be not afraid. It is the Lord! And, by the mercies of God, you know that we ought to rejoice in our troubles because "God's love has flooded our hearts."—Raymond Bryan Brown[1]

---

[1]*The Fire of Truth* (Nashville, Tenn.: Broadman Press, 1982), pp. 16ff.

ALL THINGS ARE YOURS. We need not endlessly grieve the distant villages we will never see. We need not grieve the strange flesh we will never touch, the wrongs we will never right, the ills we will never cure. I'm against quietism, but I think I have lived just long enough to learn that contentment lies in discerning the value of the things we have, long enough to understand what Saint Paul meant when he wrote, "For all things are yours; whether Paul, or Apollos, or Cephas, or the world, or life, or death, or things present, or things to come; all are yours; and ye are Christ's; and Christ is God's."—William Sloane Coffin[2]

SERMON SUGGESTIONS

Topic: Hope Fulfilled
TEXT: Jer. 31:7–14
(1) It is preceded by prayer (v. 7). (2) It is accomplished in God's providence (vv. 8–11). (3) It is the occasion of great rejoicing (vv. 12–14).

Topic: The Blessings of Christ
TEXT: Eph. 1:2–6, 15–18
(1) The blessings given (vv. 3–6). (2) The blessings received (vv. 15–18).

WORSHIP AIDS

CALL TO WORSHIP.   "From the Rising of the sun to its setting my name is great among the nations" (Mal. 1:11, RSV).

INVOCATION.   O almighty God, who pourest out, on all who desire it, the Spirit of grace and of supplication: deliver us, when we draw nigh to thee, from coldness of heart and wanderings of mind, that with steadfast thoughts and kindled affections, we may worship thee in spirit and in truth.—Book of Common Prayer

OFFERTORY SENTENCE.   "Give unto the Lord the glory due unto his name: bring an offering, and come before him: worship the Lord in the beauty of holiness" (1 Chron. 16:29).

OFFERTORY PRAYER.   Most gracious and benevolent heavenly Father, accept these our gifts as our humble effort to return unto thee a portion of thy bounty entrusted to our care. Grant unto us, O Lord, the wisdom and compassion to use these gifts offered unto thee for the care of all thy children throughout the world; in the name of our Lord and Savior, Jesus Christ.—Rodney K. Miller

PRAYER.   To thee, O God, we pray, who hast comprehended our whole life in the gospel of thy Son, Jesus Christ, who hath not left us alone with Christmas, with all its beauty and fair tradition and its sweet story; because we have to live our life with the heights above us and on the level plain. We make our roadway down through the abysses and across the gorges. And there is another side to live beside the greatness of heroism: the richness of thine own Spirit in the children of man, and we thank thee that he who came to us the incarnate Christmas, bringing to us the Christ-mass, bringing to us the very solution of the problem of

---

[2]*The Courage to Love* (San Francisco: HarperSanFrancisco, 1984).

life with its humiliation and its meagerness and its straitness—we thank thee that he bore our griefs and carried our sorrows; that it was not alone the visit of the Wise Men, but the visit of the fools, also; that it was not alone the song of angels, but the cry of the disgraced and the sorrowful and the pained. We thank thee that he heard not only the voice of the Infinite above him, but that he heard the cry of the dying thief.

Surely he hath borne our grief and carried our sorrows and knows our pathway between these experiences. We ask thee to help us to look upon it seriously, with the utmost friendship, in the atmosphere one for another, not boasting, but humble. We ask in the name of the captain of our salvation, even Jesus.—Frank W. Gunsaulus

SERMON

Topic: A Happy New Year in the Peaceable Kingdom
TEXT: Isa. 2:2–4; 11:1–9; Luke 12:22–32, 17:20–21

I. "Happy New Year." How many times have you heard these words lately? How many times have you said these words lately? Saying "Happy New Year" is a social ritual we all engage in at this time of year, with hardly a thought about the meaning of the words.

Do you remember just a few years ago? The words our public pundits were using not so long ago were *euphoria,* the *peace dividend,* the *triumph of freedom,* the *downfall of tyranny.* Those were heady days, not so long ago, when the possibility that the new year might really be one seemed very real. We had witnessed things we thought we would never see.

II. If we want to date the end of this era of good feeling, we could make a good case for August 2, 1990, when Iraq invaded Kuwait, plunging our world into yet one more international crisis. Of course, all along there has been an undercurrent of dis-ease about problems that just don't want to go away—the continuing degradation of our environment, our declining economy, the chasmlike disparity between rich and poor, the federal deficit, the savings and loan scandal, the banking crisis, and on and on.

"Happy New Year."

My wife and I went to a party December 31, 1990. If these global problems were not depressing enough, some of the personal problems of some of our friends were. One couple had a son serving in an elite combat unit in Saudi Arabia, and his prospect for survival was one of the unspoken subjects of our conversation. (He did survive.) Another couple needed to talk about the disillusionment their son, a college junior, was feeling at the greed and selfishness he witnessed among his own generation. A third couple came late because they had to check one of their sons, who was suffering a deep depression, into Our Lady of Peace.

For these friends, there was a real question whether the new year, 1991, would be happy or not. Our mood at the beginning of that particular new year was less like that of Isaiah 2 and more like that of Joel 3:9–10.

III. At that New Year's Eve party, at midnight we watched on TV as the glittering ball descended on Times Square, we kissed our spouses and hugged our friends, we blew our horns and made noise with our noisemakers, we threw streamers over the rafters of the den where we greeted that particular new year.

"Happy New Year," we said to each other when midnight struck. Then we went back to eating and drinking and the private conversations we had interrupted to greet the new year.

I sat down beside the man whose stepson was suffering from depression, and we talked. He had no explanations; neither did I. We just talked about this young man and the behavior that had led to his hospitalization. Soon my wife caught my eye, signaling that we should be leaving. I got up and said, "I hope this year will be better for you than the last one."

And he said, "It's been a good year so far."

The new year was thirty-one minutes old, and he said, "It's been a good year so far." He made a joke, and I laughed.

If anything can save us from the fears and anxieties we all feel about a new year, it's humor. I think this couple and their son will make it because my friend could see something good and something to joke about, even at that dark hour.

Someone once said that if the problem for the believer is explaining how God can be good yet the world be full of evil, then the problem for the unbeliever is explaining how an evil world can be full of so much good. In the face of a wrenching personal crisis, under the shadow of ominous world events, my friend could say something funny. He could make a joke.

Where do people get the resources to cope with the pretty unhappy new year facing them? Where will you, where will I, get the resources to cope with our new year and all of its uncertainties and threats?

IV. One of the ways the Bible answers that question is to give us an image: "the peaceable kingdom," as we have come to call it. This image is found in the book of Isaiah, where the prophet says a day will come when soldiers will beat their swords into plowshares and their spears into pruning hooks and natural enemies like the lion and the lamb will lie down in peace with each other.

This vision of Isaiah's was a vision of the future, a vision of the Day of the Lord, which was coming at some later moment in history. This vision was not true in Isaiah's day, nor was it true when the prophet Joel wrote his vicious parody of it four hundred years later. To many of us worldly wise observers of the contemporary scene, it seems no truer today than it did then. Why should we, with all of our problems, be more ready to believe in a vision of a peaceable kingdom than Joel was in 400 B.C.? Is our world really any better than his—except that we have better and more sophisticated ways to kill ourselves? Why could my friend say something funny in the face of a new year that did not promise to be all that much fun for him?

The only difference I can think of between our times and the time of the prophet Joel is that Jesus Christ has come into the world and, in coming, has claimed to bring that peaceable kingdom with him.

And in case we should mistakenly think that this peaceable kingdom is something that is going to happen some time in the future (as it was for Isaiah), a little later on Jesus says, "The kingdom of God is among you." The verb is in the present tense, not the future. The reign of God is a present reality we can experience now, not merely something we look for in a distant, far-off eschatological future.

V. This peaceable kingdom within us is not to be understood as a good feeling we have about ourselves or our world. It may not be a good feeling at all. It is not to be understood as personal salvation while the world around us goes to hell. The kingdom of God within us is manifest, rather, in the confidence we have that no matter how bad we may feel or no matter how bad our circumstances get, God is seeing to it that things are turning out for the good.

Not that things will turn out necessarily the way we want them to, but rather that whatever has gone wrong is being put right and that whatever happens—even if it's the worst we can imagine—is somehow being redeemed in God's goodness.

The peaceable kingdom of God within us is something else as well: it's the power within us to do good, to make some difference in our world for God. It is the belief that God works through us to extend this peaceable kingdom to others. It doesn't come with the guarantee that others will listen and respond with their own faith, hope, and courage. But it does come with the guarantee that God is in the work we do for this peaceable kingdom.

No matter our burden of fear or anger or hatred or anxiety; no matter what the world has done to us; no matter what we've done to the world, there is always the possibility that the peaceable kingdom can be ours. There is always the reality that nothing can keep us from this peaceable kingdom other than our own refusal to let it be.

And because all this is true, you and I and everyone else who believes that the peaceable kingdom of God has come in Christ—we can really and truly say, "Happy New Year!"—Bill Thomason[3]

SUNDAY, JANUARY 9, 2005
Lectionary Message

Topic: God Shows No Partiality
TEXT: Acts 10:34–43
Other Readings: Isa. 42:1–9; Ps. 29; Matt. 3:13–17

I. *The context of Peter's message.* The Roman centurion Cornelius was a righteous, God-fearing man, as were those in his household. He regularly demonstrated the same piety as the Jews: making generous gifts to the poor and praying sincere prayers.

One day Cornelius had a vision in which an angel of God told him his prayers had ascended to God and that he was to send for a man named Simon Peter who was in Joppa. Cornelius lived in Caesarea Maritima, a town that was about thirty-five to forty miles from Joppa. Cornelius immediately dispatched two servants and a soldier to Joppa to invite Peter to visit him.

As the messengers approached Joppa about noon the following day, Peter was praying. He became hungry, but while the food was being prepared he had an ecstatic vision of all kinds of animals, reptiles, and birds. He heard a voice telling him to eat these animals. But Peter refused, stating that he never ate anything ritually impure. The voice came again, and a third time, also saying that nothing God has created is unclean.

Almost immediately the men from Cornelius arrived, and Peter received them. They remained with him overnight. The following day Peter and the messengers accompanied by some believers from Joppa journeyed to Caesarea. They arrived at Caesarea on the fourth day.

Cornelius had invited relatives and friends to his home, anticipating Peter's arrival. Peter, noting that those assembled were Gentiles, recounted his ecstatic vision to explain why he agreed to come. He then asked why Cornelius had invited him.

---

[3]*Real Life, Real Faith* (Valley Forge, Penn.: Judson Press, 1994), pp. 98–103.

Cornelius recounted his own vision and his sending messengers to Peter. Peter preached his message sharing the gospel, and the Holy Spirit fell on all those in Cornelius's house.

Peter's message is the heart of this passage. But before we get to the message, I note one other preliminary matter.

II. *The preparations for Peter's message.* Note all the preparation shown in the passage—the way God brought the parties all together:

1. God prepared Cornelius with a vision.
2. God prepared Peter with an ecstatic vision.
3. Cornelius prepared for Peter's coming, inviting relatives and friends to be present.
4. Peter shared the gospel. He prepared the gentiles to receive the gospel and respond to God. The Holy Spirit fell on all in Cornelius's house while Peter was still speaking. The believers from Joppa were amazed that the Holy Spirit fell on gentiles.
5. These new believers were then baptized.

Perhaps these events together are to prepare the Early Church for an awareness that the gospel is for all, Jew and gentile alike.

III. *The content of Peter's message.* Peter's message is summed up in the first words of his message: God shows no partiality—God doesn't play favorites (or, in an old translation, God is no respecter of persons). The gospel is for "whosoever." "Whosoever believes will be saved." The remainder of Peter's message is arranged in a chiastic pattern (ABBA):

A. Anyone from any nation who fears God and does what is right is acceptable to God.
B. Christ was crucified and raised from the dead.
B. Christ is the one ordained by God to judge the living and the dead.
A. Anyone who believes in Christ receives forgiveness of sin through his name.

This pattern puts Christ crucified and empowered at the center of the structure, and "anyone, whosoever, all" in the outer ring. The message begins and ends with "anyone" and has Christ at the focal center.

The message Peter brought is that God's family is an inclusive family. There are no divisions on the basis of race, age, gender, national origin, language, education, social status, or any of the other divisions we often see. God's family is open to "whosoever."

In God's family, the outsider is brought in. The word *gentile* means little to us today. But to the first century Jew it represented the worst possible outsider. To the Jew of Peter's day, the world had two simple ethnic groups: "*us*" (Jews) and "*them*" (gentiles). What is our "us-them" division today? How easily we rationalize that "they-them" are different from "us"—"*they*" have different music or have a different type service. "They" wouldn't be comfortable in our worship; "they" would feel out of place with "us." Who is our "*them*" today? In his vision Peter said he had never touched anything "unclean" or "impure" before. Then by analogy he indicates that Gentiles were "unclean." Who are the unclean, the untouchables for us? Is it the murderer, the drug addict, the prostitute? Or is it a matter of race or social status? Peter learned from his ecstatic vision that there are no unclean or impure ones from God's perspective. The gospel is for "whosoever." Who is our gospel for? Are we really as open as Peter became? Do we include "them" along with "us"?

One of my favorite poems is by Edwin Markham; it is entitled "Outwitted":

He drew a circle that shut me out—
Heretic, rebel, a thing to flout.
But Love and I had the wit to win:
We drew a circle that took him in!

What size circles do we draw? Do we draw small exclusive circles that leave one out? Peter's message is that God draws inclusive circles that take "whosoever" in!—Joel F. Drinkard Jr.

ILLUSTRATIONS

SERVICE OR OFFERING?   He was too modest to mention that he had urged others to work with the elderly or with young people in trouble with the law, with drugs and drinking. In fact, he always pointed to the initiatives, activities, and good ideas of friends of his, working men who made it their business to give time and energy to others. When a local paper wanted to highlight his volunteer efforts, he insisted that he be mentioned only as part of a group. And he urged that their work *not* be called community service.

"It's more a person-to-person thing, and it's us trying to be friendly to people who aren't having the best of times. I know, it does help everyone—the community—when you go and visit the old folks, but I don't think of it as service. To me, service means, like, the military, or you're doing something you've *got* to do, or you've been *told* to do it, or you've been *sentenced* to it because you got in trouble with the law. To me, what we do is—well, it's us trying to offer something from our hearts, only we all got together, and we're organized about it."

He could have been speaking for many of the college students and older people who have the impulse to engage themselves in a broken world and find a place for their moral energy.—Robert Coles[4]

ESTRANGEMENT.   The most irrevocable expression of the separation of life from life today is the attitude of social groups within nations towards each other, and the attitude of nations themselves towards other nations. The walls of distance, in time and space, have been removed by technical progress; but the walls of estrangement between heart and heart have been incredibly strengthened. The madness of the German Nazis and the cruelty of the lynching mobs in the South provide too easy an excuse for us to turn our thoughts from our own selves. But let us just consider ourselves and what we feel, when we read, this morning and tonight, that in some sections of Europe all children under the age of three are sick and dying, or that in some sections of Asia millions without homes are freezing and starving to death. The strangeness of life to life is evident in the strange fact that we can know all this, and yet can live today, this morning, tonight, as though we were completely ignorant. And I refer to the most sensitive people amongst us. In both mankind and nature, life is separated from life. Estrangement prevails among all things that live. Sin abounds.—Paul Tillich[5]

---

[4]*The Case of Service* (Boston: Houghton Mifflin), pp. 48ff.
[5]*The Shaking of the Foundations* (New York: Scribner, 1948), pp. 157ff.

SERMON SUGGESTIONS

Topic: God's True Servant

TEXT: Isa. 42:1–9

(1) A champion of justice. (2) An example of patience. (3) An instrument of God. (4) A prototype of Jesus Christ.

Topic: Christ for All

TEXT: Acts 10:34–43

(1) His program (vv. 34–36). (2) His works (vv. 37–38). (3) His witnesses (vv. 39–41). (4) His purpose (vv. 42–43).

WORSHIP AIDS

CALL TO WORSHIP.   "Oh, that men would praise the Lord for his goodness, and for his wonderful works to the children of men! For he satisfieth the longing soul, and filleth the hungry soul with goodness" (Ps. 107:8–9, KJV).

INVOCATION.   Today, O Lord, give us such keen vision that we can see what thou dost mean to us and all thy children every day of our lives. Then help us to render to thee fitting praise in psalms and hymns and spiritual songs; in the reading and preaching of thy word, and in the offering of our very selves to thee.

OFFERTORY SENTENCE.   "For every beast of the forest is mine, and the cattle upon a thousand hills" (Ps. 50:10).

OFFERTORY PRAYER.   We are thine, O God. Thou hast created us. Thou hast redeemed us. Thou hast given us the power to gain the fruits of our labors. And now we bring as offerings of gratitude and love only what is already truly thine.

PRAYER.   Eternal God, before whom sinners cannot stand, we come humbly into thy presence. Out of the turbulence of the world, our hearts disquieted by its confusion, our lives contaminated by its sin, we come to thee. Give us an hour of insight and cleansing; grant us grace to be honest with ourselves, sensitive toward our neighbors, reverent toward thee.

We dare not come to worship thee without bringing our brother with us. Father of all men, who hast said that we cannot love thee unless we love our brother also, we would come bringing him with us in our hearts' compassion and goodwill. Before we seek forgiveness, help us to be forgiving; before we ask for mercy, help us to be merciful. Take from our hearts the hidden grudge, the secret vindictiveness, the lurking hate. Give us an inclusive spirit of sympathy and understanding. From all bigotry and prejudice of race and class, deliver us. Teach us what it means to care even for those who despitefully use us, and so abiding in love may we abide in thee.

Though we come with our brother in our sympathy, nonetheless thou seeist how alone we are. We come from the world, where men look on the outward appearance, to thee who dost look upon the heart. We ourselves hardly know the secret motives of our own lives; we are so busy in the world that we seldom meet ourselves face to face. O God, seek us out now in the inward, untrodden recesses of our souls. When we confront our severest troubles, our profound temptations, we are solitary, and when death comes, we die alone. Companion of the companionless, inner source of strength, comfort, and fortitude, deep well from which the living waters rise, be with us today.—Harry Emerson Fosdick

SERMON
Topic: What Happens When We Pray for Others?
TEXT: "You also must help us by prayer, so that many will give thanks on our behalf for the blessing granted us in answer to many prayers" (2 Cor. 1:11).

"Without prayer," wrote Thomas Carlyle, "there can be no religion, or only a dumb one." If the religion of some Christian believers is not exactly dumb, it is probably dull, lacking bite, excitement, adventure. This is particularly true in the area of prayer. In all candor, many Christians would admit that prayer to them is an exercise in boredom or a grim, mechanical duty.

The trouble may well be that their praying is both spasmodic and selfish. They pray only in a crisis, when adversity strikes, when disease threatens, when anything unwelcome invades their ordered lives. Or they pray only for themselves and their immediate family. Prayer is thus a means of obtaining things from God when other avenues are closed, and it is a means of gratifying self. No wonder such an approach to prayer becomes tedious and unsatisfying!

One way of putting zest into the life of prayer is by rediscovery of the nature and value of intercessory prayer. Prayer for others is a glorious, noble, and exciting adventure. The Bible is full of it. Turn the pages of the Old Testament. Examine the lives of the giants of faith: Abraham, Moses, Samuel, Elijah, Jeremiah, David. They were all intercessors with God for others. Or turn the pages of the New Testament. Look at Jesus Himself, our Supreme Example in prayer, as in everything else. His prayers contained much intercession. One day, alone with His disciples, He exclaimed, "Simon, Simon, behold Satan demanded to have you, that he might sift you like wheat, but I have prayed for you that your faith might not fail." How much it must have meant to Peter to know that he was being carried on the everlasting arms of that intercession.

Now all this raises a basic question: What happens when we pray for others? It is a question to be faced frankly and answered clearly.

I. *What happens when we pray for others?* I answer, first, that *something happens to us.* Quite apart from any effect of those prayed for, there is an undoubted effect on those who pray. In the book of Job, chapter 42, verse 10, there is an arresting statement: "The Lord restored the fortunes of Job, when he prayed for his friends."

Prayer for others has a transforming effect on our relationships. It changes our attitude toward people and causes. It changes ill will and dislike into good will and friendship. It changes unholy envy into holy emulation. It changes proud indifference into personal interest. Are there people who irritate you or have injured you, people you even detest and tend to shun? Pray for them. You will become more loving, patient, understanding. Let prayer take the place of criticism, hostility, and aloofness, and you will be a happier person, with a healthier mind, living in a larger, enriched world.

Prayer for others also has a dynamic effect on our actions. It is true of all prayer that, divorced from positive action, it is a sham. It is meaningless indulgence in misdirected piety. There is no use in praying for God's will and way if we are not prepared to be resolute and determined to follow His light and leading when it comes. So if we pray for those dear to us, for our friends and enemies, it will constrain us to action. As we imagine their situation and hold them before God, we shall be moved to ask: "Lord, what will you have me to do? What action can I take to get this prayer answered? Is there an apology to make, a letter to write, a visit to pay, a service to do?"

II. *What happens when we pray for others?* I answer, in the second place, that *something happens to others.* To know that you are being prayed for is a heartening, fortifying assurance.

As a son, I have cherished the unfailing prayers of my parents. As a minister, it is always humbling and strengthening to hear oneself prayed for in public.

But what of those who do not know others are praying for them? Does something happen to them? An officer on wartime operations fired a question at his padre: "Why is it that sometimes when my nerves are on edge I begin to quiet down and become as calm and collected as if I were sitting at home in the living room?" The padre replied, "May it not be that somebody is praying for you?" "Of course!" the officer exclaimed. "My mother!" William Temple put it very simply: "When I pray for my friends coincidences happen to them. When I cease to pray, the coincidences cease."

We pray believing that we are creating new channels down which the power of God can flow into the situation. We pray believing that prayer can reach out over the miles, cross continents, penetrate barriers. Something happens to others! What happens is not in our control. How it happens is not for us to speculate. Faith accepts the fact—and prays.

III. *What happens when we pray for others?* I answer, thirdly, that *something happens with God.* In our prayers of intercession we are cooperating with God, entering into partnership with His purposes. We are not inducing God to interest Himself in those for whom we pray, nudging Him in their direction. No. We are proving to God that we are concerned about them and submitting our concern to Him for purification and correction. More than that, we are actually uniting ourselves with the life of God Himself—Father, Son, and Holy Spirit—unceasingly active for the salvation and welfare of men and women.

We never pray for others—alone! We have a great High Priest and Mediator, Jesus Christ crucified, risen, and ascended. According to the Scriptures, some forty days after Christ had risen from the dead, "He ascended into heaven"—that is, He was withdrawn from the physical sight of man and is now with God the Father. What is He doing right now? He is praying for us—and with us! In that perfect, invisible world that surrounds this physical universe, our humanity is represented. There is a Man in heaven, One who understands our lot and ever lives to make intercession for us.

Every time we pray, it is as if we put into the hand of God an added instrument for the working out of His purpose. Something happens. Something happens in us. Something happens to others. Something happens with God.

Finally, we must face this question: How can we make these things happen? Sibyl Harton wrote a little classic entitled *To Make Intercession.* The last chapter is called "The Cost of Intercession." It costs! There are demands to be met if we are serious about it.

It demands *compassion.* Intercession has been called "love on its knees." If we love enough, care enough, we shall pray. Prayer for others is one way—perhaps the greatest way— of obeying the commandment to love our neighbors as ourselves.

Again, intercessory prayer demands *method.* Nobody can pray meaningfully for everybody. Our two enemies are vagueness and forgetfulness—especially vagueness. What can be expected of such generalized prayers as "God bless Canada," "God save China," "Bless the church"? They are like an unfocused lens. It is better to pray realistically and specifically for a few than vaguely and generally for many.

Once more, intercessory prayer demands *persistence.* "Men ought always to pray and not faint," said Jesus. "Unceasingly I make mention of you always in my prayers," wrote Paul. We are not designed to wear God down, as a child wears his mother's resistance down by continual asking. It is to prove by persistence our sincerity in asking, and to wait until the conviction is strong within us that our prayers are answered. This persistence in prayer is rooted in the assurance that something happens when we pray, something that may not happen if we do not pray. "No true prayer ever comes weeping home." One of our greatest hymns of praise, "Praise to the Lord, the Almighty," has this question in its second stanza:

> Hast thou not seen
> How thy entreaties have been
> Granted in what He ordaineth?

Yes! We have seen. And so we pray, and keep on praying.—John N. Gladstone[6]

SUNDAY, JANUARY 16, 2005
Lectionary Message

Topic: The Lamb of God
TEXT: John 1:29–42
Other Readings: Isa. 49:1–7; Ps: 40:1–11; 1 Cor. 1:1–9

There are only two places in the Bible where the phrase "the Lamb of God" occurs—and both are in our focal passage today. We also have a fuller explanation of the meaning of the phrase. John the Baptizer identifies the Lamb of God as the one "who takes away the sin of the world." We need to consider the context of this phrase "Lamb of God."

I. In our typical twenty-first-century image, a lamb is a sweet, innocent, cute baby sheep. They are what we know from petting zoos and from those cuddly, stuffed animals our children have. Maybe if we're of the right age we think of Sherrie Lewis and her puppet, Lamb-chop, on the children's television program. Our second thought, from the Biblical narratives, is of this innocent lamb being killed. And we're not really into this sacrifice thing. So what did the phrase "Lamb of God" connote to John the Baptizer's hearers?

II. The Old Testament background. As Christians we bring a lot of tradition to the phrase, most of which comes directly from John's pronouncement. But what would that phrase have connoted in its original usage? Clearly the first use of the phrase on the lips of John the Baptizer relates it to sacrifice—"who takes away the sins of the world." We would most likely consider some of the sacrificial texts in the Old Testament where lambs (sheep) are the common sacrificial animal. In Genesis 22 Isaac speaks of the animal for the sacrifice as a lamb: "Behold the fire and the wood. Where is the lamb for the whole burnt offering?" And Abraham's

---

[6]*Living with Style* (Burlington, Ont., Canada: Welch, 1986), pp. 95–101.

response implies the same understanding: "God himself will see to it/provide for himself the lamb for the whole burnt offering" (Gen. 22:7–8). The same Hebrew word for lamb in Genesis 22 is used in the Passover narrative (Exod. 12). Each household is to kill a lamb and rub some of its blood over the doorpost and lintel so that the death angel will pass over the household. The lamb is a sacrificial lamb. Likewise in Isaiah 53 the same word is used: the Suffering Servant is characterized "like a lamb that is led to the slaughter, and like a sheep that before its shearers is silent, so he did not open his mouth" (Isa. 53:7).

So which is John the Baptizer referring to when he calls Jesus the Lamb of God who takes away the sins of the world? Is it the Lamb sacrificed at the Passover, the Lamb slain and blood smeared over the lintel and doorpost so that the death angel would pass over the household? Yes. Is it the Lamb led to the slaughter in Isaiah 53, the Suffering Servant? Yes. Is it the substitutionary Lamb in the narrative of Abraham and Isaac, the Lamb-ram which was sacrificed in place of Isaac, the Lamb-ram God himself provided? Yes. All those images come together in the word picture John the Baptizer uses. All would have been very familiar to John's hearers.

III. And yet none of those texts and images of Lamb fully completes the message of the Baptizer. For the Lamb-ram in the Abraham-Isaac narrative was a substitute only for Isaac, not for the sins of the world. And the Lamb of the Passover only substituted for those within the individual household. Every household had to sacrifice its own lamb. And even the vicarious, substitutionary suffering of the Servant in Isaiah 53 was only for God's people, for many, yes, but in their mind-set for many in Israel: "stricken for the transgression of my people (53:8). . . . When you make his life an offering for sin (53:10). . . . The righteous one, my servant, shall make many righteous, and he shall bear their iniquities (53:11) . . . because he poured out himself to death, and was numbered with the transgressors; yet he bore the sin of many" (53:12). But John the Baptizer's message took on a new scope. The Lamb of God was not just a substitutionary sacrifice for one individual—an Isaac. Nor was he just a substitutionary sacrifice for a single household, as was the Passover lamb. Nor was he just the vicarious suffering servant sacrifice for just one people Israel, even the many that made up Israel. John saw clearly what Isaiah 53 intended—that this Suffering Servant was the sacrifice for *all* God's people. God's people weren't limited just to Israel. The "many" of Isaiah 53 became *all* in John's message. The word here is that this Lamb takes away the sins of the world. Not just the sins of some, but the sins of *all,* of *all* the world. And just a couple chapters later in this same Gospel John the Evangelist states concerning Jesus the Christ: "For God so loved the world [the cosmos] that He gave his only Son, that whosoever believes in Him—that *all* who believe in Him [anyone who believes, everyone who believes, *all* who believe]—will not perish, but will have everlasting life!" Quite a promise. Quite a Lamb!—Joel F. Drinkard Jr.

ILLUSTRATIONS

A FAMILY OFFERING.   Lamb was the familiar type of an offering to God. But this is more than a victim for sacrificial offering; for first, *the Lamb of God* is the victim whom God provides, as He provided the ram in place of Isaac (Gen. 22:8); and secondly, this Lamb Himself *beareth away the sin of the world.* In the coming of Christ, God Himself is active; He not only accepts an offering made by man, but He provides (for indeed He Himself is) the offering, and He Himself makes it. All that man has to do is to participate in this divine action. And that action is a *bearing* which has the effect of *taking away* the sin of the world.—William Temple[7]

A VERSATILE IMAGE.   The versatile image of the lamb was prominent in all three of the major traditions lying behind the ministry of John: the cultic, the prophetic, and the apocalyptic.

In all of these varied strands of Jewish usage, however, it is striking that none provides the precise antecedent of a *lamb (amnos)* that *takes away the sin of the world.* Jesus fulfilled many of the spiritual functions symbolized by the lamb in the Old Testament, yet he transcended them all. He was the Servant who suffered as a lamb (Acts 8:32–35), the true Passover sacrifice (1 Cor. 5:7), the unblemished offering (1 Peter 1:19), and the slain but conquering leader of the flock (Rev. 5:6, 12, 7:14, 17, 17:14, 22:1, 3). We cannot now determine just how many of these insights would have been clustered around the concept in the thinking of John himself. Probably the Evangelist intended the paschal allusion to be central (cf. 19:36 and Exod. 12:46). The instructed Christian reader, however, who has pondered the Old Testament and celebrated the Lord's Supper is heir to all of the multiple meanings that belong to the history of this rich symbol.—William E. Hull[8]

SERMON SUGGESTIONS

Topic: Promise and Fulfillment
TEXT: Isa. 49:1–7
Like the Lord's "Servant," Christ and his church (1) are especially chosen by God, (2) are God's secret weapon in the world, (3) are at last recognized and honored because of God's faithfulness.

Topic: What Makes Your Religious Leaders Thankful?
TEXT: 1 Cor. 1:1–9
(1) Your experience of the grace of God in Christ Jesus; (2) your expression of this grace—in a fullness of knowledge, in a completeness of ability to put this understanding into words, in the variety of spiritual gifts among Christ's people; (3) your promise as believers, sustained to the end by God's faithfulness.

WORSHIP AIDS
CALL TO WORSHIP.   "Behold, I stand at the door, and knock; if any man hear my voice and open the door, I will come in to him, and will sup with him, and he with me" (Rev. 3:20).

INVOCATION.   O Christ, we open our hearts individually to you; we open the heart of our fellowship of believers to you; and we would open the hearts of men and women everywhere to you. Grant that the intimacy of our communion with you may deepen our finest motives to serve you both here and wherever we go in this world.

---

[7]*Readings in St. John's Gospel* (London: Macmillan, 1963), pp. 23ff.
[8]In *The Broadman Bible Commentary*, Vol. 9 (Nashville, Tenn.: Broadman Press, 1970), p. 223.

OFFERTORY SENTENCE.   "Give unto the Lord the glory due unto his name: bring an offering, and come into his courts" (Ps. 96:8).

OFFERTORY PRAYER.   Loving Father, we do not always understand why we have enough and to spare when others have so little. But we do understand that we are stewards of what we have. Grant that our offerings may help supply bread where it is needed, and send forth your word, the bread of life, without which no one can truly live.

PRAYER.   Eternal God, Great Shepherd of the sheep, we look to you for all our needs. You provide our food and drink, the warmth of friendship, our health and strength, and human understanding and forgiveness. And when all these blessings are scarce, you give us courage to go on, patience to wait, and love that will not give up on you or on those who doubt us. In the best of times, we rest in you and find peace that passes all understanding. We thank you, Lord.

Even at this moment, we face testings: we are tempted to renege on the best we know, to take shortcuts to happiness, to allow those who are blind to their own needs and careless of ours to pressure us into foolish ways. May your rod of discipline keep us in right paths.

Because you are with us, we do not have to be afraid, whether of our sinful nature, of adversaries around us, or of the baffling brutalities of the world in which we live.

Bring us ever closer to you and to those who love and serve and praise you, both now and forevermore.

SERMON

Topic: The Relevance of Christ

TEXT: "What have you to do with us, Jesus of Nazareth?" (Mark 1:24)

Is Christ really relevant to the modern situation? Is Christianity not out of date for man come of age? Jesus Christ is supremely relevant to modern man. His day is not over; it has hardly begun. We have everything to do with Him, whoever we are, and for two main reasons. Because of who He is, because of His Divine Personality, Jesus Christ will not, and cannot, be casually dismissed. In Him we confront Ultimate Reality.

The other reason is to be found in the indispensability of Christ to the life of man. We may be happy, active, apparently self-sufficient, and secure in our materialism, but there exist in the depths of human nature basic needs which only Christ can satisfy. These needs are constant from age to age. What are they?

I. *There is the need for personal identity.* Contemporary man does not know who he is. This is obvious enough in his behavior.

Albert Camus, reflecting deeply on this theme, wrote in one of his books: "The world itself, whose single meaning I do not understand, is but a vast irrational. If only one could say just once, 'this is clear,' all would be saved." The good news of Christianity is that once in history the rationality of life, the purpose of God, and the identity of man have been made clear—in Jesus Christ! Jesus came to seek and to save the lost, to show man his origin and destiny in God the Father, to reveal to him what life is all about, and how it should be lived. From Him you learn that you belong to a god who made you for Himself, who loves you with an unwearying love, who suffers and forgives, who purposes to train you by the free probation of life on earth for a high calling that exceeds your wildest ambitions for yourself.

D. R. Davies was a restless, dynamic Welshman, on the search for a life worth living. He concludes his autobiography, *In Search of Myself,* by saying: "What I was searching for was my own identity, and without knowing it my search was for God. I had to give myself up exactly as I was, in the chaos of disillusion into which I had fallen, to find Him. I found Him, and became a new man."

II. *There is, next, the need for moral victory.* Modern man has mastered the atom, but he has not mastered himself. Our age has been described as one of intellectual giants and moral dwarfs. There is evidence in plenty to support this.

Look around at the world we live in. To be sure, the achievements of man are dazzlingly significant. No point whatever in denying that! There is, however, another side to be faced. The most decent of men are conscious of a civil war raging within them. We are victims of clashing loyalties and competing impulses. Sins of commission and sins of omission, the nightmare of every good man, haunt and harass us, burdening us with feelings of shame, regret, and guilt. Paul gave classic expression to this problem of the divided self, and the need for moral victory: "For the good that I would I do not: but the evil that I would not, that I do . . . O wretched man that I am! Who shall deliver me from the body of this death?" (Rom. 7:18, 24) And yet the purest, most high-minded legislator is himself tainted with the curse of sin and self. He is part of the problem, not the answer to it.

Who shall deliver us? Education, reply others. This is an old belief, at least as old as Plato. The Greeks equated sin with ignorance, persuasively proclaiming education as the only solution. It is certainly our duty to educate the mind, and Jesus Himself declared that we are to love the Lord our God with our mind as well as with the heart and soul and strength. Reason is a precious gift of God, and it must be developed and disciplined to His glory. Realism, however, compels us to recognize that the best education in the world is as powerless as legislation to lift a disillusioned, defeated soul to moral victory. The worst calamity that can befall any society, any individual, is an unholy alliance between high intelligence and low integrity.

Who shall deliver us? Christ, we reply. Where all else dismally fails, He dynamically succeeds. When we call Him "Savior" we call Him by His name. Hear the thrilling, triumphant assertion of the Christian Gospel: "He is able to save to the uttermost" (Heb. 7:25).

"What have you to do with us, Jesus of Nazareth?" I don't know about you, friend. You may be able to meet and master the enemies of your soul in your own strength; but I cannot. I need to make the victory of Christ my own. I suggest that you do too, and that is what Jesus has to do with you. "This is the victory that overcomes the world," cried John lyrically, "our faith" (1 John 5:4).

III. *There is, once more, the need for final security.* Today we tend to place an inordinate emphasis on material security. Every effort is made to protect men and women from the contingent and accidental. A measure of security is a legitimate demand for all responsible people to make, and not least those with family responsibilities.

The inevitable death awaiting us mocks the best-laid security plans. It is frivolous and, indeed, a delusion to adopt a devil-may-care or a head-in-the-sand attitude to death. It remains the grim spectre that it is, the enemy of reason, of achievement, of love. None of us can live with joy and abandon and self-sacrificing devotion until we have discovered a security that transcends death and enables us to laugh in its face. So we need Jesus Christ as desperately as our fathers needed Him. When our lives are hid with God in Christ, we are secure. When we can shout with Paul the Apostle, "For me to live is Christ, and to die is gain," we are secure. When we are sure that nothing, literally nothing, can separate us from the love of God in Christ, we are secure.

The relevance of Christ to our lives is beyond doubt. What we have to settle is the relation of our lives to Christ.—John N. Gladstone[9]

SUNDAY, JANUARY 23, 2005
Lectionary Message

Topic: Unity in Christ
TEXT: 1 Cor 1:10–18
Other Readings: Isa. 9:1–4; Ps. 27:1, 4–9; Matt. 4:12–23

No church that Paul started did he agonize over more than the church in Corinth. This was a church that often "just didn't get it." His concern is evident even from the opening words of the first epistle to the Corinthians.

I. Paul's appeal is urging, begging his brothers and sisters in Christ's name that they be of the same word (that is, in agreement), that they have no divisions, that they have the same mind and intent. Now such an appeal clearly indicates that there were divisions in the church. (You don't beg for actions not to occur unless they are occurring already!) Note Paul's words urging unity in just the first verse: "all of you," "agreement," "no divisions," "be united," "same mind," and "same purpose." This profusion of words calling for unity belies the reality that existed in the church at Corinth. The church was anything but united. There was strife, wrangling, contention in the church at Corinth. It was filled with cliques and factions. But the factions had not yet reached the point of a full breach. Paul has hopes his letter will restore unity in the church. After all, he does address the letter to the entire church at Corinth, not just one of the groups. Paul mentions at least four of these groups. Each felt their faction was the correct one. The factions were each related to one of the early Christian leaders who had apparently evangelized different individuals in the church at Corinth. Some had heard the gospel from Peter, others from Apollos, and others from Paul, and they said they thus belonged to Peter's group or Apollos's group or Paul's group. In addition to these factions, one other group said they belonged to Christ.

This last group had it right but may have been just as wrong. They were right in their theology of saying they belonged to Christ. But if they were using that theology to promote factionalism, they didn't have it right. I guess today we would say it in terms of Christian denominations: I belong to the Presbyterian Church, I belong to the Methodist Church, I belong to the Baptist Church, I belong to the Catholic Church, I belong to the Christian Church. Each church feels it has a special correctness in terms of doctrine or polity.

I grew up in a very conservative denomination. I was taught in Sunday school that my church was the only way to heaven. No other churches were truly Christian—not even other

---

[9]*A Magnificent Faith* (Hantsport, Nova Scotia, Canada: Lancelot Press, 1979), pp. 26–33.

mainline denominations. But from a rather early age I had some problems with that teaching. My brother and his wife belonged to a different tradition, although he had been raised in the same church as I had been. My mother had been raised in yet another denomination, and she had a brother who was a pastor in that denomination. And four of my cousins were also ministers in that denomination. My home church changed from that early position I was taught in Sunday school. I could treat as brothers and sisters in Christ those in other Christian traditions. Later, as a pastor, I participated in forming a new evangelical pastors' association. As a part of that pastors' association we shared in communion with ones from virtually every Christian denomination. We still had differences of doctrine and practice, but we could nevertheless break bread as fellow believers around the Lord's table.

II. Paul next asks those in Corinth the crucial question, "Is Christ divided?" The answer is obvious. No, Christ isn't divided. Wasn't then, isn't now! But the church in Corinth was certainly divided, much to Paul's dismay. And furthermore, Christ's church is woefully divided today. The division in Corinth seems to have been over personalities—Peter, Apollos, Paul. Today division is over doctrine, polity, and practice. What is the answer? Is it a new denomination? That would be, in effect, another schism, another division. Well, what about church union? A number of denominations have tried that but not too successfully. The rub comes because most churches want to keep their own traditions, doctrines, and practices. We want merger so long as the other group will adopt our (correct!) position. We can answer Paul's question: No, Christ isn't divided. But we don't have the answer to the issue of division it poses as yet.

III. Paul asks two other questions: Was Paul crucified for you? Or were you baptized in the name of Paul? Paul's point is that it was not he that was crucified for the Corinthians (or for us). Nor was it Apollos, nor Peter. Christ alone was the one crucified for our sins. Likewise the Corinthians were not baptized in Paul's name, nor Apollos's, nor Peter's. They were all baptized in one name: in the name of Jesus Christ. And so were we.

Our unity comes not from any group to which we belong. Our unity isn't just based on our race or gender or nationality or social status. All those conditions may be issues of divisiveness. Our unity can come only from Christ. And at that it isn't a matter of a local church to which we belong, or even of a denomination to which we belong. Again those may be factors that tend to divide us from our fellow believers.

What was Paul's mission in reference to the Corinthians? Was it to convert and baptize as many as possible? Was he striving to gain some convert feathers for his cap? No. Paul said his mission was not primarily to baptize new converts. He even expresses thanksgiving that he baptized only a few in Corinth (and admits he isn't even sure who all he baptized). It sounds like some were boasting about the numbers they had baptized.

Paul understands the real purpose of his ministry. His primary ministry is to proclaim the gospel, to evangelize, to share the message of the cross. He is not to preach himself or promote himself. His message is a simple one—Jesus Christ and Him crucified. What should be our priority? Is it just a matter of numbers? Are we to get into a race to see how many we can add to our church? To a divided church, Paul speaks of that gospel—not a power message on success, not a message of wealth, not even a message of worldly wisdom or philosophical sophistication. Simply the message of the cross: Jesus Christ and Him crucified. If there is anything that can unite us, it is a common faith in Christ and Him crucified—not fancy theology or rhetoric, simply the word of the cross.—Joel F. Drinkard Jr.

ILLUSTRATIONS

THE INNER SPIRIT.   Each one of us has a spirit, this power of life in us, and like breath it is not just something that is in us but something that also issues from us. Every man has the capacity, more at some times than at others, to project some of this power of his own life, his vitality, into others. It is the power literally to in-spire, breath into, and although it is invisible and intangible and cannot be put into a test tube or under a microscope it is perhaps the greatest and most dangerous power that we have.

Team spirit, group spirit, *esprit de corps* in French—all these point to the power that can be generated by a group of people and can be generated with such force that to be in the group or even just near it is to risk being caught up by it and for a time at least transformed by it, made drunk on it. The least likely person can be so galvanized by the spirit generated by the crowd at a horse race or a football game that their madness becomes his own and he finds himself one of them. Or the least likely person can be so possessed by the spirit of a mob bent on destruction that he joins in deeds of violence and hate that otherwise he would never be capable of and that leave him, once the spirit has passed, gutted and empty like a house that has been swept by flame.—Frederick Buechner[10]

CREATIVE DIFFERENCES.   A member may choose to leave a congregation over some issues, and his leaving need not be decried as destructive. There are occasions when a member clearly senses that his position and that of the body [are] clearly divergent. He may then exercise God's will in retaining the sense of unity of the fellowship by withdrawing himself. His stewardship and outlook can effectively be used by God in another place and perhaps more effectively be channeled by another congregation. Pastor and caring leaders sometimes need to bless this departure as inspired by God. Prayerful and careful evaluation of the circumstance will help determine if such is God's will.

Above all experiences of anger is withdrawal; the Spirit of God needs to be invoked as constant mediator in differences, a reconciler in distances, and a guide in new commitments. God has frequently used even the angry withdrawal by a member (sometimes a caring gesture, as we shall note yet) as a means through which he multiplies his body and achieves new unity of purpose.—Daniel G. Bagby[11]

SERMON SUGGESTIONS

Topic: Three Gifts the Christ Brings
TEXT: Isa. 9:1–4
(1) Light. (2) Joy. (3) Victory.

Topic: Dissenters
TEXT: 1 Cor. 1:10–17
(1) The real problem: competitive strife. (2) The potential solution: recognition of the power of self-denying unity given in Jesus Christ. (3) The urgency: "lest the cross of Christ be emptied of its power."

---

[10]*The Magnificent Defeat* (New York: Seabury Press, 1966), pp. 112ff.
[11]*Understanding Anger in the Church* (Nashville, Tenn.: Broadman Press, 1979), p. 142.

WORSHIP AIDS

CALL TO WORSHIP.   "We are laborers together with God: ye are God's husbandry, ye are God's building. According to the grace of God which is given unto me, as a wise master builder, I have laid the foundation, and another buildest thereon. But let every man take heed how he buildeth thereupon. For other foundation can no man lay than that is laid, which is Jesus Christ" (1 Cor. 3:9–11).

INVOCATION.   Today, O God, build us into a habitation fit for thy Spirit to indwell. We claim as the foundation of our works and worship, Jesus Christ, whom we praise and whose will and way we seek to follow, and in whose name we make our prayer.

OFFERTORY SENTENCE.   "As we have therefore opportunity, let us do good unto all men, especially unto them who are of the household of faith" (Gal. 6:10).

OFFERTORY PRAYER.   O thou who hast given us all that we have and hast made us thy own children, use our lives and material gifts for the spreading of the gospel to the ends of the earth as well as for the blessing of those already near and dear to us.

PRAYER.   Gracious Father, we humbly beseech thee for thy universal church. Fill it with all truth, in all truth with all peace. Where it is corrupt, purge it, and where it is in error, direct it; where it is superstitious, rectify it; where anything is amiss, reform it; where it is right, strengthen and confirm it; where it is in want, furnish it; where it is divided and rent asunder, make up the breaches thereof, O thou Holy One of Israel; for the sake of Jesus Christ our Lord and Savior.—William Laud

SERMON
Topic: How Long?
TEXT: Pss. 13 and 82

The cry became a trademark of the American civil rights movement. The walk to Montgomery in 1965 was concluded with a speech from Martin Luther King Jr. He described the agenda of the movement and then asked the question of the hour, "How long will it take?" He answered his own question with a spontaneous litany that came to be characteristic of his sermons:

> It will not take long, because truth pressed to the earth will rise again. How long? Not long, because no lie can live forever. How long? Not long, because you still reap what you sow. How long? Not long. Because the arm of the moral universe is long but it bends toward justice. How long? Not long, 'cause mine eyes have seen the glory of the coming of the Lord.

As effective and poetic as this theme sounds in the contemporary cry for justice, the question did not originate with King. He had a keen sense of the biblical cry for justice. "How long?" is a lament that flows with the tears of Israel. It is the question of God spoken by Moses to Pharaoh, "How long will you refuse to humble yourself before me?" God challenged

Moses, "How long will you refuse to keep my commandments?" and the people, "How long shall this wicked congregation complain against me?" It was Job's accusation to Bildad, "How long will you torment me and break me in pieces with words?" It was Isaiah's question before the holiness of God in the Temple and Jeremiah's question raised to condemn the wickedness of the nation. Mostly as a nagging complaint against injustice, the poetic question is raised some twenty times in the Psalms.

At the height of the civil rights movement and the Vietnam War, some of our folks had been put on the defensive. They were getting a barrage of complaints from their young adult children. Most of the men were well employed by large corporations. They tended to see themselves with the "establishment" rather than the revolution. I recall a comment from one of our deacons with roots deeply planted in Calvinism: "I am not sure that I can handle justice; I'll just pray for mercy." He offered a gentle protest to the protests, but he also revealed a theology of sin that was relevant to the discussion of justice: "All of us have sinned." No one of us is good enough to pass judgment on the rest of us.

I. *Lamentation is a cry for justice.* We have been strongly influenced by the movement toward the gospel of positive thinking. Norman Vincent Peale was a popular advocate of a new interpretation of Christian religion that attempts to purge all negative thinking from our minds. Robert Shuler has taken up Peale's mantle. The legitimate message here is that we become what we think. People who dwell on the negative usually get what they expect from life. We need to think positively about ourselves, our companions, and our God. Thus, we must think positive thoughts and offer positive prayers to God.

The whiny complaint of discomfort and injustice is a sign of immaturity. Children often whine to their parents about matters totally beyond the control of any human power. Our impatience and difficulty with the child's protest has something to do with our mortal limitations. Parents are constantly reminded by children that we are not gods. No matter how much we may sympathize with the discomfort of our children, parents cannot stop the rain or instantly arrive at destinations. Complaints can be understood and affirmed, but they cannot be fixed by loving parents, and the surest sign of growth and maturity in our children is their acceptance of the things parents cannot change. The "Serenity Prayer" of AA, written by Reinhold Niebuhr, is a call to maturity: "God, grant me the serenity to accept the things I cannot change; the courage to change the things I can; and the wisdom to know the difference."

At bottom, the lament of the child to a parent or our prayer of lament to God is a reflection of the deep sense of justice within us. The human conscience seems to detect meanness and injustice whether or not we have been educated or trained in ethics, especially if we are the victims.

II. *God joins the lament against injustice.* In Genesis the God of creation regrets that humans had ever been created. In the story of Noah, God lets justice roll down with the floods. Yet the flood story concludes with a rainbow of hope for humanity. Psalm 82 is God's protest against the gods. Walter Wink names the powers identified in the New Testament with the world of spiritual darkness. The "gods" are no longer religious deities represented in the pagan temples and shrines. The powers of our time are the institutions, governments, and corporations that have come to exist only for themselves with little or no concern for the future of humanity. I can well imagine God in a meeting of the CEOs, governors, and generals of our world raising the question: "How long will you judge unjustly and show partiality to the wicked?" James Muilenburg, *The Way of Israel,* notes that the God of the Old Testament exposes injustice through raising questions, like the inquiries addressing Adam and Eve: "Where are you?" and "What have you done?"

III. *Lamentation is a statement of faith.* The literature of lamentation is a legitimate expression of faith in God. Walter Brueggemann recognized a form of protest in the deep grief of the prophets for the injustice of their world. Instead of raising an army to start a revolution against the king, Jeremiah wept. He grieved publicly. He reflected the injury and hurt inflicted by injustice. His deep sobs of grief resonated throughout the kingdom and echoed down though the centuries. Grief was a means of exposing corruption in high places. In his book of Lamentations, Jeremiah, like Job, wished that he had never been born and accused God of being like a "deceitful brook." Beneath the sobs flowed a stream of faith in a righteous God who demands and gives justice.

Perhaps the greatest value in the prayer of lamentation is the value in putting words to our deepest thoughts. I learned early in ministry that churches, like families, are prone to complain when things are not going well. The first impulse is to silence the protest along with the right to speak. Often misperceptions and distortions of the facts are represented in the frustration that emerges from the pain of conflict and the hope for success in the church. I had a teacher who once advised ministerial students to keep the baptismal waters moving to silence the protests from the pews. Maybe the protest does not need to be silenced. As long as we know that our laments are not the last word, we might find the redemptive value in whining to God.

Our expectation of something better here is a vote of confidence in the justice and goodness of God. Our statement and offering to God of our deepest thoughts, however distorted, is the beginning of chance within us. Our prayer to God must always be a surrender to the will of God in which we must make ourselves available to service. Walter Brueggemann observed that the Psalms of complaint usually turn from venom to self-reflection on the words "But Thou."

Jesus' prayer of lament from the cross, "My God, why have you forsaken me?" came out of Psalm 22. The psalmist also writes: "Yet you are holy, enthroned on the praises of Israel." Psalm 13 begins with "How long, O Lord? Will you forget me forever?" and ends in trust: "But I trusted in your steadfast love; my heart shall rejoice in your salvation."—Larry Dipboye

SUNDAY, JANUARY 30, 2005
Lectionary Message
Topic: What Does the Lord Require?
TEXT: Mic. 6:1–8
Other Readings: Ps. 15; 1 Cor. 1:18–31; Matt. 5:1–12

In the TV drama *Law and Order,* Assistant District Attorney Jack McCoy prosecutes the defendants accused of heinous crimes. He is handsome, brash, and brilliant in the courtroom. He regularly seeks the maximum punishment for the accused. His cross-examination of defense witnesses picks at every inconsistency in their testimony. He relentlessly confronts the defendant. He is at his best in his summation, demolishing the defense attorney's assertions. Jack poignantly and powerfully shows the horror of the crime. He points his finger accusingly at the defendant as he intones, "And this man, the defendant, killed his victim in cold blood. No one can excuse what he has done. You, the jury, must find him guilty as charged." Rarely does Jack lose a case. The evidence is overwhelming; the defense is unable to convince the jury of any reasonable doubt. The jury quickly brings in the verdict: guilty as charged.

I. Look with me as a parallel panorama is set in the book of Micah. The passage is a legal case. The prophet Micah is the prosecuting attorney, Israel is the defendant, and the jury is composed of the mountains or hills and foundations of the earth. The movement of the passage is clear. The text starts with the reminder that the words are Yahweh's words. Micah, the prophet and prosecuting attorney, is told to stand and present his case; he is to address the hills and mountains. The hills, mountains, and foundations of the earth are an appropriate jury because they were witness to God's covenant with Israel. They know the conditions of covenant and can judge whether Israel has broken covenant or not. The legal case presented by Micah is based on charges Yahweh has made. Yahweh's charges are stated. First, Yahweh asks in what manner he has wronged Israel or how he has made Israel weary. Do the prophet's words drip with sarcasm as he asks the questions? The questions are rhetorical. They expect no answer. Yet the answer is obvious. Yahweh has done no wrong to Israel. He hasn't wearied Israel by his inaction.

II. Next, the prosecuting attorney moves to what Yahweh has done. He has brought up his people from Egypt. He has freed a people who were enslaved. He has brought them through the Wilderness Wandering and provided their leaders, Moses, Aaron, and Miriam. God continually delivered Israel. (Now we probably need an aside to remember what Israel had done through all this time. They continually murmured, complained, and rebelled against God. At every juncture, they complained, whether about the [lack of] food and water, or rebelled against Moses, or made a Golden Calf to lead them while Moses was receiving the covenant on Mt. Sinai.) What we really see is God's faithfulness alongside Israel's faithlessness.

III. In verses 6–7 the people respond to the prophet and God. One cannot be certain if their questions are sincere or not. But the exaggerated and excessive progression of the sacrifices implies that the people are disingenuous. Alternatively, the prophet may be mimicking the people—he may be answering in the way he expects the people to respond. "What sacrifice shall I bring to God?" The response is a series of increasingly extravagant sacrifices: Shall I bring burnt offerings, the typical offering brought to God? Or shall I offer year-old calves (more costly than a young animal because it has been cared for and fed for a year)? Shall I offer thousands of rams (no longer a single animal, even a costly calf, but thousands of rams, adult male sheep, a fortune in a sacrifice)? Or even tens of thousands of rivers of oil (now the sacrifice has become so extravagant that they are whole rivers of precious oil—and not merely rivers, but myriads, tens of thousands of rivers of oil)? Finally the people suggest the ultimate sacrifice: Shall I give my firstborn as the sacrifice for my sin?

IV. In verse 8 the prophet responds with God's desire: "He has told you, O mortal, what is good; and what does the LORD require of you but to do justice, and to love kindness, and to walk humbly with your God?" The sacrifice God desires is not a costly gift, no extravagant offering. What God most desires is proper relationships, both on the horizontal plane with one's fellow humans (doing justice and loving kindness), and on the vertical plane between humans and himself (walking with humility before God). The real issue isn't what we do religiously—going through all the proper motions of our ritual—but is instead how we lives our lives in relationship, our ethical and moral behavior. This message is found often in the prophets: "For I desire steadfast love and not sacrifice, the knowledge of God rather than burnt offerings" (Hos. 6:6; cf. Amos 5:21–25; Isa. 1:10–17, and others). Jesus twice uses this same message of God's desire (although quoting from Hosea 6:6 rather than Micah): "I desire mercy, not sacrifice."

V. I note from this passage a balance we often see missing from contemporary society. Those who are secular humanists agree with the need for the horizontal plane—with proper relationships with all humankind; but they omit the vertical plane. Many in the religious sphere focus almost entirely on the vertical sphere: just believe in God; that's all you need to do. But this text reminds us that both are necessary—right relationship with God that in turn also leads to right relationship with all humankind. Micah's message from twenty-eight hundred years ago is just as relevant today: "He has told you, O mortal, what is good; and what does the LORD require of you but to do justice, and to love kindness, and to walk humbly with your God?"—Joel F. Drinkard Jr.

ILLUSTRATIONS

GOD'S PROFOUNDEST WISHES.   He willeth not that any should perish, but that all should come to repentance; by repentance, to faith in a bleeding Lord; by faith, to spotless love; to the full image of God renewed in the heart, and producing all holiness of conversation. Can you doubt of this, when you remember the judge of all is likewise the Savior of all? Hath He not bought you with His own blood, that ye might not perish, but have everlasting life? Oh make proof of His mercy, rather than His justice; of His love, rather than the thunder of His power! He is not far from every one of us; and He is now come, not to condemn, but to save the world. He standeth in the midst! Sinner, doth He not now, even now, knock at the door of thy heart? Oh that thou mayest know, at least in this thy day, the things that belong unto thy peace! Oh that ye may now give yourselves to Him who gave Himself for you, in humble faith, in holy, active, patient love! So shall ye rejoice with exceeding joy in His day, when He cometh in that clouds of heaven!—John Wesley[12]

CREATIVE ASSISTANCE.   I heard the story of an old Italian artist who had lost some of his skill. One evening he sat discouraged before a painting he had just completed. He noticed that he had lost some of his touch. The canvas didn't burst with life as his previous work had once done. As he went to bed, his son heard him say, "I have failed, I have failed."

Later that evening, his son, also an artist, came to examine his father's work, and he, too, noticed that it did not reflect his father's usual work. Taking the palette and brush, he worked far into the night, adding a little touch here, smudge there, a little color here, a bit of depth, a shadow or two, some highlights. The son worked until he knew that the work would fulfill his father's vision.

Morning came, and the father descended into the studio. He stood before the perfect canvas and in utter delight exclaimed, "Why, I have wrought better than I knew!"—Gigi Graham Tchivdjian[13]

---

[12]"The Great Assize," in *Tongues of Angels, Tongues of Men* (New York: Doubleday, 1999), p. 42.
[13]Gigi Graham Tchivdjian, with Ruth Bell Graham, *A Quiet Knowing* (Nashville: W. Publishing Group, 2001), pp. 172ff.

SERMON SUGGESTIONS

Topic: God's Lawsuit

TEXT: Mic. 6:1–8 (NEB)

(1) The case for the prosecution: a wayward and ungrateful people. (2) Hypothetical reparations by the defense: bribery with good and costly deeds. (3) God's requirements: (a) to do his revealed will as prescribed, (b) to be faithful to him and to serve others from the heart, (c) to "live in humble fellowship" (TEV) with him.

Topic: Paradoxes of the Cross

TEXT: 1 Cor. 1:18–31

(1) It is wisdom. (2) It is power. (3) It is glory for God.

WORSHIP AIDS

CALL TO WORSHIP.   "Thanks be to God, which giveth us the victory through our Lord Jesus Christ" (1 Cor. 15:57).

INVOCATION.   Today we meet to worship in the assurance that in our Lord Jesus Christ, we are victorious both in this world and in the world to come. May the joy of this assurance radiate in our prayers, in our hymns, and in all our spoken and wordless acts.

OFFERTORY SENTENCE.   "Whatsoever ye do in word or deed, do all in the name of the Lord Jesus, giving thanks to God and the Father by him" (Col. 3:17).

OFFERTORY PRAYER.   Accept these our gifts, O Lord, as tokens of our mindfulness of thy presence in our lives. Grant us the will, the desire, and the love to be gracious and faithful stewards of the many blessings that thou hast bestowed upon us.—Rodney K. Miller.

PRAYER.   On the night when you were betrayed, Lord, you were giving thanks. Why weren't you bitter and anxious, as we would be? We do not give thanks when someone turns against us. We vow revenge. It takes even less than betrayal to stir our ire: if the car breaks down, if the potatoes boil dry, if we hit our thumb with a hammer, if the store misbills us, then we act as though heaven's door has slammed in our face.

Yet, on the same night that a companion turned you in, and best friends deserted you, and prominent citizens tried you in a kangaroo court, and soldiers tortured you, on that very same night—you gave thanks.

O Christ, we acknowledge that we curse more than we praise, we damn more than we thank, we grumble more than we rejoice. Give us, Christ, the smallest portion of your grace so that whatever happens to us, we shall be glad simply to have lived and to have known your love.—Thomas T. Troeger

SERMON

Topic: What Do You Want Jesus to Do for You?

TEXT: Mark 10:46–53

It is Jesus asking the question: "What do you want me to do for you?" It almost sounds like the question we hear every Christmas: "What do you want Santa to bring you?" And judging from the content of my prayers and the prayers I hear of others, our response is basically the same as the child at Christmas. We have a long list of things we want God to give us. We want our health to be wonderful, our children to be great, our friends to be happy, and the whole world to live at peace. So it is fascinating to listen to the two stories, back-to-back in Mark, where Jesus puts this question to his disciples and to the blind beggar Bartimeus.

As you remember, Jesus has told his disciples at Caesarea Philippi that He was destined for Jerusalem and there he would establish the Kingdom of God and be crucified and resurrected. He has had his run-in with Peter, who could not imagine that the Messiah of God would end up in such a mess and who told Jesus plainly that his predictions were stupid. But Jesus has insisted, and he is now on the way to Jerusalem in order to make visible the Kingdom of God.

As his disciples travel with him, they too are preoccupied with the whole exciting adventure of the revolutionary changes which will come about when Jesus makes visible his Kingdom. They do not have $87 billion to rebuild Jerusalem, but they know that there will be an upheaval. The old will be out. The new will be in. The rich will be sent away empty. The poor will be lifted up. So who is going to run this new world? The obvious choices in their mind are those who have been closest to Jesus in his ministry. They will be his transition team. James and John figure they are the best suited to be the top two administrators, and they come to Jesus and ask him to do them a favor. Jesus asks them, "What do you want me to do for you?" In this conversation it seems clear that the disciples have only one thing on their mind, and Jesus understands that they are asking him to do one particular thing for them. "What do you want me to do for you?"

James and John have a very specific and clear request. They have thought about it. They are not wanting some vague and undefined happiness or peace for Jerusalem. They want Jesus to appoint them to the two top administrative positions in the Kingdom of God. They want to sit next to the throne on the right hand and on the left. They know what they want. They want to have more power.

Jesus does not berate them or scold them for their ambition. He simply wonders if they fully understand what they are asking for. Do they really understand what is preparatory for the positions they seek? With the ambition they have for greatness, are they really able to become the kind of servants of others that would prepare them for the positions they want? The positions of leadership in the Kingdom of God are given by God to those who are servants of others. Indeed, we may have problems with the Roman Catholic church's rapid multiplication of saints; we do share with them the criteria that whether it be Mother Teresa of India or Clara Mae Ellis of Henderson, the leaders in the body of Christ rise to their places of honor by service to others. But James and John clearly knew what they wanted and asked Jesus for it.

And the road show moves on toward Jerusalem and makes its way through Jericho. As the crowd of the curious, the skeptic, and the faithful moves along the road, the blind beggar Bartimeus hears the noise and asks what is happening. Somebody in the crowd throws off the answer that it is Jesus passing by, and Bartimeus begins to act out of control. He starts screaming, "Jesus son of David, have mercy on me." Over here, hey, look at me. Jesus, son of David, over here. So often the poor and handicapped have trouble getting noticed. Bartimeus wants to be noticed. The crowd tries to hush him. Push him back. Brush him off. Get us a mayor who will keep the beggars out of Times Square. Just pretend like you don't hear him.

He is a nobody. But he keeps yelling and Jesus tells them to bring that man forward. And Jesus asks Bartimeus the same question, "What do you want me to do for you?"

It is a lesson for us to learn from Jesus that in both cases he asks them what they want. We might very well have assumed that we knew that a blind man would want to see, but Jesus asks him. Perhaps he had a blind son as well and he would want his son to see rather than himself. Jesus makes no assumptions. He does not act like he knows what they want or knows what they need more than they do. He calls them forward and asks them what they want him to do for them. He asks Bartimeus, and again there is suggested in the nature of the conversation the implication that Jesus is not looking for a laundry list of things that Bartimeus wants done. There seems to be an understanding that Jesus is asking for the one thing Bartimeus wants more than anything else in the whole world.

Bartimeus knows immediately what he wants. "I want to see." He wants to have his sight. He has spent his whole life dreaming of the possibility of sight. Sitting by the side of the road, he has had a lot of time to reflect upon the one thing he most wants. Day after day his prayers have gone up. Slowly, year by year the other things have fallen away, but always there is this one thing, *sight*. He wants to see. Give me my sight. Master, let me receive my sight. And Jesus gives him his sight.

There are so many things that fascinate us about these stories and Jesus' response. What do you want Jesus to do for you? No, not that long grocery list of little petty wants and wishes. What is the one thing that you want Jesus to give you? The disciples want power and position in the Kingdom and Jesus says, "Well, to get that you must prepare for that position by service." Bartimeus says he wants to see; he wants wholeness. He wants his one major deficit restored. He wants the one sense that he is lacking completed. He wants to be made whole. What do you want Jesus to do for you? What is the one thing needed for you?

The disciples and Bartimeus both knew very clearly what they wanted from Jesus. And in some ways it is a bit discouraging. The disciples and Bartimeus both wanted something for themselves. There is no great wish for world peace, or that all the hungry in the world might be fed. Every year we send out lots of cards and notices, and we all say so easily that our one great wish is that there would be peace on earth, but when James and John and Bartimeus are asked what is the one thing they want more than anything else it is something personal. Power and position, or healing and sight. And Jesus does not launch into some sermon about "Seek ye first the kingdom of God, and His righteousness and all these other things will be added unto you." He hears the cry of each of them and tells the disciples how they can prepare for the positions they want, and he gives Bartimeus his prayer.

What is the one thing you want Jesus to do for you? James and John and Bartimeus have rejected the temptation to use their own opportunity to talk about hurting others, about revenge. There is an old story about a feud. Two knights had been competing against each other since they were little boys. The competition and jealousy was horrible. One day one of the knights found an old bottle that, uncorked, produced a genie who told the knight that he had one wish. He could wish for anything he wanted in the world, but he needed to know that whatever he wished for himself, his rival would get double. The knight wrestled with that choice for a long time. Finally, he told the genie, I have my wish, my one wish: make me blind in one eye.

James and John and Bartimeus are beyond that point. They are deep down inside themselves where they are looking at themselves and looking at what they feel they are lacking.

They look at their lives and see something missing. We talk a lot about self-esteem and act as if we believe that all that matters is to believe that we are OK, but the story of the Scriptures is that when we look at ourselves long enough and clearly enough we find that there is a hole, a space, something missing; our picture of ourselves is missing an arm, we do not have a heart, our face has no eye, our mouth has no smile. Kindergarten teachers are trained to look at the drawings of the children to see how the children see themselves. When we look at who we think we are there is a space that we think needs to be filled with a sense of power and importance to make us complete. When we look at ourselves there are no eyes because we are so blind we cannot see. When we come before Jesus he asks us, "What do you want me to do for you? What is the piece you need me to give you to make you whole?" "Go and sell all you have and give to the poor," Jesus told one man. The Rich Young Ruler knew he needed something, but he did not know he needed to unburden his heart from his material possessions. What do you want Jesus to do for you? Salvation is the gift of wholeness. Salvation is the bringing of the gift to completion, the picture of ourselves in God's image. The gift of God's creation is that we are created in the image of God, and the picture gets distorted. Jesus asks us, "What do you want me to do for you?" What is it that you see lacking in your life that you need to have given to you by God, because you cannot give it to yourself? What is that one thing that hinders you from the joy and the fullness of life in God's kingdom? Not a long list of nice little things we would like for everybody, but that one thing that is absent from your heart. "What do you want me to do for you?"

"Master, I want to be made whole, I want to see." And Jesus said, "Receive your sight."—Rick Brand

SUNDAY, FEBRUARY 6, 2005
Lectionary Message

Topic: Dwelling with God
TEXT: Matt. 17:1–9
Other Readings: Exod. 24:12–18; Ps. 2; 2 Pet. 1:16–21

Peter and James and John want to stay right there on that mountain. And who wouldn't? Jesus' face shines like the sun, and his clothes are dazzling white. Moses and Elijah, heroes the disciples have heard about all their lives, are even there. Peter wants to freeze the moment in time. Then Peter said to Jesus, "Lord, it is good for us to be here; if you wish, I will make three dwellings here, one for you, one for Moses, and one for Elijah." But Peter's suggestion dies the death of many offered to a wiser person: it is simply ignored. Luke's version of the story offers a comment on Peter's idea: "not knowing what he was saying." Here, however, the idea just fades away because Jesus recognizes time can't be frozen. As a proverb puts it, time and the tide wait for no man.

Jesus, too, has reason to stay. Staying means not facing the dark days he senses are ahead. Staying would mean not drinking from a bitter cup. But Jesus knows that staying put is not an option. We know this, too, at least intuitively; nevertheless, we often join with Peter in saying, "Can't we just stay put for a while?"

What then are we to do with our mountaintop experiences if we can't cling to them? Even if we can't stay too long, we can still relish the time we have. Peter's timing is bad, but his impulse is good. Moses, one of the heroes with them on the mountain, has dwelt with God on a mountain before, and he stayed there for forty days (Exod. 24:18). The challenges that awaited Moses would require the strength he acquired atop the mountain with God. We, however, have a tendency always to rush ahead. Too often the next item on our to do list calls us onward when lingering is in order. We can't enjoy the highs forever, but we can relish them long enough to recharge our batteries and prepare for what lies ahead. The valleys will come soon enough, and once we reach them the fuel we acquired atop the mountain may be needed to get us through.

You may be saying that this is all well and good, but it's a moot point for you because you haven't had a mountaintop spiritual experience in quite some time. Well, if the mountain won't come to you, go to the mountain. It's true that we cannot manufacture spiritual experiences, but it is also true that we can seek them. We may need to go in search of our mountains if they do not come to us. Jesus and the disciples didn't just stumble upon the mountaintop; Jesus chose to go there and chose to bring the disciples with him. At other times in Matthew and the other Gospels he seeks out mountains as a place to escape.

If we will make the time to seek God in lofty places, we can be transformed as Jesus was there before the disciples. After all, it is not just this one place in Matthew where something important happens on a mountain. The end of Jesus' time in the wilderness is spent on a mountaintop just before he begins his public ministry (4:8). His greatest sermon is preached on a mountainside (chapters 5–7). And as he speaks to the disciples for the last time after his Resurrection, he stands again with them atop a mountain (28:16). God can transform and renew us amid the day-to-day din, but drawing aside to a lofty place may open a path for the Spirit.

Mountains are a source not only of strength but also of hope. The psalmist proclaims, "I will look unto the hills, whence cometh my strength." Two mountain ranges dominated the geography of the region, and they seem also to have dominated the psyche of the people. God, whom the psalmist frequently refers to as "the Most High," protects believers by placing them in a high place: "For in the day of trouble he will keep me safe in his dwelling; he will hide me in the shelter of his tabernacle and set me high upon a rock" (Ps. 27:5, NIV). We can find ourselves mired in the same valleys where the psalmist found his troubles, and we can join our voice with his: "From the ends of the earth I call to you, I call as my heart grows faint; lead me to the rock that is higher than I" (Ps. 61:2, NIV).

We may live more of our stories than we wish in the valley, but the good news is that we serve the Most High, the Lord of the transforming mountaintops. That other champion of the faith atop the Mount of Transformation, Elijah, knew God's power to work in the high places. After all, it was atop Mount Carmel that the prophet's great victory was won. No, my friends, Transfiguration is not something God did once. It is God's constant mission.

Look unto the hills. Draw strength and hope from the mountains. Know that the end of our story, like the end of Jesus' story, will take place atop a mountain. Hear what Revelation, the end of the biblical story, proclaims about the end of our story: "Then he said to me, 'It is done! I am the Alpha and the Omega, the beginning and the end. To the thirsty I will give water as a gift from the spring of the water of life. Those who conquer will inherit these things, and I will be their God and they will be my children.' . . . And in the spirit he carried me away to a great, high *mountain* and showed me the holy city Jerusalem coming down out of heaven from God" (Rev. 21:6–7, 10).—Chris Caldwell

ILLUSTRATION

TRANSFORMING MOMENTS.   God's transforming moments come to prepare us for something else. They are not an end in themselves. Fred Craddock tells the story of a woman who spent the day at the spa and had a complete makeover. Gliding out the door she said to herself, "I'm the new me!" Then she paused and said, "Now where was it I was going?"—Chris Caldwell

SERMON SUGGESTIONS

Topic: When God Is Not Impressed

TEXT: Isa. 58:3–9a

(1) *Situation:* religious rites and ceremonies are a normal and proper expression of faith. (2) *Complication:* these practices, however, may become a convenient, inexpensive, and empty substitute for more significant expressions of faith. (3) *Resolution:* redefine these rites and ceremonies in terms of their inner meaning and requirements, such as costly justice and demanding compassion.

Topic: Who Are the Wise?

TEXT: 1 Cor. 2:1–11

(1) People taught by the Spirit, (2) who perceive the wisdom of the cross, (3) and who let that cross argue God's case.

WORSHIP AIDS

CALL TO WORSHIP.   "How lovely is your dwelling place, O Lord of hosts! My soul longs, indeed it faints for the courts of the Lord; my heart and my flesh sing for joy to the living God" (Ps. 84:1–2, NRSV).

INVOCATION.   Lord, as we pause to worship, break in upon our lethargy, stir our hearts, motivate us anew with the things of God that for a while we may behold your glory. Amen.—E. Lee Phillips

OFFERTORY SENTENCE.   "First they gave their own selves to the Lord and to us through the will of God" (2 Cor. 8:5).

OFFERTORY PRAYER.   Creator of all, help us to be good sister and brothers in the community of faith, so that we may reach those outside the fold and enlarge that family for whom heaven is home and faith in Christ Jesus is joy.—E. Lee Phillips

PRAYER.   God of all time, place, and memory, let us never forget you have made us and not we ourselves. From lowly dust of the good earth, you blew holy breath into our being and called us forth to life.

We who had not shape were formed grandly in the gentle cradle of your master hands. We who had no image were made in your very likeness, eternal goodness beyond our best knowing. We who had no name were chosen, set apart, blessed and called your children, your people. We who had no hope of salvation were given the matchless gift of Jesus the

Christ, our Redeemer and Lord. God of bold expectation and boundless grace, we pause in time and place and remember and voice our thanksgiving and praise.

Receiving God, Lord of holiness, forgive our taking lightly your creation, overlooking the grandeur and wonder of it all; for belittling the sacred gift of life; for tarnishing your image within us; for forgetting our name and lineage, which comes surely from you even in Jesus Christ. Forgive our begrudging the joy and claim of our salvation.

We pray, God of mercy and light, for deeper understanding and experience of the sufficiency of your grace; for fresh indwelling of your power in our weakness; for wisdom and passion to know and follow the way that leads to life and wholeness. O Love that calls us, names us, blesses us, and will not let us go, we give our lives freely and gladly to you, even in Jesus Christ our Lord, in whom we pray.—William M. Johnson

SERMON
Topic: Christ Satisfies Life's Hunger
TEXT: John 6:25–40

How will all the people in the world be fed? This is a question about which serious men and women wonder today.

Scientists have said that a large part of our food may have to come from the ocean and from our homemade efforts to grow microscopic plant life called algae.

Some parts of our world are frantically anxious about the shortage of food. This should be a matter of concern everywhere. Anyone's hunger is everyone's problem.

But this problem is not new. People have never had an easy mind about food. Yet the demand for bread can become a craving passion and erase every other value of life.

Jesus had fed the five thousand, having only five loaves and two small fish. The crowd was amazed and delighted. Jesus was the man who could lead an army of Israelites against the hated Roman Empire. How unbeatable would little Israel be with a food supply that could not be exhausted!

The idea spread like fire among the people. "Let us make him king!" they said with increasing intensity. (See John 6:15.) Far from discouraging this sort of thing, the disciples appeared to go along with it, if they were not the actual instigators.

But Jesus fled alone from the mistaken mob. In the night, disciples and Master met in a dramatic encounter on the Sea of Galilee. Next day, a part of the feverish crowd located Jesus with his disciples.

I. *The hungry crowd.* Far from feeling flattered at the sight of those who pursued him, Jesus met the crowd with a sharp rebuke. Exposing their persistent materialism, he accused them of following him because they were pleased with the promise of economic security (v. 26).

Does our chief interest in Christ lie in what he can do for us in every way but spiritually? His belonging to us differs greatly from our belonging to him. We may want to "use" Christ for our selfish purposes. He wants us to be used in the eternal purpose of God.

At various times some have sought to use Christ to further their political aims, to enhance their success in the business world, or to confirm their economic views. More subtly, they have emphasized Jesus' love for sinners to the exclusion of his hatred for sin; they have welcomed him as Savior and rejected him as Lord. Perhaps most of us have sometimes tried through our prayers and actions to make him a different Christ from the Christ he is: the Christ we need.

II. *The bread of God.* Nowhere do the Scriptures condemn our labor to earn daily bread. Jesus taught his disciples to pray for their daily bread (Matt. 6:11). In fact, Paul declared that one who refuses to work is not entitled to eat (2 Thess. 3:10–12).

Even so, Jesus Christ declared as his doctrine the teaching of the Old Testament: "Man shall not live by bread alone, but by every word that proceedeth out of the mouth of God" (Matt. 4:4; cf. Deut. 8:3).

There is food worth working for. It does not decay or become unusable. It is not gone with the eating of it. This food is a spiritual blessing given by Jesus Christ. He is qualified to bestow it, for he bears the seal of God the Father (v. 27); that is, Christ is the Father's appointed representative. Therefore, the food Christ gives has to do with another world and a different kind of life. It is for the nourishment of the life of God within those who believe (John 17:2–3).

Indeed, Jesus Christ is that food. He said, "I am the bread of life" (v. 35). But this statement was the climax of a lengthy argument with the Jews (vv. 30–34). Even after the healing of the lame man and the miracle of the loaves and fish, the crowd refused to believe. These miracles did not convince the Jews. They demanded another sign, a sign which fitted their age-old ideas about the Christ.

So do we. With all of the wondrous works of God about us—in nature and in human life— we ask for one more sign that God is gracious and that Christ is true. But the most dramatic miracle possible would call for still another to satisfy the heart that will not believe.

The Jews expected the Messiah to prove his truth by bringing again manna from heaven to fall before their greedy eyes. Through Moses they had received what they termed "bread from heaven" (v. 31). Jesus said that manna was not the true bread from heaven. It was an indirect blessing of God. But the true bread came directly from heaven (vv. 32–33). Jesus had himself in mind. God gave *him* directly.

The crowd still could not see Jesus as the bread of God. With their minds yet on material things, they said, "Lord, evermore give us this bread" (v. 34). Then he confronted them with the blunt truth: "I am the bread of life" (v. 35). What the world needed then and needs now is not so much the bread that Christ can give as the bread that Christ is. Our basic need is to have our spiritual hunger met and satisfied. Yet, as Calvin said, "We are prone to seek something in Christ, other than Christ himself."

III. *Grace and decision.* When William Carey, the "father" of the modern missionary movement, was a young man glowing with his first dreams of preaching the gospel to the heathen, he tried to stimulate a group of ministers to share the burden of his heart. His efforts were rebuked by a revered, saintly preacher: "Young man, sit down. When God wants to save the heathen, he'll save them without your help or mine."

To be sure, some of the Scriptures seem to lead to such a conclusion. But the truth of the sovereignty of God in such verses is always held in balance by other verses that clearly show our responsibility. Jesus speaks of the overruling power of God (vv. 37, 39–40). But he also speaks of our responsibility of coming to him (vv. 35, 37) and of believing on him (v. 40).

God in his mercy gives bread and draws the hungry. But the hungry must respond, come, and eat. Those who refuse to be fed perish by their own folly, not by the will of God. Those who receive God's mercy receive the promise of a meaningful present life and of a triumphant and complete life hereafter (vv. 39–40), for they have within them the life of God himself. Indeed, Jesus assures us, "anyone who comes to me I will never drive away" (v. 37, NRSV).—James W. Cox

SUNDAY, FEBRUARY 13, 2005
Lectionary Message

Topic: Crucial Confessions
TEXT: Rom. 5:12–19
Other Readings: Gen. 2:15–17, 3:1–7; Ps. 32; Matt. 4:1–11

Paul lays before us two realities we cannot escape: our sin, and God's grace. Our heritage of sin runs far and wide, as far back as Adam and as wide as all humankind. And just as the power of our sins is personified in a single man, Adam, the power of God's grace is found in "the one man, Jesus Christ" (v. 15). The reality of grace does not erase the reality of sin, but Christ is the bridge from one to the other. Christ's reconciling role is a key concept within Paul, and indeed is at the heart of the whole New Testament. It is in the Old Testament, however, where we find an excellent model of how to take the theological idea of justification in Paul and apply it to our own lives.

Like Paul, the psalmist stresses the pervasiveness of sin. Three words are used for the psalmist's sins in verse 5. The NRSV translates them as *sin* (based on a Hebrew word meaning to miss the mark), *iniquity* (from a Hebrew word meaning an enduring and destructive form of sin), and *transgressions* (meaning willful disobedience in Hebrew). Where Paul points to the breadth of our sin ("all have sinned"), the psalmist points to sin's depth (in all these ways have I sinned).

Paul and the psalmist both stress forgiveness. Paul teaches us our sin is "covered" by Christ. Psalm 32 begins by declaring, "Happy are those whose transgression is forgiven, whose sin is covered," but then he goes on to remind us that just because God's grace is available to us does not necessarily mean we will move toward it. He speaks from experience: "While I kept my silence, my body wasted away through my groaning all day long" (v. 3). Sin's power "exercise[s] dominion" (v. 14) over us because we let it. Like the psalmist, we remain silent about our sin in God's presence, trying to hide our mistakes. We do the same thing in our human relationships. Something is wrong between us and another person, and we fold our arms and walk away. How many problems get resolved that way? If the relationship is strained from our mistake, then we, like the psalmist, groan under the weight of a guilty conscience rather than getting to the root of the problem. Psychology understands this. Although depression can have complex medical and emotional origins, one contributing factor can be anger turned inward upon ourselves. The weariness of depression is akin to the psalmist's strength being "dried up as by the heat of summer."

All this would be depressing indeed if there were no remedy. But of course there is. Paul identifies the power to solve the problem: "For if the many died through the one man's trespass, much more surely have the grace of God and the free gift in the grace of the one man, Jesus Christ, abounded for the many" (v. 15). Paul's gift to us is this idea, this *notion.* Too often, however, what we lack is not the notion but the *motion.* We know God will forgive, but we do not move toward him. We are like a starving person sitting in the parking lot of a restaurant.

I don't know where you stand in relation to your sin. I know you have it, because we all do. Its weight for you might be a nagging sense that something is not right between you and God, an unresolved tension that lurks in the shadows. Or you may feel like Atlas struggling beneath a world of sin, fearful it will crush you if you don't get out from under it. Whatever form the bad news of your sin takes, I present to you the good news of the gospel. "But the free gift is not like the trespass. For if the many died through the one man's trespass, much more surely have the grace of God and the free gift in the grace of the one man, Jesus Christ, abounded for the many." So let us set down the burden of our sin and follow the way of the psalmist: "Then I acknowledged my sin to you, and I did not hide my iniquity; I said, 'I will confess my transgressions to the LORD.'" Let us embrace the wise counsel of one who learned not to run from grace: "present yourselves to God as those who have been brought from death to life."—Chris Caldwell

ILLUSTRATION

In *Jim the Boy,* by Tony Earley, a young boy cuts down a corn stalk as he is hoeing. He tries to prop up the stalk but his deception is easily detected by his uncle, who says, "Jim, this was just a mistake until you tried to hide it. . . . But when you tried to hide it, you made it a lie."

We sometimes fail to come before God because we expect too much of ourselves. My best friend attended a golf tournament, and Tiger Woods hit a shot that landed right in front of my friend, who, unfortunately for Tiger, was standing in the trees. Furious, Tiger abruptly addressed the ball, smacked it out of the trees, and stomped out. He was angry because he was not playing golf like Tiger Woods, a high standard he, of course, could reach. Our mistake is beating ourselves up for not meeting impossible expectations, such as playing golf like Tiger Woods.—Chris Caldwell

SERMON SUGGESTIONS

Topic: Adam and You (First Sunday of Lent)

TEXT: Gen. 2:4b–9, 15–17

(1) Our origin: from God. (2) Our obligation: to manage God's world. (3) Our options: to obey and know God's life; to disobey and taste of death.

Topic: The Harbinger of Death and the Pioneer

TEXT: Rom. 5:12–19 (RSV)

(1) Adam's disobedience led to death for all. (2) Christ's obedience led to "acquittal and life for all."

WORSHIP AIDS

CALL TO WORSHIP.   "Oh, come, let us worship and bow down; let us kneel before the Lord our Maker" (Ps. 95:6).

INVOCATION.   Enfold us Lord, close to the heart of God, that we may catch the rhythm of the divine in a worship that is life altering. Amen.—E. Lee Phillips

OFFERTORY SENTENCE.   "And to whomsoever much is given, of him shall much be required; and to whom they commit much, of him will they ask the more" (Luke 12:48).

OFFERTORY PRAYER.   We would praise you, O Father, not only in word but in deed, for all your love in our creation and re-creation. As your children may we share with our brothers and sisters here and everywhere. And through your consecration may these gifts of monies become the bread and water of life for many. Through him who gave all.—John Thompson

PRAYER.   O God of constant newness in whom all renewal abides and all hope originates, bless us as we worship thee and pause again to ponder the possibilities of a new week.

Lead us, Lord, to hear the voices of anguish that call out to us, overtly or disguised. Let us be stilled, quiet enough to hear, and courageous enough to act. Enable us to look beneath the surface of events to human hearts and to address the needs of the soul.

Help us, O Lord, to confront the good and evil in the world and to encourage the good and shun the evil. Grant us the firmness and poise born of the Holy Spirit to confront prejudice and littleness. Attune us to truth and light. Draw us to the mind of Christ: Jesus' way of thinking, Jesus' kind of love, Jesus' illuminating light, so that our actions may radiate the presence no darkness can overcome, which saves to the uttermost.—E. Lee Phillips

SERMON
Topic: Christ Opens Blind Eyes
TEXT: John 9:24–35

"Eyes that grope, in a fog that never lifts." These words captioned a magazine advertisement that showed a man staring straight ahead of him, not seeing where he went but trusting that caution, consideration by thoughtful people, and the use of other senses might protect him.

To one who had sight, this was an appalling thing—eyes that grope, a fog that never lifts! The knowledge that there is one person so handicapped is bad enough. But how shocking it is to know that there are millions of the blind, and that many cases of blindness could have been prevented.

One day as Jesus and his disciples passed by, they saw a blind man. This man became the topic of discussion. "Why was he born blind?" The disciples assumed that he suffered because of someone's sin—his own or his parents'—for the general Jewish view was that suffering was always the direct result of sin.

But Jesus brushed aside the sin theory of the man's affliction. He said that it happened in order to give God an opportunity to demonstrate what he could do.

Then Jesus applied a common remedy, clay mixed with spittle, to the eyes of the blind man. He told him, "Go, wash in the pool of Siloam." The man obeyed and received his sight.

This miracle happened on the Sabbath day, and the Pharisees were incensed. They completely ignored the blessing that had come to the blind man. They saw that Jesus had broken their Sabbath laws. He had done three specifically forbidden things: he mixed clay; he applied spittle to the eyelids; he healed. And all of these acts violated the Jewish laws prohibiting work on the Sabbath; therefore, the Pharisees questioned the man's parents and, being unsuccessful there, confronted the man himself.

I. *The realm of the blind.* Two kinds of blindness are evident in our Scripture passage. One is physical, the other spiritual. But there are two kinds of spiritual blindness: the blindness of those who do not see and the blindness of those who *will* not see.

In addition to lack of physical sight, the man in our story was spiritually blind. But this was a temporary blindness, the condition that all humankind shares until it receives sight from Christ.

The Pharisees, however, were blind in a far more perilous way. Paul says of such: "The god of this world hath blinded the minds of them which believe not, lest the light of the glorious gospel of Christ, who is the image of God, should shine unto them" (2 Cor. 4:4).

Jesus said of the Pharisees: "Let them alone: they be blind leaders of the blind. And if the blind lead the blind, both shall fall into the ditch" (Matt. 15:14).

The blindness of the Pharisees manifested itself in two ways. First, they failed to see that human well-being is more important than laws. Actually, the laws that regulated the lives of the Jews were given to promote the physical, moral, and social health of individuals and of the community. Today it is possible so to magnify the mechanical aspects of obedience to God that the purpose of obedience is lost. In one of Dickens's stories a character become so wrapped up in the needs of the heathen that she lets her own children run wild and suffer other neglect. Just laws and noble enterprises are necessary, but they must lift, not crush.

Second, the Pharisees closed their minds to opportunities for learning what God was doing in history (vv. 29–34). It was more convenient to walk in the hard-beaten paths of custom than to strike out in new, untried directions. History was being made, but the Pharisees stood abreast and fought to stop it. Religious people, even professed Christians, may be so stubborn in their views of how God ought to do certain things that they may be found, like the Pharisees, actually fighting against God.

But there is another type of blindness that yields to the offer of healing. The blind man was willing to receive his sight. He had no vested interests that he wanted to protect by remaining blind, though it is not unheard of that some people—professional beggars and the like—prefer affliction to wholeness. The blind man thus represents the host of human beings who walk in darkness but prefer the light. Our evangelistic efforts and our missionary enterprise move forward with the conviction that there are men and women who, though blind, will respond to the opportunity to see. Again and again, we have been heartened by seeing them come to be healed.

II. *Now I see.* The Pharisees moved in on the newly healed man. They tried to place him under oath by saying to him, "Give God the praise." Then they attempted to make him confess that Jesus was a sinner (v. 24). He answered by saying that he did not know whether Jesus was a sinner, but he did know that whereas he had been blind, he now could see (v. 25).

The practical test—does the thing work?—is often a good test. If an idea succeeds or if one is able to do miraculous works, then this must be good. Or so it would seem. Jesus *did* say, "By their fruits ye shall know them" (Matt. 7:20). But he also said, "Many will say . . . Lord, Lord, have we not . . . in thy name done many wonderful works? And then will I profess unto them, I never knew you: depart from me, ye that work iniquity" (Matt 7:22–23). Therefore, even ability to work miracles does not prove one to be right with God. The same judgment would apply to Jesus. But since he was the Son of God and did the Father's will, the miracles of Jesus were one way of giving evidence of who he was and that he worked the works of God.

The man might have been right in saying that he did not know about Jesus' rightness or wrongness, but he was ready to explore the matter. This he did to the great embarrassment of the Pharisees. He argued, first, that in view of their profession to understand Moses their ignorance of Jesus was shocking (vv. 29–30); second, that God does not answer prayers of sinners, but of those that do his will (v. 31); and third, that a miracle just like this was unheard of (v. 32). Before he was through, the man had convinced himself—if he were not convinced before. He summed up his argument with the words: "If this man were not of God, he could no nothing" (v. 33).

In spite of the praise of many for Jesus, some today would join with the Pharisees in trying to mark off Jesus as a nuisance and one who does more harm than good. But the argument of the man born blind is still good.

Thus, one who has met Jesus in a vital spiritual experience might say of him: "He has done something worthwhile for me. How can one be so *apparently* wise in matters of science, ethics, and government and not see the truth in Jesus Christ? How can Jesus be so effective in human lives if God is not with him? How can his miracles in the realm of character and social relations be so characterized by goodness and love except that he works the works of God?"

The "impudence" of the man was too much for the guardians of the old ways. They excommunicated him, that is, they "churched" him (v. 34). We, too, have seen that happen in other circles. A man begins to take his faith seriously and for his pains gets dropped by some of his business friends. A woman sees the consequences of dangerous social customs and for the sake of conscience quits them, and she is no longer invited to some places. Decisions to go God's way are often costly and for a time painful, but Christians should be willing to pay the price.

III. *"Lord, I believe."* It is comforting to know that Christ does not abandon those who have found help from him in some great crisis. We must not think that one important meeting with Christ brings enough strength and health to see us through all our days. When the religious leaders cast out the man born blind, Jesus heard about it and went to him with further help.

In the healing miracle, Jesus had given the man eyes to see. Now he gave him light to see by. It was, at first, grace. It was, at this meeting, full commitment to grace.

When Jesus revealed himself to the man as the Son of God, there was an immediate response of acceptance and consecration.

Once in a time of personal grief and despair, George W. Truett talked of quitting the ministry. In his own mind, he had been "cast out." But in an unusual way, Christ came to him, saying, "You are my man from now on." And from that time this "man of God" entered upon the most fruitful phase of his ministry.

Many are the world's blind. They may see if they will. Many are those whose eyes have been opened by Christ. They will be given light, and more light, according to their willingness and their need. If we have received spiritual vision from Christ, then our Savior, the Light of the World, will not let us walk in darkness but will give to us the light of life (John 8:12).—James W. Cox

SUNDAY, FEBRUARY 20, 2005
Lectionary Message

Topic: Our Need to Follow

TEXT: Gen 12:1–4a

Other Readings: Ps. 121; Rom. 4:1–5, 13–17; John 3:1–17

Scene one: The first word Abram hears from God is, "Go." Not "How are you?" Not "Allow me to introduce myself." Just, Go. And go means leaving behind many things: a country, relatives, and his father's household. Abram is being asked not just to leave a place but to abandon powerful familial commitments to his parents and his siblings. In place of all these, God offers simply, "A place that I will show you."

Scene two: Imagine what it must have sounded like as Abram goes to have a little talk with his wife, Sarai.

ABRAM: "God spoke to me."

SARAI: "Which god? [This was a time before monotheism had really taken root.] Has this god spoken to you before? What did this god say?"

ABRAM: "We have to leave."

SARAI: "When will we get back?"

ABRAM: "Uh, I forgot to ask specifically. Maybe never."

SARAI: "Well, can you at least tell me where we are going?"

ABRAM: "God didn't say."

Scene three: Abram goes and rents the biggest U-Haul truck he can find, and they load up all they have. He and his wife climb into the front seat. At the end of the driveway, it occurs to Abram that he doesn't know if he should turn left or right.

All this on the basis of what? A promise: "I will make of you a great nation, and I will bless you, and make your name great, so that you will be a blessing. I will bless those who bless you, and the one who curses you I will curse; and in you all the families of the earth shall be blessed." On the basis of this promise and nothing more, with no pause and with no fanfare, he goes. Abram and Sarai, two people of faith, set out following God.

What do we learn about God from this story? First, God is personal. This is not the God of the deists, who winds the universe as a clock and then steps back. This God picks a single person in a specific place at a specific time and says, "I choose to work with you." Second, we learn God relates to us through promises. God could have been a puppeteer controlling every move, could have forced a relationship. But the chord that God employed to connect him to his children is a promise. Third, we learn God is faithful. We know this because we know the rest of the story: God does keep his promises to Abraham. Fourth, God is moving. God essentially says, "Follow me." Abram doesn't know where he is going. God is not showing the destination yet, and so his only option is to follow.

That's the way God's relationship with humankind began, and so it still is today. Later the people in the wilderness will follow a God who is a cloud by day and a pillar of fire by night. Three wise men will follow a star. And to this day we chase after God like a little child trying to keep up with her mother's long strides. In summary: God moves forward. We try to follow. This is the story of faith.

What more can we say about our following? First, we never really arrive at a final destination. Even Abram doesn't. Although he finds the land, the real promise is about a future he will never see. Faith, you see, is not a destination; it's a journey.

This restless God we follow keeps us moving, and this applies even to seventy-five-year-old Abram. Jesus, likewise, stayed on the move, with no place to lay his head. He was a man with a mission that called him forward. And so let this be said clearly: choosing faith—if we choose faith—means moving and following. It does not mean following perfectly. There will be times when we stumble or wander off course. Abraham makes his share of mistakes along the way, to be sure, and so will we. The Bible says, "All we like sheep have gone astray, each one to his or her own way." Indeed.

As we travel with God, there will be no maps for the journey of faith. Abram was sent to "a land I will show you." He and Sarai were given no turn-by-turn directions off the Internet. In fact they were told to leave the Rand-McNally road atlas behind. God makes no promises about what will happen on the journey. Life is unpredictable, and God does not offer to change that fact just because we follow in faith.

What God does promise, however, is that he will always travel with us. Retired pastor Hal Marchman is one of my heroes. We made lots of ministerial calls together to see people in crisis. Hal typically offered some variant of this prayer: "Lord, you never promised us we wouldn't have to go through valleys; you did promise we wouldn't do it alone."

If Abraham were here with us today, I think he'd want us to know one more thing: the journey will be fantastic! If you traveled back in time and asked Abraham, shortly before he died, if he ever regretted leaving Haran, I think we all know what he'd say: "Of course not!" That decision to follow the divine impulse and go was the moment of his transformation, the moment he really began living. The same can be said for the many followers whose stories fill this book resting on this pulpit. They followed. Not perfectly, to be sure. But they were willing to go.

God started asking us to follow with Abraham, but he never has stopped asking. God continued asking through Christ, who came to ordinary men leading ordinary lives, saying, "Why settle for just fishing? I'll make you fishers of men." Do you think any of those disciples regretted following?

And so we have two choices. One is to stay comfortable. Get a cozy spot where things seem reasonably good, then continue taking meals and sucking up oxygen until our time is up. This is the eminently reasonable choice, which is why most people opt for it.

Or? Or, go. Follow. Where to? Beats me. But I know this. God will go with you. And you won't regret the journey.—Chris Caldwell

ILLUSTRATIONS

FOLLOWING.   Following is not easy. The hardest job on a football field belongs to the defensive backs. The receivers they are defending have a map. They have a route and know where they are going. The defensive backs must follow the best they can and react quickly.

THE NEED OF A SHEPHERD.   Following is part of being in God's flock. Sheep don't know where they are going, and they do not respond to being driven from behind like cattle. They do best when they follow their Shepherd.—Chris Caldwell

SERMON SUGGESTIONS

Topic: The Anatomy of Faith

TEXT: Gen. 12:1–4a (4b–8)

(1) A demanding command. (2) An inspiring promise. (3) Decisive obedience.

Topic: What Puts Us Right with God?

TEXT: Rom. 4:1–5 (6–12), 13–17

(1) Not our good works and religious rituals. (2) But the grace of God who regards our faith as acceptable righteousness.

WORSHIP AIDS

CALL TO WORSHIP.   "It is good to sing praise to our God; it is pleasant and right to praise him" (Ps. 147:1, TEV).

INVOCATION.   Lord, we recall the words of Jesus Christ: "And I, if I be lifted up, will draw all persons to me," and we lift up Christ in worship today that all who are in need may find in him the grace and strength that redeems and edifies.—E. Lee Phillips

OFFERTORY SENTENCE.   "You are so rich in all you have: in faith, speech, and knowledge, in your eagerness to help and in your love for us. And so we want you to be generous also in this service of love" (2 Cor. 8:7, TEV).

OFFERTORY PRAYER.   O Gracious God, thou hast called us into thy kingdom of love, and we are grateful for thy call and for thy kingdom. Use these gifts to further that service in areas that are not open to us as individuals. May the joys of participation overcome the separation of distance, of language, of culture, of kind, so that we may rejoice whenever, wherever, and however these gifts are used in the name of Jesus Christ.—Richard Brand

PRAYER.   Father, you have made this wonderful world and called it good. You have placed us in a paradise of promise. We thank you for majestic hills and fertile valleys, for rivers and lakes and seas teeming with life and laden with riches, for institutions of learning and government, for the sources of technologies of human well-being. Yet, we have proven by our many failures as stewards that we must have your guidance and help; otherwise, we will turn the beautiful garden of earth into a wasteland. Forgive our delinquencies, we pray, and make life-giving streams to flow in any deserts our sins have created. Heed the madness of our greed. Help us to see the end of our prodigal ways, so that sanity may dictate what we make of both the abundances and the scarcities of your world. Grant that we may not be forever praying that our barns may be filled so that we have to build more and larger ones; rather, grant that we may pray for our bread for the day and that whatever more your providence gives us we may use as grateful and faithful stewards for the benefit of others and for your honor.

SERMON

Topic: Christ Gives Life Eternal

TEXT: John 11:17–27, 38–44

According to an old Greek story, Aurora, the goddess of the dawn, fell in love with a mortal youth. Zeus offered any gift she might choose for her lover. She requested that Tithomus might live forever. Her wish was granted, but she had made a terrible mistake. She did not ask that Tithomus be given eternal youth. Thus his eternal existence became a constant decline from vigorous strength to ever-increasing infirmity.

Eternal existence on the same terms in which we now experience life would be unbearable. But eternal life is different. It brings to our human situation a new dimension, for to have eternal life is to experience something akin to the life of God himself (John 17:3).

The Lazarus story opens the door for us. During Jesus' life, he formed many strong human attachments. Among those dearest to him were Lazarus of Bethany and his sisters, Mary and Martha. They valued his warm affection and believed in his unusual powers. Thus, when Lazarus became seriously ill, the sisters sent for Jesus, believing that he would heal Lazarus.

But Jesus would not yield to so strong a pull as even the deep friendship of the three at Bethany. He was under orders from the Father. There was a divine purpose in his delay in returning to Bethany (John 11:4).

I. *Shadow and sorrow.* When Jesus arrived in Bethany, four days had passed since the death of Lazarus. The Jews had a superstitious belief that the soul of the deceased lingered for three days about the corpse, seeking to be reunited with it. But since four days had gone by, all hope was lost. Lazarus was really dead!

Grief held the village in its grip. The sorrow of Mary and Martha was the deep sense of loss and emptiness that one knows when an intimately loved one dies. The hurt was so great that even God might be blamed. Grief can be completely unreasoning and often quite selfish. Great lessons may be learned in the time of bereavement, but great mistakes may be made also. First Martha and then Mary said, "Lord, if thou hadst been here, my brother had not died?" (vv. 21, 32).

But great waves of emotion swept over Jesus also. "He groaned in the spirit, and was troubled" (v. 33). "Jesus wept" (v. 35). "Jesus therefore again groaning in himself cometh to the grave" (v. 38). Jesus entered into the situation fully. But the onlookers—the mourners—misinterpreted the source of his deep feeling. Some regarded it as the natural reaction to the loss of one profoundly loved (v. 36). Others saw it as helpless frustration because he could not prevent Lazarus' death (v. 37). But the first reaction of Jesus came when he saw the wailing of Mary and of the Jews (v. 33). The second emotional outburst came after the Jews sarcastically stated that since Jesus had given sight to the blind, surely he could have prevented the death of Lazarus. Not mere sympathy, but grief and indignation at unbelief shook Jesus.

II. *Resurrection faith.* Here Jesus was confronted with the fact of death. What would he who had changed water into wine and had healed the paralytic and the blind do about death?

Jesus could comfort Mary and Martha with the doctrine of "the resurrection at the last day" (v. 24). Though the Sadducees did not hold to belief in a future life, the Pharisees and other devout Jews in Jesus' time believed that a day would come when the dead would be raised. Indeed, in the book of Daniel are the words: "Many of them that sleep in the dust of the earth shall awake, some to everlasting life, and some to shame and everlasting contempt" (Dan. 12:2).

The biblical view of the future life of the redeemed, therefore, is belief in resurrection. The Hebrews believed that by the power of God the redeemed one would be a complete personality after resurrection, not a soul without a body. They believed that immortality is a special gift of God.

Martha's only consolation in the loss of her brother was expressed in the words: "I know that he shall rise again in the resurrection at the last day" (John 11:24). But Jesus had more immediate hope to give Mary and Martha. When he said, "Thy brother shall rise again" (v. 23), he referred in particular to Lazarus' rising again that day. They misinterpreted Jesus' words (v. 24), but he who said "I am the resurrection, and the life" (v. 25) gave them their brother again. When the miracle was wrought, Jesus prayed aloud, so that all might know that he did the words of God and that God worked through him (vv. 41–42).

III. *The awaking voice.* In all of the miracles of the Fourth Gospel, we must read between the lines for the hidden meaning. We must remember that John calls these mighty works "signs." Jesus gave the significance of the raising of Lazarus when he said, "I am the resurrection, and the life . . . whosoever liveth and believeth in me shall never die" (vv. 25–26). The expression of "eternal life" in John's Gospel refers to a quality or kind of life that can be experienced here on earth (see John 5:24–25).

The dead are those who have not received the spiritual life that comes from God through Christ to those who believe in, love, and obey Christ, God's Son. This fact is indicated in Jesus' command: "Let the dead bury their dead" (Matt. 8:22). Paul thought of the ungodly as those "dead in trespasses and sins" (Eph. 2:1). (By way of contrast, consider the words of Paul in 2 Corinthians 5:17.)

The voice that shook the stillness of the tomb of Lazarus and raised him from the dead speaks to the spiritually entombed today. Because Christ says to us, "Come forth," we emerge from tombs of guilt and fear and condemnation. The dead are made alive!

But of those awakened souls, trembling at the edge of their spiritual tombs, Christ says, "Loose them, and let them go! They are now responsible citizens of the realm of the living. There is work to do. There are people to love. There is a world to save. This is their task" (cf. John 9:44).—James W. Cox

SUNDAY, FEBRUARY 27, 2005
Lectionary Message

Topic: Our Need to Wait Patiently
Text: Exod. 17:1–7
Other Readings: Ps. 95; Rom. 5:1–11; John 4:5–42

The people of God have just been delivered from years of captivity. Saved from slaughter at the hands of the Egyptian soldiers, fed with food that God has sent from the sky, we would expect the ancient Israelites to be a thankful and joyful people. But the Bible is the story of the people with whom God deals, not the story of the people with whom God wished to deal, and so Moses is bombarded by carping. The complaint *du jour* is a lack of water. Moses responds by saying, "Don't blame me; God's in charge, so you're really complaining about him." But the people still are not satisfied, replying, "Why did you bring us out of Egypt, to kill us and our children and livestock with thirst?"

Moses appeals to God, but not on behalf of the people, rather on his own behalf, because he fears for his life. At this point God intervenes, and the problem is solved by God's showing Moses how to produce water. The people, then, are happy. But Moses is not (v. 7); he called the place Massah and Meribah, because the Israelites quarreled and tested the Lord, saying, "Is the Lord among us or not?"

This story seems to be just another routine example of human nature causing people to act as people sometimes act. In fact, this story becomes a formative moment as God's people reflect on it. The Bible also returns again and again to this event. Psalm 95 quotes it directly. Hebrews chapters 3 and 4 quote portions of the story as well.

Given the amount of ink the Bible spends on the topic, it would seem to be saying that impatient faith is a great temptation. Surely this is no less the case for those of us who live in this world of instant gratification, with our drive-through windows and ever-shrinking attention span. Modern life hurtles forward at an ever-faster pace, but is it likely that the pace of God's work has changed all that much over the same time period? Is it likely that God is now working on a different timetable just because we are less patient? Surely this temptation is alive and well today.

Yielding to this temptation has a specific result: spiritual "hardness." In referring to this wilderness scene, the psalmist (95:8) admonishes us, "Do not harden your hearts." In Hebrews' discussion of the story, four times it refers to the hardening of the people's spirits. This hardening of the soul's arteries appears to stem not just from impatience, but also from selfishness. A fixation on "What am I getting out of this?" leads to a faith that makes demands on God, so that God's faithfulness is measured in terms of God's ability to deliver the goods; God is faithful when I am getting what I want. This is spiritual immaturity. Like impatient babies, we demand instant gratification because the world revolves around our needs.

The Bible tells us to remain steadfast in faith, even if all our wants are not being supplied. Psalm 95 says that rather than acting as the people of God did at Meribah, we should praise God: "O come, let us worship and bow down, / let us kneel before the Lord, our Maker!" Likewise, the author of Hebrews encourages us not to fail to enter into God's rest by repeating the impatience of Meribah.

Words of instruction and direction are all well and good, but this still begs the question: How are we as the people of God going to avoid the temptation that has snared so many of our sisters and brothers before us? One remedy is to practice encouragement. Hebrews 3:12–13 says, "Take care, brothers and sisters, that none of you may have an evil, unbelieving heart that turns away from the living God. But exhort one another every day, as long as it is called 'today,' so that none of you may be hardened by the deceitfulness of sin." Encouragement is an *under*valued spiritual gift. Perhaps you have known the power of a little note of encouragement sent by a fellow believer. Most churches have these quiet saints who have the gift of sending a card or making a call just when it is needed most. If self-centeredness and impatience harden our souls, then encouragement is the water that helps keep our souls supple.

The other key to avoiding spiritual impatience is simply practicing the art of waiting upon God. The best time to begin this practice, according to the Bible, is today. Psalm 95 says, "O that today you would listen to my voice." Three times, Hebrews encourages believers to wait upon the Lord *today.* This makes sense, because impatient people are busy people, and if you want to get them to start doing something, better to get them to start it right now. And so, let's do just that. Let's begin practicing patience and softening our souls a bit. Let us literally "Wait upon the Lord." Let's spend two minutes in silence—two of the ten thousand eighty minutes in this week. If you are not sure what to do during this time of silence, simply repeat to yourself the words of scripture: "Be still, and know that I am God."—Chris Caldwell

ILLUSTRATIONS

EXCUSE.   Have you ever known someone who reflected again and again upon some less-than-overwhelming moment that taught them a long-term lesson? Willy Loman, the central character in Arthur Miller's *Death of a Salesman,* repeatedly returns to the great investment opportunity he missed early in life, feeling that this moment explains his lifetime of coming up short.

IMPATIENCE.   The story of a man in a long airport line typifies impatience stemming from self-centeredness. Having waited longer than he wanted to check in at the gate, he strode past the other customers and demanded service. Reminded by the attendant that there was a line, he replied, "Do you know who I am?" The attendant, according to legend, took the microphone in hand and announced, "Excuse me, ladies and gentlemen, but we have a customer here who seems to have forgotten who he is. Is there anyone here who can help him?"—Chris Caldwell

SERMON SUGGESTIONS

Topic: Is the Lord Among Us or Not?

TEXT: Exod. 17:3–7

(1) *Situation:* Like the people of Israel, God has led and blessed us. (2) *Complication:* Like Israel, we tend to forget past blessings when present difficulties arise. (3) *Resolution:* Nevertheless, God is patient with us, accommodates to our lack of faith, and awaits our maturity.

Topic: Your Standing with God

TEXT: Rom. 5:1–11

(1) What is the subject? Peace with God. (2) Whom is it for? Those justified by faith. (3) Where is it found? At the cross of Christ. (4) How does it happen? Through being saved by Christ's life. (5) When does it happen? Now! (6) Why does it happen? Because of God's love for us.

WORSHIP AIDS

CALL TO WORSHIP.   "Be glad in the Lord, and rejoice, ye righteous: and shout for joy, all ye that are upright in heart" (Ps. 32:11).

INVOCATION.   Lord, bless our singing and praying, pervade sermon and listening, stir imagination and commitment. Be to us our mighty God and may we be obedient followers of the Christ. Amen.—E. Lee Phillips

OFFERTORY SENTENCE.   "The earth is the Lord's, and the fullness thereof; the world, and they that dwell therein" (Ps. 24:1).

OFFERTORY PRAYER.   Lord, though we have at times neglected to serve thee when asked, may we never fail to give to the church, asked or not, for we love the church for which Christ died and pray that our gifts will meet the needs of many for Jesus' sake.—E. Lee Phillips

PRAYER.   Eternal God, your power is beyond measure, your goodness exceeds our imagining, and your love defies the farthest reaches of our thoughts. As we ponder who we are, what we have done, and how we act toward you and one another, we confess that we have sinned and constantly fall short of your glory. We are in debt to you, and we know that we can never fully discharge that debt. And we are every day adding to our mounting indebtedness. With the psalmist we cry, "If thou, O Lord, shouldst mark iniquities, who could stand?" You are merciful and gracious to us, answering with your kindness even before we call to you. You girded us with grace before we knew you. While we were without strength, Christ died for us the ungodly. How can we now refuse the love that offers us free and full forgiveness, love that can remove our iniquities from us as far as the East is from the West; love that forgets that we ever sinned. O gracious and forgiving Father, reach into the darkness of our guilt, take us by the hand, and lead us into the light and promise of new life, as we trust in your sure word, for "there is forgiveness with thee."

SERMON
Topic: The Challenge of the Cross
TEXT: John 12:20–36

"Why is that plus sign up there?" asked a small boy who had heard much in his home about mathematics, but nothing about religion. He was looking at a church—the first one he had ever seen. His new governess answered, "Because it's all-to-the-good."

Once the cross had a quite different meaning. It was an instrument of torture and punishment. It was the fate of the worst criminal in the Roman world to be crucified and left hanging for the mocking passers-by to see. Now the cross is intimately related to our lives. It is at the cross that we find the meaning of Jesus Christ for us and for the world.

The cross was the greatest challenge to the life and ministry of Jesus. Early in his ministry he saw that it was inevitable. In fact, the voice of God at his baptism, "this is my beloved Son, in whom I am well pleased" (Matt. 3:17), echoed in part the passages in Isaiah that referred to the Lord's Suffering Servant. His radiant life was lived in spite of the shadow of the cross.

The cross is our greatest challenge, also. To Jesus, cross-bearing was not unique. It was the normal responsibility of every Christian, stated Jesus several times. Actually, the cross of redemption in which we boast has no meaning in our lives unless we surrender ourselves to Christ and his way. One may "survey the wondrous cross" and one must say "Love . . . demands my soul, my life, my all."

I. *A significant quest.* All the events in the life and ministry of Jesus moved toward the cross. One event was especially important. It was the coming of the Greeks to see Jesus. This indicated the future world mission of those who believed in Jesus Christ. These Gentiles were not out-and-out converts to the Jewish religion. Since their own religion did not satisfy, they had turned to the Jewish faith for a better answer to their problems. They generally practiced the Jewish moral law and worshiped the God of the Jews. They were welcomed at Jerusalem for the great religious celebrations but were not granted full rights and privileges enjoyed by devout Jews.

These men were possibly from Galilee and might have known Philip. At any rate, they approached him, saying, "Sir, we would see Jesus" (v. 21). This seemingly casual request, which could have been made out of mere curiosity, was recognized by Jesus as having critical importance for his mission in the world. It meant that now not only the Jews but also the Gentiles were being brought within the sphere of the influence and power of Christ. Closely connected with this incident in meaning are these words of Jesus: "And I, if I be lifted up from the earth, will draw all men unto me" (v. 32).

II. *The way to fruitfulness.* It was in response to the inquiry of the Greeks that Jesus said, "The hour is come, that the Son of Man should be glorified" (v. 23). At last the time had arrived when Jesus would complete the work God had given him to do on earth. Verse 23 contains a tremendous paradox. How unthinkable that the Son of Man should go down in the defeat of death!

The term *the Son of Man* is frequently used in our references to Jesus to indicate our belief in his humanity, much as we use the term *the Son of God* to indicate our belief in his deity. But as the term is used here, the Son of Man is the amazing heavenly conqueror referred to in Daniel 7:13–14.

Though some of those who heard Jesus would interpret the word *glorified* to mean "world conquest," Jesus actually meant by that term "crucified." Again and again he referred to this crucifixion as his glorification. In Jesus' words that followed, however, it was clear to his hearers that he meant that the Son of Man must die (v. 34).

The same contrast is seen in words Paul wrote in his letter to the Philippians. Paul said that although Jesus existed in the form of God, he did not regard equality with God as a thing to be seized and held onto, but instead he emptied himself of his heavenly glory. He took upon himself the form of a servant. He was made in the likeness of men. He humbled himself and obeyed God, even though it cost him his life on the cross. Because he was willing to endure such humiliation, God exalted him and permitted him by service, as well as by right, to bear the divine name (see Phil. 2:6–9).

This truth is demonstrated in the world of nature. A seed has to fall into the ground and die before it can bear fruit. Francis of Assisi, in his beautiful prayer, summed up his petition by saying, "It is in giving that we receive, and it is by dying that we are born again unto eternal life."

Thus the dimension of depth in life is reached only by living according to the principle of the cross. This principle runs through all of life.

A mother hazards her own life in giving birth to her child. A father, at the risk of his own life, defends his family. A student gives up many pursuits that are immediately pleasant in order to prepare for greater happiness and service later. A couple who marry surrender some of their independence, in order that something greater might come.

Human experience has proved true again and again Jesus' statement that any one who lives primarily to promote and defend selfish interests will lose what he tries to save. But one who gives self to the larger concerns of life, the worship of God and the service of humanism, will store up from life every worthwhile value and have it for eternity (v. 25).

III. *A voice of reassurance.* Now, all of this sounds good when explained from the vantage point of the history of humankind. But who can accept this fact in an immediate situation? Within us there is something that recoils from self-denial, from suffering, and from death. Apparently, God has given us this instinct to save us from many foolish and unfruitful decisions. But sometimes we find ourselves, in our perverted use of this instinct, fighting against God.

It was not easy for Jesus to accept the cross. Though he knew it was inevitable, he postponed it as long as he could, in view of the will of God. He did not prematurely expose himself to danger that would cost him his life. But even in the garden of Gethsemane, as the soldiers were approaching, he prayed in a final agony of withdrawal from the cross, "O my Father, if it be possible, let this cup pass from me: nevertheless not as I will, but as thou wilt" (Matt. 26:30). Here also (John 12:37) Jesus responded, first shrinking from the cross, then accepting it.

God has his own ways of showing his servants the rightness of the way they take. At Jesus' baptism, the Heavenly Father spoke reassuring words that indicated the nature of Jesus' mission in the world. At his Transfiguration, Jesus received comfort and strength from Moses and Elijah and from the words of God. After Jesus' troubled prayer and his acceptance of the cross, God's reassuring voice from heaven was heard. The people standing there heard the sound but did not understand the significance of it (v. 29).

A high school graduate talked of his college plans to prepare for the gospel ministry. When asked why he planned to enter that field, he replied, "Because I feel God has called me." The skeptical man asked further, "Did you see a light from heaven and hear a voice?" With unusual discernment, but perhaps not enough tact, the lad answered with the words of Paul, "The natural man receiveth not the things of the Spirit of God: for they are foolishness unto him" (1 Cor. 2:14).

The person who takes Christ and his teachings seriously will be thought by some people to be completely foolish. "Why are you going as a missionary and throw your life away on some ignorant savages? Why do you spend your life doing this, teaching for a pittance when a man with your brains could make a pile of money?" These questions are asked by people who, when God speaks, merely think it thunders and do not know it is the voice from heaven.

IV. *Unlimited outreach.* The universal outreach of Christ was anticipated in the Old Testament: "O praise the Lord, all ye nations: praise him, all ye people" (Ps. 117:1); "I will also give thee for a light to the Gentiles, that thou mayest be my salvation unto the end of the earth" (Isa. 49:6). Jesus referred to "other sheep" that were not of the Jewish fold and that he would bring within the circle of this care. Paul said that the gospel of Christ "is the power of God unto salvation to every one that believeth; to the Jew first, and also to the Greek" (Rom. 1:16).

Thus the millions have come from every walk of life. And none who has come in sincere repentance has been denied the mercy and help of the Savior. The ageless invitation, based on the eternal purpose of God, stands; "Whosoever will may come." First Christ was lifted upon the cross, then exalted in his Resurrection and Ascension, and now he draws to him men and women from all over the earth.

V. *Limited opportunity.* The door of religious opportunity does not remain forever open. The light of heaven does not shine forever upon each man's path. Therefore, it is urged that men and women accept Christ while the door is yet open and the light still shines (John 12:35).

Yet there are some who, like the people of Jesus' time, continue to speculate and debate when they should be choosing and believing. The people of Jesus' day expected the Messiah to be a shining hero, immune to the ills and the defeats of earth. That the Son of man should die was impossible! And they wanted to argue the point.

But Jesus avoided debate with them. He spoke of himself in terms of light—"the light." The light would soon be gone. Their opportunity was right at that time. In the darkness beyond lay only confusion, stumbling, and disaster. If they believed in the light while they yet had opportunity, they could be "the children of light" (v. 36). They could become, because of Jesus, "the light of the world" (Matt. 5:14).

Still today light goes forth from the exalted Christ. And it is yet true that many speculate and debate, evade and postpone. Rejecting the light today is as dangerous as it was in the time of Jesus. People continue to crucify Christ every day. Perhaps this is the message you need to read and hear: that Christ has been lifted up and that he is drawing you to himself.—James W. Cox

SUNDAY, MARCH 6, 2005
Lectionary Message

Topic: Jesus Heals a Man Born Blind
TEXT: John 9:1–41
Other Readings: 1 Sam. 16:1–13; Ps. 23; Eph. 5:8–14

I. *As Jesus was walking along (vv. 1–5).* According to Herschel H. Hobbs, Jesus was still in Jerusalem following the Feast of Tabernacles. "The events in this passage are the center of John's sixth sign of Jesus' deity. The 'sign' gives tangible proof to Jesus' claim of being the Light of the World. He who can drive away spiritual darkness can also remove darkness from a person's eyes."

As Jesus was walking along he saw a man who had been blind from birth. Jesus saw much more than his disciples could see. He saw a man with a genuine need. His disciples saw only a problem. They asked, "Why was this man born blind? Was it a result of his own sins or those of his parents?" One is forced to ask what was behind the disciples' question—"Who sinned, this man or his parents that he was born blind?" It appears that the man's situation or circumstance stirred only the disciples' curiosity, not their compassion. They were focused on the cause of the man's blindness when they could have been moved to action.

Jesus' response to his curious disciples was that it was not because of his sins or his parents' sins. "He was born blind so the power of God could be seen in him." Jesus then exhorts his listeners by declaring in verse 4, "As long as it is day, we must do the work of Him who sent me. Night is coming, when no one can work." "While I am in the world," he said, "I am the light of the world." According to Hobbs, Jesus' answer called for action, not analysis.

II. *Jesus' method of healing (vv. 6–7).* Jesus then spit on the ground, made mud with his saliva, and applied the clay over the blind man's eyes. Then he instructed the blind man to go and wash his eyes in the pool of Siloam. (*Siloam* means "sent".) So the blind man went and washed, and came back seeing! It is essential that one understand that neither the clay nor the washing in the pool was necessary for the healing. The healing came through the man's faith in Jesus' word and by God's power.

Jesus, who gave physical sight to the blind man, can also give spiritual sight for a person's soul. Expressing faith in the word of God and believing in Jesus are the essentials for divine intervention.

III. *The response of the crowd (vv. 8–12).* The blind man's neighbors and others who had formerly seen him begging asked, "Isn't this the same man who used to sit and beg?" Some claimed that he was. Others said, "No, he only looks like him." But he himself insisted, "I am the man" (vv. 8–9). He had been blind all of his life, and now he could see. The crowd insisted on knowing, "Who healed you? What happened?" At their request he identified Jesus as his healer. They further wanted to know "Where is he now?" (v. 12). The man responded, "I don't know where he is."

IV. *On to the Pharisees (vv. 13–23).* Then they took the formerly blind man to the Pharisees. Now, the day on which Jesus had made the mud and opened the man's eyes was a Sabbath. The Pharisees asked the man about the details of his healing, and after recounting the experience some of the Pharisees concluded, "This man Jesus is not from God, for he is working on the Sabbath." Others said, "But how could an ordinary sinner do such miraculous signs?" So there was a deep division of opinion among them. Then the Pharisees questioned whether or not he was blind in the first place. They summoned his parents, who verified that he had been born blind. Fearing excommunication, they refused to say how their son was healed. Instead, they said the Pharisees should ask their son, since he was of age.

According to Hobbs, excommunication, or as the Jews called it, "casting out of the synagogue," was a terrible thing; it cut a person off from all social, economic, and religious relationships.

V. *Summoned a second time (vv. 24–34).* The Pharisees called the man in a second time and told him, "Give glory to God by telling the truth." They told him to testify that Jesus was a sinner. He did not budge an inch in responding, "Whether He is a sinner, I do not know. One thing I do know, that being blind, now I see."

They responded (v. 26), "But what did he do? How did he heal you?" He reminded the Pharisees that he already had done so. Then he began to taunt them. Why did they want to hear it again? "You do not want to become his disciple too, do you?" The Pharisees shot back that he was Jesus' disciple, they were Moses' disciples. They knew that God had spoken through Moses. They did not know anything about Jesus.

The formerly blind man thought their response to be very strange. "He healed my eyes, and yet you don't know anything about him. Well, God doesn't listen to sinners, but he is ready to hear those who worship him and do his will" (v. 31).

Unable to refute the man's logic and personal healing experience, they still refused to believe in Jesus. So they put him out. This does not mean they cast him out of the synagogue. This would have required a vote of the Sanhedrin. They simply put him outside of their presence. They refused to acknowledge what was so plainly obvious. They refused to accept anything out of their religious comfort zone!

VI. *Spiritual blindness (vv. 35–41).*

(a) *The healed man's response (vv. 35–19).* When Jesus heard what had happened, he found the man and said, "Do you believe in the Son of Man?" The man who had been born blind responded, "Who is he, sir, because I would like to." "You have seen him," Jesus said, "and he is speaking to you!" The man responded, "Yes Lord, I believe." And he worshipped Jesus. Jesus said, "For judgment I have come into this world, so that the blind will see and those who see will become blind." In other words Jesus is saying that he has come to give sight to the blind and to show those who think they see that they are blind.

(b) *The Pharisees' response (vv. 40–41).* The Pharisees who were standing there heard him and asked, "Are you saying we are blind?" Jesus said, "If you were blind, you would not be guilty of sin; but now that you claim you can see, your guilt remains." They (like some today) thought only of physical blindness. Jesus spoke of spiritual blindness. True, they did see the evidence with their physical eyes, but while claiming to be the Jews' moral and spiritual leaders, they refused to see all that was involved (Hobbs). They valued the Sabbath institution more than they valued the man. Instead of receiving Jesus as Savior, they rejected him and called him a sinner because he healed on the Sabbath.—T. Vaughn Walker

ILLUSTRATION

COMPASSION.   One sunny day in Central park a blind man was seen tapping for attention with his cane and carrying on his chest a sign, "Help the Blind." No one paid attention to him. A little farther on another blind beggar was doing better. Practically every passer-by put a coin in his cup, some even turning back to make their contribution. His sign said: "It is May—and I am blind!"—Edmund Fuller

SERMON SUGGESTIONS

Topic: The Choice
TEXT: Deut. 30:15–20
(1) All decisions or postponements have consequences. (2) God confronts us with decisions of ultimate consequence. (3) If we choose life and commit ourselves to its requirements, blessing will follow.

Topic: Jealousy in the Service of Christ
TEXT: 1 Cor. 3:1–9
(1) Jealousy in Christian service is human, but immature. (2) The ultimate success of Christian service is the work of God, not of humans.

WORSHIP AIDS

CALL TO WORSHIP.   "Give ear to my words, O Lord; give heed to my sighing. Listen to the sound of my cry, my King and my God, for to you I pray. O Lord, in the morning you hear my voice; in the morning I plead my case to you, and watch" (Ps. 5:1–3, NRSV).

INVOCATION.   God of mercy, let our worship be vibrant, open, expectant, that as we sing and pray and listen our hearts will be shaped after the things of God. Show the compassion that Christ showed for others.—E. Lee Phillips

OFFERTORY SENTENCE.   "The earth is the Lord's and the fullness thereof; the world, and they that dwell therein" (Ps. 24:1).

OFFERTORY PRAYER.   Searching God, send this offering on its way where it will shine the greatest light in the darkest corners and reflect the power of the glory of God in the face of Jesus.—E. Lee Phillips

PRAYER.   Our hearts are glad and our spirits sing this morning, Father, as we concentrate on you. With the promise of a little child before us facing all the challenge and joy, all the change and stability of life, we cannot but be aware of the need for your presence in every life, that we might be all you designed us to become. That such may happen for us, we ask that we experience your forgiveness here today. So many times our lives could have been a garden, and we made them a desert by refusing to allow the waters of your love to penetrate our hard hearts. So much of the beautiful life you have given us we have wasted in futile worries, vain regrets, and empty fears. Rather than seeing the joy you have placed all around us, the joy of a birdsong, or the early bloom on a spring flower or the innocent face of a little child, and rejoicing in it, we have sunk into complainings that have narrowed our blinded souls. Deliver us here today from the bondage of our unchastened desires and unwholesome thoughts and bitter hatreds. Help us to conquer hopeless brooding and faithless reflection and the impatience of irritable weakness.

Increase our faith, Father, we pray. Fill us with a more complete trust in you and a more wholehearted surrender to your will. Then every sorrow will have its lining of joy. Then our weak faith will become strong. Then we shall indeed mount up with wings as eagles, we shall run and not be weary, we shall walk and not faint, and we shall go from strength to strength by your power. Let it happen, here, now in this place, Father, we pray in Jesus' name.—Henry Fields

SERMON
Topic: Broken
Text: Hos. 6:1–6

We were visiting our son's family in Seattle. We came upon an opportunity that every grandparent dreams of. Mom and Dad were to be out for most of the evening, and we were entrusted with the total care of our grandchildren—including, however unintended, complete access to all inside family information. Some of us remember Art Linkletter's entertainment of the nation with his interviews of kids who say "the darndest things." He was once asked by a reporter where he got the idea for his famous TV show and recalled a conversation with his first grade son Jack. Art asked his son, "How did you like your first week at school? Jack replied, "I ain't goin' back." Art asked, "Why not?" and Jack answered, "I can't read, I can't write, and they won't let me talk."

We were assured that Nina and Kye (ages eight and six) could direct us to their favorite restaurant and back home, but as we pulled out of the driveway, Granddad wanted complete, advanced information. I asked, "Will we get to see your school?" Nina replied with some hesitation, as she searched for the right word, "Yeah, but it's broken."

We were both amused and curious. Had there been an earthquake or structural failure that had been kept from us? We pursued information about the crisis, "How did the school get broken?" Nina learned Japanese before English. She sometimes strains to find the right English word. She is also somewhat precocious, and we were not sure whether she was straining for a word or teasing her grandparents. She tried to explain that the school was "all gone, broken down . . ."; then she stopped and said, "You'll see." She was right on both points. The school was broke, and we did see. The school was under construction. Demolition was almost complete. Large earthmoving machines stood where the building had been. The school, indeed, was broken. It was nothing but a big hole in the ground. Nina then explained that they would be bused to another school this fall, while a larger school was being constructed on the old site.

Broken is a mechanical word that finds its way into human situations. Windows break because they are brittle. Cars, washing machines, clocks, and TV sets break because they are imperfect machines that wear out or malfunction. I find something therapeutic about working on machines and sometimes envy the engineers in town. Occasionally I like to invest my time in something that can be "fixed," and I have often grieved that people and churches are not so easy.

I. *The Covenant can be broken.* We sometimes speak of a person who has had a complete "breakdown," and everyone knows from experience the meaning of a "broken heart." In school, we learn about the problems that emerge when someone "breaks the rules." I recall a newspaper article about a large Baptist convention that I attended. The reporter tossed in the old saw about the Baptist who came to town with the Ten Commandments in one pocket and a ten-dollar bill in the other. He left without having broken either. Breaking a bill is not a big deal, but a broken commandment is a moral failure that has serious consequences in the bond of trust between God and the people.

A common biblical term for the failure of God's people is to break covenant. Through Hosea, God complains about Israel: "they have broken my covenant, and transgressed my law" (8:1). The covenant bond that tied Israel to God was like a marriage. It was a bond of trust, a promise for life between two parties grounded in love and expressed in faithfulness. It was not a cold contract of rules and regulations. Always, God's bond to the people is a bond of covenant love (*hesed*): "For I desire steadfast love and not sacrifice, the knowledge of God rather than burnt offerings" (6:6).

The story of Hosea is allegory, a living parable to the covenant relationship between Jahweh and Israel. Considerable discussion has been given to the question of history. Is this a real-life parable, or a story to illustrate a point? Hosea was called by God to marry a woman named Gomer, whom he loved. Some indication of a problem emerges when names are given to each of the three children. The firstborn son was named Jezreel—a place of military disaster like Pearl Harbor. A daughter was named "no mercy," and the youngest son was named "not my people." Hosea discovers that his wife has been unfaithful, playing the prostitute. That kind of behavior tends to put a strain on the marriage bond. Hosea and Gomer are separated either because she leaves him for her lovers, or he was understandably divorced for her adultery. The marriage commanded by God seems to have been a bad idea from the start, but God sends Hosea out after Gomer a second time. He finds his beloved on the auction block and buys her back. But this is not a marriage of contracts and commerce. Hosea commits himself to winning back Gomer's love and fidelity.

Eric Rust discovered a natural connection between the Hebrew idea of marriage and the covenant relationship with God. In Genesis, God created male and female together in the divine image. Marriage brings two incomplete beings into wholeness. From the beginning the covenant between God and Israel was filled with grace and characterized by faithful love. Rust notes that the Hebrew word for God's love, *hesed,* is more than mercy or loving kindness as in the King James. God's love is marked by fidelity to promise, and God demands no less from us.

If covenant is like the commitment of love between husband and wife, sin is like adultery, unfaithfulness to the marriage promise. The broken covenant flies in the face of the eternal mercy of God. It demands punishment, divorce, destruction of the other; but at the core of God's nature is *hesed.* Like His servant Hosea, God is faithful not only to the marriage, but to the redemption of his beloved.

II. *The Covenant can be restored.* Henry Ward Beecher was the pastor of Congregational Plymouth Church in Brooklyn. He was also the brother of Harriet Beecher Stowe, author of *Uncle Tom's Cabin* and, like his sister, a committed opponent to the institution of slavery. On September 19, 1860, Beecher stood in his pulpit beside a small slave child. He challenged his congregation to raise the $800 price to buy the girl from her owner, and the congregation rose to the occasion, pledging the full purchase price for her freedom. Sixty-eight years later, in 1928, that slave child, Mrs. James Hunt, climbed back to the same spot where her fate had once hung in the balance, and she told the congregation in a quite articulate manner how she had thought that God had abandoned her that day until she heard the voice of the great preacher, "My child, you are now free!" Robert Sanders tells the story as he introduces Hosea in his book on the Prophets, *Radical Voices in the Wilderness,* and wonders about the "Everlasting Mercy" that was demonstrated in Hosea's similar purchase of Gomer from her bondage to sin. The focus of Hosea's message is not on the infidelity of Gomer but on the faithfulness of God, not on the hopelessness of sin but on the promise of a restored relationship through the grace of God. The whole story is the call in chapter 6: "Come, let us return to the LORD."

Finally, a word for my grandchildren: Nina and Kye, I can't wait to see your new school. Broken was the right word. Things we build, break. Schools get broken. Churches are sometimes broken. Families break. But God cannot be broken, and God will not stop loving us. God is faithful, and God is able to rebuild our lives even better than the construction crew will build your school. The story of the Bible is about the broken people that God keeps on loving and the unbroken promise of God. Let's make a covenant with God and with each other to be faithful as God is faithful.—Larry Dipboye

SUNDAY, MARCH 13, 2005
Lectionary Message
Topic: The Resurrection and the Life
TEXT: John 11:1–45
Other Readings: Ezek. 37:1–14; Ps.130; Rom. 8:6–11

When Jesus left Jerusalem following the Feast of Dedication, less than four months remained in his earthly ministry. Since his "hour" had not yet come, he continued to minister in Perea, east of the Jordan and away from the center of the Jewish leaders' power. Moving on his Father's timetable, he avoided those who were determined to put him to death.

In John 11 there is a visit to Bethany. The event was the death of Lazarus. This village was located about two miles east of Jerusalem on the road to Jericho. It was near enough to Jerusalem for Jesus and the disciples to be in danger, but far enough away so as not to attract attention prematurely.

I. *Lazarus becomes sick and dies (vv. 1–16).*

- Two sisters send for Jesus
- Lazarus's sickness for the glory of God
- After two days Jesus decides to go

- His disciples object
- Jesus' reply
- Jesus means Lazarus has died
- Another opportunity to believe in Jesus

Disciples: "Let's go, too—and die with Jesus"

As their brother grew sick, Mary and Martha turned to Jesus for help. They believed in his ability to help because they had seen his miracles. Any trial a believer faces can ultimately bring glory to God because God can bring good out of any bad situation.

If Jesus had been with Lazarus during the final moments of Lazarus's sickness, he might have healed him rather than let him die. But Lazarus died so that Jesus' power over death could be shown to his disciples and others who were watching. The raising of Lazarus was an essential display of his power, and the resurrection from the dead is a crucial belief of the Christian faith. Jesus not only raised himself from the dead, but he has the power to raise others.

There are unknown dangers in doing God's work. It is wise to consider the high cost of being Jesus' disciple.

II. *Jesus comforts Mary and Martha (vv. 17–37).*

- Lazarus already in his grave for four days
- Many people have come to pay their respects and console Martha and Mary
- Martha goes out to meet Jesus: "Lord, if you had been here . . ."
- Jesus: "Your brother will rise again"
- Martha: "Yes, when everyone else rises, on resurrection day"
- Jesus: "I am the resurrection and the life. Those who believe in me, even though they die like everyone else, will live again"
- "Do you believe this, Martha?"
- Mary goes to Jesus
- Mourners follow Mary
- Mary falls to Jesus' feet weeping
- Jesus is deeply moved
- Jesus weeps
- Questions by the crowd

Many agree that the home of Martha, Mary, and Lazarus was Jesus' home away from home while he was in Jerusalem and the surrounding area. But even this did not make their home immune from trouble and sorrow.

Jesus was in Perea when he received the news. A two-day delay plus a two-day journey to Bethany corresponds to the time Lazarus was dead when he received the news. It would suggest that Jesus knew Lazarus was dead when he received the news.

When Jesus arrived in Bethany he found that Lazarus had been in the tomb four days. Of necessity the Jews buried people the day they died.

True to her nature, Martha was stirring about. She was probably looking after their visitors. Martha, hearing that Jesus was coming up the road, rushed out to meet him. She expressed her faith that had he been there he would have prevented Lazarus' death.

However, her faith still held that even now whatever he asked of God would be granted.

Herschel Hobbs writes, "One cannot help but ask why this crisis should happen to such a beloved family. Each of us has asked, 'Why me, Lord?' The answer is that God does not seal His people in a trouble-proof bag to shield them from the stern realities of life."

Jesus has power over life and death as well as power to forgive sins. This is because he is the creator of life. He who is life can surely restore life. Whoever believes in Christ has a spiritual life that death cannot conquer or diminish in any way. When we realize his power and how wonderful his offer to us really is, how can we not commit our lives to him?

III. *Jesus raises Lazarus from the dead (vv. 38–45).*

- They come to the grave, a cave with a stone rolled across its entrance
- Jesus: "Remove the stone"
- He has been dead four days
- "Father, thank you for hearing me"
- "Lazarus, come out!"
- "Unwrap him and let him go"

Many of the people who were with Mary believed in Jesus when they saw what happened.

Tombs at this time were usually caves carved in the limestone rock of a hillside. A tomb was often large enough for people to walk inside. Several bodies would be placed in one tomb. After burial, a large stone was rolled across the entrance to the tomb.

Jesus' words were "I am the resurrection, and the life; he who believes in me shall live even if he dies, and everyone who lives and believes in me shall never die." These words have ministered to and increased the faith of millions who have stood in bereavement.

Now we see why Jesus delayed his coming to Bethany. The Jews had a belief that when a person died, the spirit waited three days in hope of reentering the body. If after that time it had not done so, the spirit departed. Had Jesus raised Lazarus during that three days, the Jews would have interpreted it according to their false belief. Equally false is the view of some today that Lazarus was only in a coma. There must be no question concerning Lazarus's death. He was dead, buried, and decomposing. No one could reasonably deny the enormousness of this sign.

Herschel H. Hobbs writes what joy overflowed the hearts of this little family! The sisters had buried him with deep sorrow. Now they abounded with joy. Truly, they had seen the glory of God! Many believed in Jesus.—T. Vaughn Walker

ILLUSTRATION

LAZARUS AND JESUS.   This a sign, and beyond what is apparently happening is what is really happening. It is as though one held up to the light a sheet of paper on which was written the story of the raising of Lazarus. But bleeding through from the reverse side of the paper, and clear enough to be read, is the other story of the death and resurrection of Jesus.—Fred B. Craddock[1]

SERMON SUGGESTIONS

Topic: Providence All the Way

TEXT: Isa. 39:8–13

Because God cares for his people, (1) he has a plan for them (vv. 8–9); (2) he will meet their unfolding needs (vv. 9–12); (3) they can join in a hymn of rejoicing (v. 13).

Topic: True Christian Leaders

TEXT: 1 Cor. 3:10–11, 16–23

(1) Will build on the foundation of Jesus Christ. (2) Will treat God's people as his very temple. (3) Will serve on the basis that they belong to the people who belong to Christ and that the people do not belong to them.

WORSHIP AIDS

CALL TO WORSHIP.   "Commit your way to the Lord; trust in him, and he will act" (Ps. 37:5, NRSV).

INVOCATION.   Lord, fill the depths of the searching of our souls with the wisdom and power of the living god, and shape in us a worship pleasing to our Creator and soul-enlarging to us, for Jesus' sake.

OFFERTORY SENTENCE.   "Ascribe to the Lord the glory due his name; bring an offering, and come before him. Worship the Lord in holy splendor" (1 Chron. 16:29).

OFFERTORY PRAYER.   Lord, through this offering, bring some soul to Christ, lead some saint to victory over temptation, allow some praying struggler to find peace, build the kingdom, redeem the saints, magnify the name of Jesus.—E. Lee Phillips

PRAYER.   Here we are, Father, your children, alike, yet different; a family, yet individuals; gathered from separate places, coming for different reasons, burdened with varied needs.

There are those present this morning who come with large question marks in their minds, Father. Life has dealt them a hard blow and their faith has been shaken by the circumstances they are forced to manage. In the midst of their struggle they have called for some direction, some sign that you are with them, and they have seen nothing thus far to encourage them or strengthen them in their struggle. This morning let some word be fitly spoken that will give the assurance they need or answer the nagging doubts that assail them. May these hon-

---

[1]*The Gospels* (Nashville, Tenn.: Abingdon Press, 1981), p. 141.

est and shaken souls go from this gathering today reassured of your caring because they have experienced you here in this fellowship.

There are those present this morning who have been disappointed in their fellow human beings. Trust, once so strong, has been shaken or destroyed. Loyalties have been betrayed, and right now there is the feeling that nothing can ever be the same again. Lead these dear souls to the place where forgiveness of another becomes real for them and restoration of relationships becomes a reality. May those spirits wounded by the misdeeds of another find here sufficient faith to bring about a mending of hurts, we pray.

There are present this morning those whose sins have so strained their lives that they cannot continue their journey in peace. Give them the courage to face themselves, their guilt, and their need to seek forgiveness, that they may find life worth living again. Oh, Father! Open the door of redeeming love for them this morning as we worship before you, we pray.

There are those who come this morning resounding notes of joy because of what they have experienced through faith as they have walked life's road. They have tasted its all-sufficiency and gloried in its strength. Thank you for them, Father, and may we all join their ranks ere this hour is done, we pray in Jesus' Name.—Henry Fields

SERMON
Topic: Stop and Smell the Thorns Along the Way
Text: 2 Cor. 12:1–9

Do you think the apostle Paul would have given almost anything to have a friend who could pull the thorn from his flesh and wrap his wounds? Paul longed for this thorn to be removed: "For this thorn I prayed to the Lord three times that it might depart from me" (2 Cor. 2:8). However, the thorn remained.

Why do life's roses have thorns anyway? I suppose the beautiful, sweet-smelling rose was created by God to have thorns. A rose is not a complete, whole plant without thorns.

Before we stop and smell the thorns, as well as the roses, let's begin by asking, *What was the thorn in Paul's flesh* that stayed with him like a hunting dog on the heels of a rabbit? Could it have been a physical thorn? Paul's body must have been bent over, old, and weak when he wrote these words. Listen to a few words form his diary (2 Cor. 11:24–27). It is no wonder that onlookers said of Paul, "His bodily presence is weak" (10:10). Paul probably had physical pain that constantly nagged him, as if he were daily lying on a bed of nails. Perhaps he had unhealed wounds caused by scourgings or stonings. Perhaps that is why Luke the physician was his traveling companion. We could hypothesize further concerning Paul's thorn.

Was Paul's thorn physical, emotional, or spiritual? I choose to believe that *thorn* was a catch-all word Paul used for all the difficulties and troubles that befell him during his ministry. There is not one thorn in mind here, but a principle that applies to everyone. The Greek word for thorn meant "a mode of execution or torture, a stake, unbearable pain." Paul was like one crucified: "Always carrying in the body the death of Jesus, so that the life of Jesus may also be manifested in our bodies. For while we live, we are always being given up to death for Jesus' sake, so that the life of Jesus may be manifested in our moral flesh" (2 Cor. 4:10–11).

This leads us to a second question: *Why was the thorn given to Paul?* As we have just implied, we speak here only of thorns allowed by God . . . only they have a purpose. Paul is not talking about thorns we bring upon ourselves through our own sinful devices, suggested Clarence Macartney. Paul's thorn must be linked with following God's will. Much trouble is not related to suffering for Christ, but it is self-manufactured. This was not the case with Paul's thorn.

Instead, God allows thorns, for one thing, to keep us from falling into the pit of spiritual arrogance. Paul declared, "To keep me from being too elated by the abundance of revelations, a thorn was given me in the flesh" (12:7). Thorns are given to us sometimes as a deterrent from spiritual pride. The thorns remind us of our humanity in need of redemption.

Furthermore, thorns may be given by God to aid the Christian's ministry in forwarding the cause of Christ, not hindering it. The thorn brought Paul to his knees in prayer and dependence upon God, leaving him more open to the leading of God's Spirit. The thorn never embittered Paul, and it never turned him back from his divine call. Instead, it pushed him forward as he pressed on.

Some people are inspiring because of their thorns. Helen Keller was blind and deaf, yet from her world of darkness and silence she shined a radiant light that has guided the pathways of millions of people to this day.

How can we learn to stop and smell the thorns along the way? After Paul had earnestly prayed repeatedly for the thorn to be removed from his life, God answered, "My grace is sufficient for thee, for my power is made perfect in weakness" (12:9). God gave Paul something better than what he desired; he gave him grace, the unmerited favor of God.

God's grace is sufficient for you, no matter what thorn has stabbed your life. It is sufficient for one reason, because grace helps us to endure when the thorn is not removed. We can repeat the words of Paul: "For the sake of Christ, then, I am content with weakness, insults, hardships, persecutions, and calamities" (12:10).

Naturally, no one wants a thorn in the flesh, but sometimes we have no choice but to do the best we can with one when it comes. Paul did not want a thorn in the flesh, but he found God's grace was sufficient to keep him in the race toward the finish line.

In a similar vein, God's grace is sufficient because it is the vehicle that carries God's strength to us in our times of human weakness. God assured Paul, "My power is made perfect in weakness" (12:9c). The world's strength is weak when set alongside God's power; it is like comparing an ant to an elephant.

Paul Scherer reminds us that the world and Satan are too strong for us without God's grace. We need to link our abilities with God's grace to find new power for living.

You may never know God's strength until you have been pressed to pray about something that lingers and will not leave. God's grace is sufficient to give us a different attitude toward thorns in the flesh. Paul stated that his thorn in the flesh was a "messenger of Satan to harass me" (12:9b).

We cannot always dodge the thorns, but what will we allow God to do with us despite them? Will we let the thorns get the best of us, or through God's grace will we turn Satan's barriers into God's blessings?

Jesus Christ, for our sakes, endured not one thorn, but a crown of thorns. Every thorn that pierced deeply into his skull was for you and for me. Each huge spike that was driven through his hands and feet was for you and me. Christ, too, prayed three times in the Garden of Gethsemane for the crown of thorns and the cross to be removed. God the Father could well have answered, "Son, my grace is sufficient for thee, for my strength is made perfect in weakness." Paul said it best: "For he was crucified in weakness, but lives by the power of God. For we are weak in him, but in dealing with you we shall live with him by the power of God" (13:4).

What is your thorn in the flesh? Whatever it is, take heart, because "God's grace is sufficient for thee."—Ron R. Blankenship

SUNDAY, MARCH 20, 2005
Lectionary Message

Topic: The Triumphal Entry

TEXT: Matt. 21:1–11

Other Readings: Ps. 118:1–2, 19–29; Isa. 50:4–9a; Ps. 31:9–16; Phil. 2:5–11; Matt. 26:14–27:66

I. *Introduction/background.* All four Gospels record this entry into Jerusalem. Herschel Hobbs states that is usually called Jesus' "Triumphal Entry." But was it? In the time when a victorious king or general returned to his capital city, the populace gave him a triumphal entry. He rode a white horse, symbolic of victory. Chained captives walked behind him. The throngs cheered and threw flowers upon him. And he threw coins into the crowd.

None of those elements are present in this scene. It took place before the battle (cross), not after the victory. He rode a donkey, like a king, when in peace he visited a city in his realm. Hobbs calls this Jesus' "Royal Entry." He came to offer peace and was rejected.

II. *Jesus rides into Jerusalem on a donkey.* Matthew mentions a donkey and a colt, while the other Gospels mention only the colt. This was the same event, but Matthew focuses on the prophecy in Zechariah 9:9, where a donkey and a colt are mentioned (Zech. 9:9, NLT): "Rejoice greatly, O people of Zion! Shout in triumph, O people of Jerusalem! Look, your king is coming to you. He is righteous and victorious, yet he is humble, riding on a donkey—even a donkey's colt." He shows how Jesus' actions fulfilled the prophet's words, thus giving another indication that Jesus was indeed the Messiah. When Jesus entered Jerusalem on a donkey's colt, he affirmed his messianic royalty as well as his humility.

According to Warren Wiersbe, this was the only "public demonstration" that our Lord allowed while he was ministering on earth. The result was a growing animosity on the part of the religious leaders, leading eventually to the Crucifixion of the Savior.

There were three groups in the crowd that day: (1) the Passover visitors from outside Judea (John 12:12, 18); (2) the local people who had witnessed the raising of Lazarus; and (3) the religious leaders who were greatly concerned about what Jesus might do at the feast. At each of the feasts, the people were in keen expectation, wondering if Jesus would be there and what he would do. It looked as though Jesus was actually seeking to incite a revolution and establish himself as king, but that was not what he had in mind.

Certainly Jesus was openly announcing to the people that he indeed is the King of Israel, the promised Messiah. No doubt many of the pilgrims hoped that *now* he would defeat the Romans and set the nation of Israel free.

Wiersbe asked, What did this demonstration mean to the Romans? Nothing is recorded about the Roman viewpoint, but it is certain that they kept a close watch that day. During the annual Passover feast, it was not uncommon for some of the Jewish nationalists to try to arouse the people; and perhaps they thought this parade was that kind of an event. I imagine that some of the Roman soldiers must have smiled at the "Triumphal Entry," because it was nothing like their own "Roman triumph" celebrations in the city of Rome.

Wiersbe says whenever a Roman general was victorious on foreign soil, killing at least five thousand of the enemy, and gaining new territory, he was given a "Roman triumph" when he returned to the city. It was the Roman equivalent of the American ticker-tape parade, only with much more splendor. The victor would be permitted to display the trophies he had won and the enemy leaders he had captured. The parade ended at the arena where some of the captives entertained the people by fighting wild beasts. Compared to a "Roman triumph," our Lord's entry into Jerusalem was nothing.

What did the "Triumphal Entry" mean to the people of Israel? The pilgrims welcomed Jesus, spread their garments before him, and waved palm branches as symbols of peace and victory. They quoted from Psalm 118:26, which is a messianic psalm; and they proclaimed him the "King of Israel." But while they were doing this, Jesus was weeping!

Verse 8 is one of the few places where the Gospels record that Jesus' glory is recognized on earth. Jesus boldly declared himself King, and the crowd gladly joined him. But these same people would bow to political pressure and desert him in just a few days. Today we celebrate this event on Palm Sunday. That day should remind us to guard against superficial acclaim for Christ.

The name Jerusalem means "city of peace" or "foundation of peace," and the people were hoping that Jesus would bring them the peace that they needed. However, he wept because he saw what lay ahead of the nation: war, suffering, destruction, and a scattered people.

How did the Jewish leaders respond to the "Triumphal Entry" of the Lord? As they watched the great crowd gather and honor Jesus, the Pharisees were quite sure that Jesus had won the day. They were anticipating some kind of general revolt during the Passover season. Perhaps Jesus would perform a great miracle and in that way capture the minds and hearts of the restless people. How little they really understood the mind and heart of the Master! What they did not realize was that Jesus was "forcing their hand" so that the Sanhedrin would act during the feast. The Lamb of God had to give his life when the Passover lambs were being slain.—T. Vaughn Walker

ILLUSTRATION

PROMISE AND FULFILLMENT.   Matthew places his emphasis on the character of Jesus, who termed himself gentle and humble (11:29–30), and is therefore the promised King for all the little ones, the poor and humble, who expect everything from God (5:3–5). Thus he introduces the Passion narrative. The obedience of the disciples is also part of the story; they follow Jesus' instructions to the letter and thereby contribute to fulfilling the promise.—Eduard Schweizer[2]

---

[2]*The Good News According to Matthew* (Atlanta: John Knox Press, 1975), p. 405.

SERMON SUGGESTIONS

Topic: The Taste of Death and the Life of Grace

TEXT: Heb. 2:9

(1) Jesus Christ not only died, but he tasted death as incredible bitterness and penury of soul. I would dwell on the psychology even more than on the theology of it. (2) He did so because he died for every one of us. He experienced in a divine life the universal death. (3) Yet this desertation and agony of death was a gift and grace of God, not only to us, but to him. And he knew it was so. And that faith was his victory and our redemption.—P. T. Forsyth

Topic: God Reveals Himself

(1) In historical events. (2) Through persons. (3) Supremely through one person: Jesus Christ. (4) Through the life of a community. (5) Through a book.—Robert McAfee Brown

WORSHIP AIDS

CALL TO WORSHIP.   "Let us praise God for his glorious grace, for the free gift he gave us in his dear Son! For by the death of Christ we are set free, that is, our sins are forgiven. How great is the grace of God, which he gave to us in such large measure" (Eph. 1:7–8a, TEV).

INVOCATION.   Lord, let our cheers of this day last the rest of our lives, that rejoicing may never be replaced with rejection, that the Son who comes riding into our lives may so control the desires of our hearts that we will give praises to God all our days. Amen.—E. Lee Phillips

OFFERTORY SENTENCE.   "Will anyone rob God? Yet you are robbing me! But you say, 'How are we robbing you?' In your tithes and offerings" (Mal. 3:8, NRSV).

OFFERTORY PRAYER.   Accept this offering O Lord, as today we rejoice in the coming of our Lord, riding in the Kingship he deserves and use of gifts to spread the word, that Christ died for all.—E. Lee Phillips

PRAYER.   In these early beginnings of a new spring, we come to thank you that you have kept us through the dark and quiet hours of the night and have brought us to this moment of worship. We see the beauty of the world unfolding as shrubs bud with promising blossoms; birds, gone for the winter, return with melodious song; and warmth spreads its blanket over the earth, forcing it to respond in growth and plenty. And we know once again that all nature sings and round us rings the music of the spheres.

As we worship we remember the redeeming God, who in the cross has shown us the full face of grace and forgiveness. How we need to experience forgiveness—forgiveness for the misuse of words, not honoring the call to truth, spending our wealth and power in unwise ways, belittling others with our attitudes and deeds, harboring evil toward those who trouble us, and much more. Father, cleanse us from our iniquity and make us whole. Deliver us from our foolish ways, that we may walk in the ways of truth and love after the fashion of the Lord.

Abiding Father, we pray this morning that you will cradle gently those who are grieving over the death of a loved one, those struggling with pain, those waiting beside sick folk, swaying to and fro on words of better, then worse, knowing that healing comes slowly and sometimes not at all. For all who are weary and heavy laden, cumbered with a load of care, we ask your abiding presence with them and pray for your healing touch upon them.

We pray for ourselves, a family of faith. Grant us wisdom and courage, vision and the will for right living in these days. May we be kind, one to another, tenderhearted, forgiving, affirming, and faithful as we make the journey along the road of life one with the other. We pray in Jesus' name.—Henry Fields

SERMON
Topic: A Clean, Well-Lighted Place and the Cross
Text: Ps. 22; Luke 23:33–48

I want to tell a story about a man who knew what it was to despair and wonder if there was any reason to hope.

All of his life this man had a profound sense of the presence and goodness of God. Life, as he and his family and community had known it, was hard, precarious, and uncertain. But this hardness of life could not shake his faith in God, and his faith that God was at work in the world setting right what had gone wrong. So profound was his conviction that he quit his day job and became an itinerant preacher, proclaiming this gospel of God's unconditional love.

People began to listen and began to follow him. They heard him say that the most important things were the things of the Spirit and that if we put these things first everything else we needed would be given us. He told his followers not to "worry about your life, what you will eat, what you will wear." Life is more than all that, he said. "Look at the birds of the air," he said. "They don't work, yet God takes care of them. Are you not of more value than they?"

"Consider the lilies of the field," he said; "they neither toil nor spin, yet I tell you, even Solomon in all his glory was not clothed like one of these." If God lavishes such care on something as insignificant as grass, "will he not much more clothe you—you of little faith?" God knows already what we need; and if we put the things of God first, then everything that we really need will be ours.

The faith of Jesus was an absolute, unconditional faith that God would love and sustain us and be with us, no matter what. It was an absolute faith that God wanted righteousness and justice and would be there wherever human beings courageously took a stand for the rule of God in the world. And so Jesus courageously went to Jerusalem to take a stand, to say to the Powers That Be that this is what believing in God really means.

And the Powers That Be crucified him.

Jesus had said that even we who are evil know how to give good things to the ones we love. "How much more will you, Abba in heaven, give good things to those who ask?" Yet in the Garden of Gethsemane Jesus had asked for the cup of crucifixion to pass, and God had not given him that good thing. Instead, God had given him the Cross and then he had abandoned him there, in that despairing moment when Jesus cried, "My God, my God, why have you forsaken me?"

In this moment of despair, in this moment of hopelessness, it must have seemed to Jesus that his wonderful dream of a kingdom where all would know the love and grace of God that *he* had known was finished, over, done with.

Scholars tell us that Jesus' cry of dereliction probably means that he was reciting or singing Psalm 22. This psalm taken as a whole is a portrait of the soul struggling with despair. Its first words are those awful words of abandonment by God that Matthew and Mark quote for us as the only word of Christ from the Cross. The second movement of the psalm, however, is a word of trust: a recitation of the trust Israel had placed in God and an affirmation of how that trust had been well-placed. Then the psalmist plunges once again into despair, calling himself a "worm." But then the mood turns again and the psalmist remembers God's blessings, which flood his soul with hope.

We do not know how far Jesus got into the singing of this psalm as he hung on the Cross. We do know that the psalm ends in praise of the God who delivers even the despairing from the temptation to give up hope. "He did not despise or abhor the affliction of the afflicted," the psalmist writes; "he did not hide his face from me but heard when I cried to him." And because God had heard this cry of dereliction, future generations will be told about the Lord, and proclaim "his deliverance to a people yet unborn, saying he has done it." Psalm 22 ends with this affirmation of faith.

I want to believe that Jesus did get to the end of the psalm and that the despair with which it begins is not his final word; that his final word is the psalm's word of faith and trust and hope in God *in spite* of this sense of abandonment. Jesus' despair was real, but it wasn't final.

Luke's account of the Crucifixion lends some credence to this understanding of the cry of dereliction. Luke gives us three of the seven last words of Jesus, and all of them betray his ultimate trust in God.

When first lifted up on the Cross, Jesus says, "Abba, forgive them, for they know not what they do."

Midway through the Crucifixion, he says to the penitent criminal, "Today you will be with me in Paradise."

And at the end, he cries with a loud voice, "Abba, into your hands I commend my spirit."

Whatever abandonment Jesus may have felt, I believe that at the very end he entrusted his spirit to the God of love and grace he had believed in all of his life. God had not abandoned him. God was there, with him, even at the end.

According to John's Gospel, Jesus' final words from the Cross were, "It is finished." Finished in the sense of completed. The deliverance the psalmist had spoken of hundreds of years earlier is now made perfect in Jesus. It is a deliverance that we, a people yet unborn, have known; a deliverance from all that would destroy our hope.

Is there a clean, well-lighted place where we can go when the darkness threatens us? Is there a place where we can find wholeness and human dignity in place of our dis-ease? Is there any place Hemingway's older waiter could have gone, besides a café or a bar, to find the light? Is there anything besides brandy that might have alleviated the awful ache of nothingness Hemingway's would-be suicide felt?

There is a place where we can go with all the burdens of our life: all of our failures, sorrows, guilt, disappointments, pains, uncertainty, sin, and even our despair. In this place we encounter one who is a man of sorrows and acquainted with grief, who knows even more than we what it is to despair. He does not take our burdens from us, but he does help us carry them, because he knows our burdens far better then we do. He has carried them already to the cross.

The place where we encounter this one is clean and well-lighted, and there's room enough for all of us there.

How do you find this place?

You find the clean, well-lighted place at the foot of the cross.—Bill Thomason

SUNDAY, MARCH 27, 2005
Lectionary Message

Topic: The Empty Tomb

TEXT: John 20:1–18

Other Readings: Acts 10:34–43; Ps. 118:1–2, 14–24; Col. 3:1–4; Isa. 25:6–9; Ps. 114; 1 Cor. 5:6b–8; Luke 24:13–49

I. *Introduction/background.* The greatest proof of Jesus' Resurrection is the difference it made in his followers. To explain the Christian movement on anything less than absolute, irrefutable truth would be both psychologically and spiritually impossible.

The commentary in the *Life Application Study Bible* indicates that the absence of women among the twelve disciples has bothered a few people. But it is clear that there were many women among Jesus' followers. It is also clear that Jesus did not treat women as others in his culture did; he treated them with dignity, as people with worth.

Mary of Magdala was an early follower of Jesus who certainly deserves to be called a disciple. An energetic, impulsive, caring woman, she not only traveled with Jesus but also contributed to the needs of the group. She was present at the Crucifixion and was on her way to anoint Jesus' body on Sunday morning when she discovered the empty tomb. Mary was the first to see Jesus after his Resurrection.

Mary Magdalene is a heartwarming example of thankful living. Jesus miraculously freed her life when he drove seven demons out of her. In every glimpse we have of her, she was acting out of her appreciation for the freedom Christ had given her. That freedom allowed her to stand under Christ's cross when all the disciples except John were hiding in fear. After Jesus' death, she intended to give his body every respect. Like the rest of Jesus' followers, she never expected his bodily resurrection—but she was overjoyed to discover it.

Mary's faith was not complicated, but it was direct and genuine. She was more eager to believe and obey than to understand everything. Jesus honored her childlike faith by appearing to her first and by entrusting her with the first message of his Resurrection.

II. *Jesus rises from the dead (vv. 1–9).* John related his account of the discovery of Jesus' Resurrection from the standpoint of Mary Magdalene. He allowed the presence of other women with her, as recorded by Matthew 28:1 and Mark 16:1.

It was on the "first day of the week." Literally, "the first of the Sabbaths." "The Sabbaths" so used denoted "the week." This was "early" on our Sunday morning. A comparison of the Gospel accounts shows that she and the other women started to the tomb while it was still dark and arrived there at early dawn. The stone covering the entrance to the tomb had been rolled away to let the women in to see that the tomb was empty. So Jesus was resurrected sometime prior to early dawn on Sunday morning. The stone was not rolled away from the entrance to the tomb so Jesus could get out. He could have left easily without moving the stone. It was rolled away so others could get in and see that Jesus was gone.

According to Hobbs this time element constitutes a problem for some interpreters. Noting Jesus' words about being in the heart of the earth "three days and three nights," they figure back from Sunday morning to either Wednesday or Thursday for Jesus' death and burial. We have noted that he was crucified on the "preparation" of Friday.

However, when we note the Jewish, Roman, and Greek method of reckoning time, the problem vanishes. They all considered any part of a day as an entire day. Jesus spoke in terms of that understanding. He was buried late on Friday (one day). He was in the tomb all Saturday (one day). He rose from the dead between sunset and sunrise on Sunday (one day). On several occasions Jesus said He would rise the "third day." So this is in agreement with his words.

People who hear about the Resurrection for the first time may need time before they can comprehend this amazing story. Like Mary and the disciples, they may pass through four stages of belief. (1) At first, they may think the story is a fabrication, impossible to believe. (2) Like Peter, they may check out the facts and still be puzzled about what happened. (3) Only when they encounter Jesus personally are they able to accept the fact of the Resurrection. (4) Then, as they commit themselves to the Risen Lord and devote their lives to serving him, they begin to understand fully the reality of his presence with them.

Despite Jesus' many references to his Resurrection, none of his friends remembered. Mary Magdalene "runs and comes to Simon Peter and to the other disciple whom Jesus loved." The other disciple whom Jesus loved refers to John himself. She carries the distressing news that "they have taken away the Lord out of the tomb, and we do not know where they laid him." She assumed someone had taken Jesus' body away and she did not know where it was.

In a race to the tomb, after hearing this startling news, Peter and John were followed by Mary. "And the two were running together; and the other disciple ran ahead faster than Peter, and came to the tomb first." Peter came second and Mary came in third. Being the younger of the two, John outran Peter.

John stooped and looked in and saw the linen cloth lying there, but he didn't go in. Then Simon Peter arrived and went inside. He also noticed the linen wrappings lying there, while the cloth that had covered Jesus' head was folded up and lying to the side. Then John also went in, and saw and believed, for until then they hadn't realized that the Scripture said he would rise from the dead. Then they went home.

The linen wrappings were left as if Jesus had passed right through them. The cloth that covered Jesus' head was still rolled up in the shape of a head, and it was at about the right distance from the wrappings that had enveloped Jesus' body. A grave robber couldn't possibly have made off with Jesus' body and left the linens as if they were still shaped around it.

Jesus' Resurrection is the key to the Christian faith. Why? (1) Just as he said, Jesus rose from the dead. We can be confident, therefore, that he will accomplish all he promised. (2) Jesus' bodily Resurrection shows us that the living Christ, not a false prophet or imposter, is ruler of God's eternal Kingdom. (3) We can be certain of our own resurrection because Jesus was resurrected. Death is not the end; there is future life. (4) The divine power that brought

Jesus back to life is now available to us to bring our spiritually dead selves back to life. (5) The Resurrection is the basis for the church's witness to the world.

III. *Jesus appears to Mary Magdalene (vv. 11–18).* According to John, Mary Magdalene was the first person to see Jesus after his Resurrection. After Peter and John left, she remained at the tomb. She did not yet believe that Jesus had been raised. So she stood outside the tomb weeping.

Finally, she stooped down and looked (took a sustained look) into the tomb. She saw what Peter and John had seen. But she also saw more. She saw two angels sitting, one at the head and the other at the foot, where Jesus' body had lain. "Had lain" or "was lying" means that it was lying there, but not anymore.

"Why are you crying?" the angels asked her. "Because they have taken away my Lord," she replied, "and I don't know where they have put him."

Having said this, "she turned around and beheld Jesus standing there, and did not know it was Jesus." Why did she not recognize Jesus? Since others would recognize him later, evidently it was not due to a change in appearance. Hobbs states, again, we assume it was because of her tears. Jesus asked, "Woman, why are you weeping? Who are you seeking?" Thinking that he was the gardener, Mary assumed he had removed Jesus' body. So she requested that he tell her where the body was, so she might take it away. Evidently she was thinking in terms of giving Jesus a decent burial. At this point the last thought to enter her mind was a resurrection.

Apparently Mary turned around with her back to the gardener. At this point Jesus spoke her name, "Mary." She recognized his voice! Hearing her name she "turned." This word expresses sudden action. She turned toward him and explained, "Teacher!"

"Don't cling to me," Jesus said, "for I haven't yet ascended to the Father. But go find my brothers and tell them that I am ascending to my Father and your Father, my God and your God."

Mary did not want to lose Jesus again. She had not yet understood the Resurrection. Perhaps she thought this was his promised second coming. But Jesus did not want to be detained at the tomb. If he did not ascend to heaven, the Holy Spirit could not come. Both he and Mary had important work to do.

Mary didn't recognize Jesus at first. Her grief had blinded her; she couldn't see him because she didn't expect to see him. Then he spoke her name, and immediately she recognized him. Imagine the love that flooded her heart when she heard her Savior saying her name. Jesus is near you, and he is calling your name. Can you, like Mary, regard him as your Lord?—T. Vaughn Walker

ILLUSTRATIONS

GOD'S PRESENCE.   St. John believes that everything that happens is the consequence of God's will, for what God did not will could not happen. But he is not a philosopher discussing abstractly the problem of free will; he is a deeply religious man who sees the presence of God in everything. He is aware, as the whole Bible is aware, that although it is absurd to suppose every illness or accident is an exact requital for sins committed, there is nevertheless a deep and mysterious connection between sin and suffering, as between sin and death. The power of Jesus to heal is therefore closely connected with his power to forgive sins (cf. Mark

2:1–12); the Greek verb "to heal," "make whole," is the same word as "to save" (*sozein*).—Alan Richardson[3]

A FINAL SHARING.   I believe that Christ's Resurrection was not different in kind from what we may hope for through him; that our rising will be a sharing in that Resurrection.—Geoffrey W. H. Lampe

SERMON SUGGESTIONS

Topic: The Living Christ
TEXT: Rev. 1:17–18
Faith in Christ is: (1) faith in a historical Christ. (2) Faith in a living Christ. (3) Faith in a Christ personal to each of us.—P. Y. Forsyth

Topic: Christ and the Golden Candlesticks
TEXT: Rev. 3:7–13
(1) We have the same spiritual resources and defenses that made the church in ancient Philadelphia invincible. (2) We have the confirmation of nearly two thousand years of Christian history to validate our faith. (3) We have the same divine Overseer who encouraged the faithful Philadelphians.—Charles W. Koller

WORSHIP AIDS
CALL TO WORSHIP.   "You are looking for Jesus of Nazareth, who was crucified. He has been raised." "The Lord has risen indeed" (Mark 16:6; Luke 24:34, NRSV).

INVOCATION.   Loudly would we sing our hosannas, Lord, for the tomb could not hold, nor sin destroy, our Savior. Because he lives, we too can live by faith and worship with rejoicing, which is our prayer this Easter Sunday.—E. Lee Phillips

OFFERTORY SENTENCE.   "Your life must be controlled by love, just as Christ loved us and gave his life for us as a sweet-smelling offering and sacrifice that pleases God" (Eph. 5:2, TEV).

OFFERTORY PRAYER.   Here is our resurrection offering, O Lord, one filled with gratitude and rejoicing and a prayer that it will lead many others to the one who conquered death and offers the faithful life everlasting.—E. Lee Phillips

PRAYER.   We don't really understand it, Father. Mystery surrounds the Good News of resurrection. Yet we know that you have created life and granted seasons for all things. We hear from afar the words of the ancient preacher reminding us that there is a season for all things under the sun. We understand that there is a time to be born and a time to die. We have seen that many times in our journeying through life. We even understand in part that there is a time to be reborn. We comprehend that life is renewed in this world as we commit ourselves

---

[3]*The Gospel According to Saint John* (London: SLM Press, 1959), p. 124.

to the Lord Jesus and receive his forgiveness. But resurrection is hard for us, just as it was for those who first experienced it. Maybe it is so because resurrection is not the expected experience. This morning, clear away the fog of our thinking, wipe away the mist of our doubts, and help us rejoice in the recollection of the Lord's Resurrection.

Then we shall be able to hope without fear, knowing that this little walk we take through life on earth is not the final event for us, but that there is more to come beyond the vale of death.

Then we shall be able to help, for we shall have reason to lift those who are fallen along the way and need a hand to strengthen them, so that they might journey on with renewed courage, which comes when we know that death has been swallowed up in life.

Then we shall be able to evaluate rightly and not be cumbered by the things of this world, not be tied down by the substance of life, but in the light of eternal life, see things as they are and be able to use them for the higher purposes of the Lord.

Then we shall be able to rejoice without hindrance, for we shall know that there is now nothing that can ever separate us from the love of Christ, not even death itself.

And above all we shall be able to tell good news to a world that is caught up in horror stories and depressing situations. We shall be able to love the unlovely, lift the fallen, comfort the comfortless, and declare the true day of salvation to all mankind.

Lord of the resurrection, come now among us with power, we pray in Jesus' name.—Henry Fields

SERMON
Topic: Awaiting the Spirit
TEXT: Ps. 130; James 5:7–11

I. The season of the Christian year called Eastertide is the time between Christ's Resurrection and the coming of the Spirit at Pentecost fifty days later. Eastertide is a time of waiting for the Spirit of God to become manifest in our lives.

Have you ever thought about how much of the Christian year and Christian life involves waiting? We begin the year with Advent, four weeks of preparation awaiting the birth of Christ. The Twelve Days of Christmas celebrate that birth and then give way to Epiphany. During the Ordinary Time between Epiphany and Lent, we wait for the baby born at Christmas to grow to adulthood and begin making manifest the coming rule of God in our hearts and the world. Even after Jesus begins his ministry, there is still a waiting he insists on. In Mark's Gospel Jesus sternly forbids those he has healed to reveal who healed them. And in John, one of the themes is that "the time has not yet come" for Jesus to be glorified.

That is why Lent, the next season of the Christian year, is also a time of waiting; we need to be ready for that final manifestation of God's rule, in the Cross and empty tomb, and Lent prepares our hearts and minds for this ultimate revelation of divine love.

After Easter comes Eastertide, and it too is a time of waiting. The Risen Christ, in his final appearance to the disciples, commands them to wait in Jerusalem for the Holy Spirit, God's final gift to God's people. The Spirit is welcome because the Spirit will encourage and sustain the Christian community in the time after Christ's departure and before Christ's return.

The whole of the Christian life since Jesus' Ascension has been a waiting for that return, a waiting for the eschaton, the end of all things, when history will finally come to fruition in God, and the purposes at work in our lives are finally revealed.

Waiting.

We should not really be surprised at this extraordinary emphasis on waiting in the Christian year and the Christian life. Waiting is a thread that runs through the fabric of Hebrew Scripture. If we try to pull that thread out, the whole fabric will unravel. God promises Sarai and Abram a child, and they wait twenty-five years for that promise to be fulfilled. Moses is called to liberate Israel from Egyptian bondage and spends the next forty years in the Sinai desert herding sheep, waiting for the burning bush that will reveal to him his opportunity to act. God commands Samuel to anoint the young man David to be King of Israel. But David is almost forty years old before God's promise is fulfilled. Isaiah of Babylon sees the coming Servant of the Lord who will achieve God's purposes through redemptive suffering. But six hundred years pass before that Suffering Servant appears.

II. This emphasis on waiting strikes us as extraordinary, in part at least because we are Americans, and for us waiting is almost subversive, an un-American activity. Our whole culture is predicated on the desire to do as much as possible as quickly as possible. We have invented all sorts of labor-saving devices that are supposed to save us time. We are the people who have invented instant everything: instant orange juice, instant mashed potatoes, instant replay, Minute Rice, fast food (a double oxymoron because so often it's not fast, and food it never is).

We don't like to wait in line or at stoplights. One of my pet peeves is the driver who manages to get into the left lane of the interstate and go exactly the same speed as the vehicle next to it in the right lane, making it impossible for me to go as fast as I want. Why do we want to save time? So we will have more of it to do the things we really want to do—which usually means cramming as much activity into the "saved" time as we possibly can.

(As we make plans for the summer, we would do well to remember that "vacation" comes from the same root that "vacate" and "vacant" come from. A vacation should literally be a time to empty our normal, regular activity. If we are to have a true vacation, we need to be careful about filling that time with activity that mimics our normal routine.)

Waiting.

It's not something we're good at in this country. Part of our problem is our belief that waiting is a waste of time. It seems to be a time when nothing significant happens. The important thing, after all, is what we're waiting for. If we can shorten the time it takes to get to the payoff, we feel that such a shortcut is good. This impatience to get to a desired end sometimes leads to business excesses, when decisions are often made with an eye only to the next quarter's profits and with little concern for long-term productivity and well-being (and sometimes no concern for legality). What we want—a nice return on our investment—is a good thing. If we can get that now, why wait? Now is better than later.

III. But considering this economic example gives us a clue why waiting is so important. To delay our payoff assumes that something good will happen if we wait, something better than if we did not wait. Development, growth, change—these can be better than an immediate payoff. But they take time, so we must be prepared to wait.

Time is God's creation, a necessary aspect of the kind of universe God made for us to live in. Whatever else we may say about our world, it is a world in a state of becoming, change, development. Nothing is completely inert, static, or unchanging, though some transformations may take eons to occur. Perhaps God could have created a universe that was perfect, complete at the moment of creation, one that would suffer no change ever. Perhaps God *has* created such a world, for all we know. Ours, however, is not that world. The universe God created for us is one dominated by a great fact: everything in it is being transformed into something else.

This great fact gives us a metaphor, an image, for interpreting our world and our lives. It is the image found in James 5 of the farmer patiently tending the field, waiting for the crops to grow. This metaphor of growth includes planting, cultivation, birth, maturation, and fruition as implicit elements.

I admire and respect people who can grow things. My wife and I don't have that skill. We have, instead, whatever the opposite of a green thumb would be—a "gray" thumb, perhaps, because all of the plants we've ever tried to grow have looked pretty gray just before expiring. We are like Sally, the career woman, wife, and mother in the comic strip "Sally Forth," who is contemplating a shriveled plant hanging in her kitchen and says to her husband, "This really upsets me, Ted. I watered it, I fertilized it, I gave it sunlight, and still it died."

"Some people just don't have a way with plants, Sal," Ted says.

"Hey, I even talked to it," Sally says.

And Ted responds, "Maybe 'Grow, you lousy weed!' wasn't soothing enough."

IV. We are creatures of time. That's the way God made us. We move from our past, through our present, into our future. We mark these times by the changes that occur as time passes: by comparing the way we were with the way we are now and the way we envision our various alternative futures.

One of the great things about being young is the sense of unlimited possibilities we see on our horizons. One of the sad things about growing old is the way we come to see the limits of our future. This sense of limitation comes partly because we have less time to realize such possibilities and also because we have a more realistic sense about what *is* possible. But one of the good things about growing older is that our future possibilities are more focused, more realistic, more attainable.

(They are more attainable in part because we are likely to have more economic resources. Remember the scene in the movie *Fried Green Tomatoes* where Kathy Bates is cut out of a parking space at a shopping center by two younger, sexier women? Bates begins ramming their car with hers while they look on helplessly, aghast at the thousands of dollars of damage she inflicts. When she's through, Bates rolls her window down and says triumphantly, "You may be younger, but I've got more insurance.")

Our essential involvement with time explains why we must learn to wait and why the Christian year is full of so much waiting. Christian discipleship is, in part, a school of waiting where we learn how to take into account our past, present, and future. The past has been determined and can't be changed. It also determines much of our present. Past circumstances, events, and decisions have made us who we are today and have ruled out possibilities that might have been real had those circumstances, events, and decisions been different.

My father hoped I would become a professional baseball player, because he loved baseball and would have liked to play professionally himself. When I announced that my future plans lay in another direction, he was disappointed. His hopes for my baseball career were not very realistic. In any case, whatever possibilities might have been mine when I was eighteen are no longer real, now that I am well past the minimum age for AARP membership, in part at least because of choices made when I was eighteen.

If the past determines our present, then the present is the moment we are given to determine the future by the choices we are now making. The future is the field out of which the real possibilities we can choose are growing. We explore this field of possibilities without imagination and select those we most want to realize. The decisions we make now are limited, of course, by the determination of the past. But the future is not completely determined. It is still open within the limitations set by past circumstances, events, and decisions.

V. Christian waiting is not like waiting in line at the bank or waiting for an income tax return. It is not like treading water. Christian waiting is not passive. Instead, it is an active waiting in which we prepare for what will be and ready ourselves for the coming of God's Spirit. The Christian year, with its emphasis on waiting, is a discipline for us to follow as we are being transformed from what we have been into what we will become through the present moment of our decisions and actions. The Christian year is a time of preparation and decision making, guided by the future possibilities we have imaginatively envisioned. It is a time of cultivation in anticipation of a future harvest.

As Christians, we believe God has a future for us. We envision what futures are possible, and we begin to discern—sometimes clearly, but more often than not through a glass darkly—which of those futures might be God's future for us. Our active waiting consists in our preparing for that future by seeing what it requires of us now. What actions do we need to take now to see that future realized? What attitudes and skills do we need to be developing now, so that when God's future is ready for us, we will be ready for it?

Our waiting may be a corporate waiting, when we as a Christian community wait for God's future (calling a new minister, for example, or resolving some denominational crisis). Or the waiting may be very personal—a waiting for the lab report from the doctor, or waiting for that person we long to know as a friend to respond to our overtures of friendship and love. In such waiting, there are two general questions we always need to ask. First, what in our past can we affirm as still viable for our future? Second, what in our past must we now be ready to give up in order to realize God's future for us?

We always want our waiting to end sooner rather than later. We are always impatient to get on with things. But God's time for us, like God's time for Sarai and Abram, Moses and David, may require later rather than sooner. Our waiting may be short or long. In either case, our waiting is sure, because the One we are awaiting is the Spirit of God, who is Lord of past, present, and future.

"God may not come when we want God to, but God always comes in time." We can therefore have confidence in our future, both as a Christian community and as individuals.

We are awaiting the Spirit of God, and God always comes in time.—Bill Thomason

SUNDAY, APRIL 3, 2005
Lectionary Message

Topic: A Unique Inheritance
Text: 1 Pet. 1:3–9
Other Readings: Acts 2:14a, 22–32; Ps. 16; John 20:19–31

Crown Prince Carl Philip of Sweden was born to be king. His parents and the nation rejoiced in May 1979 that they had an heir to the throne. It was probably a matter of relief to King

Carl XVI Gustav that his second child was a boy; his own parents had four daughters before finally producing the necessary male heir. The king was *not* pleased, therefore, when the Swedish Parliament changed the constitution's law of agnatic succession in December 1979. This meant a reigning monarch's eldest offspring, male *or* female, would become heir to the throne. Sweden now has Crown Princ*ess* Victoria, born two years before her brother. For seven months, Carl Philip possessed an inheritance that was his by birth and by law. Then his inheritance was taken from him—probably forever.

It's hard to lose something you thought was promised to you or yours by right, whether you're a king or a commoner. People displaced from their own land, surprised and angry relatives when a will is read, travelers finding that their hotel reservation has been disregarded, all these evoke the feeling of injustice and thwarted expectation. But Christians have an advantage over others when it comes to their inheritance. What is promised to them is guaranteed. Nothing can take it away from them. Their confidence in what has been pledged for the future sustains them in the present. This is what the writer of 1 Peter is reminding his readers in today's epistle lesson.

I. *Our inheritance is like no other.* The ironic thing about most inheritances is that the "lasting worldly goods" don't last. The treasures that have been left me by loved ones are precious to me, but eventually both they and I will wear out. My great-grandmother's wedding ring becomes thinner and more fragile each year I wear it. The Persian rug will one day fall prey to moths or mildew or simple wear and tear. Even a royal throne can be destroyed, and one kingdom overtaken by another. But our inheritance as Christians is "imperishable, undefiled, and unfading," as this morning's text puts it. We are heirs to eternal life, to heaven, to the salvation of our souls. This inheritance has no shelf life. It won't spoil or wear out or decline in value. We are heirs to something that will last forever and ever, as Paul reminded the Christians in Thessalonica. He wrote, "since we believe that Jesus died and rose again, even so, through Jesus, God will bring with him those who have fallen asleep . . . the dead in Christ will rise first, then we who are alive, who are left, shall be caught up together with them in the clouds to meet the Lord in the air; and *so we shall always be with the Lord.*"

No one can take this inheritance from those who put their faith in Jesus Christ. God's promise has been made, and no human or government can undo or revoke it. This is cause for rejoicing!

II. *Our inheritance comes through the Risen Christ.* The text says, "we have been born anew to a living hope through the Resurrection of Jesus Christ from the dead." Our hope and our inheritance find their source in the Redeemer who died on the cross and was raised on the third day. The Gospel reading for this morning is testimony to that. The early disciples were hiding fearfully behind closed doors—without apparent hope, because they assumed their Master was dead. They seem to have been a sort of Jesus Memorial Society until the Risen Lord appeared in their midst. Thomas's transformation happened as he, too, came to believe when Jesus presented proof of his bodily Resurrection. 1 Corinthians reminds us emphatically: "If Christ has not been raised, your faith is futile and you are still in your sins. . . . If for this life only we have hoped in Christ, we are of all people most to be pitied. But in fact Christ has been raised from the dead, the first fruits of those who have fallen asleep."

Not long ago I saw a clever bumper sticker that read: "No Christ—no hope. Know Christ—know hope." Our inheritance and our hope come through believing in the Messiah who died for our sins and promised, "I go to prepare a place for you."

III. *Our future inheritance sustains us now.* Heirs of eternal life are not immune to difficulty in this life, as the New Testament regularly reminds us. Before he went to the cross, Jesus said to his disciples, "In this world you have tribulation; but be of good cheer, I have overcome the world." In Acts we read of James being beheaded, Peter thrown in prison, Paul being flogged and shipwrecked, and Stephen being stoned. The author of 1 Peter also acknowledges that "for a little while you may have to suffer various trials." Yet in nearly every case, we find disciples rejoicing in spite of tough circumstances. Why is this? One answer is found in the text itself: "for *a little while.*" Whatever ordeal befell them, they knew it would not last forever. God's sovereignty and goodness would have the last word. Their inheritance was sure. Another answer is that they realized that in their suffering they had a share in the redemptive work of Christ, and a chance to glorify Christ. Paul gave thanks when writing to the Philippians, because he could see that his imprisonment had worked to advance the gospel.

We cannot give our inheritance to another person, or borrow someone else's inheritance. As the old saying puts it, you can't ride to heaven on your granddaddy's coattails. But thanks be to God, our confidence in times of suffering may ultimately bring others to faith, that they too may become members of the household of God and heirs to eternal life. This is cause for joy!

A few years ago a dear friend of mine died, leaving me a large share of his estate and making me executor of his will. After the funeral I stood in his home and tried to decide which of his possessions to have shipped to my house in Chicago, and which things I could fit in my suitcase. Because I had visited this friend many times, nearly all the objects around me were familiar. Many were beautiful, and most had pleasant associations. I found myself wishing I could take far more than was practical, given the size of my house and the cost of shipping. I realized that what I wanted more than the inheritance was my friend himself. I was trying to hold on to *him* through the earthly goods he had left to me.

The most precious thing we receive from God in Christ is not eternal life, as wonderful as that is. Our inheritance is beyond price because we receive *Jesus himself,* crucified and risen and alive. The relationship with him, unbroken and unending, is an inheritance we can share with others without having any less of him for ourselves.—Carol M. Norén

SERMON SUGGESTIONS

Topic: This Is the Gospel Truth!

Text: Acts 10:34–43

(1) The good news is for all, Jew and Gentile alike. (2) The good news centers in Jesus Christ—what he was and what he did. (3) The good news is the subject of our preaching and witness, and forgiveness of sins is its object.

Topic: The Great Escape

Text: Col. 3:1–4

Escaping the gravitational pull of earthly desires (1) is based on the Easter victory of Christ, (2) requires "the expulsive power of a new affection" (see Gal. 5:16, 22), (3) enjoys a security the world does not know and cannot appreciate, and (4) anticipates a glorious future with Christ.

WORSHIP AIDS

CALL TO WORSHIP.   "Is it nothing to you, all ye that pass by? Behold, and see if there be any sorrow like unto my sorrow, which is done unto me, wherewith the Lord hath afflicted me in the day of his fierce anger" (Lam. 1:12).

INVOCATION.   O God, the sufferings of our Lord Jesus Christ overwhelm us, as we survey the wondrous cross. Help us this day to see in the depths of his sacrifice the depths of thy love.

OFFERTORY PRAYER.   God of grace, we know that you are able to do exceedingly abundantly above all that we ask or think. Though we also know that we cannot outgive you, help us to know if we are giving as we are able and grant us the faith and willingness to give as we ought.

PRAYER.   Almighty and most gracious heavenly Father, we cry out to you from the very midst of our need and imperfection. We are perishing, O Lord; rescue us from our unbelief. We are hungry, O Lord; feed us by the milk of your Word. We are sinful, O Lord; cleanse us of our iniquities. We are often too weak to control our tendency to sin, and our pride and selfishness seize control of our lives. We then lose sight of the path that you would have us follow. We most humbly ask, O Lord, that your Spirit will enter our lives anew to guide us, to heal us, and to sustain us. We pray that your presence will dwell continually in us and that your grace will abound ever more strongly in us. Make us whole, O Lord, that we may completely conform to the image of your Son, Jesus Christ. Enter this day into the lives of those of our number whose lives have been complicated and disrupted by the stress of illness and loss. Grant unto those persons and their families the courage and resources that they may creatively cope with the difficulties that beset them.—Rodney K. Miller

SERMON
Topic: When Life Falls Apart
TEXT: Job 1–2

If you could ask God one question, and you know he would give you the answer, what would you ask? Pollster George Barna surveyed a cross-section of adults, asking that question. The number one response was, "I'd ask God why there is pain and suffering in the world."

There is no more perplexing subject than the problem of pain. I want you to turn in your Bibles to the book of Job, which is the classic biblical treatise on the subject of suffering. I want to survey the life of Job in a series I am calling Life Is Hard, but God Is Good.

First, *bad things happen to good people.* The first thing the Bible teaches us about Job is that he was a good man.

One of the first lessons the Bible teaches us through Job is that bad things are going to happen to good people. The Bible says, "The rain falls on the just and the unjust." If the righteous were exempt, our motivation and obedience would be totally selfish. We'd try to be good to avoid getting hurt.

Second, *nothing bad will occur in your life without God's permission.* Some of the painful experiences that happen to us in life are the result of Satanic attacks.

Another lesson we learn from Job is that nothing can touch you that God does not allow. Your suffering does not actually mean that God is upset with you or that God is punishing you. Your suffering may be Satan attacking you, or you're just experiencing the inevitable consequences of living in a fallen world where everyone hurts. You can be sure that God is very much aware of your pain and will not allow you to experience more than you can bear.

Why does God permit any struggle? Why doesn't he make all life smooth and easy? Sometimes God permits us to go through sufferings to mature us. Sometimes God lets us go through pain to comfort others. God permits us to suffer to test us. Sometimes God permits suffering to allow people to appreciate what Jesus endured. God gave Satan limited permission to attack Job, to mature him, to enable Job to comfort others, to prove his faith genuine and to appreciate what Christ would go through for him one day.

Third, *a key to endurance is worship.* Life suddenly started to completely fall apart for Job. He was worth millions, and suddenly everything that could possibly go wrong went wrong. Cattle rustlers, lightning strikes, enemy raids—within minutes Job had lost everything, and in a day when there was no insurance coverage. One moment he was one of the wealthiest men in the east; the next he was penniless.

But even though Job grieved, he worshipped God. He did not shake his fist at God and curse him as Satan had predicted. Instead, he worshipped God saying, "Everything I have belongs to God anyway; I am still going to trust him. May the name of the Lord be praised."

Fourth, *your experience is not unique.* Job's story was not finished yet. Just when it seemed it could not get worse, it did. Satan isn't all-knowing. He didn't understand he had already played his trump card. You cannot hurt a man any worse than taking his children away. So God permitted Satan to attack Job's body, and Job broke out with painful sores; the King James calls them boils from his head to his toes. The closest family member he had, his wife, turned on him.

Here is a lesson to learn—your experience is not unique. Others have overcome adversity and you can, too. No matter how bad you have it right now, your suffering is not worse than Job's. He lost all his wealth and all ten of his children, his health was broken, and his wife turned on him. Yet he held on to his faith. Job said, "Though he slay me, yet will I hope in him" (Job 13:15). No matter how bad you have it, there is someone who had it worse than you and yet maintained his faith.

Earlier I listed four reasons why God allows suffering: to comfort, to test, to mature, and to help us appreciate the sufferings of Jesus. But there is one other reason why God permits pain: it keeps our focus on heaven. C. S. Lewis said, "Our Father refreshes us on the journey with some pleasant inns but will not encourage us to mistake them for our home."

Pain keeps our focus on heaven and not on earth. It's a reminder that this world is not your home. You're not to get too comfortable here.

We think that the worst thing that can happen is for us to experience pain. The worst thing that can happen to us is to resist Christ.

If you have Christ, he promises there will come a day when there will be no more sorrow, no more pain, no more death, no more tears. If you resist him, there will come a day when the fire is not quenched and the pain never quits hurting.—Bob Russell

SUNDAY, APRIL 10, 2005
Lectionary Message

Topic: Life on the Inside

TEXT: Acts 2:14a, 36–41

Other Readings: Ps. 116:1–4, 12–19; 1 Pet. 1:17–23; Luke 24:13–35

A popular movie of the midnineties, *Four Weddings and a Funeral,* depicted a group of single young adults as they attended the rites of passage noted in the film title. At the third wedding reception, an older man in the group expressed frustration that they were always attending someone else's wedding. He exhorted them to "be fruitful and multiply," that is, find the right person and tie the knot. The end of the story suggests that each of them did, eventually. The values reflected in the film do not present a Christian understanding of marriage or weddings. However, the movie does make one point in common with this morning's reading from Acts: a commitment is understood only from the inside. Merely hearing the words does not effect a change. Something else has to happen.

How many times have you or I attended a wedding, watching and listening as vows are made and a couple pronounced husband and wife? We are familiar with the order of service, the lines about "for better, for worse, for richer, for poorer, in sickness and in health." But seeing and hearing on their own do not make the people in the pews married. They have not entered that commitment. Something else is needed.

Something else was needed by the crowd that gathered to hear Peter preach on the day of Pentecost. Today's reading is the introduction and the tail end of the sermon. Much of what was said in between was a reminder of Scriptures that the listeners already knew. There were familiar with the prophecy of Joel. They would have recognized the quotations from the Psalms. Many of them had heard Jesus speak during his earthly ministry. But the "penny hadn't dropped." The words alone did not make them disciples of Jesus Christ. Two things were lacking: the outpouring of the Holy Spirit, and their openness to receive.

I. *Readiness to enter.* It is interesting to note the differences between the readiness of the listeners in Acts 2 and the readiness of the disciples in the Emmaus Road encounter, found in today's Gospel reading. In Acts, the Holy Spirit was poured out on the apostles, manifested as tongues of flame and the ability to witness to the mighty works of God in various languages they didn't know. This Spirit-empowered speech moved some in the crowd to respond to Peter's sermon with the question, "What shall we do?" It made them open to believe in the Risen Lord and enter a committed relationship. In Luke, however, the unknown stranger opened the Scriptures to the disciples and explained all things pertaining to the Messiah *before* they invited him to stay and break bread with them. The Spirit was invoked in the thanksgiving over the meal. At that point, the Spirit enlightened them to see that the one who took bread, gave thanks, broke it, and gave it to them was the same Lord who had broken bread with them at the Last Supper. They "received" the good news of the Resurrection. They believed in the Risen Lord and entered into a new relationship with him.

II. *Once inside.* Those in the crowd who asked the apostles, "Brethren, what shall we do?" were open to a new relationship, but they didn't know what it would mean, or how to enter it. There are many outside the church today who are not sure how to become a Christian or what it means. Do they have to sign a commitment card? Are they required to give up drinking, dancing, going to movies, or playing the lottery? Do they raise their hands or put them on the TV screen while a televangelist prays? Peter's answer was much simpler; he said, "Repent, and be baptized every one of you in the name of Jesus Christ for the forgiveness of your sins; and you shall receive the gift of the Holy Spirit." *Repentance,* in this context, means being sorry for rejecting and crucifying the Messiah. *Being baptized* is undergoing a symbolic cleansing or rebirth with water and invoking the name of Jesus Christ. It is entrance into a new relationship—not just with Christ, but with the community of disciples. Being inside means living under Christ's authority and ownership. And *receiving the gift of the Holy Spirit* is being equipped for service and witness in Jesus' name.

Being inside does not have the connotations of imprisonment that we usually associate with the phrase. Instead, it means freedom from bondage to old ways. Those who were open to Peter's invitation found it meant fellowship, the joy of meals together, times of prayer, and spreading the gospel.

III. *Are you inside—or just a spectator?* Of course, not everyone who heard Peter preach and saw the tongues of flame and recalled the Scriptures he quoted made the commitment. Acts 2:41 reports that "those who received his word were baptized," implying that others did *not* receive the word. They were still outside, only spectators at an event more historic and world-changing than any wedding, however grand.

Where do you find yourself in the crowd that day? Are you living on the inside of a new relationship with God through Christ, or have you been closed to the possibility? The good news is that, like a loving suitor, Jesus Christ still waits for you to say yes. By grace, you can become his—and you will discover for yourself a new life that you may have heard about, but until now have only seen from the outside. Thanks be to God.

"There is a sense of course in which God *can* be known in our hearts, but the God of the Bible, the God revealed in the living Christ, also stands over against us in our 'hearts.' We do not take him captive in our hearts. Indeed *he* may take *us* captive in our hearts, and then perhaps we can know the peace of God which passes all understanding. But it is precisely beyond our understanding because God, if Christ is the clue to his nature, is different. He is surprising, like appearing as a stranger along the dusty road to Emmaus."[1]—Carol M. Norén

SERMON SUGGESTIONS

Topic: The Voice of Experience of God

TEXT: Isa. 50:4–9a

(1) It is encouraging. (2) It is grounded in obedient suffering. (3) It is self-authenticating.

Topic: A Redeeming Pattern for Prideful People

TEXT: Phil. 2:5–11

(1) Pride is listed as first of the seven deadly sins. (2) Pride works all kinds of mischief in the Christian community. (3) Jesus Christ, who had the highest credentials and rights, set the example of "self-emptying" for the sake of others. (4) God will reward self-humbling with satisfactions that self-seeking could never achieve. (5) Therefore, work toward the attitude of Christ (vv. 1–5).

---

[1]Edmund Steimle, *God the Stranger,* reprinted in *The Minister's Manual for 1999,* p. 87.

WORSHIP AIDS

CALL TO WORSHIP.   "Grace to you, and peace, from God our Father, and from the Lord Jesus Christ" (Phil. 1:2).

INVOCATION.   We thank you, our Father, for the fellowship of the gospel, for your gracious work among us present here today, for the promise of the fulfillment of your purpose through us. Strengthen us in that good work by all that is said and done in this service of worship. For your name's sake.

OFFERTORY SENTENCE.   "If you are eager to give, God will accept your gift on the basis of what you have to give, not on what you don't have" (2 Cor. 8:12, TEV).

OFFERTORY PRAYER.   Gracious Lord, no true offering is ever too small for your notice or ever too large for our earthly well-being. May we give remembering the widow's mite and Jesus' yielding of his all to you. So we bring to you the fruits of our labors and the produce of your grace. In the name of him who loved us and gave himself for us.

PRAYER.   O God, you have heard our prayers. Many times you have spared our lives and delivered us from temptation. Your hand is never shortened that you cannot save. Even when we felt forsaken, we were not alone.

We love you because you did first love us. We have received redemption in your Son, who loved us and gave himself for us. Through the years, we have been blessed by your providence. Every moment of our lives, we are upheld by your grace.

Give to us, we pray, a greater awareness of your many gracious acts toward us. Then let thanksgiving rise to our lips and gratitude sanctify our lives.

SERMON

Topic: When Pain Is Prolonged (Job)

TEXT: Job 1–2

Job's life fell apart. It seemed that everything that could possibly go wrong went wrong for him.

He began the day as a multimillionaire, but through a series of bizarre events he lost everything and ended the day totally broke. But then something worse happened. A tornado hit the house where his ten children were partying, and all ten were killed. He was devastated. Then his health broke.

Job became afflicted with boils from head to toe, and there was no relief from his physical anguish. His wife, the one close relative he had left, sneered, "Why don't you curse God and die!"

But Job didn't. He was a man of great integrity and held onto his faith. At that point Job must have thought, "At least it can't get any worse than this; I've survived the most horrible blows life can dish out. I'll soon begin to feel better and rebuild my life."

But Job was in for an experience that few people understand until they go through it. Deep wounds take a long time to heal.

The most severe test of life is not the immediate crises but the prolonged pain that follows. We're going to survey the middle section of the book of Job, a section that Jill Briscoe in her commentary calls God's waiting room. I want us to learn three important lessons that I hope will encourage us to be faithful to God when we go through deep, ongoing suffering.

First, *when you go through prolonged pain, most friends will not understand or continue to sympathize with you.*

The most important thing you can do when you have a friend who is hurting is make contact. Sometimes you choose not to because you don't know what to say. It's not nearly as important that you say the right thing as it is that you be there to reaffirm your love and concern. You're tempted to pretend nothing has happened and ignore it. That doesn't help at all.

Job's friend's reactions sound strange, but actually it was probably helpful. They wept with him and sympathized with him. They didn't make small talk and pretend it wasn't so bad. They didn't say, "You'll have other children, you're such a financial genius that you will become a millionaire again within a year or two." Instead, they sat in silence for seven days. They didn't say a word because they saw how great was his suffering.

Eventually they did speak up. When they tried to comfort Job and get to the bottom of his situation, they really bombed.

When you go through prolonged pain, you need to understand that most of your friends will not understand, and they will lose sympathy for you.

Second, *when pain is prolonged, God often will be silent and seem very distant.*

Job still believed God even though he was hurting.

One of the most difficult tests of faith is to wait for God when answers don't come. How do you react when you pray for relief and God is silent? When life falls apart and pain is prolonged, and there is no sign that God even hears your prayer, what do you do? That's when you have to rely on God's promises, not on signs or feelings.

Third, *when pain is prolonged, you will probably experience anger, and your bitterness will disappoint you.*

We praise Job for his faith, but he battled doubt, bitterness, and depression because his pain was ongoing.

When Job's pain was prolonged, he battled bitterness toward God, resentment toward his friends, despair toward life, even thoughts of suicide. When you are really down, Satan will plant thoughts of self-destruction in your mind and try to convince you that everyone would be better off if you ended it all. That's never the right solution. That's never God's will. That's never a shortcut to peace. When you despair in life, even for a long time, trust that somehow God's promises will hold true—"All things work together for good to those who love God."

I find it encouraging that the New Testament refers to Job as a man of faith and perseverance. As in Job's case, God understands and even expects us to battle doubt and despair when life falls apart.

When you battle bitterness, it's important that you hold onto your Heavenly Father rather than burst from his arms and run. Accept what you get as an assignment from God. Go through the spiritual disciplines even though it seems perfunctory at times. Be realistic. You may be in it for the long haul. Remember there will be a greater reward for you in heaven for your endurance. We are promised an eternal reward commensurate with our faithfulness in this life. For those who have suffered a great deal yet remained faithful, for those who have been persecuted for their convictions, there is a promise of great reward in heaven someday.

Sometimes there is nothing we can do but wait and hope. Sometimes the concluding chapter on earth has a happy ending. But even if there is no happy ending on earth, there is a final chapter yet to be written in heaven. There, God has promised he will wipe away all tears from our eyes and make all things new. Sometimes in the midst of pain there is nothing we can do but hope for that eternal experience.—Bob Russell

SUNDAY, APRIL 17, 2005

Lectionary Message

Topic: The Sincerest Form of Flattery

TEXT: 1 Pet. 2:19–25

Other Readings: Acts 2:42–47; Ps. 23; John 10:1–10

During the 1990s in Chicago, one item of clothing more than any other could be seen on children and teens playing basketball: a Bulls jersey with Michael Jordan's number twenty-three on it. Drive by any outside basketball court and you would see at least two or three kids wearing this jersey, even if they were playing on opposing teams. The number twenty-three did not signify who the wearer *was*; it indicated that the wearer wanted to "be like Mike."

Such imitation is commonplace. Not only do teenage girls mimic the vocal and dress style of pop stars like Britney Spears; we see political candidates emulating the speech patterns and strategies of admired predecessors. Homemakers try to replicate Thanksgiving dinner as Martha Stewart would make it. It seems to be human nature to imitate others.

I. *Imitation to gain power.* The Bible has more than one example of someone imitating someone or something else in order to gain an advantage. When Jacob wanted to get the blessing that Isaac intended for Esau, the first-born twin, Jacob put on Esau's clothes and put kidskin on his neck and hands to mimic his brother's hairiness (Gen. 27). Laban disguised his elder daughter, Leah, to look like her younger sister, Rachel (Gen. 29), and gain another seven years' labor from Jacob. We might even say that at Pentecost, the gift of tongues gave the apostles the ability to imitate native speakers from other lands, and thus proclaim the gospel with more power than if they had spoken only their own dialect.

We see imitation to gain power in the church, too. Sometimes this is a worthy emulation, and other times not. A Peter Jennings special, *In the Name of God,* documented some of the contemporary Willow Creek "wannabe" ministries: preachers or congregations aiming for the same amazing growth (and church budget) as one of the nation's best-known megachurches. But contemporary music and skits before the sermon do not transform the life of a church any more than putting on a number twenty-three jersey makes a person able to play basketball like Michael Jordan.

II. *Imitation to become or surpass the model.* A more laudable form of imitation is striving to *become* like one's model, not simply resemble him or her. An academic surgeon I know describes what is evidently a common method in teaching how to perform various medical procedures: "watch one, do one, teach one." A doctor learns by imitating, and others learn by imitating that doctor. Someone who is serious about wanting to "be like Mike" will practice constantly, watch videos that demonstrate techniques, get coaching, and hope perhaps to become an even better player than Jordan.

This imitation in order to become like one's model is also biblical. In Luke 10, we read of seventy of Jesus' followers going out and trying to minister and preach as he did. They announced "the kingdom of God is come near to you" and bid peace on whatever house they entered. In Mark 6, we read that Jesus commissioned the twelve and sent them out to preach repentance and heal and cast out demons—just as Jesus himself did. Paul acknowledged that he was himself striving for perfection but exhorted the church at Philippi, "Join in imitating me, and mark those who so live as you have an example in us." The mother of James and John wanted her sons to become like Jesus through association, in terms of sharing his glory, when she asked if they could sit at his right hand and at his left in the kingdom (Matt. 20:20–23). In all these examples of imitation, the person doing the striving seeks some gain for himself or herself: skill, praise, game, and so on. But there is another kind of imitating to be found in the Bible, and today's reading from 1 Peter offers this radically different model.

III. *Imitation that pleases God.* The first letter of Peter proposes a course of action that is counter to our instincts and cultural values. It exhorts us to imitate Jesus Christ—not in working wonders or being enthroned in glory, but in suffering. Imitate Jesus; refrain from sin. Imitate Jesus; when reviled, do not revile in return. Imitate Jesus; when attacked, do not retaliate or threaten. This is the imitation to which we are called, and the example Jesus set. This is imitation that pleases God.

This seems a strange and undesirable model to follow, but as we contemplate the lives of the early Christians it begins to make sense. The Bible never asks us to pursue opportunities for suffering—but it does acknowledge that persecution and injustice were problems in the early church. This morning's text, with its call to imitate, turns suffering inside out. The pain inflicted on followers of Jesus was meant to silence them. But by keeping Jesus in mind as their model, their endurance and gentleness bore witness to the gospel. Their imitation of Christ in the midst of suffering became a window through which onlookers could see the Savior himself.

The apostles understood this and learned to endure and praise God. It says in Acts 5:41 that they rejoiced that they were counted worthy to suffer dishonor for the name (of Jesus). Paul gave thanks that he was imprisoned and shared in Christ's suffering, because he could see God using it to further the spread of the gospel.

Few of us in North America are subject to the cruelties and martyrdom of the early church, or those suffered by Christians in other parts of the world. Yet even in the small injustices and unfair treatment that come our way, our God can have the last word when we imitate Jesus' response to those who persecuted him. It may not bring us public acclaim or prizes, but it does give glory to our Lord.

A visitor to Las Vegas is sure to encounter an entertainer doing shows there, regardless of when one travels there. In Vegas and elsewhere, there are people who make their living as Elvis impersonators. Wearing a pompadour hairstyle and, more often than not, a bejeweled white jumpsuit, the impersonators mimic the King's body language, accent, and music. Their success depends on how convincing the imitation is. As Christians, we too are to imitators of our King. We are not distinguished by clothing or speech pattern, but by our behavior. Although our imitation may not bring us applause from the world, it does promise the approval of our God.

"Posterity weaves no garlands for imitators," wrote Johann Christoph Friedrich von Schiller in 1798. His point is well-taken. Christians who imitate their Redeemer today often reap derision or incredulity from those outside the faith. Their striving to emulate Jesus brings glory—or garlands, if you will—to their Lord.—Carol M. Norén

SERMON SUGGESTIONS

Topic: The Drama of the Ages

TEXT: Acts 2:14a, 22–32

(1) Act I: The eternal plan of God. (2) Act II: The revelatory life of Christ. (3) Act III: The hostile response of the lawless. (4) Act IV: God's last word (see v. 36).

Topic: All of This Is Ours

TEXT: 1 Peter 1:3–9

(1) Our hope. (2) Our inheritance. (3) Our security. (4) Our testing. (5) Our sustaining motivation.

WORSHIP AIDS

CALL TO WORSHIP.   "Hear, O Lord, when I cry with my voice; have mercy also upon me, and answer me. When thou saidst, See ye my face, my heart said unto thee, Thy face, Lord, I will seek" (Ps. 27:7–8).

INVOCATION.   God of wisdom, no problem is too hard for you; so we bring to you our vexing needs, asking you to take over those things that are more than we can manage. Today we pray for answers or for patience to live bravely with what we cannot understand.

OFFERTORY SENTENCE.   "He who supplies seed to the sower and bread for food will supply and increase the harvest of your righteousness" (2 Cor. 9:10, RSV).

OFFERTORY PRAYER.   Gracious Lord, grant that through all of our giving we may be enabled to give more, so that blessing from thee may be enjoyed everywhere.

PRAYER.   O thou who art the source of all life and the light of all seeing, we acknowledge with joy and reverence that the world is thy creation, and that life is thy gift. Lift up our thoughts from the littleness of our own works to the greatness, the majesty, and the wonder of thine, and teach us so to contemplate thy glory that we may grow into thy likeness. May that love be real to us through which we can call thee our Father. Teach us the meaning of thy grace: to love in the presence of hate; to forgive in the face of malicious slander; to celebrate life in the presence of death; to be a light-bearer in the midst of darkness. As the oyster takes a grain of sand and turns it into a pearl, may we be as creative in using the irritation that comes to us in fashioning a life to reflect thy glory. May the promise of thy love be realized in all of our relationships. May we not turn from the cross but deny ourselves to choose thy will in all of life. O Father, the mystery of intercessory prayer, we cannot fully fathom. But our hearts cry out in behalf of others, for we sense the intimacy with which our lives are set—that no one lives and dies unto himself. For youth in their aspirations to make a better world, and for parents in their desire to be responsible to their sons and daughters, we pray understanding and love, so that high idealism may be nurtured to responsible action. For those in mature years we pray the fulfillment of thy purpose in all of the uniqueness of their personalities and opportunities. Encourage those in bereavement with a grasp of the meaning of eternal life and an awareness of thy love from which even death cannot separate. Bless those who are ill and the families which anxiously await their recovery.

From the celebration of thy presence in this place may we be enabled to celebrate thy presence in the peculiar circumstances in which each of our lives is set in the days coming. In all things may we discover the greatest joy in life is to do thy will and that in thy service is perfect freedom.—John Thompson

SERMON
Topic: When God Appears (Job)
TEXT: Job 1–2

Job demanded that God explain himself.

Why did God allow him to endure so much pain? He wasn't perfect, but he was more righteous than others whose wealth hadn't been stripped, children hadn't been killed, and health hadn't been broken. Why was he the victim of so much suffering and injustice? Job didn't deserve that, so he specifically requested an audience with God, but there was no reply. "I cry out to you, O God, but you do not answer; I stand up, but you merely look at me" (Job 30:20).

Most of us have felt that way at times. We've gotten angry with God for allowing us to hurt, and we've demanded an explanation. Even though God has warned us that his ways are not our ways, we try to make sense of it all. We demand an explanation for broken relationships, financial hardships, premature deaths, brutal wars, and physical pain. Like Job we cry out, "Where are you, God?"

We are going to look at Job 28, where God speaks directly to Job. Finally, after hours of shallow dialogue and frequent disagreements with his friends, God appeared and spoke directly to Job. In this final section, there are several practical principles that will help us remain faithful to God through difficult times.

I. *God humbled Job and reminded him Who was in charge.*

God challenged Job: Who are you to question me?

I'm God; you're man. I'm the Creator; you're the created being. I'm omniscient; you're limited to your understanding.

He called Job's arguments "words without knowledge." They sounded ludicrous to God. So God said, "Brace yourself like a man; I am going to question you." This admonition to "brace yourself like a man" means brace yourself like a warrior; we're going head-to-head in intellectual combat here.

Then God asked Job a series of seventy questions. Here's the first lesson we learn from God's response: God is in charge of the universe, so develop a servant's heart.

Here's a fact we often miss, but it is so important in coping with trouble: the universe doesn't revolve around us. God is in charge. We're his creation, not vice versa. He's not our servant. Once you accept that he's in charge, your attitude about your problems changes. When we understand this is God's world and we exist to bring honor to him, we quit complaining and start making the most of our circumstances.

II. *God will provide answers in his time. Be willing to wait.*

If I asked you to tell me about the book of Job, what would you say?

It tells about the terrible sufferings of Job. So many bad things happened to such a good man to show that being good doesn't exempt us from pain.

What about Job's friends? You'd say, "They give long, drawn-out speeches trying to explain to Job why he is suffering, and they all conclude he is a sinner."

What does the book of Job say is the answer to suffering? What would you say? You would be hard-pressed to answer. The most notable thing about the book of Job to me is the absence of explanations.

But I can think of two reasons why God does not answer the question. First, maybe it's because we're not capable of comprehending the answer. If God gave us the answer, it would probably involve so many centuries and so many people, and be so complex, that we wouldn't grasp it. We'd say, "God, are you talking to me?"

So he says, trust Me and wait until eternity, and I'll explain it.

The second reason he doesn't give us the answer is that maybe it would ruin the test if we knew the answers in advance. The book of Job teaches us not to expect simple answers. When we're involved in difficulty, we trust that God's will is to be done.

God provides answers in his time—be willing to wait—even until eternity, if necessary.

III. *God will make all things right in the end. Keep trusting in him.*

Job repents. But what does he repent of?

The first chapter describes him as blameless, so he doesn't repent of the way he raised his children or the way he made his money or the way he treated his wife. He repents of his attitude toward God. He repents of his limited understanding of who God is. He repented of his many complaints against God.

Here's the final lesson from Job: God will make all things right in the end. Keep trusting him. Life may be hard, but God is good and he will bless you in the end. Sometimes you may have to wait until eternity before God settles up. But many times God blesses in this life as well as in eternity.

Job learned that though life is hard, sometimes cruel, in the end God is good. Satan's most vicious attack wasn't against Job, but against Jesus. He was perfect. He didn't deserve any pain at all. But Satan's agents ridiculed him, lied about him, brutalized him, and crucified him. God took the cross, the instrument Satan intended for evil, and used it as a means of salvation, forgiveness, and hope for all mankind.

Three days later, God raised Jesus from the dead and exalted him above all names. What Satan meant for evil became God's greatest triumph. If we place our trust in him and not our good works, he will save us because he is God and we are not!—Bob Russell

SUNDAY, APRIL 24, 2005
Lectionary Message

Topic: Many Mansions

TEXT: John 14:1–14

Other Readings: Acts 7:55–60; Ps. 31:1–5, 15–16; 1 Pet. 2:2–10

A few days after actress Katharine Hepburn died, a cartoon tribute appeared on the editorial page of the *Chicago Tribune*. It showed an angel holding a sheet of paper with "Katie" written on it and calling happily through the pearly gates, "Guess who's coming to dinner?!" It was clever to use the title of one of Hepburn's best films in that way, and it accurately reflected the esteem in which our culture held the actress. However, it suggested widely held beliefs about heaven that have little to do with Christian faith or Scripture. We should thank God things *aren't* the way that cartoon depicted them.

After all, would you want your death or arrival in heaven to be a surprise to God? Would you want some people to be treated as more important than others? Would you want your earthly accomplishments—or shortcomings—to be the basis for determining whether heaven is your destination? Would you want your stay in heaven to be as brief as an evening dinner party? Of course not. We believe that God and heaven are not like that, because Jesus has told us otherwise.

I. *Our place is already prepared.* In the familiar passage of Scripture we heard a few moments ago, Jesus said to his disciples, "In my Father's house are many mansions/rooms; if it were not so, would I have told you that I go to prepare a place for you? And when I go and prepare a place for you, I will come again and will take you to myself, that where I am you may be also." In these three verses, we were given a very different impression of heaven—and "impression" it is, in contrast to the stark, unambiguous lines of a cartoon drawing. Jesus spoke of many mansions or many dwelling places, a figure of speech suggesting that the scope of heaven is beyond our imagining. Those who have gone on bus tours around Hollywood celebrity homes have seen earthly mansions—places so big you wonder how a family could use that much space. When Jesus spoke of "many mansions," he didn't mean heaven is a gated community with big fancy houses for everyone there. He meant that the Father's house is large enough to accommodate all who belong to him, and the riches of God are beyond our comprehension.

The Redeemer said, "When I go to prepare a place for you, I will come again and will take you to myself." The death of Christians does not catch Jesus by surprise. On the contrary, he prepares for them their inheritance through his own death and Resurrection. His Holy Spirit is with them in the hospital room, the workplace, at church, and at home. Christ's followers live in fellowship with the Lord they love, and that fellowship is unbroken, for at death he takes them to himself. Because they believe in the One who promises "I will never fail you nor forsake you," Scripture promises that one day they shall see the Savior face to face.

II. *Our Lord will lead His people there.* Many of us have felt—or still feel—the question posed by Thomas in John 14:5: "Lord, we do not know where you are going; how can we know the way?" The sting of death is real, whether we mourn someone who is no longer present in the body or we contemplate our own mortality. We do not fully understand the words of Jesus, or perhaps they seem at odds with the picture of heaven presented by television shows or popular songs and even, at times, by religious leaders. In times of crisis, such as the one Thomas and the apostles faced, or sorrow, as we grieve over the death of someone we love, cartoons or wishful thinking aren't enough. To us Jesus says, *"I am the way, and the truth, and the life; no one comes to the Father but by me."* Our hope is not in our ability to understand precisely what those many mansions look like; our hope is in the one who is preparing them. Our consolation is not in comprehending what the next life will entail, but rather in relying on the one whose will is ever directed to his children's good. For Thomas and for us, assurance does not come by the physical proof of the marks of the nails in the Risen Savior's hands; assurance comes in believing in the one whose hands were scarred for us, the one who forgives our sins and will raise us to eternal life. We don't have everything spelled out for us in minute detail. The author of John's Gospel writes elsewhere, "Beloved, we are God's children now; it does not yet appear what we shall be, but we know that when he appears we shall be like him, for we shall see him as he is. And everyone who thus hopes in him purifies himself as he is pure" (1 John 3:2).

Several years ago, I had occasion to spend several months in a foreign country that I didn't know much about. I tried to read up on the place. I bought maps and made sure my passport was in order. There was some anxiety at the prospect of going and being separated from family and friends here at home. As the day of departure drew near, I wondered, "What will this be like? Am I ready? Will I be OK?" But one thing made all the difference: I had a friend who was waiting there for me. He knew the country well. I had confidence that he would welcome me and make sure I was all right. Brothers and sisters, Jesus is the one who has prepared a place for you and me, and for all who seek his friendship and believe in him. We do not have a blueprint of heaven, but we know the architect. Put your trust in him, and he will lead you to the heavenly mansions waiting for all those who confess him as Lord.

During a conversation about growing older, a woman said to me, "Whenever I wonder what my husband will look like when he's an old man, I just look at his father." The resemblance between the two, even with thirty years' difference in age, was remarkable. This is not an uncommon occurrence. I attended an event at a church I had been part of many years earlier and was delighted to see a familiar face approaching me. "Georgia!" I exclaimed, "it's so good to see you again." The woman shook her head. "Georgia is my mother; I'm Deanna, her daughter."

The many mansions that Jesus promises his followers are still ahead of us, not yet visible to our sight. But we enjoy a foretaste of what heaven will be like when we worship Jesus Christ in fellowship with others.—Carol M. Norén

SERMON SUGGESTIONS

Topic: When the Spirit Prevails
TEXT: Acts 2:42–47
(1) Structured disciplines will follow. (2) Spontaneous expressions will follow. (3) Evangelistic outreach will follow.

Topic: The Problem of Pain
TEXT: 1 Pet. 2:19–25
(1) Pain is inevitable; all suffer sooner or later. (2) Some pain is deserved; we may foolishly invite it. (3) Some pain is unjust; we may suffer willingly for the sake of Christ our example. (4) Suffering may advance the cause of God and bless the lives of others.

WORSHIP AIDS
CALL TO WORSHIP.   "I had fainted, unless I had believed to see the goodness of the Lord in the land of the living. Wait on the Lord: be of good courage, and he shall strengthen thine heart" (Ps. 27:13–14).

INVOCATION.   God of Abraham, Isaac, and Jacob, lay before us today some great task. Give us the assurance that you will go with us in it, and by your grace it shall be done. Speak, Lord, for your servants are listening.

OFFERTORY SENTENCE.   "Thanks be unto God for his unspeakable gift" (2 Cor. 9:15).

OFFERTORY PRAYER.   Gracious Father, we confess that we live because of many gifts, and our hearts are cheered when others think of us. But words would fail us to express the magnitude of the gift of your Son. Let your love tell us how we ought to give.

PRAYER.   Dear Lord and Master of our lives, we are here today because we know that we need to be here. You alone have the secret of life, its living, its true significance. All of us have tried so many other things, but without the joys we think ought to be a part of life. The more we have surrounded ourselves with friends, the more lonely we have become. The more we have possessed, the more insecure we feel. The harder we have struggled and worked, the more we seem to miss. You are our last resort! Without you, there is really no difference between having and being without. Permeate us now, Heavenly Father, with your Spirit so that our whole being is refashioned and we see and think and hope with a different rhythm to our lives. Teach us to order the priorities of life after your order rather than those of men. Teach us to love with the divine gift rather than for our own selfish purposes. Teach us to strive for others rather than for ourselves. Give us the inner peace that comes from commitment and faith, and enable us to possess the gift of serenity that comes from hope in your presence and power. Thanks be to you Father, Son, and Holy Spirit, for eternal life that dwells with each of us even now.—Harold C. Perdue[2]

SERMON
Topic: Value and a World of Change
TEXT: John 20:10–18

I. We live in a world of change, a world in transition. The old world we were born into has ceased to exist, and the new world that our children and grandchildren will inhabit is not yet here, though from time to time we get a glimpse of its outlines. The world has always, of course, been changing. It has never been static. The world is dynamic, its one unchanging constant being change. The difference, however, between our experience of change and that of earlier generations is the rapid rate at which the change now occurs. Statisticians tell us (how they know this I can't say) that human knowledge has doubled in the past ten years. There is twice as much knowledge now as there was ten years ago.

With increased knowledge comes increased power; we can do things today that we couldn't do ten years ago because of this exponential growth in knowledge. Doctors announce daily new breakthroughs that hold the promise of eradicating, or at least controlling, our most dreaded diseases. Change is therefore good when it promises us conquest over some threatening feature of our world. Yet, ironically, change itself can be a threat. Our world of rapid change upsets our equilibrium because we are not sure what the future is going to be like, and that uncertainty is upsetting because if we don't know what the future will be like we can't be sure we will be able to cope with it when it gets here.

But there is another reason why we fear change, why change threatens us. Change threatens what we value most. Change threatens not only our ability to cope with the future but also our discernment of what we ought to live for, what we ought to consider important and

---

[2]*Pulpit Digest.*

worthy of our time and energy and effort. We fear that in the process of change something of real value may be lost.

The academic world of the university and graduate school (which is largely responsible for the rapid expansion of our knowledge and therefore our power, and therefore the rapid rate of change today) has noted this threat and responded in various ways. The introduction to a popular textbook in ethics, for example, states that one of the purposes of studying ethics is to discover new values to replace the old values that have failed us.[3] Medical students today take courses in medical ethics that raise issues doctors of a few generations ago never faced.

But the perception that real, significant values are threatened by our world of rapid change is not confined to the ivy-covered halls of academe. It is widespread in the marketplace as well. It explains (in part at least) the rise of reactionary social, political, and religious movements in our century. Fundamentalists, for example, are afraid that free and critical investigation of the Bible, using the most up-to-date techniques and drawing on our best knowledge, will somehow destroy the authority of the Bible (which to them is perhaps the greatest value).

Think of Moslem fundamentalism in Iran, the Marxist Puritanism of Pol Pot in Cambodia, the reactionary dictatorships of Latin America. Catholic churches that offer the Latin Mass have so many parishioners respond that they often turn worshipers away for lack of room. Some Episcopal congregations have broken ties with their church because they do not approve of recent changes in Episcopal polity.

Change is threatening, at least in part because we fear that something we value will be lost.

II. Change is a threat, but it is also a fact and will not go away. We know that the world of the future will be different in significant ways from the world of the past. Furthermore, we know that one day our world will undergo the ultimate change: total destruction when the sun in its last stages of existence explodes into a supernova and incinerates the earth and all that is in it. Think about what that means for things we value. Think about the things that will be gone in that final conflagration.

Gone: Michelangelo's *David, Moses,* the *Pietà,* the Sistine Chapel; da Vinci's *Last Supper* and the *Mona Lisa.*

Gone: the Acropolis in Athens, the skyline of New York City, the Golden Gate Bridge, the Taj Mahal, Shakertown at Pleasant Hill, Kentucky.

Gone: the Declaration of Independence, the Constitution of the United States, Lincoln's Gettysburg Address and the Second Inaugural, the United Nations Declaration of the Rights of Man.

Gone: the music of Beethoven, Bach, Brahms, and the Beatles; Mozart, Haydn, Ralph Vaughan Williams, and Simon and Garfunkel.

Gone: the movies of Ingmar Bergman and Federico Fellini, Orson Welles, David Lean, and Stanley Kubrick.

Gone: the novels of Dickens and Dostoyevsky and Tolstoy and Balzac and Trollop and Stern.

Gone: *Moby Dick, Huckleberry Finn,* and *The Scarlet Letter.* Gone: the poetry of Kits and Byron and Shelley and Wordsworth and Robert Frost.

Gone: Greek drama, Shakespeare, the Bible; the words of Plato and Aristotle, Augustine, Aquinas, Hume, and Kant; Luther, Calvin, Barth, and Tillich.

---

[3]Raziel Abelson and Marie-Louise Friquegnon, *Ethics for Modern Life,* 2nd ed. (New York: St. Martin's Press, 1982), pp. 4–5.

Gone: everything Thomas Merton, C. S. Lewis, and Frederick Buechner ever wrote.

Gone, all gone. All lost. Everything we value most highly as the epitome of what is best in our culture will one day be gone.

III. This total destruction of all that we value is (we hope) in the far future, millions and millions of years away. Yet in our reflective moments we must somehow come to terms with this fact intellectually. Why should we value these things if one day they will all be destroyed? Why should we value anything at all if it ends in death and destruction?

Some people have, in fact, come to this conclusion that nothing we value is permanent, so we should value only what is pleasing to us, though transitory. Eat, drink, and be merry, for tomorrow we all die. (If not tomorrow, then the day after.) There is nothing to live for, so let's live for nothing. This is what I call "cosmic despair," and it paints a pretty grim picture of human existence.

There is another, different attitude of despair we might adopt. I call it *heroic* cosmic despair. It embodies the despair we experience when we realize that anything we value has no permanence, but it does not degenerate into the eat-drink-and-be-merry variety. No, the one who despairs heroically still clings to the values we all share—truth, beauty, goodness, justice—but does so as an act of heroic (though ultimately futile) defiance against an indifferent, or possibly malevolent, universe. The hero of cosmic despair says, in effect: "I know that what I value will not last. It will one day be destroyed. I know that truth, beauty, justice, goodness are doomed in the last analysis to be frustrated and thwarted. But I thumb my nose at the universe and its indifference. I will continue to live my life in accordance with these values, even though I know I'm doomed to defeat." No one put this attitude better than Bertrand Russell, in an early essay entitled "A Free Man's Worship":

> That man is the product of causes which had no prevision of the end they were achieving; that his origin, his growth, his hopes and fears, his loves and his beliefs are but the outcome of accidental collocations of atoms; that no fire, no heroism, no intensity of thought and feeling can preserve an individual life beyond the grace; that all the labors of the ages, all the devotion, all the inspiration, all the noonday brightness of human genius are destined to extinction in the vast death of the solar system, and that the whole temple of man's achievement must inevitably be buried beneath the debris of a universe in ruins—all these things, if not quite beyond dispute, are yet so nearly certain that no philosophy which rejects them can hope to stand. Only within the scaffolding of these truths, only on the firm foundation of unyielding despair, can the soul's habitation henceforth be safely built.[4]

No one had a keener sense about social and political justice than Russell. No one worked harder to make the world a better place than he did. Yet he did so believing that all of his efforts would eventually come to naught. "Unyielding despair," he says, must be our attitude, the only "firm foundation" on which to build our lives.

Living in an age of transition threatens us because it threatens what we value most. We know that one day our earth and everything in it will be destroyed. We may respond like the

---

[4]Bertrand Russell, *Why I Am Not a Christian and Other Essays on Religion and Related Subjects* (New York: Simon and Schuster, 1957), p. 107.

reactionary and try to hold change back, or pretend that it is not there. Or we may respond with cosmic despair—in its nihilistic or heroic forms. If these were our only choices, I hope I would opt for heroic cosmic despair like Russell's.

But we have not yet said all there is to say about the future, change, and threats to what we value.

IV. John 20 portrays Mary Magdalene as one threatened by cosmic despair. Her world has crumbled. What she valued most—her relationships to Jesus—has been destroyed by death. She is sorrowful and grief-stricken. She weeps. The Risen Christ approaches her, and she doesn't even recognize him. Her cry is the cry of despair: "The one who meant the most to me, the one whom I loved the most, is gone. He's dead. I'll never see him again. And I don't even know where his body is so that I can honor his memory." She is saying that what she most valued has been taken from her and that she no longer has anything to live for.

Jesus speaks her name, and with the one word she realizes that he is not dead but alive and standing before her. What she cherished most in this world has not been destroyed after all. In joy she reaches out for Jesus to take hold of him and never let him go. But Jesus stops her. "Do not cling to me," he says, "for I have not yet ascended to God." Then Jesus gives Mary a commission: "Go and tell my brothers that I am ascending to God." Mary is ordained to be the first witness to the Resurrection. She is ordained to be the first evangelist, the first bearer of Good News. So Mary goes to the disciples and says, "I have seen the Lord!" Her message is that what they all valued most in this world had not been destroyed or taken from them after all.

V. This is Good News. But there is more to Jesus' message than this. There is also the command to accept the fact of change: "Do not cling to me," Jesus says to Mary, when she reaches out to grab hold of Jesus and never let him go. "What I have meant to you has not been lost," Jesus is saying, "but what I have meant to you is being changed. I am ascending to God. So you must not try to cling to me, to hold on to what our relationship was. If you truly want to preserve my value to you, then you must let the old relationship go and accept the new reality of my Resurrection. Nothing essential between us has changed. But there are changes, and you must accept them, or you will run the risk of losing everything."

The Resurrection of Jesus shows that what we value most, if it is what we ought most to value, persists through change. What we value changes, but nothing essential is lost. I do not know how this can be. I do not know how the value of great works of art and literature and music will be preserved. I do not know how people we have loved—parents, children, friends—continue to be real values after the death of their bodies. I have confidence, how-ever, that value—our highest and best values—is preserved, though transformed. I have this confidence because this is what happened to Jesus. Jesus died. But death did not destroy him. He lives, and he is still with us as our highest value.

Therefore, we need not despair that our work for goodness and beauty and justice is in vain, whether or not we are successful. In some way that we cannot fathom, God will make sure that what we do will be of lasting value. We can have confidence that even the small-est act of rightness makes some difference and will not be lost. But if we cling desperately to the old embodiments of value, we will miss the new. Faith in Christ means the willingness to let go of the past in order to have the future. It means the willingness to undergo the trans-formation from something old to something new, something wonderful. We must lose in order to find.

"All's lost," Godric says at the end of his life, as he realizes that he is about to die and finally meet God face to face. But then he says, "All's found."[5] Godric had to give up his life in order to find it. Another saint put it this way: "If anyone is in Christ, there is a new creation; everything old has passed away; see, everything has become new!" (2 Corinthians 5:17).—Bill Thomason[6]

SUNDAY, MAY 1, 2005
Lectionary Message
Topic: Getting Acquainted with the One True Living God
TEXT: Acts 17:22–31
Other Readings: Ps. 66:8–20; 1 Pet. 3:13–22; John. 14:15–21

I have twice visited where the Apostle Paul stood on the Areopagus in Athens and looked down some 370 feet at the Agora. The first time, my wife and I followed our guide up the little known Panathenic Way, where, two and a half millennia ago, ancient Greeks took their carts containing bulls to the sacrificial altars of the Parthenon. From 500 B.C., Athens became the "Golden Age" intellectual and cultural center of the ancient world, and it has powerfully affected Western civilization. Alfred North Whitehead, a noted philosopher in his own right, claims that all philosophy since then is merely a footnote to Plato.

"All the Athenians and the foreigners who lived there," Luke tells us, "spent their time doing nothing but talking about and listening to the latest ideas" (17:21). Except for the sacrificial bulls and oxcarts, it sounds a lot like many of the political, philosophical, and religious discussions in our postmodern age. Like us, they were very religious. They even built an altar and inscribed it "To an Unknown God," in case they missed one. Although he was greatly distressed that Athens was full of idols, Paul respected them enough to begin where they were as he shared the good news of Christ: "Now what you worship as something unknown I am going to proclaim to you" (17:23).

However, Paul was careful not to present his message about God as one more god among many. He proclaimed him as the one and only true God, and his inspired view of the universe as the only true one. Though his concern for people led him to begin where they were, he was not concerned about being politically correct. The Epicureans and Stoics who heard him had to realize that their worldview and his clashed rather than coincided. Paul knew that how you relate to God and how you view your world make all the difference.

I. There are areas where we have no control about how we relate to God. They are true whether we believe them or not, whether we ignore them or not.

God is the one true and living God. He does not live in temples made with hands: "And he is not served by human hands, as if he needed anything, because he himself gives all men life and breath and everything else" (17:25). We are God's offspring; he is not ours. He is not made of gold or silver or invented in the gray matter between our ears (17:29). The core of

---

idolatry is to try to trade places with God and remake him in our image. He is not our cosmic servant created to please us.

God is the Creator of the universe. He made the world and everything in it, including all men and women, and he sustains it by his power and authority.

God's presence is everywhere. The theologians say it this way: he is omnipresent. He is not far from anyone of us: "For in him we live and move and have our being" (17:28). Though we ascend the highest mountain, he is there. Though we descend into the deepest sea, he is there. We cannot get away from God no matter how hard we try.

God is a God of love and mercy: "From one man he made every nation of men, that they should inhabit the whole earth; and he determined the times set for them and the exact places where they should live. God did this so that men should seek him and perhaps reach out for him and find him, though he is not far from each one of us" (17:27, 28). If we are searching for God, Paul's message will enable us to find him.

God is the judge of all men and women. He has set a day when he will judge the world with justice by his Son, whom he has appointed and credentialed by raising him from the dead (17: 31).

God is the one true and living God; he is the creator of the universe; his presence is everywhere; he is a God of love and mercy; and he is the judge of all men and women—whether we know it or not, whether we believe it or not.

II. There are areas of our relationship with God where we can make choices.

We have a choice about our service. Paul could have simply lived a moral life during his stay in Athens and waited for the next ship out. He did not do that. He knew what he believed about God, and he knew that what one believes about God makes all the difference. We find him in the synagogue reasoning with the Jews and God-fearing Greeks. Later he is in the marketplace reasoning with whoever happens to be there, including the learned philosophers of the day. If we do not use our God-given gifts to share the gospel, who will? How will they hear unless we tell them?

We have a choice about our salvation. He commands all people everywhere to repent. We can choose to put our faith in God's son, repent of our sins, and obey the gospel; or we can refuse to do so and be condemned by his righteous justice.

Luke tells us that there were three reactions to Paul's presentation of the gospel. There always are. Some mocked and sneered. Others put off making a decision until another hearing. Still others gave their hearts to Christ and obeyed the gospel. At least four, maybe more, became believers: Dionysius the Areopagite, a woman named Damaris, and a number of others.

Those same three choices are yours today: to reject the gospel, to put him off until it is more convenient, or to accept him gladly. What you do about that will make all the difference.—Wayne Shaw

ILLUSTRATION

KNOWLEDGE OF GOD.   The richest man in the world, Croesus, once asked the wisest man in the world, Thales, "What is God?" The philosopher asked for a day in which to deliberate, and then for another, and then for another, and another, and another—and at length confessed that he was not able to answer; the longer he deliberated, the more difficult it was for him to frame an answer. The fiery Tertullian, the early church father, eagerly seized upon this incident and said it was an example of the world's ignorance of God outside of Christ.

"There," he exclaimed, "is the wisest man in the world, and he cannot tell you who God is. But the most ignorant mechanic among the Christians knows God, and is able to make him known unto others."—Clarence Edward Macartany

SERMON SUGGESTIONS

Topic: God Is Accessible
TEXT: Acts 17:22–31
(1) The quest for God (or a god) is universal (v. 22). (2) Such a quest can lead to frustration and desperation (vv. 23a, 24–25). (3) Yet God has made himself accessible (vv. 23b, 26–31; see also Heb. 1:1–4).

Topic: Your Defense as a Christian
TEXT: 1 Pet. 3:13–22, especially verse 15b. (1) Expect to give account of your Christian convictions. (2) Live what you profess. (3) Make your point with consideration of the feelings of others.

WORSHIP AIDS

CALL TO WORSHIP.   "I sought the Lord, and he heard me, and delivered me from all my fears" (Ps. 34:4).

INVOCATION.   Lord God, we are reminded this day that the Savior who was obedient unto death and victorious in Resurrection also ascended into heaven, from whence he will one day come. All we need is found in Christ, who completed what he began and ever works through the Holy Spirit to complete in us a mighty salvation until we meet again.—E. Lee Phillips

OFFERTORY SENTENCE.   "And the King shall answer and say unto them, 'Verily I say unto you, Inasmuch as ye have done it unto one of the least of these my brethren, ye have done it unto me'" (Matt. 25:40).

OFFERTORY PRAYER.   Open our eyes, O Lord, and let us see the good that our gifts may do. Help us to minister to the hidden Christ in everyone. To that end, bless us with increasing awareness and openness of heart.

PRAYER.   Oh God, who has ordained the seasons of the year and also the seasons of our lives, we praise you for the steadfastness of your love and mercy, which support us in every season and time of life. Help us now to open ourselves to the gift of your presence, which will transform our very existence. Where there is fear, give courage; where there is anxiety, give peace; where there is loneliness, give companionship. Let the mind of your Son Jesus become our mind as well, drawing us into fellowship and commitment and service. In a world that grows daily more difficult and complicated, lead us into simplicity of heart and soul. As others contend for place and possessions, make us joyful with relationships. Where the paths that we must walk become steep and narrow or overgrown with briers and weeds, hold our hands lest we stumble. Reveal yourself especially to those who suffer grief or illness, that they may be encouraged by a deeper knowledge of you. Help us to hear your Word for each of us as we wait before you in reverence and love.—John Killinger

SERMON
Topic: God Has a Purpose for Your Life
TEXT: Isa. 55:11

The best illustration of this is in Genesis 1: God spoke, and it was so. And it was good. What happens when the God of the universe speaks to you? It is so, and it is good. If the God of the universe spoke all the heavenly hosts into being, including the sun and the moon, and if he spoke and created the whole world, what can he do when He speaks to you? Any path that the God of the universe selects has eternal dimensions. Some directions seem so very obscure; in the eyes of the world, it might seem that you haven't amounted to much. But there are no small assignments with God.

Our problem is that we've become so self-centered. We've got to become God-centered. You can tell whether you have moved from relationship to religion by how you respond when God speaks to you. Many of us are familiar with Jeremiah 29:11: "For I know the thoughts that I think toward you" (NKJV). What happens when God thinks toward you? "As I have thought, so shall it come to pass" (Isa. 14:24, KJV). God says the same thing to you. He's also going to say, "They are thoughts of peace and not of evil, to give you a future and a hope" (see Jer. 29:11).

What do you do when you're convinced that God has set some thoughts toward you? The Lord says: "Then you will call upon Me and go and pray to Me, and I will listen to you. And you will seek Me and find Me, when you search for Me with all your heart. I will be found by you, and I will bring you back from your captivity" (Jer. 29:12–14, NKJV). Does God know your life right now? Does he have thoughts toward you? Every thought of God toward every child of God is for a hope and a future, for good and not for evil. Go to him and pray to him. Seek him with all of your heart. This means you're going to seek him until God chooses to reveal what his thoughts are toward you. Sadly, God's people often say, "I understand this, but I haven't the faintest idea of how to go about it." I could say, "You have the same book I have. Those verses have been there all along. Have you read them?" Because once I see the nature of God and the ways of God toward my life, I can set my heart and my life in the path of God's activity. When you hear God say something to you, you should take a different attitude. If God says something to me, then it is already in the process of being accomplished. Have you sensed that maybe your life is at a strategic moment—that God has for you something far more significant than what you've been experiencing, but you can't put your finger on what it is? That's OK. He has his finger on what it is. God is actively at work in your life, speaking to you. When God speaks, he's announcing what he has purposed for you, and what he purposes, nobody can turn back. I've heard many a person say to me, "Henry, I just feel so sure that God wanted me to do this, but my church didn't respond." I've replied, "What's that got to do with Almighty God?" They start to tell me all the reasons why something turned back the hand of Almighty God. The enemy has deceived them. When the God of the universe speaks, there is nothing—no combination of principalities, powers, kingdoms, dominions, or names in heaven or under the earth or on the earth—that can ever thwart his purposes. The purposes of God can be thwarted only if we don't believe him. We look at circumstances and say, "God, if only you knew." He says, "I know! If only *you* knew!" All the circumstances arrayed in front of us are as nothing to God. Most of us are not living in that truth. The enemy has convinced many of God's people that there's just too much against

God's plan to make it happen in their lives. But would you settle in your heart for the thought that God's Word is true, that what contradicts God's Word is a lie, and that when God speaks it is so? Learn how to walk with him, so that he has an unhindered opportunity to express his Word to you. Be willing to wait until he does.—Henry Blackaby

SUNDAY, MAY 8, 2005
Lectionary Message
Topic: The Difference It Makes That Jesus Ascended Back to Heaven
TEXT: Acts 1:6–14
Other Readings: Ps. 68:1–10, 32–35; 1 Pet. 4:12–14, 5:6–11; John 17:1–11

Only a few events in history have affected every man and woman who ever lived. Sometimes they go unnoticed at the time. The Ascension of Jesus back to heaven is one of those events. It still affects our lives today. It was meant to.

The last words of Luke's Gospel record the Ascension of Jesus, and they are full of blessing and joy. "When he had led them out to the vicinity of Bethany," Luke says, "he lifted up his hands and blessed them. While he was blessing them, he left them and was taken up into heaven. Then they worshiped him and returned to Jerusalem with great joy. And they stayed continually at the Temple, praising God" (Luke 24:50–53).

How strange! When two people in love part, there is no joy. When close friends realize they will never see each other again, there is no joy. When the family is separated by death, there is no joy. Yet the disciples returned to Jerusalem rejoicing with a new strength and power immediately after seeing their Risen Lord disappear in the clouds. Why? Because of the lasting consequences of Christ's Ascension and exaltation.

I. *Christ sends the Holy Spirit to comfort and counsel us.* Shortly before the events of his Crucifixion, Resurrection, and Ascension, Jesus tells his disciples that he is going to leave them in order to prepare a place for them. Sensing their deep sadness because of his words, he adds, "It is for your good that I am going away. Unless I go away, the Counselor will not come to you; but if I go, I will send him to you" (John 16:7). The work of the Spirit is to bring glory to Christ by making the events of his earthly ministry real to his followers and by guiding them into all truth (John 16:13). Jesus has mentored them for three years. Now he is about to turn them loose to carry out his mission for the church in the power and counsel of the Holy Spirit.

II. *Christ reigns in glory today at God's right hand as Lord of the church.* Luke's two writings deserve to be read together because they tell the whole story of Jesus' ministry. The Gospel of Luke is about Jesus' earthly ministry; Acts is about Jesus' heavenly ministry as he leads his church from God's right hand—a place of absolute power and authority. Paul puts it this way: "And God placed all things under his feet and appointed him to be head over everything for the church, which is his body, the fullness of him who fills everything in every way" (Eph. 1:22).

III. *Christ is always present in the midst of his people.* We have Jesus' promise: "For where two or three come together in my name, there am I with them" (Matt. 18:20)—two or three, two or three dozen, two or three thousand, Christ is there. Matthew closes his Gospel by giving us Jesus' promise in the last words of his Great Commission: "And surely I am with you always, to the very end of the age" (Matt. 28:20). No longer limited by time or space, Christ can be with all believers everywhere at the same time. Take the Lord's Supper, for example. We are told that as often as we eat the bread and drink the cup, we proclaim his death until he comes (2 Cor. 11:25). True, we remember his death at his table, but we do it in the victorious presence of the Risen, ascended Lord. It is his presence that makes "holy communion" holy. We in Christ and Christ in us are the hope of glory. Paul calls this "glorious riches" (Col. 1:27).

IV. *Christ's Ascension is vital to the evangelistic task of the church.* Immediately before ascending into heaven, Jesus gave his disciples their mission. "But you will receive power when the Holy Spirit comes on you," he said, "and you will be my witnesses in Jerusalem, and in all Judea and Samaria, and to the ends of the earth" (Acts 1:8). After he said this, he was taken up before their very eyes, and a cloud hid him from their sight (Acts 1:9).

Ten days later, on the Day of Pentecost, the apostle Peter stood up with the eleven and included the Ascension in the core of his gospel. Jesus was crucified for our sins, raised on the third day, and exalted to God's right hand. God has made him both Lord and Christ, and he reigns with the Father. When they cried out, "Brothers, what shall we do?" he told them, "Repent and be baptized, every one of you, in the name of Jesus Christ so that your sins may be forgiven. And you will receive the gift of the Holy Spirit" (Acts 2).

What the people of this world need more than anything is the forgiveness of sins and God's power to help them live a victorious Christian life. One reason the apostles witnessed with such power was that they remembered two men in white suddenly standing by their side and asking them, "Why do you stand here looking into the sky? This same Jesus, who was taken into heaven, will come back in the same way you have seen him go into heaven" (Acts 1:10, 11). This is the reason they worshipped him and returned to Jerusalem with great joy praising him (Luke 24:52, 53). They believed that no matter what happened to them in the meantime, they would see him again. And so will we.—Wayne Shaw

SERMON SUGGESTIONS

Topic: Getting on with God's Business
TEXT: Acts 1:6–14
(1) A troublesome question: times and seasons. (2) The substantive issue: worldwide witness. (3) Essential preparation: concerted prayer.

Topic: Expectation and Admonition
TEXT: 1 Peter 4:12–14, 5:6–11
As faithful Christians (1) we expect in some ways to suffer for our commitment, (2) we must follow proven tactics for handling threats to our obedience, and (3) we may depend on God for strength to fulfill our calling.

WORSHIP AIDS

CALL TO WORSHIP.   "Whatsoever ye do in word or deed, do all in the name of the Lord Jesus, giving thanks to God and the Father by him" (Col. 3:17).

INVOCATION.   O God, open our hearts to thee, that we may be led by thy Spirit to render to thee true worship. Receive, we pray, the words from our voices, the gifts from our hands, and the service from our daily living.

OFFERTORY SENTENCE.   "Where your treasure is, there will your heart be also" (Matt. 6:21).

OFFERTORY PRAYER.   Lord, we have professed to have surrendered our all to you. Help us to know if it is really true or if there are still miles to travel in our stewardship, and then strengthen our true desires to make what we are and what we have available for your service.

PRAYER.   Gracious Lord, our heavenly Father, we pray for our homes, those most precious and important of all human institutions. In them are fashioned the health of society, the hope of the future. Give us the joy of shared forgiveness, the mercy and life of shared love. Help us learn the fine art of disagreeing without bitterness, of being angry without destructiveness and hurt, of forgiving without vengeance. Then our love shall be like that of Christ and our homes a fitting place for your spirit to dwell. We ask this in Christ's name but for the sake of us all.—Paul D. Simmons

SERMON
Topic: It Takes Two
TEXT: Deut. 7:6–14

Don and Helen McNeely were our pulpit guests a few years ago in service with missions. Helen and my wife had been friends for several years before our marriage. The McNeelys, also newly married, visited in our seminary apartment in Fort Worth, Texas, on several occasions during our three years of study at Southwestern Seminary. Their son and our daughter were born in the same year. They were serving a church in the Washington, D.C., area, and Helen made several visits to Fort Worth on the way to her family in south Texas. She was captive of the mystique of the Capitol, and she often talked about the young family and handsome president in the White House. I recall one particular visit when Helen arrived full of excitement about having been included in a presidential prayer breakfast. With awe that might be described as reverence, she told how the president had walked past their table close enough for her to reach out and touch—but she didn't. I was impressed.

The semester after the Kennedy assassination, I took a class in Christian ethics under a very young associate professor, Bill Pinson. Pinson was a friend and seminary classmate of Bill Moyers, the newly installed press secretary for President Johnson. I recall the day Pinson came into class with the excitement of a small child on Christmas morning. He had received an invitation from Moyers for a visit to the White House that included a night in one of the White House guest rooms. After the visit, an entire class period was devoted to a play-by-play description of this experience of a lifetime.

To this day, I have never touched or spoken personally with a sitting president. Furthermore, I have never had a personal letter or phone call from the person who fills the highest office in the United States. My parents received a note of congratulations on the celebration of their fiftieth wedding anniversary from President Carter, but they did not take it too personally. We somehow assumed that the president had not really taken note of our big family celebration in Fort Smith, Arkansas. In fact, we were not absolutely sure that he had ever really noticed Fort Smith or Arkansas. I am still amazed at the film shown several times during the Clinton administration of a teenage Bill Clinton shaking hands with President Kennedy at the White House. Every president is in some sense *my* president, but not quite on the level with *my* family or *my* friend. To receive personal notice by the president, you have to be very wealthy or very powerful, or do something very noteworthy.

I have never had access to the president of the United States, and I suspect that I would also be ecstatic about a close encounter with the person who sits at the top of the world. The kind of personal relationship most of us have—or do not have—with the president serves to illustrate something of the importance of the covenant relationship Israel had with God.

I. *You are chosen.* The covenant with God was two-sided, between a personal God and the people of Israel, a corporate covenant with strong personal responsibilities. God took notice of individual persons named Abraham, Moses, and David. God took the initiative to establish a personal bond not only with these great men but with all of their descendants forever. God chose the nation Israel. God rescued the people from slavery in Egypt and brought them to the land of promise. The Hebrews were set apart from the rest of humanity. To be holy is to stand in contrast. Holiness is a perpendicular line cutting across the ordinary plane of life. A holy people are a special people with a special role to fulfill in history. Israel took their election personally and seriously, as well they should, but they were reminded that they did not earn the right or privilege of a special role in history. God is not like kings and politicians who play to power, who tend to be interested in people primarily for what they have to offer in return. God's election of Israel did not add up. They were not the most numerous of peoples. They were not big and important. All that they were and all that they had was grace—the gift of God. God chose them because God loved them. God's covenant was never a cold contract for mutual service and protection. It was always a bond of love between a personal God and a nation of persons.

Election has often followed the line of Calvin's doctrine of predestination, which makes us pawns in the hands of history. Biblically, election is a loving, personal choice by a personal God totally immersed in the *hesed,* steadfast love of God. I got a clue to this side of election while working as a lifeguard and swimming instructor in my high school and early college years. Several of the guards had worked with a delightful child, adopted as an infant by a couple in their late forties. From infancy the boy had taken to water like a fish; so from the age of three his parents paid the freight on private swimming instruction. He knew that he was an adopted child, but he had been carefully taught that he was chosen. "Natural parents have no choice," he would proudly announce. He was picked by his parents after he was born. He was obviously loved and felt wanted by his doting parents.

II. *Know God.* Genesis 4:1 reports that Adam knew Eve, and she conceived and bore Cain. The Hebrew word *Yada* is not limited to the marital relationship that leads to children; the application throughout the Old Testament reminds us of the intimate, personal nature of the relationship between God and the people.

Because God had chosen Israel, the people were called to respond by knowing that *JHWH* your God is God. The monotheism of Israel is something like the monogamy of Christian marriage. As God had a choice among the peoples of the earth, the Jews had a choice among the gods of the nations. The *sola* of the Reformation—faith alone, grace alone, Christ alone, and Scripture alone—has roots in the jealousy of God's love for Israel. The Jews were to know who God is in distinction from all the alternative gods of their neighbors, and they were to be devoted to God alone. As God is faithful and loving, the people need to be faithful and loving. With the strong personal commitment of the marriage covenant, the people were to know God and be faithful to God.

Rabbi Abraham Heschel called God's covenant with Israel at Sinai "the decisive moment in Israel's history." It initiated a new relationship between God and the people: "God became engaged to a people." When the people accepted the covenant, they "became engaged to God."

The religion of Israel and its development in the person of Christ was a personal religion of relationship. Most of the battles in church history over issues of theology, definitions of heresy and orthodoxy, miss the central issue of the nature of our walk with God. We do not know God as we know facts and control nature. We know God as we know one another, in personal love and commitment, and we look toward the day with Paul when we will know as we are known.

III. *Be responsible.* The ball is in our court. God initiates covenant. God seeks us out and loves us as God's own people, but the covenant is incomplete without a human response. The big "therefore" of the covenant is the message that this is a three-dimensional faith. To picture God as the big guy in the sky who makes the rules and runs the world is a distortion of the picture of God in the Bible. Indeed, Heschel wrote that the Bible is the word of God and of the human, a record both of revelation and response, and we are not done at the distance of tipping our hats to the superpower of the universe. Because God is love, the only way we can respond is in kind. Jesus said it best in the announcement of the Great Commandment: love God with all that you are and love one another as yourself.—Larry Dipboye

SUNDAY, MAY 15, 2005
Lectionary Message

Topic: Pentecost—Birthday Party Time

Text: Acts 2:1–21

Other Readings: Num. 11:24–30; Ps. 104:24–34, 35b; 1 Cor. 12:3b–13; John 20:19–23 or John 7:37–39

Today is Pentecost Sunday. Perhaps we would do well to remind ourselves why it is so important to us as members of the church. The Jews had a long history of keeping Pentecost. Sometimes called the Festival of Weeks because it was a week of weeks (seven weeks) plus one day, Pentecost is fifty days after the Sabbath of the Passover. Historically, it had two purposes: to celebrate the giving of the Law to Moses on Mount Sinai and to present the first fruits of the barley harvest before God. It came at the right time. The weather was beautiful, travel was pleasant, no one worked on Pentecost because it was a holiday, and the streets of Jerusalem were often crowded with more people than at Passover—many of them God-fearing internationals. There was a festive spirit in the air; it was religious party time.

But this Pentecost was different from all the others. What happened on that day became the turning point of history and gave birth to the church. God used that Pentecost to bring newness to planet earth.

I. *New power.* Shortly before his Ascension into heaven, Jesus told his disciples to wait in Jerusalem until they received the promised gift: the baptism of the Holy Spirit. Ten days went by, and they were all together in one place. Then the miracle happened: "Suddenly a sound like the blowing of a violent wind came from heaven and filled the whole house where they were sitting. They saw what seemed to be tongues of fire that separated and came to rest on each of them. They were filled with the Holy Spirit and began to speak in other tongues as the Spirit enabled them" (Acts 2:2–4). Everyone heard them in their own language. A few made fun of them, accusing them of being drunk. But many others who had also heard the sound of fierce wind and seen flaming tongues of fire were amazed, including the disciples, who knew that this mighty miracle had come from God. Pentecost means the gift of new power for Christ's disciples.

II. *New message.* It came from the Father, was credentialed by the Spirit, and focused on the Son. Peter led into his sermon by answering his accusers. "These men are not drunk," he said. "This is what the Prophet Joel wrote would happen when God poured out his Spirit on all men and women." Then he quoted King David's prediction that the Messiah would come. Our faith has its roots in Old Testament history. It is not a fly-by-night cult founded by a Johnny-come-lately charismatic leader.

Christ is the core of Peter's Pentecost sermon. He accuses them, along with wicked men, of crucifying Jesus, whom God had accredited by miracles, wonders, and signs. They are guilty of murder, but God raised him from the dead because death cannot hold him. Further, God exalted him to his own right hand in glory and power. The message of Pentecost is that Christ died for our sins, was buried, rose on the third day, and ascended to God. No one else can atone for our sins: "Salvation is found in no one else, for there is no other name under heaven given to men by which we must be saved" (Acts 4:12).

In answer to their question, "Brothers, what shall we do?" Peter gives us a double command and a double promise. If we repent and are baptized, Christ will forgive our sins and give us the gift of the Holy Spirit. More than anything else, we need cleansing from our sin and the power of God in our lives to help us overcome. This promise is "for all whom the Lord our God will call," and the plea is for us to "save ourselves from this corrupt generation." The choice is ours; eternity hangs in the balance.

III. *New community.* "Those who accepted his message were baptized, and three thousand were added to their number that day." Peter had made the Good Confession months before: "You are the Christ, the Son of the living God." Jesus responded, "On this rock I will build my church, and the gates of Hades will not overcome it" (Matt. 16:18). On Pentecost his promise came true; the Church was born. "Church" is what happens to us when we are saved from our sins and are given the gift of God's Holy Spirit. We become a part of his spiritual family—the household of God. Today we remember our roots and celebrate the Church's birthday. If Christ died for the Church, then it must be important to him that we be a part of it.

IV. *New purpose.* We label it the Great Commission. In Matthew's Gospel, Jesus says, "All authority in heaven and earth has been given to me. Therefore go and make disciples of all nations, baptizing them in the name of the Father, and of the Son, and of the Holy Spirit, and teaching them to obey everything I have commanded you" (28:18–20). In the Gospel of John, Jesus says, "As the Father has sent me, I am sending you" (20:21). Luke mentions it twice: "The Christ will suffer and rise from the dead on the third day, and repentance and forgiveness of sins will be preached to all nations, beginning at Jerusalem" (Luke 24:45–47) and "But you will receive power when the Holy Spirit comes on you; and you will be my witnesses in Jerusalem, and in all Judea and Samaria, and to the ends of the earth" (Acts 1:8). We have our marching orders.

Happy birthday, Church! The best is yet to come; Christ promised to return for us. In the meantime, "Stand firm. Let nothing move you. Always give yourselves fully to the work of the Lord, because you know that your labor in the Lord is not in vain" (1 Cor. 15:58).—Wayne Shaw

ILLUSTRATION

W. E. Sangster has a sermon on Pentecost that he calls "Drunk and Mad." Peter answered the charge of being drunk, and Paul defended himself before Festus and Agrippa against the charge that he was mad. Sangster asks if we are exuberant, cordial, and infectiously gay enough, would anyone accuse us of being drunk? Then he argues that Christianity gives the real euphoria of the Holy Spirit, the real sanity; it is the world that is mad. Discerning men and women have seen it getting more insane for years. Vital Christianity is the most joyously sober and sane thing in the world.—Wayne Shaw[1]

SERMON SUGGESTIONS

Topic: When the Holy Spirit Is at Work
TEXT: Acts 2:1–21
(1) The gospel is fitted to each individual's need. (2) Witnesses come from every quarter.

Topic: Unity and Diversity in Community
TEXT: 1 Cor. 12:3b–13.
(1) The unifying confession (v. 3b). (2) The diversifying service (vv. 4–11). (3) The confirming explanation (vv. 12–13).

WORSHIP AIDS

CALL TO WORSHIP.   "Seek the Lord and his strength, seek his face continually" (1 Chron. 16:11).

INVOCATION.   O Lord, we know that you are mighty and we are weak, but we take heart, knowing also that your strength is not only the power to make the mountains tremble, but also and especially the power of love. We come to you with trust, relying on your strength to do in and through us what we could never do in our own power. So fill us with renewed faith, hope, and love.

OFFERTORY SENTENCE.   "Upon the first day of the week let every one of you lay by him in store, as God hath prospered him" (1 Cor. 16:2).

OFFERTORY PRAYER.   God of grace, you have prospered each of us with enough to give at least a token of that with which you have blessed us. Help us to measure out our gifts by what we have received and by our fitting gratitude.

PRAYER.   Our Father, we know that you love us. No gift of yours could be greater than the gift of your Son, the revelation of your love and the means of our salvation. Yet some of

---

[1]Wayne Shaw, *These Things Abide* (London: Hodder and Stoughton, 1939), pp. 133–141.

us come before you perplexed. We have prayed for one thing and received another or nothing at all. We have expected abundant life, yet life became for us pinched and frustrated. Nevertheless, you have promised your help to those who cry to you. Grant that we may not look so longingly at doors closed that we cannot see other doors opening before us. Give us the grace to accept, if it is your will, some lesser good that we may discover at least to be what is best of all. Let us not be afraid to struggle with you in our disappointments, assured that you sometimes inspire us to pray bold, believing prayers that may seem to be defiant even to you. Yet may we always be prepared to say, "Not my will but yours be done."

SERMON
Topic: Beware of the Lilliputians
TEXT: Gal. 6:7

Series: The Bitter Harvest I

Most of us probably remember *Gulliver's Travels,* by Jonathan Swift, as a children's story, since abridged editions for juveniles have often been published. In actuality, this masterpiece was the most brilliant as well as the most bitter of Swift's biting satires. Divided into four parts, the account tells how its hero, Lemuel Gulliver, embarked on a series of travels to remote nations, only to be cast up on some strange land as the result of calamities such as shipwreck. Book one takes him to "a voyage to Lilliput," where he awakens to find himself fettered to the ground by a horde of six-inch-high Lilliputians who view him as the Man-Mountain.

Swift was insisting that his fellow-citizens needed to awaken from their slumbers and realize that they had been hamstrung by a multitude of minor threats long ignored or dismissed as inconsequential: "avarice, faction, hypocrisy, perfidiousness, cruelty, rage, madness, hatred, envy, lust, malice, and ambition. . . ."[2] Swift saw Great Britain as a giant of a nation immobilized by a swarm of Lilliputian sins that could corrupt its future.

Let us inquire whether this strange tale remains a parable of our time as well.

I. *The strength of Lilliputian sins.* With advances in microtechnology, we have learned that there are a host of tiny, even invisible, kingdoms that constitute the very foundations of physical reality. In this realm of the miniscule lies the invisible dust that gives color to a sunset, the viruses that can cause an epidemic, and the pollens that can activate our allergies. Also in the domain of the unseen lie a host of bacteria, the most dominant form of life on earth, plus all manner of quarks and x-rays. As Sue Hubbell put it in writing about the Lilliputian order of things, "We humans are a minority of giants, stumbling around in a world of little things."[3]

The potency of the petite is at work in the moral world as well as in the physical world. In Galatians 6:7, for example, Paul stated with categorical finality a law learned from nature: "Whatever you sow, that you will reap." In other words, spiritual issues often begin as tiny

---

[2]Jacques Barzun, *Introduction to Jonathan Swift, Gulliver's Travels* (New York: Oxford University Press, 1977), p. xvi.

[3]Quoted by Mark Rozzo, "Get Small," *New Yorker,* Apr. 3, 2000, p. 20, from Sue Hubbell, *Waiting for Aphrodite* (New York: Houghton Mifflin, 2000). See also Joseph A. Amato, *Dust: A History of the Small and the Invisible* (Berkeley: University of California Press, 2000); Wayne Biddle, *A Field Guide to the Invisible* (New York: Henry Holt, 2000); and Ivan Amato, *Stuff: The Materials the World Is Made of* (New York: HarperCollins, 1997).

as a seed. We usually depict evil in grandiose terms, such as a dragon with a pitchfork, horns, and tail, whereas we ought to visualize it as the sowing of microscopic spores in the soil of life.

II. *The strategy of Lilliputian sins.* Not only are tiny sins powerful, but they are also seductive because their very size leads us to let down our guard. We know that we are not perfect; thus we assume that a little mischief, a modest amount of hanky-panky, is not only permissible but inevitable in life. Sin uses this assumption to steal into our lives when our defenses are down, convincing us that there is nothing to worry about precisely because we are dealing only with gremlins that can easily be brushed aside.

Seldom are we confronted with clear issues painted black or white. More often, our decisions are compounded out of innumerable choices, each so small that it goes unnoticed. Rarely do we turn a corner or choose a fork in the road at one decisive moment.

Many of us suppose that we can easily conquer the "little" (venial) sins, whereas the "big" (mortal) sins may prove too hard to handle. I suspect that just the opposite is nearer the truth. Faced with monstrous evils, such as murder or rape, we are seldom tempted and our choices are usually clear. It is when the gremlin sins begin to infiltrate that we prove most vulnerable. After all, no one will rebuke us, or arrest us, or cause us any problems if our sins seem to be insignificant.

III. *The significance of Lilliputian sins.* Because we assume that we can "handle" a mere handful of sins, particularly of the modest variety, just as we can handle a few drinks without getting drunk, preachers tend to get accused of legalism when they warn against apparently trivial patterns of conduct. The lesson of the seed is that small beginnings may have a significance all out of proportion to their size!

To generalize from decades of pastoral counseling: the alcoholic never sets out to become captive to a bottle; he only wants to sip on a social drink. The unwed mother never intends to become a parent without a partner; she only bargains for fleeting pleasure in a moment of ecstasy. The embezzler never seeks to bankrupt his company; he only "borrows" some needed funds that he fully intends to repay as the company prospers. Sin never shows us the consequences of our compromises. Instead, it poses as a harmless midget so that we will simply shrug and not bother to banish it from our lives.

The key question to ask in beginning to build a life of integrity is, What invisible influences are at work in the very air that you breathe? Ask yourself: How many bad influences are slowly but surely tying down your spirit so that it will no longer soar? Don't let six-inch Lilliputian sins keep you from finishing the journey of faith to which God called you.—William E. Hull

SUNDAY, MAY 22, 2005

Lectionary Message

Topic: "The Great Commission: An Exercise in Love"

TEXT: Matt. 28:16–20

Other Readings: Gen. 1:1–2:4a; Ps. 8; 2 Cor. 13:11–13

Friendship love is the most powerful force in the universe. When the British author Charles Lamb was asked how he was able to weather his grave adversities, he replied simply, "I had a friend." The friendship of Jonathan and David in Scripture is ageless and classic. Scripture simply says, "David loved Jonathan as his own soul."

But these are pale expressions of love compared to Jesus' love for his disciples when he told them, "I call you no longer servants but my friends" (John. 15:15). He had convinced them of two realities: "I am the Son of God and I am your friend." John the Baptist prized that friendship so much that he declared, "He must increase and I must decrease," and the apostle Paul wrote, "I count all things as loss to gain Christ."

Christ's friendship love is the biblical context for the Great Commission. Notice how it illuminates our text.

I. *The might of Christ's friendship love.* "All authority in heaven and on earth," he said, "has been given to me" (Matt. 28:18). How much is that? Paul tries to describe it in these words: Christ is the image of the invisible God, the firstborn over all creation. All things were created by him and for him, and in him all things hold together. He is supreme in everything, and God was pleased to have all his fullness to dwell in him (Col. 1:15–20). Isn't it marvelous that the power behind the universe is not some cold, impersonal force, but friendship love?

II. *The measure of his friendship love.* He pays us his highest compliment by trusting us to disciple the nations. He has no plan B. But he also measures our love for him by our response to his commission.

He tells us, "Therefore go." These words can also be translated "Going" or "As you go." Both meanings fit the Church's commission. Wherever we go, we are to share the good news by our words and our example. But he calls some for special ministries in special places. Christ knew that all of us need to "gossip" the gospel wherever we go, and some of us need to go where the gospel has never gone.

We are to "disciple the nations." Having been discipled, we are to disciple others by first introducing them to Jesus and then teaching them to follow him. This command reaches around the globe. It requires more of us than simply making disciples where we live. It includes everyone God loves, and that means all the people in the world. Jesus' last words to his disciples before he ascended into heaven were to "disciple the nations." World mission is not optional. It is at the heart of the Great Commission.

We are to "baptize them in the name of the Father and of the Son and of the Holy Spirit." Baptism is much more than a ritual to initiate converts into the Church. We are baptized in the name of God the Father, Son, and Holy Spirit. In baptism we become the Father's child. We are buried with the Son in the likeness of his death, burial, and Resurrection. We receive the gift of the Holy Spirit indwelling in us to help us live the Christian life. He has no one to carry out the Great Commission except those of us baptized in his name.

We are to teach his disciples to obey everything he has commanded us. We must teach the important doctrinal truths and ethical principles of Scripture, and we must also teach as Jesus did—by example. For three years, he poured himself into his disciples' lives and then turned them loose to change the world. We are to entrust what we have been taught to reliable men and women who will be qualified to teach others who, in turn, will teach others also (2 Tim. 2:2).

III. *The meaning of his friendship love.* "And surely I will be with you always, to the very end of the age" is not only reserved for heaven. It means that he assures us of his presence with us now as we go about carrying out his commission.

I learned long ago that if I wanted to get close to my father, the way to do it was to get side-by-side with him in the work he loved most to do. I have also learned that if I want to get close to my heavenly father, the best way for me to do it is to be about the work of discipling the nations.

He puts the Great Commission on the strongest possible motive—do we love him enough to obey him? If we love him, we will keep his commandments (John. 14:15). He will be with us always. The question is, Will we always be with him?—Wayne Shaw

SERMON SUGGESTIONS

Topic: The God of the Temple and Church

TEXT: 2 Chron. 36:14–23

(1) He keeps his promise in faithful love. (2) He causes his name to dwell in special places. (3) He hears the prayers of his people who turn to him in faith.

Topic: The Secret of Christ

TEXT: Eph. 3:4–10

(1) What it is (v. 6). (2) How it became known (v. 5). (3) Who its ministers are (vv. 7, 9).

WORSHIP AIDS

CALL TO WORSHIP.   "He shall call upon me, and I will answer him; I will be with him in trouble; I will deliver him, and honor him" (Ps. 91:15).

INVOCATION.   We are here today, gracious Lord, not only to praise you but also to call on your name. Some among us may at this very moment feel the pain and loneliness of deep trouble. Let this service of worship bring reassurance of your promised help.

OFFERTORY SENTENCE.   "All the law is fulfilled in one word, even in this: Thou shalt love thy neighbor as thyself" (Gal. 5:14).

OFFERTORY PRAYER.   O God, as we see what we can do for one another and for others outside our church by our giving, we rejoice that our offerings do not have to be a matter of law and demand, but an expression of love and caring. Deepen our love for neighbor, and help us to find practical ways of expressing that love.

PRAYER.   Accept, O Lord, our thanks and praise for all that you have done for us. We thank you for the splendor of the whole creation, for the beauty of this world, for the wonder of life, and for the mystery of love. We thank you for the blessing of family and friends, and for the loving care that surrounds us on every side. We thank you for setting us at tasks that demand our best efforts, and for leading us to accomplishments that satisfy and delight us. We thank you also for those disappointments and failures that lead us to acknowledge our dependence on you alone. Above all, we thank you for your Son Jesus Christ: for the truth of his Word and the example of his life; for his steadfast obedience, by which he overcame temptation; for his dying, through which he overcame death; and for his rising to life again, in which we are raised to the life of your kingdom. Grant us the gift of your Spirit, that we may know him and make him known; and through him. At all times and in all places, may we give thanks to you in all things.—Book of Common Prayers

SERMON
Topic: The Vitality of Evil
TEXT: James 1:5

Series: The Bitter Harvest II

The first sermon in this series looked at a text that seemed to speak only of seed time and harvest (Gal. 6:7). But hidden between the sowing and the mowing is a vital connective link: the growing! The planting begins very small, but what it produces ends very large. The farmer who starts out with his crop in a bag will end up with his crop in a barn. Jesus spoke of the proverbial capacity of a seed to increase thirtyfold, sixtyfold, and a hundredfold (Mark 4:8).

This neglected factor speaks to the power of sin to proliferate. Evil has a latent strength to multiply, a built-in capacity to escalate, to achieve momentum, and thus to spread far beyond its original bounds. Our text today speaks to that truth (James 1:15).

I. *Sin is personal rather than impersonal.* We like to think of evil in terms of a set of rules ("Don't do this or that!"), or a code of conduct, or a theory of depravity. The key distortion is to keep the concept impersonal so that sin will be something that we sit around and think about. As long as sin is impersonal, we can keep it at arm's length. Many reject the existence of a personal Devil because, if evil were alive, that would change the ground rules for dealing with "it."

But arguing about whether the Devil is "personal" may well be the Devil's shrewdest strategy for deceiving us. After all, no one has ever seen a "literal" Satan, and so the issue seems moot. But it really isn't, because sin does come to us in terms that are personal rather than impersonal. The Devil, whatever his or its reality may be, wears a human face. Because of this "incarnational" aspect, sin is always more than a rule or a theory. Perhaps God chose to come to us "in flesh"—that is, as a human being—because flesh is the way in which his adversary engages us. Human influences, not abstract ideas, are the weapons of warfare by which spiritual battles are won or lost. Adam did not agonize over a rule; he bit into an apple offered by Eve. Samson did not stumble over a theory; he allowed Delilah to play with his locks. David did not succumb to a concept, but to Bathsheba taking a bath before his very eyes. Peter did not wilt before a definition of iniquity, but before the tauntings of a servant girl. Notice how many masks evil is able to wear! This personal factor helps to explain the power of sin to seduce, for a person can disguise the issues so as to make them seem benign or even beneficent.

In every temptation, there is far more than meets the eye. Sin wears many subtle disguises. How much easier it would be if evil grew horns and tail and confronted us with pitchfork in hand, for then we would know who the enemy is. But no, because temptation comes in and through people, it may strike at any moment, when and where we least suspect it, with all of the craftiness and tenacity of which we are capable. The culprit may turn out to be our wife (Eve), our girlfriend (Delilah), our employee (servant girl), or even a fellow disciple (Judas)! What this "lineup" of villains proves is that sin can crop up anywhere and anytime by anybody.

II. *Sin is active rather than inactive.* In the Bible, there are many vivid images for evil: it is likened to leaven in a lump (Matt. 16:6), to a wolf on the prowl (Matt. 10:16; John 10:12), to a voracious bird of prey (Mark 4:4), and to an army arrayed for battle (Eph. 6:12). Galatians 6 begins with a warning that sin is like a swift runner who can "overtake" a person. Common to all these images is a view of sin as active rather than inactive. Evil is no inert "skeleton in the closet" but is a vital, dynamic force.

Our minds and hearts are not like a closet that is dark, closed, and locked tight against the world. Instead, they are like a seething, fermenting, open cauldron full of fears, ambitions, jealousies, frustrations, sorrows, guilt, and pride. Once sin plunges into that swiftly moving stream, it never stands still again. Because of this, we cannot control the consequences even of our most minor compromises.

Why do we so tragically underestimate the potency of our sins? Just as interest compounds when we leave it in the bank, so sin compounds when we leave it in the swirling mix of passions that rule the human heart.

How swiftly sin escalates! Men gather to grumble about a grievance, and soon a riot is under way. Nations watch in horror as diplomatic incidents become occasions for world wars. Friendly football rivalries degenerate into pitched battles. "Harmless" gossip spreads until a career is ruined. Petty bickering poisons a marriage until divorce is the only recourse. On every hand, we see how some trivial incident mushrooms to engulf those who paid no attention to it at first. Therefore a crucial question to ask in making every moral decision is, To what does it lead?

Some things are neither right nor wrong in themselves; nor is the situation decisive to determine their worth. Thus they must be judged by their *consequences* (for example, drinking, smoking, dancing, playing cards). Always we must ask, What processes are being set in motion? What attitudes are being formed? What relationships are being developed? In these gray areas, it is not the seed that is sown but the crop that is grown that matters most.

III. *Sin is organized rather than chaotic.* One of our most foolish mistakes is to assume that evil just pops up from nowhere, each little temptation isolated from the next. The Biblical view is that sin is much smarter than that. Satan represents the cunning mastermind that meshes together separate compromises into collective corruption that gives evil far more power than it would otherwise have. One way evil escalates is by becoming systematic; that is, it becomes institutionalized, taking on a corporate nature as "principalities and powers." The whole becomes far mightier than its several parts.

Think of the vast collective forces that seem masterminded to win reluctant concessions from us. Giant corporations string out the decision-making process through so many echelons that no one individual in the chain of command feels any personal responsibility for the outcome. Vote buying becomes so commonplace that conspirators against the very fabric of democracy simply shrug and say, "It's the system." This is just the point: it is the system, and evil systems can become so powerful that they crush the individual conscience.

Our text speaks of the growth that ensues from the union of temptation and desire. Sin that begins no larger than a tiny sperm or egg conceives a baby who finally becomes a full-grown monster called death (James 1:15). Our first sermon in this series taught us to look at little things when seeking to be on our guard against sin. This second message underscores the importance of looking at those little things in terms of how much capacity they have for growth.

Sin can spread fast once its seed finds fertile soil. Be not deceived by small beginnings. To adapt a similar phrase: The seeds of sin may grow slowly, but they grow exceedingly large!—William H. Hull

SUNDAY, MAY 29, 2005
Lectionary Message

Topic: Proud of the Gospel

TEXT: Rom. 1:16–17

Other Readings: Gen. 6:9–22, 7:24, 8:14–19; Ps. 46; Rom. 3:22b–28 (29–31); Matt. 7:21–29

"I am proud of the gospel" is the positive way of saying what the apostle Paul meant when he wrote to the church at Rome, "I am not ashamed of the gospel." What is this gospel that he was so proud of? The word means "Good News." But good news about what? In Romans 1:1 he says he was "set apart for the Gospel of God"; that would have to include "the Father God who reconciles us to Himself, the Son of God crucified for our sins, and the Holy Spirit of God who gives us abundant life." This good news about God is good news from God. Elsewhere Paul gives us the core of the gospel: "For what I received I passed on to you of first importance: that Christ died for our sins according to the Scriptures, that he was buried, that he was raised on the third day according to the Scriptures, and that he appeared to Peter, and then to the Twelve" (1 Cor. 15:3, 4). The apostle John gives us a wonderful one-verse summary tucked away in his Gospel: "For God so loved the world that he gave his one and only Son that whoever believes in him shall not perish but have eternal life" (3:16). Christ is the center of the gospel.

But why should we be proud of the gospel? These two verses, Romans 1:16–17, are extremely important because they announce the theme of the entire letter to the Romans, and in them he gives us several reasons why we should be proud of the gospel.

I. *The gospel's awesome power.* It is God's awesome power to save us. The good news is so good because our bad news is so bad. In Romans 3:23 he says that "all have sinned and fallen short of the glory of God," having just argued that all Gentiles are lost because they have not even lived up to their own standards, and all Jews are lost because they have not lived up to the law that God revealed to them in the Old Testament. We are all sinners, but Christ died for our sins and rose from the grave to gain victory over sin and its penalty—death. He tells us in chapter 6, verse 23, "For the wages of sin is death, but the free gift of God is eternal life through Christ Jesus our Lord." That is Good News.

The gospel also has the power to transform us. We died to sin, were buried with Christ in baptism, and were raised with Christ to live a new life (6:4). "Therefore, I urge you, brothers," he pleads, "in view of God's mercy, to offer your bodies as living sacrifices, holy and pleasing to God—which is your spiritual worship. Do not conform any longer to the pattern of this world, but be transformed by the renewing of your mind. Then you will be able to test and approve what God's will is—his good, pleasing and perfect will" (12:1, 2).

II. *The gospel's universal scope.* God includes the whole world—Jew and Gentile, Greek and non-Greek, wise and unwise, you and me—in the gospel (1:14). It may be a difficult stretch for us to include every nationality, race, color, gender, degree of education, and social status in our commitment to the gospel, but it is God's stretch.

Nowhere is it better illustrated than in how the church at Rome is instructed to treat Gentile and Jewish differences over food (Rom. 14). All roads led to Rome, and Christians of various nationalities came from all over the Roman Empire. Though begun by Jews who returned to Rome after participating in the birth of the church in Jerusalem, the church at Rome, William Barclay tells us, was predominantly Gentile by the time Paul wrote his letter. How do Jewish Christians eat a fellowship meal with their Gentile brothers and sisters in Christ when many of the foods are so different and are forbidden for the Jew by Old Testament law? The answer is, "The man who eats everything must not look down on him who does not, and the man who does not eat everything must not condemn the man who does, for God has accepted him" (14:3). Christ expects diversity in his church, but he condemns division.

III. *The gospel's unique claim.* It is *the* power of God for salvation to everyone who believes (1:16). It may not be politically correct in our inclusive and relativistic world, but the Bible knows only one way to be saved: through the gospel of Christ. The apostle Peter agrees: "Salvation is found in no one else, for there is no other name under heaven given to men by which we must be saved" (Acts 4:12).

The Roman letter is about world evangelization. The gospel saves everyone throughout the world who believes the gospel (1:16). But all must respond in "the obedience that comes from faith" (1:5). To demonstrate our obedience to the gospel, we turn from our sins, are buried with Christ in baptism, and rise to live a new life (6:4). God justifies us (puts us right with himself) through our obedient faith, and as Christ's justified ones we live all our days trusting God wherever he leads. Everyone needs to hear and obey the gospel to be saved. Our priority as the church is to send and take the gospel to the whole world.

"I am proud of the gospel," says the apostle Paul. How proud of the gospel is your church? How proud of the gospel are you? What are you doing about it?—Wayne Shaw

ILLUSTRATION

Without knowing it, a Chinese friend in Indonesia gave me an illustration of the difficulties that different ethnic groups have in enjoying table fellowship with one another. In casual conversation she talked about her two favorite delicacies when eating chicken: eyeballs and brains. I let her know that it would work out perfectly in any meal I shared with her; she could eat not only her portion of chicken eyes and brains but mine as well.—Wayne Shaw

SERMON SUGGESTIONS

Topic: The Fugitive

TEXT: Gen. 28:10–17

(1) The problem: Circumstances may cause one to find oneself in a lonely, apparently God-forsaken path. (2) The solution: in the crisis time, God may manifest himself to us in some unusual way or comfort us through faith in his promise and presence.

Topic: The Great Difference

TEXT: Rom. 5:12–19

(1) Because of Adam, we are pronounced guilty. (2) Because of Christ, we are pronounced not guilty.

WORSHIP AIDS

CALL TO WORSHIP.   "Love must be completely sincere. Hate what is evil, hold on to what is good" (Rom. 12:9, TEV).

INVOCATION.   Eternal God, as you have raised your Son, Jesus Christ, from the dead, make our spirits alive to you and to one another, so that we may render to you the worship and service due your holy name.

OFFERTORY SENTENCE.   "Keep your life free from love of money, and be content with what you have; for he has said, 'I will never fail you nor forsake you'" (Heb. 13:5, RSV).

OFFERTORY PRAYER.   Our Father, help us keep our lives, including our relationship to money, in true perspective. Grant that our decisions will always be made remembering what is right and who is faithful.

PRAYER.   O thou that dwellest in the heaven, and whose heart is in the earth; thou that wert once a man of sorrows and acquainted with grief, but now art ascended on high, a Prince and a Savior, reach forth to us this morning that sovereign and reviving joy which thou hast and dost impart, and which all thine may have if they are united by faith to thee. Care, and labor, and sickness, and anxieties, and disappointments, and the whole round and turmoil of earthly experience overshadow us. As birds in deep forests forget to sing when the morning is coming, not knowing in the twilight that the whole air above the forest is full of daylight, so we are silent and voiceless, though thy glory flames above. Help us to fly into that upper air where all the beauty of thy presence is, where thou art, and where we shall be undisturbed by those sluggish thoughts that hold us down, those envious and corrupt thoughts which mar the purity of the soul. Deliver us from the power which holds us to the earth and makes us earthy. Give us more of the vital power of divine inspiration in those elements which unite us together and make us the heirs of immorality.

We beseech of thee, O Lord! that thou wilt this morning draw near to every one of us. We hate our hatreds; we hate our prejudices; we hate our selfishness; we hate all those corrupt ways, and all those compliances with the world's corrupt ways, which our weakness too often leads us to. We have, today, in thy presence, such a thought of manhood in Christ Jesus that we look upon our real and worldly selves with shame and can scarcely believe that men who are competent to form such ideas of themselves—bless so high and Christlike—do walk in a way so burdened, in a way so full of imperfection and sin and unloveliness. When we fain would follow thee, who dost breath peace and give forth joy, how often do we find ourselves bringing forth anger, and seeking cruelly to hurt! Thou that dost love thine enemies, are we thy followers, who hate our fellow men, even those that were slaughtering thee; and cannot we forgive those who have reached but a little way to disturb our worldly peace and outward prosperity and interest? How shall we call ourselves thine, if we cannot forgive as we are forgiven? How are we the children of the Lord Jesus Christ, if our hearts are fountains of bitterness and are not fountains of love, with all its sweet and blessed fruit?

Grant, we beseech of thee, O Lord! that we may be changed, and be no longer carnal, nor follow the law of the beasts that rend and ravage. Grant that we may be born into thee, and that we may have that higher beneficence which becomes the sons of God. Teach us that gentleness, that deep peacefulness, which they have whose souls are staid upon thee. From all the fluctuations of our passions, from the disturbance of pride, from hungerings after the fantastic follies of vanity, deliver us. Grant unto us that subtle fidelity, that fealty to thy name, that hearty and thorough love of thee, that childlike docility, that leaning and yearning on thy bosom which shall make us indeed thine own children.—Henry Ward Beecher

SERMON
Topic: Reaping the Whirlwind
Text: Hosea 8:7

Series: The Bitter Harvest, III
The comic Fred Allen once quipped, "Most of us spend six days a week sowing wild oats and then go to church on Sunday and pray for a crop failure."[4] But the crop will not fail! Evil carries its own built-in consequences that cannot be denied. We started this series with Galatians 6:7, which announced the law of the harvest as a categorical imperative: "that shall he also reap." In the second installment we saw how James 1:15 altered the image from agricultural to biological: "and sin, when it is full-grown, brings forth death." Now, in Hosea 8:7, sowing and reaping are related to a weather image: "sow the wind . . . reap the whirlwind."

These are strong words indeed, in all of our texts. Note the way in which each image points to an unavoidable tragedy. Galatians 6:8 speaks of reaping "corruption," James 1:15 of bringing forth "death," and Hosea 8:7 of standing grain that "has no heads." What begins as a gentle breeze can quickly swell to gale force, carrying everything before it to devastation, such as the tornado that ripped through Louisville, Kentucky, on April 3, 1974, crushing whole houses to rubble in an instant.

The common conviction uniting these texts is that of an awful increase in evil leading to an inexorable judgment. Even though the concept is tainted today ("judgmental" being a response viewed as unworthy of God), Scripture insists that accountability cannot be avoided. Judgment may be delayed, but this is only a sign that its consequences are gathering strength. Finally, a verdict on our deeds will not be denied, no matter how hard we try to wish it away. What does this mean about our life under God?

I. *The certainty of judgment.* Take one last look at a Biblical quartet of characters. At first, Adam only wanted to learn about good and evil, then to hide from God, then to blame his wife. But none of these evasions worked. Instead he got banishment from Eden, alienation from God, and a lifelong struggle with guilt. Samson eventually regained his strength in captivity as his hair grew back, but by then he was so embittered that he pulled down wreckage on himself and his tormentors. Peter finally got the campfire crowd off his back, only to hear the cock crow thrice, to see the forlorn look of his Master, and to go weep in despair as a broken man. Judas, revolted by the tragedy he had triggered, tried to give back the thirty pieces of silver and call off the deal, but, failing to turn back the clock, cast his own life into the void by committing suicide.

Notice what these four lives had in common: all were utterly helpless to postpone or mitigate the judgment that finally fell upon them. All got a far greater dose of tragedy than they

---

[4]Cited in *Pulpit Digest* (May-June 1980), p. 18.

would have ever bargained for in the beginning. All of their status and strength were of no avail when the verdict was declared. Once the fateful process was launched, they lost any ability to bargain for a better deal by promising to make amends.

So it is with us. Reciprocity is built into the universe. If we topple the first domino and set in motion a chain reaction, finally the last domino will fall as well. There is a law of cause and effect operating just as inexorably in the spiritual sphere as in the physical. Making decisions is like a sowing. Living out those decisions is like a growing. Harvesting the results of those decisions is like a mowing. We are *response*-able, significant enough for our choices to have ultimate consequences.

II. *The equity of judgment.* One reason why we recoil from judgment is that so often it seems unfair or even capricious. How many times do we humans judge in anger or frustration? Our verdicts are skewed by prejudice. To be judgmental often means to be harsh and punitive rather than reasonable and constructive.

But the Biblical insistence is that God's judgment is just, guaranteed by the unity of root and fruit. As Jesus clearly taught, it is only what we sow that we eventually reap.

Punishment is not a stray thunderbolt hurled from heaven. God has better things to do than to spank his naughty children. Rather, we grow the grapes of wrath that set our teeth on edge. Whatever we decide that our lives *will* be, God simply decrees that they *must* be. We alone determine the judgment that we deserve.

Forget the old fire-and-brimstone metaphors if you must. It would be hell enough just to live for eternity with the mess that we have made in this life. Think how awful it would be if we had to live with a harvest of all our shallow thoughts, our petty jealousies, our selfish deeds, our idle gossip. What if eternity simply multiplied our self-inflicted heartaches by infinity! What kind of seed am I now sowing? What kind of fruit is now growing? What kind of wind is now blowing? God will be fair with us, even generous with us, by giving us thirtyfold, sixtyfold, even a hundredfold whatever we have sown.

III. *The ministry of judgment.* But why should it be this way? Why won't God answer our prayers for a crop failure? Why can't he be at least a little bit permissive or even indulgent with us?

First, because only this kind of consistency gives any dignity to our decisions. Suppose grapes did grow on a thorn tree (Matt. 7:16); then why bother to plant and tend a vineyard? Just so, if we could harvest love from indifference, or truth from thoughtlessness, or strength from indulgence, then it would make no difference what we decided or how we lived. Life would become a game of chance, a lucky or unlucky roll of the dice, a farce played by clowns.

Second, judgment gives ultimate seriousness to what we decide to do. This makes us both responsible and accountable; hence we become actors rather than puppets in the drama of life. Once our decisions really matter, life is no longer endlessly cyclical and repetitious but rather linear and forward moving because what has already been serves as a sure foundation for what is yet to be.

Third, we learn the nature of moral reality from the instruction offered to us by divine indictment. "This is judgment," says John 3:19, that "light is come," a light beckoning us from the darkness of evil. Just as parents use discipline to teach a child how to avoid danger, so God chastens those whom he loves (Heb. 12:5–6) lest they become careless in dealing with spiritual threats.

The answer of the gospel is not that of crop failure: "For he that soweth to his flesh shall of the flesh reap corruption" (Gal. 6:8a). Rather, the gospel offers an opportunity to sow different seed: "but he that soweth to the Spirit shall of the Spirit reap life everlasting" (v. 8b). Paul had just given detailed commentary in the preceding chapter on the "works of the flesh" in contrast to the "fruit of the Spirit" (Gal. 5:16–25). The issue is not whether seed will grow; that is as certain in life as it is in nature. The only issue is which kind of seed each of us will choose to grow.

The best way to choke out the bitter harvest is to grow a better harvest in its place. Look closely at your life. What kind of seed are you planting there? Each act of prayer, Bible study, and worship is a tiny seed indeed, but think of its potential for growth! Deeds of love and mercy are so inconspicuous that we are tempted to view them as insignificant; but tended faithfully, they can make the heart bloom like flowers opening to the sun. The key is to "not grow weary in well-doing" (Gal. 6:9a), to "not lose heart" (Gal. 6:9b), for it is as certain as the immutable laws of the universe that *"in due season we shall reap."* Take care how you tend the garden of life!—William E. Hull

SUNDAY, JUNE 5, 2005
Lectionary Message

Topic: Altars in a Strange Land

TEXT: Gen. 12:1–9

Other Readings: Ps. 33:1–12; Rom. 4:13–25; Matt. 9:9–13, 18–26

God guides us on a journey through life toward the place that is prepared for us, a house not made with hands, eternal in the heavens. There is a place at the end of our journey that we can call home after we've finished our journey. We set up altars as we journey to this home, altars that show those around us who it is that has given us the promise.

I. *A different kind of altar.* When the Canaanites gathered around their sacred oak at Moreh, they found an altar to a God they did not know. This altar was different from the pillars they erected to get the attention of their gods.

Canaanite religion was practical. As farmers, their lives depended on the uncertainties of nature. They did what they could to cajole the gods who they believed controlled the elements.

In the fall the fields needed a steady rain to bring a good harvest, so before the rains were due they would go to their sacred places, where they would sacrifice bulls, burn grain, and perform rituals to get the attention of Baal, the god who controlled the clouds. They would flatter him into opening the sky so their crops would get water. If the harvest was a good one, they would return to the sacred place and erect a stone monument so Baal would know they noticed his generosity.

In the spring, the farmers would try to get the attention of Ashtoreth, the fertility goddess. They would encourage the goddess to grant fertility to their crops and their herds by engaging in rituals with cultic prostitutes who sold their services as a way of getting Ashtoreth's attention.

Abram's faith was different. Instead of trying to get his God to make his life easier, Abram had left a good life in Haran to set off into a strange land because his God told him to go.

When Abram was seventy-five, an age when most people are settling down and reflecting on what they have accomplished, Abram left his roots behind and headed for an unknown place.

God promised Abram not only land but also that he would be the father of a great nation. Abram and his wife, Sarai, must have given up hope for children long ago, but God told him that, at the age of seventy-five, he would have a son and his descendants would populate the land where God was leading him.

So the Canaanites must have been amused when this senior citizen appeared out of nowhere and erected an altar to his God in their holy place.

He did not set up the altar to appease his God or to cajole a favor. He erected it because he had received a promise that he would inherit a land (although he could not say when) and a promise that he would be the father of a great nation (although he was childless at age seventy-five).

The last the Canaanites at Moreh saw of Abram, he was wandering off with his wife and nephew with servants, herds, and flocks in tow. Word came back to them that he had set up another altar to his God in the south, between Bethel and Ai.

II. *A new altar.* Two thousand years later, Jesus traveled up and down the land God promised to Abram. He was the Messiah, the one God had promised to free Abram's descendants from their captors.

The altar where Jesus made sacrifice was in a strange place, on a hill where the Romans executed criminals. His altar was not a pile of stones where someone might sacrifice a goat or a lamb, but a cross where he himself was sacrificed. His altar was unlike any other before or since. It was not a place where human beings tried to reach up to God. It was a place where God reached down to human beings.

The promise God gave through Abram was that the patriarch's name would live on in his offspring. The promise God gives through Jesus is that all who believe in him will live forever. God kept the promise to Abram. God keeps the promise given to us through Jesus.

III. *The altars we raise.* God sends us on a journey through a land where altars are raised to cajole the gods of our culture. Sex is used not to entice a good harvest but to sell cars and clothes and cigarettes. Faith is something you have in a mutual fund with a good track record, not in a God you cannot see.

We raise altars to God, who sends us on a journey through this land. Ours are not altars of stone but altars of faith, testimonies to the God who was true to Abram and is true to us. We trust God to be faithful in the promise that God will bless us, protect us, and lead us home.

But right beside the monuments to the gods of this land, the gods of consumerism and pride and self-reliance, we set up our altars to the God of Abram.

In a world that values rugged individualism and disdains those who cannot make it on their own, we bear testimony to our God whenever we reach out to a person who cannot make it on his or her own.

In a world that says look out for number one, we erect an altar to our God whenever we give of ourselves to those in need.

In a world that is so private that people blush if you talk about your faith, we set up a monument to God every time we tell a friend what God means to us.

Abram erected altars as he journeyed in faith through a strange land. What altars have you erected to God in your journey home?—Stephens G. Lytch

ILLUSTRATION

Albert Schweitzer was a professor of theology in Europe, an authority on Bach, and an accomplished musician. When he was about the age of Abram, God called Schweitzer to leave his country and his kindred and his father's house and go to a foreign land. Schweitzer did not have to go to Gabon in West Africa to receive the promise. The promise was already his, the promise of eternal life that Christ sealed when he rose from the dead. Schweitzer went to Gabon to raise an altar to God. He did not raise an altar of stone or of sacrifice, but an altar of mercy and compassion, a hospital where people were healed and loved in the name of Jesus Christ.—Stephens G. Lytch

SERMON SUGGESTIONS

Topic: Why the Good News Is So Good

TEXT: Acts 10:34–43

(1) It tells of the love of God for all peoples. (2) It shows the love of God in action in Jesus of Nazareth. (3) It provides witnesses who offer God's forgiveness of sins to everyone who believes in Jesus Christ.

Topic: The Gospel According to Paul

TEXT: 1 Cor. 15:1–11

(1) Christ died for our sins. (2) Christ was buried and was raised on the third day. (3) Christ appeared to many. (4) Christ appeared to the chief persecutor of the church and by grace made him an apostle.

WORSHIP AIDS

CALL TO WORSHIP.   "Let the people praise thee, O God; let all the people praise thee. O let the nations be glad and sing for joy: for thou shalt judge the people righteously, and govern the nations upon earth" (Ps. 67:3–4).

INVOCATION.   Lord, does your glory dwell in this place? Is your name honored as it should be by all of us gathered here? Does your Spirit live in our hearts so that the thoughts we think, the deeds we do, the decisions we make, the relationships we establish, the words we say, the goals we set all reflect that you are our only God, that we love you and each other? Are we brave and honest enough to worship you so that you come first in our lives? Are we ready to let go of the trivial and insignificant and second-rate, and seek first, with all our being, your kingdom of righteousness and love?

What do we look like, Lord, as you look upon us? Do you weep over us, as Jesus wept over the holy city of Jerusalem because so many refused to accept the time and manner of their visitation by you; because so many insisted that in order for you to be their God you had to appear and conduct yourself according to their way of thinking? Or do the very heavens rejoice because we here are prepared to do anything except to forsake, disappoint, disobey, deny you?

O Lord, our God, be pleased with our worship of you this hour, as with our lives we resolve, being helped and led by your Spirit, to praise you in all things, not just today but in each tomorrow you give us.—Gordon H. Reif

OFFERTORY SENTENCE.   "He who supplies seed to the sower and bread for food will supply and multiply your resources and increase the harvest of your righteousness" (2 Cor. 9:10, RSV).

OFFERTORY PRAYER.   Lord of all, accept these contributions to the Church in the name of our Elder Brother, Jesus, for wherever light is needed in darkness, and hope is needed in struggle, and love is needed in despair, through the Holy Spirit of truth.—E. Lee Phillips

PRAYER.   Eternal God, our Father, we thank you for your justice and your love in which we have come to believe. Your love gives us hope and comfort when your justice reveals our sin. Your justice gives us hope and comfort when your love for all humankind is forgotten by the cruel and greedy.

Forgive us our sins and redeem us from any part we may have in adding to the sufferings of thy children. Redeem us from insensitivity to their needs. Raise up those who will put principle above profit, peace above war, and you above all.

We pray now for all of the institutions and persons that make you real in our world, for churches that faithfully teach the gospel, for missionaries who take Christ to the ends of the earth—and to the darkest corners of our crime-ridden cities—for parents who by their wise and faithful love put a face on God for their children, for gentle friends who do not forget in the worst of times to say a good word for Jesus Christ.

We pray especially for those whose homes have been struck with tragedy, for those who suffer the loss of family and friends, the anguish of shattered faith, the dread of an uncertain future. Help them all find you even when they can find no immediate answers.

And now grant that we who are gathered here for worship may open our hearts for some new hint of your will for our lives, for some new concern for others, first for those with whom we live and work and play, and also for those we hardly know, but to whom we can be a blessing.

SERMON
Topic: The Dynamic of the Cross
TEXT: 1 Cor. 1:18–25

An ancient legend tells of a large tree in the forest; it prayed that when the time came for it to be cut down, it would become part of a palace or a ship, or might in some way point toward God. When the day came that the mighty tree fell to the woodsman's axe, some of its branches were used to build a common stable where was born the fairest Babe in all creation. A sturdy part of the old tree became the main stem of a small sailing vessel that plied the waters of Galilee, while on the deck stood One who said, "I have come in order that you might have life—life in all its fullness." Part of the wood became a cross, an instrument of death, on which this finest of young men was to be nailed and tormented until he died. Ever since, the cross has pointed to the sky and beyond, in fulfillment of earth's fondest hopes. The apostle Paul writes of it in our Scripture.

In the biblical story, when sin intervenes it creates a barrier between us, our God, our neighbor, and even our own best self. The venerable Adam and Eve story with its forbidden fruit makes that plain. In the New Testament letter to the Hebrews, the author uses the imagery of a foot race to represent sin as the heavy weight that could cost us the victory in the race of life.

God in the cross meets our sin with a flood of forgiving, cleansing, redeeming love. Never forget that the very first prayer of Jesus from the cross is about his tormentors: "Forgive them, Father! They don't know what they are doing." Here is the ultimate disclosure of God's suffering for our sin.

The cross is the eternal exposure and condemnation of all that crucifies Christ, and therefore hinders the fulfillment of God's purpose in the world.

The cross brings judgment on good people and their shallow or selfish motives. Remember that Jesus was not put to death by the bad guys or the bums in the Jerusalem society of the day. They were respectable folks, pretty much in charge of the morals and ethics of the community, law-and-order officials, soldiers who were just doing their duty, officials of the religious establishment, probably a good number of the people who were at the city gate to welcome their long-hoped-for Messiah but who turned quickly against him when he refused to lead them in revolt against their Roman overlords. The cross speaks to good people like these.

Many today amass riches at the expense of the poor and often try to influence public officials to manipulate the tax system for their benefit. Then there are otherwise good people who sell handguns to anyone who has the cash, or cheat on examinations, or sign and disregard the oath to tell the whole truth on their income tax statements, or sneak life-shortening tobacco products to kids.

Over the centuries, the cross has demonstrated its power to make giants of mere mortals. Perhaps in part this is because they have sensed that not only are they responsible for the cross, but they have a continuing responsibility to it. Certainly the flame of the Spirit enlivened the hearts of the discouraged disciples after they had lost their leader at Calvary but now at Pentecost sensed that he was alive in their midst. Their sudden awareness that he was Christ crucified but undefeated was the dynamo that energized the heroes of the early church.

I know a man in our own American Baptist family who shares the same spirit that energized Albert Schweitzer. I have enjoyed the hospitality of his home on two occasions in recent years. Dr. Sheldon Downs served until his retirement for well over thirty-five years as resident physician-surgeon and Christian friend to hundreds and hundreds of Garo tribespeople, recent descendants of active headhunters, living peacefully now in Tura, a town that nestles in the bend of the Brahmaputra River in Northeast India. He is known and revered by almost every resident of Tura, for he has been family doctor to the whole town for more than a third of a century. We have talked of his occasional sabbatical visits back home in the states, where he sometimes attends national medical society conventions and visits with professional colleagues he has known over the years. They have their fancy cars and usual creature comforts, and sometimes they wonder aloud why Sheldon chooses to live and work in a faraway, strange land almost completely lacking in comforts his colleagues back home enjoy. He tells me that he wouldn't trade his life, with its joys and challenges, for all the Cadillacs and fancy homes they could offer. I believe his life has been touched by the dynamic of the cross.— George W. Hill

SUNDAY, JUNE 12, 2005
Lectionary Message

Topic: Faith Without Limits

TEXT: Gen. 18:1–15 (21:1–7)

Other Readings: Ps. 116:1–2, 12–19; Rom. 5:1–8; Matt. 9:35–10:8 (9–23)

I. *Getting to know God.* The way you get to know people is by noticing the things they do over and over. After a while, their actions give you a good idea about their character, and you begin to know what you can expect of them. Each story in the Bible tells us something about God. As we become familiar with God through the Bible, we become more adept at recognizing God when God is at work in our lives.

One thing we see God doing throughout the Bible is making something out of nothing. At the beginning of time, God took nothing and made the universe out of it. God took dust from the earth and fashioned human beings. God took a couple who were almost one hundred years old and gave them a baby. God took the dead body of Jesus and breathed life into it on Easter. Romans 4:17 summarizes what the Bible tells us about God: "God . . . gives life to the dead and calls into existence the things that do not exist." God takes nothing and makes something out of it. God takes those things that seem useless and makes them important. God takes those who are last and makes them first.

So often the things God does defy common sense. That's one reason so many people have trouble trusting God. That's why Sarah laughed. Sarah was hiding behind the tent flap, listening to Abraham talk to three strangers who had stopped by for lunch. One of them said, "I will surely return to you in due season, and your wife Sarah shall have a son." The story goes on: "So Sarah laughed to herself, saying, 'After I have grown old, and my husband is old, shall I have pleasure?'" Of course she laughed. Wouldn't you?

That's the way it is with God. The way God acts doesn't always make sense to our usual way of thinking. 1 Corinthians 1:22 and 25 says, "we proclaim Christ crucified, a stumbling block to Jews and foolishness to Gentiles. . . . For God's foolishness is wiser than human wisdom, and God's weakness is stronger than human strength."

II. *Trusting the God we know.* So there's something that seems unreasonable about committing our lives to God, as unreasonable as a woman in her nineties having a baby. To trust God enough to give our lives to God requires a leap of faith. It's like a child standing on the edge of a swimming pool, terrified to go in the water, whose mother is standing there in the water with her arms stretched out, calling his name. She smiles and assures him it is all right. Jumping into the water goes against everything the child's instinct and reason tell him. But he trusts his mother, so he steps off the edge, knowing she'll catch him as she has promised.

The Bible is filled with stories of those who trusted in God and found God to be faithful. Abraham trusted God would be faithful to God's promise to make him the father of a great nation. Joseph, whose brothers sold him into slavery, trusted that God would bring good out of his brothers' treachery, even as he languished in Pharaoh's prison. He trusted that God was with him, even as he faced death on the cross.

At the heart of faith is the conviction that nothing is impossible for God. God's promise to Abraham was the promise of a son, and faith is what kept Abraham going when there was no reason to believe he and Sarah would ever have a child. That's not God's promise to every-one. There are plenty of couples who desperately want to have a child, and in spite of all the advances of medicine they have had to accept the fact that their dream is not going to come to pass. It doesn't eliminate the disappointment or the sorrow of not having a child, but faith gives assurance that God is still with them and that God will use their marriage in other ways to make God's world a better place.

III. *Living in confidence.* Faith that God is actively involved in the world gives us confi-dence. It allows parents to entrust their children into God's care as they leave home, confident that God will see them through the temptations and challenges of those first years away. Faith gives us the conviction to continue to stand up for what is right and good and fair, even when it seems we are the only ones who care. Faith is what gives us courage to face death, know-ing that the same God who brings life out of death has promised us eternal life.

The story of Abraham welcoming those three strangers shows how faith often works. When Abraham invited them to partake of his hospitality, he did not know the three men were God. He was expressing the attitude of openness and welcome that characterizes a per-son of faith. He gave freely from what he had to those who needed food and shelter from the heat of the day. He got joy from giving, just as God gets joy from giving freely to us. It was through his openness and hospitality that God gave a blessing.

Faith balances our desire to hold onto what is familiar and trust what we have experienced with the assurance that God is waiting to give us better things than we can even imagine. Faith is what lets us step outside of ourselves, trusting God to be as faithful to us as God was to Abraham and Sarah. Faith knows that God has no limits. God can bring into being what-ever God needs to keep God's promises. God made a couple in their nineties parents. God makes sinners righteous. Just think what God can make out of you and me.

ILLUSTRATIONS

The medieval mystic Meister Eckhart said that faith is like looking at the sun and then look-ing elsewhere. Everywhere you look you see the sun. As we learn about God's character through those stories in the Bible, we develop the ability to identify God when we see God at work in the world today.

Martin Luther King Jr. was sustained by God's presence in the difficult days of the civil rights movement:

> One year after being called to Dexter Avenue Baptist Church . . . King was chosen to be the spokesperson for the Montgomery Improvement Association. Shortly after assuming his role as community leader and activist, King started receiving phone calls threatening his life and the lives of his wife and children. One night a caller ordered him to leave town in three days or risk having his home firebombed. Unable to sleep, King went into the kitchen hoping to find some relief in a warm cup of coffee. He sat at his kitchen table wrestling with the meaning of his pre-sent crisis and came face-to-face with the fact that he could lose his newborn daughter or wife at any moment.
>
> Looking deep within himself, King bowed his head and prayed, "Lord I'm down here trying to do what's right. I think I'm right. I think the cause we represent is right. But I'm weak now.

I'm faltering and I'm losing my courage." At that moment King heard a voice saying, "Stand up for righteousness. Stand up for justice. Stand up for truth and 'Lo, I will be with you even till the end of the world.'" From then on, King was sustained by God's promise to be with him.[1]

SERMON SUGGESTIONS

Topic: The Good News of the Law

TEXT: Exod. 20:1–17

(1) What God has done for us (v. 2). (2) What we can do for God (vv. 3–10). (3) What we must do for one another (vv. 11–17).

Topic: A Saving View of Christ

TEXT: 1 Cor. 1:22–25

To know Christ: (1) we might try the path of reason, but that is insufficient. (2) We might seek the evidence of miracle, but that is inadequate. (3) If we bow before his cross in faith, the foolishness of the cross becomes wisdom, and the weakness of the cross becomes power.

WORSHIP AIDS

CALL TO WORSHIP.   "Lord, thou hast been our dwelling place in all generations. Before the mountains were brought forth, or ever thou hadst formed the earth and the world, even from everlasting to everlasting, thou art God" (Ps. 90:1–2).

INVOCATION.   Lord, our Creator and our God, open us in our worshiping to bow the will to your leading. Open us in our thinking to bow the mind to your teaching. Open us in our choosing to bow the heart to your loving.—E. Lee Phillips

OFFERTORY SENTENCE.   "The Lord said to Moses, 'Tell the Israelites to make an offering to me. Receive whatever offerings any man wishes to give'" (Exod. 25:1–2, TEV).

PRAYER.   Father, we thank you for thy tender care: for your strong defense of thy people across the ages, in spite of "dungeon, fire and sword"; for your forgiving grace that has often restored the sinning and undeserving; for your call to service that has made us partners with you in your work of your kingdom; for your presence in our lives and the reassurance that where we are and what we are doing are significant in your sight. Forgive us for our sometimes silent bitterness, as well as our whining complaint, when faith and gratitude could transform the desert into a garden. Give us today a renewed sense of your purpose for each individual life, and put us every one to our worthwhile, even if unrecognized, duties, and may we discharge them with freedom and joy.

SERMON

Topic: The Man of God at Prayer

TEXT: Heb. 4:14–5:4

No man dares to pose as an authority on prayer. I speak to you as a theological professor. For better or worse, that is who I am. Professors may strike the "didactic pose" on many less-

---

[1]Prince Raney Rivers, "Living by the Word: Promise Keeper," *Christian Century* (May 22-29, 2002), p. 17.

important topics, but none of us knows prayer half as well as the apostle Paul, who himself said, "We know not how to pray." We, as professors, can only turn with our most reticent and timid student and say to the Lord Jesus Christ, "Lord, teach us to pray," for the life of prayer begins with a confession of ignorance, the simplicity and openness of a child hungry to be taught.

James Stewart tells of a group of theological students in a Scottish university. They firmly believed that their Hebrew professor, if he prayed at all, did in truth and in fact say his prayers in Hebrew. A few of them had repeatedly heard this legend and decided to see for themselves if it were so or if this were just a part of the Apocrypha. One evening, therefore, they crept to the edge of his window and waited until the old Hebrew teacher knelt beside his bed to pray. Much to their chagrin, instead of hearing Hebrew intoned to the Lord, they heard him say:

> Gentle Jesus, meek and mild,
> Look upon a little child;
> Pity my simplicity;
> Suffer me to come to Thee.
> Loving Jesus, gentle Lamb,
> In thy gracious hands I am;
> Make me, Savior, what thou art,
> Live thyself within my heart.

We know not how to pray as we ought to pray, then. A certain kind of ignorance is a precondition of prayer—the ignorance of an observing audience that is left when we enter our place of privacy and close it behind us; a left hand that is ignorant of even the right hand's motions of prayer. Such poverty of spirit is a hunger and thirst after God.

But the average professor or student is likely to see his prayer life and his study life as enemies rather than friends. One reason for this is that true study and true prayer call for many of the same habits and disciplines. For instance, the person who writes a paper or reads a book must temporarily deprive himself of the company of others. The question is, "Can he stand being alone?" Being alone with God in prayer calls for this same discipline. Both in study and in prayer, we have gone a long way if we can successfully resist the temptation to go knock on our neighbor's door, to call him or her on the telephone. Somerset Maugham was asked the secret of his writing ability. He said: "Placing my posterior extremities in a chair and resisting the first fifteen temptations to get up." However we do it, we must have the courage both in our prayer and study—courage that only Christ can give us—to withdraw from the crowd and pray. It takes courage for us to leave the seeming safety of the chatter and cacophony of noise, to hush the many contending voices enough to meet ourselves and to become a self before God.

Not only does the Protestant minister's prayer life share much in common with his or her study life, but the minister's spousal relationship is inseparable from prayer life. What can be said of the minister is equally true of the layperson, if indeed we see all men and women with a priestly relation to God. First Peter 3:7 underscores (albeit in language we moderns must adjust to) the intimate bond between our prayer life and our relationship with our wife or husband: "Likewise you husbands, live considerately with your wives, bestowing honor on the woman as the weaker sex, since you are joint heirs of the grace of life, in order that your prayers may not be hindered" (RSV). There may not, as the truism puts it, be any atheists in foxholes, but one cannot say that of preachers' homes. Our inconsiderateness and inability to think of our wives or husbands as joint heirs of the grace of life are often a hindrance both to their prayers and to ours. Candor and Christian integrity, though, bring the beauty of holiness into the unhindered relationships of prayer we can have with God and with our life partners.

W. R. Inge, English clergyman and writer, who was dean of St. Paul's Cathedral for many years, tells of the relationship of prayer between his wife and him. He says that just before the birth of their first child, his wife wrote that although she knew the future was uncertain for her, she was content because she knew that not even death could separate them. He did not have access to his wife's writings until after her death. In his book *Diary of a Dean,* Inge also recalls that his wife said that she could not begin to express what he had meant to her or what she had learned from him. Her calm trust prior to this experience shows, however, something of what their relationship had been.[2]

But such relationships of prayer require internal honesty. We must dare to shed shame and drop our self-evading defenses. When we are alone before God, there is no one left to deceive but ourselves. We cannot—by confessing how we really feel, think, act, and are—add to God's knowledge of us. Dark and stringent hostilities come—with humor, I hope—to the pinpoint of our awareness. Back in the days before we saw the crippling power of hidden dishonesty in the inner life, I used to think that the harsh imprecations of the Psalms should never be read, that maybe they were of a lower order of inspiration and really should have been left out of the Bible. But the Bible, especially the Psalms, is a cleansingly honest book. The prayers of the psalmist in the same breath can say "I hate them with perfect hatred: . . . Search me, O God, and know my heart; try me, and know my thoughts. And see if there be any wicked way in me, and lead me in the way everlasting" (Ps. 139:22–24).

But ordinarily we are not so candidly honest with ourselves. We may even avoid this internal honesty by being harsh, inconsiderate, blunt, and tactless with other people. This is real sickness. More candor with ourselves in prayer leads to considerateness of others.

But such candor and internal honesty is not self-generated. We cannot with safety face ourselves alone. As Nietzsche so rightly said, "If we saw the whole truth at once, it would kill us!" Another way of saying it is, "No man can see God and live." Our hearts, therefore, are filled with fear at the thought of facing and knowing ourselves. As the psalmist says, "When I thought to know this, it was too painful for me" (Ps. 73:16). We dare not attempt self-knowledge alone. It is not possible nor safe, for as Calvin said, "No man can survey himself without forthwith turning his thoughts toward God." Then it is not safe, because we are destroyed by insight that we must bear alone. We cannot bear our burdens alone. Fear overwhelms us.

Christ stands with us as our advocate and burden bearer. In him "we have not a high priest that cannot be touched with the feeling of our infirmities, but one that hath been in all points tempted like as we are, yet without sin" (Heb. 4:14–15, ASV).

Let us, therefore, cease to talk about prayer and pray. Let us come to the throne of grace that we may obtain mercy in time of need.—Wayne E. Oates

---

[2]New York: Macmillan, 1949, p. 187.

SUNDAY, JUNE 19, 2005
Lectionary Message

Topic: From the Outside Looking In

TEXT: Gen. 21:8–21

Other Readings: Ps. 86:1–10, 16–17; Rom. 6:1b–11; Matt. 10:24–39

One thing that makes the Bible such a powerful book, a book you keep coming back to again and again, is how it can surprise you. You think you have it pretty well figured out, but then you come across a story like the one about Abraham and Sarah and Hagar. This is a story that draws you up short and takes your breath away because it is so different from what you might expect in the Bible.

God can use stories like this to shake us up. We develop assumptions about the way God should do things, assumptions that usually mirror how we would run the world if it were ours to control. Every once in a while we have to be reminded that God does not always conform to how we think things ought to be. This story challenges us to reconsider our view of outsiders, those different from us. For those who feel they are on the outside, it offers a word of hope and encouragement.

I. *Our treatment of outsiders.* The story of Abraham, Sarah, and Hagar makes the movie *Indecent Proposal* look almost decent. Abraham and Sarah could not have children, so Sarah told Abraham to have a child by Sarah's servant, an Egyptian woman named Hagar. Abraham and Hagar had a son named Ishmael. Eventually Abraham and Sarah had a son, whose name was Isaac. One day, when Isaac was a little boy, Sarah saw him playing with his half-brother Ishmael. The jealousy that had been brewing in her flashed. Sarah demanded that Abraham send Hagar and Ishmael away.

One might expect the Bible to report that Abraham told Sarah, "We should all get along." Instead, Abraham gets up early one morning, lifts his son Ishmael onto Hagar's shoulder and sends them out into the wilderness with nothing more to sustain them than a skin filled with water. That is not exactly the kind of parenting we want to celebrate on Father's Day.

This story is shocking because Abraham does not exhibit the behavior we try to teach our children. It grates against our civility and open-mindedness. But if you have ever been on the outside looking in, this story may not sound so foreign. It portrays a realistic picture of what it is like to be out of the mainstream. If you have ever felt cut off, wandering, not sure how you are going to make it from week to week, feeling people treat you as though you are not up to par, you might be able to identify with Hagar. Anyone who has ever been told, either outright or in a subtle and indirect way, "You're not one of us" knows that what Hagar experienced is not so unusual.

This is a story for anyone who has ever felt on the outside. It is for children and teenagers who feel shut out because they are not old enough. It is for anyone who has ever felt out of place in church because of something in his or her past.

II. *God's treatment of outsiders.* The really surprising thing about Hagar and Ishmael is not how those outsiders were treated by those on the inside. What is surprising is the way God treated them. God treats outsiders a lot differently from how we usually treat them. When we are on the inside, we tend to think that what we see and experience is the norm for everyone else.

Hagar's story shows that the Israelites were not the only ones for whom God cared. The central story in the Bible is the story of God's relationship with Israel. The Israelites are the insiders in the Bible. The story of Hagar and Ishmael is a reminder to those insiders that God is not confined to them. God looked out for Hagar and Ishmael. They wandered in the wilderness until their water gave out. Hagar placed her son under a bush to shelter him from the direct heat of the sun as he was dying. As she cried in despair, an angel of the Lord came to her and said that God had heard her son's voice. God was going to bless Ishmael by making him the father of a nation. Then God opened Hagar's eyes and she saw a well. She and her son drank and survived until they settled in the land of Paran. The last we hear of Ishmael, he has grown into a strong hunter and married a woman who is an Egyptian, like his mother. God is caring for the outsider.

There is something about human nature that needs to know who is inside and who is out, who is our friend and who is our foe. We feel compelled to identify those with whom we have things in common and those who are different. But God's goodness cannot be contained to one group, even if it is the group God has chosen to be God's own. Sometimes God surprises us by showing us that those whom we thought were so obviously on the outside are really the insiders, and those who thought they were in do not have it made quite as they thought. This God whom we worship is not confined to doing things the way we think they ought to be done. That would be a pretty small God to worship.

ILLUSTRATIONS
Our neighbors Harold and Sally were agnostics. The only time they ever went to church was for a wedding or the funeral of a friend. Harold and Sally were content in their nonbelief, but they were good people. They were far more involved in the affairs of our town than I was. They were advocates for strong schools and a good library. It was important to them that our town had adequate housing for low-income residents so you would not have to be wealthy to live there. When their daughter, Amanda, who was also outside the church, graduated from college, she moved to Africa to work with a relief agency that serves children.

These neighbors were not Christians, but God worked through them. I still pray that they will believe in Christ and join his church because I know God wants them to enjoy a relationship with Christ. But Harold and Sally are a humbling reminder to me that God's work cannot be confined to those of us who are on the inside.

William Willimon writes about a friend of his who went on a tour of Russia in the 1970s with an ecumenical group of church leaders. When his friend came back, he lamented, "The church in Russia is irrelevant. It has no one in it but old ladies." The church of Jesus Christ appeared to be dying off because it had no insiders, no one with power or influence or the vigor of youth. It had only little old ladies, people with no clout who were outside the mainstream.

When communism collapsed, the churches began to burst at the seams. New churches opened every day. People flocked to the church looking for meaning and purpose in life. Who kept those churches alive through the decades of persecution when religion was irrelevant to anyone who wanted to get ahead in the communist regime? Little old ladies, people outside the mainstream. It makes you wonder who was really on the inside and who was on the outside.[3]—Stephens G. Lytch

---

[3]William Willimon, *Peculiar Speech* (Grand Rapids, Mich.: Eerdmans, 1992), p. 90.

SERMON SUGGESTIONS

Topic: Because God Is the Almighty

TEXT: Gen. 17:1–10, 15–19

(1) I must live my life to please him. (2) I can expect his blessing to follow my obedience. (3) I should be prepared for divine surprises.

Topic: The Father of Us All: Abraham

TEXT: Rom. 4:16–25

(1) We are the heirs of his blessing. (2) He is the example for our faith.

WORSHIP AIDS

CALL TO WORSHIP.   "Behold, how good and pleasant it is for brethren to dwell together in unity" (Ps. 133:1).

INVOCATION.   We thank thee, O God, for the faith that draws us together in love, a love that proves that we have passed from death to new life in Christ. Grant that we may share that faith with gratitude, with humility, and with patience.

OFFERTORY SENTENCE.   "And he said unto them, Go ye into all the world, and preach the gospel to every creature" (Mark 16:15).

OFFERTORY PRAYER.   Lead us, Lord, to that openness of spirit and generosity of heart that never loses sight of the cross of Christ and never stops giving in his name.—E. Lee Phillips

PRAYER.   I thank you for him who satisfies the deepest impulses of my nature. He is the only man who ever really lived: gentle, yet brave; confident, yet humble; wise, yet simple; meeting life with calmness, trouble with fortitude, hate with forgiveness; disloyalty with magnanimity, and crucifixion with faith. He has given to my life a Savior, a meaning, a movement, a challenge, a promise. I know assuredly that somehow the life, ministry, and living again of Jesus is where it's at!

What's new? Life is, when love is renewing it day by day. Jesus taught and demonstrated that we can live in the perennial springtime of your love. Hallelujah! Love never gives up. It is always looking for ways to be constructive. It is imaginative, above all else. Though it is crucified, even death cannot destroy it. It keeps coming back. Love perseveres.

Above all else, may we participate in this love, for it is the fulfillment of all things. Life is ever new, for it is the life of the *living* God—shared, celebrated. To love and keep on loving is to live a life that not even death can destroy.

What manner of love you have bestowed upon us, O Father, that we should be your children. Thank you!—John Thompson

SERMON

Topic: How Can We Be Sure?

TEXT: Ps. 23:6

This sermon is intended especially for those who are not sure about their religion. They participate in it, but they have no inner certainty about it. They may say something like this to themselves: there may be a God, and there may not be. I am not sure. There may be some great purpose in life, and there may not be. I cannot be certain. There may be life after death, sometimes it looks as though there were, and there may not be. I am not sure. So they travel in the twilight of uncertainty, staggering between their intellectual doubts and their emotional desires. They walk, so to speak, the tightrope of an open mind.

Yet they are by no means happy about their lack of assurance.

I. One thing must be said at the outset: you never can have the same kind of assurance in religion that you can have in some other realms of experience. There are some things that you are sure of because you can prove them. For instance, you can be sure that two parts of hydrogen mixed with one part oxygen make water because, when you put them together, you have water. There are scores of things in life that you are sure of because they are demonstrable. You can prove them as you can prove a problem in arithmetic.

But there are other things you are sure of in spite of the fact that you cannot prove them. For example, when a teen falls in love with someone, the parents, concerned for the youth, are very likely to ask, "Are you sure you are in love with this person?" The teen will say something like this: "All I know is that I am more sure of that than anything else in the world." The youth cannot prove it (it is beyond demonstration) and yet is absolutely certain of it. Likewise, when we look at a dogwood tree in full bloom we are likely to say something like this: I am sure that that is beautiful and I am sure that beauty is real. Ask me to prove it, and I cannot. It may simply be the strange reaction of the chemicals in my body to a particular arrangement of natural elements that I choose to think are beautiful. Nevertheless, I am sure of it as I am sure of little else.

So, when we say, "Surely goodness and mercy shall follow me all the days of my life; and I will dwell in the house of the Lord forever," we cannot prove it. Yet when we begin the sentence with the single word *surely*, we know we are as certain of it as of the fact that the sun will come up tomorrow morning, and our life rests upon it as surely as a building rests upon its foundation.

So if you are looking in your religion for the kind of assurance that you have in the realm of demonstrable, provable things, I must tell you that you will never find it. Some people are not sure of their religion today because they have tried to approach it by the one-way street of the intellect.

II. Now, where does that kind of assurance come from? It is the kind of assurance we want. In the first place, it is handed down to us from the generations who have gone before us. A child's first assurances are most likely to be the assurances of the child's father and mother.

For it is true, is it not, that our deepest and most basic assurances we inherit from those who have gone before us, and it is not surprising for us to see that our first religious assurances are those of our ancestors, the ones that have been forged on the anvil, to use a trite expression, of experiences down through long generations of human history. We are members of a family that, by and large, has been sure, in spite of many facts indicating the contrary, that there is within this whole complex situation that we call human life a purpose.

Likewise, we are the children of a family that has been sure Jesus is the personification of the divine. They have expressed it in a number of ways. They have had different kinds of evidence to support the assurance, but by and large our family has been sure of it. They have been sure that life has a height and depth not comprehended completely by the calendar. They have been sure that individuals have a dignity worthy of our respect, for it is the dignity derived from the Creator, God. They have been sure of all these things. Of course, they have had their doubts and their questions, but we inherit those subconscious, deep, racial, social assurances that have been handed down from generation to generation.

So I say in the first place that those of you who are looking for assurance in your religion must not turn too quickly and with impatience from your heritage, all the great body of faith that has come down to you.

This assurance, however, must then be verified by the facts of personal experience. No assurance, no matter how much we may want it, can long be sustained if it is contrary to fact.

God made himself known in various times, places, and degrees to His people. We had to revise what we inherited from the past in the light of the facts of our own knowledge, which have happened more than once.

Other things that we inherit from the past are verified and confirmed and amplified by the facts of our own experience, and this to my mind is one of the greatest satisfactions in life. For example, to be told by your family, by the great Christian family that has gone before you, that there is a purpose in life and all the extraneous and apparently irrelevant strands really can be woven together to make a pattern, to be told this is one thing, but then to go through the deep waters of life yourself, facing all the contradictions and acknowledging all the things that seem to point to the fact that life is chaos, and suddenly realizing, because you feel it in your own life, that there is some purpose toward which all the avenues of your own personal existence converge, that there is a pattern slowly and painfully emerging, and that beyond your personal life there is a purpose that holds together, drawing them as a magnet draws steel, all the fragments of life, to feel this yourself and to verify it yourself in your own experience is one of the great moments in an adult's life. The heritage of the past has been confirmed by the experience of the present.

In much the same way, some people receive as their heritage the teaching of Jesus, and as obedient children they accept it and come to a period in their life when suddenly the teaching becomes alive because they see it working.

But in the absence of complete proof, and there never is complete proof in these things, the evidence is never completely in; it is finally confirmed, this assurance we are speaking of, by the desire of the human heart.

Here, then, is someone who is sure of God and all that we mean by God—purpose, mind, meaning, love, goodness—sure of it. There are not enough facts to prove it or to demonstrate it to the world. We want the assurance of purpose, we want life to be good, we want it to make sense, and so we go out with no fact proving to the contrary—yet without enough facts to prove our case, believing because in our heart of hearts we want to believe.

This is where our assurance of things unseen finally is bound to rest. Do not be afraid of the things you sincerely desire. Do not hold back from believing in the things you want to believe in; make the ground of your assurance that citadel of the human heart where your greatest desires dwell.—Theodore Parker Ferris

SUNDAY, JUNE 26, 2005
Lectionary Message

Topic: A Test of Faith

TEXT: Gen. 22:1–14

Other Readings: Ps.13; Rom. 6:12–23; Matt. 10:40–42

I. *What kind of God?* What kind of God would do such a thing? Abraham had waited a lifetime to have a son; he had staked all he had on his faith that God would be true to God's word. How could God watch as Abraham saddled his donkey, cut the firewood, and walked for three days toward Moriah; as he unloaded the wood from the donkey, laid it on the boy's back, took the fire and knife in hand, and climbed the mountain? How could God stand the silence of those footsteps, broken only when Isaac asked, full of innocence and trust, "Father, here is the fire and the wood, but where is the lamb for the burnt offering?" What kind of God could watch as Abraham gathered stones to build an altar, placed the wood in order, bound the boy with cords and laid him on the pyre, as the father reached out his hand and took the knife and raised it high above his head to plunge it into the flesh of his son? What kind of a God is that?

And what kind of man was Abraham? How could Abraham do it? How could he raise a knife over his son, his only son, the son he loved?

II. *We try to domesticate God.* This story is an embarrassment to moderate people, to us who run from excess and paint our pictures of God in bright, pastel shades. Most of us are easygoing about our religion. We worship God for what we get out of it. We confess our minimal sins and give God what we consider a reasonable return, but we try to be careful not to go overboard with it.

God whom we worship so carefully is the same God who told Abraham to sacrifice his son. What does that tell us about God? What does that tell us about ourselves? Maybe our revulsion at Abraham's sacrifice is not an indictment of Abraham's zeal or God's demand. Maybe our horror is an indictment of us. Maybe we do not take God seriously enough.

How hard we try to domesticate God. We would be more comfortable with Abraham if he stood up to God, if instead of replying, "Here I am," he said, "No. I will not give you my son. He is mine to protect and to rear. I will not give him back." We would understand if Abraham were willing to sacrifice almost anything to God but drew the line at his son. But God asked Abraham, "Will you trust me with the gift I have given you, the most precious thing in your life?"

III. *What God asks of us.* Now, you and I know as we read the story that it was a test. The Bible makes it clear from the start, when it says, "God tested Abraham." God forbade human sacrifice, and Abraham knew that. That's what made his obedience all the more remarkable. He was willing to lay aside even his understanding of right and wrong to be obedient to God.

Sadly, there are people today who believe God asks for human sacrifice. They are the people who with all good intentions say to a bereaved parent, "God needed your child in a better place," or "God is doing this to you to strengthen you." The message underneath that well-intentioned attempt at comfort is "God made your child die." There was only one son God asked as a sacrifice: God's own son, who died on the cross. God put Abraham to the test, not because God kills innocent people but to show us the kind of faith God demands.

This story of Abraham is not a story of child sacrifice but a story of faith, faith that offers God's most precious gifts back to God. But why are we appalled at that? If we take seriously the vows we make before God, we might shudder at what God asks us to do as much as we shudder at the command God gave Abraham. Every one of us who has professed our faith in Jesus Christ has made a commitment to God as radical as Abraham's. On that day we gave our lives back to God, not as burnt offerings but as living sacrifices. We put all our possessions and all our relationships not on an altar but on a cross and committed everything we love to God as surely as Abraham committed Isaac.

The breathtaking thing about the kind of faith God requires is that when we give back to God the most precious gifts we have received, when we return them trusting that God will provide, God multiplies our blessings many times over. Abraham offered Isaac to God, and God gave him back with this promise: "Because you have done this, and have not withheld your son, your only son, I will indeed bless you, and I will make your offspring as numerous as the stars of heaven and as the sand that is on the seashore. And your offspring shall possess the gate of their enemies, and by your offspring shall all the nations of the earth gain blessing for themselves." Jesus said it another way: "Those who find their life will lose it, and those who lose their life for my sake will find it."

What kind of God is this? This is a God who demands all that we have and gives back more than we can ever imagine, who asks everything of us and gives us himself.—Stephens G. Lytch

ILLUSTRATION

The Chronicles of Narnia by C. S. Lewis is a series of fantasies about some children who enter a strange and wonderful world as they are playing in an old wardrobe. One of the characters in the *Chronicles* is a lion named Aslan, who is a figure for Christ. In this passage from the book, "The Silver Chair," one of the children named Jill confronts the lion by a sparkling brook.

"Are you thirsty?" said the Lion.

"I'm dying of thirst," said Jill.

"Then drink," said the Lion.

"May I—could I—would you mind going away while I do?" said Jill.

The Lion answered this only by a look and a very low growl. And as Jill gazed at its motionless bulk, she realized that she might as well have asked the whole mountain to move aside for her convenience.

The delicious rippling noise of the stream was driving her nearly frantic.

"Will you promise not to—do anything to me, if I do come?" said Jill.

"I make no promise," said the Lion.

Jill was so thirsty now that, without noticing it, she had come a step nearer.

"Do you eat girls?" she said.

"I have swallowed up girls and boys, women and men, kings and emperors, cities and realms," said the Lion. It didn't say this as if it were boasting, nor as if it were sorry, nor as if it were angry. It just said it.

"I daren't come and drink," said Jill.

"Then you will die of thirst," said the Lion.

"Oh dear!" said Jill, coming another step nearer. "I suppose I must go and look for another stream then."

"There is no other stream," said the Lion.[4]—Stephens G. Lytch

SERMON SUGGESTIONS

Topic: Mighty Deeds, Great Expectations

TEXT: Deut. 4:32–40

(1) God has done great things for his people. (2) God expects great things from his people.

Topic: Round About to the Triune God

TEXT: 2 Cor. 13:5–14

(1) God touches our lives with grace through Jesus Christ his Son. (2) This acquaintance leads us to experience of the love of God as Father. (3) Consequently, we have fellowship with God and one another at the deepest level through God's Holy Spirit.

WORSHIP AIDS

CALL TO WORSHIP. "And God said, 'Let there be light'; and there was light" (Gen. 1:3, RSV).

INVOCATION. God of light, God of truth, God of Spirit, shine upon us with blessing, engage our minds with understanding, warm our hearts with your own self, so that we may worship you with our total being. Make us ready for every duty of the day and for every challenge of the future.

OFFERTORY SENTENCE. "For God so loved the world that he gave his only Son, that whoever believes in him should not perish but have eternal life" (John 3:16).

OFFERTORY PRAYER. Our Father, if we are ever inclined to be miserly toward you and your kingdom, may we take again the measure of your generosity toward us and all the world. Let the love you have bestowed on us flow on through our generosity and our deeds.

PRAYER. O God, we come to you through the clouds of mystery and unknowing to call you Father. As our Lord Jesus Christ has lived among us and loved us, taught us, and even died for us, we know what you are like. We trust in your care for us; we look to you for guidance; we know that nothing can separate us from your love. Yet we have sometimes doubted in the day what we have felt most deeply in the dark of night. We have at times almost willingly given in to temptations that we have at other times stoutly resisted. We have even acted as if you had forsaken us. If we have today or yesterday or even at this very moment in any fashion betrayed you or presumed on your love, forgive us. Restore to us an alert and steady awareness of your redeeming presence. Help us grow in your grace and knowledge. Let our lives, even as the life of our Lord, give helpful glimpses into your heart. May something in us—some daring faith, some courageous act of obedience, some expression of self-giving

---

[4]C. S. Lewis, "The Silver Chair," in *The Chronicles of Narnia* (New York: HarperCollins, 2001), pp. 557–558.

love—remove from a friend, a neighbor, or an enemy any dread of your power, any questions of your justice, or any fear of your truth, for you are our Father.

SERMON
Topic: The Heresy of Orthodoxy
TEXT: 2 Tim. 1:13

John A. Mackay, in his *Preface to Christian Theology,* uses an expression that I want to use as the subject of this message: "The heresy of orthodoxy." He is not responsible, however, for the content of this message.

I do not like to use theological labels, although it does seem necessary to do so at times. One problem with such labels is the fact that they mean different things to different people at different times. They are always relative. This is certainty true of the terms *heresy* and *orthodoxy.* The heresy of one generation is frequently the orthodoxy of the next. Another problem is that each of us is inclined to have his own standards of orthodoxy. We tend to consider heretical anything with which we disagree.

Orthodoxy becomes heresy when the orthodoxy test is wrongly applied. This may be done by making things that are of secondary importance the primary test of orthodoxy. This happens when a person gets his or her values out of focus or balance or when he or she attaches primary or supreme value to the secondary. There may be an orthodoxy of the secondary, but we should always recognize that it is secondary.

I hesitate to give illustrations since some of you will tend to argue with me. It may be, however, that a couple of specific examples will help you understand more clearly what I mean.

One illustration, more prevalent a generation or two ago than at the present time, is God's relation to creation. It is of major importance for one to believe that in the beginning was God and that "without him was not any thing made that was made" (John 1:3). The time and the method God used in his creative work is of secondary importance. Many people, however, in the past and some even today would make these matters a final test of orthodoxy. When such importance is attached to that which is secondary and that which is uncertain, orthodoxy has become heresy.

Another example of the possible heresy of orthodoxy that is more relevant today is related to the millennium. There are many who make one's view concerning the millennium the final test of orthodoxy and the basis of fellowship. A belief in the triumphant return of the Lord is primary; the relation of the return to the millennium is of secondary importance.

The rise of millennial fellowships seems to me to attach entirely too much significance to the millennial question. What would happen to any group of Christians if there were not only a premillennial fellowship but also an amillennial fellowship, a postmillennial fellowship— if enough postmillennialists could be found—and an agnostic-millennial fellowship composed of the great host of believers who do not know what they believe concerning the millennium but who look for the return of the Lord? One's view concerning the millennium may be of considerable significance, but it definitely is not of primary importance when compared with many of the great doctrines of the faith. When it is raised to a place in the scheme of orthodoxy out of proportion to its importance, such at least borders on heresy.

Orthodoxy also becomes heresy if the orthodoxy test is applied to methodology. Some methods of Christian life and growth, and the fact that those methods have been generally accepted and almost universally used by the churches, help to explain the growth, vitality, and strength of some groups today. Unity of methods has been particularly evident in the area of evangelism, in educational organizations and programs, and to a lesser degree in financial policies.

Although there is strength in uniformity, there is real danger if churches seek to maintain uniformity by pressure or ostracism. How tragic it will be if there is developed an orthodoxy of methods, and individuals and churches are considered heretical if they do not conform to the generally accepted pattern. The test of orthodoxy does not belong in this area, and if applied it will strike at two of the basic concepts of the Baptist way of life: the competency of the individual soul and the freedom of the local congregation.

Orthodoxy becomes heresy when it interferes with the search for truth. Orthodoxy interferes with the search for truth when orthodoxy as such is the final test of truth. How unfortunate if we accept a thing as true simply because it is considered orthodox. Also, how tragic for us and for the cause of truth if our first question, as we search for truth, is whether or not it is orthodox. The supreme question should be, Is it true?

Orthodoxy also interferes with the search for truth if it erects artificial barriers in that search. The creative mind must be free from external restraints. It must be free from the fear of truth. The creative Christian mind is a disciplined mind, working under the guiding impulse of the divine Spirit with a deep sense of its responsibility to mankind in general but to God in particular.

Could it be that some Christian groups have not contributed their share of creative scholarship because they have been too much under the constraints of heresy hunters? Is there a danger that we will develop a Baptist scholasticism, freedom within prescribed limits? The only limits that should be set in the search for truth are the limits of truth itself.

Again, orthodoxy may interfere with the search for truth by giving a premature or false sense of finality in the search. Orthodoxy is heresy when it closes minds to new truths and new insights. There is always the danger that orthodoxy will become too self-conscious and dogmatic. We should remember that even in the areas of basic importance we have not begun to fathom all the truth. Even the apostle Paul said, "Now I know in part" (1 Cor. 13:12).

How tragic for anyone or any group or denomination to imagine that they know all there is to know about any area of divine truth. When we, as individuals or as a denomination, think that we have discovered about all the truth there is to know, we begin to stagnate and die. The open-minded attitude toward truth is particularly important for a democracy, political or spiritual. A democracy cannot survive if it loses the ability of self-criticism. It will not retain this ability unless its face is set in the direction of new truth and fresh insights.

Orthodoxy becomes heresy when it is substituted for consistency of life. An extreme emphasis on orthodoxy frequently includes an orthodoxy of practice as well as an orthodoxy of belief. There tend to be certain forms and ceremonies that must be adhered to and practiced. There is an inclination to substitute this orthodoxy of belief and practice for genuine Christian living. This tendency has been a continuing problem. The prophets, particularly those of the eighth century, faced it. The children of Israel in their day combined theological orthodoxy with faithful observance of the formal requirements of their religion, and with personal injustice, immorality, and public scandal. The prophets cried out against this combination. They stated frankly that profession was no substitute for practice, nor ritual for righteousness. They proclaimed, in tones that have reached down through the centuries, that no man can be right with the holy and righteous God and at the same time wrong with his fellow man.

Jesus faced the same problem. The Pharisees of his day were the orthodox party, yet Jesus called them "blind guides," "whited sepulchers," and "hypocrites." They might outwardly appear righteous, but within they were full of hypocrisy and iniquity. They might be unusually faithful in tithing—a thing they should have done—but they had left undone weightier or more important matters such as justice, mercy, faith, and fidelity. These who were so orthodox in belief and in practice bound heavy burdens on men, but they would not "move them with their finger." These self-righteous religious leaders were the only ones for whom Jesus had any words of condemnation.

This tendency to substitute orthodoxy for basic morality and practical Christian living is prevalent in the contemporary period. Some of the most unscrupulous, dishonest, immoral preachers are loudest in proclaiming their orthodoxy. Someone thoroughly at home in the use of the best research methods needs to make a study of this rather perplexing and entirely too prevalent phenomenon.

Are we guilty, to any degree, of substituting orthodoxy for everyday Christian living? If so, we should hear the Master say, "This you ought to have done, but not left undone the weightier, the more important matters."

There is a great truth in Mackay's statement that it is much easier "to be a Calvinist or a Lutheran or a Thomist than to be a Christian!" We could just as truthfully say, "It is much easier to be a Southern Baptist, even an orthodox one, than to be a real Christian."—T. B. Maston

SUNDAY, JULY 3, 2005
Lectionary Message

Topic: Oh, Wretched Me!

TEXT: Rom. 7:15–25a

Other Readings: Gen. 24:34–38, 42–49, 58–67; Ps. 45:10–17; Matt. 11:16–19, 25–30

Unfortunately chapter 7 of Romans ends and interrupts the thought. If the early church had lost everything after chapter 7, the Roman Epistle would be a disappointment. (I'll let you in on a secret: chapter 7 describes the problem, while chapter 8 reveals the solution.) Fortunately, we have chapter 8. We'll explore the problem today and the solution next week, I promise.

Chapter 7 closes: "What a wretched man I am! Who will rescue me from this body of death?" It reminds me of the Elephant Man, John Merrick, a wonderful, intelligent, artistic man trapped in the body of a monster. A strange disease twisted and deformed his body. Ugly on the outside but sterling within, he was both beauty and the beast.

Thus Paul laments being trapped in a body determined to sin. He seems to cry, "I'm a good guy trapped in a sin suit, and I can't find the zipper!" "If I can overcome this body, I can escape death."

I wish I could preach this passage without using the *S* word, the nastiest three-letter word in the Bible. All the ugly four-letter words derive from it. It's spelled *S-I-N*; it begins with the "sss" of a snake, and "I" am "n" the middle of it. No generation likes to hear it.

Seeker-sensitive churches try not to say the *S* word. They don't want to offend outsiders who come to church for the music and multimedia lessons. But we can't escape the *S* word because our text for today is about sin. Sin is a vast problem: why we think, feel, and act the way we do.

I. *It was true for Paul.* He wrote: "I do not understand what I do . . . it is no longer I myself who do it, but it is sin living in me. What a wretched man I am." He almost chants again and again, "It's sin!" On the one hand, it's discouraging; if the apostle had this problem, what chance do I have? On the other hand, it's encouraging because he speaks from common experience.

Three prolific Bible writers, Moses, David, and Paul, were all murderers! Moses killed an Egyptian; David contracted the death of a loyal officer; and Saul, later Paul, persecuted early Christians to death. Each sinned big time.

Jesus' apostles John and James lobbied him to sit on his right and left hand in the coming kingdom. Jesus explained he could not allow it; "These places belong to those for whom they have been prepared" (Mark 10:40). Who were the two most prominent apostles? Who sits on Jesus' right and left in the kingdom? Historically, Peter and Paul! But even Peter showed himself a coward and liar who denied Jesus, and Paul presided at the stoning of the martyr Stephen. The worst of the apostles rose to dominant positions.

Decades later, Paul wrote Romans confessing how sin continued to be a problem for him. If it was true for Paul then—

II. *It is true for everyone.* Paul began Romans (1:16–17) with: "I am not ashamed of the gospel, because it is the power of God for the salvation of everyone who believes: first for the Jew, then for the Gentile. For in the gospel a righteousness from God is revealed, a righteousness that is by faith from first to last, just as it is written: "The righteous will live by faith."

Scholar Paul Achtemeier helps us understand how Romans is not the logic of doctrine but the logic of history. The logic of doctrine goes like this: "Don't do that!" "Why not?" "Because I said so." Mom's rule was, Don't play with matches, but I did anyway. So much for rules.

The logic of history is, "See what happens when you do that?" "Yes! I got burned; I won't do it again." The logic of history is more persuasive than the logic of doctrine.

Allow me to summarize the historical logic of Romans 1–7 in three sentences. Paul explained how God created the world; humans worshiped the creation rather than the Creator; the Creator gave them permission to sin but they would be judged and die for it, and then gave the law that identified sin, making it more sinful; people were helpless until righteous Jesus died for them, doing what they could not do for themselves. Logically, sin was the problem of the past, and it's the problem of the present. We're not righteous, but God regards us so because of Christ's atonement, our faith, and His grace. Whew! How's that for a lightning summary?

I still meet people who are surprised to learn they're not right with God as they are. "Wretched me" describes two groups. One is the human race outside the grace of God through Christ. "Wretched me" also describes the flesh-versus-spirit struggle all Christians experience.

Some theologians believe Paul spoke for the first man, Adam, who lived without laws except for one little rule: "Don't eat the fruit from this tree" (Gen. 3:1). He ruined creation for everyone! Why didn't Adam put a minefield around the tree of the knowledge of good and evil? Why didn't he erase it from every map and guidebook? Why didn't he dose the tree with poison? Is it Adam who says, on behalf of us all, "O wretched me"?

Others believe Paul spoke for the entire human race in first person singular. Collectively, humanity complains, "I can't do what I want to do. Oh, wretched we!"

Sigmund Freud attempted to explain why humans think, act, and feel as they do, often contrary to their good sense, safety, and best intentions. He created his personality theory of the id, ego, and superego, insisting people are driven by a desire for pleasure. Where did he gain his theory? From observation of patients, Jewish mysticism . . . and the book of Romans. There's a spiritual dimension to the human cry, "Oh, wretched me."

So if Paul and everyone else can complain "Oh wretched me," then—

III. *It is true for me.* Some of you in the audience are Christians and some are not . . . yet! Both groups of us admit with Paul, "For what I want to do I do not do, but what I hate I do."

First-century Roman religions were gnostic, believing in a dual reality. They took the spiritual reality and the material reality for granted. But they are completely separate.

By their logic, "As long as my heart's right my body can do what it wants." Paul stated it this way: "So then, I myself in my mind am a slave to God's law, but in the sinful nature a slave to the law of sin" (7:25b). This is not the solution, folks; it's a problem. The Christian's solution is coming in chapter 8.

When I was five years old my mom bought me a snowsuit to play in. It was heavily padded with a hood, and it had snaps (this was before zippers) up the front and down the legs. She dressed me warmly and then stuffed me into the snowsuit, added mittens and rubber boots, and sent me out to play. How could I make a snowball when I couldn't get my hands together? I fell down and couldn't get up! She finally rescued me and gave my precious little snowsuit away.

This illustrates my spirit, trapped in a restrictive body. I can't do what I want to do. But I'm more than a spirit. I'm a human being; part of me is spiritual and part of me is physical. A spirit with no body is a spook, and a body with no spirit is a corpse. I want all of me to be right with God. Help me, Jesus! Oh, wretched me!

The sermon stops here. Storytellers call this a cliff-hanger ending. Like the old movie serials, or an Indiana Jones epic, there is a solution to the *S* word. The next sermon is about the rescue of wretched me. If you can't stand the suspense, you might read Romans 8, how God redeems us body and soul, now and forever. It's the best chapter in the New Testament.

Christians, as you go from here, be assured that Christ's atonement is total, generous, and forever. Pray this prayer each day: "Thank you, God, for looking at me through 'Jesus' colored glasses."—David Beavers

SERMON SUGGESTIONS

Topic: The Finishing Touches
TEXT: Jer. 31:31–34
God's new covenant: (1) The outreach of it is universal. (2) The experience of it is personal. (3) The result of it is redemptive.

Topic: Our High Priest
TEXT: Heb. 5:7–10
(1) His fervent prayers. (2) His poignant suffering. (3) His perfect Saviorhood.

WORSHIP AIDS

CALL TO WORSHIP.   "For they got not the land in possession by their own sword, neither did their own arm save them: but by thy hand, and thine arm, and the light of thy countenance, because thou hadst a favor unto them" (Ps. 44:3).

INVOCATION.   Despite our sinfulness and unworthiness and that of our forebears, O Lord, you have given us this good land in which to live. Grant that on this day and in the future we may confess our sins as a people and as individuals and dedicate ourselves anew to the ways of truth and right that make us genuinely free.

OFFERTORY SENTENCE.   "By love serve one another. For all the law is fulfilled in one word, even in this; thou shalt love thy neighbor as thyself" (Gal. 5:13b–14).

OFFERTORY PRAYER.   Let love have its way, O God, as we bring our offerings to your altar. May love abound toward institutions, causes, and individuals through our giving.

A LITANY.   Almighty God, giver of all good things: we thank you for the natural majesty and beauty of this land. They restore us, though we often destroy them. *Heal us.*

We thank you for the great resources of this nation. They make us rich, though we often exploit them. *Forgive us.*

We thank you for the men and women who have made this country strong. They are models for us, though we often fall short of them. *Inspire us.*

We thank you for the torch of liberty that has been lit in this land. It has drawn people from every nation, though we have often hidden from its light. *Enlighten us.*

We thank you for the faith we have inherited in all its rich variety. It sustains our life, though we have been faithless again and again. *Renew us.*

Help us, O Lord, to finish the good work here begun. Strengthen our efforts to blot out ignorance and prejudice, and to abolish poverty and crime. And hasten the day when all our people, with many voices in one united chorus, will glorify your holy Name.—*The Book of Common Prayer*

SERMON

Topic: "Nobody Ever Died of Old Age"

TEXT: Ps. 71:5–12; Philem. 1:8–10

Aging is a natural part of life. If we did not age, then we would all remain infants, retarded in the process of life, limited in experience and awareness. We should be thankful for aging.

As we begin to think about getting older, we have certain fears. We have fears about the loss of health. "Will I stay healthy?" The fear of illness and suffering is a paramount fear. As we age, our motor skills do slow down. We have no promises that we will always be healthy. Sometimes we may get sick and suffer. That too is a part of life.

Others are concerned about their financial security. Will I have enough money put aside to support myself and my spouse when I become older? Others are concerned about independence and usefulness. Will I continue to be useful and find something worthwhile to do? There are fears about desolation from the death of a loved one, and loneliness. Others are concerned about whether or not they will be a burden to their family. We all have different kinds of fears as we age. These questions are a natural part of the concerns we all have about the aging process itself.

Let me suggest that you do some inner reflection as you work at your construction. Ask yourself—whatever age you are today—some questions: "What do I want to be five or ten years from now? Where do I want to be?" Think about this not just in terms of where you are living, but in terms of what kind of expectations you have for yourself. "How will I reach my goal? How will I maintain myself financially? Who will be with me? Who do I want with me, if possible? What will I be doing that is useful and worthwhile?"

One factor that is basic in your life's construction is your attitude. The way a person sees himself or herself is essential. Remember the importance of yourself. You are special. You are unique. You are your best gift to others. There are some people who die at thirty-nine but are not buried until seventy-nine. You have seen these folks. They have simply quit living. They have turned their attention toward death instead of life. Our attitude can make all of the difference.

Some buy into the myths about aging. These myths state that the elderly can't do anything. They are not useful or are senile. Don't buy into that view of life. A positive attitude can make the difference in being a healthy person.

I read about a study that Karl Menninger did of eighty-eight senile, psychotic patients at the Topeka State Hospital. He said that most of these people had been there for more than ten years, one had been there for fifty-eight years. A young doctor and a therapeutic team of cheerful nurses, aides, social workers, and psychiatric residents were assigned to that ward. They gave careful individual attention to the patients. They began to instigate birthday parties and other activities. They played music, turned on the television sets, brought in pets, and did all kinds of other things for them. At the end of a year the results were dramatic. Dr. Menninger said that of the eighty-eight patients, only one was still bedfast and only six were incontinent. Twelve patients had left the hospital to go live with their families; six had moved out to live alone; four were in comfortable nursing homes; and only five had died. Four returned to the community as self-supporting adults. Most of these so-called hopeless persons, once they had a different atmosphere around them, developed a different attitude and changed remarkably.

In our text for today, the psalmist declares that God is my Rock, strong fortress, and refuge. Note how many times the personal pronoun is used in this psalm: *I, my,* and *me.* Here is the prayer of an old man who expresses his laments and makes his confession, but voices his assurance of God's presence with him, even in his aging years and the distresses around him. He trusted God as a youth and has served God all his life (71:6).

Although an older person's motor activities may slow down, there is no reason why one cannot continue to excel in other areas despite one's age. Many have. Golda Meir became the prime minister of Israel at seventy-one. Konrad Adenauer was first elected chancellor of West Germany at seventy-three and served for fourteen years. Grandma Moses began painting at seventy-nine and was still painting beautiful folk art at one hundred. Goethe wrote *Faust* when he was eighty. John Wesley preached until he was eighty-eight. At eighty-three, William Gladstone was elected prime minister of Great Britain for the fourth time.

The list could go on: Thomas Edison, J. C. Penney, Norman Vincent Peale, George Burns, Lena Horne, Thomas Jefferson, Col. Harland Sanders, Julia Childs, John Forsythe, Jessica Tandy, and hundreds of others who have been productive into advanced age.

Don't buy into the myth that you can't do something after a certain age. Some of the most profound discoveries, paintings, books, music, inventions, and so on have been produced by people in the later years of life.

Let's go another step; let me encourage you to cultivate new chapters in your life. We are always moving from one chapter to another in our lives. We are always saying good-bye to something.

Life is made up of good-byes, but that doesn't mean life is over. Find a new chapter. Live creatively in the chapter you have now, where you are, with whom you are. Live in the moment you have; don't be merely a window shopper.

Second, continue educating yourself. Stretch your mind. Continue to learn, because you never reach the point where you can't learn. You might learn a new language, or study an area you know nothing about. Continue to educate yourself.

Let me encourage you, maybe, to spend more time with your family. You could find time to do some traveling. Let me encourage you to consider taking up some new projects.

You could experience the rich life of a volunteer. Church and community organizations always need volunteers. The opportunities are endless: Sunday school teacher, docent at a museum, library assistant, tutor, translator, teacher's aide, visiting in a nursing home, shut-in, and so on.

You might also deepen your religious life. Ah, we have all been so busy we haven't had time for our spiritual development. Maybe in your senior adult years you could put some special emphasis on growing spiritually and deepening your faith.

Or you might even get a new job. There are some people who retire and then take another job. Another unexpected chapter, or one sought after, may open up for them. Who says that when one chapter ends, life is over? Find a new chapter.

Finally, let me encourage you to continue growing. Continue growing through the journey of life. Even if your health is not good—hopefully you will stay well, but even if it isn't, keep growing. There are always some things you can do. Don't rest on your oars.

There is an awful lot we can learn from older people. Older people have gone through many experiences in life, good and bad, sad and happy. They have seen a variety of dimensions of life. They know many causes and effects. We can continue to learn from them. Their wisdom about the past and our history should not be forgotten. We ought to be open and responsive to continue learning from those who have learned much.

Each of us needs to continue reaching. Each of us needs to be striving and stretching to grow further. We need to be learning more. We need to be laughing more. We need to be praising more, just as the psalmist in our text did. He was able to praise God no matter what the circumstances of life were.

We need some new stories to tell our children and grandchildren. Some of the stories that we often tell them are growing-up stories—"what it was like when I grew up." Many of us take our grandchildren or children on our knee and tell them stories about what it was like for us growing up. Now we may need some growing-down stories. These stories could come from people who are older, who might tell us what life is like in the senior adult years. They can tell us some of their expectations, and what life has really been like. Maybe we could learn more from them about how to live in the "twilight years." But remember, no one fully arrives in life. We are always seeking to be more than we are. Keep on reaching.—William Powell Tuck

SUNDAY, JULY 10, 2005
Lectionary Message
Topic: Living in the Spirit's Jurisdiction!
TEXT: Rom. 8:1–11
Other Readings: Gen. 25:19–34; Ps. 119:105–112; Matt. 13:1–9, 18–23

Frederick Douglass chronicled his escape from slavery in 1838: "It was the custom in the State of Maryland to require the free colored people to have free papers—with the name, age, color, height, and form of the freeman described, together with any scars or other marks which could assist in identification. Hence many slaves could escape by personating the owner of one set of papers."[1]

Douglass, disguised as a sailor, was on a train from Baltimore to New York when the conductor asked for his free papers. Douglass said he had a seaman's protection with an American eagle on it that would carry him around the world. The merest glance at the paper satisfied the conductor; had he looked more closely the papers described a very different-looking person. He boarded the train a slave but stepped off a free man.

The difference between confinement and freedom is only a matter of jurisdiction; a criminal in one area is a hero in another. If a child steals something, it isn't a crime; why not? The child did it but there is no guilt. It's a jurisdiction of innocence.

Today's sermon is a sequel to last week's message, where Paul posed the question, "What a wretched man I am! Who will rescue me from this body of death?" (Rom. 7:24). He answers in 8:11b: "He who raised Christ from the dead will also give life to your moral bodies through his Spirit who lives in you. By dying [with Christ] to what once bound us, we have been released from the law so that we serve *in the new way of the Spirit*" (7:8). Paul goes on to reveal the now-and-future benefits of living in the Spirit.

I. *The spirit and our present.* Spiritually, we live in the jurisdiction of the Spirit. Notice how the mood of Romans changes abruptly from frustrated anxiety to joyful confidence because of one word: Spirit! Spirit occurs only eight times in chapters 1 through 7 and only five times after chapter 8. Spirit occurs twenty-two times in Romans 8, so that one is often named "the Spirit chapter."

It's obvious the apostle means the Holy Spirit, third person of the Trinity, given to every new disciple of Jesus. This is not about spiritual gifts (prophesying, tongues, miracles); it's the gift of the Spirit as an indwelling presence.

Therefore, there is *now no condemnation for those who are in Christ Jesus.* Criminal trials rely on three types of evidence: witness, forensic, and confession. Imagine you're on trial on "Court TV" and everyone knows you are guilty because every form of evidence proves it. Judge knows, jury knows, prosecution knows, public knows it. The judge takes one look at your defense attorneys and raps out, "Not guilty—you're free to go!" You've received a bench pardon (not innocent, but declared not guilty). Why? Your advocates are Jesus and the Spirit.

All the guilt you once mourned doesn't count in this court. The wretched me is now the new me under new jurisdiction. This is legal language; those guilty under the old laws are not guilty under the law of the Spirit. In God's eyes, because of Christ's atonement and the

---

[1] "My Escape from Slavery," *Century* magazine, 1881.

gift of the Holy Spirit, you are innocent. God doesn't look at us as we are but sees us through the blood of Jesus. You've heard the phrase "looking at the world through rose-colored glasses"? God looks at us through "Jesus" colored glasses.

Now we're also living under Spirit control; "The mind of sinful man is death, but the mind controlled by the Spirit is life and peace." Control, or *hupotasso* in Greek, means to rank under, a military term. What we can't control, the Spirit can.

Grandfather worked his land with horses—enormous, powerful animals who never needed reins or a whip. He hitched them to a plow or harrow, draped the reins over his shoulders, and drove them with quiet words: *gee, haw, back, giddy-up,* and *whoa.*

I was only eight years old but allowed to drive the team home one day after a hot day in the fields. I sat on the wagon seat with Uncle Matt, enjoying my illusions of control. As we came down the road the team saw the barn and creek and their trot became a dead run! I knew the wagon was about to turn over and pulled on the reins with all my strength, "Whoa, whoa, whoa!" Uncle Matt did nothing but take the reins in his experienced hands and the team sensed it, slowed immediately, and resumed a sensible trot.

With Spirit control, you are still you and the Spirit is still the Spirit. Most times you do quite well; at other times life is too much for you, and the Spirit takes the reins. It's a different way of living, thinking, feeling, and being right with God. Right now, in the present, we're under Spirit's control and jurisdiction.

II. *The spirit and our future.* Wretched me cried out to be delivered from a dying body. Death is the common end of every human being. Different religions propose creative solutions. Ancient Egyptians preserved the bodies of the dead, convinced this gave them eternal life. Ancient Hebrews were pragmatic about it, believing you live on through your children; "When you die you're dead all over, just like Rover!" Buddhists proposed that each spirit merges with all the other spirits, like streams flowing into the sea, where all become God. Reincarnation insists our spirit lives again and again in different bodies through the ages. Spiritualism claims the spirit lives on in an ideal spiritual world where a body is unnecessary.

Christians believe we will be resurrected in new and wonderful bodies. Every Easter we celebrate proof of it, Jesus Christ. We have all kinds of evidence, confessions, forensic, and reliable testimony. "Wretched me! Who will rescue me from this body of death?" The answer: "But if Christ is in you, your body is dead because of sin, yet *your spirit is alive* because of righteousness. And if the Spirit of him who raised Jesus from the dead is living in you, *he who raised Christ from the dead will also give life to your mortal bodies through his Spirit, who lives in you* (8:10–11).

The early church celebrated Easter every Sunday. Celebrate it now! Be convinced that eternal life has already begun in you. It's the result of Christ in us and power of the Spirit. Your task this week: read the last chapter of Matthew, Mark, Luke, and John. Read 1 Corinthians 15:12–24. It's about the Spirit and your future.

Realize now that you are living in the jurisdiction of the Spirit, where you are not guilty, nor condemned.

We close with Frederick Douglass's first experience in free territory of New York:

On my way down Union Street I saw a large pile of coal in front of the house of Rev. Ephraim Peabody, the Unitarian minister. I went to the kitchen door and asked the privilege of bringing in and putting away this coal. "What will you charge?" said the lady. "I will leave that to you, madam." "You may put it away," she said. I was not long in accomplishing the job, when the dear lady put into my hand *two silver half-dollars.* To understand the emotion which swelled my heart as I clasped this money, realizing that I had no master who could take it from me— *that it was mine—that my hands were my own. . . ."*

Douglass lived the rest of his life in the jurisdiction of freedom.—David Beavers

SERMON SUGGESTIONS

Topic: The Career of the Called

TEXT: Isa. 50:4–9a

God raises up from among his people individuals who represent both God and his people— but especially God. (1) God teaches these special servants and gives them relevant words for the people. (2) These servants often suffer indignities from those they are called to bless. (3) Yet these servants, sustained through all trials, are at last vindicated by their God, even as Jesus triumphed and has received the name above every name.

Topic: Seeing Others from the Proper Angle

TEXT: Phil. 2:5–11

(1) We are fittingly grateful for blessings and privilege that others might not share. (2) Yet we should be willing to surrender all to God's will for his glory and the good of others. (3) In it all, we can be assured that God will give suitable rewards and recognition in his own time and ways.

WORSHIP AIDS

CALL TO WORSHIP.   "Enter into his gates with thanksgiving, and into his courts with praise: be thankful unto him, and bless his name. For the Lord is good; his mercy is everlasting; and his truth endureth to all generations" (Ps. 100:4–5).

INVOCATION.   Guide us in our worship, O Lord, by our sense of your marvelous grace. Capture again our wandering hearts and make all that we can become praise and glorify you.

OFFERTORY SENTENCE.   "Serve the Lord with gladness" (Ps. 100:2a).

OFFERTORY PRAYER.   In the name of the God of creation, the Son of redemption, and the Spirit of conviction, we give with joy and dedicate with delight this offering of our substance.— E. Lee Phillips

PRAYER.   O God, in whom we live and move and have our being—we are yours by right of creation; we are yours because you have forgiven and redeemed us; we are yours, for you are sustaining us day by day. To know whose we are is to know who we are. How often we play God to ourselves and especially to others, when our high calling is to live out the fullness of our humanity even as Jesus lived out the fullness of his humanity. We have come here to find self—it is so easy to get lost in the world. How we need to hear your Word spoken from the beginning—in the very nature of creation and in the very nature of our creation, that we may gain or regain direction, perspective, values for our lives! One who lived life out in its depths and in its heights is saying, "What does it profit a man or a woman if he or she gain the whole world and lose the self"; what shall a person give in exchange for the self? In Christ you call us not to be gods but to be ourselves—to be the person you have created us to be. It is in obedience in a loving, trusting relationship with you as Father that we fulfill our true estate as your sons and daughters. It is the meaning and mystery of life that in our humanity—in our humanness—we are temples of your Holy Spirit.

"Once we were no people but now we are your people; once we had not received mercy, but now we have received mercy, that we may declare the wonderful deeds of him who called us out of darkness into his marvelous light." As the called-out ones, *ecclesia*, the church, we are gifted with your love in Christ to one another and to all others. May we embrace of your love those who suffer sudden tragedy that they may experience the comfort, the strength, the courage, the hope that only you can give. May we be responsible in love in all of our relationships, that we may declare your deed in Christ, who teaches us to pray as a family together: [The Lord's Prayer].—John Thompson

SERMON
Topic: Fruitful Suffering
Text: 2 Cor. 1:3–11

We are a remarkable society. We have fire insurance and even insurance to cover glass breakage, theft, and water damage. There is only a remote chance that our house will burn down or we will be robbed, perhaps one chance in a hundred. But one thing is almost certain: suffering in one form or another awaits us. This is, I would guess, between 95 and 100 percent probable. Yet, we do nothing to insure ourselves against it. Isn't it far more important to be inwardly prepared and to stand the test of our sufferings than at some time to collect a few hundred dollars' insurance claim?

We act most foolishly. We put all suffering away from ourselves and try not to think about it. We make the life of our children as easy as we can. We put our seriously sick in the hospital; they don't die in our homes anymore. When we read in Gottfried Keller's *Green Henry* about what the dying of the grandmother meant to him and the whole family in a bygone generation, then we realize what we have lost. Death is now changed into a friendly hospital room where the relatives see nothing but flowers, chocolates, and a person who smiles for half an hour. We suppress all thoughts of suffering, with the result that our anxieties flutter beneath the surface and work their way into neuroses and nightmares.

And now this morning Paul stands before us. Like a trumpeter who blows full force into his trumpet, he begins with a loud, joyful song of praise, blaring it forth with the first note: "Blessed be the God and Father of our Lord Jesus Christ, the Father of mercies and God of all comfort." Paul knows more about suffering than most of us (or all of us). Not long before, in Ephesus, he had already written off his life. We do not know for sure what the trouble was. Apparently he lay in prison awaiting beheading; or he could have had a serious illness. It might seem to us that a man can be joyful and praise God easily enough if his suffering is all over and done with. But the truth is that repeated persecutions, imprisonments, and scourgings lay in wait for Paul. Just a few weeks or months later, he writes in the Epistle to the Romans that he dies daily. Why does he say this? Because he has to reckon with death every day he lives. So Paul has learned how to rejoice from the ground up. Why can't we learn something of that with him?

If we do not see where his thoughts and everything else in his life begin, we cannot fathom Paul's joy. When he says "God" he means "Father of Jesus Christ," "who raises the dead." Paul does not begin his way of thinking and his living with his own self. He does not begin with his own sufferings, with all the good times and bad times he has known. He does not begin with his own faith, with the comfort of that faith that would enable him to overcome everything. Paul does not imagine that he is to be pitied because manifold evils befell him and evil persons treated him shamefully. And he does not imagine that he is to be admired because his faith is strong and he is brave. He believes that he himself, Paul, is not the least bit important, but that God is inconceivably important. And certainly not just any God, but the god who makes Easter happen!

Now do you understand why Paul rejoices so loudly in such a dreadful time? Easter has taken place. For Paul, things often went well, and often badly. Paul is often strong and brave in faith and often without courage and at the end of his rope. But God remains the same. Easter remains. When I cannot believe it and find myself in the Slough of Despond, Easter is still true, and God is still the Father of Jesus Christ—the one who wakes the dead. Every Sunday morning reminds us of that morning when Resurrection, not death, won the victory.

But of course this awareness of Easter and this life derived from the Easter event must be practiced. Nobody ascends Mount Rosa with skiers without practicing the fundamentals of skiing for a long time beforehand. What awaits us in the near or distant future is infinitely more than a Mount Rosa. It may be a sickbed. Or it may be the coffin of a loved one. Death it surely is. Even if we keep on dodging it, since we do not think about it until our mental faculties are almost gone, it is quite certain that God awaits us and will question us about what we have built our life upon. Then eternity will depend on whether we have so practiced trusting him and his power that we can face the last judgment.

The *first thing* that Paul has learned and practiced is to believe in the God "who comforts us in all our afflictions so that we may be able to comfort those who are in any affliction, with the comfort with which we ourselves are comforted by God." In the very hour in which the Risen Christ appeared to him, Paul knew that Christ was sending him to all men as his messenger. One cannot believe in Easter at all without immediately becoming to some extent accessible and open to all other men. Whenever the Risen One encountered his disciples, he sent them out into the world. Paul knew that immediately. But in years of suffering, he learned how even his suffering was always borne for the sake of others also. If he had not found such comfort for his own pressing need, how could he have passed on to others genuine comfort—real consolation and encouragement? He understood that all suffering can become the source of a veritable river, which flows on and on, growing on, growing perennial fruit all along its banks.

Before I decided on my vocation, when I was between sixteen and eighteen years old, a young pastor in Basel went through a difficult time of suffering. He never spoke to us about it. We only knew that his engagement of five years was broken. But during that time what he said to us about the gospel, though he did not directly connect it with his own problem, had such power and authenticity that it lived on in me. I do not know whether I would have become a pastor apart from what happened to him. The young pastor has long since died, apparently never suspecting what a creative and nourishing stream would flow from his suffering.

Paul dares to call his suffering *Christ-suffering*: "For as we share abundantly in Christ's suffering, so through Christ we share abundantly in comfort too. If we are afflicted, it is for your comfort, which you experience when you patiently endure the same sufferings that we suffer. Our hope is unshaken, for we know that as you share in our sufferings, you will also share in our comfort." Paul is quite right! Suffering does become Christ-suffering when it is gone through in his footsteps. It matters little whether it overtakes us directly on his account, perhaps with some kind of persecution, or with an illness or something like that. Only this makes a difference: whether the Lord Christ takes it into his hands and makes something grow out of it. That is what has actually happened in Paul's case.

The *second thing* Paul has learned is that it is primarily suffering that causes the church rightly to be the church, for the church learns through suffering to take intercession seriously: "You also must help us by prayer, so that many will give thanks on our behalf for the blessing granted us in answer to many prayers." Not only the *intercession* but also the *thanksgiving* that follows is very important. Who knows how many among us have received the commission to suffer for the sheer purpose of learning to pray as much as we can, to ask and be thankful not only for our own selves, but for others also?

Many times we have to suffer very acutely until we finally quit being like a crustacean that sits in its hard shell and is always alone with its own self, caring for nothing going on around it. Isn't there a special kind of religious hard shell? Some have never observed that God is always God for all others, and that he is not nearly so interested in the life of our individual souls as in the birth of a community in which individuals think about others and practice this concern continually in intercession and thanksgiving. God is incomparably interested in that. When I came from the university to my student parish, a very unfortunate Toggenburger farm wife, who faded away little by little through many weeks and was about to leave behind her husband and children, did me a very great service. It was nothing more dramatic than that she calmly endured, and that the gospel and prayer became authentic and powerful through what she was and did.

And one *last thing* has become clear to Paul: "For we do not want you to be ignorant, brethren, of the affliction we experienced in Asia; for we were so utterly, unbearably crushed that we despaired of life itself. Why, we felt that we had received the sentence of death; but that was to make us rely not on ourselves but on God who raises the dead; he delivered us from so deadly a peril, and he will deliver us; on him we have set our hope that he will deliver us again." In suffering, God has helped him actually to understand what Easter is. We might even say: actually to understand what "God" means. He had to come so far that he was at the very end of his tether. He had given up his life for lost. And then he really understood what it means to have a God who raises the dead.

As a rule a man is inclined to think quite theoretically: "A car might run over me on my way home from church, but it probably won't happen." Even so, he thinks by nature in his subconscious: "It hasn't happened yet, it will not actually happen, and I won't have to begin thinking about death for a long, long time." However, Paul has been brought so close to death that he can no longer push it aside. For that he is wholeheartedly thankful to God. He has seen not death alone, but also God, who raises the dead, and his vision is clearer than ever before.

My dear brothers and sisters, let me now conclude with something unusual. The gentleman in whose house it is my privilege to live here in Zurich and whose task I am permitted to carry on at the university spoke to me several months ago. As I visited Gottlob Schrenk in Arosa, he told me that the most important thing to him was not his rapidly approaching blindness or his many other infirmities, but the reality of God, which has become clearer and clearer. In such a case a man may see into realities that he scarcely dreamed for so long as he was preoccupied with his many everyday problems. In a brusque, almost austere calm, the octogenarian in the highlands imparted to me this sentence: God is real, the God who is the Father of Jesus Christ and for that reason the Father of mercies and the God of all comfort, the God who raises the dead.[2]

SUNDAY, JULY 17, 2005
Lectionary Message

Topic: Being Co-Heirs
TEXT: Rom. 8:12–25.
Other Readings: Gen. 28:10–19a; Ps. 139:1–12, 23–24; Matt. 13:24–30, 36–43

Now if we are children, then *we are heirs—heirs of God and co-heirs with Christ,* if indeed we *share in his sufferings* in order that we may also *share in his glory.*

Picture this scene. The heirs of a wealthy woman gather for the reading of her will. They won't look at each other; anxious jealousy and resentment are thinly disguised. One thinks, "I should get it all!" Another, "she should get nothing." Another, "I'm so distantly related I'm grateful for anything." Another, "why am I here, I hardly knew her?"

The family lawyer observes the dynamics, old and young, calm and desperate, humble and proud. He opens the document before him and, remembering his deceased client, smiles from the pleasant memories of her goodness and generosity. He gestures for attention.

"You are all here today because you are co-heirs of this last will and testament. Each of you is included. And there is so much money, so many securities, trusts, lands, and titles to share, not one of you will be able to spend your inheritance in your lifetime."

In our text, the apostle assures us we are heirs of God, co-heirs with Christ. Because of him we are in the will. Our sermon explores two benefits of being related to Christ.

I. *You are children of God.* Paul emphasized our obligation to live by the Spirit in verse 12. Then he elaborated on the work of the Spirit and Christ in us (8:14): "those who are led by the spirit are children of God." We glibly prayed earlier in our service, "Our Father who art in heaven." God is our Father.

References to God as Father are few and far between in the Old Testament. One psalmist prayed (Ps. 89:26b): "You are my Father, my God, the Rock my Savior." But it was Jesus who taught us to address God as Father. Now Paul reminds us, "You received the *Spirit of sonship.* And by him we cry, Abba, Father" (Rom. 8:15). Abba is best translated as "Daddy."

---

[2]Eduard Schweizer, *God's Inescapable Nearness,* translated by James W. Cox (Waco, Tex.: Word Books, 1971), pp. 77–83.

My father's name was Zep, but if I addressed him as "Zep" or "Father" he might chuckle. He was "Dad!" He referred to his father as "Pa." Others use "Poppy," "Daddy," "Papa," "Da," all informal diminutives of "Father."

My half-brother was thirteen years older than I. He called my mother, his stepmother, "Gert," so I did too. "Gert" meant "Mom" to me from the time I began to talk. Don't think I didn't raise some eyebrows of disapproval. But "Gert" was my affectionate term for mother.

We're allowed intimacy with our parents and with God as our heavenly parent. Maybe we should pray, "Daddy who is in heaven." Address God as "Daddy" during your intimate devotions, and you'll enter a new dimension of spirituality.

How did we become children of God? Paul alludes to our adoption in verse 32 and made a bold statement in Ephesians 1:4–6: "For he chose us in him before the creation of the world to be holy and blameless in his sight. In love he predestined us *to be adopted as his sons* through Jesus Christ, in accordance with his pleasure and will—to the praise of his glorious grace, which he has freely given us in the One he loves."

Roman adoption was more complicated than our modern system in that it brought a person under the power of a father (a woman couldn't adopt, for even her own children weren't in her power). The result was a legal authority of father over son, usually not a "Daddy." Adoption was strictly controlled by government because of citizenship and inheritance issues. For example, an adopted son couldn't marry his adopted father's daughter because she was now his sister, but he was not the son of the adoptive mother. Paul explains our relationship to God in legal terms but redefines God as our Abba. We qualify to inherit from our Father. The apostle John explained our relationship to God differently, as being born of God: "Everyone who believes that Jesus is the Christ is born of God, and everyone who loves the father loves his child as well" (1 John 5:1). So which are we, born or adopted? Both! God takes no chances.

A Christian is doubly a child of God with all the benefits, so then, *you are co-heirs with Christ* (8:17). A business man of my acquaintance called the children and grandchildren together after his wife's funeral. He explained how the couple's will had two parts. "You receive one part now. When I die the second part will come to you. You are all in the will." Each child and grandchild received a handsome sum of money, which was only a hint of what was to come. Paul barely lifts the curtain but gives us an exciting glimpse of our share of Christ's inheritance: *first, we inherit his suffering* (v. 17). Church history verifies what Paul promised. Jesus made it clear we will be persecuted for his sake. In the news, at the time of this writing, in India: Christians are concerned they could be the next group targeted for ethnic cleansing. In Georgia: old USSR officers of the former KGB burst into apartments of Adventist Christians and confiscated leaflets and Bibles. In Afghanistan: under the existing constitution only certain religious groups are specifically offered protection under the law, excluding Christians. In Uganda: the Lord's Resistance Army, a cult-militia led by Joseph Kony, continues to terrorize the Christian community of northern Uganda and southern Sudan.

All the apostles understood and accepted suffering for Jesus' sake. They believed Christ's suffering didn't end at Calvary but continues in his body, the church. Suffering for Christ is like a baton passed from one generation to the next. It's our lot as co-heirs of Christ.

II. *We inherit his glory (v. 17).* Moviegoers rarely sit through the credits after "The End" centers on the screen. Theatergoers remain in their seats to applaud and cheer everyone in the cast, until last, the star appears. For the star the applause and cheers are strongest, because he or she deserves the glory. Sometimes the star will point to the director or author, and insist the musicians stand to share the glory.

Jesus sits at the right hand of God; his name is above all names; his is the honor and glory that he will share with us. Paul told the Thessalonians, "He called you to this through our gospel, that you might share in the glory of our Lord Jesus Christ" (2 Thess. 2:14). The apostle Peter promised, "And when the Chief Shepherd appears, you will receive the crown of glory that will never fade away" (1 Pet. 5:4).

III. Finally, *we inherit his resurrection (v. 23).* Many of you made your own will, leaving to loved ones things of value you can't take with you. One of my students designed a poster with a hearse pulling a U-Haul trailer. The caption reads, "Maybe you can take it with you!" As co-heirs with Christ we live on with our inheritance.

Romans 8:12–15 is good news to read regularly. Put the ribbon in your Bible at that place. Then memorize verse 17: "Now if we are children, then *we are heirs—heirs of God and co-heirs with Christ,* if indeed we *share in his sufferings* in order that we may also *share in his glory."* Our sermon set out to explore the benefits of being related to Christ. First, we are children of God. Then, we are co-heirs of Christ. Don't neglect to address God as "Daddy" in your prayers.

All through this sermon's preparation a hymn of Harriet Buell hummed in my mind: "My Father is rich in houses and lands, he holdeth the wealth of the world in His hands. Of rubies and diamonds, of silver and gold, His coffers are full, He has riches untold. I'm a child of the King, a child of the King, with Jesus my Savior, I'm a child of the King."

Sing the hymn aloud with me now in response to the message.—David Beavers

SERMON SUGGESTIONS

Topic: God's Blessing of His People
TEXT: Isa. 60:1–6
(1) Comes in the fullness of time. (2) Brings obligation to reflect God's glory. (3) Is rewarded with astounding influence.

Topic: Epiphany
TEXT: Eph. 3:1–12
(1) The mystery of Christ hidden. (2) The mystery of Christ revealed. (3) The mystery of Christ proclaimed. (4) The mystery of Christ experienced.

WORSHIP AIDS

CALL TO WORSHIP.   "O magnify the Lord with me, and let us exalt his name together" (Ps. 34:3).

INVOCATION.   Tune our hearts, O God, to sing your praise. We love you because you first loved us, and we wish for all the universe to join us in praise of you. Purify our hearts, so that we may worship you today and serve you tomorrow in spirit and in truth.

OFFERTORY SENTENCE.   "God was making all mankind his friends through Christ. God did not keep an account of their sins, and he has given us the message which tells how he makes them his friends" (2 Cor. 5:19, TEV).

OFFERTORY PRAYER.   Lord, make this message effective at home and abroad through our faithful personal testimony and through our faithful financial stewardship.

PRAYER.   O God, Creator of all good, if we are honest we have to confess that we are wealthy. Though we may be poor in the world's goods, as people count wealth, we have, each of us, overwhelming riches: our human heritage, our national treasures, the natural beauty of this world, the gift of friends, and of others who love us. Life itself we have received from you, as well as our personal gifts and potentials. Greater than any other gift is the gift of your Son and all the treasures of truth and life that come to us through him. Whenever we are tempted to imagine that any of our blessings have come simply because of what we have done or deserve, deliver us from the evil of ingratitude, and help us to acknowledge you with joy as the Source and Goal of all that we are and have.

SERMON
Topic: "Christians Unashamed"
TEXT: Rom. 1:8–17

In Paul we see a person of extraordinarily sensitive conscience, a Roman citizen and a Christian. Like other men and women of sensitive conscience down the ages, Paul found much in his world about which to be ashamed. In light of his loyalty to Christ he was ashamed of himself and some of his friends. He was ashamed of the incessant squabbles in the churches he founded. He found himself ashamed of the excess of Roman civilization—its shabby morals, its patent injustices. Yet amid all these matters making him ashamed, Paul treasured one thing of which he was not ashamed. As he wrote in introducing himself to the church at Rome, "I am not ashamed of the Gospel of Christ."

I suspect there are some of us here this morning who stand somewhat with Paul. Who among us does not harbor any number of things of which we are ashamed? On the personal level, who is not ashamed of all the time she has wasted? Who is not ashamed of the numerous times his temper has gotten away from him; of all the letters left unanswered; the friends and loved ones taken for granted? Who is not ashamed of the enormous sums spent on self-indulgence; of the times we fail to do what we know is right; of letting down our best selves? Who is not ashamed of being ashamed of the gospel? I dare say few of us are not ashamed of ourselves in one way or another.

Yes, on a larger scale, I suspect some of us find ourselves ashamed of our churches, the quality of life in our cities, the monumental social wounds in our country. Yet, amid all the troubles, the failures of will, the betrayals of self of which we have to be ashamed, I pray this morning you and I may testify with Paul: "I am not ashamed of the Gospel of Christ, for it is the way unto salvation for those who have faith." This is one of the ringing witnesses of the New Testament, something we can all stand and glory in. I want to reflect on it for a few moments this morning. Inevitably, like Paul, this will be a somewhat personal statement.

I. In the first place, I am not ashamed ours is a gospel of truth born of faith. I am not ashamed to tell you I trust an Eternal One whose character, whose presence, whose existence, whose impact on us and our world is revealed to us—hear that? *revealed to us*—in the decisive, creative, compassionate, explosive story of Jesus of Nazareth, the Christ.

Through the story of Jesus Christ we see a God whom Jesus compares to a father losing us, his beloved children, to skewed loyalties and to messed-up lives; a father losing us to searches for meaning, leading again and again to dead ends; a father losing us to quick and easy routes to self-gratification leaving us all the more empty. We see a God who waits for us to return to our senses, to surrender ourselves finally to the divine acceptance and forgiveness itself dying to embrace us and welcome us home.

I am not ashamed of a gospel that through the story of Jesus Christ affirms an inclusive, barrier-free human community. When Jesus tells of a Samaritan caring for a stricken Jew, he blows to smithereens the walls we build between one another. He discloses a God who will not be stuffed into the prison of being male or female, nor into the imperial claims of any nation, nor into the ethnic chauvinism of any race, nor into the doctrinal constraints of any religion. For the God of Jesus Christ the barriers of sex, or race, or nation, or religion we perversely equate with Divine warrant and entitlement—those barriers of God are already down. We have only to rejoice as if always at a global wedding reception celebrating our love for one another and God's love for us.

Yes, I am not ashamed of a gospel grounded in Resurrection. For the good news is simply that for the God of Jesus Christ—this God of Hope—there exist no dead ends. Indeed, I trust that light through all seeking to quench it, that life through all pressing to destroy it, that love through all threatening to crush it—I trust the God of Hope who bears us through all of this, opening new doors, forging new possibilities, promising finally, whatever may be, our God will never let us go.

I am not ashamed of faith in such a gospel.

II. But in addition to being unashamed of faith in God's good news, I am also unashamed of the gospel's unblinking attitude toward sin. The New Testament is no Pollyanna when it comes to the human condition. We need look no further than the cross at the center of this room to catch a glimpse of our capacity for evil. All our modern attempts to attribute our massive human problems to ignorance, or psychological maladjustment, to hormones or environmental conditions—whatever; our counting on cures ranging from education, to drugs, to social planning, to psychotherapy—you name it; all of this appears finally as a bland distortion of something running much deeper in and through us. Sin deceives us by giving us good reason for doing bad things. The New Testament is not ashamed of seeing human nature as somehow corrupted; nor does it avoid saying that we might be most corrupt when we consider ourselves most innocent.

But that potent understanding of who we are does not end there. For the good news, the gospel, deals directly with this terrible human problem. The cross shows us how deeply we may fall into self-deception and violence, but it shows us as well the very vehicle and power for our deliverance. The cross shows us the nature of our sin, but at the same time it shows us the invincible love, grace, and forgiveness of God.

My friends, I am not ashamed of a gospel revealing human nature at its worst while at the same time—mysteriously, marvelously, redemptively—demonstrating the loving power of God at its best.

III. Lastly, I am not ashamed of the courage of the gospel. Jesus gave his life over to it; he gave his death up to it. Paul found the gospel so persuasive and exciting he underwent shipwreck, beatings, and jail in its service. Peter, who had more to be ashamed of than many of us, found the gospel the towering fact of his life, driving him to a missionary vocation leading finally to death, so it is said, on a cross, upside down.

So I say to you this morning, the courage of the gospel is something of which we can never be ashamed. It sustains people through loss and grief.

I am not ashamed of a gospel proclaiming and practicing the mutuality of our humanity and our common destiny as children of God in the face of xenophobia, racism, homophobia, culture wars, virulent nationalism, and social injustice; a gospel compelling men and women to go to jail for the cause of peace; a gospel abhorring the sickness of our cities not less so than the sickness in our hearts. I am not ashamed of a gospel with the courage to require much of those who possess much, of a gospel enabling us to love others more than life itself.

So we close with this confession, and I pray you can share it.

I am not ashamed of faith in gospel.

I am not ashamed of a gospel that shows me who I really am, and how God, as Paul Claudel remarked, "can write straight with crooked lines."

I am not ashamed of the courage of the gospel. Yea, "I am not ashamed of the Gospel of Jesus Christ, for it is the power unto salvation for those who have faith."—James W. Crawford

SUNDAY, JULY 24, 2005
Lectionary Message

Topic: All Good Things
TEXT: Rom. 8:26–39
Other Readings: Gen. 29:15–28; Ps. 105:1–11, 45b; Matt.13:31–33, 44–52

Our sermon is a reconsideration of what may be the most misquoted idea in the New Testament—misquoted because it makes too much of too little. I first memorized these words from the King James Version: "And we know that all things work together for good." Those ten words are a needlepoint saying crocheted and mounted in a frame in many homes.

"All things work together for good" is as quotable as John 3:16 and Genesis 1:1. "Yessir, I broke my leg on the first day of harvest but then we all know how 'all good things work together for good,'" etc.

It's the theme of the dedicated optimist as well as the subjective lament of a victim of a tragedy. It's the conclusion of people who suffered hardship and fought their way back to happiness. "All things work together for good!" But we misquote when we isolate the saying from the rest of its sentence: "to them that *love God,* to them who are *the called* according to his purpose."

Realists understand from observing history that not everything works out for the good. What good came from the assassination of four presidents: Abraham Lincoln, James Garfield, William McKinley, and John Kennedy? What good came from the Holocaust? What good came from the Black Death which snuffed out three hundred million Europeans in three hundred years? What good came from my little sister contracting rheumatic fever?

So we're to read it this way: "In *all things God works* for the good of those who love him, who have been called according to his purpose." It's not God making everything work out just for me and my good. It is God working out all things for the good of his chosen people. Our text uncovers three important truths about God.

I. *God works through history.* The NIV reads, "And we know that *in all things God works for the good* of those who love him, who have been called according to his purpose." God brought about a cosmic good from all things, both good and bad, that ever happened.

Romans 8:28 is the conclusion of the first eight chapters of the Book of Romans. Paul insists only God could accomplish anything good from our tragic history. From the first chapter he reminded readers how God made the world, but the creation worshiped the creature rather than the Creator. God's wrath was then expressed by permission to sin, and those who sinned had to die. God later gave the Law which increased sin and guaranteed judgment. But finally God intervened by sending Jesus Christ, who atoned for the sins of all. By the Holy Spirit we live under a new spiritual jurisdiction. Ultimately Christ's atonement will result in resurrection and life.

Earlier in Romans he explained in detail how God foreknew and predestined a people, called them, justified them, loved and glorified them. Only God could work out all the mess of human history to a good ending.

Along the way God provided some object lessons to help us. Take, for example, Joseph, who went from a pampered son of Jacob to an Egyptian convict to being Pharaoh's right hand man. Joseph's story was the human dilemma in miniature. Creation had it all, lost all, and God made it right in the end. For another object lesson, read the Book of Esther.

While traveling in the mountains of Tennessee, I visited a church and was invited to lunch by the pastor. After our meal we toured the beautiful little mountain town and he told me a strange story. Not many years before, a block or two from town center, a truck backed into a huge propane tank and ruptured it, releasing a deadly, explosive cloud. The powerful white mass grew until a spark set it off, an enormous blast. The school bus barn next door, with all the buses, was destroyed; several mobile homes on a sales lot nearby. Every window in the business district was shattered. The Christian church and the Baptist church were heavily damaged. It was like a bomb in the worst place possible.

But no one was killed or seriously injured. The school district received a new barn and a new fleet of buses. The trailer lot was restored. The churches were repaired and the downtown shopping district sported a bright, modern facelift. The pastor rubbed his chin and observed, "All in all, it was the best thing that ever happened to this town!" (I didn't say it but I thought, *not for the insurance companies.*)

We hear these true stories and marvel that they have a happy ending. Paul writes a happy ending for all those who love God, and we gain some theological insights here.

First, there are forces against us. "Who shall separate us from the love of Christ? Shall trouble or hardship or persecution or famine or nakedness or danger or sword? As it is written: For your sake we face death all day long; we are considered as sheep to be slaughtered."

Second, evil is at work and its business is to create tragedy, death, illness, and disappointment. Part of our world is only happy if it can make the rest of us miserable. Every idea that benefits society is countered by one that corrupts it. For example, the Internet was a wonderful idea, but it's corrupted by pornography and viruses.

Third, some people suffer while others do not. Pessimists say, "Saints always suffer while scoundrels rarely sneeze." But God doesn't work out all things in this life. Creation is moving toward a moment when God will have the final word. Our text uncovers the truth of God working through history, and it is this:

II. *God is for us.* My home town had only one radio station, WLBH, and we were faithful listeners. Every day "the man on the street" was featured. A large microphone was dangled by its cord from the second story studio to the announcer standing on Broadway. He interviewed passers-by with his question of the day. He had a knack for choosing some genuine characters. I would love his job. What would be my question today? How about, "What does God really think of us?"

Some insist there is no God, so God doesn't think. Others accept there is a God, but the Divine lost interest in us after creation. Many see God like a great stone face out in the darkness, hoping to catch us in our mistakes. A few might regard God as an ocean, and we're drowning in the stormy waves. How do you believe God thinks of us? Fools? Sinners? Failures? Worthless? My favorites?

Paul wrote, "What, then, shall we say in response to this? If God is for us, who can be against us?"

A psalmist sang, "Many, O LORD my God, are the wonders you have done. The things you planned for us no one can recount to you; were I to speak and tell of them, they would be too many to declare" (Ps. 40:5).

Think of God like a soccer mom, paying the fees, buying a uniform and equipment, driving the kids to the game, and then standing on the sidelines cheering for her offspring. Especially if the kid makes a mistake. Of all the people in the crowd, Mom's on my side.

If you gain anything from our passage from Romans, have the confidence that God is for you, cheers for you, tends your wounds, protects your back, and loves you without reservation. God works through history, God is for us, and:

III. *God is not yet finished.* I like Bible stories with no ending because I can imagine my own. The rich, young ruler changes his mind, gives away everything, and follows Jesus. Pontius Pilate retires from politics, becomes a believer, and starts a church. The Samaritan woman at the well? She overcomes her bad reputation and starts a home for orphans. My stories have happy endings.

Paul looks into the future in chapter 11 and promises, some day, the gospel will finally bring the Jews to faith in Christ. He prophesied, "And so all Israel will be saved" (Rom. 11:26). That's a happy ending.

He also predicted, "For I am convinced that neither death nor life, neither angels nor demons, neither the present nor the future, nor any powers, neither height nor depth, nor anything else in all creation, will be able to separate us from the love of God that is in Christ Jesus our Lord" (Rom. 8:38–39).

Your homework this week is to remember the three truths (God works through history, is for us, and is not yet finished) and look for object lessons, like Joseph, which illustrate them. Share your discoveries with me when next we meet.

Also, when you remember this sermon, realize we didn't try to exhaust the text. We plugged it like a watermelon and withdrew a succulent idea: "In *all things God works* for the good of those who love him, who have been called according to his purpose." All good things are ours because God, who is for us, is working through history, and isn't finished with us yet.—David Beavers

ILLUSTRATION

TESTIMONY.   As many of you know, I was born and raised in this wonderful church. When I was eleven, I made my profession of faith and was baptized. About two years ago, my mother had many complications with her ulcerative colitis. For many months, she was in and out of many hospitals and having multiple surgeries. On December 17, 2001, we took my mom to the hospital, where she nearly passed away during the middle of the night. I have never seen that much pain in my entire life and I couldn't bear to watch my mom suffer. Fortunately, she came out of emergency surgery and recovered. It is a blessing that she is with us today, but at that time my faith started to diminish. I doubted my faith and my God. I suddenly realized God works in many different ways. This time he worked through the people of this church. Through those many months of struggle you stood by our side, supporting us. On Sunday, we preached about circles within a church. Today, I believe that this church has formed a circle. You, my church family, restored my faith when I was lost; you prayed for a person in need, you supported my family when we were weak, and you comforted us when we were afraid. This, the church family, has taught me a valuable lesson: love and care for those around you, no matter what, and the power of Christ will be shown through your eyes into those who need it. I challenge all of you to continue that circle and uplift those around you, because the power of the church family is a great and powerful thing.——Stephen Lin

SERMON SUGGESTIONS

Topic: When God Began to Create
TEXT: Gen. 1:1–5
(1) He had a purpose. (2) He met an obstacle. (3) He conquered the chaos and darkness.

Topic: Signs of the Spirit's Presence
TEXT: Acts 19:1–17
(1) Vital knowledge. (2) Valid baptism. (3) Variety of testimony.

WORSHIP AIDS

CALL TO WORSHIP.   "O send out thy light and thy truth: let them lead me; let them bring me unto thy holy hill, and to thy tabernacles. Then will I go unto the altar of God, unto God my exceeding joy" (Ps. 43:3–4a).

INVOCATION.   Eternal God, out of the noisy world and the strife of tongues we come to this quiet place to worship thee. Far from us thou never art, but by the insensitiveness of our own hearts we keep thee distant. In this hour of opportunity grant us the grace of receptiveness that into responsive souls we may welcome thee.—Harry Emerson Fosdick

OFFERTORY SENTENCE.   "There is neither Jew nor Greek, there is neither bond nor free, there is neither male nor female: for ye are all one in Christ Jesus" (Gal. 3:28).

OFFERTORY PRAYER.   Almighty god, Creator of all people, Father of people of every race and nation and color, grant that our love may know no artificial bounds and barriers in our stewardship. Forgive us our smallness of mind, our pinched and selfish hearts, our bloated opinions of ourselves and our kind, and give us the graciousness that belongs to Christ and all who truly love him and obey him.

PRAYER.   Almighty God: in whose goodness we have been created, in whose love we have been redeemed, in whose presence we worship, and in whose name we pray, as with the psalmist and all creation, we praise your holy name.

We enter to worship, O God, having been pushed to and back by the ways of the world and the events of the week. We come bruised and shaken by hard and crushing blows; we come encouraged and made glad by new expressions of hope and possibility. We come weary and tired, worn by the roundness of routine and sameness. We come expectantly and receptively, open to your grace and power. We come defeated and cynical, jaded by repeated failures and dreams gone bad. But we are here, O God, and we want to truly be your people.

Accepting God of forgiveness and fresh start: like Jesus we have been tempted at all levels; unlike Jesus we have given in and sinned and need your pardon. Accept our confession as we receive your forgiveness.

Lord of giving and goodness: with forgiveness warm in our hearts, we become persons of gratitude. We give thanks, O God, for simple things: for a cup of ice on a hot day, for squirrels playing on the church lawn, for a day with no fever, for courage to live in the face of death; for a step with no pain, for children who came to Bible school as strangers and leave as friends; for nameless parents who lend and entrust their children to our safekeeping and gentle nurturing, for teachers who give generously of heart and spirit and mind to tell of your love and pass on the faith; for the delightful sights and sounds of Bible school, for your love that will not let us go.

Lord of life, be thou our vision and hearing and speaking this day as we worship and serve thee.—William M. Johnson

SERMON
Topic: "So You Want to Be a Christian?"
TEXT: Luke 14:25–33

Do we church people really know what we are in for? Do we have any idea what we have taken on? I ask these questions because the answer might help us to get our bearings, discover what we are really all about. These questions confront us year in and year out.

The question comes, as Luke put it, from Jesus himself. Remember the passage we read just a moment ago? Luke sets his narrative amid what we might consider an enthusiastic religious revival. Word of our Lord's ministry spread like wildfire. Wherever Jesus went, he drew crowds: a cross-section of society—zealous patriots, crippled bodies, parched souls, the curious, the trendy, the skeptics, some hangers-on, some wishful thinkers. You see, Jesus changes people. Confused lives become integrated; wasted lives were salvaged; defeated lives set again toward radiant, victorious living. Rumors spread about a prophet finally arriving who would pry freedom from Roman tyranny, lay the religious traditions. A bandwagon for Jesus started to roll.

But what do we see in this narrative? We see Jesus leading this clamoring, fervent mob toward Jerusalem. Suddenly he turns, stops them in their tracks, pauses: "Do you know what you are doing?" he asks. "Do you know what it means to hook on to my cause? Do you know where you are headed? Have you any idea what this campaign will cost you? I'll tell you. Following me will force rough choices. You will face terrible conflict. To build the world as Love would have it may put your closest personal relationships on the line. To surrender yourself to the sovereignty of Jesus Christ may risk ties as close as those of father and mother, of spouse and children, and yes, even one's own death. To follow me means a reorientation of loyalties, a new configuration of priorities, a new definition of first things first. Have you counted the cost? Do you know what it takes? Which of you desiring to build a tower does not first calculate the cost in order to ensure your finishing the job? A hole in the ground with a partially built foundation and no superstructure is a sad and shabby wreck, a joke and mockery. If you're not ready for the risks of the gospel, your discipleship could turn into a laughingstock. Or which of you, setting out for a battle, knowing that your enemy comes at you with twice as many troops and threatens to wipe you out, how many of you will not measure the risk and sue for peace before the massacre begins?"

"So you want to be a Christian? Better not start if you are not ready for the challenge; better quit now if you can't see through to the finish."

I have to tell you, a passage like this really shakes me up. It reminds me again that we discover at the heart of the New Testament the story of one whose efforts at showing us what our life together could be like and what it would take got him nothing but the contempt of the religious establishment and the resistance of the political regime. The mission of Jesus got him a cross.

And I think that is what it got Luke's church, too: crucifixion. That is why Luke includes this vivid imagery in his Gospel. Luke's church, fifty years after Jesus' death, instead of finding itself an evangelical marvel, successful and growing, finds itself under siege. To become a member of Luke's church, instead of garnering public respect and a sound bite on television, leads to rejection, to persecution, to the lions in the coliseum. Luke's little community finds itself ostracized because it believes cultural, religious, and ethnic antagonists—in Luke's time, Jew and Gentile—could make it together in one body. Luke's community finds itself under governmental suspicion, if not investigation and arrest, because it refuses to pay its ultimate allegiance to Caesar and his empire and instead confesses Jesus Christ and the world he envisions as their ultimate loyalty. It finds itself struggling with the terrible reality of families wounded or broken because some family members decide they will climb on board the Jesus movement and as a consequence their families simply disown them.

You see, Luke describes the circumstance in his own church. When people join it they have to make tough choices. And because the risks of discipleship and its costs are so high a lot of folk, after their initial enthusiasm, drop by the wayside. Remembering Jesus' images, Luke compares the dropouts to pathetic, crumbling, unfinished towers; he says they appear like generals stupidly going into a major battle leading a tiny contingent of ragtag troops unprepared for the rigor of battle, ready only for the slaughter.

Do you see why this passage shakes me up? I feel it may be aimed directly at us. Surely the point is clear: churches and ministers are past masters at covering up the cost of discipleship. We know the cost Jesus paid. We know he offers us opportunity no less risky, dangerous, and demanding.

Can we build the tower? Can we fight the battle? We have children who know nothing of the gospel, whose steady diet is television junk, sitcom trash, cinema violence, and we provide a church school for them one hour a week. You don't think we've got a battle on our hands?

In this suffering world, where children starve; women suffer untold humiliation, abuse, and violence; where social inequity proliferates; where vengeance seems to rule the nations, can we in the churches move the world with a social gospel, ourselves prepared like a general deploying his army for the ongoing struggle of justice and reconciliation? And yes, friends, as we augment our tower's foundation, as we gather our troops, will we make the individual financial investments worthy of ourselves and of a high commitment to the one who put his death on the line for us? Will we be a laughingstock, or soldiers of the cross?

So then, it is great to see you in church. I am glad you are here. Is it because we want to be Christians? I hope so. But, careful. We don't want to be tower builders who start and then abandon a barren hole in the ground and get laughed out of town. We don't want to be monarchies underestimating the devastating power of the enemy, overrun before we can lift a finger, forced feebly to surrender to the enemy. So let's take a good look at the promise and the peril of discipline, and God grant we see it with courage and joy to the end!—James W. Crawford

SUNDAY, JULY 31, 2005

Lectionary Message

Topic: "Seeing God and Living to Tell About It"

TEXT: Gen. 32:22–31

Other Readings: Ps. 17:1–7, 15; Rom. 9:1–5; Matt. 14:13–21

A: APPROACH

I'm not proud of it, but I lost track of my sister for almost twenty years. The family gathered for my mother's funeral, my sister and I returned home, each of us moved two or three times. You know how it happens.

There was no animosity between us, but neither knew where the other was. I tried to locate her through relatives and the Internet but didn't know if she was alive or dead. She was on my prayer list, though, and I began to pray to hear from her. Perhaps I should have prayed for it earlier because her son called me early one morning; then she was on the line and the years fell away. We live three thousand miles apart, and we planned for a reunion next Spring. This leads us into the Bible text for today.

B: BIBLE

Read Genesis 32:22–32. The twin brothers were separated for two decades because of trickery and deceit. Jacob cheated and stole from Esau, his twin brother, and they will meet tomorrow. What will happen?

I don't like Jacob very much at this point. He is a conniving little thief who lives by his wits and deception. His name means "Tripster." Esau has every reason to be suspicious of Tricky Jake, even after twenty years, and to tell the truth, I'm on his side. But God favored Jacob over Esau for a reason.

Jacob was on his way to a family reunion, no mother Rebekah to protect him this time. No father Isaac to negotiate for him. He sent his two wives and dozen kids and everything he owned on ahead to meet Esau. And that night, all alone, he wrestled for his life.

Some commentators insist the wrestling match was nothing but a dream. Was it a nightmare? Who was "the man," his opponent? If a dream, maybe Jacob wrestled with himself, or his brother Esau. If it was no more than a dream, why was Jacob crippled by it the next day?

Jacob said he wrested with God. We refer to it as a "theophany," or manifestation of God by actual appearance. Some early scholars insisted Jacob wrestled with Christ himself, a "Christophany." Jacob struggled with God, in some form. They saw, heard, spoke, and touched each other. A common belief of the ancients was that if you see God you will die. Jacob was amazed he lived through it.

Moses, who wrote this story, shared a similar experience on Mt. Sinai when he heard the voice of God from a burning bush: "I am the God of your father, the God of Abraham, the God of Isaac and the God of Jacob." At this, Moses hid his face, because *he was afraid to look at God*" (Exod. 3:6). Moses, like Jacob, asked to know His Name and saw God. Jacob and Moses were two people who could say, "I saw God and lived to tell about it."

The next day Jacob limped away from his encounter with God to an encounter with his brother, Esau. He was a different man though, with a new name, Israel. Israel means "wrestles with God." He walked away with a blessing: a great nation descended from him, the Israelites.

The brothers met in peace and were reconciled. Jacob brought rich gifts for his twin. "But Esau said, 'I already have plenty, my brother. Keep what you have for yourself.' 'No, please!' said Jacob. 'If I have found favor in your eyes, accept this gift from me. For to see your face is *like seeing the face of God*, now that you have received me favorably'" (Gen. 33:9–10).

Once he saw God he recognized the Divine in other ways. What are we to make of this story? Why did Moses tell it? The Bible story leads us to some conclusions.

C: CONCLUSIONS

First, *wrestling with God was always a problem for Israel*, the man and the nation. The New Testament lesson for today is Romans 9:1–5:

> I speak the truth in Christ—I am not lying, my conscience confirms it in the Holy Spirit—I have great sorrow and unceasing anguish in my heart. For I could wish that I myself were cursed and cut off from Christ for the sake of my brothers, those of my own race, the people of Israel. Theirs is the adoption as sons; theirs the divine glory, the covenants, the receiving of the law, the temple worship and the promises. Theirs are the patriarchs, and from them is traced the human ancestry of Christ, who is God over all, forever praised! Amen.

Christianity began with the Israelites, who carried it to the nations. It was a struggle for them because the Mosaic system was almost part of their genetic code. Even when the Jerusalem temple was erased and the Jewish people were scattered everywhere, still they wrestled with God, clinging to the old law, hoping for a Messiah.

Romans, chapters 9 through 11, is not anti-Jewish. It's a loving concern for Israel with a promise that God isn't finished with them. Yet, Israel wrestles with God.

Second, *wrestling with God is the universal human condition*. Researcher Thomas Reeves reported nine of ten Americans have never doubted the existence of God; they pray and believe God loves them. However, they believe truth is relative and "religious authority" lies in the believer, not the Bible or church. George Gallup discovered 44 percent of Americans are unchurched. Cyberfaith is only warming up, whereby fifty million people rely solely on the Internet for their faith-based experiences. People of faith are wrestling with God!

Then there are those without any faith. Pagan religions. Atheists. The unreached. Those who live in the mainstream of life, rejecting any religious influences that might change them. They wrestle with God who loves them! So we must conclude:

Third, *wrestling with God is my problem*. Can't we each admit this? Wretched me! What Christ wants of me I resist. What I don't want to do, I do. Thank God he wrestles with me to shape me into the person he wants me to be.

Something happened to Jacob that night by the Jabbok. He was given a better name and walked with a limp for the rest of his life, but he faced the new day as a changed man. I believe it was something of a conversion by which God took the rascal he was and redeemed him.

One of my fourth grade classmates was bigger and stronger than I, and we got into an angry wrestling match over something. It went on for what seemed an hour; neither of us won nor lost. We both tried and tried but finally quit from exhaustion. I was small and tough but I simply couldn't beat . . . her!

Wrestling with God is good for us. We can't pin God, but good comes from it. We're renewed, renamed, and rewarded. The conclusions provoke us to make some decisions.

D: DECISIONS

Decide to reconcile with someone who was once important to you but is now lost to you; a sibling, child, friend, or church member. Today's a good day for reconciliation. Like Jacob, send a gift in advance and quit wrestling with your pride, anger, or fear.

Decide to make the most of wrestling with God. It keeps you out of trouble. It demonstrates how God intervenes in your life. Jesus enjoyed contending with the disciples, and he still does.

Decide to look for the face of God during and after a difficult situation. Like Mary Magdalene at the garden tomb, "I have seen the Lord." And the disciples that Sunday night, "we have seen the Lord." And Paul on the Damascus road, you might exclaim, "I have seen the Lord!" This realization often occurs after a crisis. Expect it.

We close our sermon with the poetry of Job, another who wrestled with God. "Oh, that my words were recorded, that they were written on a scroll, that they were inscribed with an iron tool on lead, or engraved in rock forever! I know that my Redeemer lives, and that in the end he will stand upon the earth. And after my skin has been destroyed, yet in my flesh I will see God; I myself will see him with my own eyes—I, and not another. How my heart yearns within me! (Job 19:23–27).—David Beavers

SERMON SUGGESTIONS

Topic: The Urgency of Preaching

TEXT: John. 3:1–5, 10

(1) Seen in god's persistent call. (2) Seen in God's imminent righteous judgment. (3) Seen in god's compassionate deliverance.

Topic: Advice for a Time of Crisis

TEXT: 1 Cor. 7:29–35

(1) Devotion to our Lord is of first importance. (2) Unusual circumstances may dictate unusual ordering of our lives. (3) Each person must decide what is individually best for personal fulfillment, the common good, and the doing of God's will.

WORSHIP AIDS

CALL TO WORSHIP.   "The Lord is my strength and my shield; my heart trusted in him, and I am helped: therefore my heart greatly rejoiceth; and with my song will I praise him" (Ps. 28:7).

INVOCATION.   We praise you, O Lord, and rejoice and continue to look to you for your help. And we do this just now, even as we seek your Spirit to guide our worship.

OFFERTORY SENTENCE.   "Set your affection on things above, not on things on the earth" (Col. 3:2).

OFFERTORY PRAYER.   Because we love you, O Lord, we now bring to you these offerings. May our love for you never wane but grow more and more toward the perfect day. And may that love, translated into joyous stewardship, bring many to know our Savior.

PRAYER.   O God, thou art Life, Wisdom, Truth, Bounty, and Blessedness, the Eternal, the only true Good. Our God and our Lord, thou art our hope and our heart's joy. We confess, with thanksgiving, that thou hast made us in thine image, that we may direct all our thought to thee and love thee. Lord, make us to know thee aright, that we may more and more love and enjoy and possess thee. And since, in the life here below, we cannot fully attain this blessedness, let it at least grow in us day by day, until it all be fulfilled at last in the life to come. Here by the knowledge of thee increased, and there let it be perfected. Here let our love to thee grow, and there let it ripen; that our joy being here great in hope, may there in fruition be made perfect.—Adapted from St. Anselm

SERMON
Topic: Philadelphia, Brother Love
TEXT: Gen. 50:15–21

Nothing sells like a good family feud. They are mirrors to the little bumps and bruises that most of us carry around in our memories. Family tension is basic to the popularity of the parable of Jesus about the prodigal son, the forgiving father, and the resentful elder brother. I suspect that sibling conflict is a big part of our fascination with the entire story of Israel. We are often reminded these days that the Mideast conflict, now in global proportions, began with resentment in Abraham's household between Sarah and Hagar, projected onto their sons Ishmael and Isaac. The family feud continued in subsequent generations. The story of Joseph and his brothers reflects something of the family competition between their father, Jacob/Israel, and their uncle Esau. The story of family in Jewish life is a strange love-hate relationship. There is no existence without family. One's essential identity is wrapped up in the family system. To be cut off from family was to be cut off from life. Yet the family story is always the story of struggle, not only with the threat from outside but from the threat within. Real families at the root of the biblical story are works in progress, with at least as much reason for embarrassment as for pride. You have to keep in sight that the story of Joseph is the family scandal behind the Twelve Tribes of Israel.

Joseph is the favorite son of Israel. To be fair, much of the tension between brothers is created by the father's favoritism as well as by Joseph's childish arrogance. The angry resentment of the older brothers is not improved by the prized coat given by father Israel to Joseph, or by the act of sending the son, perceived as a child of leisure, to check on the work of his brothers. The brothers act out their anger first by a plot to reenact the Cain and Abel story of brother killing brother. Finally they agree to sell the boy into slavery to allow fate to take its course. They lie to their father about the death of their brother and then carry the guilt of their secret into their own families. Joseph, the dreamer of dreams and interpreter of dreams, ends up in Egypt. Through his wonderful insight into dreams, he rises to a high government office in the court of the pharaoh. A drought brings the brothers to Egypt to beg for food, and the tables are turned. Now in the place of complete control and the power of life and death, Joseph weeps at the sight of his younger brother Benjamin and plays games of cat and mouse with the other brothers. Finally Joseph reveals his identity, and the entire family is moved to Egypt.

The continued tension between Joseph and his brothers becomes evident at the death of Israel. Assuming that Joseph will get his revenge after the death of their father, the brothers plead for mercy and offer themselves as servants to Joseph. The sibling bond proves greater than the family secret, and the book of Genesis ends in *philadelphia*—not the city, but the brother love for which the city was named. I would like to say that they all lived happily ever after, but the saga of the family continues with new scandals requiring constant grace.

Grace flows out of the providence of God. The Joseph story is lauded as the best literary product of Genesis, far above the other stories of the Patriarchs. Edwin Good calls the story "the irony of Providence." Joseph finds in the evil deeds of his brothers both the means to save his family and the fulfillment of the will of God. All along, Joseph is portrayed as a dreamer. He seems to live in a fantasy world of his own imagination, yet his vision of the direction of history and the ways of God is far superior to the surface evidence available to the naked eye. Joseph's gift of insight into the meaning of history and the purpose of God leads to compassion toward his brothers. Joseph knows better than anyone else that God has a future for this family. The bond of love must rise above the desire for revenge. Justice is served through forgiveness rather than punishment of the brothers. In the end, we get this glimpse of the gospel in the Old Testament because Joseph is able to see the providence of God at Work even in the evil done to him.

In *The Different Drum,* M. Scott Peck claims Maundy Thursday as the most important day of the Christian calendar. He passes on Easter and Christmas in favor of the revolution in relationship that occurred when Jesus washed the feet of his disciples and gave new meaning to the bread and the cup of the Passover. "Here this man already on top—who was rabbi, teacher, master—suddenly got down on the bottom and began to wash the feet of his followers. In that one act Jesus symbolically overturned the whole social order." Then Peck cites Keith Miller's book *The Secret Love* to note that the successful evangelism of the early church was not in miracles performed or the great organizational ability of the institutional church. The pagan world was attracted to a community of inordinate compassion and love for one another. The world followed the scent of love, into the gospel of Christ.—Larry Dipboye

SUNDAY, AUGUST 7, 2005

Lectionary Message

Topic: Lessons Learned at the Feet of Deity

Text: Matt. 14:22–33

Other Readings: Gen. 37:1–4, 12–28; Ps. 105:1–6, 16–22, 45b; Rom. 10:5–15

When one is in the presence of deity, one can never be certain about what is going to happen. God is often in the business of doing the unexpected and the unusual. Just when you think you have him figured out, he surprises you and takes things in a direction that stuns and amazes. Sometimes you walk away, scratching your head, asking, "What just happened?" Other times you are driven to your knees in awe and worship because of the lessons you just learned at the feet of deity.

This is exactly what happened to the disciples after Jesus fed the five thousand and then took an early morning walk *on* the Sea of Galilee. They learned some very valuable lessons at the feet of deity, at the feet of the Son of God.

I. *Learn from Jesus the importance of solitude (vv. 22–23).* Jesus has performed one of his greatest miracles, the feeding of five thousand men.

This is the only miracle, besides the Resurrection, recorded in all four Gospels. All told, the number must have been close to twenty thousand! John 6:16 provides a valuable insight: because of this miracle "they were about to come and take him by force and make him King." What an opportunity! What a decision. The time is right. He is their man. He is the Messiah, God's Son. God said so himself (Matt. 3:17). What an opportunity to bring in the Kingdom and avoid the cross. What will he do? What would you do?

(a) *Take time to pray. Immediately* he sent the disciples away and on ahead. *Made* is a strong word, meaning to compel or urge. Perhaps they were caught up in the fervor of the crowd. He also sent the crowds away. What would he do now? Verse 23 tells us: "He went up on the mountain to pray." The crowd wanted to make him king. He wanted to talk to his Father. Satan was again tempting him (cf. Luke 4:13) to take the easy and popular route to the Kingdom (cf. Matt. 4:8–9). Jesus determined to seek the face of his Father and the place of prayer.

(b) *Find a place of privacy.* Verse 23: "He went up . . . by himself to pray" and "He was alone there." Prayer is best done where you will not be distracted or disturbed, where you can give your full attention to talking and listening to your heavenly Father.

All of us face times of opportunity and crisis. Crucial and important decisions have to be made. What will you do? Jesus teaches us to find a place of solitude, a place of prayer and a place of privacy.

II. *Learn from Peter the essence of salvation (14:24–31).* The text indicates that the disciples were to go on ahead of Jesus until he was free from the crowds; he would then join them, but after he had spent some time alone in prayer. However, his prayer time went on much longer than anticipated. The disciples apparently decided not to wait any longer and started across the lake on their own. This would be another occasion for them to learn a lesson at the feet of deity.

(a) *Keep your focus on Jesus.* We suddenly find the disciples in the middle of the sea (many furlongs from the shore). The waves are tossing the boat, torturing it, tormenting it, harassing it! The disciples were in serious trouble and they knew it. In the midst of the storm, the Savior suddenly appears. Following Roman time it was the fourth watch, somewhere between 3:00 and 6:00 A.M. For a brief moment the disciples fall into an error that afflicts so many. They fail to see Jesus for who he really is. The text says they were troubled, fearful, and screaming. We really can't blame them. They needed to get their focus. Jesus is not a ghost, a phantom (the Greek word is *phantasma*). Nor is he some fictional creation or ancient fable. No! He is God in the flesh who walks on the land or the waves of the sea with equal ease.

Seeing their fear, Jesus speaks to them: "Be of good cheer!" (present imperative) "Take courage. It is I." (the Greek *ego eimi*) "I am! Do not be afraid." (the Greek *me,* negation, with the present imperative) "Stop being afraid." The *I am* statement is bracketed with imperatives for emphasis and to highlight it as the reason for his words of encouragement. Echoes of Exodus 3:14 linger in the background. He does not explain *where* he has been, *why* he is there, or *how* he got there. What was important was he was there and he spoke words of encouragement. He will do the same for you! Keep your *focus* on Jesus. He will be there when you need him.

(b) *Keep your faith in Jesus.* Peter knows this voice, and it is a voice he can trust. Emboldened by his Lord's presence, Peters acts with great courage and asks the Lord, "Command me to come to you *on the water.*"

Our Lord, as he always does, honors Peter's faith. He commands him, "Come."

Peter then does what no normal human being has ever done before or since: he walks on the water. What courage! What faith! But it is only for a moment. Suddenly, and we don't know why, *he took his eyes off Jesus.* Suddenly the storm had his attention more than the Savior. Fear gripped his heart, his eyes were on the storm, and he began to sink; the Savior is so near, yet death is beginning to engulf him. Down, down, down he goes.

Peter turned to his only hope, our only hope. He turned to Jesus and cried, "Lord, save me." Peter must have been close. Jesus simply stretched out his hand and caught him. Still a valuable lesson was in the offering as Jesus kindly chided him, "O you of little faith, why did you doubt?" Why? He forgot two important lessons that are the essence of salvation: Keep your focus on Jesus, and keep your faith in Jesus.

Only he can keep you from sinking into the stormy waves of sin and trouble that can destroy you.

III. *Learn from the disciples our response to the Savior (vv. 14:22–23).* When one is in the presence of deity, the supernatural, the unexpected is to be expected. And yet, an important question naturally presents itself: What will be our response? The disciples teach us two important lessons.

(a) Only Jesus is worthy of our worship. Jesus steps into the boat and the storm stops. But the stilling of the storm is not the climax of the story. It is the disciples' response. Who is this who can walk on water? Calm the sea? Feed twenty thousand? He must be God, for only God is worthy of our worship. The disciples' response is entirely appropriate. They came, fell down, and worshipped him.

(b) Only Jesus is worthy of our confession. The disciples spoke as they worshipped, "Truly you are the Son of God." Exactly what they meant by this at this time we can't be sure. The Gospels are quite clear and honest in their depiction of the disciples. They understood in degrees; theirs was a growing understanding of who Jesus was that would reach full fruition only after the Resurrection. Still, even now they knew this one is different than anyone we have ever known before. He has a relationship with God like no other. He must be God's Son. Only later would they understand the full impact of their confession, but already they were headed in the right direction.

IV. *Conclusion.* There is a wonderful song in some of our hymnals. I can't be certain, but it sounds like the writer was reflecting on this passage of Scripture when he penned these words.

Stanza One
I was sinking deep in sin, far from the peaceful shore.
Very deeply stained within, sinking to rise no more.
But the Master of the sea heard my despairing cry.
From the waters lifted to me, now safe am I.

Stanza Two
Souls in danger look above, Jesus completely saves.
He will lift you by His love, out of the angry waves.
He's the Master of the sea, billows His will obey.
He your Savior wants to be, be saved today.

Chorus
Love (the Son!) lifted me! Love lifted me!
When nothing else could help, Love (the Son!) lifted me.
Love lifted me! Love lifted me!
When nothing else could help, Love lifted me.

When Peter was sinking in the depths of the sea, he cried to the Lord and was saved. If you are sinking in the depths of sin, cry to the Lord and he will save you.—Daniel L. Akin

SERMON SUGGESTIONS

Topic: Who Speaks for God?
TEXT: Deut. 18:15–20
(1) Not the pagan diviners (see 18:9–14). (2) Rather, only those who faithfully pass on the very will and Word of God.

Topic: This Liberty of Yours
TEXT: 1 Cor. 8:1–13
(1) Can deliver you from superstitions, and that is commendable. (2) Can puff you up with pride, and that is dangerous. (3) Can cause a weaker Christian to stumble, and that is unthinkable.

WORSHIP AIDS
CALL TO WORSHIP.   "He that hath an ear, let him hear what the Spirit saith unto the churches" (Rev. 2:29).

INVOCATION.   Speak now to us, O God. Tell us again of thy loving judgment, which ferrets out the wrong in our lives, to make life better and happier for us all. Tell us again of thy judging love, which brings to life again the dying embers of neglected faith, to give new purpose and drive to our futile wanderings. And may we carefully listen as thou dost speak to us.

OFFERTORY SENTENCE.   "Bring ye all the tithes into the storehouse, that there may be meat in mine house, and prove me now herewith, saith the Lord of hosts, if I will not open you the windows of heaven, and pour you out a blessing, that there shall not be room enough to receive it" (Mal. 3:10).

OFFERTORY PRAYER.   Almighty and most benevolent heavenly Father, bless the giving of these gifts as a symbol of our renewed dedication to thy service. Consecrate our resolve to respond more readily to the leading of thy Holy Spirit, that we may live lives of greater devotion and more fruitful service.—Rodney K. Miller

PRAYER.   Almighty God, in whom alone we live, we turn in all our need to thee, the fountain of our life. Thou hast made all things dependent upon thee for their existence, and thou hast made our hearts so that they fail without the inspiration of thy presence. Forgive us if, knowing this, we have been careless about that which should be our chief concern, if we have taken no pains to establish a life of communion with thee, if we have not hungered and thirsted after righteousness. We have been slack in prayer, careless in living, until we have found glory departing from the earth and thy rest from our hearts. We thank thee that thou dost never withdraw thyself from us without our knowing that the Spirit of God has departed. Thou makest us quickly to cry after thee. O visit us early with thy mercy, satisfy us with thy self, for thou art our God. Bind us to thee with the bond of an endless love. Find us in the wilderness, lead us to where fountains of living waters flow, shepherd us where flowers everbloom. Bring us in sight, most gracious One, of the cross, at once life's mystery and life's healing. And may our foolish wandering and false self-worship come to an end this day. Hold us, for thou art stronger than we. Forgive us, for thou art kinder than we dare to be.—W. E. Orchard

SERMON
Topic: Jesus Prayed for This
TEXT: John 17:1–11, 20–21

We have had the high privilege this morning of listening to one of the greatest prayers in all history. Indeed, we have listened in on "the Lord's prayer." As important as it is—and its importance is too great to be exaggerated—it is given to the disciples and later followers of Christ so that we might have a pattern for prayer. We do need a model for the kind of communication that flows between ourselves and God—prayer. So in the most succinct style, Jesus taught his disciples to pray.

Yet, if there is anything in Scripture that deserves to be called the Lord's Prayer, it is this prayer contained in the seventeenth chapter of John. We hear about Jesus praying all through the Gospels. When there is a big decision to be made, Jesus prays. When the press of the crowd is too much, he goes apart to a quiet place and he prays. But we are not usually privy to the words that Jesus prays. So here in John's Gospel there must be some great significance for us, because we are allowed to hear this prayer. What a prayer it is. He prayed that his glory would be fulfilling God's will and that God's glory would be giving him strength to continue to be obedient throughout. Then in verses 9 through 19, Jesus prays for his immediate followers, the disciples.

Yes, they were a ragtag group that fell down, that sometimes denied, that sometimes didn't believe; but these would receive the power to turn the world upside down. Jesus prays for them. Jesus prays for us. Jesus prays for you and me.

This is the prayer of his life. *He prays that we might be one.* Can this be the most important thing in the world? He says that if we truly begin to look, act, and behave as one, the world around us will believe.

Do you begin to glimpse the miracle of being one? Not of trying to look, act, and behave as if we are all cut out with a giant cookie cutter. Rather that we are one because we are one in Christ. Jesus here says, "As my father and I are one" over and over again. In chapters 14, 15, 16, and now in the seventeenth chapter, it is clear that Jesus knows he can't do a thing without the power of the Father. He committed himself to knowing the Father well, so that God's work may be done.

Somewhere along the line we recognize a desire for what God created for us, a sense of value and purpose.

Sin, in part, is wanting to feel worthy and accepted but trying to find a short cut. So we learn how to do it at the expense of another. "You are out and I'm in." We do it in families, in churches, in communities. "You are a tongue speaker, so you are out. I'm not a tongue speaker, I'm in." "I'm a tongue speaker, I'm in, you're not, you are obviously out." When we run out of ways, we discover more ways.

What is the key for celebrating and accepting the great gift of creation and salvation that God has given us, while calling forth the uniqueness of those around us? Jesus died. He died to those prerogatives that would hold on to his claims. He was one in the Father, and now through the Holy Spirit that is promised, we are able to be one in him.

If you want a good commentary on this prayer, look up 1 Corinthians 12. It talks about the body as one organism. The hand can't say, "I'm tired of being a hand. You don't get nearly the credit being a hand you get in being a foot. I'm out of here." The more we discover that we are one in Christ, the more we discover the unique beauty of the other members of the body.

One of the great Bible words we can't fully translate from the Greek into English is usually rendered "patience." The idea behind the word is that God gives us the staying power when things are really tough.

It is more than recognizing other's gifts. It is even more than appreciating them. It's *needing* them.

The glorious good news is that Jesus prayed in and to the power of the spirit to make us one. Through that same spirit, we recognize, appreciate, and confess our need for all who are part of Christ's body. Can there be a greater witness to the truth of the gospel than being the answer to Jesus' prayer for unity?—Gary D. Stratman

SUNDAY, AUGUST 14, 2005
Lectionary Message
Topic: Will the Real You Please Stand Up?

TEXT: Matt. 15:10–20

Other Readings: Gen. 45:1–15; Ps. 133; Rom. 11:1–2a, 29–32; Matt. 15:21–28

We live in a world that gives a lot of attention to *the externals* of life. What kind of house do you live in? What kind of car do you drive? How much money do you make? What is your net worth?

Jesus would hear this and shake his head in disappointment. Why? Because Jesus knows what really matters is not the *externals* but the *internals*. Jesus knows that the real you is who you are on the inside.

Jesus was engaged in a sharp and heated conversation with the scribes (teachers) and the Pharisees (v. 1). The point of contention was ceremonially washing hands when you eat.

They were convinced that the truly spiritual would go through this ritual. Jesus used this as an occasion to rebuke them in very strong terms for placing their traditions above the clear commandments of God (vv. 3–6). In fact, He calls them hypocrites and says their hypocrisy was prophesied by Isaiah (Isa. 29:13, vv. 7–8). However, Jesus decides to press the issue because of its importance in defining what true spirituality is. He calls for the multitudes and makes clear who the "real you" really is. Jesus is emphatic that we understand that real faith and devotion to God is not a matter of religious form; it is a matter of the heart.

I. *The real you is who you are on the inside (15:10–14).* What is the essence of true spirituality and godliness? This is a conversation everyone needs to hear.

(a) *It is a matter of your heart (15:10–11).* Jesus calls the multitudes to listen in on the debate. He ushers forth a twofold command: "Hear" and "Understand" (imperative).

Defilement, or spiritual uncleanness, is a matter of the real you, the you who lives on the inside. Spiritual or moral pollution is not a matter of washing your hands or what you eat. No, what matters is what is in your heart, because what is in the heart will eventually come out of the mouth; what is on the inside will eventually come out, for all to see.

In 1 Samuel 16:7, the Lord says to Samuel as he begins his inspection of Jesse's sons, "Do not look at his appearance or at his physical stature. . . . For the Lord does not see as man sees; For man looks at the outward appearance, but the Lord looks at the heart."

(b) *It is a matter of your father (15:12–13).* The disciples evidently were taken aback by what Jesus said. The Pharisees certainly were. The text says they were offended (the Greek for *scandalized* is used) by what he said. Had they heard him correctly? Jesus assures them that they had and provides an analogy to drive home the point. Those who major on the externals and ignore matters of the heart prove that God is not their heavenly (spiritual) Father. They will be uprooted, destroyed in judgment. In John 8:42–47, Jesus reminds us that we are either children of God or the children of the devil. There is no third category.

(c) *It is a matter of your eyes (15:14).* Jesus uses a second image or analogy: the folly of a blind man trying to lead others. Because they prided themselves on knowing and obeying the law, the scribes and Pharisees described themselves as "guides of the blind." Jesus denounces them in strong language and says the persons who are really blind are they. Let them alone (aorist imperative). They are "blind" (four times in this verse) and they will lead others with them into a ditch (in NIV, a pit) of destruction. They are blind, willfully blind.

II. *The real you will be revealed on the outside (15:15–20).* Peter, acting as spokesman, asks Jesus to explain the parable (v. 15). Jesus expresses shock, amazement, and perhaps grief at this question and asks, "Are you still without understanding? (NIV, "are you still so dull?") One has to wonder if there were times when Jesus felt like a total failure. Still, he presses on and provides for the disciples and for us important insight into what real and genuine spirituality is.

(a) *Pay great attention to the things that matter most (15:15–19).* After hearing Peter's question (v. 15) and expressing his disappointment (v. 16), Jesus explains further the main point he made in verse 11.

Steeped in religious legalism, formalism, and ritualism as taught by the religious leaders of their day, the disciples, as well as the common people, struggled to hear, see, and understand what real godliness and spirituality is. Jesus realizes this, and so he expands his explanation. Food goes in the mouth, into the stomach, is digested, and the waste eliminated ("is cast into the latrine or drain").

In contrast, some things do come up from within and out of the mouth that defile you, that pollute your life. Its source? The heart, the real you on the inside. Ceremonies, rituals, other external practices; baptism, giving, church attendance, these are not the things that prove you are God's child. Some people do all of these things and are lost. It may be hard to understand given our tendency to measure spirituality by the things we do, but the bottom line is, "What is the condition of your heart?"

From your heart will inevitably come out what is in it. Generally following the latter portion of the Ten Commandments, Jesus notes seven examples (his list is not exhaustive) that an evil heart will produce:

1. Evil thinking
2. Murders
3. Adulteries
4. Fornications
5. Thefts
6. False witnesses
7. Blasphemies

Jesus' point is simple. Guard your heart, for what a person truly is *will be seen* by what he says and does. If your heart is a toxic waste dump, rest assured it will leak out. It is corrosive and it will seep through the walls of your heart and out into the open for all to see.

(b) *Pay small attention to the things that matter a little (15:20).* The thing that defiles and corrupts a man or woman is not unwashed hands, but an unwashed heart. Should we give attention to matters of religion? Sure, and with a view to cultivating religious practices that honor God and help us grow in the grace and knowledge of the Lord Jesus Christ. Jesus said in Matt. 5:9, "Blessed are the pure in heart, for they shall see God." Jesus said in Luke 6:45, "A good man out of the good treasure of his heart brings forth good; and an evil man out of the evil treasure of his heart, brings forth evil." It really is a matter of the heart. Make certain yours is a heart that belongs to Jesus, for from it the real you will stand up.—Daniel Akin

ILLUSTRATIONS

HAPPINESS.   Does your happiness reside in your circumstances or in yourselves? Important as circumstances are, I insist that the fount of happiness must be from God in ourselves. As my ministry lengthens and widens, I can look back and remember being intimate with men and women in the most varied circumstances, and I say plainly that an adequate income, and a pleasant house, and kindly neighbors, and a decent job, cannot of themselves produce happiness. I have known men who possess them all, and yet were miserable.[1]

REVIVAL.   All our exits may become entrances. The human capacity to take whatever life dishes out and to come back is never to be underestimated. How amazing it is, knowing we are all going to die anyhow, that we are so determined to live as well as we can, no matter what. For all our little deaths, we defy our fate and come to life again and again, and yet again.

---

[1]W. E. Sangster, *Westminster Sermons, Vol. 2* (London: Epworth Press, 1961), p. 31.

Daily, we redeem ourselves in unspoken rituals of renewal. Daily, we get up and go to work in the construction business of building and repairing and remodeling a life.

The ritual of revival has many names: "born again" and "healing," or simply "getting our act together." Whatever the name, however large or small the act, the urge to reassemble the fragments of our lives into a whole is the same.[2]

SERMON SUGGESTIONS

Topic: In Combat with God

TEXT: Gen. 32:22–23

(1) Jacob's need: a sense of identity and purpose. (2) God's provision: a new name and purpose revealed in spiritual struggle.

Topic: What Your Baptism Means

TEXT: Rom. 6:9–11

(1) That you have died to sin and buried the old life. Has the old life lessened its grip on you? (2) That you have been raised with the living Christ and now "walk in newness of life." Have new desires, loves, and aims awakened in your life, which clearly come from God?

WORSHIP AIDS

CALL TO WORSHIP.   "Since then we have a great high priest who has passed through the heavens, Jesus, the Son of God, let us hold fast our confession. For we have not a high priest who is unable to sympathize with our weaknesses, but one who in every respect has been tempted as we are, yet without sin. Let us then with confidence draw near to the throne of grace, that we may receive mercy and find grace to help in time of need" (Heb. 4:14–16, RSV).

INVOCATION.   O God, we come to you with boldness this day, not because we are worthy, but because you have assured us that we may come, that mercy is available, and that our needs will be met. Give us a fresh vision of our Savior, our great high priest, who sympathizes with all our weaknesses and has power to strengthen us at our most vulnerable points.

OFFERTORY SENTENCE.   "Every good gift and every perfect gift is from above, and cometh down from the Father of lights, with whom is no variableness, neither shadow or turning" (James 1:17).

OFFERTORY PRAYER.   We thank you our Father, for your many gifts which have continued to bless us in spite of our unworthiness. Help us to learn from you how to be faithful, in season and out of season.

PRAYER.   Most gracious and benevolent heavenly Father, heal the many pains, doubts, and frustrations that daily assail us. Enter into our lives with thy empowering presence that we may know thy comforting and sustaining Spirit. Help us to be the persons that thou hast

---

[2]Robert Fulghum, *From Beginning to End* (New York: Villard Books, 1995), pp. 232–233.

created us to be through the putting aside of our pride, egotism, selfishness, indifference, and fear, which drive us from thee. Create in us, O Lord, clean hearts that are capable of loving thee with ever greater constancy and devotion. Grant that our healing, given through thy Spirit, may help us to reach out in a spirit of love and fellowship to those about us. Give unto us, O Lord, the courage and commitment to share of ourselves with those in distress, despair, and need, that we may truly be thy hands in this thy world.—Rodney K. Miller

SERMON
Topic: Promises to Keep
TEXT: Eccl. 5:2–5; Deut. 23:21–23

> The woods are lovely, dark, and deep,
> But I have promises to keep,
> And miles to go before I sleep,
> And miles to go before I sleep.[3]

With these hauntingly beautiful words, Robert Frost called us to remember the overriding importance of keeping promises. Life is full of appealing diversions and distractions, but they must not be allowed to compromise our prior commitments. The writer of Ecclesiastes lifted this principle to the level of a religious imperative (5:4–5) which summarized the warning of Deuteronomy 23:21–23. Indeed, the entire twenty-seventh chapter of Leviticus is an appendix that spells out just how carefully religious vows are to be honored.

I. *The importance of promises.* We begin with the inherent nature of a promise. Some words are merely "descriptive"; that is, they are verbal symbols representing an external reality. But promises are "performative," which means that they do not merely report on some action or disposition but are an action in themselves—"operative speech," which seeks to call into being that which it describes. Our vows *do* something; they *make* promises which have a value and life of their own. Even God cannot ignore his promises because, once uttered, they establish a covenant with his people (for example, Rom. 3:2–4, 4:21, 9:6–8). That is why we acknowledge the binding power of promises by saying, for example, "His word is his bond."

Therefore, to make a promise is to lay a claim on my very being; it is to place upon myself a new obligation to become, as Will Willimon put it, "a trusted one, one who is reliable, faithful, dependable in the midst of life's vicissitudes . . . I find myself transformed, redone, converted in my promising."[4]

That is why our text has such hard words about unpaid vows (Eccles. 5:5). Why is no vow better than an unpaid vow? Because a forsaken pledge compromises character. It exposes the speaker as unfaithful. A broken promise is just that—broken! It leaves one with no true past by allowing each new situation to supersede and thereby sweep away the resolves of yesterday. It leaves one with no true future because there is no way to define priorities and make them stick.

---

[3]Robert Frost, "Stopping by Woods on a Snowy Evening," in Edward Connery Lathem (ed.), *The Poetry of Robert Frost* (Austin, Tex.: Holt, Rinehart and Winston, 1968), pp. 224–225.
[4]William H. Willimon, "Promises to Keep," *Quarterly Review*, 1981, *1*(5), p. 38.

Think, for example, of how the entire business world would collapse if the contracts offered as surety were not binding. Or how the justice system would be fatally undermined if testimony sworn on oath could not be trusted. Or how diplomacy would be impossible if nations could not be counted on to honor their treaties. Without reliable promises the future becomes utterly unpredictable, subject to every whim of circumstance.

Does all this mean, therefore, that we are obligated to fulfill every promise in literal fashion no matter how much the future may change? No; precisely because vows are so sacred, our text warns us repeatedly against uttering them lightly (Eccles. 5:2, 4, 6). The principle is clear: we are under no obligation to honor foolish oaths; rather, such thoughtless avowals should never be uttered in the first place.

Let it be clear that the only vows worth keeping are those consistent with the character of God and with his intentions for humankind.

Jesus perfectly united the Biblical concern to honor every worthy vow with its equal concern to avoid every unworthy vow. Negatively, he abolished all efforts to use sacred symbols as a guarantee of the oaths we utter (Matt. 23:16–22). If God is everywhere, then every word we speak should be "on oath" before the judge of the universe. This means that there is no need to swear oaths because every word should be backed by our incorruptible integrity and thus have no need to be propped up by pious phrases (Matt. 5:33–37; cf. James 5:12). What this means positively is that we are never to speak any "idle" or "careless" words (Matt. 12:26). Rather, once every word becomes a sacred trust, then we will keep promises because they are worth keeping and, in so doing, learn the meaning of self-respect, character, and trust. In the spirit of the Sermon on the Mount (Matt. 5:37), we are to say yes to worthy vows and mean it, say no to unworthy vows and mean it, and thus never let our mouths lead us into sin (Eccles. 5:6a).

II. *The keeping of true promises.* In light of these clarifications, let us look now at the role of promises in three of the most foundational institutions of society: the home, the state, and the church.

The home. At the heart of a wedding service is a set of promises between two people, vows freely exchanged by mutual consent in the presence of witnesses. The marriage is actually *made* as a new reality by virtue of each taking the other "as my wedded husband/wife." The service is, above all else, a public declaration of "promises to keep"!

But today this emphasis on a voluntarily pledged lifelong covenant has shifted to the passing mood of subjective feelings. To be sure, each will deeply disappoint the other many times before their lifelong pilgrimage is complete, which is why they made a realistic promise to cherish each other "for better *or for worse.*"

The wedding service never promises that a couple will always "feel romantic," nice as that is, or that they will be able to resolve all of their differences in amicable fashion. Rather, it invites two people to declare that they will always belong to each other and, by that declaration, to actually begin the process of becoming truly "one." To be sure, such a promise entails high risk, and the courage needed to carry it through must come as a gift of God.

The nation. According to the Declaration of Independence, our country was founded not because England wanted to set us free or because circumstances were propitious but because a sturdy band of patriots vowed: "we mutually *pledge* to each other our lives, our fortunes, and our sacred honor." That covenant is renewed by citizens to this day every time we salute the flag and say, "I *pledge* allegiance. . . ."

Today we are reaping the bitter fruits of citizen apathy. What is urgently needed today is the rebirth of old-fashioned patriotism, the kind that is ready to make a courageous pledge rather than wait in line for a political handout.

Some of our ablest citizens never stand for public office because the necessities of campaign financing dictate that they serve only a handful of special interests rather than all the people. When the United States began, it had nothing but a future built on promise rather than preferment. To ensure that future, come what may, is still our greatest challenge!

The church. Jesus came with a promise: "Follow me and I will make you to become . . ." (Mark 1:17). Our response of faith is a freely given vow of undying loyalty. To commit is to promise that we will leave behind a shadowed past and begin to live differently in the future. It is to enter into covenant with God regarding what that promised future is to be like, a future shaped by the Kingdom of God rather than the kingdoms of this world. Faith says, "I am yours—come what may!" It binds us to Christ with ties thicker than blood.

How glibly we forget those promises, justifying such unfaithfulness by saying that the church just doesn't "mean much" to us anymore, that we are not "getting" anything out of its various activities. This attitude is demonstrated particularly in the lives of those who violate their vows by giving nothing of themselves in terms of time, energy, or resources. Others try to justify themselves by complaining that the church is forever making demands: attend! give! serve!

Christianity is undermined and scandalized far more by the defaults of its own than by the doubts of agnostics or the disbelief of atheists. To forsake our faith commitments, which are surely the most serious promises that we ever make, is literally to commit an act of infidelity that strikes at the root of our integrity.—William E. Hull

SUNDAY, AUGUST 21, 2005
Lectionary Message

Topic: The Church Will Prevail
TEXT: Matt. 16:13–20
Other Readings: Exod. 1:8–2:10; Ps. 124; Rom. 12:1–8

When one surveys the life of Jesus of Nazareth, there are several particular moments that stand out like majestic mountain peaks that cause one to stop and gaze. There are, of course, the twin peaks of the incarnation or virgin birth and his Crucifixion/Resurrection. There is the experience of his baptism, which is closely followed by another mountain peak, his temptation by the devil. To these we could add the Sermon on the Mount (Matt. 5–7), the feeding of the five thousand (Matt. 14:13–21), his Transfiguration (Matt. 17:1–8), the raising of Lazarus (John 11), and his Ascension (Luke 24; Acts 1).

But there is another major happening we need to examine, one that is particularly relevant in our day. The event was the occasion of Peter's great confession of Jesus, "You are the Christ, the Son of the living God," and our Lord's wonderful promise, "I will build my church, and the gates of Hades shall not prevail against it." This is a promise we desperately need to hear today.

This text is a bedrock for the church of the Lord Jesus Christ. It is essential both for our message and our methods.

I. *The church must ask a great question (16:13–15).* Jesus takes his disciples away from the crowds to the far northern area of Caesarea Philippi, twenty-five miles north of Galilee at the base of Mt. Hermon.

Jesus was aware of both the popularity and the confusion that swirled about who he was. He understood clearly something we need to understand as well.

(a) *Many people try to answer the question of Jesus (16:13–14).* Jesus gathered his disciples together for a theological seminar. He put before them a question ("the question") everyone must consider and answer: "Who do men say that I, the Son of Man, am?"

Their response is interesting and reveals something of the variety of opinions already developing:

- John the Baptist: risen from the dead, the view of Herod Antipas (Matt. 14:2)

- Elijah: a forerunner to the Messiah who is still to come, as prophesied in Malachi 4:5–6

- Jeremiah: a prophet of authority and compassion who wept and suffered over the nation of Israel

- One of the prophets: someone important who boldly preached the Word of God in the face of opposition

All of these answers were honoring, yet no group was confessing him as Messiah. These answers fell short of the truth of who he really is. It is possible to hold Jesus in high esteem, to think well of him, and still get it wrong.

(b) *You personally must answer the question of Jesus (16:15).* Hearing the results of popular opinion polls concerning his identity, Jesus turns the question in the direction of his disciples. I want to know what you think. "Who do you say that I am?" This question that Jesus puts to his disciples he likewise puts to us. It is inescapable. We must personally answer the question of Jesus.

II. *The church must announce a great confession (16:16–17).* We have come to a moment of truth. Peter, as he often did, steps forward to speak on their behalf. Impetuous and often guilty of speaking and acting without thinking (see vv. 22–23!), Peter gets it right this time and answers the question with words that resound in the heart of every believer who has met the Lord Jesus.

(a) *You must have an accurate conviction about Jesus (16:16).* "You are the Christ, the promised Messiah of Hebrew Scripture, the Son of the Living God." Here is a confession that is a turning point in the life of the disciples and world history. Jesus is the Christ, God's Messiah, but (there is no way to overstate what he adds), "You are the Son of the Living God." Peter no doubt did not grasp all that this means, but he gets a grade of 100 for his answer. To affirm that Jesus was the Messiah was correct, but that he was the very Son of God, deity in human flesh, was a truth of enormous significance.

(b) *You must have a divine revelation about Jesus (16:17).* Jesus affirms Peter and his words, and then he tells him how it came to him. "Blessed [happy] are you Simon, son of Jonah, you did not come to this on your own ability and insight, but in grace, *My Father,* who is in heaven revealed it to you." No mere mortal being could arrive at this on his or her own.

The effects of the Fall and sin have so blinded human beings we could never see it without divine enablement.

The Father drew Peter to Jesus and opened his eyes.

III. *The church must answer with a great mission (16:18–20).* Jesus blesses Peter and affirms his great confession. He then takes things forward and provides the church with a promise that will free her to serve her Lord with radical devotion.

(a) *We are a spiritual building (16:18).* Jesus declares to Simon Bar-Jonah, "You are Peter (*Petros*), and on this rock (*petra*) I will build my church. . . ." Few statements in Scripture have provoked more debate throughout the history of the church than this one. What did Jesus mean by "this rock"? Five views stand out when we survey the interpretive playing field:

1. The rock is *Peter* (the classic Roman Catholic position).
2. The rock is *Peter's confession* ("you are the Christ, the Son of the Living God").
3. The rock is *Jesus Himself* (1 Pet. 2:5–8, after all, teaches that he is the chief cornerstone).
4. The rock is the *revealed truth* in general of Jesus' teaching.
5. The rock is *Peter* as representative of *all the apostles.*

I am convinced there is some genuine and legitimate complementarity to these views. Jesus is addressing *Peter and his confession.* It identifies who Jesus really is as the cornerstone of his spiritual building, the church. Moreover, Protestants should not overreact to Roman Catholicism's papacy. Peter indeed plays an unprecedented role in the early stages of the church's birth and growth. He is *primus inter pares* ("first among equals"), and on the foundation of such men Jesus did built his church.

(b) *We engage in spiritual battle (16:18).* The church of the Lord Jesus is a spiritual building called to engage a spiritual battle. The enemy is clearly marked in the latter part of verse 18: Hades. Hades represents the strength and stronghold of Satan, the kingdom of darkness and death. When the Son of God came into this world he launched an all-out assault as he invaded enemy territory. The church is his bride, his body, his building, and his battalion. We are to be on the offensive, taking the battle to the enemy, attacking its gates.

(c) *We conduct spiritual business (16:19–20).* Jesus makes one additional promise and then adds a word of warning. Jesus promises his disciples and his church the keys of the kingdom. The keys represent authority and the power to exclude or allow entrance into the kingdom. However, Jesus is quite clear where authority ultimately resides. What takes place on earth has its origin in heaven. The use of the future periphrastic perfect should be rendered: "Whatever you bind on earth *shall have been* bound in heaven, and whatever you loose on earth *shall have been loosed* in heaven."

The same gospel that compels some to enter the kingdom of heaven drives others away. Yet what we do on earth has already been determined in heaven. What Peter, the apostles, and we do by welcoming people into the kingdom who confess Christ, or by excluding people who reject him, is simply the outworking of God's plan laid out in heaven.

Jesus concludes this theological seminar with a warning not to tell that he is the Christ. Why? The time will come when bold, worldwide proclamation is in order. Now, nationalistic zeal and feverous messianic expectations cloud the picture. The kind of Messiah that he is will require a cross, something he will now begin to explain (16:21–23). Events leading to that event are not to be short-circuited.

IV. *Conclusion.* Peter's confession that Jesus was the Christ, the Son of the Living God, did not receive a warm reception in the first century. It eventually led to Jesus being nailed to a cross. Peter's confession does not receive a warm welcome in the twenty-first century either. In a day, very much like the first century, where pluralism, inclusivity, and tolerance are the expectations of the culture, we cannot and should not expect that people will applaud this message. However, it is the truth, and an empty tomb stands as a monument to it. Who is Jesus? I will tell you what I believe: "He is the Christ, the Son of the Living God." On that great confession, the church will prevail.—Daniel Akin

SERMON SUGGESTIONS

Topic: Surviving Unpopularity
TEXT: Ps. 69:6–15
(1) Unpopularity may be for God's sake. (2) Surviving unpopularity is possible through self-denying love for God's sometimes undeserving people and through trust in God's help and justice.

Topic: When God's Spirit Dwells in You
TEXT: Rom. 8:9–17
(1) You will recognize God as your own Father. (2) You will be a fellow heir of God with Christ.

WORSHIP AIDS
CALL TO WORSHIP.   "Awake, awake; put on thy strength, O Zion" (Isa. 52:1).

INVOCATION.   Eternal God, our heavenly Father, you have given us every reason to rejoice. You have forgiven us of our sins through our Lord Jesus Christ. You have strengthened us in time of temptation. You have led us in marvelous ways all the days of our lives. Help us now to cast aside our fears, confess our unacknowledged sins, look to you for guidance, and praise you with all that is within us. For the sake of your glorious name.

OFFERTORY SENTENCE.   "Give, and it shall be given unto you; good measure, pressed down, and shaken together, and running over. . . . For with the same measure that ye mete withal it shall be measured to you again" (Luke 6:38).

OFFERTORY PRAYER.   Gracious Lord, give us generous hearts, not holding back through fear or selfishness, but imitating your blessed example in our prodigality of love.

PRAYER.   O God, we who are bound together in the tender ties of love pray thee for a day of unclouded love. May no passing irritation rob us of our joy in one another. Forgive us if we have often been keen to see the human failings, and slow to feel the preciousness of those who are still the dearest comfort of our life. May there be no sharp words that wound and scar, and no rift that may grow into estrangement. Suffer us not to grieve those whom thou hast sent to us as the sweet ministers of love. May our eyes not be so holden by selfishness that we know thine angels only when they spread their wings to return to thee.—Walter Rauschenbusch

SERMON
Topic: A Tough Gospel for Tough Times
TEXT: Various

Shortly after September 11, 2001, somebody scribbled on a wall in Washington, "Dear God, save us from the people who believe in you."[5] Can we trust a priest not to be a sexual predator? Can we invest our retirement savings through a Baptist Foundation without having it squandered by fraudulent practices? Is it any wonder that the number of acknowledged "believers" who are skipping church in America rose from 14.3 million in 1990 to 29.4 million in 2001?[6]

So let us be honest: getting people to accept our faith for the right reasons is a tough sell today. But we also have a tough gospel equal to the challenge of this hour. Vague religious generalities will no longer suffice, but we have a fighting chance if we are willing and able to commend the very core of our faith, those distinctive beliefs that make it unique. From the beginning, Christianity was startlingly new, so much so that it challenged all of the religions of its day, even the one out of which it emerged. There were many "gods" and many "lords" in the Graeco-Roman world (1 Cor. 8:5), but Christianity refused to be limited by any of them. Three foundational realities set our faith apart then, and these are the same three realities on which we must stake everything today.

I. *The Christ.* The claim that "Jesus is Lord" (Rom. 10:9), that Christ is divine, that deity has become incarnate in human life, represented a revolution in our understanding of God. God did not delegate the task of dealing with our dilemma but got personally involved himself. In Jesus of Nazareth, divine love stooped to conquer the loveless heart. Make no mistake: he was not man becoming God but was God becoming man. Thus to emphasize the deity of Jesus is to claim that we have a Christlike God, for, as Jesus himself put it, "He who has seen me has seen the Father" (John 14:9).

But Christ gave us not only a revolutionary new understanding of God but an equally revolutionary new understanding of humanity. If God could be fully and completely "in Christ" (2 Cor. 5:19), then he can also be "in us" (v. 17) as we are reconciled to him (v. 18). For centuries we supposed that, because God was "high and lifted up," he could never be truly in our midst. But Jesus made God radically accessible by becoming who we are, a flesh-and-blood human being at a particular time and place.

That being true, Christian salvation came to be understood in terms of Christ living God's life with us, in us, and through us. It was necessary for him "to learn obedience through what he suffered" (5:8), to accept God's will in Gethsemane only after "offering prayers and

---

[5]Cited by Maureen Dowd, "Sacred Cruelties," *New York Times*, Apr. 7, 2002, p. 15-WK.
[6]Cited by Alfred Lubrano in *Philadelphia Inquirer* from American Religious Identification survey of 2001, reprinted in *Birmingham News*, Apr. 12, 2002, p. 1-H.

supplications with loud cries and tears" (5:7), to run his race by faith from start to finish (12:2). It is a living relationship that Christ patterns with us on a daily basis, bonding his spirit with our spirits so that we now live "in Christ" and he lives "in us."

When you go to prospects, do not offer them religion or reputation, mysticism or morality, divinity or decency. Instead, *offer them Christ* as the living presence of a God who is willing to become incarnate in their lives. Your witness is first and foremost neither an explanation nor an exhortation, but a sharing of Christ!

II. *The cross.* The climax of the life of Christ was not a royal triumph but a bloody cross. In our day, the followers of Christ are those who believe that evil does not have to remain forever entrenched, that its power can be broken by sacrificial love, that the best is yet to be for those willing to live out of the future rather than the past. In a nutshell, the cross is a willingness to die to the old so that we may be born to the new.

This radical break with things as they are is focused first on the self. There are many things in each of us that need to die and be buried for good: bad habits, poisoned attitudes, petty jealousies, competitive pride. To "deny self" as the way to take up our cross (Mark 8:34) does not mean that we deny the self *something* but rather that we abdicate self-rule and replace it with Christ-rule. Baptism is a powerful demonstration of our commitment to die to the old so that we may live to the new.

There is also a social dimension to this lifestyle of renunciation. Christ taught his followers to love their enemies, to see the potential in every person, even if they be publicans, centurions, or Samaritans. But society never likes to have its petty prejudices exposed; thus it often fights back against those who champion the dignity and rights of every person.

Therefore, when you witness, do not offer your prospects human power but divine weakness, not material success but spiritual struggle, not a victory to be celebrated but a war to be fought. Accepting Christ is not the way that one avoids the conflicts of life; rather, it is the way by which one commits to fight on the right side.

III. *The church.* Because the church was born on a cross, it became the opposite of an elite religious society. Its members were recruited not because they were the most respectable citizens in the community but because they were willing to repent and start life all over again. Everyone wants to associate with the brightest and the best, the fewer the better. By contrast, Paul said of the church, "Not many of you were wise according to worldly standards; not many were powerful. Not many were of noble birth; but God chose what is weak in the world to shame the strong. God chose what is low and despised in the world, even things that are not, to bring to nothing things that are, so that no human being might boast in the presence of God" (1 Cor. 1:26–29).

Despite our many frailties, the commonality that we share in Christ results in a blessed fellowship forged by love that is utterly free of competition and exploitation. Paul called it "the unity of the Spirit in the bond of peace" (Eph. 4:3). Ultimately, it is a fellowship in which we are *loved* apart from any merit in ourselves (1 John 4:10–11).

The unity of believers in Christ creates a profound sense of identity that transcends all of the status systems of earth. Here there is no superiority based on ethnicity, nationality, gender, or social standing. In this way the church anticipates and foreshadows the Kingdom of God, even though the church is only a broken reflection of the Kingdom in this world, always standing in need of renewal and reformation. The church is God's earthly beachhead where the reconciliation that will one day extend to the entire universe has just begun to be realized (Col. 1:18–20).

Therefore, in your offer to prospects, do not promise them membership in a club limited to the spiritually elite, but invite them to join fellow strugglers who fall down and get up, who take two steps forward and one step backward, who often rail to reach their highest resolves because they now aspire to more than ever before. Do not promise that the sermon will always be powerful, or the music beautiful, or the pews comfortable. Rather, offer them the chance to become a colony of heaven (Phil. 3:20), a countercultural force for change on earth, God's avant-garde in a world that prefers to wander in the wilderness rather than to claim the Promised Land.

According to this tough gospel, becoming a Christian means at least three things: first, practicing the presence of Christ at the core of one's being through prayer, worship, Bible study, and fellowship. Second, it means taking a stand, marching to the beat of a different drummer, resisting the mass appeals of the marketplace, forever pulling up weeds in the garden of one's soul, determined to leave the world a better place than we found it. Third, it means finding reinforcement in the company of like-minded believers, not because they are better than others, not because they have suddenly become free of failure, but because of a conviction that if God can save the likes of them, then he can save anybody, including me!—William E. Hull

SUNDAY, AUGUST 28, 2005
Lectionary Message
Topic: What Does a Real Christian Look Like?

TEXT: Rom. 12:9–21

Other Readings: Exod. 3:1–15; Ps. 105:1–6, 23–26, 45c; Matt. 16:21–28

We live in a day when finding authenticity is more and more of a challenge. So many things are now imitation. Add to that the outright fraud and deception that is more often the rule than the exception, and it is easy to become cynical and skeptical.

This condition is not altogether surprising in the world. It is, however, a tragedy when it takes place in the church. Unfortunately, the church has been influenced by the world more than the world has been influenced by it. If we were brutally honest, we would have to admit there are too many "imitation" Christians who think, talk, and live *not a whole lot differently* from their lost neighbor and coworker.

The situation is so desperate we now struggle to answer a basic and fundamental question: "What does a real Christian look like?" Beginning with chapter 12, Paul discusses the transformed life (12:2). The transformed life is a surrendered life in which we present our total self to God as a living sacrifice, being transformed daily by a renewing of our minds. This life results in a radical metamorphosis that becomes the very life of Christ in and through us. Paul challenges us to live our lives for Jesus in three specific ways.

I. *Love others sincerely (12:9–13).* Here are marching orders for the soldiers of Jesus Christ. This is God's will and expectation for us in our daily lives. Paul begins with sincerity, pointing out what we should love and also what we should hate.

(a) *Hate what is evil (12:9).* Paul starts with what is most important: love. He tells us love should be sincere, genuine, without hypocrisy. Real love is a matter of the heart, not the face. Masking your real feelings and intentions with superficial niceties is an act, a charade.

"Abhor" what is evil. The word has the idea of "shrinking from." A real Christian will not be passive or indifferent about evil. He or she will hate it, be repulsed by it.

Complementing hatred for evil, we will cling to what is good. We will join firmly to those good things as defined by Scripture.

(b) *Honor others (12:10).* "Be kindly affectionate to one another with brotherly love." This command addresses how we treat one another in the family of God. Jesus teaches us in John 13:35, "By this all will know that you are my disciples, if you have love for one another."

"In honor give preference to one another" echoes the words of Philippians 2:3. With an attitude of genuine humility we should honor or esteem others ahead of ourselves.

(c) *Serve the Lord (12:11).* The three commands of this verse are closely connected. "Not lagging in diligence" speaks to the sin of laziness. We are not to be seduced into slothfulness. The flip side of laziness is fervency. Paul challenges us to be zealous, to burn like a vibrant flame in spirit. What is the goal of such fervency, zeal, and passion? "Serving the Lord." As a slave to our Savior, we are to bring all of our life under his lordship.

(d) *Rejoice with hope (12:12).* We do not live as Christians in despair and dread. We have a hope, a settled confidence in the sovereign plan and purpose of our God. We can rejoice continually in hope, regardless of the circumstances that surround us.

We can be patient under the load of tribulation, the "pressures of life." All of this is possible as we wrap all things in prayer, telling him that even when we cannot trace his hand, we can still trust his heart.

(e) *Care for fellow believers (12:13).* Two very definite and practical actions will mark the Lord's church: giving and hospitality. Those who are hurting and who are a part of our fellowship should have their needs met by us. Wise policies, principles, and procedures should certainly guide us in this area, but we dare not neglect it.

Showing hospitality means we take the initiative in graciously and generously opening our home to others. The author of Hebrews reminds us, "by so doing some have unwittingly entertained angels" (Heb. 13:1).

II. *Bless others graciously (12:14–16).* Paul shifts gears but continues his comprehensive exam. Living under the lordship of Jesus Christ does not leave out any area of our lives.

(a) *Be kind in what you say (12:14).* Paul commands us to bless and not to curse. Paul understands the power of the spoken word to build up or tear down.

Paul clearly has in mind those who oppose us, our enemies. His words reflect those of Jesus in Matthew 5:44. Be kind in what you say, even if you don't receive a similar word in return.

(b) *Be kind in what you do (12:15).* Verse 15 gives us insight into the depths of the depravity in our heart. John Chrysostom probably got it right when he said the command to rejoice with those who rejoice is placed first because it is more difficult to do! In Phil. 4:11, Paul says, "I have learned, in whatever state I am, to be content." Contentment in Christ will free you to rejoice when good things come to others, and to weep when things are not so good as well.

(c) *Be kind in how you think (12:16).* The key to the Christian life is the mind. Again and again Scripture drives home this truth:

- Proverbs 23:7: "As a man thinks in his heart so is he."

- Romans 12:2: "Be transformed by the renewing of your mind."

- Philippians 2:5: "Let this mind be in you which was also in Christ Jesus."

Paul's words are again reflective of what he wrote to the Philippians (2:3–4). Four words of instruction address our thought life.

"Be of the same mind" points us in the direction of harmony and unity, but not uniformity. People are different and God has gifted us differently (cf. 12:3–8), yet there will be a oneness of mind as we honor and esteem one another above ourselves (v. 10).

"Do not set your mind on high things" addresses the sins of pride and arrogance. Treat well those who are under you and cannot aid your agenda. "Do not be wise in your own opinions." Do not let yourself be deceived in cultivating an empty opinion of yourself.

III. *Live with others peaceably (12:17–21).* How we respond to our enemies is a telltale sign of the genuineness of our faith and devotion to Christ. First Peter 2:23 reminds us that when our Lord was scourged and crucified, "He [who] was reviled, did not revile in return, when he suffered he did not threaten, but committed himself to him who judges righteously." Here is the pattern for our response as well.

(a) *Always do the good thing (12:17–18).* We should not retaliate with evil against evil. When we are wronged on the personal level, we must fight against the urge to get even. Respond in such a way that all men will see the grace of God in your response. Pursue peace with everyone. Peace will not always be possible, but if not, do not let the failure be laid at your feet.

(b) *Always trust the good God (12:19–20).* Paul recognizes the difficulty of doing what he is saying, and so he tenderly addresses the Roman church as "beloved." He then grounds his argument in his ultimate proof: the sovereignty, providence, and justice of God. We are not to avenge ourselves, take matters into our own hands. We are instead to give place, space, and time to wrath, the wrath and judgment of God. Why? Paul cites Deuteronomy 32:35: "'Vengeance is mine, I will repay,' says the Lord." God says place the fate and destiny of your enemies in my hands, not yours.

In verse 20 Paul cites more Scripture in support of his position, drawing upon Proverbs 25:21–22. If your enemy is hungry, feed him; thirsty, give him a drink, "for in so doing you will heap coals of fire on his head." Just as believers are to refrain from revenge because God will judge (v. 19), so they are to be kind and do good because it is God who will punish their enemies.

(c) *Always pursue the good end (12:21).* Paul's closing word in this passage is short and concise. Christians must not let the evil that comes their way master them and overpower them. No, we are to master evil and overpower it with good. We can do this when we accept by faith that our God is a righteous and just judge who will make right every wrong and set straight every evil.—Daniel Akin

SERMON SUGGESTIONS

Topic: The Call of God

TEXT: Exod. 3:1–12

(1) It comes to the undeserving. (2) It may come in a strange way. (3) It comes in the context of genuine need. (4) The implications and responsibilities may seem overwhelming. (5) The god who calls promises his presence.

Topic: Why Suffering Can Be Discounted
TEXT: Rom. 8:18–25
(1) Because an incomparable destiny awaits us. (2) Because God is at work even now to bring all things into harmony with his glorious purpose.

WORSHIP AIDS

CALL TO WORSHIP.   "If we say that we have no sin, we deceive ourselves, and the truth is not in us. If we confess our sins, he is faithful and just to forgive us our sins, and to cleanse us from all unrighteousness" (1 John 1:8–9).

INVOCATION.   Today, Our Father, may we learn the meaning of our new standing with you: darkness past, and the true light shining. Help us to live out of that new light where love prevails, and to turn away from the old darkness, where hate festers and prejudice grows. This we ask for the sake of him who loved us and commanded us to love one another.

OFFERTORY SENTENCE.   "It is written, he that had gathered much had nothing over; and he that had gathered little had no lack" (2 Cor. 8:15).

OFFERTORY PRAYER.   O Lord of our lives, as our material blessings multiply, grant that the grace of giving may be increased. May we sustain no spiritual loss because of an abundance of material goods, nor may we fail of your grace when the fig tree does not blossom, and no fruit shall be in the vines. At all times and in all conditions may we be your faithful stewards.

PRAYER.   O Thou, who didst lay the foundation of the earth amid the singing of the morning stars and the joyful shouts of the sons of God, lift up our little life into thy gladness. Out of thee, as out of an overflowing fountain of love, wells forth eternally a stream of blessing upon every creature thou hast made. If we have thought that thou didst call into being this universe in order to win praise and honor for thyself, rebuke the vain fancies of our foolish minds and show us that thy glory is the joy of giving. We can give thee nothing of our own. All that we have is thine. Oh, then, help us to glorify thee by striving to be like thee. Make us just as pure and good as thou art. May we be partakers of the divine nature, so that all that is truly human in us may be deepened, purified, and strengthened. And so may we be witnesses for thee, lights of the world, reflecting thy light.—Samuel McComb

SERMON
Topic: When the Going Gets Tough
TEXT: 1 Sam. 1:4–20; Mark 13:1–8

Occasion: After the California Fires
John Wesley, the founder of the Methodist movement, late in his life was asked to sit for a portrait. If your vision of Wesley is like mine, that must have been very difficult for him to do, because my vision of Wesley is he was a man always on the move. For him to sit for a while so that a portrait might be painted of him I am sure was pure grief for the man. But he used the time to reflect on his own life and all the changes that had taken place in his life.

He wrote in his journal the following words of reflection: "Behold what frailty we in many may see. His shadow is less given to change than he."

Wesley makes the point that everything in life changes. Except for the possibility of our shadows, everything else is in transition. As we move through the years, don't we know that to be true?

There is a whimsical report made about Adam when he left the Garden of Eden. Supposedly he turned to Eve as they were exiting the garden and said, "Eve, we are living in a period of rapid social change." That is probably the most positive spin he could put on the changes they were experiencing.

We too live in a period of rapid social change. What we have discovered in the last few weeks is that crises impel that change even faster forward. The crises of our experiences with the fires in this county have impelled us to new directions and new experiences that we could not have imagined. There are certain kinds of responses that are necessary to a crisis, whether it be an individual crisis, something within a person's own life, or something like we have experienced, something that covers residents of a whole county.

Our responses fall into two categories. One would be immediate response. It has been well documented that in this county the immediate response to the fire was a very positive one. Many people found many ways to help those in need. The help has been so extensive that in many of the centers around the county there is still an overwhelming number of resources waiting to be picked up, but there no longer seems to be any need. Many of the food items donated have had to be given to others, or thrown away, because there was not the kind of need that matched the response. We have met the immediate need well.

The second category is long-term response. How do we address that? There are two qualities that are essential in responding to long-term need. They are patient openness and resiliency. Let me give you an illustration of what I mean.

There is a family that some of us on the staff know who had a cabin up in the Julian area. It burned in the fires. The family was in grief for a period of time following the fire. This location, this building, this second home, had been a very precious place for that family. There were a lot of memories associated with that structure. There was grief and sadness in the family. But then slowly something began to happen. First one member of the family, and then others, spoke up and said, "The future is open. Are we going to rebuild? If we do choose to rebuild what will we build? Will we build something just for us, or will we build something for others as well? What does God want us to do with this occasion?"

In process theology, one of the postures that is most important for understanding process thinking is that we need to be open to the possibilities that God is bringing our way, even though we can't see them. That is what this family was doing. They are open to possibilities that they can't even imagine right now, but they trust that God is bringing their way. What is necessary for long-term needs? A patient openness and resiliency.

We see that so well in the person of Hannah in the Old Testament passage today. Hannah is a person who suffered dramatically for a long period of time in her life. Listen to the description of Hannah again. She is one of two wives of Elkanah. Right there you can see crisis looming on the horizon. Two wives; one husband. It's a crisis. Second, she has no children, and the other wife, Peninnah, does. Thirdly, Peninnah never lets Hannah forget it. She is constantly riding her, teasing her, and demeaning her because she is childless. Fourth, when Hannah goes to Shiloh to pray in the temple, Eli the priest mistakes her prayers for drunkenness and chastises her. Hannah responds to the priest by saying, "Do not consider me a worthless woman. I have been praying through suffering for many years."

Hannah could have responded in revenge to Peninnah. Hannah could have lost her faith in her interchange with the priest. But neither of those things happened. Hannah approached life with a patient openness and resiliency, offering herself to God, not knowing what it was that God was bringing her way. When she finally received a son, she offered her son to God. Samuel becomes one of the great prophets of Israel and the last of the Judges. His role in the whole history of Israel is a key one.

Hannah knows what to do when the going gets tough: patient openness and resiliency. We know what the word *resilient* means. It means rebounding, springing back or jumping back. I also consulted *Webster's Third International Dictionary*. The following definitions of *resiliency* were included: "It is the capacity to withstand shock without permanent deformation or rupture; tending to regain strength or high spirits after weakness or depression." A second definition is the one I really like: "It is the capacity of a strained body to recover its size and shape after deformation, especially when the strain is caused by successive, compressive stresses."

Does that sound like some of your days: successive, compressive stresses? Yet look, you are here this morning! You are a resilient people. Rejoice and be glad. Hannah knew successive, compressive stresses in her life, and yet she was open to what it was that God was bringing to her.

We had a trainer from the United Methodist Committee on Relief in town. His name was Gordon Knuckey. He talked about resilient people. He defined them in these ways. Resilient people have a lot of patience. They recognize that there is no quick fix. They know the tincture of time. Remember tincture of iodine? This is the tincture of time. They accept support from others. They value community. They are self-reflective. They have a spiritual foundation. They know survival is an ongoing process. What we need for the long-term is patient openness and resiliency.

Gordon Knuckey was one of the United Methodist Committee on Relief representatives in New York City right after September 11, 2001. He said there too the response to the emergency was overwhelming. Resources came from around the world. People in the United States traveled to New York to help. There was an overwhelming immediate response to the need of those three-thousand-some families after the Twin Towers fell.

However, he said the overwhelming need came about six months later when they finally discovered that some ten thousand service personnel had been put out of work by the collapse of the two towers. Those people had no resources to live on. The general public was now ready to put the disaster behind them. They wanted to move on. They wanted to think about other things. He said that it was left to the church, and to the church's emergency response teams, to help those ten thousand people. There are still representatives of churches in New York City to this day helping those folks with this ongoing need. He warned us that in our community the same would be true. Six months, eight months, a year from now, new needs will crop up of which we have no idea at the present time. We will need to respond to those. We need patient openness and resiliency.

One of the examples of resiliency came from one of the families in our church who lost their home. This week they discovered another family who also lost their home but were not insured. The first family gave the second family one thousand dollars. That's resiliency, in the midst of your own grief and sense of loss to reach out in strength and compassion to someone else.

We had a visitor last week, one of our extended family, from Los Alamos, New Mexico. Remember, they went through wild fires a couple of years ago. He said the long-term need will be the critical determiner of the character of our community. It is how we respond long-term that will show who we really are.

When Jesus and the disciples come out of the temple, the disciples turn around and look at the huge stones and large buildings. Jesus has just told them not to be taken in by appearances. Here they are, probably their first time in Jerusalem, looking around. They are like hillbillies from Galilee. They are trying to drink it all in at once. They see all this and they are amazed by it. Jesus says, "All this will be destroyed." Their immediate response is, "When will that be?" Jesus says, "The question is not when. The question is what will we do? How will we be ready?" Then he said to them, "We must continue to live and preach the gospel." In other words, we must continue to love and care for each other, even in times of great crisis. That does not change.

Simone Weil, the famous French philosopher, theologian, and social critic, in her book, *Waiting for God,* uses the world *affliction.* In times of affliction it feels like God is absent. When God is absent, so often we no longer love from our souls, because who is there to love if God is no longer here? Yet it is truly in those times that we need to continue to love, because as we continue to love, then God will be able to fill us with whatever it is God has for us in the future.

What is necessary when the going gets tough? Patient openness, resiliency, living the gospel, living love with each other.

John Innis is our bishop in Liberia. Liberia has been in civil war for fourteen years. The country is almost totally destroyed. Bishop Innis wrote in one of our periodicals recently about a conversation he had with one of his pastors in the Camphor area. The pastor's name is Albert Barchue. In their conversation the bishop asked Albert, "How is it in your area?" Albert answered, "Bishop, it is very hard. The rebels have come in. They occupy our homes. They don't let us go outside. There is no food in the stores, but we can't even go out to gather food. When we find food they take it away from us and eat it themselves. We are dying for lack of food and medication. We are physically hungry, but Bishop, we are spiritually filled. The church still continues to meet and to worship. We praise God and love each other. When we find food we share it with all who are hungry."

What do we do when the going gets tough? Patient openness, resiliency, and we live the gospel we know. We act as Christ in the world.

R. S. Thomas was a priest in the Church of Wales. Leslie Griffiths, who spoke here last month, knew him very well. Thomas was not only a priest but also a poet. In the 1960s, he wrote very dark poetry that reflected the mood of the times, especially in Great Britain and in the United States. He reflected the mood of all those disenchanted with life. He spoke to people's needs. He was widely read, especially in the British Isles. In one of his poems, called "Threshold," he says, "When you come to the point of life where it is the bleakest, what do you do?" Then he offers this suggestion. "We follow the model of Michelangelo's Adam, and we reach out trusting there is a reciprocating hand."

What do we do when the going gets tough? Patient openness, resiliency, and we trust there is a reciprocating hand. Thanks be to God.—Jim Standiford

SUNDAY, SEPTEMBER 4, 2005

Lectionary Message

Topic: Confrontation That Preserves Community

TEXT: Matt. 18:15–20

Other Readings: Exod. 12:1–14; Ps. 149; Rom. 13:8–14

In the evangelical Christian world today there is a widely heard call for a return to accountability within the Christian community. Scripture calls for such accountability and prescribes the spirit and methodology for resolving interpersonal conflict, as well as confronting and correcting members of the body of Christ as necessary. Unfortunately, when "church discipline" is misunderstood and biblical prescriptions are misapplied, misappropriated zeal for fidelity to scriptural mandates may destroy lives and threaten the unity among Christians for which our Savior so fervently prayed in the seventeenth chapter of John's gospel. To ignore the need for accountability and restoration of erring brothers and sisters is to forsake a vital scriptural mandate; to wield Scripture as a sword to destroy those who are falling is to violate the prevailing law of love and grace. Today's scriptural lesson from Matthew's Gospel instructs us concerning a mode of accountability through loving confrontation that emerges from, and preserves, a true spirit of community.

I. *Christian confrontation counters conventional wisdom.* Jesus consistently commanded behaviors that fly in the face of commonly held assumptions. The common wisdom says retaliate; Jesus says turn the other cheek. The prevailing notion is that we should disdain or even hate our enemies and be justified in seeking their demise; Jesus says we should love and pray for them. The book of common behavior prescribes resistance to unreasonable or seemingly oppressive demands and expectations; Jesus says we are to go the extra mile as a response of grace (Matt. 5:38–44).

So too, Jesus' command concerning Christian confrontation and mutual accountability flies in the face of the common wisdom. Most folk would imagine that, having been offended (hurt, sinned against, wronged) by another, as the offended party we are justified in waiting for the approach of the offender as the initiator of the process of reconciliation ("He hurt me, so, of course, he should come to me to make things right!"). Not so, according to our Lord. In our passage for today, Jesus says, "When your brother sins against you, [you] go and show him his fault" (v. 15a, NIV, my parenthetical insert). The first step toward addressing the pain and division caused by a disruption in fellowship between believers is for *the offended party to initiate restoration of fellowship* through a personal approach to the offender. Jesus teaches this same principle in Luke 17. This is a challenging model that calls for obedience to Jesus' command that we love one another as he has loved us (John 15:12, NIV). Though it is we who have sinned against God, it is God who has taken the loving initiative to restore our fellowship with Him (Rom. 5:6–8, NIV). We are no less obligated to seek reconciliation and, in the spirit of Christ's love, be initiators of the process. Notably, this first step is very personal and private. The offense is between two parties and the reconciliation efforts draw those directly affected toward a restoration of relationship. Ideally, the matter is resolved at this stage, and all is well in the body of Christ (v. 15b, NIV). But what if the problem persists . . . what then?

II. *The rift that ripples.* Jesus anticipates and answers that "what if" question: "But if he will not listen, take one or two others along." Unresolved personal conflicts are potential catalysts for wider conflict in the body of Christ. As such, what is first an interpersonal matter becomes a small group process and then, if still unresolved, an issue for the whole congregation. Jesus' directive presumes the interlocking relations present in community. The members of the body are to be concerned with any threat that the interpersonal problem may lead to larger rifts. The unrepentant offender is demonstrating a hardness of heart that belies the profession of a sinner saved by grace.

Having been the beneficiary of God's gracious plan of reconciliation, how then can any of us refuse to reconcile with others? (see Matt. 18:22–35). The formation of a small group to approach the rebellious member of the family specifically ensures the integrity of the process: "take one or two others along, so that every matter may be established by the testimony of two or three witnesses" (v. 16, NIV). Broader perspectives and wider accountability demonstrate both fairness and resolve. Still, the matter is approached at the most intimate level beyond that suggested by the stage-one, directly personal confrontation that failed to produce reconciliation. The desire is to restore, not to indict. This is not a lynch mob but a redemption-minded coalition of concerned brothers and sisters.

The final stage in this process of accountability is brought to bear only when the more private and personal approaches have failed to restore peace in the body and between its members. The one who insists on clinging to some selfish personal interest, intransigently resisting the loving attempts first of the one he or she has offended and then of several other concerned brothers or sisters and finally rebelling against the collective outreach of the whole congregation, may ultimately accrue unto himself or herself exclusion from the community.

This tragic state is not imposed by some formal action as much as it has become a reality because of the disintegration of community. Because the unrepentant one has shown no regard for, nor participation in, community efforts to be reconciled, the resulting state is one of detachment. There is no reason any longer to imagine that this rebel desires to be treated as family. He has accrued unto himself the results of his stubborn rejection of the community's proffered embrace. What a man sows, he reaps (Gal. 6:7, NIV).

Yet, to abandon this individual entirely is not mandated by this text. Instead, the relationship now shifts from the familial estate of a member of the body to the state of those still outside the body. The "pagan or tax collector" referred to in verse 17 is also loved by God and should be the object of the church's concern and evangelistic outreach, as should this now-excommunicated fugitive from grace. The church is not gleefully to wash its hands of the matter, but from a collective grieved spirit doggedly pursue this wanderer with the same grace-filled passion evident in the heart of God as described in Hosea: "How can I give you up, Ephraim? How can I hand you over, Israel? . . . My heart is changed, all my compassion is aroused" (Hosea 11:8, NIV).

III. *All in love.* This teaching of Jesus falls between two passages that serve to provide a helpful context. In verses 12–14, Jesus paints the beautiful picture of the compassionate shepherd, ever seeking those sheep that wander from the fold, rejoicing when they are recovered. The passage following our passage for today (vv. 22–35) highlights the great debt that God has forgiven and our responsibility to be compassionate as well. All of our efforts to confront and restore are to be as loving, patient, and persistent as those that God has engaged toward us in love. After all, "love covers over a multitude of sins"! (1 Peter 4:8).— Michael A. Wyndham

ILLUSTRATIONS

CONSEQUENCES.   According to an illustration attributed to Marabel Morgan, posted on www.SermonIllustrations.com, Don Shula has said that it was his coaching practice to confront every mistake, no matter how seemingly small, made by a player in practice: "We never let an error go unchallenged. If ignored, errors multiply. With my children I have sometimes let errors slide, because I did not want another confrontation. But uncorrected errors do multiply. You will have to deal with their consequences at some point; you might as well face them on the spot." These are principles that translate well to errors in the body of Christ and the necessity of confrontation and restoration where possible.

RESTORATION.   A few years ago an angry man rushed through the Rijks Museum in Amsterdam until he reached Rembrandt's famous painting *Nightwatch.* Then he took out a knife and slashed it repeatedly before he could be stopped. A short time later, a distraught, hostile man slipped into St. Peter's cathedral with a hammer and began to smash Michelangelo's beautiful sculpture *The Pieta.* Two cherished works of art were severely damaged. What did officials do? Throw them out and forget about them? Absolutely not! Using the best experts, who worked with great precision, they made every effort to restore the treasures. By his sovereign grace God can bring good out of our failures, even out of our sins![1]

SERMON SUGGESTIONS

Topic: A Miracle of Deliverance

TEXT: Exod. 14:19–31

(1) The story: God saved his people Israel by dramatic acts of his providence, and Israel's oppressors perished. (2) The meaning: (a) God uses natural means to accomplish his purposes. (b) Yet such acts must be seen as works of the care of God. (c) These phenomena are rightly regarded with reverent awe by those who benefit and with fear by those who oppress.

Topic: A Heart Aflame

TEXT: Rom. 9:1–5

(1) Because of a great heritage and great promise. (2) Because of a great God and a great salvation.

WORSHIP AIDS

CALL TO WORSHIP.   "Behold, I stand at the door, and knock: if any man hear my voice and open the door, I will come in to him, and will sup with him, and he with me" (Rev. 3:20).

INVOCATION.   O Christ, we open our hearts individually to you; we open the heart of our fellowship of believers to you; and we would open the hearts of men and women everywhere to you. Grant that the intimacy of our communion with you may deepen our finest motives to serve you both here and wherever we go in this world.

---

[1]Attributed to Charles Swindoll, *The Quest for Character* (Multnomah, p. 49), at www.SermonIllustrations.com.

OFFERTORY SENTENCE.   "Give unto the Lord the glory due unto his name: bring an offering, and come into his courts" (Ps. 96:8).

OFFERTORY PRAYER.   Loving Father, we do not always understand why we have enough and to spare when others have so little. But we do understand that we are stewards of what we have. Grant that our offerings may help supply bread where it is needed, and send forth your word, the bread of life, without which no one can truly live.

PRAYER.   Eternal God, Great Shepherd of the sheep, we look to you for all our needs. You provide our food and drink, the warmth of friendship, our health and strength, and human understanding and forgiveness. And when all these blessings are scarce, you give us courage to go on, patience to wait, and love that will not give up on you or on those who doubt us. In the best of times, we rest in you and find peace that passes all understanding. We thank you, Lord.

Even this moment, we face testings: we are tempted to renege on the best we know, to take shortcuts to happiness, to allow those who are blind to their own needs and careless of ours to pressure us into foolish ways. May your rod of discipline keep us in right paths.

Because you are with us, we do not have to be afraid, whether of our sinful nature, of adversaries around us, or of the baffling brutalities of the world in which we live.

Bring us ever closer to you and to those who love and serve and praise you, both now and forevermore.

SERMON
Topic: The Golden Rule
TEXT: Luke 6:27–36

A story is told about a Gentile inquirer who came to see Hillel, the famous Babylonian Jew who presided over the Sanhedrin, or supreme court of the Jews, about the time Jesus was born. Hillel was the greatest lawyer of his time, with a reputation for wisdom and fairness. The fellow who sought his counsel, on the other hand, was something of a smart aleck who thought he could discredit Hillel by asking a shrewd question. Once in the company of the great man, this fellow requested that he be taught the whole law, everything he needed to know concerning ethical conduct, while he stood on one leg. His assumption was that this was an impossible assignment and Hillel would have to admit inadequacy. The reverse was true. To the smart aleck standing on one leg Hillel answered, "What is hateful to you, do not to thy neighbor. That is the whole law. The rest is but commentary; go and learn." One source says that this questioner then became a disciple of Hillel's, so impressed was he by this reply.

"What is hateful to you, do not to thy neighbor." From Jesus' lips this sage advice was given a positive twist. Said Jesus, "In everything, do to others as you would have them do to you." He then added, "For this is the law of the prophets." A common or colloquial version of this teaching says simply, "Do as you would be done by."

We call this the Golden Rule. It was not new or original to Jesus or Hillel. Lao-tzu, Confucius, Plato, Philo, and the Old Testament all expounded the Golden Rule in one way or another, usually in its negative form. This directive summarizes ethical behavior by describing how people are to live and get along with each other. The implied question is, "How do you wish to be treated?" Answering that, we quickly perceive how we are to treat others in return. Understanding and empathy come into play, for in effect we put ourselves in someone else's place. We see things from that person's point of view and recognize what the appropriate response needs to be. It is a "golden" rule because it signifies the very best. Here is valuable advice, rich in meaning, content, and application.

Of special interest is the realization that it was the revered Jewish lawyer, Hillel, who called the Golden Rule the whole law. Hillel emphasized restraint, calling people to refrain from doing hateful or hurting things to others. Jesus, with his positive statement about doing to others as you would have them do to you, prompted his listeners to take the initiative, expressing actions of goodness and helpfulness. For Jesus, the essence of righteousness forever is the constructive doing of good; it is not the negative avoidance of evil. Active, outgoing deeds of love and service become the norm.

From a purely human point of view, Jesus has given us a tough assignment. Taking initiatives in promoting all that builds up life, all that aids and encourages our neighbors, all that is good and affirmative puts a heavy load upon us. An Indian chief bluntly said of the Golden Rule, "It is impossible. It cannot be done. If the Great Spirit that made man would give him a new heart, he could do as you say, but not else." The chief was exactly right; Jesus' teaching proves to be a reach that exceeds our grasp.

Writer G. K. Chesterton recognized this and wryly observed that Christianity has not been tried and found wanting, but it has been found difficult and so never tried. The context of the Golden Rule as we read it in Luke's Gospel includes these further teachings of Jesus: "Love your enemies, do good to those who hate you, bless those who curse you, pray for those who abuse you."

This concentration on doing good regardless of the circumstances is a bigger order than most people seem willing to accept. When you and I feel stymied or overwhelmed by the Golden Rule, it probably is because we leave out the Man who spoke it. Apart from Jesus and the power of God to create new and right hearts within us, the whole law is totally beyond implementation. Doing to others as we would have them do to us is achievable only when we turn to Jesus and say simply, "O Lord, give what you command. Enable us to fulfill your high call." Jesus gives what he commands. Let us not leave Jesus out of the equation.

Now and again, someone emerges in our experience who demonstrates the meaning of these things. Jesus' incredible ideal becomes lived out in the daily activity of certain individuals and virtually everyone is aware of their special contribution.

Henry Drummond said, "There are some men and women in whose company we are always at our best. Here are sanctifiers of souls; here, breathing through common clay, is heaven." These persons have given us glimpses of what practicing the Golden Rule with its heroic love can mean. For those of us lagging behind, Jesus—who set the goal as high and far—has compassionate understanding, provided our desire is in his direction. And provided we ask for that new heart, that new and right spirit within. Granted such a transforming orientation, you and I can begin in everything to do to others as we would have them do to us. Moreover, as Hillel said, "That is the whole law. The rest is but commentary; go and learn."— John H. Townsend

SUNDAY, SEPTEMBER 11, 2005
Lectionary Message
Topic: God's Action and Human Reaction
TEXT: Exod. 14:19–31
Other Readings: Ps. 114; Rom. 14:1–12; Matt. 18:21–35

The story of the crossing of the Red Sea is among the most widely known stories in Scripture. Believers, nonbelievers, and agnostics alike know the basics: Charlton Heston stretches out his staff and millions of extras scuffle through a path in the midst of roiling waters, temporarily suspended in midair by special effects artists. Right? Of course!

It is true that the Hollywood depiction of this event has served to burn an image into the minds of millions. Historical-critical scholars would have another version, calling into question the literal historicity of some of the fundamental features of the story. Conservative evangelical scholars would offer an apologetic supporting the facts as recorded. All of these treatments are worthy of consideration for the serious student of God's word. In the present case, however, it is not the particulars of the event that I wish to engage. Rather, it is one prominent truth that emerges from the account—namely, that when God acts, people react. Sir Isaac Newton's Third Law of Motion asserts that for every action, there is an equal and opposite reaction. In this passage we observe a similar spiritual law: "When God acts, humans have reactions, seldom equal and more often opposite."

I. *God acts.* Whatever else one may say about this record, it must be universally acknowledged that this Scripture attests to God's action. Though various readers of the text have viewed the specific elements from critically varying perspectives, all agree that this story is integral to the faith history of the Judeo-Christian tradition. At the very least, it affirms that God acts on behalf of those who trust and worship Him. This in itself is a miracle from any perspective. The psalmist's question is profound: "What is man that you [God] are mindful of him, the son of man, that you care for him?" (Ps. 8:4, NIV, parenthetical insertion mine). The core truth of the entire corpus of Scripture is that there is a God who shows himself kind, merciful, and redemptive toward humanity, as astounding as this may be! In this passage of Scripture, we read of God's powerful actions in preserving and delivering his people as they move toward the fulfillment of a divinely appointed destiny. God, in his sovereignty, is able to accomplish his purposes in our lives and to bring us safe to the promised places set before us. No force is able to deter the ultimate actualization of God's plan for his people. Always wisely and with divine intention, God acts.

II. *Humans react.* When God acts, humans react. When God does something, humans respond to it. Sometimes humans react by denying that there is a God behind whatever has happened. Sometimes humans see what God has done and question whether what he has done is good, wise, or right. Sometimes humans see what God does and, in response, ascribe to God various attributes, good or bad. Sometimes God acts and folks claim that what they perceive is God's favor toward one group as opposed to some other group. Sometimes God acts and some people tremble while others rejoice. Sometimes God acts and humans fail even to notice, which is a reaction, albeit passive.

In this story, God acts and people react. In verse 25, we read that as the Egyptians faltered in the muddy wake of the Israelite procession, they cried, "Let's get away from the Israelites!

The Lord is fighting for them against Egypt" (NIV). Their pursuit had indeed begun when they reacted to God's deliverance of his people from Egypt by stubbornly refusing to accept the finality of God's work on behalf of his people. Their response was one of self-preservation and dismay. God is against us and we are doomed, they surmised. There are still many people today who recognize that there is some deity at work but who believe that this deity is out to get them. They see God as an arbitrary and cruel force who acts maliciously in ways ranging from the mundane to the cosmic: it is this God who strikes them with acne before the prom while also causing, or at least allowing, famine, disease, and injustice. If Pharaoh had accepted God's revealed will in the beginning, there would have been no plagues. But his heart was hardened. If the Egyptians had relented and repented, they might well have enjoyed prosperity, even as they did through all of the years they lived peacefully with the Israelites in their midst. The Ninevites responded before God's promised action and were renewed. God was not out to get the Egyptians; he was out to protect and bless his people! The Egyptians, out of self-interest, sought to thwart God's plan and learned the hard way the consequences. The great teacher Gamaliel wisely counseled those who in the first century sought to thwart God's plan for the church, that such action was vain and placed them at odds with the sovereign of the universe (Acts 5:33ff, NIV). To react to God's acts by resisting, or fleeing, is to miss the grace that God offers to those who acknowledge his sovereignty and seek his face.

The Israelites did so. We learn in verse 31 that the Israelites responded to God's actions thusly: "the people feared the Lord and put their trust in him and in Moses his servant" (NIV). This was one of Israel's finest hours. The chapter that follows this story records a time of community praise and celebration as the people joyfully reacted to God's saving action on their behalf. Now, we know that Israel had low moments of doubt and disobedience as well, but only when they failed to acknowledge God's will as good and accept it for their lives without reservation. When we acknowledge God and praise him for those things he does in our lives, we please him and find peace for our souls. We may not always grasp the significance of his acts, and we will certainly have times when we are troubled and confused by unfolding circumstances beyond our understanding. But those who trust him and acknowledge the goodness of God's acts are blessed with deeper intimacy with him and inexplicable peace even in the midst of life's most threatening times. Standing on the banks of whatever obstacle flows across our paths, we may trust that God will act to guide us over and see us through. With the sage we can attest: "Trust in the Lord with all your heart and lean not on your own understanding, in all your ways acknowledge him and he will make your paths straight" (Prov. 3:5–6).

III. *When God acts, how do you react?*. The passage today is about God's great act of deliverance and the reactions of those who experienced it. The Israelites, though not without some hesitancy, followed God's lead and crossed over on dry ground. Delivered, they acknowledged God and rejoiced. The Egyptians, in the face of God's action, feared and recoiled, resisting God's revelation of himself as they had done since Moses first came to say, "Let my people go" (Exod. 7ff).

When God acts, how do you react? Do you accept God's action, trusting his wisdom and goodness, or do you flee, doubt, and recoil? By God's grace, may we grow in our capacity to acknowledge the goodness of God's nature and his acts and joyfully experience the benefits of yielding to his will in our lives.—Michael A. Wyndham

ILLUSTRATIONS

FRUITS OF FAITH.   In 1996, the community surrounding our church in the southern sector of the Louisville metro was devastated by a tornado, or perhaps several tornadoes. As I spent time working my way around the neighborhoods in the aftermath, I was struck by the reactions of the "victims"; some were praising God for life and limb, seeing his grace in what had been spared, while others vented their pain and frustration with anger or disillusionment toward God or whatever other force they imagined responsible for the devastation. Though I am not sure that my observations are entirely accurate, I am sure that at last generally I found those whose lives had reflected trust in God before the storm also saw his grace manifested in the storm's aftermath.

DIVERGENT RESPONSE.   Jesus' life and actions evoked incredibly divergent responses. When he taught concerning the cost of discipleship, many stopped following. Responding to Jesus' query as to whether the disciples would also leave him, Peter said, "Where else can we go? You have the words of life!" When Jesus performed miracles, some said, "He has a devil!" even as others said, "Who is this man that even the winds and waves obey him?" When Jesus asked the disciples to report on public perceptions of him, they said, "Some say you're John, some say Elijah or some other prophet." Jesus asked, "What about you? What do you think?" Peter answered, "You are the Christ, the Son of God!" Even as he died, some spit on him, while another confessed, "Surely, this man was the Son of God!" How astonishing that even God's clear and complete act of revealing himself in the incarnate Christ evoked, and continues to evoke, such widely varying response!

SERMON SUGGESTIONS

Topic: A Day of Remembrance
TEXT: Exod. 12:1–14, especially verse 14
(1) Then: In the history of redemption, God has invested certain days with special meaning.
(2) Always: Regular observance of special memorial events has continued to keep alive the sources of spirituality. (3) Now: The call is to recovery of former vitality through rededication to the most meaningful devotional habits.

Topic: More Than Conquerors
TEXT: Rom. 8:37–39
(1) The powers that threaten us. (2) The love that gives us victory.

WORSHIP AIDS

CALL TO WORSHIP.   "Lord, who shall abide in thy tabernacle? Who shall dwell in thy holy hill? He that walketh uprightly, and worketh righteousness, and speaketh the truth in his heart?" (Ps. 15:1–2).

INVOCATION.   Spirit of holiness and peace! Search all our motives; try the secret places of our souls; set in the light any evil that may lurk within, and lead us in the way everlasting. Take possession of our bodies. Purge them from feebleness and sloth, from all unworthy self-indulgence, that they may not hinder, but help the perfection of our spirits. Take possession of our wills that they may be one with thine, that soul and body may no longer war against each other, but live in perfect harmony, in holiness and health. Wake us as from the sleep of death, and inspire us with new resolves, and keep us blameless in body, soul, and spirit, now and ever. Let thy light fill our hearts more and more, until we shall become in truth the children of light, and perfectly at one with thee.—Samuel McComb

OFFERTORY SENTENCE.   "He which soweth sparingly shall reap sparingly; and he which soweth bountifully shall reap also bountifully" (2 Cor. 9:6).

OFFERTORY PRAYER.   O God, you did not spare your own son, but gave him up for us all. Your daily mercies are beyond our counting. May our joyous giving reflect something of the prodigality of your giving.

PRAYER.   O thou great Father of us all, we rejoice that at last we know thee. All our soul within us is glad because we need no longer cringe before thee as slaves of holy fear, seeking to appease thine anger by sacrifice and self-inflicted pain, but may come like little children, trustful and happy, to the God of love. Thou art the only true Father, and all the tender beauty of our human loves is the reflected radiance of thy loving kindness, like the moonlight from the sunlight, and testifies to the eternal passion that kindled it.

Grant us growth of spiritual vision, that with the passing years we may enter into the fullness of this our faith. Since thou art our Father, may we not hide our sins from thee but overcome them by the stern comfort of thy presence. By this knowledge, uphold us in our sorrows and make us patient even amid the unsolved mysteries of the years. Reveal to us the larger goodness and love that speak through the unbending laws of thy world. Through this faith, make us the willing equals of all thy other children.

As thou art ever pouring out thy life in sacrificial father-love, may we accept the eternal law of the cross and give ourselves to thee and to all men. We praise thee for Jesus Christ, whose life has revealed to us this faith and law, and we rejoice that he has become the firstborn among many brethren. Grant that in us too, the faith in thy fatherhood may shine through all our life with such persuasive beauty that some who still creep in the dusk of fear may stand erect as free sons of God, and that others who now through unbelief are living as orphans in an empty world may stretch out their hands to the great Father of their spirits and find thee near.—Walter Rauschenbusch

SERMON
Topic: Approaching the Fire
TEXT: Heb. 12:18–29

Roland Bainton's classic biography of Martin Luther, *Here I Stand,* tells of the young Luther's search for peace with God by entering the priesthood and submitting to the discipline of an Augustinian order. After a year as a novitiate, the young Luther took his vows and was allowed to preside in the Mass. Bainton recalled Luther's fear in first approaching the Table of the Lord. "The terror of the Holy, the horror of Infinitude smote him like a new lightning bolt, and only through a fearful restraint could he hold himself at the altar to the end."

Bainton observed that the secular idea of God in our age knows nothing of this kind of religion. In part, Luther's dread came from his childhood image of a mean and capricious god, the enemy of humanity easily offended if sacred places were violated or magical formulas mispronounced. Luther had also inherited the fear of ancient Israel before the Ark of God's presence; the God who inhabited the storm cloud by day and the fire by night in the Exodus. His was the God of Sinai into whose presence Moses could not enter with unveiled face. He was like Moses before the burning bush. He was on holy ground that required acts of submission, like removing his shoes, and an attitude of listening to the Word of God.

I. *Worship God in the splendor of holiness.* We do not switch gods when we turn the pages of our Bibles from the Old to the New Testaments. The word of the gospel in every generation is a call to worship the holy God revealed to us in the word of Scripture, from the Word of God in creation to the Word become flesh in Christ. We dare not forsake the experience of reverent awe before God repeated throughout the story of Israel. When Isaiah went to the Temple to pray at the death of King Uzziah, his vision of God was accompanied by the chorus of angels, "Holy, holy, holy is the LORD of hosts, the whole earth is full of his glory" (Isa. 6); and he was bowed by the contrast between his own sinful nature and the holiness of God: "I am a man of unclean lips . . . yet my eyes have seen the King, the LORD of hosts!"

The entire book of Hebrews is written to Jewish Christians, calling them out of the past and into the new covenant with God in Christ. The problem in Hebrews is with a people who refuse to move forward. It is a call to go with Abraham on the journey of faith, to risk all to follow Christ. Although the contrast between the covenants is real, the connection is also essential. The Old Testament is the foundation for understanding our gospel, and we are at a loss to fathom the depths of faith without an understanding of the journey of the saints who have gone before us—saints like Abraham, Sarah, and Moses. Thus we are led to visit two critical mountains in the Jewish journey, Sinai and Zion. We are reminded, "You have not come to something that can be touched." Not only the people but Moses was terrified at the presence of God on the mountain. Whatever else God was to the Jews, God was holy.

Gordon Clinard tried to get across to his seminary preaching class that we were handling fire in the ministry of worship. H. Guy Moore was Clinard's pastor at the Broadway Baptist Church in Fort Worth. I visited the church and saw the magnificent building. The place was different from any church I had ever seen. The character of the building and the service of worship was often ridiculed by seminary students as an Episcopal Baptist Church, but my experience of God in that place was also different from the ordinary trip to church on Sundays. Clinard's pastor told him that he never reached for the doorknob to enter that sanctuary of worship that he did not feel a grip of fear. He was charged with the responsibility of the Word of God for that hour. He had a sense of being on holy ground. After a few years of reaching for that door in other places, I began to understand.

II. *Worship is also celebration.* In stark contrast with the dread and fear of Sinai, we are called to Mount Zion, to the festal gathering of the heavenly Jerusalem, to a kingdom that cannot be shaken. The author of Hebrews (4:16) had already issued a call to boldness: "Let us therefore approach the throne of grace with boldness, so that we may receive mercy and find grace to help in time of need." The gospel of grace is an open door before the holy God. Through Christ, we are encouraged to approach God not because of our merit or achievement but because Christ has led the way. We have a high priest who intercedes before this holy God and who has revealed for all time that God's holiness is wrapped in "love divine, all loves excelling."

The Hebrew Christians were reminded that the celebration of God is also rooted in Jewish experience. The trip to Jerusalem for the great Jewish festivals was like a family vacation.

In the Psalms, approaching the Temple, the dwelling place of God, was a call to exuberant joy: "Make a joyful noise to the LORD, all the earth. Worship the Lord with gladness; come into his presence with singing" (100). We are called out of the gloom and darkness of Sinai to the celebration of the joy in Jerusalem. Every experience of worship ought to be a call to joy in the God of our salvation. Every prayer ought to contain the word of thanksgiving and praise to the God of every good gift. To be worship, our gathering as church must always include praise to God.

As a child, I had trouble with being quiet anytime, especially in church. Life was all about fun and games, and the serious stuff in church did not meet me where I lived. I was in serious trouble more than once for wiggling when I was supposed to be still or talking when I was supposed to be quiet. Of course, these were problems I had in school as well as in church. Being serious just did not fit into my agenda, and I welcomed the suggestion that came through to me in my teens that church is a place of joy, and worship is celebration. We never want to communicate to our children that God is gloom and doom or that worship is terror. Reverence before God is far from a negative spirit.

III. *Worship is more than celebration.* We are called to "offer to God an acceptable worship with reverence and awe." With maturity comes the realization that we do not live on mountaintops of perpetual song and dance. The call of reverence in worship acknowledges that "God is a consuming fire." The nature of God calls us to reverence. The popular reference in song to "the man upstairs" just does not fit with the holy God of either Sinai or Zion. All worship must recognize the nature of God beyond the stretch of our highest imagination. If God is God, then we find ourselves, with Moses, removing our shoes before the burning bush and, with Isaiah, acknowledging that we are among the people of unclean lips. Reverence has nothing to do with self-hatred or flight from the presence of God. Reverence is the call to stunned awe before the splendor of God's holy nature.

The nature of life calls us to reverence. Life is more than celebration. I asked a guest in our church, Kara Jean Porter, to speak to us today. When we were remembering our experiences together in our church in St. Louis twenty-eight years ago, she refreshed our memory of the time when she almost lost her child and the church dared to approach God in intercessory prayer. As I remember with Kara Jean the roller coaster of emotions, the sheer terror and the stunned joy, I commented, "This is what the church is about." Of course, we rejoiced that the child survived without any serious impact on his mental or physical ability, but something even greater happened that day. We were young and learning what it means to be church, and we learned that day to approach God in reverence and awe. More than healing, we had a life-changing experience of the holy presence of a loving God.—Larry Dipboye

SUNDAY, SEPTEMBER 18, 2005
Lectionary Message

Topic: Lessons from a Murmuring Mob

TEXT: Exod. 16:2–15

Other Readings: Ps. 105:1–6, 37–45; Phil. 1:21–30; Matt. 20:1–16

My father loves God's word and has taught it to others in his Sunday school classes throughout his adult life. He has a gift for forming vibrant images in the minds of those who listen to his treatment of the biblical text. This story from Exodus evokes an image in my mind every time I read it, an image he first planted when I was a child. You see, Dad is also a big fan of the old B-Western flicks. You know, the Hoot Gibson, Lash LaRue variety. Most of those films told pretty much the same story and had fairly interchangeable scenes. One common scene was the "murmuring mob." A group of weather-beaten cowboys are sitting in the bar, listening to a lively piano ditty, playing cards, and having a generally fine time, when in strolls the stranger. Dead quiet descends on the place until someone approaches him and suspiciously inquires, "What can we do for you, Stranger?" "Oh nuthin' much," he replies, "I'm just gettin' the lay o' the land around here. I'm Ben Carson. I just bought the Johnson place. Plan to herd some sheep out there." As sure as Cassidy Hops-a-Long, this sheepherder's revelation of his un-American intentions to eschew cows in favor of sheep is going to be greeted by an unintelligible but easily discernible MURMUR, MURMUR, MURMUR. The murmuring mob scene may be repeated several more times before the hero kisses the sheepherder's daughter as the credits roll.

My Dad always said that the persistent grumbling of the mob of Israelites as they wandered in the desert must have sounded a lot like that. Our passage today centers on the murmuring mob scene.

I. *Murmuring over memories.* To set the scene, we remember that the Israelites were slaves in Egypt, bending low under heavy burdens. God heard their cries for help and sent Moses to lead them out of Egypt and toward the Promised Land. As we join the journey today, the multitude of Israelites has recently seen God's power displayed in the dividing of the Red Sea, allowing their final escape from Pharaoh's army. Almost immediately on the heels of the rejoicing on the other side of the sea, there are two incidents of complaining, of which this is the second. At Marah, they murmured about the lack of water and God provided. Now they are as far as the Desert of Sin, and their patience is again wearing thin. Lights, camera—CUE THE MURMURING—action!

Funny what a little hardship can do to one's memory. The Israelites are not far removed from their experience of slavery and their cries for help, but now, as they reflect back on that time, they remember it almost fondly! "What are we doing in this God-forsaken wilderness? In Egypt we sipped stew by the fire in our family rooms, and here we are with sand in our shoes and nothing in our bellies. Oh, for the good old days in Egypt!" MURMUR, MURMUR, MURMUR.

It would be funnier if it weren't so tragic . . . and so like so many of us. Having pastored churches for about twenty years now, I am quite familiar with this phenomenon. Somehow, there always seems to be some Golden Era in the past of so many of God's folk. In that time in the church's past, the pastor was blameless, the singing superb, the youth program energetic but spiritual, and the sanctuary would hardly hold the throngs. This same condition seems to be common among individuals as well. Ah, how fond the memory of one's past: strong, confident, good-looking, and suave, we did stride like the heroes of old through the land of Back Then. For some reason, it is the now that most commonly prompts us to grumble. Even if it's better now than it was then, it's not now as good as it could be, or not as wonderful as we hoped it would be when we looked ahead to now from then. So we grumble. We find reasons, to be sure: I weigh too much. My house is too small. My closet is too empty. My children are too demanding. My job is too meaningless. Our church is too small. Our this is too that. My this is too the other thing. It will never be as good again as it once was. So we murmur, we grumble.

II. *God has heard your grumbling.* Israel grumbled and God heard. Just as God heard when they cried out in misery—real misery—in Egypt, he heard when they whined in the wilderness. How patiently God hears! He did not chastise the Israelites despite their faithlessness. He just heard and acted to meet their needs. How gracious is our God! God would have been justified in pointing out all he had already done for them, how pitifully self-centered they were, how little they trusted in God to know and meet their needs. Later in Exodus, God does vent his anger over the continual murmuring and faithlessness of his people (chapter 32), but not yet, not at this juncture. God is longsuffering, and patient.

Ostensibly, the Israelites murmured because they were hungry. The fact is they grumbled every chance they got, for any convenient reason. The root of their grumbling was not particular circumstance, but rather a fundamental lack of trust. They lived in fear and uncertainty, provoked by every slight obstacle to imagine the worst was upon them. They seemed to be ever seeking proof that God was still there and worthy of their trust. Sound familiar? I squirm a bit when I read this story, and maybe you do as well. All too often, I'm not so different from these murmuring mobsters. Sometimes I shrink back from following God's lead into unknown places, no matter how great the promise of those places, preferring instead security, even if the security is in a place without promise. Sometimes, when I do step out, I cry constantly to God, panicking if I sense that he is not near, especially when the path bends toward a dark shadowy place beyond which I am unable to see. Sometimes my cry crosses the line between the cry from Egypt and the whining in the wilderness. At these times, my cry is not a desperate plea for help from the only source where help may be found; it is, rather, the hollow whimper of a faithless grumbler. Either way, God hears. Thank God he patiently hears, but I am sure that when I grumble, God is saddened and sometimes angered. When I grumble I fail to acknowledge that God is worthy of my trust, compassionate to care and able to provide.

III. *God's response: just enough and not too much.* So, God heard their faithless murmuring. God's response was to provide, but to do so in a way that would advance Israel's growth toward a more mature faith. He would send them more than enough bread and meat for each day, but they were to gather *only enough for the day.* Would they trust that God would provide tomorrow? Or would they fearfully grab all they could, trying to ensure adequate provision for the future while they had the chance?

When Jesus taught his disciples to pray (Matt. 6:9ff), he taught them the same lesson. Jesus said we should pray for our *daily* bread, trusting that the God who provided yesterday, and whom we are petitioning for provision today, will also be there for us tomorrow. Like the Israelites, we must trust God for today.

Most of the Israelites learned the lesson, but if we read beyond our passage of today, we learn that some gave in to the temptation to faithlessly hoard for tomorrow. The process of learning to trust—and not to murmur—is not an easy one and is not mastered without persistence and growth through experience, sometimes through the experience of failure. This is a lesson worth learning, as attested by the apostle Paul, who, after enduring all sorts of circumstances, was able to affirm that he had learned to be content in whatever circumstance (Phil. 4:11, paraphrased). This level of trust is the secret to contentment that will quiet the murmuring mobster within each of us.—Michael A. Wyndham

ILLUSTRATIONS

TRUST.   On learning to trust God's nature: it seems that this passage also prompts me to another fond, and instructive, memory of an experience with my dad. Growing up in south

Alabama, one of the rituals of autumn (to the slight degree there is anything like autumn on the Gulf Coast!) was raking pine needles from the shallow roof of our ranch-style house. When I reached the age of about five, my dad took me up on the roof with him while he tackled that chore. He sat me down at a safe point far from the edge, and I was thrilled to take in the view from that dizzying perch. An agile and athletic man, when he finished his work he leapt nimbly to the ground. Then he stretched up his arms and instructed me to jump to him. Now, he was a bit over six feet tall and the roofline at its edge only perhaps eight-and-a-half feet from the ground. So for me to jump to his reaching arms was to negotiate only a foot or less of distance. It may as well have been a freefall from thirty thousand feet. Such was my fear. "I don't know if you can catch me," I cried.

"You're right," Dad said, "I'm asking you to do something you have never done before and you don't know if I can catch you. But, you do know that *I love you and would not ask you to jump if I could not catch you.*" That's all it took. I jumped.

He caught me. I knew he would, because I trusted his very nature.

PROBLEMS.   "Don't complain and talk about all your problems—80 percent of people won't care and the other 20 percent will think you deserve them." (Attributed to Mark Twain on www.SermonIllustrations.com)

SERMON SUGGESTIONS

Topic: Our Daily Bread
TEXT: Exod. 16:2–15
(1) Need and disenchantment. (2) Grace and provision.

Topic: Arguing for God
TEXT: Rom. 11:13–16, 29–32
(1) God desires the salvation of all people, Jews and non-Jews alike. (2) God's strange ways are designed to achieve the salvation of both Jews and non-Jews with utter faithfulness to his purpose.

WORSHIP AIDS
CALL TO WORSHIP.   "Whatsoever things are true, whatsoever things are honest, whatsoever things are pure, whatsoever things are lovely, whatsoever things are of good report; if there be any virtue, and if there be any praise, think on these things" (Phil. 4:8).

INVOCATION.   O God, as we strive to achieve our place under the sun, grant us the wisdom to trace the steps of our Lord Jesus Christ in his servanthood and grant us the courage to follow him. To that end, give us a new vision of true greatness as we wait before thee.

OFFERTORY SENTENCE.   "God is able to give you more than you need, so that you will always have all you need for yourselves and more than enough for every good cause" (2 Cor. 9:8, TEV).

OFFERTORY PRAYER.   Gracious Lord, thou hast given us all things to enjoy, to share with others, and to make us better and more useful servants of thine. Now deepen our love, open our hands, and help us to know the joy of a cheerful giver.

PRAYER.   O Jesus, we thy ministers bow before thee to confess the common sins of our calling. Thou knowest all things; thou knowest that we love thee and that our hearts' desire is to serve thee in faithfulness; and yet, like Peter, we have so often failed thee in the hour of thy need. If ever we have loved our own leadership and power when we sought to lead our people to thee, we pray thee to forgive. If we have been engrossed in narrow duties and little questions, when the vast needs of humanity called aloud for prophetic vision and apostolic sympathy, we pray thee to forgive. If, in our loyalty to the church of the past, we have distrusted thy living voice and have suffered thee to pass from our door unheard, we pray thee to forgive. If ever we have been more concerned for the strong and the rich than for the shepherdless throngs of the people for whom thy soul grieved, we pray thee to forgive.—Walter Rauschenbusch

SERMON
Topic: Respect for Wealth
TEXT: James 2:1–17

According to the great columnist Walter Lippmann the purpose of the Christian church is to lay down the law to everybody as to what they are supposed to do. There is just too much crime. There is just too much lack of discipline. There is just too much permissiveness, and the preachers of this country had better get on the tick and start preaching the Word of God. In one of his columns Lippmann said, "Fundamentally the great churches are secular institutions; they are governments preoccupied inevitably with the regulations of the unregenerate appetites of mankind. In their scriptures there is to be found the teaching that true salvation depends upon internal reform of desire. But since this reform is so very difficult, in practice the Churches have devoted themselves not so much to making real conversions, as to governing the dispositions of the unconverted multitude." That is what the Church is supposed to be: the policeman of society telling people what is right and wrong and telling them what is to happen if they don't obey God.

Lippmann is not the only one who believes that. Harold Macmillan, a former prime minister of Great Britain, in a conversation with David Frost on TV, said in his country it was the job of the clergy, the state-sponsored clergy, to tell the people what was right and wrong and what happened if they did not do right. There are still lots of people who think that our society is slowly sinking into a moral quicksand, and that decay is caused by the failure of preachers to preach the commandments of God. Supposedly we need a much stronger voice in the pulpit saying, "Thus sayeth the Lord," and a second sermon that sounds for all the world like Maude on the old TV program when her husband violated one of her rules, "God is going to get you for that, Walter."

I have no problem with that. This is a moral universe, and there are eternal realities against which we beat our heads and destroy ourselves. There are God-created, God-given, God-maintained absolutes, and we need to lift them up before the people so that all people may find that sense of joy, the feeling of fitness, that sense of in the groove; the absence of resistance and twistedness, the rush of delight that comes with the perfect golf swing, the excitement of when the bass strikes the line, the satisfaction when the tenon fits the mortise, when life moves in congruency with the will and purpose of God. God is Lord of life and Sovereign over history, and there are disappointments, pain, and suffering where we strive to live in opposition to the will and purpose of God. Yes, we need to declare that loudly, consistently, and boldly.

So let us pick up right here where James reminds his Christian congregation that God has given them a new commandment; this is the will and law of God, that you love one another as you love yourself, and that you love God with all your heart, mind, and soul. To disregard this law and purpose of God is to court conflict, pain, suffering, and divisiveness. To be obedient to the Law of God to love one another as you love yourself will express itself in worship in the equality of all people in the congregation. "Show no partiality as you hold the faith of our Lord Jesus Christ."

"To love your neighbor as yourself," as James has reminded us that God has commanded, requires tremendous discipline. It will express itself in many different ways in the public arena, but James says that one of the most obvious ways the discipline of loving our neighbors as ourselves will show up in worship is that there will be no favoritism. And James knows exactly where we are most likely to be weak, where our greatest temptation will come. When a rich person walks in the door, we will be much more likely to smile, offer them a bulletin, invite them to sit next to us, or even perhaps to take our favorite pew, than we would be to welcome the person in dirty clothes who has not had a bath in a week. It requires immense discipline and devotion to God to live out this policy of no partiality to anyone, especially the rich.

Reynolds Price, whom many of you enjoy as a writer, writes from the perspective of a believer and a follower of God. But Price has declared often in publications that he does not go to worship regularly because he thinks that every time he goes his presence disrupts the flow of worship. The congregation gets all excited that they have a famous writer in attendance; people stare at him and do not turn their eyes upon Jesus. We need a lot of discipline and practice to be able to obey and observe the implication of no favoritism in worship if we are true to the commandment to love God and to love our neighbor as ourselves.

One Sunday morning, while I was working at First Presbyterian Church in Raleigh, about 10:00, before worship, one of the ushers answered the phone. On the other end was one of the advance people for a candidate for president of the United States, who happened to be in Raleigh over the weekend. The caller was calling to see if we would be willing to have the candidate attend worship. The caller knew that we were broadcast live to most of Eastern North Carolina and was wondering what we would say to the idea of the candidate showing up for our worship service. The usher was taken aback, and all he could think of to say was that worship was at 11:00 a.m. and all were welcomed. The candidate did not come. We heard later that they were hoping for a little more response on our part. They were looking for a little more favoritism. They were thinking about being recognized by the preacher, or asked to stand and acknowledge the greeting of the congregation, or invited to come forward and say something. "Worship is at 11:00 A.M., and all are welcome." It takes the Holy Spirit or discipline to be able to say that. We all agreed that had the advance person called on Friday and talked with us about it, we would have been much more tempted to find a way of accommodation.

Have some discipline in worship. Show no partiality, no favoritism to the rich or famous. James knows us so well and knows how tempted we will be to fawn all over the rich and powerful. But that is because we do not know the value of the faith stories and the faith journeys of the poor. "Has not God chosen those who are poor in the world to be rich in faith and heirs of the kingdom which he has promised to all those who love him?" To show partiality to the wealthy of the world is to display a failure to value the things of the spirit and the witness of God's power in the lives of others.

The fellowship of worship has to be a gathering where we come to praise God's love and mercy for all. It is the place where we affirm that all have fallen short of the glory of God and all are forgiven by the mercy of God. We are all equal before the cross, and to show partiality is to deny the very foundation upon which we gather. It is to go back to making the evaluations about people on the basis of the standards of the world. This week the Internet had as one of its lead stories a list of the ten richest men under forty years old. The world shows partiality on the basis of riches; the company of saints is to have the discipline to show no partiality in worship. First come, first served. All of us standing on the same level at the throne of God.

This is the new commandment given to us by the love and grace of God as that grace lived and moved among us in Jesus Christ: that we love God with all our hearts, minds, and souls, and that we love our neighbors as ourselves. In worship that means no partiality or favoritism to any. And the judgment of God upon us is that where we fail in that commandment, we find divisions. We find hostility. We find jealousy. We find competition. We find apathy. We find behavior problems in those who want to be noticed and appreciated. We find the kind of collapse and disintegration of society that we are complaining about.

There is in the Christian faith a great demand for discipline of our hearts and minds. There is a great need for us to surrender our hearts and minds to the spirit of Christ so that we might be given the strength to grow and discover how to love equally all those who are our neighbors. It is not easy, and it is not always obvious to us. There is the story in Mark's Gospel of the conversation Jesus had with a Syrophoenician woman. The woman, an outsider, one of the Other kind of people, comes begging Jesus for help with a demon in her daughter. Jesus says he cannot help her. He has come to bring the grace of God to the children of God. He has come to the Jews. He cannot be taking the gifts he has for the Jews and giving it to the Samaritans. Jesus speaks as if God has a partiality for the Jews. The woman does not flinch. She does not back away. She absorbs her insult of being called a dog without response. She says, "But even dogs get to receive the crumbs on the floor." And Jesus realizes that indeed God's grace is for this Samaritan woman even as it is for the children of Israel. His favoritism is not necessary. It is not appropriate. It is not needed. God has enough for all to receive some. He sends her home with the assurance that her daughter is well.

Jesus says it is his new commandment, that you "love one another as I have loved you." "That you love the Lord your God with all your heart, mind and soul, and that you love the neighbor as you love yourself." And where we do not find the power or the discipline to live by the standard, God does get us, God lets us live in the world of our own distinctions, our partialities, our favoritism, where Jew and Arab kill each other, where our favorite American soldiers try to impose our will on Iraqi people, where blacks and whites fight over who is getting the largest piece of the college admission pie, where we scramble for who gets the cheapest gas and biggest tax cut. It is our mission, our work, to share with the world the God-given absolutes and to threaten them with the consequences. We can live in the spirit and grace of Jesus Christ with the heart to love God and to love our neighbor, or we can live and suffer in the chaos of our fractured, hostile, and petty world. It is our job to say that to the world.— Rick Brand

SUNDAY, SEPTEMBER 25, 2005
Lectionary Message

Topic: How Would Jesus Think?

TEXT: Phil. 2:1–13

Other Readings: Exod. 17:1–7; Ps. 78: 1–4, 12–16; Matt. 21:23–32

In recent years, many modern Christians have rediscovered Charles Sheldon's paradigm for Christian ethics, "What Would Jesus Do?" The phrase has been popularized on T-shirts, bracelets, bookmarks, and bumper stickers. It's a pithy phrase that, if taken seriously, is a meaningful guide for Christian living. It occurs to me that action always has its ground in attitude. How we act proceeds from how we think and how our basic core is oriented. Right action is the result of right attitude. This marvelous passage in Paul's affectionate letter to the church at Philippi teaches us that to act like Christ we must, to borrow another popular phrase, have an "attitude adjustment." In other words, if we are to do as Jesus does, we must have the mind of Christ. When we have the attitude of the Savior, our behaviors will mirror his pattern of behavior. So how would Jesus think? What is the attitude of the Savior? What is that mind of Christ to which we aspire? Let's turn our attention to the latter half of this passage.

I. *A hymn about him.* Verses 6–11 are arranged in such a way as to suggest to many scholars that they actually may have composed the first, or one of the first, hymns of the church. Whether or not this is the case, this subset of our reading does form a beautiful and powerful Christ-centered reflection. Following the admonition in verse 5 that we as believers should have the "attitude" (as translated in the NIV) of Christ, this poetic section describes that model of attitude as seen in the life of Jesus. The attitudinal attributes of Jesus revolve around his willingness to act selflessly. Though he might have clung to his preincarnate sovereignty, he opted to deny his own interest in favor of humanity, taking on the form of a servant and ultimately suffering an ignominious death as an act of obedience to the Father's will. He was selfless (holding the interests of others above his own), humble (willing to assume any station necessary to advance the interests of the other), and obedient (submissive to the will of God the Father in attitude and action). The five verses before, and the two verses following, this central hymn call on us to emulate the actions of Jesus. Thus the necessity of understanding and assuming the attitude that was the ground of Jesus' behavior. We are also to be selfless, humble, and obedient so that our behaviors will be Christlike.

II. *The results of having the mind of Christ in us.* The fruit of Christ-mindedness is described in verses 1–4. Even as Christ was one with the Father, we are called to be like-minded, unified in purpose. This is not a call for lockstep conformity with one another in every opinion, but rather agreement in our desire to seek to live with one another cooperatively in the spirit of Christ. Jesus prayed also for this unity of heart and soul among believers in the great priestly prayer recorded in John 17. Jesus' prayer sets a high standard indeed for our unity: "I pray also . . . that all of them may be one, Father *just as you are in me and I am in* you . . . *so that the world may believe that you have sent me*" (John 17:20–21). Our very witness in the world can be no greater than our unity; the world's belief hinges on our like-mindedness.

We are also told to be, like Jesus, other-centered rather than self-centered. Paul urges the Philippians to avoid selfish motivations and to look "to the interests of others," considering others "better than yourselves" (vv. 3, 4). This is perhaps the most challenging admonition in Scripture and is central to the example and teaching of Jesus. Just as Jesus suffered selflessly in order that we might receive the saving benefit of his death, so we are called to "deny ourselves and take up the cross and follow [Jesus]" (Matt. 16:24, NIV). Jesus says we are to love as we have been loved by laying down our lives for our friends (John 15:12, 13, paraphrased from NIV). There is no greater love than this!

Finally, we are to have attitudes of obedience leading to acts of obedience even as Jesus submitted himself to God's purposes by his death on our behalf. Paul assures the Philippians that God is working in them "to will and to act according to his good purpose," and as such they are called to continue being obedient in persistently living out God's call on their lives, "working out their salvation with fear and trembling" (vv. 12–13, NIV). Those who have the mind, the attitude, of Christ live obediently, submitting themselves to the will and purposes of God.

The next time you purpose to do as Jesus would do, make sure you are careful to think as he would think! When our attitudes are like those of Jesus, the Christ-likeness of our actions will follow!—Michael A. Wyndham

ILLUSTRATIONS

LIKE CHRIST.   When told that a newspaper writer had likened him to an apostle, Adoniram Judson replied, "I do not want to be like a Paul, or any mere man. I want to be like Christ! I want to follow him only, copy his teachings, drink of his spirit, and place my feet in his steps. Oh, to be like Christ!"—Source unknown (www.SermonIllustrations.com)

CHOICE.   Everything can be taken from a man but one thing: To choose one's attitude in any given set of circumstances, to choose one's way.—Viktor Frankl, concentration camp survivor (www.SermonIllustrations.com)

SERMON SUGGESTIONS

Topic: The Glory of the People of God
TEXT: Isa. 61:10–62:3, RSV
(1) It is a blessing to be hoped for, though not yet achieved. (2) It will be a blessing from God, though requiring the integrity of his people.

Topic: Our New Status
TEXT: Gal. 4:4–7
(1) Its basis. (2) Its confirmation. (3) Its privileges.

WORSHIP AIDS
CALL TO WORSHIP.   "Lord, I have loved the habitation of thy house, and the place where thine honour dwelleth" (Ps. 26:8).

INVOCATION.   O God our Father, make this truly a house of prayer today. May we call upon you in the confidence that you do hear us. May we surrender to you our selfishness and greed so that nothing will hinder our prayers.

OFFERTORY SENTENCE.   "Bear ye one another's burdens, and so fulfill the law of Christ" (Gal. 6:2).

OFFERTORY PRAYER.   Most gracious heavenly Father, we thank you for the many gifts that we have received of your bountiful and benevolent hand. We humbly and lovingly return unto you a portion of that which you have bestowed upon us. Accept these our gifts, O Lord, as a symbol of the consecration of our lives and means for the coming of your Kingdom.—Rodney K. Miller

PRAYER.   O Infinite Source of life and health and joy! The very thought of thee is so wonderful that in this thought we would rest and be still. Thou art Beauty and Grace and Truth and Power. Thou art the light of every heart that sees thee, the life of every soul that loves thee, the strength of every mind that seeks thee. From our narrow and bounded world we would pass into thy greater world. From our petty and miserable selves we would escape to thee, to find thee the power and the freedom of a larger life. It is our joy that we can never go beyond thy reach: that even were we to take the wings of the morning, and fly unto the uttermost parts of the earth, or were we to make our bed in hell, there should we find signs of thy presence and thy power. Wherever we may go thou art with us, for thou art in us as well as without us. We recognize thee in all the deeper experiences of the soul. When the conscience utters its warning voice, when the heart is tender and we forgive those who have wronged us in word or deed, when we feel ourselves upborne above time and place, and know ourselves citizens of thy everlasting Kingdom, we realize, O Lord, that these things, while they are in us, are not of us. They are thine, the work of thy Spirit brooding upon our souls.—Samuel McComb

SERMON
Topic: Now Is the Hour
TEXT: Rom. 13:8–14

The cartoon "Frank and Ernest" shows the two little guys in an art gallery looking at sculptures. They are standing with a puzzled look before a display labeled "Procrastination." Among the carefully crafted figures in the background, the object of their attention is a large, square block of uncut stone.

We prefer to brush off the problem with humor. At a time when it seemed that everyone was getting into an exercise program, a friend told me that whenever he had the urge to exercise he would lie down and rest until the urge passed.

The little button showed up in church one Sunday morning. It was a round, yellow, metal tag with the letters "TUIT" printed in the center. I took the bait and asked what the button meant and was informed that this is "a round tuit," as in, "whenever I get around to it."

Procrastination has its own creed: if anything is worth doing, it has already been done. All deadlines are unreasonable regardless of the amount of time given. If at first you don't succeed, wait till next year. Never put off until tomorrow, what you can avoid forever. The procrastination club has never gotten around to organizing, but the members meet once a year at the shopping center on Christmas Eve.

The question hangs in Romans: Could God be a procrastinator, and has Christ left us here with this mess forever? The message of Paul to Roman Christians was, "It is now the moment for you to wake from sleep." The delayed parousia, the return of Christ, had taken the urgency out of the gospel message. Day after day the first Christians looked at the heavens for the return of Christ, and all they saw was the same sun rising and setting. Christ had come and gone. Rome was still in charge of the world, the darkness of evil continued to prevail, economic instability continued to create fear of the future, friends continued to die. While waiting for the final justice of God to be established in the new political reality called the Kingdom of God, injustice ruled. The church was beginning to fall asleep at the wheel of history. Christians struggling to make the transition from the Jesus of history to the Christ of eternity were beginning to give up. Maybe the man who was born in Bethlehem and died in Jerusalem has left the stage of history forever.

Paul has a pattern in his epistles. Paul always moves from theology to ethics, from the big ideas about God to the practical application of the gospel. After Christmas and the confrontation with the wonderful theology of the incarnation of God in Christ, we need to answer the most practical question of all: So what?

I. *Wake up to the new day.* Jerry and I shared an apartment for over two years at Baylor. He was later the best man in my wedding. We learned to live with each other's peculiar interests and preferences and remained friends after Jerry's graduation, in spite of the close-quarter drill. Jerry owned a luxury item for students of our day, an alarm radio. I had a travel alarm clock that worked rather well, but Jerry had a problem with the sound of an alarm clock. It fell somewhere between the scream of a cat and fingernails on a chalk board for him, so he agreed to set the radio for whenever I wanted to get up, just to keep me from using the alarm clock. I don't know of anyone who enjoys being awakened out of a sound sleep, and I suspect that Jerry's distaste for alarms came form unpleasant memories of a history of rude awakenings.

Carolyn wisely equipped both of our children with their own alarm clocks. She did not want them to associate her with the pain of waking up every morning.

In spite of the pain, Paul was sounding an alarm. It was characteristic of his preaching in other epistles. Christians lived between the time of the incarnation of God in Christ and the time when God will be all and in all. The Thessalonian church battled despair in waiting for the return of Christ, and the apostle assured them that friends and loved ones who had gone before them in death would be first in the final resurrection. But the problem of delay was not only about questions of death and resurrection; it was about lifestyle and behavior. Shall we live on the watch, believing in the certain return of Christ potential in every sunrise? Shall we go to sleep in Zion, resting on the featherbed of past commitments and old confessions of faith? Shall we rest on the laurels of what God has done in Christ, passively waiting for God to work it out?

The same word for time, *kairos,* is found in the message from Mark that began our journey into Advent. Jesus came preaching that the time is fulfilled. The time was ripe for the rule of God in the hearts and lives of God's children. The time was ripe for the Christ to be born, for the light of God to dawn in the darkness of the Roman world of pagan inhumanity. The time is ripe to live out the gospel to break through the political and social corruption of the age. It's time to wake up and to turn on the lights.

II. *Love one another.* John Paul Carter was a classmate in seminary. He tells of growing up in Dallas getting his haircuts at a shop that had a shoeshine stand in the corner run by an African American man who entertained the shop with a joyful spirit and sharp wit. His statement of faith was on a tag he wore on his jacket: "While you wait—Jesus saves." As John grew up and responded to the calling of God to Christian ministry, he found a companion in the journey across the barriers of race and age. As he told the story, John observed the truth in the message that we live in the meantime. While you wait for your ship to come in, to grow up, to finish school, to get your dream job or big promotion, to find your perfect mate and be blessed with your perfect children, or perhaps to reap the reward of life in retirement, remember that Jesus saves. In the meantime, God is among us in Christ. The incarnation is more than a Christmas theology to be dusted off for December sermons. God is incarnate in God's people. The church is the body of Christ, and life is what happens while you are waiting for something else.

While you wait, hear the Word of God in Christ. The Law of God is fulfilled in the role of love. The practical rule of life comes down to the ethics of love applied to the real life-and-death situations of this world.

Living in the heyday of the great Roman Empire, one of the practical questions that Paul addressed in Romans 13 was how to live under a government that seems so alien to the gospel of Christ. Augustine lived to witness the decline and fall of Rome. Some three centuries after Paul, Augustine committed his faith in Christ, reading the words of Romans 13: "not in reveling and drunkenness, not in debauchery and licentiousness, not in quarreling and jealousy. Instead put on the Lord Jesus Christ, and make no provision for the flesh, to gratify its desires." In his mind he heard the voices of children calling for him to open the Scriptures and read, and he turned to the message of Paul to the Romans. He shared the passage with his friend Alypius, and both made a life-changing commitment in Christ. After they were baptized, Augustine vowed to leave the darkness of sin behind to live out his days in service to God. His new faith led to priesthood and eventually the office of bishop.

The Bishop of Hyppo left a legacy of writings that rival the apostle Paul in influence on subsequent generations. As Christ put on the flesh and blood of humankind to reconcile us to God, let us put on Christ to reveal his love to the world.—Larry Dipboye

SUNDAY, OCTOBER 2, 2005
Lectionary Message

Topic: Rejected

TEXT: Matt. 21:33–46

Other Readings: Exod. 20:1–4, 7–9, 12–20; Ps. 19; Phil. 3:4b–14

Who could have known how things would turn out for Jesus? In Matthew's account of the approaching passion of Jesus Christ, the events leading up to that moment are quite remarkable. In the opening sentences of the chapter (vv. 1–11), Jesus is given a royal welcome into the holy city of Jerusalem. The crowds flocked to the trail that Jesus would follow and offered up to him the kind of praises often reserved for royalty or dignitaries.

Matthew is quick to introduce us to the inconsistent ethos of the crowd. One moment they embrace Jesus as a welcome prophet, but by the next day their adoring welcome has turned to outright rejection of the one sent by God. With the echoes of revelry still in the air, Matthew doesn't want us to miss the utter rejection that lies just around the bend.

The sequence of events is critical to note. Upon Jesus' arrival into Jerusalem, he immediately entered the Temple, where he disavowed the secular methods of the moneychangers and the merchants. As if to say that in his Kingdom every thing is topsy-turvy, Jesus proceeded to "turn the tables" in the Temple (vv. 12–17). The action and impact of his arrival in Jerusalem has yet to be fully realized. The next day Jesus cursed the fig tree (vv. 18–22), returned to the Temple, where once again he tangled with the religionists about his authority (vv. 23–27), shared an intriguing parable about two sons with varying degrees of commitment to the Kingdom (vv. 28–32), and then ultimately unveiled his role in God's revelatory process.

The parable of the vineyard is essentially a condensed version of God's self-revealing nature to humanity.

I. *The owner reveals his provision through the image of the vineyard (v. 33).* Everything that could be and should be provided was offered in the vineyard, including a protective hedge, functional winepress, and a tower (cf. Isa. 5:1–7). On the surface, every provision imaginable was present. There was, however, one element completely lacking in the vineyard. The owner was not physically present or available. The owner was at a distance. Thus it was impossible for the tenants to know or develop a relationship with him.

Many view their relationship with God in the same vein. Believing that God is a distant and benevolent ruler, they prefer to look to a God of distance, not a God of intimacy. Yet the very essence of this parable of Jesus is to clearly reveal God's desire not to be heard from a distance but to be experienced up close and personally.

II. *The owner entrusted his purpose to the servants (v. 35).* The trusting owner in the parable graciously (or was it naïvely?) offered the privileges and responsibilities of actual property ownership to the tenant farmers. Clearly believing them to be responsible and trustworthy, the owner left town to visit another country. Still the owner did not abdicate full authority to the tenants, for when the harvest time was near he sent his servants to the property to secure his rightful portion of the harvest.

At this point in the story, things turn ugly. Those whom the owner sent to harvest his fruit were savagely attacked, leaving one dead. Rather than exact rightful revenge, the ever-patient owner sends yet another group of servants to the vineyard, and once again the same results occur.

By virtue of this teaching parable, Jesus is clearly implicating those who have not accepted the authority of those prophets and representatives of God who had preceded his earthly ministry. They were sent by God to tend to the vineyard, and their welcome was brutal and far from welcoming.

III. *The owner reveals his priority through his son (v. 37).* Believing that the respect due the owner will be afforded to his son, the owner sends one final representative to the vineyard. The tenants, however, did not look upon the moment as ripe with opportunity to respect the owner; rather, they saw it as ripe with vulnerability, and they seized the son and killed him, with the bizarre logic of believing that if they killed the son, the grieving father would actually give *them* the inheritance.

The intention of Jesus is remarkably clear. The father has extended himself in every imaginable way, but the recipients of his grace fail to recognize his benevolence. Indeed, says Jesus, "the very stone which the builders rejected has become the chief corner" (v. 42; cf. Ps. 118:22–23).

The ministry of Jesus was subject to great ridicule and rejection. There was, however, no greater rejection than that of his own people. Upon hearing these indicting words, the Scripture indicates that the chief priests and Pharisees understood the aim of Jesus' parable. They understood that the language of rejection was being leveled at them.

Rejection continues, does it not? The chief corner stone is no more welcome in our homes and hearts as he was in ancient days.

SERMON SUGGESTIONS

Topic: On Eagle's Wings

TEXT: Exod. 19:1–19, RSV

(1) God chooses a people. (2) God delivers these people. (3) God works through his elect for the blessing of all people.

Topic: Behaving as a Christian Should

TEXT: Rom. 12:1–13, especially verses 1 and 2

(1) What we must do: (a) offer ourselves to God; (b) let ourselves be transformed. (2) How we can do it: by the mercies of God. (3) To what end will we do it: to know and do the will of God.

WORSHIP AIDS

CALL TO WORSHIP.   "If he then be risen with Christ, seek those things which are above, where Christ sitteth on the right hand of God" (Col. 3:1).

INVOCATION.   Almighty God, our Father, who brought again from the dead our Lord Jesus Christ, help us to live the lives of those who have been raised with him to walk in the newness of life. Give us high aspirations in all things, and lift our thoughts above everything that would keep us from fulfilling thy purpose for us.

OFFERTORY SENTENCE.   "Whatsoever ye do, do it heartily, as to the Lord, and not unto men; knowing that of the Lord ye shall receive the reward of the inheritance; for ye serve the Lord Christ" (Col. 3:23, 24).

OFFERTORY PRAYER.   O Lord our God, who givest liberally and upbraidest not, teach us to give cheerfully of our substance for thy cause and Kingdom. Let thy blessing be upon our offerings, and grant us to know the joy of those who give with their whole heart, through Jesus Christ our Lord.—*Book of Common Order*

PRAYER.   O thou who are our maker and our God, the giver and sustainer of life, we would bless thy name at all times. Thy praise would continually rise from our grateful hearts.

We thank thee that thy power extends beyond man's prowess and achievements, that our towers never do quite touch the sky, that always thou art more than we have thought or preached thee to be.

We thank thee that a fall of snow can hobble a mighty city, that strong headwinds can slow our jets and make us late, that heavy rains can force a cancellation of public events, that high seas command the respect of our sturdiest oceangoing ships.

In short, we thank thee, God, for everything and anything that humbles us before the mystery of life and keeps us from the folly of worshiping the works of our hands. Thou alone art God, and together we would bless thy holy name.—Ernest T. Campbell

SERMON
Topic: Through the Eyes of Jesus
TEXT: Matt. 16:13–16

I grew up in the Deep South, and it saddens me to say that in that culture I took for granted there were differences between people that ultimately had implications for their value in society. When I was growing up, the word *black* or *white* said everything about a person. It was the determining category in terms of where people could live, where they could go to school, what they could do socially, and for the most part what they could do with their lives.

In 1960, John Howard Griffin authored a book titled *Black Like Me*. Griffin used special medication to darken his skin, and then he traveled the Deep South as a black man in the latter days of legal segregation. The "Negro" Griffin encountered separate facilities, hate-filled stares, and job options limited to menial labor. I can still remember the impact that book had in my family when my father read it. The book helped turn our family around in our attitudes about race.

When we respond to another person primarily through a characteristic we see in him or her, then we have reduced the person to that characteristic. He or she has ceased to be a person! We have turned the person into an object! Our response is based primarily upon whether or not the characterization we have made is seen by us to be negative or positive. Even when we see the characteristic positively, and we relate to the person in a favorable manner, we are still treating him or her as an object and not as a whole person. The ongoing tragedy of our human saga is that we are forever confusing adjectives and nouns. Adjectives have to do with some fact of a person's make-up. Adjectives are descriptive of one thing about a given individual, but not inclusive of the whole person. We are forever taking words that are simply descriptive of one aspect of a person and elevating them into the primary thing that we see when we think of that person. Still today, there are many ways in which we limit the lives of others around us by narrowly defining them rather than seeing them as persons very much like ourselves. The truth is that God does not look upon any of us in terms of a particular characteristic. God looks at the very essence of our being!

Some years ago, I heard a sermon on the "genius of our Lord." The preacher said that one characteristic of the "genius of Christ Jesus" was that he always knew the difference between adjectives and nouns when it came to relating to others. He knew the difference between characteristics of the person and the true being of the person. Jesus illustrates this by saying to his disciples, "You have been hearing lots of things about me. Tell me what other people think about me." And they said, "Some say John the Baptist, but others say you are like Elijah, or Jeremiah, or one of the prophets." Then he said to them, "You have been with me now for some time. Tell me, who do you say that I am?"

Simon Peter did not confuse characteristics about Jesus with the very essence of Jesus' Being. Peter said to Jesus, "You are the Messiah, the Son of the Living God." Peter used the one word that was definitive of Jesus. It was the word that summed up what he was in his most essential being, and Jesus honored Peter's recognition of his true Being.

The Gospels contain account after account of how Jesus related to others in the same manner. He saw them in their essential wholeness, and not by any descriptive characteristic. Jesus calls us to this same higher level of living our humanity. He invites us to join him in seeing the true essence of wholeness of every person we encounter.

How can we get past the -isms and "qualifications" we allow to come between us? How can we be true to this high calling of our Lord? Ralph Sockman, a respected, longtime Methodist pastor and teacher in New York City, said something that I think can be helpful to us. He said God has given us not one set of eyes, but three! The eyes of the body, the gift of physical sight ("What does this object or person look like?"). The eyes of the mind, the gift of insight ("How does my experience of this person fit with everything else I have experienced?"). The eyes of the heart ("Why does this person exist? What is the meaning of this person as a part of God's creation, and one for whom our Lord gave himself?").

In a novel written just after World War I, *All Quiet on the Western Front,* there is an episode where the German army and the British army are engaged in an intense battle. A German soldier dives into a foxhole to get out of the line of fire, and to his great surprise he finds it already occupied by a British soldier. Immediately sensing he is in the presence of the enemy, he grabs for his bayonet, but then he sees that the British soldier is far too wounded to fight. He has a gaping wound where once his stomach was. It is very clear the man is almost at the end of his life. The British soldier is fumbling for something in his breast pocket. The German soldier, realizing that he is not under attack, reaches over and unbuttons the British soldier's pocket, and out fall two photos. One is a picture of a young woman with two babies, and the other is a picture of an older couple. He realizes that these are the family of this stricken soldier. He takes the photographs and holds them so that the British soldier can see them. He looks at them longingly, and then the British soldier squeezes the German soldier's hand in that universal gesture of gratitude, and he dies. The German soldier lies there in the foxhole, thinking about what that experience means. His commanders taught him that the British solder is his enemy. The adjective *Britisher* has become a noun meaning "enemy," but he has discovered a commonality.

Human being is the noun underneath the adjective *enemy,* and he realizes there is something more important about the other soldier than the fact that he wears a British uniform. Suddenly, the other soldier is a person just like him! Suddenly, he sees the British soldier through the eyes of his heart, and it makes all the difference in the world to him how he relates to his former enemy. Once he sees himself as no longer in danger, he is able to see another human being, just like himself. He also has a wife with two small children at home, and he carries a picture of his parents in his breast pocket. He also is vulnerable to being wounded.

We are sometimes like the German soldier, fearful that we are in danger, and blinded to the commonality we all share as human beings.

We are not in danger! These differences between ourselves, which can at times evoke the strongest levels of negative emotion and fear, are not differences that will hurt us. With the eyes of the heart, we can look beyond particular qualities of another person. When we look beyond mere characteristics, we see all people in God and God in all people. It is with the eyes of the heart that we finally know the difference between adjectives and nouns. If we are bold to say, with Simon Peter, that Jesus is the Christ, the Son of the Living God, and we are one body in him, then we do have a higher calling. Christ can open the eyes of our hearts to see each person as coming from the hand of God and therefore sacred!

"O Christ, who again and again opened the eyes of the blind, open the eyes of our hearts that we might see others as you have seen us."—Dick Brown

SUNDAY, OCTOBER 9, 2005

Lectionary Message

Topic: Up Close and Far Away

TEXT: Exod. 32:1–14

Other Readings: Ps. 106:1–6, 19–23; Phil. 4:1–9; Matt. 22:1–14

The children of Israel were growing anxious. Their leader, Moses, had been up the mountain too long and they began to doubt his leadership and God's presence. The people leaned upon Moses as a trusted confidant, leader, and friend. But now he had deserted them at the base of Mt. Sinai and they were afraid. They were riddled with questions: Would he return? How long would he be gone? Their inquiring minds wanted to know.

I. *An absent leader (v. 1).* Moses had scaled the heights of Mt. Sinai to meet with God (19:20ff). His absence, however, for over forty days caused great unrest and consternation among the people of God. Like children whose parents are out of their physical sight, the anxious Israelites panicked, thinking they had not only been abandoned by Moses but also been abandoned by God. For what seemed an eternity, the children waited and wondered about their well-being. The insecurity in the camp hovered over them like a thick cloud. The most pressing issue was not the leadership of Moses. The issue was his absence. And in response to his absence they veered off the path of faithfulness.

II. *A new leader and a new god (vv. 2–6).* With the great uncertainty that permeated the camp, the children of Israel turned to Aaron and demanded that a new god be formed.

Something intriguing occurred at this point. The children of Israel uttered a twofold cry for help. They needed the physical presence of their leader, Moses, and they desired the spiritual presence of their God. In their moment of anxiety, the people were willing to make an unholy substitution. They were willing to exchange Aaron for Moses, and a golden calf for Yahweh. Clearly they were motivated by selfish immaturity rather than devout loyalty to God.

This unholy exchange reminds me of the title of a book written several years ago by Tony Campolo, *Who Switched the Price Tags?* That very question is the issue facing the people of God. Who would exchange the steadfast grace of God for a puny deity crafted from used jewelry? Yet ultimately that is what happened.

In the frenzy of this troubling moment, Aaron ordered the people to contribute jewelry to the cause of crafting a new god, and a golden calf was formed. The extent of the rebellion against Almighty God cannot be overestimated. The forgetful and rebellious children, however, were willing to abandon their God (who they believed had abandoned them) so that they could create a god with their fingerprints upon it. They needed a presence in the absence. They desired a god with handles—a deity on their own terms. Aaron led the rebellious people and promised "There are your gods who brought you out." In the shadow of Mt. Sinai the gods were forged and an altar was built. The next morning there were offerings and orgies. It was an unholy episode for a supposedly holy people.

III. *An old leader advocates for a broken people (vv. 7–14).* Moses, the old leader, was camped in the presence of God atop Mt. Sinai. Little did he know that the very people whom God entrusted to his leadership had betrayed his legacy and forsaken their god. It is astonishing to note that in one fell swoop everything sacred and holy within the children of Israel was forfeited.

God proceeds to inform Moses of the betrayal of the people (v. 7). God's anger over the rebellion is kindled to the point he wants to destroy all of the people, with the exception of Moses. Moses quickly resumes his posture as leader, for he engages God in an intriguing argument or defense on behalf of the rebellious people. His defensive is passionate and at times confrontational. In this face-to-face dialogue, Moses the man dares to challenge the integrity of Almighty God. He has the audacity to ask God why he is so angry with his own people. With deep conviction Moses implores God to "repent" his vindictive thoughts and not destroy the rebellious children.

Certainly God does not repent in the traditional manner in which we employ the term. He has not sinned or rebelled, but if so, against whom? He is God. Rather, the passage takes us behind the scenes of the unique and privileged relationship that Moses enjoys with the Almighty. The biblical writer wants us to understand how favored Moses is in the sight of God—so favored in fact that God listens to the reasoning of his impassioned servant (vv. 11–14).

It is a terrible thing when we exchange loyalty and fealty to the true God in order to create a god based upon our own desires. The consequences are dire and the lack of fulfillment makes it all the more futile.—Danny West

ILLUSTRATION

GOD'S SILENCE.   In her Lyman Beecher lectures at Yale University, Barbara Taylor Brown addresses the issue of God's silence. She recalls an incident in her pastoral ministry in which she spends time with a grieving widower. In conversation with the sorrowful soul, the questions are raised: "Is God more at home in silence than in word? Is the moment of most profound silence the moment of God's most profound presence?"[1]

> *Hearing*
> The idols have ears but do not hear. . . .
> So unlike you, for all your hearing. . . .
> So like us, ears but do not hear.
> You have endlessly summoned us: shema
> Listen,
> Listen up,
> Pay attention,
> Heed,
> Obey,
> Turn. . . .[2]

SERMON SUGGESTIONS

Topic: When a People Is Special to God

TEXT: Exod. 19:1–9

(1) God delivers them. (2) God gives them a holy task. (3) God stays in touch with them.

---

[1]Barbara Taylor Brown, *When God Is Silent* (Boston: Cowley, 1998), p. 72.
[2]Walter Brueggemann, *Prayers of Walter Brueggemann: Awed to Heaven, Rooted in Earth* (Minneapolis: Fortress Press, 2003), p. 53.

Topic: The Good of Government

TEXT: Rom. 13:1–10

(1) It is authorized by God. (2) It is for our good. (3) Its aims can be better achieved through love than through law.

WORSHIP AIDS

CALL TO WORSHIP.   "The righteousness of thy testimonies is everlasting: give me understanding, and I shall live" (Ps. 119:144).

INVOCATION.   All-wise God, spread the glory of the hope of life eternal into every open heart today. Stir to new heights of faith and new depths of commitment all who name the name of God and pray to do thy will.—E. Lee Phillips

OFFERTORY SENTENCE.   "Although the fig tree shall not blossom, neither shall fruit be in the vines; the labor of the olive shall fail, and the fields shall yield no meat; the flocks shall be cut off from the fold, and there shall be no herd in the stalls: yet I will rejoice in the Lord, I will joy in the God of my salvation" (Hab. 3:17–18).

OFFERTORY PRAYER.   God of mercies, help us to rejoice as readily in the difficult times as in the days when everything runs smoothly. We know that we can rejoice, because you are in final control of all things, and you can make the banes of today the blessings of tomorrow. Keep us from embarrassment or reluctance in our giving, though our gifts be small, and multiply our little, as the loaves and fishes, for the good of others.

PRAYER.   Eternal God, deep beyond our understanding and high above our imagining, we worship thee. We thank thee that we cannot comprehend thee, for if thou couldst be caught in our nets, if we could run the lines of our weak thought around thy being and thy ways, then wert thou too small a God. We glory in thy greatness and thy depth beyond our comprehension.

As we lift our petitions, spoken and unspoken, before thy mercy seat, we think of all souls, praying to thee around the world. Across all the lines of race and creed and nation, our sympathy goes out to them today. We are one brotherhood of man upon the planet. God forgive us that we have made of it so ill a place, when peace and brotherhood, justice and equity and goodwill might have had their habitation here. Shame us out of our waywardness and ill will, we beseech thee, and beginning with ourselves let us seek thee in Christ, that, as a fire spreads, so the contagion of Christ's Spirit may kindle all mankind.

Especially we beseech thee for some soul here hard bestead, his back to the wall, fighting some temptation, all but overthrown by anxiety of estate, grieving for the waywardness of those dearly loved, brokenhearted with bereavement at their death. Come thou, beyond our power to pray for them, close to all needy souls. We thank thee that we do not need to stay defeated; that we can be reborn transformed, redeemed from defeat to victory. Grant that triumphant experience to some souls here today.

We ask it in the Spirit of Christ.—Harry Emerson Fosdick

SERMON
Topic: Take a Look at the Foundations
TEXT: Matt. 7:24–27; 1 Cor. 3:11; Ps. 19:14

"Let the words of our mouths and the meditations of our hearts be acceptable to you, O Lord our Rock and our Redeemer."

When I was about five years old, my brother was watching me while my mom was away shopping. We were outside playing, and I was skipping and jumping and fell flat on my face. I hit my chin on the sharp edge of our concrete porch. Blood was pouring. My brother scooped me up and ran the three blocks to our doctor's office. I never will forget being held down as they sewed my chin back together. I was yelling and crying. Billy was trying to hold me and comfort me. To this day I have a huge scar across my chin that you can't see, but it's there. When I touch it I remember as if it were yesterday. I don't remember the pain exactly, but I remember the experience of the pain.

Scars always have a story, don't they? And most of our scars are not physical. But all the same, when we touch them or when they are touched emotionally, we remember and often react.

There was a really fine churchman, devoted. If church was open he was there, taught Sunday school, served on the vestry, was the treasurer. He was congenial, generous with his time and money, always looking for ways for the church to take care of those in need. But there was one place! Anytime Alcoholics Anonymous was mentioned—and they used the church a lot—he would say "That bunch of worthless drunks," and he would always vote against them.

One night after a meeting, a friend confronted him about his remarks. He was defensive: "I have the right to my opinion." "Sure you do, Bill, but it's not like you—you are one of the finest Christian men I've ever known. Why do you hate them so much?"

He walked away not sharing the story.

And the story? Bill grew up in a blue-collar family. He was bright and made great grades, and he wanted to go to college. But he was the oldest. When he graduated from high school he had to go to work to support the family. When his younger brother came along, the money Bill had earned, along with his mom and dad's scrimping and saving, sent his brother to college, where he mastered in partying and drinking and got so good at it that he dropped out of college and made it his career and ended up on the street. He was found dead in a railroad boxcar.

What's inside Bill, what's inside us, is foundationally part of us whether we know it or not. Others often see more than we can because they see how we act and react. They hear our hurt often spoken as anger and animosity; they hear our pain often expressed as prejudice.

It's like when Lois and I moved into our house. We noticed that our porch railing was rickety and wobbly. It was kind of floating in air, not touching in places. There were a few cracks in the porch too. I didn't think much of it until a builder came and quickly diagnosed what never occurred to me: my porch had fallen.

So we dug it out, and sure enough, the concrete lintels had crumpled and decayed, and the support was not there to hold the porch up. In fact, it was so serious that our porch could have torn away and done thousands of dollars in damage to our home.

In the same way, when our behavior or attitudes or responses—our emotions—are about to rip our house, our building, apart, what do we do? Wisdom says that you take a look at the foundation.

When we really look and examine the cracks, the walls and ceiling and the roof and railing that make up our life, too often all that we want to do is surface work: patch and paint, learn some new technique, find a new interest, follow a new leader; but when the problems and the hurts and wounds still remain, as they always remain, then maybe, just maybe, we've got a foundation problem.

Jesus, in today's Gospel, says, "If you do, there's only one solution: you gotta dig in and let God in." Because God will and does come so often—most often—as a person acting in kindness and sanity and honesty and grace in the midst of our trouble.

A priest friend was serving a small rural church. One night the phone rang: a mother of three small children had died. Her husband had no family. She had a sister somewhere up north. The priest helped make all the arrangements.

On the day of the funeral the family came early to the funeral home. The sister had arrived from Boston. She was a serious-looking woman, matronly in dress and manner. She stood back as the children made their way to her sister's casket before it was closed for good. They were amazingly composed as they stepped to their mother's body, but when the oldest started to cry, they all did. Their crying became wailing as their grief poured out.

A woman in the congregation got up and physically began to move them away from the casket, telling the children, "Get a hold of yourselves, your momma is with Jesus."

That's when the sister stepped forward, pushing the woman back: "I'll take care of the children." She gently put her arms around them. "Can I say a prayer with you?" They knelt together.

Over the next days and months the children were not more than an arm's length away from their newfound aunt. In fact, they were that close for the rest of their lives.

The experience was foundational for those children. How can we measure the loss of a mother at such a young age? But don't miss what they learned: that their grief was not only OK but absolutely appropriate, that their feelings were OK, that tears and brokenness are part of life, that love and understanding and relationships help us face and overcome even the largest of life's obstacles.

Today Jesus wants us to see that the love and understanding—the relationship—we need is God.

What did you learn? What have you learned along the way about life and living? What cracks, what scars, still betray the wounds that lie beneath? It is never too late to take a look at the foundation. It's never too late for a little reconstruction. It's never too late for God.—John Ross

SUNDAY, OCTOBER 16, 2005
Lectionary Message

Topic: Grace in the Shadows
TEXT: Exod. 33:12–23
Other Readings: Ps. 99; 1 Thess. 1:1–10; Matt. 22:15–22

The shoe was clearly on the other foot. Moses had been rightfully angry at the obnoxious and rebellious behavior of the children of Israel while camped at the foot of Mt. Sinai. It was as if they had completely forgotten about their God and misplaced all loyalty to his provision.

Moreover, not only had the Israelites seemingly forgotten their commitment to God, they had apparently even forsaken their God, as evidenced in the creation of their own gods. If one god won't satisfy the hunger, roll up the sleeve and create another god. It was no big deal to the people. In their moment of spiritual amnesia, they believed that any god would do.

In fairness, however, it is important to remember that the people of God were truly perplexed. That perplexity provided the foundation for the real life-and-faith issues that surfaced among the people. They had legitimate questions about their own well-being and about the leadership of Moses. He ascended Mt. Sinai and stayed what seemed to his followers an inordinately long time. So in their fear and out of weakness, the cry of the people of God was in essence, "Who will be with us? Who will guide us? Are we alone and abandoned in the wilderness?" Lest we forget, none of us are above those moments of self-doubt and spiritual crisis. Many of us have cried out to God in moments of his holy silence. It was no different for the children of Israel, and it was no different for Moses.

I. *Moses was plagued by the very same issues of companionship and abandonment that his people experienced: he needed to know that God was available to him (vv. 12–13).* As perplexing as it seems, Moses was now asking the very questions the people were asking. He needed assurance that God would accompany him and be with him. It is a classic case of "like people, like leader." After all that Moses had experienced with God, after the miles of journey with God and under God, Moses was still requesting that God prove his presence.

II. *Moses demanded more than a spiritual presence; he insisted on a glimpse of the holy (v. 18).* It was an audacious request. Moses, the man, dared look to the heavens and demand a view of the Almighty. Many of us find it hard to fathom that a mere mortal could ever dare challenge God's authority in the way that Moses did, but the incident is a clear reminder of the favor that Moses enjoyed and the intimate manner in which the leader approached God. There is a conversational tone to the dialogue. It is as if two old friends are sitting on a bench enjoying lively conversation. What a refreshing reminder of the kind of relationship that God desires of his children.

Underneath the rhetoric, however, was a sense of hunger and insecurity that Moses possessed. A relationship of faith and trust was ultimately not enough for Moses. Although the Israelites demanded a god on their own terms, Moses in many ways required the same. He wanted to catch of glimpse of his God. No, he *needed* to catch a glimpse of his God!

III. *There was a moment of grace in the shadows (vv. 20–23).* God eventually responded to the demands of Moses. Not because God is held hostage to any demands but because he understands our quirks and our desires. He understood that Moses the man needed assurance. Believing that he could not live without seeing the glory, Moses asked God to reveal himself, and God did. Reminding Moses that "you cannot see my face and live" (v. 20), God sheltered the leader in the crevice of a rock by the shadow of his hand and allowed Moses to see "my back, but my face you shall not see" (v. 23).

God's powerful presence shadowed the moment and offered Moses an ever-so-slight glance of the image of God. God's protection was an ever-present sense of hope and shadowing comfort.—Danny West

ILLUSTRATIONS

GOD'S PRESENCE.   In his classic work *The Word of God and the Word of Man*, Karl Barth reminds us that congregational listeners come to worship with a deep and abiding hunger to hear something from God. They need more than just an oral event. They crave the very presence of God. The cry "God is present" must be affirmed in the lives of the people. Barth says, "They want to find out and thoroughly understand the answer to this question: Is it true?"[3]

PRAISE.   Gardner C. Taylor once preached, "I think it takes a saint, maybe more than a saint, not to be jolted, staggered, when something happens that looks bad . . . panic is the mood that belongs to somebody that does not have a way out."[4]

SERMON SUGGESTIONS

Topic: The Least God Expects
TEXT: Exod. 20:1–20
(1) The motivation (vv. 1–2). (2) The mandate (vv. 3–17). (3) The mystery of the mountain (vv. 18–20).

Topic: The Basics of Christian Tolerance
TEXT: Rom. 14:5–12, especially verse 12
(1) Each of us is accountable to God. (2) Yet we are inclined to judge each other's way of serving God. (3) However, we have an obligation to be helpful and supportive (v. 13).

WORSHIP AIDS
CALL TO WORSHIP.   "Jesus answered and said unto him, if a man love me, he will keep my words: and my Father will love him, and we will come unto him, and make our abode with him" (John 14:23).

INVOCATION.   Today, our Father, increase our love for thee, that we may know more of thy infilling presence and in turn share in a greater way with the world the Good News of thy salvation.

OFFERTORY SENTENCE.   "The silver is mine, and the gold is mine, saith the Lord of hosts" (Hag. 2:8).

OFFERTORY PRAYER.   What we bring to thy treasury, O God, we bring with an awareness of our stewardship. Help us to reflect on every aspect of our living, working, and saving, to the end that we shall make our lives richer toward thee.

PRAYER.   O Lord, amid all threats to our security we look to thee to protect us. We would not dictate the terms of thy providence. Thou knowest what is best. If our loyalty to thee means that we shall be misunderstood, disliked, or even persecuted, then give us the grace to bear patiently and creatively this burden of our obedience. Doubt grant that we shall never, through lack of love or lack of courtesy or lack of tact, bring on ourselves needless burdens and all them thy will.

As we look back across the years of our lives, we can see how, again and again, we have been spared through thy mercy. Thou hast, again and again, set our feet upon a rock and put a song on our lips. Give us the faith to feel that solid foothold and sing that song even before

---

[3]Karl Barth, *The Word of God and the Word of Man* (trans. Douglas Horton; New York: HarperCollins, 1957), pp. 104–108.
[4]*The Words of Gardner Taylor* (vol. 3, Valley Forge, Pa.: Judson Press, 2000), p. 83.

the deliverance comes. For it befits us who believe in thee to stand firmly and sing joyfully even before the fruition of our salvation. So renew our hearts in praise and gratitude.

SERMON
Topic: The "Common Cold" of God's People
TEXT: Exod. 17:1–7

Moses named the place Massah ("the place of testing") and Meribah ("the place of arguing") because the people of Israel argued with Moses and tested the Lord saying, "Is the Lord going to take care of us or not?" This church is too small; why, we haven't seen a new face in here for ages. What we need is some people who'll be really committed, like that church over on so-and-so road. Why can't we ever seem to get ahead of the game? Our church budget's been every shade of the color spectrum, save black. There aren't any young people in this church, and there's nothing for the kids to do. Are we ever going to pay down that debt? "Is the Lord going to take care of us or not?"

After serving as an elder for thirty years, as church treasurer for twenty-five, and as a Sunday school teacher for eighteen, a man wanted to know why God hadn't stepped in to prevent him from having quadruple bypass surgery. A woman's mother had been one of the founders of the congregation and worked her fingers to the bone to help raise funds for the new social hall. So what she wanted to know was why God hadn't prevented her mother from suffering from such crippling arthritis. "Is the Lord going to take care of us or not?"

Last week the company closed its door; it didn't matter whether you'd worked for four or forty years, they just locked the door behind you. Each month it seems that your checkbook teeters on the brink of placing you in bankruptcy court, and you fear that they'll soon come to repossess the car. Or you're absolutely certain that there must've been some mistake on the part of the doctor who read the X ray; you couldn't possibly have cancer, you're only twenty-four years young. Or the pediatrician told you that your child would soon lose her hearing, and now, while holding her tiny hand, you walk to the car in a kind of daze. "Is the Lord going to take care of us or not?"

So Moses cried out to the Lord, "What shall I do with this people? They are almost ready to stone me." The people of God demanded bread, and God gave them the bread of heaven ("manna"). The people of God demanded meat, and God provided them with a sky black with quail. Following God's provision of quail, the people demanded water, and God provided for them streams in the desert. The Israelites quarreled and tested the Lord, saying, "Is the LORD going to take care of us or not?"

The other day, as I passed by Light Hall on my way to the kitchen, the children of the day care were gathered at tables for their lunch. I paused in the hallway when I overheard the attendant say, "Everyone put your hands together for prayer. Now, we'll say the prayer together." With voices as smooth as velvet I heard the children say: "God is great, God is good, and we thank him for our food; by his hand we all are fed; give us now our daily bread. Amen." As they tore into their lunch bags and boxes I head a cacophony of whining and complaint: "Mom forgot my chips!" "I didn't get any cake!" "Where's the apple? My mom said there's an apple!" A lesson from the mouths of little children.

In the story from the Book of Exodus, and in the chapters that precede it, we're told that Israel desired meat and God provided quail, Israel desired bread and God provided *manna*,

Israel desired water and God provided a stream in the desert. In each case, following the provision of what was needed, the text says that the people complained. Well, actually and more accurately, the passage read this morning says they *grumbled* and *complained*. There's an important distinction between a complaint and a grumble.

A complaint sounds like the four-year-old insisting that she simply *must* use the bathroom at the next rest stop. Grumbling is the fact of the same child, with the lower lip pushed forward, and the knee constantly pounding at the back of the driver's seat, because dad *refused* to stop for ice cream. The biblical storyteller is making a similar distinction. A complaint is a warranted claim to some basic necessity; grumbling is an attitude of bad faith normally associated with the denial of something of lesser significance.

Now honestly, I wish that I could simply say that this is the issue that's central to the Old Testament lesson. Unfortunately, that's not the case. As important as the distinction between complaining and grumbling is to the storyteller, that's not what's at issue in this account. To discover the concern the storyteller wants to address, we need to turn back to chapter 16. The issue is not so much grumbling nor complaining, as it is disobedience. Disobedience not as an act of defiance, but rather a failure of faith *as trust* in God's wanting only the best for his people.

The issue becomes evident in the scene in which the manna from heaven is provided in response to Israel's request for bread. Moses commands that the people gather their manna for six days; they're to gather enough for seven days, because they're forbidden to go out and gather the manna on the Sabbath day. But, says the storyteller, "Some of the people went out anyway to gather food, even though it was the Sabbath day." And God responded, saying: "How long will these people refuse to obey my commands and instructions? . . . Do they not realize that I have given them the seventh day, the Sabbath, as a day of rest? That is why I give you twice as much food on the sixth day, so there will be enough for two days. On the Sabbath day you must stay in your places. Do not pick up food from the ground on that day."

It helps to understand why disobedience is the issue, when we contrast the bread of Egypt with the bread of heaven.

Egypt was the place where bread could be gotten only in exchange for hard labor. In Egypt bread was given only as the reward for being productive. In Egypt, bread was only and always received with fearful anxiety; each day the Hebrew slave would fearfully wonder whether his or her hard labor would meet with the taskmaster's approval, and therefore qualify for the daily distribution of this basic necessity for survival.

On the other hand, this bread of heaven was a gift from a gracious God. As a gift it was intended to break that bondage to fear, abuse, exploitation, and anxiety associated with life in Egypt. Israel failed to understand that God would not demand something in return for the provision of life's fundamental needs. They also failed to understand that what God wanted in return was the love and worship of his people, freely given. In other words, God would not be to Israel a demanding tyrant; nor would he serve as a useful means to their expressed ends. God desired to enter and share a relationship.

Israel's willful disobedience manifested their unwillingness to trust that God is in fact a good and gracious Lord, who provided what they needed solely on the basis of his benevolent heart. Buried deep within their mistrust is the problem that continues to haunt the people of God in each and every generation of believers. It's the problem I refer to in the title of this sermon as the common cold of God's people.

We tend to judge God on the basis of how well or poorly he responds to our expressed desires or our deepest needs. It's determining God's goodness in terms of God's effectiveness. In other words, we often judge God's love and care for us in terms of his apparent willingness or reluctance to meet that which we perceive to be our most urgent need or our most pressing problem.

But that's to fall into the same trap as Israel. On this issue, the insight offered by Anne Graham is on the mark. If you'll recall, she said, "How can we expect God to give us his blessing and his protection when we demand that he leave us alone?" It seems to me her insight implies that although we expect God to bless and provide, we deny any other relationship whatsoever. It's an understanding of God that smacks of practicality: Where God is useful, we'll call on him, and expect a favorable response; but let's not talk about a relationship of reciprocity, trust, service, or obligation.

Throughout the ages, the Christian Church has endured some pretty serious setbacks, due to some very serious illnesses. Sicknesses of the soul-full kind. Sicknesses like the suggestion to get rid of the Old Testament God; sicknesses like Church leaders hopping in and out of bed with kings and princes and other political expedients; sicknesses like the denial of the divinity of Jesus; sicknesses like Martin Luther's unfortunate mingling of the gospel with a strong dose of anti-Semitism; or sicknesses like wrapping Christ's cross in the flag and calling it "Christian patriotism." The church has suffered more than its fair share of soul-full sicknesses.

But none has been more threatening and done more damage to the body of Christ than the common cold of the contemporary Church. This is the one symptom: Judging God on the basis of his unwillingness to bless and protect us, regardless of the nature of our relationship with him. God, simply because he's God, should not allow people to suffer; should not allow children to die of starvation; should not allow terrorists to pursue their twisted ends; should see to it that we are blessed with all the necessities and even the benefits of life—regardless of whether or not we've responded in love, devotion, and worship to God's call to enter into a relationship that is reciprocal.

"Is the Lord going to take care of us or not?" The answer to that question cannot be found in some calculated formula. The answer will never be found by a simpleminded measure of the sum total of good or bad things that happen to us in the course of this life. It can only and always be answered by those who willingly embrace the relationship God desires. The question can also be answered by those determined, in faith, to believe the historical record: God has and will provide; God's heart is saddened by the suffering we sometimes must endure as the consequence of sin's disruption of our world; and God's love is without limit. Amen.—A.J.D. Walsh

SUNDAY, OCTOBER 23, 2005
Lectionary Message

Topic: An Appeal to Integrity
Text: 1 Thess. 2:1–8
Other Readings: Deut. 34:1–12; Ps. 90:1–6, 13–17; Matt. 22:34–46

Paul was under attack. But then again, that was nothing new. Everywhere he went, everything he tried resulted in the same outcome: criticism. Often the attacks were physical in nature, resulting in imprisonment and harsh treatment. In this passage, however, the attacks were verbal and highly confrontational. The old apostle was accused of being a charlatan and a pretender of faith.

Many believed that Paul's spectacular conversion experience (Acts 9:1–9) resulted in the stimulation of a massive ego. Certain critics alleged that Paul enjoyed the spotlight and was motivated for all the wrong reasons. Still others believed that Paul was a master manipulator who parlayed his considerable rhetorical abilities into a following of individuals who were duped into a belief system by the apostle's "golden tongue."

Paul can do nothing right. So in the face of this harsh criticism and intense scrutiny, he writes to the church hoping to clear the air of the allegations made against him.

I. *A ministry of scars (vv. 1–2).* Paul reminds his readers of the intense pain that he endured for the cause of Christ. Recalling the events that occurred in Philippi (Acts 16:19–40) that resulted in harsh beatings and painful imprisonment, Paul defends the integrity of his ministry against those who hurled verbal stones. As if the painful beatings were not enough from which to recover, now Paul finds himself in a situation of attempting to ward off those who deliberately wanted to cast aspersion against the essence of the apostle himself.

II. *A ministry of integrity (vv. 3–7).* Paul understands that the stakes are high in this battle. This ministry to which he was called is not based upon his own credential or authority but rather is from God. He attempts to remind his Thessalonian audience that his work is about God and not about Paul. He passionately proclaims the truth of Christ, but he is ever cautious to not allow "his" words to interfere with the word of Christ.

For Paul the essential ingredient in his preaching ministry is that of integrity. He does not need to call upon gimmicks or outrageous shenanigans to deliver the gospel message. There are many today who resort to outlandish and bizarre events in order to prop up the good-news message. The message of the gospel needs no such influence. Paul understands that the message is to be proclaimed with integrity, and the integrity of the gospel itself then makes its presence known. It is not about "words or flattery" (v. 5) but about authentic ministry in the name and under the authority of Almighty God.

III. *A ministry of God (v. 8).* Paul's ultimate appeal in the face of the unrelenting criticism is an appeal to the highest of all authorities: God himself. In other words, Paul is in essence saying, "If you have a problem with me, place the blame on God, not on me. It was God who called me and it was God who authorized my ministry."

The final testing ground for all of our lives is our willingness to be under the wing and shadow of God. With all of the complexities of Kingdom service, it is vital that our lives and our ministry be connected to the power of God. Ridicule will come. Hard days will follow. But Paul reminds us that even in the midst of scars and criticism his ultimate loyalty is to God.

ILLUSTRATION

I once served a church in a community that was often inundated with other churches luring its children away by the use of bribery. It was not uncommon for this church itself to saturate neighboring towns with church buses that bribed the children to church by taping dollar bills to the seats of the bus. Why must we pollute the pure message of Christ with bribery and less-than-honorable tactics? If it is indeed the gospel of good news we declare it to be, it will hold up under pressure when all other voices are silent.—Danny West

SERMON SUGGESTIONS

Topic: God's Amazing Patience
TEXT: Exod. 32:1–14

(1) Then: the story of the making of the golden calf. (2) Always: it is a recurring theme of the Scriptures that God forgives and restores his erring and unworthy people. (3) Now: we get turned aside to many modern idols—money, fame, power, etc.—despite God's goodness and will for us, and yet he awaits our return with amazing patience.

Topic: To Be in Heaven or to Be Here?
TEXT: Phil. 1:21–27

(1) A dual destiny (vv. 21–22). (2) A dubious desire (v. 23). (3) A divine decision (vv. 24–26). (4) A disciple's duty (v. 27).

WORSHIP AIDS

CALL TO WORSHIP.   "Honor the Lord with thy substance, and with the first fruits of all thine increase: so shall thy barns be filled with plenty, and thy presses shall burst out with new wine" (Prov. 3:9, 10).

INVOCATION.   We have been blessed, O God, beyond all that we could ask or think. Beyond all material things, we have been enriched in the more important matters of spirit. We would pray for our daily bread, but realizing that we do not live by bread alone, we would pray that we might receive thine own self—known, loved, and obeyed—for what thou art: God of love and grace.

OFFERTORY SENTENCE.   "Walk in love, as Christ also hath loved us, and hath given himself for us an offering and a sacrifice to God for a sweet-smelling savor" (Eph. 5:2).

OFFERTORY PRAYER.   With this offering, Lord, we bring a harvest of gratitude for the health and wealth we enjoy, the wisdom and instruction we receive, the friendships and fellowships we experience. Allow these tokens of the fruit of our land to merge into the fruit of thy Spirit in proclaiming the gospel of salvation.

PRAYER.   O God, we thank thee for life, and all the beauty and the wonder of it, for the people that we have known and loved, and for the rare opportunities that we have had to enter into the deeper things of life. Forgive, O God, our triviality, and overlook our foolish ways. Help us to deepen and cultivate our understanding of primary things, things that come first, and then give us the will and the grace to make this nation strong that it may endure and that it may not go the way of others into exile and oblivion.—Theodore Parker Ferris

SERMON

Topic: Throw It Down; Pick It Up; Raise It High
TEXT: Exod. 3:11, 13, 4:1–5, 17, 14:15–16; 2 Cor. 12:1–10

We fear the thing that weakens us because we think that our pathway to success depends on our greatest strength. So in the face of hardship, we clench our fists, we set our faces like flint, and we determine to go it alone.

Men and women all over the world are dealing with lost limbs, lost lovers, lost innocence, and lost opportunities. But some are learning the power of God's gospel paradox: the thing that seeks to destroy you is the very thing that can save you.

You will recall that, though Moses was born a Hebrew, he was providentially given to the royal court of the pharaoh to be reared a prince. But as he learned of his identity, and as he watched his Hebrew kinsmen being oppressed, he tried to become the captain of his own soul. He killed an Egyptian. That crime sent him on a forty-year pilgrimage to Midian, in the southeastern part of the Sinai Peninsula in the Arabian wilderness. There, among the sons of Midian and Ishmaelites, this royal son of the court, this painfully misunderstood man, learned that he was not in fact the captain of his own soul.

It is there, in Midian, with this refugee named Moses, who would become the greatest leader of a nation in all of human history, bowing before the God of Abraham, Isaac, and Jacob, God who is speaking from a burning bush—it is there that we learn some important lessons for our lives tonight.

I. *God puts up with our excuses for a while, but he eventually gets to the bottom of what's ailing us ("What's in your hand?").* In Exodus 3 and 4, God is calling Moses to go back to Egypt and lead the Hebrews out. Moses balks. I would say that this man is facing one of the greatest challenges in all of his life. He may have prayed for deliverance (we don't know), but when it comes he is crawfishing out of it. It is always hard to walk through divinely opened doors. They are scary. It is scary for Moses to imagine going back. So, he balks: *"Who am I?"* (3:11); *"Who are you?"* (actually, in 3:13, Moses wonders what he will say to the children of Israel when they ask, "What is his name?"); "But what if they don't believe me?" (4:1).

It is at this point that God has had enough. Instead of striking him dead, which I might have done, he graciously begins to deal with Moses. There have been what we might call "presenting issues," and there are real issues. God is about to deal with the real issues. So the Lord asks Moses, "What is in your hand?" And Moses answers, "A rod."

In that one exchange between God and Moses, we have the key for the rest of the story of the deliverance of Israel. Moses' salvation and Israel's salvation and the advance of the One True Faith—which would lead to salvation for the ends of the earth—are hanging on this dialogue.

You see, God knows, of course, precisely what is in Moses' hand. And so does Moses. It used to be a scepter of Egypt. But now it is, as I heard one preacher call it, just a "sheep stick." Here is the symbol of what has become of the prince of Egypt. He stands before the Lord with a staff to lead bleating, stinking sheep out in the Midianite wilderness. In that answer, "A rod," we see God moving Moses to see the very symbol of his sin, his pain, his abandonment, his failure. God cuts through the excuses and gets to the heart of Moses' problem. Moses is a failure. He has taken matters into his own hands and now he holds a sheep stick.

When Jesus deals with men and women during his earthly ministry, we see the same thing. Rich young men and women, ambitious zealots, opportunists, faithless fanatics, and political wannabes all bring their issues to the Lord to hear him respond to them with a question. The questions of God always force us to look at ourselves. Our excuses are not accepted. They are shown to be just excuses. The Lord always leads us to see his greatness and our need of his greatness.

Moses has run to Midian and stayed there for forty years. But time and distance do not stop God from coming to him. God has a plan for Moses, but first God has to get to the problem with Moses. It maybe that tonight the Lord is so dealing with you.

II. *God always wants us to take what's ailing us and offer it to him.* First of all God tells Moses to throw it down ("Cast it on the ground"; 4:3).[5]

When we come to the Lord with our heartaches, our painful memories, our health, and the one debilitating event in our lives, the answer is always the same: "Throw it down!" Because when we release that thing that is stopping our service to God, God transforms it. "Throw it down!"

But look at what's next: pick it up! ("Reach out your hand and take it by the tail"; 4:4.)

The rod become a serpent. It is not wise to pick up serpents. The other day my son and I were watching the Crocodile Hunter and he was hunting—not crocs, as he is fond of doing, but venomous snakes. He found one he wasn't sure about and warned viewers like me, "If you are unsure, best to leave it alone." He didn't need to tell me that. Well, God tells Moses to pick up the snake. When he does, you know what happens: it turns back into a rod. But the truth is that something has changed. When Moses throws that rod down it turns into exactly what it is: a very dangerous, venomous thing that could kill Moses. That is what our secret sins and our hidden agendas do to us. They are killing us. They prevent us from enjoying the life-giving joy of serving the Lord Jesus. But when we give them to the Lord, we see them for what they are. Then we must pick it up! In admitting our sin to the Lord, the thing that would otherwise hurt us is transformed. Now it is still a rod, it is still a handicap, it is still a painful memory, it is still that business failure or that relationship failure; but now it is, through faith in God's power, a sign of his power.

It leads us to the next command: raise it high! ("Take this rod in your hand," 4:17; and "Lift up your rod," 4:16.)

In verse 17, God tells Moses, "And you shall take this rod in your hand with which you shall do the signs." Later, in chapter 14, when the mightiest army in the world is on one side and the Red Sea is on the other, when Israel is in between a rock and a hard place, that old rod holds the key to victory. It is as if, when the great trail comes, the Lord is saying, "Moses, the rod! The rod, Moses!" And the sea parts and a nation is saved by raising the testimony to God's salvation high.

You see, that is what it is all about. That rod is a testimony. The way the Lord wants you to be a witness is not to rely on your ingenious giftedness and your deep intellect. It is to raise up the testimony of God's power in your life . . . I think of 2 Corinthians 1:3–7: the Lord is calling you to "throw it down, pick it up, and raise it high!" Lift up his grace in your life. This is your power. This is your strength. There are a lot of us wondering how we will get out of the bind we are in. We are praying that God will raise up a person like you to lift up his grace and help us to see that our salvation is in him.

III. *Conclusion.* Moses learned that the rod, the symbol of his failure, would become the sign of his salvation. 2 Corinthians 12:1–10 shows that Paul's problem, his debilitating thorn in the flesh, became the place where Jesus Christ met him. In Paul's weakness, Christ was made strong. Like Moses, like Paul, this is what we must learn as well.

Whatever it is with you—the thing that is breaking you—when you offer it to the Lord, it is the very thing that brings you his grace.

---

[5]I once heard an old preacher use the three points "throw it down, pick it up, and raise it high" as his points, and I offer them tonight. I would quote him, but he used it from someone else. I think these points are now part of the "textus receptus" of preachers!

So "Throw it down! Pick it up! Raise it high!" Minister out of brokenness, not self-sufficiency. In your weakness, Christ is made strong. When Christ is made strong, people are saved.—Michael A. Milton

SUNDAY, OCTOBER 30, 2005
Lectionary Message

Topic: Dry Waters
TEXT: Josh. 3:7–17
Other Readings: Ps. 107:1–7, 33–37; 1 Thess. 2:9–13; Matt. 23:1–12

The very notion of dry waters is beyond the realm of possibility. Rational souls know that the idea of something wet being something dry is preposterous at best. It is outside of the boundaries of those things in our world that are logical and acceptable. Yet in the drama of the journey of the children of Israel the preposterous becomes much the pattern.

One of the recurring themes in the texts of Joshua is that of leadership. Indeed, the opening lines of the book of Joshua confront the continuity of leadership among the people of God. Following the death of Moses, God spoke to Joshua and appointed him as the successor to Moses (1:1–6). Joshua inherited the mantle of leadership from Moses. There was a clear and compelling link between these two men, but as in all transitions there is an element of uncertainty. What differences of style will emerge? Will this person direct us in the same manner as his predecessor? The children of Israel had previously struggled with this very question. Even under the hand of Moses they were concerned with matters of stability and presence. Here they are confronted with yet another leadership change. In spite of the constant threats and changes, one thread of consistency remains: the presence of God. Just as God accompanied Moses, he vowed to walk with Joshua, too (1:5).

Under the leadership of Joshua, the people of God find themselves camped on the banks of the Jordan River. They set up camp and prepare for entry into the land of promise. The people are instructed to wait for the Ark of the Covenant to head the processional, and at that point they are to follow after.

This remarkable passage is the culmination of a wonderful and often mystical journey. The children of Israel darted in and out of the will of God for years, and yet the journey continued. At times they rebelled outwardly against God, and yet the journey continued. At last the wandering is over but the journey is still before them. After the years of dusty caravans and wilderness wandering, the people stand at the edge of the thunderous Jordan. God has led them from wilderness to water.

I. *It is a journey that started with God (v. 7).* God reminds Joshua (as he often reminded Moses) that his presence is with his leadership and with those who follow. God informs Joshua that after all of the years of wandering and detour, the moment of triumph is at hand. The Scripture says, "This day I will begin to exalt you in the sight of all Israel. . . ." The land of destiny is within sight and the moment for which the people hunger is just ahead. But that moment of fulfillment is solely dependent upon the initiative and leadership of God.

II. *The journey is marked by extraordinary faith (v. 8).* The instructions to the priests and religious leaders are quite remarkable. God's instruction to the ark bearers is to "stand still in the Jordan." What an unusual request. Gather up your leaders, hoist the Ark of the

Covenant upon your shoulders, and go stand in the river. At this juncture of the journey, there is nothing else for the people to do. Having traveled to this point in the journey, this is certainly not the time to question God. The days of inquiry are past. It is time for action.

III. *The journey is consummated by obedience (vv. 9–17).* The commands of God are already remarkably complex. To the religious leaders he says, "Go stand in the Jordan." But the invitation continues and the plot thickens. Next God requests that the people choose a representative from each of the twelve tribes who will accompany the leaders. God then says to the children, "As soon as your leaders proceed into the Jordan, be ready to follow. For the waters will part and stand in a heap" (v. 13). And it happens just as described. The people follow one by one into the Jordan. The water stops flowing and the Scripture tells us that they walk on "dry land" (v. 17).

It is a journey upon dry waters. Consumed by faith and driven by the zeal to possess a new land, God's people journey in faith to their home.

Only God could arrange for a wilderness people to cross a raging river on dry land. It is but a reminder of his continued interest in their well-being and representative of the lengths he will go to prove it.

It is a story of dust to dust. The Israelites started their journey in the dust of the wilderness and they end their journey in the "dusty" waters of the Jordan. That kind of event just might be God's sneaky way of reminding them that they too were formed from the dust (Gen. 2:7), and to the dust they will eventually return.

ILLUSTRATION

"Not all who wander are lost" (J.R.R. Tolkien).—Danny West

SERMON SUGGESTIONS

Topic: On Seeing and Not Seeing God

Text: Exod. 33:12–23

(1) Moses intercedes with the Lord. (2) Moses seeks the guidance and blessing of God for himself and God's people. (3) Moses receives the promise of the Lord's presence. (4) The promise is realized when Moses and the people go forth on pilgrimage. (5) God gives this favor on his own initiative. (6) God grants to Moses only a glimpse of himself, but enough to confirm his promise.

Topic: A Symphony of the Spirit

Text: Phil. 2:1–13

(1) The aim: humility. (2) The example: Christ Jesus. (3) The energizing: God at work.

WORSHIP AIDS

CALL TO WORSHIP.   "Worship the Lord in holy array; tremble before him, all the earth!" (Ps. 96:9, RSV).

INVOCATION.   O God, our loving Father, teach us today what to be thankful for, even if at the present moment our problems, our pain, or our need might lead us to believe that we have no cause for thanksgiving. Let thy Spirit open our eyes to thy unfailing goodness.

OFFERTORY SENTENCE.   "Upon the first day of the week let every one of you lay by him in store, as God hath prospered him" (1 Cor. 16:2).

OFFERTORY PRAYER.   Grant, O Lord, that not only what is taught in church but also what is presented in the offering may flow out of a pure heart, a good conscience, and a sincere faith.

PRAYER.   Holy and merciful God! What are all our words, and what would our most fervent thanksgiving and praises mean compared with what you have done, are doing, and will still do for us and with us—compared with the new covenant, in which we all may already take our place?—compared with the grace by which you will put your law within us and write it upon our hearts? Enter our hearts! Clear away whatever might prevent you! And then speak further with us, lead us further along your path, the only good path: even when after this we once more separate, to return each to his own solitariness and tomorrow to his work.

So further your work outside this building also, and in the whole world as well. Have mercy on all who are sick, hungry, exiled, or oppressed. Have mercy on the powerlessness with which nations, governments, newspapers, and alas! even the Christian churches, with which *all* of us face the sea of guilt and trouble in the lives of present-day humanity. Have mercy on the lack of understanding because of which many of the most responsible and powerful of men see themselves driven to play with fire and conjure up new and greater dangers.

If your word were not at hand, what would be left for us to do but despair? But your word in all its truth *is* at hand, and so we cannot despair, and we may and indeed we want to feel assured, so that even if the earth is moved under our feet, all things in their entire course are in your strong and loving hands, and at the very last we shall be allowed to see that you have reconciled us and our dark world to you, and that you have already brought its salvation and its peace despite all men's arrogance and despair: in Jesus Christ your son, our Lord and Savior, who died and rose again for us and all men.—Karl Barth

SERMON
Topic: Is Reformation Past Tense?
TEXT: 1 Pet. 2:1–10

Today is Reformation Sunday. Now, that statement is not likely to generate a great deal of spontaneous enthusiasm, and little if any interest. Most of us know that the Reformation had something to do with the reforming or the renewal of the Christian Church, and that Luther, Calvin, and others helped to set this force for change in motion. But that's not enough to grasp our attention on a crisp fall morning. Perhaps we are not all that interested in history. You may even agree with Henry Ford's famous assessment that "history is bunk." You may remember the church of Flip Wilson and Brother Leroy, the Church of What's Happening Now! That's the church we are interested in: be up to date, be contemporary, speak not of the sixteenth century. To put it in an even more direct term, we did not come this morning to hear a history lecture. We came to worship (or find) a living God. You and I have come to receive wisdom and courage for the living of *these* days.

Yet is it not one of the rules of living, as well as of sport, that we must often take a step back before we can move forward? Could it be that the great ideas of the Protestant Reformation feed gnawing, spiritual hunger in the twenty-first century? Can such a truth as the *priesthood of all believers* become again more than words for us, as it was for Luther and those who heard him? What a difference it made to men and women to believe that before God all are equal. It is not a faith for the elite; *by grace we are saved.* I am freed from sin, but also free to be a priest to my brother and sister, and they to me. Christianity is not a spectator sport.

Bud Wilkinson, the architect of so many winning football teams at the University of Oklahoma, had an oft-quoted definition of *football*: it's fifty thousand people who are in desperate need of exercise, sitting and watching twenty-two men who are in desperate need of rest. Doesn't that sound like the church? We become spectators and summon the few to do our praying, proclaiming, and priesting for us. What has become of the priesthood of all believers?

In an article in *Newsweek* entitled "Power to the Laity," it was suggested that the days of a spiritual energy crisis in the Church may be challenged by a New Reformation. If that's true, then the first mark of a true Reformation will be an authentic *recovery* of a lost, or misplaced, biblical truth. In this case, I mean a universal priesthood. Malachi describes for us the duties of the priest: to teach, to practice the faith, and to minister to or serve the people. Malachi also mourns the results of an unfaithful priesthood: the people of the land are disillusioned. They stumble and fall.

Jesus confronts a similar situation in his day. The religious leaders are busy measuring the people's responsibility. Their narrow, legalistic code of some 615 laws is a burden to the common man or woman who wants to obey God. What's more, these leaders will not, Matthew tells us, lift their little fingers to relieve the burdens of their brother and sister who need to experience forgiveness, acceptance, love. Jesus goes beyond criticism. He gives us a new model of leadership and priesthood. This priest is not only one who stands before God for others, but the one who leads us into new and abundant life by becoming a servant. If we lead people out from darkness, despair, anxiety, it will be as humble servants.

Now, if that's truth that needs to be recovered from the Bible, the next step is to reform it—recast it into terms that can be understood in our times. Being called to be priests to each other can first have a tremendous effect on the structure of the Church. It will be seen in the way we act toward one another; the marks of status in our fellowship will begin to disappear. Unfortunately, it is a mark of modern Protestantism that we place so much emphasis on the pastor as superstar. Once he or she arrives, then our worship, stewardship, and witness will be what it should be. People will be visited and encouraged, and injustices corrected. Of course pastoral leadership is important, but in focusing on that call do we miss hearing our own call as priests of our God (Rev. 5:10)? You and I are members together of equal rank in that priesthood, and according to the Reformed tradition there is no hierarchy among equals.

The *Newsweek* article ends by saying that "the best of the new breed of laity seem bent on transforming churches into places where members can minister to each other and to the world—which is presumably what Jesus intended in the beginning." That statement is right on target; as priests we will minister to each other and serve people in the secular precincts where we lead our lives. Our priesthood begins in servant ministries in the Church, in the care of members of sensitive ministry, praying and standing by the side of one person or a whole committee. Second, the aspect of a priesthood of all believers that has been most neglected in the modern Church is that our ministry is not limited to what we do here on Sunday mornings or at committee meetings. The real evidence of our ministry is how we are enabled to live in the places away from here. In our gathering, are we refreshed and challenged to live a life of humble service? That is the vocation of the priest. What your office, family, club, or school cries out for is not the priest who calls attention to his status or her piety. No, true priesthood will mean at times laying down your own ego needs, the tribute you deserve, the attention you demand so another may come to life in a new way.

If our churches are to overcome the spiritual power shortage and cease neglecting the opportunity to be priests to one another, we must not only *recover* the biblical message and *re-form* it for our community, but finally we must come to a sense of personal *renewal.* The priesthood of believers cannot wait for someone else to begin. There is a prayer used by Chinese Christians that begins, "Renew your Church, O Lord, and let it begin with me." The Church can be transformed if we recover our lost heritage. You remember Jesus' charge against the religious of his day. They did not raise a finger to lift the burdens of their brothers and sisters. It is the true priests who know the power of even their finger to lift others in times when they cannot lift themselves. In these past few weeks, I have observed people in this church helping lift others through times of grief and loss. I have watched people here this morning minister to those who felt like strangers in an alien land. The example of some in this congregation has taught others of us what it means to be a steward, giving not of the leftovers but from the top of God's gracious bounty. Yes, priests are lifters of burdens.

When we really begin to exercise our priesthood, we will be pointers as well. Paul Tillich has said that the Church should be like John the Baptist in Grunewald's painting; there his whole being is in the finger with which he points to the cross. When we become servants, not self-promoters, we are priests. Even without words, we are pointing to the one servant-leader who leads us away from wanting always to be served and honored. It is still his loving presence that enables us and others to do the impossible: to seek the lesser place, to move beyond self-interest. If in and through Christ, that's what we have to offer, why are we so shy to be his priests?—Gary D. Stratman

SUNDAY, NOVEMBER 6, 2005
Lectionary Message

Topic: Taking Responsibility for Our Lives
TEXT: Matt. 25:1–13
Other Readings: Josh. 24:1–3a, 14–25; Ps. 78:1–7; 1 Thess. 4:13–18

Weddings, by their very nature, make good material for movies. In thinking of weddings, *Father of the Bride, Four Weddings and a Funeral,* and *My Big Fat Greek Wedding* immediately come to mind.

In orchestrating a wedding, so many things can go wrong and often do—a member of the wedding party gets lost and can't find the church; some members party too late the night before; the bride trips and falls on her dress; or the groom passes out at the altar. The list is endless. Despite everyone's best intentions, almost invariably there is someone in the wedding party who finds it difficult to be prepared. The key word here is *prepared.* To pull off a big wedding, one has to plan and prepare for months in advance.

I. Jesus draws on wedding imagery to make a point about *spiritual* preparedness and readiness. As we read the parable of the Ten Bridesmaids, or Ten Virgins as some translations render it, we are puzzled by some of the wedding customs of the day. Why did the bridesmaids not know the precise time the wedding was to start? Why did the groom finally decide to come for the bride at midnight? How could the five foolish bridesmaids find a place of business open at midnight to buy oil for their lamps?

It helps to know a little bit about wedding customs of the period. In ancient times, wedding celebrations often went on for days. After an initial time of festivities, it was the custom for the groom to go to the home of the bride's parents to get his bride. Young girls (bridesmaids) and other guests would then accompany them to the home of the groom's parents, where the wedding feast proper would take place. But no one really knew when the groom would come for his bride.

We have read the story of how five maidens took oil lamps, as well as extra oil, in case the bridegroom tarried. Five others took their lamps with only what little bit of oil they had in them; they took no extra oil with them. As the bridegroom tarried, their lamp oil ran out, leaving them in the dark. When they called upon the other five to share their extra oil with them, they refused, stating that they only had enough for themselves.

Well, this story is an allegory chock full of symbolism. In the early church, the parable was used to emphasize the need of being ready for the expected return of Jesus, despite his apparent delay. The parable warns of the futility of trying to prepare when it is too late. Once the Lord comes for us, it is too late to make preparations.

The bridesmaids represent the Church. In the Church, only some are really prepared. In the membership of the Church, there are saints and there are some nonsaints, or saints who are saints in name only. What will count in the end is not whether one has said "Lord, Lord," but whether one has demonstrated deeds worthy of discipleship—deeds of love and mercy in Christ's name and for his sake. Many who say "Lord, Lord" are to be excluded from the kingdom because they do not have the required deeds of discipleship. The right confession without the right character is ultimately fraught with folly and ends in disaster.

The oil represents one's spiritual preparations. It is important for us to know that in the Jewish tradition—from which and to which Matthew was writing—oil is often a symbol of good deeds. That little tidbit of information helps put the parable in perspective. In Matthew readiness or spiritual preparedness is "living the life of the kingdom."[1] So the parable is a warning to be spiritually prepared, spiritually ready. It sounds a warning that each of us must make provisions for his or her own spiritual well-being and destiny. I cannot give you any of my spiritual oil, and you cannot give me any of yours. *Each of us must individually take responsibility for our own life.*

II. Taking individual responsibility for one's life was a message that Joshua preached approximately one thousand years before Christ. At a pivotal point in Israel's history, Joshua called his people to make a commitment to serve the Lord in sincerity and faithfulness. Joshua called the people to fear or revere the Lord above everything else in their lives. The Israelites apparently assumed that they could serve God and at the same time serve the other gods worshiped by the nations around them. Joshua insisted that a choice be made, that nothing less

---

[1] *New Interpreters Bible Commentary*, vol. 8, p. 451.

than complete faithfulness would suffice. The Israelites testified that they wanted to serve the Lord and only the Lord. So Joshua led the people in a covenant ceremony and set up a stone as a witness and reminder of the covenant they had made.

A decision is required of us as well. Each and every one of us must make a conscious choice to serve or not serve the Lord. "Choose this day whom you will serve" is the call we hear again and again. In this timeless exhortation, Joshua reminds us, as he reminded the Israelites, that we owe our allegiance to the God who has brought us to where we are today. The call includes putting away the many other gods that would distract us from following the one and only true God. Life is always confronting us with choices—allegiance to God or allegiance to materialism; support of war or of making peace; being spiritually minded or being secularly minded.

One of the problems with our world is too many people have not taken responsibility for their lives. Too many have been lax in their duties. Too many have banked on the spiritual reserves of parents or grandparents, thinking righteousness can be passed down much like genetic traits. But it doesn't work that way. All of us must take responsibility for our own lives and spiritual destinies.

None of us wants to come to the end of our days and, as with the five foolish bridesmaids, hear the Lord say, "Truly I tell you, I do not know you."—Randy Hammer

ILLUSTRATIONS

COVENANT MAKING.   I cannot help but think of the Salem Covenant, that beautiful church covenant drafted by the first congregational church that was officially organized on American soil in 1629, by the Christians of Salem, Massachusetts. The Salem Covenant reads: "We covenant with the Lord and one another; and do bind ourselves in the presence of God, to walk together in all his ways, according as he is pleased to reveal himself unto us in his blessed word of truth." Because of its timeless beauty, countless churches of the Congregational Way have adopted some form of the Salem Covenant as their own church covenant and statement of faith. Whether it be the Salem Covenant or Joshua's, "As for me and my household, we will serve the Lord," or some other commitment of faith, it is imperative that we make a deliberate, conscious choice to serve God and God alone, and that we make the necessary provisions for our spiritual well-being and destiny.—Randy Hammer

A CONSCIOUS CHOICE.   Though we may baptize our children into the faith or dedicate them to God, we must never forget that we have a responsibility to help them in making a conscious choice to follow and serve the Lord.—Randy Hammer

SERMON SUGGESTIONS

Topic: Transfer of Power
Text: Num. 27:12–23
(1) Moses saw the future but was not to lead in it (vv. 12–14). (2) Moses cared for the people he had led and sought for them a suitable leader (vv. 15–17). (3) Yahweh, the Lord, chose Joshua, upon whom Moses conferred some of his own authority, and Joshua stood ready to lead at the proper time.

Topic: On Toward the Goal

TEXT: Phil. 3:12–21

(1) By humility (vv. 12–13a). (2) By forgetting the crippling past (v. 13b). (3) By reaching toward the future (v. 14). (4) By trusting in the Lord Jesus Christ for our ultimate transformation (vv. 20–21).

WORSHIP AIDS

CALL TO WORSHIP.   "O give thanks unto the Lord; for he is good; for his loving-kindness endureth forever" (Ps. 118:29).

INVOCATION.   O Lord, our Lord, give us to know again today the reality of thy near presence in this hour of worship. Let us seek thee, desire thee, think of thee, and be obedient to thy revelations, for our good and thy glory.—E. Lee Phillips

OFFERTORY SENTENCE.   "And to whomsoever much is given, of him shall much be required; and to whom they commit much, of him will they ask the more" (Luke 12:48).

OFFERTORY PRAYER.   You have given much to us, Father, not because you love us more than others but because you have entrusted us with a stewardship. We remember that it is required of a steward that he be found faithful. Help us to be faithful stewards of your good gifts. Amen.

PRAYER.   This is the day that you have made. Thank you, God. May we receive it in all its uniqueness. It is unlike any other day that we have ever lived. May we appreciate its freshness. No matter what yesterday may have been, the creative power of your Spirit is with us making all things new. May we have the discernment to see what *new* thing you are doing in our day and the willingness to be an instrument in the coming of your kingdom.

O the *wonder* of this day: your glory manifest in the mystery of your presence in all the world about us and in us: "Earth's crammed with heaven/And every common bush afire with God." May we approach all the opportunities of today with reverence and rejoicing.

Thank you, Father, for one another. May we be understanding of each other in our foibles and encourage one another to strength. Help us to comprehend more sincerely what it means to be members of the body of Christ. We all have not the same office, but your Spirit equips us for ministry according to our gifts. How great that we can complement one another and that the fullness of your love can be manifest in and through our life together!

We would pray for each other; may your love reach out through us to touch the life of each member of our church family. May we seek out those closest to us and minister according to their need. May those who are shaken because life has been so difficult gain poise to handle creatively whatever life holds for them. Where the ache of loneliness persists, minister the balm of Gilead—the sense of your presence. May those walking through the valley have the faith to say, I will not fear, for thou art with me. Free those who are ill from fear and anxiety, that they may be open and trusting to receive the health of your healing grace.

Grant to us who are citizens of this community, state, nation a sense of responsibility for our share in the democratic processes. May we earnestly seek for good government, exercising our influence responsibly. May we pray and work for the coming of your kingdom, that all peoples may be one family, as you ordain. In the name of him in whom word and deed are one and who teaches us to pray and live.—John M. Thompson

SERMON
Topic: Those with Us
TEXT: 2 Kings 6:8–23; Heb. 11

"From ghoulies and ghosties, long-leggitie beasties, and things that go bump in the night, Good Lord deliver us" runs an ancient Scottish prayer. I used to have it, framed. It hung heavy in the hall outside quiet bedrooms for years, 'til it went bump in the middle of one dark night all by itself and fell loudly to the floor. Shorter and longer leggitie beasties in my house lay paralyzed in their beds. "Good Lord, deliver us," we prayed.

Halloween is just past. Grinning pumpkins and scary costumes at our doors were survivals of days long before Christianity, when northern Europeans lit fires against autumn's dark, wore masks, and offered treats to ward off tricks by ghosts that threatened them—so they believed—with diseases, accidents, and bumps in the night.

Then Christianity came and said people need fear those ghosts no more. For abroad in the world was another ghost, or spirit. This ghost, a holy one, was Lord of hosts and ghosts and fearsome things. Its steady light waits deep, the Christians said, in very darkest night.

From earliest times, the church set days aside to remember special people, like Patrick or Andrew, whose lives let God's holy ghost light through. But also, right from the start, there was a day to honor less famous folk, their names forgotten maybe, who, while briefly here, hallowed God's spirit in their lives ("hallowed be thy name" they prayed). They were strong in their places over lesser spirits that threatened them—spirits that surround us still, and sometimes scare us in the day as well as night.

From the beginning, this was called All Hallows Day, later on, All Saints. For a thousand years its celebration was set on November first. But annual autumn rituals weren't given up. Ghosts reduced to size, the masks, and pumpkin lights could be enjoyed now for their own pleasure. Because we scare so easily, the time chosen to make fun of them was All Saints' Eve. All Hallows Ev'n, it used to be called—halloweven, hallowe'en—the night before All Saints' Day, when Christians remember again the power of God's spirit in the world.

So, still in the month of All Saints, we remember again what the Bible calls "the great cloud of witnesses" (Heb. 12:1) and the story of the boy who feared the hostile forces threatening all things good (1 Kings 6:8–23). "Alas, my master, what shall we do?" he cried. Elisha, the man of God seeing the worst of terrors were themselves outflanked by God's strong spirit, said, "Fear not; those who are with us are more than those who are with them." "Open the boy's eyes," he prayed, "that he may see." If the boy didn't quite see what Elisha saw, he at least saw Elisha—enough to cope with that night's terror anyway.

I. *"Those who are with us."* It's a matter of restoring perspective, of pushing back narrowed horizons where long-range plans look only five years ahead, and a war only sixty years away seems ancient history. The Bible has nothing to do with such shortened visions. It swings us in great concentric circles back to the swirling days of creation itself, and forward again to when the earth will become a single-family home. It declares that our flying days between are held by a strong and caring spirit who values each of us in our time and knows our separate names by heart.

In All Saints' time, at least for a moment, we're catapulted into that broader context. We remember again we're not marooned here on the whirling earth, at the mercy of things that go bump in the night. "Alas my master, what shall we do?" "Do not be afraid," we hear again today. "Those who are with us are more than those who are with them." We're not alone, after all.

That's the basic religious question, of course—not this or that doctrine but, Is the world meaningless? Are we really alone? Some people say so. Both before and after the horror of September 11, we've all had (and will have) days and nights when we suspect they're right. But there've been other days too when suddenly—watching a three-year-old asleep in her bed, or reading about someone in the crumbling building waiting back with a wheel-chaired stranger while stairways filled with smoke—we know there's something beyond us going on in this amazing world, some long purpose beyond the reach of terrorists, which we catch sight of now and then, and of which we're a part.

Everywhere and always, often in the midst of terror, people have found themselves lifting up their hearts and lives in response to this mystery or presence—in sometimes beautiful, sometimes distorted ways. In the church's family that spirit shows itself in Jesus of Nazareth, and people who down the years have responded in his name. That's why we call him Christ—not because that's his last name but because, for us, Jesus brings God's spirit into view, enough of it if not to understand then at least to trust and follow.

"The Lord opened the eyes of the young man," the old story says. Things that went bump in the night were outflanked. The boy was no longer afraid. So in our turn, in All Saints' after-glow, we remember in Jesus' name that there's a spirit stronger than the dark that holds us all.

II. *We're not alone, and we're not the first.* We remember all the saints this month—the whole, long line of those who've gone before and marked the way for us, the ones who died, too young, in wars, the ones who built this place for us, firmed it with their faith, and then moved on, and others we know in other places, whose names and faces we remember—my grandfather and yours, who maybe made no headlines, but whose lives let shine through—people who stood firm in their day when things went bump in the night, who reached for us, frightened in the dark. We couldn't see everything, but we could see them, and it was enough.

Though they're gone, it's not like autumn leaves; they're still around. They inhabit what one prayer calls "that invisible world all round us in which dwell those whom our earthly eyes can no longer see, and our earthly hands no longer touch, but with whom we are for-ever linked by ties of memory and love." That prayer was written by my own minister years ago, where I grew up. He was close to me; he is still close, though he's been gone for fifty years. His prayer went on to thank God for "the great cloud of witnesses before whom we run what remains of our race here, who encourage and assist us in the running, and amongst whom are faces familiar and well beloved."

There are holy times, when we're more open than others—when defense and poses relax, and we know God's spirit surrounds not just us but all those through whom it ever shone, especially ones whose faces we still see and know.

My mother, I know, often sensed my father in the room, though he'd been gone for fif-teen years. Thirteen years ago she died, at the age of ninety-four. That night, his picture fell off the wall; a startled nurse ran from the room. Myself, I had a dream that night, or soon after, that though her fast-clicking heels stopped when my father went, and arthritis stuck her to a chair, she walked beside me down a hall and turned and looked at me. "I'm all right," she said, and smiled.

Still, though Joyce and I visit her grave and sometimes plant flowers, she's not there, we know, but with the saints—all saints. They make a context for us; they remind us nobody starts from scratch here—not in our lives, not in this church, not in our world. They've been breathed back into God's nearer presence; they still breathe with us and help us breathe as well.

We're not alone, we remember today. There are those who are with us. God's spirit wraps us round; so do those people we love, through whom the Spirit shone.

III. *There's more.* Waiting just beyond our view are what our aboriginal brothers and sisters call "the ones coming toward us." What is this miracle? Our tiny blue earth whirling on through empty space is pelted daily with babies. Out of what mysterious, undiscouraged spirit do they come? Like dew in the morning, they arrive in our dull midst, bearing grace. They center us; they make frozen faces smile in buses and supermarket lines. They embody in our midst futures undreamed of yet by any politician, pundit, or parent. They come toward us this morning (descending unheralded, on Jerusalem, Washington, Islamabad, and Kabul) with surprising blessings from God's future for this earth.

When my youngest granddaughter reaches my age, the twenty-first century will be three-quarters gone. Touching her, I touch a future I'll never see but can be part of now—God's future, which warps round us and holds us, as Jesus held the children. He took them in his arms and blessed them. "Except you become like little children," he said, "you cannot enter the kingdom of God" (Mark 10:15). You'll be left wearing pretend costumes to scare away the dark—dressing up to look wiser, more certain, more religious than anyone your size could possibly be. You'll lose touch with God's future, which is coming. You'll work too hard, as though it all depended on you. You'll be terrified by things that go bump in the night.

So in All Hallows' afterglow, in the shadow of September's awful dark—on the fearful edge of whatever looms ahead—pumpkins wilted and costumes put away, shaken and fragile this year as never before—we come once more to this serene, renewing place. Once again "steals on the ear again the distant triumph song" of all the saints.

"Those who are with us are more than those who are with them."—Bruce McLeod[2]

SUNDAY, NOVEMBER 13, 2005
Lectionary Message

Topic: Maximizing Our Potential
TEXT: Matt. 25:14–30
Other Readings: Judg. 4:1–7; Ps. 123; 1 Thess. 5:1–11

One of my favorite poets is Robert Frost. The first poem of Frost's that I ever read, "The Road Not Taken," is still one of my all-time favorites. Its visual images of yellow leaves on a wooded path made a lasting impression upon the mind.

---

[2]*Sunday Morning at Captiva Chapel by the Sea* (Toronto: Kelly McLeod, publisher, 2003), pp. 10–15.

I have always read the lines of that poem in terms of Frost's decision to take the path of being a poet rather than following the well-worn path of being a farmer. But recently I saw Frost's words in a different light. By taking the road less traveled, Frost reveals his decision to step out on faith, to be different, to take a risk. Such is what all of us are faced with every now and again—the decision to step out on faith, to be different, to take a risk.

I. Stepping out on faith and taking a risk is at least part of the message that we find in the parable of the talents. One of the first things that surprises us about this parable is the value of the talents that were entrusted to the slaves. A talent's value was equivalent to fifteen years' worth of wages for a common laborer. So the one who received five talents received an amount equal to seventy-five years' wages for a laborer of that day. That's a lot of money.

On the one hand, the parable speaks of the necessity of responsible action. We are called upon to not squander what we have been given. But on the other hand, the meaning of "good and faithful [trustworthy] slave" is active responsibility that takes initiative and risk.

God, symbolized by the property owner, is generous. God's gifts, talents, and resources to us are abundant. As with the servants in the parable, each of us, as a recipient of God's gifts and graces, is faced with the decision of how to best use our time and talents to God's glory and for the betterment of the world around us. Talents and potential are to be used—God expects increase. We are called to use every gift, every talent, every opportunity, and every resource that is available to us so that we might become the persons we were created to be. This is our high calling.

II. Using every gift, talent, opportunity, and resource also applies to churches. As we have heard this parable preached over the years, generally it is applied to one's individual talents, whether that talent be teaching, singing, administrating, or what have you. Surely that is a lesson to be taken from the parable, as we have seen.

But today I would like to encourage us to try looking at this parable in a different light, as it pertains to church growth. Let us read this parable through "church-growth eyes." God bestows gifts, talents, resources, and potential upon churches just as God does upon individuals. True, some churches seem to have more opportunity and potential than others.

But from those that have been given more opportunity and potential, more is expected in return. Remember in the parable that the servant who received five talents was expected to make a least five more. The one who received two was expected to make at least two more. And the one who received a single talent was expected to make at least one more. The level of service that is expected of us is based on what we have received.

God expects growth, increase, and advancement of the kingdom in and through the Church. As with the servants in the parable who were given the talents, we are not to be content with the way things are. God expects more of us than just survival and hanging onto the status quo. We must be willing to take some risks. The greater the risk, the greater the possible reward. Those who take risks and end up with gain are given more.

To look at that through church-growth eyes, church growth begets more church growth. Once you get on a church-growth roll, it can be like the snowball effect. More growth and momentum leads to more growth and momentum. "To all those who have, more will be given."

The reverse is just as true. The sad truth of the matter is churches that do not make use of their resources and potential lose members to other churches. In recent years, many congregations in mainline denominations have suffered membership loss because while they did not make good use of their God-given resources other churches have taken their members.

The natural tendency for churches that begin to decline is to draw inward and, out of fear, cut back on programs and ministries. Such actions can start the so-called death spiral that begins spinning out of control. Just as growth begets growth, cutbacks in ministries and services beget more cutbacks, loss of a few members leads to the loss of a few more members, and so on. Congregations cannot let fear lead them to hoard their resources and cut back on programs and ministries (or, to put it in the parable's terms, bury their talents). Such is the beginning of the end. To cut back services, programs, and ministries is to commence the long, painful process of killing a church.

But we should be committed to a *growing* church. Our concern should not be cutting back, but adding to and moving forward so that we may do what God is calling us to do in this time and place.

Well, whether we are talking about our individual lives or the life of our church, one thing is certain: God's call to us is to step out on faith and sometimes take a risk, use all our talents and resources, make good use of every opportunity, and be all that we were created to be. In short, we are called to maximize our God-given potential.

Sometimes, as with Robert Frost, it means something like facing a fork in the road and taking the less traveled path. And sometimes that can make all the difference.—Randy Hammer

ILLUSTRATIONS

MAKING AN EFFORT.   "Better to try all things and find all empty, than to try nothing and leave your life a blank."—Charlotte Brontë

CALLED TO BE.   The call upon each of us, as Ralph Waldo Emerson saw it, is *to be*. What God expects of us is to be all that we have been created to be. "There are resources in us," Emerson contended, "on which we have not drawn."[3]

SERMON SUGGESTIONS

Topic: The Incompleteness of Life

TEXT: Deut. 34:1–12, especially verse 4

(1) Not only Moses' life but every life is flawed and incomplete. (2) Despite our sin and limitations, God intends for us abundant and eternal life in Christ both here and hereafter (see John 10:10, 17:13).

Topic: The Lord Is Near

TEXT: Phil. 4:1–9, TEV

Therefore, (1) be joyful in your union with the Lord; (2) show a gentle attitude toward everyone; (3) do not worry about anything, but ask God for what you need, with a thankful heart; and (4) God's peace will keep your hearts and minds safe.

WORSHIP AIDS

CALL TO WORSHIP.   "Thanks be to God, which giveth us the victory through our Lord Jesus Christ" (1 Cor. 15:57).

---

[3]"Divinity School Address"

INVOCATION.   Today we meet to worship in the assurance that in our Lord Jesus Christ we are victorious both in this world and in the world to come. May the joy of this assurance radiate in our prayers, in our hymns, and in all our spoken and wordless acts.

OFFERTORY SENTENCE.   "Whatsoever ye do in word or deed, do all in the name of the Lord Jesus, giving thanks to God and the Father by him" (Col. 3:17).

OFFERTORY PRAYER.   Accept these our gifts, O Lord, as tokens of our mindfulness of thy presence in our lives. Grant us the will, the desire, and the love to be gracious and faithful stewards of the many blessings that thou hast bestowed upon us.—Rodney K. Miller

PRAYER.   On the night when you were betrayed, Lord, you were giving thanks. Why weren't you bitter and anxious, as we would be? We do not give thanks when someone turns against us. We vow revenge. It takes even less than betrayal to stir our ire: if the car breaks down, if the potatoes boil dry, if we hit our thumb with a hammer, if the store misbills us, then we act as though heaven's door has slammed in our face. Yet on the same night that a companion turned you in, and best friends deserted you, and prominent citizens tried you in a kangaroo court, and soldiers tortured you, on that very same night—you gave thanks.

O Christ, we acknowledge that we curse more than we praise, we damn more than we thank, we grumble more than we rejoice. Give us, Christ, the smallest portion of your grace so that whatever happens to us, we shall be glad simply to have lived and to have known your love.—Thomas T. Troeger

SERMON
Topic: How to Use Your Money
TEXT: James 5:1–6

This morning I'd like for us to consider how to handle the wealth God has given you.

You might say, "I don't have any wealth." Yes, you do. If you own your own home, you are in the top 5 percent of the world's population. If you have changes of clothing and options about what kind of food to eat from your pantry or refrigerator, you are a very wealthy person. Now, your income may not be great, but still we in America, in comparison with most of the world, are wealthy. Therefore, it is important for us Americans to look very carefully at this issue of how we are going to handle our money.

I. *The wrong uses of our wealth.* Let's look first at the wrong uses of our wealth. What are we not supposed to do with our money?

(a) *Don't hoard it.* Hoard means to stockpile it, just accumulate it, using it for nothing but just to see the pile grow higher and higher. It's wrong. Notice what the Scripture says there in verse 3: "You have hoarded wealth. . . ."

God's word is indicting those who simply accumulate it with no purpose, no holy commitment, just gather more and more. Perhaps you've read stories of elderly people who have passed away and everyone thought they were poor, but then under the mattress was found thousands of dollars, or something buried in the back yard, or a bank account revealed these folks were quite wealthy but they never used their money for anything. Not for themselves or anybody else! How silly. How wrong.

In New Testament times, people hoarded their wealth in several forms. Some would hoard their harvest. You remember Jesus' indictment of the rich fool whose harvest was so abundant that he had plenty to share with those in need, but his decision was so self-centered that he said, "I'll just build bigger and bigger barns." Jesus condemned him for that decision. Why? Because it was so self-centered. He was just hoarding his wealth, thinking of nothing but to build a bigger barn.

Sometimes people in the first century hoarded their clothes. They accumulated clothes and sometimes would parade in the marketplace or temple in their brightly colored garments as a show that would bring glory to themselves. Sometimes people would hoard precious jewels or metals in order to accumulate, but do nothing with it. How about us?

Are we guilty of hoarding something? Maybe. If you are just gathering money and using it for no one, then God is speaking to you. How about our clothes? Do we hoard clothes? Do you have clothes in your closet you don't wear? We all do, don't we? They just get dusty. You don't use them. You just collect them. That is hoarding.

How about your pantry? Are there some food items in the back of your pantry shelves that you haven't seen in three or four years? How about in your refrigerator?

I think the Scripture is saying, if you just accumulate, it will deteriorate. Therefore, don't hoard it.

(b) *Don't steal it.* Don't steal from others to get wealth (v. 4). In the first century, workers would go to the marketplace. They would be hired at the beginning of the day and paid at the end of the day. The owners of the land would come there to hire the workers. It was not uncommon for the workers to go out into the fields and sweat all day and toil. Then at the end of the day a corrupt landowner could simply look over the work and say, "I don't like what you did. I'm not going to pay you today." The worker would go home unpaid. It was a way corrupt owners would benefit themselves at the expense of those who really had needs. That's why this verse indicts such behavior. "The wages you failed to pay the workmen who mowed your fields are crying out against you." God is mindful of those who have been mistreated. God is mindful if we do not use our blessings in the right way. We need to be aware of that. We must not steal. I think most of us don't. But it is true that whenever people cheat on their taxes, or don't pay their debts, or don't give quality work for time being paid, that is in effect stealing.

There is a third way we shouldn't use our money. We shouldn't hoard it. We shouldn't steal it, and—

(c) *We must not waste it.* Look at verse 5: "You have lived on earth in luxury. . . ." We must not waste our money. God is very concerned when we waste resources that he has given us. Now, that happened in the first century, and it happens today. People waste a lot.

Did you read the story about the corporate executive who is in trouble with the law? It came out in the process of this litigation that he organized a celebration of his birthday, and the price tag for his birthday was a million dollars. The million-dollar birthday! Think of how many people could have been helped if that person had simply chosen to have an average birthday party and used the rest for the glory of God.

Consider the pro boxer, Mike Tyson. He had great skills, achieved great fame, and amassed a great fortune. In his boxing career, they estimate he has earned $333,000,000 and has wasted all of it. Today he has almost nothing. How sad! His skills have now waned. His energies are deteriorated, and he has nothing. How wasteful.

But as we point our finger at folks like that, I think we also need to consider ourselves. In what way do we waste money? How are we wasting some of the blessings God has given us?

Christmas is coming. It is primarily a spiritual season, right? But in America, it is so materialistic. Many people waste so much money on gifts that people don't need, and on things that they cannot afford, and they miss the spiritual meaning of the season. Do not let the Christmas season be a season of waste for you and for your family. Don't waste God's resources.

(d) *Don't abuse it.* In verse 6, look at the way in which it can be abused: "You've condemned. . . ." This is a reference to the way in which corrupt, wealthy people in the first century would bribe judges to get the decision in court that would favor them. It would often result in oppression of the poor and sometimes even in condemnation of the innocent—the abuse of wealth.

I think that God's Word is saying to you and to me, to us who have so many blessings, to be sure that we don't use them in the wrong way.

Now, let's look at the other side, the positive side. How are we to use our wealth, our money?

II. *The right uses of our wealth.* Let me suggest four things.

(a) *Save your money faithfully.* Proverbs 21:20 says, "The wise man saves for the future but the foolish man spends whatever he gets." Proverbs 30:24 says, "Consider the ant, how it stores up for the winter." Saving is important. God's word encourages it. Are you saving some of your money? The average American saves 4 percent of his or her income. The average European saves 16 percent and Japanese 25 percent. Why do Americans save so little? Maybe we are so focused on the *now.* Maybe we are so materialistic that we only think about things instead of people and causes and the Lord's will. It is important for us to save.

John D. Rockefeller amassed a great fortune. He had a formula for his life that could be helpful for us. It's the 10–10–80 rule. Ten percent tithe to the Lord first, off the top. Ten percent saving. Eighty percent spending for what you need. Not a bad formula. That might be a good thing for you to practice. It's very important for us to learn to live on less than we make.

One person used this as a formula for life: Use it up, wear it out, make it do, or do without. Not bad!

You know what the biggest enemy of your savings really is? Advertising. We see this advertisement on TV and we think to ourselves, How can I possibly do without that really pretty thing I think I need? The advertisers have us in their grip.

It's important for us to remember our security is not in our money and the things we can buy. Our security is in the Lord, Jesus Christ. Remember what Paul said to the Philippian Christians: "And my God will meet all your needs according to his glorious riches in Christ Jesus" (4:19). That's where our security is. That's what is important. Save your money faithfully. And second—

(b) *Invest your money wisely.* It's good for us to invest. Proverbs 13:11 says, "Wealth from gambling quickly disappears. Wealth from hard work grows." Investing is important. Saving and investing is good. In Jesus' parable of the talents, the two people he praises are those who invest. The person he condemns is the person who chooses to simply bury his blessings. So I think it is important for us to exercise financial planning and control. It's good to save and invest, as long as we don't hurt ourselves. I've known some people who have simply tried to amass a fortune, but they have made themselves unhealthy. Proverbs 23:4 says,

"Don't wear yourselves out to get rich!" Have the wisdom to show restraint. I think it is good to save and invest, as long as it doesn't hurt your family. In other words, don't deny them in order to build up your portfolio.

Maintain balance in your life. Life is much more than material.

There is a verse of Scripture that helps us maintain balance, 3 John 2: "Beloved, I wish that you may prosper and be in health even as your soul prospers." Now, that's balance! Notice the verse. "I wish that you may prosper"—that's financial or material. "And be in health"—that's physical. "Even as your soul prospers"—that's spiritual. Maintain balance.

Third, if you want to use your money rightly—

(c) *Spend your money carefully.* Proverbs 21:5 says, "The plans of the diligent lead to profit as surely as haste leads to poverty." It's good to plan. It's important for you to think about this.

On this day, as we culminate our stewardship campaign, we are going to come to the front and lay our estimate of giving cards on the altar. I hope it is coming as a result of our praying and planning this week. It's important to spend our money carefully. It is so easy to get into debt. We have to be careful about that. You've probably gone in to buy something that cost quite a bit of money. A person says, "Aw, come on and buy it. You can pay for it in sixty easy payments." Is there any such thing as an easy payment? I don't think so. I think every payment is hard, don't you? Sometimes it is necessary to make payments on something; pay it off quickly. Spend your money carefully. There are so many Americans who are in credit card slavery, indebted to the point that they almost never pay off the interest! That's sad. Be very careful.

I have found a principle about money that holds true. Our outgo will always equal or exceed our income, no matter how much we make. Haven't you found it to be that way? Therefore, we have to exercise control. One person said, "Our yearning capacity always exceeds our earning capacity." Be careful what you yearn for.

Proverbs 27:23 says, "Riches can disappear fast, so watch your interest closely."

(d) *Give your money generously.* If you practice control and planning with what you have, then you will be in a position to give generously as God wants you to give.

Listen to Proverbs 11, verses 24 and 25: "One man gives freely yet gains even more. Another withholds unduly but comes to poverty. A generous man will prosper. He who refreshes others will himself be refreshed." It's a biblical principle that if we are faithful to the Lord we will find blessings that we can share and be generous with, and we will receive blessings in return. You know the biblical principle, "Give and it will be given unto you." "Whatever a person sows that he will also reap." But focus on that which is most important. Jesus said in Matthew 6:20, "Store up for yourselves treasures in heaven." Now, how do you do that?

Treasures in heaven are the people whose lives you influence for the Kingdom! Just think: through your praying, witnessing, and giving, people will experience the Lord Jesus. They'll trust him as Savior. They'll be in heaven, and one day you'll get to see some folks who are there because of you.

An important question we need to answer is, How many people will be in heaven because of you and because of me? What is your answer to that? That's a powerful question, isn't it?

How exciting it is that as we pray we are touching the world, and people are going to be changed for the Kingdom because of that. As we witness people, are going to be changed for the Kingdom.

We have said John 3:16 many times.

Did you notice in that verse that God so loved that he gave? Great love results in generous giving. Do you really love the Lord? Do you really love him? If you do, you will give generously. It is a direct linkage. Great love leads to generous giving. Let's use our money in the right way, to the end that God will be glorified and that souls will be brought into the kingdom forever.—Ronald Murray

SUNDAY, NOVEMBER 20, 2005
Lectionary Message

Topic: Thanks in All Circumstances

Text: Eph. 1:15–23

Other Readings: Ezek. 34:11–16, 20–24; Ps. 100; Matt. 25:31–46

It is said that some thieves once attacked Matthew Henry, the famous Bible scholar and commentator of an earlier century, robbing him of his wallet and money. Henry later wrote of the experience in his diary: "Let me be thankful first because I was never robbed before; second, although they took my wallet, they did not take my life; third, because, although they took my all, it was not much; and fourth, because it was I who was robbed, not I who robbed."

I. Such is an exemplary attitude of thanksgiving—the ability and willingness to give thanks in any and all circumstances. So it appears to have been with the apostle Paul, who testified that he had learned to be content and give thanks in any and all circumstances.

The Letter to the Ephesians is a good illustration of this fact. When the apostle wrote this letter, he was in prison because of his service to the Lord (Eph. 3:1, 4:1, 6:20). The apostle felt that he was suffering for the sake of those to whom he was writing (3:13). Yet this letter, from beginning to end, is written in the spirit of thanksgiving. He opens the letter by saying, "Let us give thanks to the God and Father of our Lord Jesus Christ!" (1:3, TEV). He rejoices in the manifold blessings that are ours through Christ. Paul notes that it is right to give thanks for those who bless our lives, as the Ephesians had blessed his life. "I do not cease to give thanks for you as I remember you in my prayers," he assures his readers (1:16). Instead of careless words coming from our lips, there should be words of thanksgiving (5:4). Finally, it is right and proper to give thanks to God "at all times and for everything" (5:20).

It is easy to be thankful when times are good and all is going well and someone reminds us of our need to be thankful. During good times, we can give thanks for the faith and love that grace our lives. We can give thanks for the hope we have, the wealth and glory of our heritage, and the greatness of power open to us who trust God.

But the truly thankful are those who, like biblical commentator Matthew Henry and the apostle Paul, can give thanks in spite of adverse circumstances. Even in the most unpleasant circumstances, if we look hard enough there is still much for which to be thankful.

II. It seems that the Plymouth Pilgrims also had the ability and willingness to give thanks in any and all circumstances. At this time of year, we are reminded of that little group of religious separatists who made their way from Holland to America aboard a small ship called the *Mayflower* in search of religious freedom. The Pilgrims suffered one trial and tribulation after another in the course of the journey that brought them to America. First of all, some of them were imprisoned because of their faith and quest for religious freedom. Then families were separated, as some of them were able to set sail while others had to stay behind. Then one of the sea captains they hired to bring them to America tricked them and ran off with their money. Another ship on which they loaded all their personal belongings began to sink and they had to return to port, unload, and wait for another ship. This necessitated their leaving Europe much later in the year than they had planned. In the course of their voyage, they faced violent crosswinds and fierce storms at sea. Many of them were afflicted with seasickness. Upon arriving in America at the coast of what is now Cape Cod, Massachusetts, they found themselves in a strange land in the dead of winter, lacking shelter against the elements and winter cold. Many of the Pilgrims died of cold and exposure that first winter on American soil. Yet the following November, the few Pilgrims who survived held a thanksgiving feast, or harvest festival. Plymouth Governor William Bradford issued a proclamation: "And, therefore, I, William Bradford (by the grace of God today, and the franchise of this good people), governor of Plymouth, say—through virtue of vested power—ye shall gather with one accord, and hold in the month of November, thanksgiving unto the Lord." Tradition says ninety-one Indians, or Native Americans, who had helped the Pilgrims survive their first year were invited to the feast, which may have included boiled pumpkin, a type of fried corn bread, fish, berries, watercress, lobster, dried fruit, clams, venison, and plums.

But here is the question: How could the Pilgrims possibly have been in the spirit to give thanks, when many of their loved ones—children, wives, husbands, or parents—had recently been laid to rest in the cold earth? The answer, I believe, lies in understanding the nature of thanksgiving and the reasons for offering it. Real thanksgiving is appropriate in any and all circumstances. Even in difficult times such as what the Pilgrims endured, there is cause to give thanks.

Author Daniel Defoe, in that classic book *Robinson Crusoe*, observes "that it is very rare that the providence of God casts us into any condition of life so low, or any misery so great, but we may see something or other to be thankful for; and may see others in worse circumstances than our own."

As we gather this season around Thanksgiving tables laden with the fruits of the earth that symbolize to us all the gifts of our Creator, let us remember our Pilgrim fathers and mothers who initiated this great tradition. But let us also remember the lesson that the apostle Paul and the Pilgrims taught us: thanks can be given, even following times of adversity. Real thanksgiving is offered in any and all circumstances.—Randy Hammer

ILLUSTRATIONS

HYMN OF THANKS.   Psalm 100 has been called "the banner hymn of the Reformed tradition." A great reformation hymn, "All People That on Earth Do Dwell," is based on this psalm.[4]

GOD IS STILL GOD.   The psalmist reminds us that in spite of what is going on about us, God is still God, we are still God's people, God is good, and God's steadfast love endures forever. Psalm 100 is quite appropriate for the Thanksgiving season since it is a hymn of thanksgiving that was sung by a procession of worshippers who were entering the gates and court areas of the temple for a service of thanksgiving and presentation of their offerings. Religious

---

[4]*New Interpreters Bible*, vol. 4, p. 1079.

pilgrims from various locales gathered to acknowledge God's worldwide rule. They were eager to confess God's providence over all of life. The message of Psalm 100 is at the same time profound and simple: God made us, God rules the world, and we belong to God. Therefore God deserves our thanksgiving and praise.—Randy Hammer

ACKNOWLEDGE THE GIFTS.   None of us enjoys giving our time and talents in service, doing nice things for others, or giving gifts if our service or kind gestures or gifts are never recognized or acknowledged with a word of thanks. You know how you feel when you've racked your brain to think of the perfect gift for someone, braved the Christmas shopping crowds and shopping mall parking contests, and stood in a long line to pay for that gift, only to have it opened and tossed aside on Christmas morning without a word of thanks or acknowledgment. How must God, who lavishes so many gifts upon us, feel when we take for granted so many gifts and graces without a single word of thanksgiving or gratitude?—Randy Hammer

SERMON SUGGESTIONS

Topic: A Marriage Made in Heaven
TEXT: Ruth 4:4–17
(1) According to human custom. (2) According to divine providence (see Matt. 1:3–16).

Topic: The Word You Hear
TEXT: 1 Thess. 2:9–13, 17–20
(1) It is the word of a human being—a fatherly word lived as well as spoken. (2) It is the Word of God—a demanding word at work in believers. (3) It is a word that brings ultimate joy to the messenger.

WORSHIP AIDS
CALL TO WORSHIP.   "Jesus answered and said unto him, if a man love me he will keep my words: and my Father will love him, and we will come unto him, and make our abode with him" (John 14:23).

INVOCATION.   Lord of all bounty, expand our soul in the depths of appreciation as today we are reminded that every good and perfect gift is from above. In the name of him who keeps on giving, Christ Jesus, our Savior.—E. Lee Phillips

OFFERTORY SENTENCE.   "For God is not unrighteous to forget your work and labor of love, which ye have shewed toward his name, in that ye have ministered to the saints, and do minister" (Heb. 6:10).

OFFERTORY PRAYER.   Lord, make us so grateful for all we have been given that we will joyously share of our bounty that others may be blessed as we have been blessed, through Jesus Christ our Lord.—E. Lee Phillips

PRAYER.   Eternal Spirit, thou dwellest in light unapproachable, beyond the power of our thought to comprehend or our imagination to portray. Yet thou art revealed to us in the order of the world we live in, in the truth our minds discover, in the inward presence of thy Spirit, and above all in Christ, thy Son. With reverent hearts we worship thee.

We would bring our fragmentary lives into the presence of thy wholeness. We would bring our transient thoughts into the light of thine eternity. We would bring our restless spirits into the calm strength of thine everlasting purpose.

See what complaints we have brought into thy sanctuary against the circumstances that have fretted us, against the human friends who have failed us, against the enemies who have wronged us, and even against the justice of thine order that has hurt us. Teach us, nevertheless, we beseech thee, to search our own lives, to see that each man is his own destiny, that each soul is its own heaven and its own hell. Send us back into our own souls to find there, by thy grace, peace and power and adequacy to conquer life. May we be victors and not victims.—Harry Emerson Fosdick

SERMON
Topic: Good News for Bad Times
TEXT: Isa. 40:11

Are these times bad times? Are these times of hope or hopelessness? Father Matthew Fox, in his book, *Original Blessings,* argues: "The comfort of consumerism and the violence of militarism dominate our times and make us a people with little or no hope." The late Erich Fromm once wrote: "Those whose hope is weak settle for comfort or for violence."

A hopeless world leads us to worship at the altar of geocide, ecocide, and biocide. Geocide is the destruction of the Earth by war. Ecocide is the destruction of the air, the water, and the ecosystems of creation. Biocide is the destruction of all animal and plant life by humans. On his deathbed, Fromm, an eminent psychologist, asked his friend Robert Fox a penetrating question. Said he, "Why is it, Bob, that the human race prefers necrophilia to biophilia?"

In plain words, he asked why we prefer the love of death more than love of life. Why do we value greed more than generosity, hostility more than helpfulness?

I answer Fromm by saying humankind loves death more than life because humans worship the creation rather than the Creator, a world minus God. The Creator equals a world where the creatures become the highest values in the society. When creatures replace the position of authority that belongs only to God, ecocide, biocide, geocide, and genocide grow out of diseased human souls and from a psychological cancer called egocide. Egocide is simply the sickness of the human ego. Egocide manifests itself in two forms: (1) the ego is degraded so that people feel as unworthy and evil as animals who roam the jungle; and (2) the ego is inflated so that people see themselves as little gods superior to nature and other human beings. Egocide is when people ignore God and do what pleases them. Egocide is bad news for bad times.

Let me illustrate an example of egocide. In an Oakland, California, hospital, a wealthy patient is neglected by her only child. This child visits the mother only now and then. When she sees her sick mother, she says: "I'd visit you more, but I am busy raising money for charity." Only a sick ego would put charity above mother. Without mother, there would be no, I, you, he, or she.

Maybe theologians are at fault for only emphasizing the masculine nature of God. God has the nature of both father and mother. Listen to Isaiah 42:14: "I [God] groan like a woman in labor. I suffocate. I stifle" (*Jerusalem Bible*).

In Isaiah 66:13 God says, "Like a son comforted by his mother will I comfort you" (*Jerusalem Bible*).

Meister Eckhart, the mystic, wrote: "What does God do all day long? God gives birth. From all eternity God lies on a maternity bed giving birth."

Like a father, God protects and provides for us. Like a mother, God comforts and consoles us. Egocide rejects God and says: "I am the master of my fate. I am the captain of my soul." But egocide is bad news for bad times. Is there good news for bad times? Hear the Word of God that comes to us through Isaiah!

"O Zion, that bringest good tidings, get thee up into the high mountain, O Jerusalem, that bringest good tidings, lift up thy voice with strength; lift it up, be not afraid; say unto the cities of Judah, Behold your God!" (Isa. 40:9).

These words were spoken to people who had been in Babylonian captivity for seventy years. They were an oppressed people with a poor self-image. Their egos were diseased and damaged. They saw themselves as helpless and powerless. They made their homes in the valley of defeat. Their environment was one of decay. Their lives were hopeless.

But the Divine Word to them was a command. Move upward into the high mountain! H. Beecher Hicks Sr. said that attitude determines altitude. Giants in attitude dwell on the high mountain of possibility. Citizens of Zion must believe in themselves because God believes in them.

This text informs the church to have a positive self-image. You are Zion! You are Jerusalem! You must dwell on the high mountain! You have good news! You are good news for bad times! You must make a difference in this world! At the Allen Temple Leadership Conference in December 1983, Hicks said that God is risking the spread of his message and mission on Earth to the church. If the church fails, God has no other plan.

"Lift up thy voice with strength; lift it up, be not afraid; say unto the cities of Judah, Behold your God!" (Isa. 40:9).

A man was hurt in an accident at work. The call went out, "Get a doctor; get a doctor!" The hurt man cried, "It is too late for a doctor! Is there anyone who can tell me about my soul?"

A layperson commented to a pastor, "There were three hundred of us ready to help the man with his body; but there was no one to help him with his soul!" The pastor replied, "You could have helped him; you didn't have to preach! You could have knelt beside him and told him what the Lord means to you! You could have prayed for him!"

The layperson confessed: "I started to kneel beside the man and do just as you said. Then I saw those who know me as I really am. And my life closed my lips!"

Can you speak words of life in these bad times? Can you utter the truths of God to hungry souls questing for liberation from spiritual famine? There are people living on the outskirts of hope. They need to hear Zion's voice. There are bewildered travelers stumbling in the darkness. They need light from Jerusalem in order to find their way! Get up from self-pity! Get up from dejection! Get up from despair! Get up into the high mountains of visibility! Speak out so the world can hear you!

Speak with the strong voice of conviction! Speak with the pure voice of sincerity! Tell the good news! What is good news? "He shall feed his flock like a shepherd. He shall gather the lambs with his arm, and carry them in his bosom, and shall gently lead those that are with young" (Isa. 40:11).—J. Alfred Smith Sr.

SUNDAY, NOVEMBER 27, 2005
Lectionary Message

Topic: Ready or Not
TEXT: Mark 13:24–37
Other Readings: Isa. 64:1–9; Ps. 80:1–7, 17–19; 1 Cor. 1:3–9

As children we often played a game called Hide and Seek. One of us would stand at home base—some centrally located place in the middle of the house if we were playing indoors, or a big tree if we were playing outdoors—and shutting our eyes would count to one hundred while all the other children ran and hid. At the end of counting to one hundred, the person who had counted and was "It" would yell, "Ready or not, here I come." And then he or she would go in search of the other children. The first one to be found was It for the next go-around, and he or she would then have to go to home base and shut his or her eyes and count to one hundred and then go hunting for all the other children in their hiding places. Obviously no one wanted to be It perpetually. But you wanted to be ready when the person who was It came in search of you.

I. An ancient hope and prayer of God's people was that God, like a divine It, if you will, might come in search of them; that God might come to find them and save them. Down through the centuries, this hope and the prayer of God's people that God would come and intervene in the affairs of the world and bless them grew ever stronger. We see this longing and prayer not only in the psalms but also in the Hebrew prophets.

By the time of John the Baptist and Jesus, this longing for God to come and intervene in the affairs of the world was at a fever pitch. Both John the Baptizer and Jesus came preaching a gospel of readiness. Much that we find in the Gospels is on the theme of being ready for God's coming.

However, by the time of Jesus, the expectations had shifted from expecting God to come to expecting the coming of the "Son of Man," the one appointed by God to make things right in the world. The Son of Man as one anointed by God is a term about which we are not totally clear. But we do know that in the early days of Christianity Jesus came to be identified with the Son of Man and seems to have even taken that title on for himself.

II. In the early church there was the expectation that Jesus, as the Son of Man, would make a visible return in the clouds of heaven, at which time the true believers would be separated from those who were not believers, or who were believers in name only. The early Christians, including the apostle Paul, expected a physical, visible return of Jesus any day. As time passed, and as Jesus did not visibly return, hopes of such an immediate physical return grew dim and the church began to make concessions in its teaching. In other words, some quarters of the church began to think of the return of Jesus in other ways—in a more spiritualized way. That is why we see a much different theology and approach in the Gospel of John than we do in Matthew, Mark, and Luke.

But the emphasis remained: everyone needs to be ready to meet the Lord when he does come, regardless of how that coming might be. In one sense of the term, the Lord comes every time someone leaves this life and journeys to the next. That is to say, if we were to die today from a massive heart attack, or a car accident, or some kind of natural disaster, then the Lord would come for us today. For as John quotes Jesus in his Gospel, "If I go to prepare a place for you, I will come again to receive you to myself, that where I am there you may be also" (John 14:3). So the gospel message that we read time and again is to be ready, be alert, keep awake, for the Lord might come for us at a time when we least expect it.

III. Well, many centuries ago the Christian Church fathers decided that the four weeks before Christmas would be a good time not only to celebrate the Lord's coming in its varied manifestations but also to emphasize the need for spiritual preparedness and readiness. The word *Advent* itself means "coming" and refers to the coming of the Lord—his first coming as a baby, his coming in Spirit at Pentecost, his coming in Spirit to present-day believers, and his future coming when we leave this life. During the four Sundays and weekdays prior to Christmas we concentrate on getting ready for the coming (comings) of the Lord. That's a theme of Advent—getting ready, being prepared for the coming of the Lord.

That takes us back to Hide and Seek. Another part of the game I failed to mention earlier was that if you stayed in your hiding place you eventually wanted to be found. You didn't want to be forgotten about and be left in a dark closet or under a scratchy bush for very long. You wanted to be hid well when the person who was It called "Ready or not, here I come," but down deep inside you also wanted to be found and not be left there.

Isn't that what Advent is all about? We want God, like a divine It, to come looking for us and find us. We want to be found. The good news is, this is what God has done in the coming of Jesus Christ. God has come searching for us and has found us.—Randy Hammer

ILLUSTRATION

READY OR NOT, HERE HE COMES.   Are you a puller or a backer? That is, when you drive into a public parking spot, say, for instance, at the grocery store, do you pull into the space or back into the space? Some years ago, Ernest, a friend of mine, shared how he had observed that when parking in a single-row parking spot, some people just whip right in and get out of the car, whereas other people very carefully and mindfully take their time to pull forward and then back into the spot so that the front of their car is pointed in the direction they need to go when they leave. Thus the question, are you a puller or a backer?

My friend Ernest philosophized a little and wondered if the way people approach a parking spot has anything to do with the way they approach life in general. In other words, are people who take time to very carefully and mindfully back into a parking space any more apt to be more prepared in their lives in general than people who pull in quickly, taking no thought for when it is time to leave? Could it be that backers are preparers and pullers are procrastinators? The idea may be trivial and the connection nil. However, there is something to be said about cultivating a habit of being ready and prepared.—Randy Hammer

SERMON SUGGESTIONS

Topic: When the Lord God Is Shepherd

TEXT: Ezek. 34:11–16

(1) He seeks his scattered sheep. (2) He provides for his gathered sheep. (3) He judges the oppressive sheep.

Topic: The Reign of Christ

TEXT: 1 Cor. 15:20–28, RSV

(1) The fact—in his Resurrection. (2) Its nature—the subjection of all things under him. (3) Its limits—until Christ is "subjected to him who put all things under him."

WORSHIP AIDS

CALL TO WORSHIP.   "O Zion, that bringest good tidings, get thee up into the high mountain; O Jerusalem, that bringest good tidings, lift up thy voice with strength; lift it up, be not afraid; say unto the cities of Judah, Behold your God" (Isa. 40:9).

INVOCATION.   O thou Beginner of our yesterdays, Mystery of our today, and Hope of our tomorrows, we acknowledge in humility and gratitude our dependence on thee. Help us this morning to prepare our lives for the birth of thy love in us. We pray in the name of him who came to us in love, even Jesus Christ our Lord.—Donald W. Musser

OFFERTORY SENTENCE.   "But to do good and to communicate forget not; for with such sacrifices God is well pleased" (Heb. 13:16).

OFFERTORY PRAYER.   God of grace, we feel that we hardly make any sacrifice so great as the compensations when thou hast opened our hearts in love and generosity. We know that thou lovest a cheerful giver and that we are loved. May others find the joy of thy boundless love because of our giving.

PRAYER.   Eternal God, Lord of all seasons, this time of thanksgiving has turned our hands and hearts upward to you in gratitude. We have remembered your generous call and blessing upon us, and we give thanks. Forever God, Lord of all time, with grateful and open spirits we embrace now this holy moment in time: Advent. It is a season for silence, for preparing, for waiting, for expecting and receiving the wondrous gift of the Christ. O come, O come Immanuel, and in our hearts, do dwell.

Gracious God, Master of kind forgiveness, we confess that our lives are not ready to receive this best gift. Our hearts are in the wilderness, so cleanse us from our rebellious wandering. The rough spots of our lives plead for the smoothness of your tender healing. Our crooked ways yield to your mending, in making straight our paths. Bring low our mountains of pride and prejudice, and lift up our valleys of despair and defeat. Merciful God, cleanse our wounds of sorrow with your pure joy and clothe us in your certain and abiding hope, Jesus Christ our Lord.—William M. Johnson

SERMON

Topic: Advent Gifts: The Gift of Consolation
Text: Luke 21:25–36; Joel 2:30–32

The frightening prospects of an apocalyptic intrusion into our world—even prospects of apocalyptic destruction of our world—have become more real in *our* consciousness, perhaps, than with most any other civilized generation since the Enlightenment.

Today, the most well-informed, the most highly educated, the most experienced among us know—and not based on any superstitious nonsense—that the world could end with precisely the kind of horror described by prescientific visionaries whose feelings about what might happen to the world were recorded in what became Holy Scripture. You'll be kept awake if you think about these things too much—not just here but even at home in your own bed.

Could our world really be destroyed in such a horrible way? You know well the answer to that question, and nuclear weaponry is just one of the ways we could destroy ourselves and our earth. It would also be grisly, wouldn't it, if we polluted ourselves to death or burned ourselves up by damaging the ozone layer beyond effectiveness? Any of these things could happen.

Many of the Old Testament prophets spoke of this "day of the Lord" when, "because of their wickedness, God would punish other nations, Israel, Judah, or all the inhabitants of the earth."[5] The prophet Joel, for one, heard God saying: "I will show portents in the heavens and on the earth, blood and fire and columns of smoke. The sun shall be turned to darkness, and the moon to blood, before the great and terrible day of the Lord comes."[6]

The *signs* to which Luke refers are disturbances of various sorts, and they are associated by him (as by other New Testament writers) with the Second Advent of Jesus Christ—that is, with the reappearing of Jesus Christ in human history at the end of time, which is a basic New Testament belief.

Because human life is and always has been subject to unexpected tragedy and calamity, and because they are often associated biblically with the end of the age in which we live, Luke admonishes his readers: "Be on guard so that your hearts are not weighed down with dissipation and drunkenness and the worries of this life, and that day catch you unexpectedly, like a trap. For it will come upon all who live on the face of the whole earth. Be alert at all times, praying that you may have strength to escape all these things that will take place, and to stand before the Son of Man [that is, Jesus Christ]."[7]

Good advice.

Whether or not you associate such events with God's intentionally bringing this age to a close on the "Day of the Lord" or at the "Second Coming of Jesus," these things *could* come to pass.

God created the heavens and the earth and their inhabitants; there never has been a time since creation that God has not continued to be with us, and this will be true until the end of life as we now know it, even until the end of this age.

In the midst of these bleak and sobering thoughts, can you find any reason for hope or encouragement? Actually, you should be able to see it here, for what Luke intends to deliver— and the prophet Joel too, for that matter—is not a burden for fear but a *gift of consolation*. Did you hear it? Will you receive it?

The Christian season of Advent is all about the coming of the Christ into this world: the word becoming flesh, the coming of Christ into our lives in the manifold ways that happens, *and* the reappearing of our Lord into human history. Wherever Jesus comes, things are shaken up; everything about his life confirmed that, so we shouldn't be surprised. But there is much more to the story.

Luke said that when the worst is happening, when the world is coming apart at the seams, when "these things begin to take place, stand up [he said] and raise your heads, because your redemption is drawing near."[8]

---

[5]"Judgment, Day of," *Harper's Bible Dictionary* (San Francisco: HarperSanFrancisco, 1985), p. 516.
[6]Joel 2:30–31, NRSV.
[7]Luke 21:34–36, NRSV.
[8]Luke 21:28, NRSV.

The word we have translated as "redemption" means deliverance, and in this context it means deliverance from "hostility, suffering, persecution, danger, and the threat of death."[9] When hostility and suffering and persecution and danger and the threat of death are over-powering, *stand up and raise your heads, because your redemption is drawing near.*

Dear friends, this is an Advent gift for you; it is the gift of consolation. It is the gift of hope when all you can feel is hopelessness. When life is doing its worst to you, when your dreams and securities are shattering to the point that you believe there can be no future for you, when everything in and around tells you to give up, lift up your head. You are a child of God, and your deliverance is at hand.

What we have in our biblical lessons today is the assurance that evil and disaster cannot ultimately overcome us; God will not stand for that. Although God has placed us in a world in which scientific and circumstantial randomness are operative and in which the effects of human freedom prevail, there are limitations, and there are boundaries. What we can know, therefore, is that God has not forsaken us, that God has not lost control, that we will some-how triumph. The fearsome circumstances that surround us may or may not be signaling the end of the age; God is the same. Be ye therefore consoled.—David Albert Farmer

SUNDAY, DECEMBER 4, 2005
Lectionary Message

Topic: The Gospel Debut
TEXT: Mark 1:1–8
Other Readings: Isa. 40:1–11; Ps. 85:1–2; 2 Pet. 3:8–15a

"The beginnings of the gospel of Jesus Christ, the Son of God." Thus begins the Gospel of Mark. There are no shepherds in the field, no angels in the sky, and no baby in the manger. Just the stark reality of it all: "the beginnings of the gospel. . . ." The fullness of time has come.

Mark's Gospel, like the other three, was written with a twofold intention: first, to provide a lasting account of the origin of the gospel message, what had been floating around as oral tradition since the first Easter; but second, to set forth the message itself so no one would be confused about Christianity's claims.

I. *The gospel debut declares the dawn of a new day.* Perhaps we can't fathom the mystery of the incarnation, but still we know that in Christ's coming something of eternal conse-quence, something everlastingly meaningful, has come our way. As the New Testament era unfolded, hundreds of years had passed since a well-defined prophet had come to the scene. Now two decisive characters appear—and in the same generation: John the Baptist and Jesus of Nazareth.

John came as a shocking wake-up call to a people grown weary and complacent. His auda-cious lifestyle surely placed him on the fringe of society. What a sight he must have been, dressed in camel hair, eating locusts and washing them down with honey. He was a rugged

---

[9]Ray Summers, *Commentary on Luke* (Waco, Tex.: Word, 1972), p. 163.

man. But his message was even more bizarre. To people who believed they were God's elect, who had all the questions answered in the law, who for hundreds of years had found comfort in their unique relation to God—to these people, John declared with emphasis their need for repentance. There the gospel began.

It is still there that the gospel begins. In fact, Jesus used the same text, "Repent for the Kingdom of God is near," in his first sermon. Repentance, the call to a new level of honesty with God and decisive living based on that new honesty, lies at the heart of the gospel message. It is indeed the great need for this neurotic generation in which we live.

II. *The gospel debut also identifies Jesus Christ with our humanity.* A question often asked is, Why was Jesus baptized? If baptism proclaims publicly the death of sin's hold on us, and Jesus was sinless, why was he baptized? Perhaps no single answer will suffice, but two reasons appear certain. First, Jesus heard John's preaching calling the nation to repentance. Something within that message resonated with the growing awareness of his divine mission, and he felt compelled to identify with it. But second, there was the identification Jesus had with the whole of the human race. Jesus was sinless, but we're not. In baptism Jesus entered into the human predicament. He sided with us and not against us! The baptism of Jesus was the open and public dramatization of the good news given to all people.

In the Advent season, we are forced by love's design to see the multicultural, multinational, multiracial face of Jesus. The distinctions we honor melt away in view of Christ's human appeal. Before the One whom the Father called "My beloved Son," the heavenly affirmation spoken at Jesus' baptism, we all bow. No place of favoritism exists there! Then follows the ordination formula from Isaiah 42:1, "in whom I am well pleased." Jesus Christ is the Suffering Servant of Isaiah sent forth to establish justice in the earth. He is the King, the Messiah, whose only throne would be a cross. He is the savior of all people.

III. *In the gospel debut, we are made aware of Christianity's radical reality.* The community of faith who first read this document needed to hear its word of hope. They were, as many suppose, a persecuted people situated in and around Rome near the time of the Neronian persecution—still only thirty years away from Jesus' death. Times were hard—and faith made a difference. Faith still does!

Mark interrupts the flow of his story to tell us of Jesus' trip to the wilderness to be tempted by the devil. There is trauma there, but as the scene ends Jesus finds solace as "angels minister to him." Even God's only Son suffered temporary horror. But victory came in the end. As God was with Christ, so God is with us. Yet we must maintain constant vigil. Every lamp must be trimmed, as he would later say. We must gird our loins and be ready for the struggle of a lifetime. We cannot be complacent in faith, for too much is at stake. We can't remain neutral. Weak faith and accommodated values will not carry the day.

Crucial choices are necessary in each age of the church, whether first century or twenty-first century. Will we truly follow the one rejected on earth but approved in heaven, the one crucified in time but victorious in eternity?—Lee McGlone

SERMON SUGGESTIONS

Topic: When God Comes

Text: Isa. 40:1–11

(1) He brings a message of comfort (vv. 1–5). (2) He asserts the trustworthiness of his Word (vv. 6–8). (3) He demonstrates both strength and tenderness (vv. 9–11).

Topic: Why the Delay?

TEXT: 2 Pet. 3:8–15a

The Lord delays his coming because (1) he does not reckon time as we do, (2) he is gracious and forbearing, and (3) he is preparing to re-create the universe.

WORSHIP AIDS

CALL TO WORSHIP.   "Oh, Lord, rebuke me not in thy wrath: neither chasten me in thy hot displeasure. For thine arrows stick fast in me, and thy hand presseth me sore" (Ps. 38:1–2).

INVOCATION.   God of the promise, on whom we rely for life and its meaning: we confess that we have sinned against you by abandoning hope, by failing to accept your promises, by relying on ourselves to be both the sources and the object of our own faith. Forgive us, we pray, and once more open our hearts to your mercy, our minds to your promise, our hands to our neighbor in need. In this season of hope, restore us to faith in your providing care and your guiding love.—E. Paul Hovey

OFFERTORY SENTENCE.   "And when he looked on him, he was afraid, and said, "What is it, Lord?" And he said unto him, "Thy prayers and thine alms are come up for a memorial before God" (Acts 10:4).

OFFERTORY PRAYER.   Generous Lord, through what we give today may others be introduced to the good news of Jesus Christ and the joy of doing thy holy will.—E. Lee Phillips

PRAYER.   Surrounding God, Lord and Father of all nations, gathered with believers around the world, we raise our prayers of adoration and praise. Eternal God of everywhere, because beautiful feet have stepped upon mountains all over your world, your kingdom is greater than we know or understand. Author of all glad tidings, we give thanks today for those who have and are giving themselves to spreading the good news of Jesus Christ. May we in all our steps to share glad tidings in service, in praying, in giving—be found generous and faithful.

Our Father of the Prince of Peace, allow us not to overlook the tie between tidings of good news and tidings of peace. Jesus Christ is our salvation and our peace, and in him we find love that conquers fear, trust that overcomes falsehood, joy that fades our sorrows, hope that endures our despair, and peace that passes all understanding. In grateful response, free us to be people of light and redemption to a dark and lost world. O God of eternal presence, this Advent Sunday of peace, may our feet be beautiful too.—William M. Johnson

SERMON

Topic: One Man's Testimony

TEXT: 2 Tim. 1:12

No one, however great, can tell us all the answers. At our wisest and best, as Isaac Newton said, we are like a boy playing on the seashore, now and then finding a smoother stone or prettier shell than ordinary—but with the vast ocean of truth undiscovered before us. Paul was a genius—"a Socrates in thought, a Garibaldi in action"—but he frankly confessed: "We know in part. . . . Now we see through a glass, darkly" (1 Cor. 13:9, 12, KJV). Mystery surrounds us.

Here, however, is one thing we can know beyond any shadow of doubt: "I know whom I have believed." In this memorable phrase the apostle explains his own terrific impact on history. His thought and theology have repeatedly been the means of rekindling the fires of faith in days of apostasy and despair.

How do we account for Paul's continuing influence? The answer is here: he knew what, and whom, he believed. He could give a convincing personal reason for the hope that was in him.

I want, in this sermon, to offer one man's testimony—my own reasons for holding to Jesus Christ as Savior and Lord.

"I know whom I have believed." This is what Christianity essentially is: a relationship to a Person. It is not a cloudy, nebulous theory; a dreary philosophy; or a grim, forbidding collection of rules and regulations. It is a thrilling personal allegiance to the living Christ of God.

What precisely do I find in Christ? What does it really mean to know him?

I. I find in Christ *the truth about God.* A man can believe in God apart from Jesus Christ. Millions do, for one reason or another. Intellectual atheism has little attraction for the majority of people, posing as it does more questions than it appears to answer.

"If men have no God," said Martin Luther, "they must have an idol." Man's groping ideas of God have ranged from the crude, revolting, and grotesque idol of the savage to the cold, abstract First Cause of the philosopher. Today in our materialistic society the evidence suggests that men must recognize some Ultimate. It may be a sophisticated substitute god—mammon, the state, technology, self, or an ideology—but it is the god they finally believe in.

More important than the question of God's existence is that of his character.

The supreme claim of the Christian faith is that God has revealed the truth about himself in Jesus Christ, and that truth is summed up in one constantly reiterated word: "Father." From the beginning to the end of his ministry, Jesus proclaimed and incarnated the fatherhood of God. "He who has seen me," he said, "has seen the Father." The nature of Ultimate Reality is not a vague abstraction—a life force, a principle of causality—but a Father who loves us each one as though there were but one of us to love.

This revelation of the divine fatherhood, at its deepest and richest, was given to mankind in Jesus Christ, and in him alone. It is the most revolutionary truth in the universe, if only we grasp its terrific implications. It brings God near to us. It assures us of his intimate knowledge of every man. It means that behind all the mighty forces shaping our destiny, all the enigmas and tragedies of life, there are at work wise and loving purposes. Christ is the revealer to men of such a God and the guide of men to such a God. He gives us the right to become children of God. He enables us to say with all the conviction of personal experience: "I believe in God the Father Almighty, maker of heaven and earth."

II. I find in Christ *the clue to the meaning of life.* Millions of our contemporaries have searched desperately for some purpose in life, for some satisfying interpretation of life. Many, broken in the disappointment of their searching, slide back toward nothingness, claiming that there is nothing to be found and that the whole sorry scheme of things is empty and absurd. They may have plenty to live *with,* but they have nothing to live *for.* They "haven't a clue."

A significant name given to Christ in the New Testament is "the word of life." What is a word? It is a clue to the idea in mind. It is an articulated thought. As the word of life, Jesus Christ is the clue to the meaning of life. In him we discover not only what God is like but what God purposes for the world and for us. This is not a claim, not for one moment, that faith in Jesus Christ answers all our questions or solves all the terrible enigmas arising out of "the giant agony of the world." Never in this life shall we have that kind of certainty. But it is to claim that Christ gives us the clue we need.

We learn, for instance, how life should be lived. Moreover, we learn from him what life is all about. This world is "a vale of soul-making." We are here to do the will of God, to be trained for our eternal destiny as his sons and daughters by the disciplines of life. We are here to seek first his kingdom with our time, talent, and treasure. We are here to fashion a Christ-like character, to face all our experiences—in the incredible but exalting conviction that the day will come, as a great preacher once said, when the angels themselves will see us coming up the slope of heaven and say: "Look at that man, that woman, how like Christ!"

III. I find in Christ *the secret of moral victory.* We know how we ought to live. We know, in our best moments, how we want to live. It is the power we lack. Nowhere in literature has our fundamental need been more eloquently expressed than by Paul himself: "For I do not do the good I want, but the evil I do not want is what I do. . . . Wretched man that I am! Who will deliver me from this body of death?" (Rom. 7:19, 24).

The answer of ten thousand times ten thousand is that Christ is the deliverer. His name is Savior—not merely teacher, example, or hero. He breaks the power of canceled sin. He sets the prisoner free. He forgives sin and gives the guilty conscience peace. He does more, far more; by the indwelling presence of his Holy Spirit he gives us the power to achieve a permanent victory over the most sordid, stubbornest of the sins that haunt and harass us. "It is no longer I who live," said Paul in another memorable passage, "but Christ who lives in me" (Gal. 2:20).

IV. I find in Christ *the assurance that death is defeated.* There is nothing stupider than the popular modern evasion of pretending death is not a fact. A faith to live by must be a faith to die by; for death is the last enemy, the final contradiction, full of pathos and mystery and solitude.

That is why in the end man clamors for an assurance that death is defeated, that beyond death there is life and hope and fulfillment, reunion with those we have loved and lost awhile. The philosophy of materialism leaves us unsatisfied and unhappy—it is so bleak and barren. The human spirit does not readily accept the verdict that the end will be final extinction: "ashes to ashes, dust to dust," and eternal darkness. Jesus Christ alone gives us the assurance we need. To be sure, there are various philosophical arguments advanced in support of immortality that leave Christ out. They are not entirely irrelevant. They are powerless, however, to create the certainty that throbs in the heart of the man who can say, "I know whom I have believed."

We rest our hopes on certainties—an empty tomb and a risen Christ who has "shattered thy myth of death's invincibility" and brought life and immortality to light. It means that the life everlasting can begin here and now for all who enter into fellowship with Christ. We receive it as a present possession. It is a new quality of life, a new dimension of life, a death-resistant life, a foretaste of the experience awaiting us on the other side of the grave. "We have passed out of death into life," cried the men of the New Testament; and this is the testimony of all who know whom they have believed.[1]

---

[1]John N. Gladstone, *The Valley of the Verdict* (Toronto: Welch, 1968), pp. 17–27.

SUNDAY, DECEMBER 11, 2005

Lectionary Message

Topic: Called to Joy

TEXT: 1 Thess. 5:16–24

Other Readings: Isa. 61:1–4, 8–11; Ps. 126; John 1:6–8, 19–28

Most of us have had bad days. On those days, nothing seems to go right. Frustration rises high. Those days may come even in high and holy seasons like Advent—and perhaps they come even more often and more powerfully at such times. These are natural and very human expressions. Yet because we are followers of Christ, another attitude rises high in the holy season. The apostle summarizes the demand in two brief words: "Rejoice always."

I. These are hard words to put into practice. In fact, they appear to be impossible. How can anyone, in the face of whatever circumstance, maintain an attitude of joy? Yet as this year's Advent season continues, we are reminded that joy is our high calling. Is Paul a naïve dreamer? Does he heap up words without clear thinking? Is his instruction here so heavenly minded that it has no earthly value?

Perhaps the answer is yes and no. The apostle was indeed an intellectual giant who dwelt often in the world of ideals. Many scholars have suggested that he believed sincerely that heaven was coming soon and that Jesus Christ would arrive for a Second Advent during his lifetime. In light of such an imminent return of Christ, whatever sorrows or horrors we have to bear become bearable. So he could say, because the time was short, "rejoice always."

The answer is also no because Paul was one who understood the ways of this world. He had not led a sheltered life. Suffering was a real part of his existence. Beaten, left for dead, shipwrecked, imprisoned—these were the lot of his Christian experience. The instructions he left to the churches of his day were forged in the white-hot furnace of personal experience.

Whether the answer is yes or no, one thing seems absolutely sure. Paul was not intending to lay a guilt trip on his earliest readers—nor on us as we read it today. "Be joyful or else" is not the tone intended here. We should note that there are a number of Christians who have been taught, and who in turn teach others, that we must always feel happy, and that to feel otherwise is evidence of small faith and to be corrected with an altered mind-set. Such negative thinking makes joy an oppressive emotion, adding guilt to already sagging spirits. True joy and rejoicing comes in another way.

II. The "joy" that does come to us "always" is the kind rooted in the gift of God's grace. It's not a matter of our feelings, so often high or low, rising or falling, depending on the prevailing winds that blow—sometimes with us, sometimes against us. No, true joy is deeper than human experience.

Verse 24 of today's text helps put this in perspective. True joy comes as gift. It comes from Christ: "The one who calls you is faithful; he will do it." Only in Christ, and with Christ's help, are we able to rejoice always. Since Christ is always with us, there is no call for acute and overwhelming despair. Just the opposite is true. When lived in the light that Christ brings us, darkness cannot win. When life is rooted in knowing Christ, in discovering our niche within it, and in faithfully living out of that eternal relationship each day, all of life can truly become joy.

Perhaps we can see ourselves here. It is possible to live life efficiently but without joy. Many will go through Advent attending to all the details but miss the joy. We are reminded frequently by our psychologists and counselors that the week following Christmas is the most difficult week of the year for hurting people. It is often called the holiday paradox: "Joy seems everywhere, but it's not there for me!" Then there are those who face grievous circumstances but are not overwhelmed by them. An inner strength rises up from the deep reservoirs of faith sufficient for the hour. They have found the living presence of Christ to be enough. A gentle and genuine character exists within, framed after the character of our Lord, which cannot be shattered. They have received the gift of Christ's joy. We are indebted to them for sharing life with us.

III. So on this Sunday in Advent, can we, will we, receive the gift of Christ's joy? Joy isn't a virtue we intentionally reach out to claim. If we do, surely we will miss it. Joy comes to us as a by-product of faith. It comes with the territory of belief. It arrived in the fullness of time just as God intended. It came long ago in the night of the sacred birth. Just as surely it comes again as God's noble intention is birthed anew in every believing heart. This gift isn't intended for only a few. It is for all—even for you.

> O Come, Thou Dayspring, come and cheer
> Our spirits by thine Advent here;
> Disperse the gloomy clouds of night,
> And death's dark shadows put to flight.
> Rejoice! Rejoice!
> Emmanuel shall come to thee, O Israel.—Lee McGlone

SERMON SUGGESTIONS

Topic: The Insecurity of Wealth
TEXT: Mark 1:17–27
(1) Our ignorance of our true self. (2) The love of Christ for such people. (3) The immense danger of trusting false securities.—Adapted from J. C. Ryle

Topic: Our Own House of Prayer
TEXT: Matt. 6:6
(1) Room 1: The room in which we affirm the presence of god. (2) Room 2: The room in which we praise, thank, and adore God. (3) Room 3: The room of confession, forgiveness, and unloading. (4) Room 4: The room set aside for affirmation and reception. (5) Room 5: The place for purified desire and sincere petition. (6) Room 6: The room of intercession for others. (7) Room 7: The big room at the top of the house, set aside for meditation.[2]

WORSHIP AIDS
CALL TO WORSHIP.   "With joy shall ye draw water out of the wells of salvation. And in that day shall ye say, Praise the Lord, call upon his name, declare his doings among the people, make mention that his name is exalted" (Isa. 12:3–4).

---

[2]Leslie D. Weatherhead, *A Private House of Prayer.*

INVOCATION.   Lord of us all, Lord of all things, we can praise you because you have done marvelous things for us, and every day is the outworking of your salvation that we have come to know in your Christ. Let our joy radiate forth and commend to others what we find in you.

OFFERTORY SENTENCE.   "Forget not to be kind and liberal; for with that sort of sacrifice God is well pleased" (Heb. 13:16, Montgomery).

OFFERTORY PRAYER.   Gracious God, Grant that our generosity may match our feeling of compassion for others, and that kindness may always inspire our gifts.

PRAYER.   We praise thee, our heavenly Father, who hast made thyself known to us as a God of light and love and truth and strength. We gather to rejoice in thee who hast called us to worship and praise thee who hast asked that we become colleagues in the great work of thy hands in the world. We invoke thy blessing upon our assembling ourselves together, that in the fellowship of common faith and purpose each may find strength from all. Let thy Holy Spirit bind us together in singleness of purpose and devotion and enterprise in the Spirit of Christ.

We thank thee for the revelation of thyself as the light that can overcome the darkness, as the hope that cannot be destroyed, as a love that is invincible, as a goodness that gives us eternally a pattern for living, for the revelation of thyself in Jesus Christ that gives to our life its light, its direction, its meaning, and its strength.

We praise thee. We thank thee for that wonderful love that did not shrink from the costly sacrifice of Calvary. We thank thee for thy outreach for us while we are yet unworthy. We thank thee for thy tender and forgiving mercies, gathering up in thy fatherly care all thy people, not because they deserve it but because thy Name is Love.

Now in this Advent season we rejoice in thy coming into this world in the person of Jesus Christ that we might know the wonders of thy grace and thy truth. Grant that each of us may truly behold thy glory in this sacred time. May our minds be brightened and our spirits strengthened as we rejoice in the Babe of Bethlehem—the light that brings us to fresh hope. Grant that through all the busy activities of this season we may see him. May all that we do become sacramental because we do it in his Spirit and in his name, and for his sake.

Wilt thou grant to all of our people thy holy peace. Bless all who are sick and those who are in sorrow. Be with all troubled spirits and anxious minds, and bless the people of thy world everywhere; and may we hold all the world in our hearts.—Lowell M. Atkinson

SERMON
Topic: The Humanity of God
TEXT: Ps. 103:13

People from the very beginning have asked, What is God? We cannot see him; we cannot touch Him; we can only describe Him in terms of something that He is like. The Bible is one answer to that question. And the Bible began by saying that God is like the most powerful thing that we know. For certainly, our first and primary impression of God is the dynamic, vitalizing energy that makes things go. Now for people who lived in a desert, the most powerful, the most awe-inspiring thing that they knew was a volcano in eruption, and so the Bible began by saying that God is like a volcano. He is like a cloud of smoke by day and a pillar of fire by night. There in that tremendous dynamic power they found the first clue to the likeness of God. But as they lived more deeply and experienced life more completely, they began to see that the power they were surrounded by was directed toward a purpose. It was not just power running rampant; it was power directed toward roses, and suns, and stars, and the building of a nation, toward the formation of a character. Furthermore, they discovered that not only was power directed toward a purpose but it was felt as a presence. When they were going through deep waters they felt as thought someone were with them, undergirding them, supporting them. When they went through great experiences of ecstasy and exhilaration, they felt as though someone were there and said, "Surely the Lord is in this place and I knew it not."

Now, power plus purpose plus presence equals person. There is nothing that you and I know in the whole universe except a person that combines those three things, power and purpose and presence, and so the writers of the Bible said this: You ask what God is. We cannot see Him; we cannot touch Him; we can only tell you what God is like. God is not a person, but God is more like human personality with all its self-consciousness and its direction toward purpose, with all of its gathering together into a presence that we can know and feel. God is more like that than anything else we know, and when they looked around them they saw that human personality was at its best when it was stripped of all its pettiness and when they were asked what God was like—" 'Like as a father pitieth his children' even so the Lord." That is something of what the Bible means by faith in a personal God.

Look now for a moment at our own situation. The times, to be sure, have changed. We are staggered as we face the prospect of interstellar space and light years, and it seems to us many times that the universe has become too big to be personal. We feel something the way Darwin felt after he had made his discoveries of the long prehistoric past of mankind. He wrote this: "Sometimes I feel a warm sense of a personal God, and then—it goes away."

Before we settle down in that mood, we would do well to remember two things. First, granting all the changes that have taken place in the universe and in our understanding of it, we as human beings have not changed very much. We are very much like the people who found the God who was like a father. When we need a God, we need the God of the Bible.

When our hearts are overflowing with gratitude and all life seems to be rising toward one great peak of happiness, we are never satisfied to cry out: "Bless the Cosmic Ether, O my soul and everything that is within me bless its holy name." That does not ring true at all. Our gratitude overflows to a personal source of all the benefits and blessings of our lives. Indeed, we may discuss God in impersonal terms, and we do over and over again, but when we get right down to God we need and find the same God that the Bible found.

The other thing that we would do well to remember is this: in spite of all the changes that have taken place in our understanding of the universe there is one thing that has not changed, although sometimes it may appear to have done so. The most powerful thing we know in life is the power of personality.

Some people have been much impressed by the fact that life seems to be driven along its way by impersonal economic forces. Granted the power of atomic energy, when you compare it with the moral purpose that exists at least potentially in humans, the capacity to discover that energy, to release it, and, if we will, to control it and direct it toward creative ends, which in the long run is greater: the energy or the human that directs it? Which is the power that really influences the lives of men and women for better: the power of the Roman legion, or the power of the crucified personality that was in Christ Jesus?

So we come right back to where the Bible began, when we try to interpret our experience of God and try to describe Him in some kind of language that is least inadequate. We say that the best, the greatest, the most powerful thing we know in life is the power of personality, and God certainly, whatever else He may be, must be something like that. We find in the Bible a kind of ladder pitched between the things that we can see and the things we cannot see. On it humans have climbed from power through personality to God. They began in a very primitive sense with the eruption of a volcano—God was like that; they ended on the highest rung of the ladder, when they said that God is more like personality than anything we know. So Paul wrote to the Colossians, "To us there is but one God, the Father." That, I am convinced, for those of you who are sophisticated and for those of you who are simple-minded alike, that is the God that you need. When you come up against God, that is the God you find, and when you search all the avenues of your reason that is the God you see out there in the mysterious spaces of the universe, and you kneel down in the presence of that God and thank Him for those who first said, "Like as a father pitieth his own children; even so the Lord." That is about as near to God as we can ever get. Outgrow Him? Grow more and more up to Him![3]

SUNDAY, DECEMBER 18, 2005
Lectionary Message

Topic: The Shout of a Mother to Be

TEXT: Luke 1:47–55

Other Readings: 2 Sam. 7:1–11, 16; Rom. 16:25–27; Luke 1:26–28

Someone has said, "I'm glad Christmas is only one day a year. I couldn't stand any more of it than that." I wonder: If Christmas is so hard, why do we bother? Perhaps the songs of Christmas, especially this one from Luke's Gospel, Mary's song, the "Magnificat," will help us see why we bother. When its spirit touches ours the groan may well become a shout—the shout of a mother to be.

I. Mary's song declares that God is with us in this life. "My soul doth magnify the Lord and my spirit rejoices in God my Savior." Mary is the sign saying that our religion is not about theological propositions that molder in the dust of decay, nor about mysterious, cold, and dry ceremony that takes the best out of us. No, it's about life. It's about giving birth, and growing, and living, and loving, and dying. Mary keeps us connected with the human and the divine.

The response of the Christian church to Mary has been quite varied. For some she is highly venerated. For others she is greatly ignored. Because of both extremes, the example of true faith that Mary is has been missed by most of us. But we must not forget her and her example of faith discovered lived out. P. T. Forsythe, decades ago in his book on creative theology, said that "faith is not something that we possess. Faith possesses us." That's why we remember Mary. Her song declares the grace of God come to her, and to her nation, and her

---

[3]Theodore Parker Ferris, *Selected Sermons* (Boston: Trinity Church, 1976), pp. 104–110.

response to that grace. She could have said no to all this—but she didn't. She said yes and as a result we sing her song: "My soul doth magnify the Lord."

II. Mary's song declares that God's work gets done when ordinary people hear God's voice and obey. She sang, "He has regarded the low estate of his handmaiden. For behold, from henceforth, all generations will call me blessed for he has done mighty things for me." In the minds of many, the example of humble faith lived out quietly, though obediently, is a sign of weakness. We would rather have a strong and powerful personality as our model of faith. Instead of Mary, some would rather choose John the Baptist. He was strong and forceful, wore animal skins, and lived off the land. His muscles were rock hard. His booming voice echoed choice invective. He appears as quite the hero.

But Mary's strength was quiet. The trek to Bethlehem wasn't an easy one, but she did it. The joys of the birth were short-lived. Soon she and the baby were rushed off to Egypt to escape the horror of the hate-filled Herod. Then followed the years of love for her son she could never really understand. In the end, she endured the torture of seeing him crucified. And she maintained stable faith in it all. She was quite a woman.

You see, Mary is one of us—a struggler in the faith. But it's the struggle, and the response of faith to the struggle, that inspires our spirits today. This was a most perplexing situation. She was not yet fully married, but betrothed to be married, and she was pregnant. She was told by an angel that the child was begotten by God. She knew that—but who would believe such a thing? What was Joseph to think? Soon another angel told Joseph the same thing— but how was he to understand it all? What would the neighbors think? You can see that this is a rather unstable situation. In the midst of her obvious concern, Mary treks off to visit her older cousin Elizabeth in an attempt to make sense out of it all. There, face to face with Elizabeth, really faith to faith, she found the strength she needed. "Mary," Elizabeth said, "your faith has brought you to the right place and your faith will see you through. There will be nothing that will come up against you that you can't handle."

III. Mary's song declared that the dreams of faith are never ended—as long as we dream God's dream. "His mercy is on those who fear him from generation to generation. . . . He has shown strength with his arm . . . he has scattered the proud . . . put down the mighty . . . exalted those of low degree . . . he has filled the hungry with good things. . . . He has helped his servant Israel."

Both Matthew and Luke are careful to remind us that the birth of Jesus was unique—one of a kind, a virgin birth. That it was a virgin birth is important for us, but not just for the sake of the fact of it. It's important because true faith, the kind of faith that empowers through life, is always virgin-born. Faith that delivers us from our ultimate doubts and weakness and fear doesn't come from parents or friends. Parents and friends may well prepare the way for faith—but they can't make faith happen. Faith comes when we discover God for ourselves.

My dear Christian friends, is this not what the incarnation is all about? It is about God breaking into our world in a new and decisive way. God comes to us through Christ. During Advent, we relive the expectant waiting for his arrival. When he comes he breaks the bonds that hold us captive. He awakens within us the smoldering candle of love. Sin is forgiven. Grace is received. Life—our own, that of our families, our church, yea, our world—is forever changed. To God be the glory; great things he hath done.

That surely will bring from our lips more than a collective groan. We join with Mary the mother to be and shout, "My soul doth magnify the Lord."—Lee McGlone

SERMON SUGGESTIONS

Topic: A Promise Only the Messiah Can Fulfill

TEXT: 2 Sam. 7:8–16

(1) The word to David. (2) The word concerning Jesus Christ (Phil. 2:5–11).

Topic: Why We Bless God's Name

TEXT: Rom. 16:25–27, NEB

(1) He has brought us to faith, (2) through the gospel of Jesus Christ, (3) thus making our standing sure.

WORSHIP AIDS

CALL TO WORSHIP.   "And the angel said unto them, Fear not: for, behold, I bring you good tidings of great joy, which shall be to all people. For unto you is born this day in the city of David a Savior, which is Christ the Lord. . . . Glory to God in the highest, and on earth peace, good will toward men" (Luke 2:10–11, 14).

INVOCATION.   Come again, O Lord, in the way we most need thee, for we come rejoicing that long ago divinity was robed in baby's flesh and all prophecy was fulfilled. Open us to thy incarnational ways in the need of others, giving faith a face not unlike our Messiah's!— E. Lee Phillips

OFFERTORY SENTENCE.   "For God so loved the world, that he gave his only begotten Son, that whosoever believeth in him should not perish, but have everlasting life" (John 3:16).

OFFERTORY PRAYER.   Lord of hosts, take the small beginning of this offering and so fill it with thy might and power as to do great things for thee, even as once a newborn baby grown to manhood did.—E. Lee Phillips

PRAYER.   O God, we have learned to say the word *Advent* but have failed to recognize your coming to us: Help us to know the healing balm of a silent night, but give us grateful hearts for *music* that pierces the silence. Thank you for the genius of a Beethoven, able to ring the infinite changes of four simple notes; for carols ancient and modern, singing of new birth; for off-key renditions of "Jesus Loves Me," which speak volumes; for the joy that has come from participation in school orchestras, marching bands, choirs, and choruses; for the mysterious music of the spheres in our cosmos; and yes, God, for the song that cannot be stilled even in a world often bent on war: "Give Peace a Chance." In the name of the Prince of Peace we pray for those who need a saving reminder of God's gift, which passes all understanding. Comfort and sustain us and others who have suffered loss today. Lord of Resurrection, we thank you that you come in seasons of darkness as well as light. Come to those who are sick or alone when the rest of the world seems to speak of health, family, and joy. Come to us who feel inadequate, with your strength. Come to us who feel resentment, with your healing and forgiveness. Come to us who are rushed and harried, with your calm. Come to us now and always through the Christ who taught us to pray, saying, Our Father. . . . —Gary D. Stratman

SERMON
Topic: Your Capacity for Joy
TEXT: Isa. 12:2–6; Phil. 4:4–9

In one of John Cheever's novels, a group of Christmas carolers have ducked into the parson's for hot chocolate and a continuation of their singing. As they begin to sing "Joy to the World" one person reacts in a way that goes beyond the sentimental or nostalgic: "It was Mrs. Coulter's favorite, and it made her weep. The events in Bethlehem seemed to be not a revelation but an affirmation of what she had always known in her bones to be the surprising abundance of life. It was for this house, this company, this stormy night that He had lived and died. And how wonderful it was, she thought, that the world had been blessed by a savior! How wonderful it was that she should have a capacity for joy."

How wonderful indeed that we have a capacity for joy. That may be one of the great understatements contained in modern literature. Think of it. Joy is not something that can be pursued like happiness or packaged like an image. It can only be tasted ("Taste and see that our Lord is good"). The tangy sea breeze, the crisp snap of an apple, taste and see life is good; when that happens we are not pursuing or packaging; we are accepting a gift. Joy is a gift of God's creation.

The apostle Paul was steeped in the tradition of a God who created the world in an expulsive moment of joy. It was good—it was oh so good. His creation, and especially the creature made in his image, was to exhibit this ethos of joy. When we create, whether it be decorations for the tree, presents for folks in the nursing home, or a poem for a Christmas letter, it can be done in joy. We can create without resenting the time given or worrying about the response given. Franz Joseph Haydn said, "When I think of God, my heart is so full of joy that notes dance and leap, as it were, from my pen. And since God has given me a cheerful heart it will be easily forgiven me when I serve him with a cheerful spirit."

We are created with the same great capacity for joy. Yet something has gone wrong. For often we feel like Lucy of the *Peanuts* cartoon strip who was "created to be a fussbudget." We seem adept at seeing the down side of people and events. A complaining, critical spirit so easily replaces a cheerful spirit. We come to expect the monotonous and the dreary. I heard of a woman who yelled at her husband after he slammed the door at the conclusion of a fight: "You'll be back; how long do you think you'll be able to stand happiness?" Doubting our capacity for joy is not difficult. Here is a man who will not get excited about anything because he knows he will be disappointed. There is a woman who has been severely disappointed; she has been "looking for joy in all the wrong places."

Yet we have been created with an amazing capacity for joy. Even though our experiences of joy have been fleeting and incomplete, they bring with them a *yearning for more*, a yearning for the sources of all joy. Paul is writing this letter from prison, and yet he is filled with joy. This was not always the case. We know of his unrelenting joyless legalism and persecution of those who followed Christ. Then when he was present at the stoning of Stephen there must have been something haunting about the undying joy of Stephen. I believe it left Paul yearning for the source of that joy. In more ordinary days, think of driving along and tasting the beauty of the earth, of life until you hear your own unprogrammed praise: My God, how beautiful! Think of the embrace of one you love and the joy is so full you want to cry. Think of the day the doctor says we can't even find the tumor and you want to hug everyone you can find.

C. S. Lewis has said that all wonderful experiences of joy "are not the thing itself, they are only the scent of a flower we have not found, the echo of a time we have not heard, news from a country we have not yet visited." Even the best but foretastes of a greater joy. Sometimes we settle for a lot less than these: "fooling about with drink and sex and ambition when infinite joy is offered, like an ignorant child who wants to go on making mud pies in a slum because he cannot imagine what is meant by the offering of a holiday at sea." We settle for a lot less than that for which we were intended.

Mrs. Coulter was right. How wonderful it is that we have been blessed by a Savior. She helps us understand why Paul could in the gloom of prison rejoice and insist that others rejoice. For it is clear, true joy does not grow from physical health or safety, affluence or prestige, the presence of family or friends. It is rooted and grounded . . . *in the lord.* Our joy is not in singing "the old familiar carols, a cozy fire, the nostalgia of Christmas" past. Our joy is rooted and grounded . . . *in the lord.*

This is the key to what Paul is saying: joy must have a source. For Paul, that source is Jesus Christ, the exalted Lord of heaven. "He is at hand," Paul says. Even for the Christian, every experience of joy points forward to a day of greater joy than we can presently know or understand, the future "day of the Lord." Yet Paul is also saying that the very presence of our Lord even in times of suffering and sorrow is joy. It is the same joy that makes heaven and is heaven here and now. This is eternal life that you know God and the one whom he has sent.

It was for your house, your company, he lived and died.

Joy to you and me, the Lord has come; let us receive our King.

Amen.—Gary Stratman

SUNDAY, DECEMBER 25, 2005
Lectionary Message

Topic: Christmas Misunderstood
TEXT: Luke 2:1–14 (15–20)
Other Readings: Isa. 9:2–7; Ps. 96; Titus 2:11–14

Some of the simplest things in life are difficult to understand. We hear a lot, but often we interpret wrongly. Christmas Day, the blessed culmination of the Father's love, is often misunderstood.

I. We misunderstand Christmas by assuming we don't need God's gift. Luke began his account with this: "In the days of Caesar Augustus." Well, what was it like in the days of Caesar Augustus? It was the time of the most marvelous peace the world had ever known, the Pax Romana. Augustus, born Gaius Octavius, at the age of thirty-three was named successor to Julius Caesar. Later the Roman Senate voted him the title God and Savior. It was the beginning of a glorious regime. His birthday was declared a holiday. Every city had its shrine to the new emperor. It seemed then that the world had everything it needed. There was no warring, no massive poverty. There was peace on earth. Why then would any other God think of sending a gift into this world of plenty? How foolish! Silly God. The world didn't need another gift.

But there it was. In the days of Caesar Augustus, when the world seemed quite self-sufficient, God came to give his only Son. Did you hear? In the days of Caesar Augustus, when the world was basking in peace, in prosperity, in power, in commercial success, in fact, in a world very much like our own—into that world God came to give the gift of himself. Foolish God. This must be a gag gift. We don't need what you have to give. Or so we say.

You can see how easy it is to misunderstand Christmas.

II. We misunderstand Christmas because it seems to have come in the wrong package. It's not that the people of Luke's day were not anticipating an in-breaking of God. They were. They had been waiting for a long time. But they never dreamed the gift God would send to the earth would look like this. Remember the promise of Isaiah: "Oh, that you would rend the heavens and come down! That the mountains would tremble before you!" (Isa. 64:1). "God," Isaiah said, "if you are going to do something in this world, it needs to be bigger than anything we've ever done ourselves. It needs to rock the world."

But what does God do? He sends a baby, of all things! Powerless even to care for itself. Babies have to be fed and burped and diapered. And babies cry all night. Is it any wonder that Isaiah would write, "Who has believed our report?" Who *could* believe it?

What we really want is for God to be to us like a giant Santa Claus, giving to us what we want for Christmas: good health, wealth, happiness. But God makes no such promises. God still will be God, giving us what we need and not what we want. We need God's Presence, his compassion, his companionship, loyalty, hope, faith, and love. It began with a tiny baby, a gift in the days of Caesar Augustus that seems way out of place. And if we don't take care, we'll miss it again. It's easy to misunderstand Christmas.

III. What makes it even easier to misunderstand Christmas is that God seemed to send his gift to the wrong people. To whom was the gift first announced? He sent his gift to shepherds out in the field around Bethlehem. But get this: in the day when Jesus was born, shepherds weren't thought of as good guys. In fact, shepherding was one of the six professions the rabbis warned their people against entering. Shepherds were thought not to be honest. A shepherd couldn't give testimony in a court of law, for it was believe they were incapable of telling the truth. Shepherds weren't even allowed to enter the temple or synagogue. They were thought to be thieves. They were thought to be a hopeless lot. But then look! How silly God is! Doesn't God know any better? Why would he send his angels to sing the Hallelujah Chorus to folks who can't even read music? But he did. God sent the wrong gift, in the wrong package, to the wrong people.

Let me ask you this: Do you suppose God is somewhere else this morning other than at church? Could God be there in the AIDS ward of a hospital among dying patients? Could God be in a crumbling inner-city apartment, amidst the poverty? Could he be in the city jail? Can God be somewhere else in a setting not nearly as beautiful as our sanctuary? Could be.

There it is. The Christmas story—so easily misunderstood. The gift was wrong. The package was wrong. The gift was given to the wrong people. So wrote an unnamed poet:

Thou shalt know Him when He comes,
Not by any din of drums,
Nor by anything He wears,
Neither by His crown,
Nor by His gown.
No—we know Him by His love.—Lee McGlone

SERMON SUGGESTIONS

Topic: The Day of the Lord—Bad News, Good News

TEXT: Zeph. 17:12–18

(1) The bad news: the proud and the oppressors will receive the consequences of their evil ways. (2) The good news: the field will be cleared for God to do a new thing.

Topic: If We Belong to the Day

TEXT: 1 Thess. 5:1–11, NEB

(1) The "day of the Lord" will not take us by surprise. (2) We will be prepared for whatever comes, by faith and love and by our hope of salvation. (3) We will hearten and fortify one another.

WORSHIP AIDS

CALL TO WORSHIP.   "The angel said unto them, Fear not: for, behold, I bring you good tidings of great joy, which shall be to all people. For unto you is born this day in the city of David a Savior, which is Christ the Lord" (Luke 2:10, 11).

INVOCATION.   Amid the world's darkness, O God, we seek a star which will give us hope and guide us on our way. Our days are troubled with the portents of despair, and the counsels of men have increased our anguish. Turn us from ourselves, lift our vision beyond our earthly empires, and let the dayspring from on high visit us. If the pilgrimage be long, sustain us by thy strength until we are made strong in the innocence of Bethlehem's Child.—Samuel H. Miller

OFFERTORY SENTENCE.   "When they were come into the house, they saw the young child with Mary his mother, and fell down, and worshiped him: and when they had opened their treasurers, they presented unto him gifts; gold, and frankincense, and myrrh" (Matt. 2:11).

OFFERTORY PRAYER.   Lord, Most Holy, accept our Christmas offering, as we who are recipients of the Bethlehem birth and a Calvary hope come to thee through our faithful advocate, King Jesus.—E. Lee Phillips

PRAYER.   Blessed Lord, who hast caused the dayspring from on high to visit us, to give light to them that are in darkness and in the shadow of death and to guide our feet into the way of peace, we pray that the Spirit of goodwill may so fill the hearts of all of us who call ourselves Christians that our love may reflect the Light of the World, drawing all men unto him. Especially do we pray for the homeless, and friendless, the forgotten by all men, those who spend this day in prison, those whose rejoicing is unhallowed by any true consecration to thee so that they know nothing of the great joy of possessing the Savior, those for whom the day recalls memories of happier times now gone by, those who are lonely for loved voices hushed in death, those who have lost an earlier faith, and all who wish they could believe the message of this day but find themselves unable. Grant that we who have learned the truth of the good tidings and have found in Jesus our Savior deliverance from selfishness, distrust, and fear may carry the gladness of this season throughout the year, rejoicing evermore because of thine unspeakable gift in him.—Henry Sloane Coffin

SERMON
Topic: Christ's Song: A Love for All Seasons
(Occasion: Christmas Eve Communion)

What I want us to remember is the song that Christ sang at Christmas. Now we know that Christ has something to do with Christmas. We are warned, "Don't take Christ out of Christmas." But that's not our danger because we know that he is the reason we celebrate it. Our danger is that we can get so busy with preparations for it that unconsciously we might nudge him to the edges of our Christmas celebration and miss the true significance of what Christmas is about. It is about a love that's for all seasons, a love that meets all our needs forever. It's a song in three parts.

I. *The first stanza begins with a birth.* Christmas is a reminder that God has come to be where we are. Into the midst of all of our lives, our confusion, our suffering, the trouble of this world, God has come to pitch his tent right next to us. He has come to look us, as it were, in the face to say, "I know you. I know who you are and what you need. I have not forgotten you."

At Christmas God has sent us a gift, wrapped with our names on it, addressed just to you or to me. As we open it, it is Christ. As I see him, the angels sing what God wants me to know. "I love you and I will love you forever." That's a song worth hearing. With shepherds and Wise Men, we should join together in worshiping this precious Christmas gift.

II. *The second stanza is a song about death.* Babies do grow up. Christ left that cradle and became a man. As he went about doing God's will, he got into trouble with the religious leaders. They would not have fellowship with sinners; he ate with them. They were judgmental of sinners; he forgave them. They lived hypocritically, playing at religion; Christ was the man who had integrity of word and deed. He was what he said. They loved only a few; he loved them all. They asked for a cheap price to pay: keeping the rules. He came calling for total commitment of life: it was the only way to live.

It's no wonder that, finally, a cross had to be lifted up. This tiny baby boy who had grown up to be the man Jesus had to be crucified.

When Christ died on that hill (which was a garbage dump), it was his way of telling us how much he understood us. He had come to live in our shoes and to face what we face. There is nothing in the world that you and I can face that Christ has not already faced himself. Suffering? He knows that. He hung from a cross and knew the physical and the mental suffering of that. Loneliness and rejection? He knows that too. The crowds turned away from him; his own disciples left him, and on the cross he felt forsaken by God. He was alone.

Doubt? He wrestled with it, asking the Father to remove the cross. Misunderstanding? He was really misunderstood not only by the crowds and his disciples but by his own family, who thought he was crazy. And death? He faced it too. Christ comes to look us in the face to say, "Look, I know the way to live; and if you follow me, I will give it to you." And we tell him, "But look, it's too tough, too difficult; it hurts. We run into too many problems. You don't understand." He turns and says, "But I do understand. I was there. I walked through it. I faced it. I know how to come through it because I did it. If you trust me, I will help you come through it too. I understand."

That's where the baby who came chose to dwell, in the midst of human suffering, human hurt, human need. He dwells where we are. We can know that each step of the way we go, there is a God who understands the pain and the struggles as well as the joy. He so loved us that he went through it all himself so we would know we are understood. Let us always thank him for that.

III. *Stanza three is a song about resurrection!* You know that if Christ had not been raised from the dead, we would not have Christmas to celebrate. If he had not been raised, he would have just been another good man who died, a memory but not a Savior. Christmas is a joy to us because Christ grew up to be the Savior who conquered all that would defeat us. He conquered suffering. We don't understand suffering, but how we detest it. We wonder how we can get through it. But he did. He is a Christ who conquered sin. Sin is so powerful; it drags us down and destroys us. It can even cause us to crucify the Son of God. But he defeated that. And death! We don't like to think of that. It seems to be so final. We all have a date with death, but how we fear it. But he conquered that!

This is the joy of Christmas: Easter. We can't have Christmas without Easter. Easter and now Christmas mean that those who face suffering, who face difficulty, who are struggling under insurmountable burdens have a Savior who knows the way to help us triumph over it. Easter and now Christmas mean that in our struggle with sin there is forgiveness for our failures. There is strength and courage to get up and try again. Easter and now Christmas mean that death is not our end but a door that leads to that which is beyond. What is beyond we do not know. *Who* is beyond we do know. This Christ who came is there. He is a Christ who sets us free. Nothing can stop us because nothing could stop him.

That's what it all means. Christ, now and forever! If we don't remember that and worship him, then no matter what tomorrow brings it will not be enough. I hope that you have remembered. We need to hear this in the world in which we live. It's a world that speaks not so much of Christ, not so much of hope, not so much of love, but we know better because Christ is here.[4]

---

[4]Hugh Litchfield, *Preaching the Christmas Story* (Nashville, Tenn.: Broadman Press, 1984), pp. 79–84.

RESOURCES FOR CONGREGATIONAL MUSIC

BY PAUL RICHARDSON

The hymns have been chosen for their relation to the Scripture readings for each service. They are not merely compatible with the theme of the pericope but reflect the particular language, imagery, or content of the passage. Several choices are provided for some readings, while others have no readily accessible companion in the hymnic literature. Sometimes the scriptural link, though evident, is not that of traditional usage (for example, "Joy to the World," typically sung at Christmas, is a paraphrase of Psalm 98 and is listed with that reading for Easter Vigil). The use of a familiar text in a different context can prompt new awareness of both Scripture and hymn.

Because hymn texts have often been altered, even in their first lines, the author's surname or the source is provided as an aid to location. No judgments are made as to authenticity of attributions, nor are preferences expressed for particular translations. The texts are listed in alphabetical order within each grouping.

A dozen hymns appear three or more times during the year, identified in connection with multiple passages. Learning and repeating them in their various relationships offers a way to expand a congregation's enduring repertory for worship and devotion. These hymns are:

"A Hymn of Glory Let Us Sing" (Venerable Bede; also translated "Sing We Triumphant Hymns of Praise")
"Ah, Holy Jesus" (Heerman)
"Alleluia! Sing to Jesus" (Dix)
"And Can It Be That I Should Gain" (Wesley)
"God It Was Who Said to Abraham" (Bell)
"God Who Stretched the Spangled Heavens" (Cameron)
"Lift High the Cross" (Kitchin and Newbolt)
"Like the Murmur of the Dove's Song" (Daw)
"Man of Sorrows, What a Name" (Bliss)
"O Love, How Deep, How Broad, How High" (Thomas à Kempis; also translated "O Love, How Vast, How Flowing Free")
"Rejoice, the Lord Is King" (Wesley)
"We Know That Christ Is Raised and Dies No More" (Geyer)

If a hymn is widely published, no source is cited. For those found in only one of the hymnals listed below, that book is indicated using these abbreviations:

BH *The Baptist Hymnal* (Nashville: Convention Press, 1991)
CH *Chalice Hymnal* (St. Louis: Chalice Press, 1995)

HWB *Hymnal: A Worship Book* (Elgin, Ill.: Brethren Press, 1992)

NCH *The New Century Hymnal* (Cleveland: Pilgrim Press, 1995)

PH *The Presbyterian Hymnal* (Louisville: Westminster/John Knox Press, 1990)

RS *RitualSong: A Hymnal and Service Book for Roman Catholics* (Chicago: GIA, 1996)

UMH *The United Methodist Hymnal: Book of United Methodist Worship* (Nashville: United Methodist Publishing House, 1989)

WC *The Worshiping Church* (Carol Stream, Ill.: Hope, 1990)

Particular mention must be made of *Hymns for the Gospels* (Chicago: GIA, 2001), an anthology of texts chosen specifically for use with the Gospel readings for most Sundays in the three-year lectionary. Because of its focus and function, this collection is cited with the abbreviation HG for every relevant text, even if it also appears in one or more of the hymnals.

Another collection of hymns directly related to the lectionary is Carol Doran and Thomas H. Troeger's *New Hymns for the Lectionary: To Glorify the Maker's Name* (New York: Oxford University Press, 1986), which contains hymns for each Sunday of Year B, the cycle that begins in Advent 2005. These hymns, some of which are also found in the hymnals listed above, are marked with NHL. Troeger's texts (without Doran's settings) are also found in his subsequent anthology, *Borrowed Light: Hymn Texts, Prayers, and Poems* (New York: Oxford University Press, 1994).

Hymns identified with the Psalm readings are closely related to the corresponding text, in keeping with the design of the Revised Common Lectionary, which intends that the Psalm itself be a response to the first lesson. Because numerous recently published resources, including many hymnals, provide brief responses for use with the reading or chanting of the Psalms, none are cited here. Rather, all hymns listed in connection with the Psalms are metrical versions; that is, they are in traditional multistanza hymn form. Many of these come from *The Presbyterian Hymnal.* A more extensive collection of stanzaic Psalm settings is found in the Christian Reformed Church's *Psalter Hymnal* (Grand Rapids, Mich.: CRC, 1987), which contains metrical versions of all 150 Psalms.

Those who would use hymns not found in their own congregational hymnal are reminded of the obligation, both legal and ethical, to observe copyright law. Each of the collections cited provides clear information about copyright owners and agents. Two services make available a wide range of this material without great cost or complex paperwork. They are Christian Copyright License International (17201 N.E. Sacramento St., Portland, OR 97230, www.ccli.com) and LicenSing: Copyright-Cleared Music for Churches (Logos Productions, 6160 Carmen Ave. East, Inver Grove Heights, MN 55076–4422, www.joinhands.com).

CHRISTMASTIDE

January 2

Jeremiah 31:7–14 [none]

Psalm 147:12–20 "Now Praise the Lord, All Living Saints" (Anderson) PH

Ephesians 1:3–14 "Christ, from Whom All Blessings Flow" (Wesley) NCH; "Come, Let Us All Unite to Sing" (Kingsbury) HWB; "Here, O Lord, Your Servants Gather" (Yamaguchi); "May the Grace of Christ Our Savior" (Fawcett); "My God, Accept My Heart This Day" (Bridges) NCH; "Redeemed, How I Love to Proclaim It" (Crosby); "Sing Praise to the Father" (Clarkson) WC; "To God Be the Glory" (Crosby)

John 1:(1–9) 10–18 "Christ Is the World's Light" (Green); "Christ Is the World's True Light" (Briggs); "Christ, Whose Glory Fills the Skies" (Wesley); "Hark! the Herald Angels Sing" (Wesley); "O Come, All Ye Faithful" (Wade); "O Word of God Incarnate" (How); "Of the Father's Love Begotten" (Prudentius); "Word of God When All Was silent" (Stuempfle) HG; "Your Word Went Forth and Light Awoke" (Stuempfle) RS

Or, for the *Feast of the Epiphany:*

Isaiah 60:1–6 "Arise, Shine Out, Your Light Has Come" (Wren) UMH; "Arise, Your Light Is Come" (Duck); "Keep Awake, Be Always Ready" (Clyde) NCH; "Rise, Shine, You People" (Klug) UMH
Psalm 72:1–7, 10–14 "Hail to the Lord's Anointed" (Montgomery); "Jesus Shall Reign Where'er the Sun" (Watts)
Ephesians 3:1–12 "Let There Be Light" (Piper) WC; "Ye Servants of God, Your Master Proclaim" (Wesley)
Matthew 2:1–12 "Angels from the Realms of Glory" (Montgomery); "As with Gladness Men of Old" (Dix); "Bright and Glorious Is the Sky" (Grundtvig) HWB; "Brightest and Best of the Sons of the Morning" (Heber; also found beginning "Hail the Blest Morn"); "Famed Though the World's Great Cities Be" (Shanley) HG; "From a Distant Home" (traditional Puerto Rican); "Midnight Stars Make Bright the Sky" (Chinese) PH; "On This Day Earth Shall Ring" (*Piae Cantiones*); "Sing We Now of Christmas" (traditional French); "The First Noel the Angel Did Say" (traditional English); "The Magi Who to Bethlehem Did Go" (Juncas) NCH; "We Three Kings of Orient Are" (Hopkins); "What Child Is This, Who, Laid to Rest" (Dix); "When Christ's Appearing Was Made Known" (Sedulius) HWB; "Wise Men, They Came to Look for Wisdom" (Idle) WC

EPIPHANY
January 9
Isaiah 42:1–9 "God, Who Stretched the Spangled Heavens" (Cameron)
Psalm 29 "The God of Heaven Thunders" (Perry) PH; "Worship the Lord in the Beauty of Holiness" (Monsell)
Acts 10:34–43 [none]
Matthew 3:13–17 "Lord, When You Came to Jordan" (Wren; a later version begins "What Was Your Vow and Vision"); "Mark How the Lamb of God's Self-Offering" (Daw) NCH; "O Radiant Christ, Incarnate Word" (Duck) NCH; "Songs of Thankfulness and Praise" (Wordsworth); "What Ruler Wades Through Murky Streams" (Troeger) NCH; "When Jesus Came to Jordan" (Green) HG; "When John Baptized by Jordan's River" (Dudley-Smith) RS

January 16
Isaiah 49:1–7 [none]
Psalm 40:1–11 [none]
1 Corinthians 1:1–9 [none]
John 1:29–42 "All Glory Be to God on High" (Decius); "Wild and Lone the Prophet's Voice" (Daw) HG; "Sing of Andrew, John's Disciple" (Daw) HG

January 23
Isaiah 9:1–4 "Awake from Your Slumber" (Schutte) RS; "Child of Mercy, Child of Peace" (Haas) RS; "Lord, Today We Have Seen Your Glory" (Balhoff) RS; "Now Bless the God of Israel" (Duck) NCH; "To Us a Child of Hope Is Born" (Morison) HWB
Psalm 27:1, 4–9 "God Is My Strong Salvation" (Montgomery); "The Lord Is My Light and My Salvation" (Bouknight) RS
1 Corinthians 1:10–18 [none]
Matthew 4:12–23 "Dear Lord and Father of Mankind" (Whittier); "Jesus Call Us, O'er the Tumult" (Alexander); "Lord, You Have Come to the Lakeshore" (Gabaraín); "Two Fishermen, Who Lived Along the Sea of Galilee" (Toolan); "You Call to Us, Lord Jesus" (Patterson) HG

January 30
Micah 6:1–8 "Come, Live in the Light" (Haas) RS; "What Does the Lord Require" (Bayly)
Psalm 15 "Lord, Who May Dwell Within Your House" (Webber) PH
1 Corinthians 1:18–31 "Darkness Is Gone" (Bell) RS; "Here Hangs a Man Discarded" (Wren) CH; "O for a World Where Everyone" (Winter); "Sing, My Tongue, the Glorious Battle" (Fortunatus)
Matthew 5:1–12 "Blessed Are the Persecuted" (Bergen); "Blessed Are the Poor in Spirit" (Edwards) NCH; "Blest Are They, the Poor in Spirit" (Haas) RS; "Mixed Like Weeds in Wheatfields" (Daw) HG; "Oh, Blessed Are the Poor in Spirit" (anonymous); "O How Blest Are the Poor in Spirit" (Avery and Marsh) WC

February 6
Isaiah 58:1–9a (9b–12) "Break Forth, O Beauteous Heavenly Light" (Rist)
Psalm 112:1–9 (10) [none]
1 Corinthians 2:1–12 (13–16) "Ask Ye What Great Thing I Know" (Schwedler); "Blest Be the Dear Uniting Love" (Wesley) UMH; "Eye Has Not Seen" (Haugen) RS; "In This World Abound" (Yuya) HWB
Matthew 5:13–20 "Christian, Let Your Burning Light" (Coleman) HWB; "Renew Your Church, Her Ministries Restore" (Cober) WC; "Take Us As We Are, O God" (Daw) HG; "This Little Light of Mine" (Negro spiritual); "You Are Salt for the Earth, O People" (Haugen); "You Are the Seed That Will Grow a New Sprout" (Gabaraín)

Or, for *Transfiguration:*

Exodus 24:12–18 [none]
Psalm 2 "Why Are the Nations Raging" (Anderson) PH
2 Peter 1:16–21 "Christ, Whose Glory Fills the Skies" (Wesley); "For Your Holy Book We Thank You" (Carter) WC; "How Brightly Beams the Morning Star" (Nicolai; also translated "O Morning Star, How Fair and Bright"); "Powerful in Making Us Wise" (Idle) WC; "Word of God, Across the Ages" (Blanchard) BH; "Word of God, Come Down on Earth" (Quinn) RS
Matthew 17:1–9 "Christ upon the Mountain Peak" (Wren; a later version begins "Jesus, on the Mountain Peak"); Jesus, Take Us to the Mountain" (Vajda) NCH; "O Wondrous Sight, O Vision Fair" (anonymous, Latin); "Swiftly Pass the Clouds of Glory" (Troeger) PH; " 'Tis Good, Lord, to Be Here" (Robinson) RS; "Transform Us As You, Transfigured" (Dunstan) HG; "We Have Come at Christ's Own Bidding" (Daw) NCH

LENT

February 9

Ash Wednesday

Joel 2:1–2, 12–17 "Deep Within, I Will Plant My Law" (Haas) RS; "Again We Keep This Solemn Feast" (Gregory) RS

Psalm 51:1–17 "Have Mercy on Us, Living Lord" (Anderson) PH; "Have Mercy in Your Goodness, Lord" (Webber) WC

2 Corinthians 5:20b–6:10 "God, Our Author and Creator" (Daw); "O Sun of Justice, Jesus Christ" (anonymous, Latin) RS

Matthew 6:1–6, 16–21 "Again We Keep This Solemn Feast" (Gregory) HG

February 13

Genesis 2:15–17, 3:1–7 "For Beauty of Meadows, for Grandeur of Trees" (Farquharson); "God Marked a Line and Told the Sea" (Troeger); "God of Adam, God of Joseph" (Kaan) RS; "Thank You, God, for Water, Soil, and Air" (Wren)

Psalm 32 "How Blest Are the People Possessing True Peace" (Woollett) WC; "How Blest Are Those Whose Great Sin" (Anderson) PH

Romans 5:12–19 "Christ Is Risen, Christ Is Living" (Martínez)

Matthew 4:1–11 "Forty Days and Forty Nights" (Smyttan) NCH; "Jesus, Tempted in the Desert" (Stuempfle) HG; "Lord, Who Throughout These Forty Days" (Hernaman); "Mark How the Lamb of God's Self-Offering" (Daw) NCH; "O Love, How Deep, How Broad, How High" (Thomas à Kempis; also translated "O Love, How Vast, How Flowing Free")

February 20

Genesis 12:1–4a "God It Was Who Said to Abraham" (Bell) RS

Psalm 121 "I to the Hills Will Lift My Eyes" (*The Psalter*, 1912); "Unto the Hills We Lift Our Longing Eyes" (Campbell) NCH

Romans 4:1–5, 13–17 [none]

John 3:1–17 "Alone and Filled with Fear" (Stuempfle) HG; "As Moses Raised the Serpent up" (NCH editors) NCH; "For God So Loved the World" (Whitney) BH; "For God So Loved Us, He Sent the Savior" (Rische) HWB; "God So Loved the World" (Lippen and Opfer) NCH; "To God Be the Glory" (Crosby)

February 27

Exodus 17:1–7 Christ Is the Mountain of Horeb" (anonymous) NCH; "Guide Me, O Thou Great Jehovah" (Williams); "I Hunger and I Thirst" (Monsell) HWB

Psalm 95 "O Come and Sing Unto the Lord" (*The Psalter*, 1912) PH; "Come, Sing with Joy to God" (Duba) PH; "Many and Great, O God, Are Thy Ways" (Renville); "Come, Let Us Praise the Lord" (Dudley-Smith) WC; "O Come, Loud Anthems Let Us Sing" (*New Version*) HWB; "To God with Gladness Sing" (Quinn) RS

Romans 5:1–11 "Ah, Holy Jesus" (Heerman); "And Can It Be That I Should Gain" (Wesley); "Lift High the Cross" (Kitchin and Newbolt); "One Is the Race of Mankind" (Clarkson) WC; "What Wondrous Love Is This" (traditional American)

John 4:5–42 "Crashing Waters at Creation" (Dunstan) NCH; "I Heard the Voice of Jesus Say" (Bonar); "Like the Woman at the Well, I Was Seeking" (Blanchard) CH; "The First One Ever,

Oh, Ever to Know" (Egan) UMH; The Thirsty Cry for Water, Lord" (Stuempfle) HG; "When, Like the Woman at the Well" (Downing) NCH

March 6

1 Samuel 16:1–13 "God of the Prophets" (Wortman) NCH

Psalm 23 "My Shepherd Will Supply My Need" (Watts); "The King of Love My Shepherd Is" (Baker); "The Lord's My Shepherd, All My Need" (Webber); "The Lord's My Shepherd, I'll Not Want" (Huber); "The Lord's My Shepherd, I'll Not Want" (*Scottish Psalter*)

Ephesians 5:8–14 "As Sons of the Day and Daughters of Light" (Idle) WC; "Awake, Awake, Fling off the Night" (Peacey) HWB; "Awake, O Sleeper, Arise from Death" (Haugen) RS; "Awake, O Sleeper, Rise from Death" (Tucker); "Each Morning Brings Us Fresh Outpoured" (Zwick) HWB; "I Want to Walk As a Child of the Light" (Thomerson); "This Little Light of Mine" (Negro spiritual); "We Are Marching in the Light of God" (anonymous, South African) RS

John 9:1–41 "All Who Love and Serve Your City" (Routley); "Amazing Grace, How Sweet the Sound" (Newton); "He Healed the Darkness of My Mind" (Green) RS; "Jesus the Christ Says, 'I Am the Bread'" (traditional Urdu) NCH; "Lord, I Was Blind; I Could Not See" (Matson) WC; "No Sign to Us You Give" (Stuempfle) HG

March 13

Ezekiel 37:1–14 "Let It Breathe on Me" (Lewis-Butts) NCH

Psalm 130 "Out of the Depths to Thee I Raise" (Luther); "Out of the Depths I Cry to You on High" (*The Psalter,* 1912) WC; "From the Depths of Sin and Sadness" (Jabusch) HWB; "Out of the Depths I Call" (*New Version*) NCH; "Out of the Depths, O God, We Call to You" (Duck) NCH

Romans 8:6–11 "God Himself Is with Us" (Tersteegen; also translated "God Is Here Among Us"); "O Spirit of God, O Life-Giving Breath" (Niedling) NCH

John 11:1–45 "I Am the Bread of Life" (Toolan); "Jesus the Christ Says, 'I Am the Bread'" (traditional Urdu) NCH; "Lord, I Was Blind; I Could Not See" (Matson) WC; "Martha, Mary, Waiting, Weeping" (Stuempfle) HG; "Up from the Earth and Surging Like a Wave" (Cooney) RS; "When Grief Is Raw" (Wren) HWB; "When Jesus Wept, the Falling Tear" (Billings); "Why Has God Forsaken Me" (Wallace)

March 20

Liturgy of the Palms:

Matthew 21:1–11 "A Beggar-King Comes Riding" (Stuempfle) HG

Psalm 118:1–2, 19–29 "Open Now Thy Gates of Beauty" (Schmolck); "This Is the Day the Lord Hath Made" (Watts)

Or, *Liturgy of the Passion:*

Isaiah 50:4–9a [none]

Psalm 31:9–16 "God of Our Life, Through All the Circling Years" (Kerr); "God of the Ages" (Clarkson) WC; "In You, Lord, Have I Put My Trust" (Reissner) PH

Philippians 2:5–11 "A Hymn of Glory Let Us Sing" (Venerable Bede; also translated "Sing We Triumphant Hymns of Praise"); "Alas! And Did My Savior Bleed" (Watts); "All Authority and Power" (Idle) WC; "All Hail the Power of Jesus' Name" (Perronet and Rippon); "All Praise to

Thee, for Thou, O King Divine" (Tucker; also found beginning "All Praise to Christ"); "At the Name of Jesus" (Noel); "Christ, Who Is in the Form of God" (Koyzis) HWB; "Creator of the Stars of Night" (anonymous, Latin); "Emptied of His Glory" (Johnson, Cloninger, and Fettke) BH; "Jesus Came, the Heavens Adoring" (Thring); "Jesus, the Name High over All" (Wesley) UMH; "Let All Together Praise Our God" (Herman) HWB; "Man of Sorrows, What a Name" (Bliss); "Morning Glory, Starlit Sky" (Vanstone) UMH; "My Lord of Light, Who Made the Worlds" (Idle) WC; "O Love, How Deep, How Broad, How High" (Thomas à Kempis; also translated "O Love, How Vast, How Flowing Free"); "Of the Father's Love Begotten" (Prudentius); "Praise the God Who Changes Places" (Wren) RS; "Sing Praise to the Father" (Clarkson) WC; "Thou Didst Leave Thy Throne" (Elliott)

Matthew 26:14–27:66 "A Purple Robe, a Crown of Thorn" (Dudley-Smith); "Ah, Holy Jesus" (Heerman); "An Upper Room Did Our Lord Prepare" (Green); "As He Gathered at His Table" (Richardson); "Before the Cock Crew Twice" (Pjeturssen) HWB; "Calvary" (Negro spiritual); "Christ at Table There with Friends" (Miller) NCH; "Go to Dark Gethsemane" (Montgomery); "Hark! The Voice of Love and Mercy" (Evans) WC; "He Never Said a Mumbalin' Word" (Negro spiritual); "Here in Our Upper Room with You" (Robinson) HWB; "How Great Your Mercy, Risen Lord" (Stuempfle) HG; "Jesus Took the Bread" (Duck) NCH; "Kneeling in the Garden Grass" (Troeger; for the stations of the cross) RS; "Lord Christ, When First You Came to Earth" (Bowie) PH; "Man of Sorrows, What a Name" (Bliss); "My Song Is Love Unknown" (Crossman); "O Love, How Deep, How Broad, How High" (Thomas à Kempis; also translated "O Love, How Vast, How Flowing Free"); "O Sacred Head, Now Wounded" (anonymous, Latin); "Rest, O Christ, from All Your Labor" (Stuempfle) HG; "Son of God, by God Forsaken" (Stuempfle) HG; "Take and Eat" (Quinn and Joncas) RS; "Throned Upon the Awful Tree" (Ellerton) PH; "To Mock Your Reign, O Dearest Lord" (Green) UMH; "Were You There When They Crucified My Lord" (Negro spiritual); "Why Has God Forsaken Me" (Wallace) PH

March 21
Monday of Holy Week
Isaiah 42:1–9 "Earth and All Stars" (Brokering); "God, Who Stretched the Spangled Heavens" (Cameron)
Psalm 36:5–11 "Thy Mercy and Thy Truth, O Lord" (*The Psalter,* 1912)
Hebrews 9:11–15 "Alleluia! Sing to Jesus" (Dix)
John 12:1–11 "Said Judas to Mary, 'Now What Will You Do'" (Carter) NCH; "Savior, an Offering Costly and Sweet" (Parker) NCH

March 22
Tuesday of Holy Week
Isaiah 49:1–7 [none]
Psalm 71:1–14 "From Time Beyond My Memory" (Perry) HWB
1 Corinthians 1:18–31 "Ask Ye What Great Thing I Know" (Schwedler); "Here Hangs a Man Discarded" (Wren) CH; "Lift High the Cross" (Kitchin and Newbolt); "O for a World Where Everyone" (Winter); "Sing, My Tongue, the Glorious Battle" (Fortunatus); "We Know That Christ Is Raised and Dies No More" (Geyer)
John 12:20–36 "Before the Fruit Is Ripened by the Sun" (Troeger) HG; "In the Bulb There Is a Flower" (Sleeth); "Lift High the Cross" (Kitchin and Newbolt); "O Jesus, I Have Promised"

(Bode); "The Work Is Thine, O Christ" (Preiswerk and Zaremba) HWB; "Unless a Grain of Wheat" (Farrell) RS; "When Christ Was Lifted from the Earth" (Wren) BH

March 23

Wednesday of Holy Week

Isaiah 50:4–9a [none]

Psalm 70 [none]

Hebrews 12:1–3 "Alas! And Did My Savior Bleed" (Watts); "Awake, My Soul, Stretch Every Nerve" (Doddridge); "For All the Saints Who from Their Labors Rest" (How); "Guide My Feet" (Negro spiritual); "I Want to Walk As a Child of the Light" (Thomerson); "May the Mind of Christ My Savior" (Wilkinson) WC; "The Head That Once Was Crowned with Thorns" (Kelly); "They Did Not Build in Vain" (Luff) NCH

John 13:21–32 [none]

March 24

Holy Thursday/Maundy Thursday

Exodus 12:1–4 (5–10), 11–14 [none]

Psalm 116:1–2, 12–19 "O Thou My Soul, Return in Peace" (*Murrayfield Psalms; The Psalter, 1912*) PH; "I Love My God, Who Heard My Cry" (Watts) NCH

1 Corinthians 11:23–26 "According to Thy Gracious Word" (Montgomery); "Bread of the World in Mercy Broken" (Heber); "By Christ Redeemed, in Christ Restored" (Rawson) WC; "Christ at the Table There with Friends" (Miller) NCH; "For the Bread Which You Have Broken" (Benson); "In Remembrance of Me" (Courtney); "It Was a Sad and Solemn Night" (Watts) NCH; "Lord, You Give the Great Commission" (Rowthorn); "The Bread of Life for All Is Broken" (Lew; also translated "O Bread of Life for Sinners Broken"); "When You Do This, Remember Me" (Campbell) CH

John 13:1–17, 31b–35 "An Upper Room Did Our Lord Prepare" (Green); "Here in Our Upper Room with You" (Robinson) HWB; "How Pleasant It Is and How Good" (Knepper) HWB; "Jesu, Jesu, Fill Us with Your Love" (Colvin); "Jesus a New Commandment Has Given Us" (Loperena) NCH; "Jesus Took a Towel and He Girded Himself" (Waddell); "Lord, Help Us Walk Your Servant Way" (Stuempfle) HG; "Love Is His Word" (Connaughton) RS; "Praise the God Who Changes Places" (Wren) RS; "There Is No Greater Love, Says the Lord" (Joncas) RS

March 25

Good Friday

Isaiah 52:13–53:12 "Ah, Holy Jesus" (Heerman); "Alas! and Did My Savior Bleed" (Watts); "I Lay My Sins on Jesus" (Bonar); "Kind and Merciful God" (Leech) WC; "Man of Sorrows, What a Name" (Bliss); "O Lamb of God Most Holy" (Decius); "O Sacred Head, Now Wounded" (Bernard of Clairvaux); "Prepare the Way of the Lord" (Taizé); "Sing, My Tongue, the Glorious Battle" (Fortunatus); "The Royal Banners Forward Go" (Fortunatus); "Who Would Ever Have Believed It" (Iona) CH

Psalm 22 "Why Has God Forsaken Me" (Wallace); "Amid the Thronging Worshipers" (*The Psalter, 1912*) WC; "O My God, O Gracious God" (Iona) NCH

Hebrews 10:16–25 "Let Us Draw Near! The Blood Is Spilt" (Clarkson) WC; "Lord, Teach Us How to Pray Aright" (Montgomery) WC; "What Is This Place Where We Are Meeting" (Oosterhuis)

John 18:1–19 "A Purple Robe, a Crown of Thorn" (Dudley-Smith); "Ah, Holy Jesus" (Heerman); "At the Cross, Her Station Keeping" (Jacopone da Todi) RS; "Before the Cock Crew Twice" (Pjeturssen) HWB; "Calvary" (Negro spiritual); "Go to Dark Gethsemane" (Montgomery); "Hark! the Voice of Love and Mercy" (Evans) WC; "He Never Said a Mumbalin' Word" (Negro spiritual); "Kneeling in the Garden Grass" (Troeger; for the stations of the cross); "Lord Christ, When First You Came to Earth" (Bowie) PH; "My Song Is Love Unknown" (Crossman); "O Love, How Deep, How Broad, How High" (Thomas à Kempis; also translated "O Love, How Vast, How Flowing Free"); "O Sacred Head, Now Wounded" (anonymous, Latin); "Rest, O Christ, from All Your Labor" (Stuempfle) HG; "Son of God, by God Forsaken" (Stuempfle) HG; "There Is a Fountain Filled with Blood" (Cowper); "Throned Upon the Awful Tree" (Ellerton) PH; "'Tis Finished; the Messiah Dies" (Wesley); "To Mock Your Reign, O Dearest Lord" (Green) UMH; "Were You There When They Crucified My Lord" (Negro spiritual)

March 26
Holy Saturday
Job 14:1–14 [none]
Psalm 31:1–4, 15–16 "God of Our Life, Through All the Circling Years" (Kerr); "God of the Ages" (Clarkson) WC; "In You, Lord, Have I Put My Trust" (Reissner) PH
1 Peter 4:1–8 "Born of God, Eternal Savior" (Lowry) NCH; "Christian Hearts, in Love United" (Zinzendorf; also translated "Heart with Loving Heart United")
Matthew 27:57–66 "Rest, O Christ, from All Your Labor" (Stuempfle) HG

EASTER VIGIL
Genesis 1:1–2:4a "All Things Bright and Beautiful" (Alexander); "Come and Give Thanks to the Giver of Life" (Janzen) HWB; "Creating God, Your Fingers Trace" (Rowthorn) PH; "Creator of the Universe" (Forbis) BH; "For Beauty of Meadows" (Farquharson); "God Created Earth and Heaven" (traditional Taiwanese); "God, Creation's Great Designer" (Huber) NCH; "God of Many Names, Gathered into One" (Wren) HWB; "God of the Earth, the Sky, the Sea" (Longfellow) HWB; "God of the Sparrow" (Vajda); God That Madest Earth and Heaven" (Heber; there are various stanzas by others, the most appropriate of which for this service, by Hosmer, are in PH); "God Who Made the Earth" (Rhodes) BH; "God, Who Stretched the Spangled Heavens" (Cameron); "God, You Spin the Whirling Planets" (Huber); "I Sing Th'Almighty Power of God" (Watts); "Many and Great, O God, Are Thy Ways" (Renville); "Mothering God, You Gave Me Birth" (Janzen); "O Day of Rest and Gladness" (Wordsworth); "O God, Great Womb of Wondrous Love" (Loewen) HWB; "O God Who Shaped Creation" (Reid); "O Lord of Every Shining Constellation" (Bayly) PH; "On This Day, the First of Days" (anonymous, Latin) RS; "Songs of Praise the Angels Sang" (Montgomery) HWB; "This Is the Day When Life Was First Created" (Kaan) RS; "Your Word Went Forth" (Stuempfle) RS
Psalm 136:1–9, 23–26 "We Thank You, Lord, for You Are Good" (Dunn) PH; "Let Us with a Gladsome Mind" (Milton); "The World Abounds with God's Free Grace" (Mehrtens) PH; "Give to Our God Immortal Praise" (Watts) WC; "We Give Thanks unto You, O God of Might" (Haugen) HWB
Genesis 7:1–5, 11–18, 8:6–18, 9:8–13 "Great Is Thy Faithfulness" (Chisholm); "Sing of Colors" (Mexican folk song) NCH

Psalm 46 "God Is Our Refuge and Our Strength" (*The Psalter,* 1912); "God, Our Help and Constant Refuge" (Anderson) PH; "A Mighty Fortress Is Our God" (Luther)

Genesis 22:1–18 [none]

Psalm 16 "When in the Night I Meditate" (*The Psalter,* 1912); "You Are All We Have" (O'Brien) RS

Exodus 14:10–31, 15:20–21 "At the Lamb's High Feast We Sing" (anonymous, Latin) RS; "Come, Ye Faithful, Raise the Strain" (John of Damascus); "Lead on, O Cloud of Presence" (Duck) HWB; "The Day of Resurrection" (John of Damascus); "This Holy Covenant Was Made" (Dunstan) RS; "When Israel Was in Egypt's Land" (Negro spiritual)

Exodus 15:1b–13, 17–18 [same as for Exodus 14, immediately above]

Isaiah 55:1–11 "All You Who Are Thirsty" (Connolly) RS; "Come, All of You, Come" (anonymous, Laotian) UMH; "Come and Let Us Drink of That New River" (John of Damascus) RS; "Ho, Everyone Who Thirsts" (Haugen) RS; "O Let All Who Thirst" (anonymous) HWB; "Seek the Lord While He May Be Found" (O'Connor) RS; "Seek the Lord Who Now Is Present" (Green) UMH; "Word of God, Come Down on Earth" (Quinn) RS

Isaiah 12:2–6 "Surely It Is God Who Saves Me" (Daw); "With Joy Draw Water" (McKinstry) NCH

Proverbs 8:1–8, 19–21, 9:4b–6 [none]

Psalm 19 "God's Law Is Perfect and Gives Life" (Webber) PH; "Nature with Open Volume Stands" (Watts); "O Sing Unto the Lord" (Rosas); "The Heavens Above Declare God's Praise" (Webber) PH; "The Stars Declare His Glory" (Dudley-Smith) RS

Ezekiel 36:24–28 "Deep Within I Will Plant My Law" (Haas) RS

Psalms 42 and 43 "As Deer Long for the Streams" (Webber) PH; "As Pants the Heart for Cooling Streams" (*New Version*)

Ezekiel 37:1–14 [none]

Psalm 143 "When Morning Lights the Eastern Skies" (*The Psalter,* 1912) PH

Zephaniah 3:14–20 [none]

Psalm 98 "New Songs of Celebration Render" (Routley) PH; "To God Compose a Song of Joy" (Duck); "Joy to the World! The Lord Is Come" (Watts); "Sing a New Song to the Lord" (Dudley-Smith); "Sing a New Song Unto the Lord" (Schutte) RS

Romans 6:3–11 "All Who Believe and Are Baptized" (Kingo) HWB; "Baptized in Water" (Saward); "Come, Holy Spirit, Dove Divine" (Judson); "I Believe in You, Lord Jesus" (Wine) HWB; "Lift High the Cross" (Kitchin and Newbolt); "See the Splendor of the Morning" (Feliciano) HWB; "This Is the Spirit's Entry Now" (Harbranson) UMH; "Wash, O God, Your Sons and Daughters" (Duck) CH; "We Know That Christ Is Raised and Dies No More" (Geyer)

Psalm 114 [none]

Matthew 28:1–10 "Christ Has Arisen" (Olson) HWB; "Christ Is Risen, Christ Is Living" (Martínez); "Christ Who Left His Home in Glory" (Kolb) HWB; "Low in the Grave He Lay" (Lowry); "O Sons and Daughters, Let Us Sing" (Tisserand); "The Sun Was Bright That Easter Dawn" (Stuempfle) HG; "Thine Is the Glory" (Budry); "We Welcome Glad Easter" (anonymous) BH

EASTERTIDE
March 27
Easter Day

Acts 10:34–43 [none]

Psalm 118:1–2, 14–24 "Open Now Thy Gates of Beauty" (Schmolck); "This Is the Day the Lord Hath Made" (Watts)

Colossians 3:1–4 "Alleluia! Alleluia! Hearts to Heaven" (Wordsworth); "Rejoice, the Lord Is King (Wesley)

John 20:1–18 "I Come to the Garden Alone" (Miles); "O Mary, Don't You Weep, Don't You Mourn" (Negro spiritual) UMH; "On This Day, the First of Days" (anonymous, Latin); "The First Day of the Week" (Green) BH; "The Sun Was Bright That Easter Dawn" (Stuempfle) HG; "Thine Is the Glory" (Budry); "Woman, Weeping in the Garden" (Damon) CH

EASTER EVENING

Isaiah 25:6–9 "Christ Jesus Lay in Death's Strong Bands" (Luther)

Psalm 114 [none]

1 Corinthians 5:6b–8 "Christ Jesus Lay in Death's Strong Bands" (Luther)

Luke 24:13–49 "Be Known to Us in Breaking Bread" (Montgomery); "Daylight Fades in Days When Deathless" (Scagnelli) RS; "God in His Wisdom, for Our Learning" (Dudley-Smith) HG; "In the Breaking of the Bread" (Hurd and Downey) RS; "Jesus, Sovereign, Savior" (Kirkland) NCH; "Jesus, Stand Among Us" (Pennefather); "Joy Dawned Again on Easter Day" (anonymous, Latin) NCH; "Lift up Your Hearts, Believers" (Dunstan) HG; "O Sons and Daughters, Let Us Sing" (Tisserand); "O Thou Who This Mysterious Bread" (Wesley) UMH; "On Emmaus' Journey" (Stuempfle) HG; "On the Day of Resurrection" (Peterson) UMH; "On the Journey to Emmaus" (Haugen) RS; "Sing of One Who Walks Beside Us" (Wright) CH

April 3

Acts 2:14a, 22–32 "Christ Is Risen! Shout Hosanna" (Wren) HWB; "His Battle Ended There" (Colvin) WC; "Wake, the Dawn Is Now Full Rising" (Miller) CH

Psalm 16 "When in the Night I Meditate" (*The Psalter*, 1912); "You Are All We Have" (Schutte) RS

1 Peter 1:3–9 [none]

John 20:19–31 "Breathe on Me, Breath of God" (Hatch); "Chosen and Sent by the Father" (Clarkson) HG; "Jesus, Sovereign, Savior" (Kirkland) NCH; "Jesus, Stand Among Us" (Pennefather); "Not with Naked Eye" (Damon) NCH; "O Sons and Daughters of the Lord" (Tisserand); "Show Me Your Hands, Your Feet, Your Side" (Dunstan) HG; "These Things Did Thomas Count as Real" (Troeger) NCH; "We Walk by Faith and Not by Sight" (Alford)

April 10

Acts 2:14a, 36–41 [none]

Psalm 116:1–4, 12–19 "O Thou My Soul, Return in Peace" (*Murrayfield Psalms; The Psalter*, 1912) PH; "I Love My God, Who Heard My Cry" (Watts) NCH

1 Peter 1:17–23 "I Lay My Sins on Jesus" (Bonar)

Luke 24:13–35 [same as for Easter Evening, above]

April 17

Acts 2:42–47 "Come, O Spirit, with Your Sound" (Dalles); "Filled with the Spirit's Power" (Peacey); "Let Us Break Bread Together" (Negro spiritual); "Wake, the Dawn Is Now Full Rising" (Miller) CH

Psalm 23 "My Shepherd Will Supply My Need" (Watts); "The King of Love My Shepherd Is" (Baker); "The Lord's My Shepherd, All My Need" (Webber); "The Lord's My Shepherd, I'll Not Want" (Huber); "The Lord's My Shepherd, I'll Not Want" (*Scottish Psalter*)

1 Peter 2:19–25 "Deep Were His Wounds, and Red" (Johnson) PH; "I Lay My Sins on Jesus" (Bonar)

John 10:1–10 "O Thou, in Whose Presence My Soul Takes Delight" (Swain); "Savior, Like a Shepherd Lead Us" (Thrupp); "We Cannot Own the Sunlit Sky" (Duck); "You, Lord, Are Both Lamb and Shepherd" (Dunstan) HG; "You Satisfy the Hungry Heart" (Westendorf)

April 24

Acts 7:55–60 [none]

Psalm 31:1–5, 15–16 "God of Our Life, Through All the Circling Years" (Kerr); "God of the Ages" (Clarkson) WC; "In You, Lord, Have I Put My Trust" (Reissner) PH

1 Peter 2:2–10 "Built on the Rock, the Church Doth Stand" (Grundtvig); "Christ Is Made the Sure Foundation" (anonymous, Latin); "Christ Is Our Cornerstone" (anonymous, Latin) HWB; "Christ's Church Shall Glory in His Power" (Idle) RS; "Come, O Spirit, Dwell Among Us" (Alford); "For Builders Bold, Whose Vision Pure" (Stuempfle) RS; "O Christ the Great Foundation" (Lew); "Our God Has Built with Living Stones" (York) BH; "To Worship, Work, and Witness" (Lambdin) BH; "We Are Called to Be God's People" (Jackson); "We Are God's People" (Leech); "What God Ordains Is Always Right" (Rodigast) WC

John 14:1–14 "Christ Is the World's Light" (Green); "Christ Is the World's True Light" (Bayly); "Come, My Way, My Truth, My Life" (Herbert); "God Is Love—His the Care" (Dearmer) WC; "Heart and Mind, Possessions, Lord" (Sangle) HWB; "Here, O Lord, Your Servants Gather" (Yamaguchi); "I Know That My Redeemer Liveth" (Pounds); "I Received the Living Lord" (anonymous) RS; "Jesus a New Commandment Has Given Us" (Loperena) NCH; "Jesus the Christ Says, 'I Am the Bread'" (traditional Urdu) NCH; "O Christ, the Way, the Truth, the Life" (Merrill) CH; "O Jesus, I Have Promised" (Bode); "Thou Art the Way; to Thee Alone" (Doane); "To Go to Heaven" (anonymous, Swahili) HWB; "We Come, O Christ, to You" (Clarkson) HG

May 1

Acts 17:22–31 "God, Our Author and Creator" (Daw); "He Comes to Us as One Unknown" (Dudley-Smith)

Psalm 66:8–20 "Let All the World in Every Corner Sing" (Herbert); "Lift up Your Hearts to the Lord" (O'Connor) RS; "Glory and Praise to Our God" (Schutte) RS

1 Peter 3:13–22 "Thy Holy Wings, O Savior" (Sandell-Berg) UMH

John 14:15–21 "For Your Gift of God the Spirit" (Clarkson) HG; "Love Divine, All Loves Excelling" (Wesley); "Peace I Leave with You, My Friends" (Repp) NCH

May 5

Ascension

Acts 1:1–11 "A Hymn of Glory Let Us Sing" (Venerable Bede; also translated "Sing We Triumphant Hymns of Praise"); "Alleluia! Sing to Jesus" (Dix); "Christ High-Ascended" (Dudley-Smith) WC; "Hail the Day That Sees Him Rise" (Wesley); "Hail Thee, Festival Day" (Fortunatus); "Up Through Endless Ranks of Angels" (Vajda) WC

Psalm 47 "Peoples, Clap Your Hands" (Patterson) PH; "A Hymn of Glory Let Us Sing" (Venerable Bede; also translated "Sing We Triumphant Hymns of Praise"); "Alleluia! Sing to Jesus" (Dix); "Give Thanks for Life" (Murray) NCH; "Lord of the Church, We Pray for Our Renewing" (Dudley-Smith) WC; "Rejoice, the Lord Is King" (Wesley)

Ephesians 1:15–23 [none]

Luke 24:44–53 "Alleluia! Sing to Jesus" (Dix); "Hail the Day That Sees Him Rise" (Wesley); "Lift up Your Hearts, Believers" (Dunstan) HG; "A Hymn of Glory Let Us Sing" (Venerable Bede; also translated "Sing We Triumphant Hymns of Praise"); "To Worship, Work, and Witness" (Lambdin) BH; "Up Through Endless Ranks of Angels" (Vajda) WC

May 8

Acts 1:6–14 "A Hymn of Glory Let Us Sing" (Venerable Bede; also translated "Sing We Triumphant Hymns of Praise"); "Alleluia! Sing to Jesus" (Dix); "Christ High-Ascended" (Dudley-Smith) WC; "Hail the Day That Sees Him Rise" (Wesley); "Hail Thee, Festival Day" (Fortunatus); "Up Through Endless Ranks of Angels" (Vajda) WC

Psalm 68:1–10, 32–35 [none]

1 Peter 4:12–14, 5:6–11 "Be Not Dismayed, Whate'er Betide" (Martin)

John 17:1–11 "For All the World" (Clarkson) HG

PENTECOST

May 15

Numbers 11:24–30 [none]

Psalm 104:24–34, 35b "Bless the Lord, My Soul and Being" (Anderson) PH; "Many and Great, O God, Are Thy Ways" (Renville); "O Worship the King, All Glorious Above" (Grant)

Acts 2:1–21 "Come Down, O Love Divine" (Bianco da Siena); "Come, Holy Ghost, Our Souls Inspire" (Maurus); "Come, O Spirit, Dwell Among Us" (Alford); "Come, O Spirit, with Your Sound" (Dalles); "Filled with the Spirit's Power" (Peacey); "Fire of God, Undying Flame" (Bayly); "God, You Have Moved upon the Waters" (Haugen) RS; "Hail Thee, Festival Day" (Fortunatus); "Let Every Christian Pray" (Green); "Like the Murmur of the Dove's Song" (Daw); "Lord of the Church, We Pray for Our Renewing" (Dudley-Smith) WC; "O Breath of Life, Come Sweeping Through Us" (Head); "O Christ, the Great Foundation" (Lew); "O Holy Dove of God Descending" (Leech); "O Holy Spirit, Making Whole" (Tweedy); "O Spirit of the Living God" (Tweedy); "On Pentecost They Gathered" (Huber); "Spirit of God, Unleashed on Earth" (Arthur); "Spirit of God Within Me" (Dudley-Smith) RS; "This Is the Day When Light Was First Created" (Kaan) RS; "Wake, the Dawn Is Now Full Rising" (Miller) CH; "When God the Spirit Came" (Dudley-Smith); "Wind Who Makes All Winds That Blow" (Troeger)

Or:

1 Corinthians 12:3b–13 "Christ, from Whom All Blessings Flow" (Wesley) UMH; "Come, Holy Ghost, Our Souls Inspire" (Maurus); "Forward Through the Ages" (Hosmer); "God of Change and Glory" (Carmines) NCH; "Many Are the Lightbeams from the One Light" (Cyprian of Carthage); "One Bread, One Body" (Foley); "We Are Many Parts" (Haugen) RS

John 20:19–23 "Breathe on Me, Breath of God" (Hatch); "Chosen and Sent by the Father" (Clarkson) HG; "Jesus, Sovereign, Savior" (Kirkland) NCH; "Jesus, Stand Among Us" (Pennefather); "O Sons and Daughters of the Lord" (Tisserand)

Or:

John 7:37–39 "Crashing Waters at Creation" (Dunstan) HG; "I Heard the Voice of Jesus Say" (Bonar)

May 22

Trinity

Genesis 1:1–2:4a [same as for Easter Vigil, above]

Psalm 8 "How Great Our God's Majestic Name" (Dudley-Smith) BH; "Lord, Our Lord, Thy Glorious Name" (*The Psalter,* 1912); "O How Glorious, Full of Wonder" (Beach) NCH; "O Lord, Our God, How Excellent" (Anderson) PH

2 Corinthians 13:11–13 "Lord, Dismiss Us with Your Blessing" (Fawcett); "May the Grace of Christ Our Savior" (Newton)

Matthew 28:16–20 "All Authority and Power" (Idle) WC; "Go, Make of All Disciples" (Adkins); "Go to the World" (Dunstan) RS; "Go Ye Therefore and Teach All Nations" (Patillo) RS; "Lo, I Am with You" (Iona) CH; "Lord, You Give the Great Commission" (Rowthorn); "O Holy God, Whose Gracious Power" (Huber) NCH; "Tell It! Tell It out with Gladness" (Harkness) HG; "You Are the Seed" (Gabaraín)

May 29

Genesis 6:9–22, 7:24, 8:14–19 [none]

Psalm 46 "God Is Our Refuge and Our Strength" (*The Psalter,* 1912) PH; "God, Our Help and Constant Refuge" (Anderson) PH; "A Mighty Fortress Is Our God" (Luther)

Romans 1:16–17, 3:22b–28 (29–31) "One Is the Race of Mankind Under Sin's Condemnation" (Clarkson) WC; "To God Be the Glory" (Crosby); "What Mercy and Divine Compassion" (Hiller) HWB

Matthew 7:21–29 "Deliver Us, O Lord of Truth" (Stuempfle) HG; "My Hope Is Built on Nothing Less" (Mote)

June 5

Genesis 12:1–9 "God It Was Who Said to Abraham" (Bell) RS; "The God of Abraham Praise" (Daniel ben Judah Dayyan)

Psalm 33:1–12 "Righteous and Just Is the Word of Our Lord" (García) UMH

Romans 4:13–25 [none]

Matthew 9:9–13, 18–26 "For the Faithful Who Have Answered" (Dunstan) HG; "Heal Us Emmanuel, Hear Our Prayer" (Cowper) UMH; "Immortal Love, Forever Full" (Whittier); "O Jesus Christ, May Grateful Hymns Be Rising" (Webster); "There Was Jesus by the Water" (Grindal) NCH

June 12

Genesis 18:1–15 (21:1–7) "God It Was Who Said to Abraham" (Bell) RS

Psalm 116:1–2, 12–19 "O Thou My Soul, Return in Peace" (*Murrayfield Psalms; The Psalter,* 1912) PH; "I Love My God, Who Heard My Cry" (Watts) NCH

Romans 5:1–8 "Ah, Holy Jesus" (Heerman); "And Can It Be That I Should Gain" (Wesley); "Come, Holy Spirit, Heavenly Dove" (Watts); "Creator God, Creating Still" (Huber); "Great God of Wonders" (Davies) HWB; "I Will Sing of My Redeemer" (Bliss); "Lift High the Cross" (Kitchin and Newbolt); "What Mercy and Divine Compassion" (Miller) HWB; "What Wondrous Love Is This" (traditional American)

Matthew 9:35–10:8 (9–23) "And Is the Gospel Peace and Love" (Steele) HWB; "Come, Labor On" (Borthwick); "How Buoyant and Bold the Stride of Christ's Friends" (Troeger) HWB; "O Christ Who Called the Twelve" (Stuempfle) HG

June 19

Genesis 21:8–21 [none]

Psalm 86:1–10, 16–17 [none]

Romans 6:1b–11 "All Who Believe and Are Baptized" (Kingo) HWB; "Alleluia! Alleluia! Hearts to Heaven and Voices Raise" (Wordsworth); "Baptized in Water" (Saward); "Baptized into Your Name Most Holy" (Rambach) NCH; "Christ the Lord Is Risen Today" (Wesley); "Come, Holy Spirit, Dove Divine" (Judson); I Believe in You, Lord Jesus" (Wine) HWB; "I Know That My Redeemer Lives" (Medley); "I'll Shout the Name of Christ Who Lives" (Vin-luan) NCH; "Lift High the Cross" (Kitchin and Newbolt); "Wash, O God, Your Sons and Daughters" (Duck) CH; "We Know That Christ Is Raised and Dies No More" (Geyer)

Matthew 10:24–39 "O Christ, Unsheathe Your Sword" (Stuempfle) HG; "Take up Thy Cross and Follow Me" (McKinney); "Take up Your Cross, the Savior Said" (Everest); "Who Now Would Follow Christ in Life" (*Ausbund*) HWB; "Why Should I Feel Discouraged" (Martin)

June 26

Genesis 22:1–14 [none]

Psalm 13 "How Long, O Lord, Will You Forget" (Woollett) WC

Romans 6:12–23 "God Is Love, Let Heaven Adore Him" (Rees) WC; "Lord of All Being, to You Be All Praise" (Winslow) WC; "Make Me a Captive, Lord" (Matheson)

Matthew 10:40–42 "Where Cross the Crowded Ways of Life" (North); "O Christ, Unsheathe Your Sword" (Stuempfle) HG [a weak match]

July 3

Genesis 24:34–38, 42–49, 58–67 [none]

Psalm 45:10–17 [none]

Romans 7:15–25a "Go Forth, O People of God" (Gabaraín); "In the Stillness of the Evening" (Ellingsen) HWB; "Make Me a Captive, Lord" (Matheson)

Matthew 11:16–19, 25–30 "Are You Weary, Heavy Laden" (anonymous, Greek) WC; "Come, All of You" (anonymous, Laotian) UMH; "Come to Me" (Joncas) RS; "Come to Me, All You Weary" (Young) RS; "Come to Me, O Weary Traveler" (Dunstan) HG; "Come Unto Me, Ye Weary" (Dix); "Come, Ye Sinners, Poor and Needy" (Hart); "I Heard the Voice of Jesus Say" (Bonar); "O Let All Who Thirst" (anonymous) HWB

July 10

Genesis 25:19–34 [none]

Psalm 119:105–112 "Lamp of Our Feet" (Barton) HWB; "Thy Word As a Lamp Unto My Feet" (Grant) UMH

Romans 8:1–11 "And Can It Be That I Should Gain" (Wesley); "O Spirit of God, O Life-Giving Breath" (Niedling) NCH; "God Himself Is with Us" (Tersteegen; also translated "God Is Here Among Us"); "Jesus, Thy Blood and Righteousness" (Zinzendorf) WC

Matthew 13:1–9, 18–23 "A Sower's Seed Fell on a Path" (Stuempfle) HG; "Almighty God, Your Word Is Cast" (Cawood) NCH; "You Are Salt for the Earth, O People" (Haugen)

July 17

Genesis 28:10–19a "As Jacob with Travel Was Weary One Day" (traditional English) WC; "Nearer, My God, to Thee" (Adams); "We Are Climbing Jacob's Ladder" (Negro spiritual)

Psalm 139:1–12, 23–24 "Search Me, O God" (Orr); "You Are Before Me, Lord" (Pitt-Watson) PH
Romans 8:12–25 "Christ Is Coming! Let Creation" (MacDuff); "In the Bulb There Is a Flower" (Sleeth); "O Spirit of God, O Life-Giving Breath" (Niedling) NCH; "Spirit, Come, Dispel Our Sadness" (Gerhardt) HWB
Matthew 13:24–30, 36–43 "Christ Will Come Again" (Wren) NCH; "Come, Ye Thankful People, Come" (Alford); "Faith and Truth and Life Bestowing" (Dudley-Smith) HG

July 24

Genesis 29:15–28 [none]
Psalm 105:1–11, 45b [none]
Romans 8:26–39 "Eternal Spirit of the Risen Christ" (Christierson); "In Solitude, in Solitude" (Duck) NCH; "Like the Murmur of the Dove's Song" (Daw); "Prayer Is the Soul's Sincere Desire" (Montgomery)
Matthew 13:31–33, 44–52 "The Kingdom of God" (Grindal); "The Reign of God, Like Farmer's Field" (Dufner) HG; "We Plant a Grain of Mustard Seed" (Matney) NCH; "When Jesus Came Preaching the Kingdom of God" (Green) RS

July 31

Genesis 32:22–31 "Come, O Thou Traveler Unknown" (Wesley)
Psalm 17:1–7, 15 [none]
Romans 9:1–5 [none]
Matthew 14:13–21 "Break Thou the Bread of Life" (Lathbury); "They Came, a Milling Crowd" (Stuempfle) HG

August 7

Genesis 37:1–4, 12–28 [none]
Psalm 105:1–6, 16–22, 45b [none]
Romans 10:5–15 "How Shall They Hear the Word of God" (Perry); "Immortal Love, Forever Full" (Whittier)
Matthew 14:22–33 "I Sought the Lord, and Afterward I Knew" (anonymous); "Your Hand, Though Hidden, Guides Us" (Stuempfle) HG

August 14

Genesis 45:1–15 [none]
Psalm 133 "Behold the Goodness of the Lord" (Anderson) PH; "How Good a Thing It Is" (Seddon) HWB; "O Look and Wonder" (Sosa) CH
Romans 11:1–2a, 29–32 [none]
Matthew 15:(10–20) 21–28 "Here, Master, in This Quiet Place" (Green) HG

August 21

Exodus 1:8–2:10 "In Egypt Under Pharaoh" (Carlson) NCH
Psalm 124 "Now Israel May Say, and That in Truth" (*The Psalter*, 1912)
Romans 12:1–8 "All for Jesus! All for Jesus" (Sparrow-Simpson) WC; "Come, All Christians, Be Committed" (Lloyd); "Like the Murmur of the Dove's Song" (Daw); "Lord of All Good, We Bring Our Gifts to You" (Bayly) WC; "Lord, Whose Love Through Humble Service"

(Bayly); "Take My Life, and Let It Be" (Havergal); "There Are Many Gifts" (Shelly) HWB; "We Praise You with Our Minds, O Lord" (McElrath)
Matthew 16:13–20 "Let Kings and Prophets Yield Their Name" (Daw) HG

August 28
Exodus 3:1–15 "Deep in the Shadows of the Past" (Wren) PH; "God It Was Who Said to Abraham" (Bell) RS; "God of Many Names, Gathered into One" (Wren) HWB; "The God of Abraham Praise" (Daniel ben Judah Dayyan); "When Israel Was in Egypt's Land" (Negro spiritual)
Psalm 105:1–6, 23–26, 45c [none]
Romans 12:9–21 "Christian Hearts in Love United" (Zinzendorf; also translated "Heart with Loving Heart United"); "Help Us Accept Each Other" (Kaan); "Sister, Let Me Be Your Servant" (Gillard; found with various opening lines; sometimes titled "The Servant Song"); "Your Ways Are Not Our Own" (Bayler) NCH
Matthew 16:21–28 "Take up Thy Cross and Follow Me" (McKinney); "Take up Your Cross, the Savior Said" (Everest); "Who Now Would Follow Christ" (Ausbund) HWB; "Would I Have Answered When You Called" (Stuempfle) HG

September 4
Exodus 12:1–14 [none]
Psalm 149 "Give Praise to the Lord and Sing a New Song" (The Psalter, 1912)
Romans 13:8–14 "Awake, O Sleeper, Rise from Death" (Tucker); "Sleepers, Wake! A Voice Astounds Us" (Nicolai; also translated "Wake, Awake, for Night Is Flying"); "Spirit of Jesus, If I Love My Neighbor" (Wren) NCH
Matthew 18:15–20 "Built on the Rock the Church Doth Stand" (Grundtvig); "Christ Has Promised to Be Present" (Whitney) HG; "Draw Us in the Spirit's Tether" (Dearmer); "The Lord Is Here" (Dudley-Smith) WC

September 11
Exodus 14:19–31 "Crashing Waters at Creation" (Dunstan) NCH; "Guide Me, O Thou Great Jehovah" (Williams); "In Egypt Under Pharaoh" (Carlson) NCH; "Lead on, O Cloud of Presence" (Duck) HWB
Psalm 114 [none]
Romans 14:1–12 "Jesus, I Live to You" (Harbaugh) NCH; "Living and Dying with Jesus" (anonymous, Croatian) HWB; "O Lord of Life, Wherever They Be" (Hosmer) HWB; "O Savior, for the Saints" (Mant) NCH; "When We Are Living" (anonymous and Escamilla; also translated "If We Are Living")
Matthew 18:21–35 "Forgive Our Sins As We Forgive" (Herklots); "Help Us Accept Each Other" (Kaan); "Help Us Forgive, Forgiving Lord" (Stuempfle) HG

September 18
Exodus 16:2–15 "All Who Hunger, Gather Gladly" (Dunstan); "Glorious Things of Thee Are Spoken" (Newton); "Guide Me, O Thou Great Jehovah" (Williams); "This Holy Covenant Was Made" (Dunstan) RS
Psalm 105:1–6, 37–45 [none]

Philippians 1:21–30 "Jesus, I Live to You" (Harbaugh) NCH; "Living and Dying with Jesus" (anonymous, Croatian) HWB; "When We Are Living" (anonymous and Escamilla; also translated "If We Are Living")

Matthew 20:1–16 "Come, Labor on" (Borthwick); "For the Fruits of All Creation" (Green) HG

September 25
Exodus 17:1–7 "Christ Is the Mountain of Horeb" (anonymous) NCH; "Guide Me, O Thou Great Jehovah" (Williams); "I Hunger and I Thirst" (Monsell) HWB
Psalm 78:1–4, 12–16 [none]
Philippians 2:1–13 [same as for March 20, above]
Matthew 21:23–32 "Welcome, All You Noble Saints" (Stamps) HG

October 2
Exodus 20:1–4, 7–9, 12–20 [none]
Psalm 19 "God's Law Is Perfect and Gives Life" (Webber) PH; "Nature with Open Volume Stands" (Watts); "O Sing unto the Lord" (Rosas); "The Heavens Above Declare God's Praise" (Webber) PH; "The Stars Declare His Glory" (Dudley-Smith) RS
Philippians 3:4b–14 "All That I Counted As Gain" (Joncas) RS; "Awake, My Soul, Stretch Every Nerve" (Doddridge); "Before the Cross of Jesus" (Blanchard); "God, You Spin the Whirling Planets" (Huber); "In the Morning When I Rise" (Negro spiritual); "Open, Lord, My Inward Ear" (Wesley) HWB; "This Is a Time to Remember" (Leech) WC; "When I Survey the Wondrous Cross" (Watts)
Matthew 21:33–46 "Christ Is Made the Sure Foundation" (anonymous, Latin); "Christ Is Our Cornerstone" (anonymous, Latin) HWB; "Salvation! There's No Better Word" (Green) HG

October 9
Exodus 32:1–14 [none]
Psalm 106:1–6, 19–23 [none]
Philippians 4:1–9 "I Would Be True" (Walter); "Rejoice, the Lord Is King" (Wesley); "Rejoice, Ye Pure in Heart" (Plumptre)
Matthew 22:1–14 "As We Gather At Your Table" (Daw) HG

October 16
Exodus 33:12–23 [none]
Psalm 99 [none]
1 Thessalonians 1:1–10 [none]
Matthew 22:15–22 "Baited, the Question Rose" (Daw) HG

October 23
Deuteronomy 34:1–12 [none]
Psalm 90:1–6, 13–17 "O God, Our Help in Ages Past" (Watts)
1 Thessalonians 2:1–8 [none]
Matthew 22:34–46 "If All You Want, Lord, Is My Heart" (Troeger) HG; "Jesus a New Commandment Has Given Us" (Loperena) NCH; "Lord of Creation, to You Be All Praise" (Winslow) WC; "We Praise You with Our Minds, O Lord" (McElrath)

October 30
Joshua 3:7–17 [none]
Psalm 107:1–7, 33–37 "Jesus, Thou Joy of Loving Hearts" (Bernard of Clairvaux); "Now Thank We All Our God" (Rinkart)
1 Thessalonians 2:9–13 [none]
Matthew 23:1–12 "The Virtue of Humility" (Dufner) HG

November 6
Joshua 24:1–3a, 14–25 [none]
Psalm 78:1–7 [none]
1 Thessalonians 4:13–18 "By Christ Redeemed, in Christ Restored" (Rawson) WC; "How Blest Are They Who Trust in Christ" (Green); "Jesus Lives and So Shall I" (Gellert); "O Lord, My God, When I in Awesome Wonder" (Hine); "O When Shall I See Jesus" (Leland) WC; "Rejoice, the Lord Is King" (Wesley); "When Peace, Like a River, Attendeth My Way" (Spafford)
Matthew 25:1–13 "Keep Your Lamps Trimmed and Burning" (Negro spiritual) NCH; "Rejoice! Rejoice, Believers" (Laurenti) PH; "Sleepers, Wake! A Voice Astounds Us" (Nicolai; also translated "Wake, Awake, for Night Is Flying") HG

November 13
Judges 4:1–7 [none]
Psalm 123 [none]
1 Thessalonians 5:1–11 [none]
Matthew 25:14–30 "God Whose Giving Knows No Ending" (Edwards); "Lord of Lords, Adored by Angels" (Vajda) HG

November 20
Christ the King
Ezekiel 34:11–16, 20–24 [none]
Psalm 100 "All People That on Earth Do Dwell" (Kethe); "Come, Rejoice Before Your Maker" (Baughen) RS
Ephesians 1:15–23 "A Hymn of Glory Let Us Sing" (Venerable Bede; also translated "Sing We Triumphant Hymns of Praise"); "Alleluia! Sing to Jesus" (Dix); "Give Thanks for Life" (Murray) NCH; "Lord of the Church, We Pray for Our Renewing" (Dudley-Smith) WC; "Rejoice, the Lord Is King" (Wesley)
Matthew 25:31–46 "As We Gather at Your Table" (Daw); "Brothers and Sisters of Mine" (Morse) HWB; "Christ's Is the World in Which We Move" (Bell) RS; "For the Fruits of All Creation" (Green); "God of Day and God of Darkness" (Haugen) RS; "Here Am I" (Wren); "Let Your Heart Be Broken" (Leech); "Lord, Whose Love in Humble Service" (Bayly); "Our Savior's Infant Cries Were Heard" (Troeger) WC; "Standing at the Future's Threshold" (Gregory) NCH; "Stir Your Church, O God, Our Father" (Price); "The Church of Christ, in Every Age" (Green); "There's a Spirit in the Air" (Wren); "We Turn Our Eyes to Heaven" (Stuempfle) HG; "When the Poor Ones Who Have Nothing" (Olivar and Manzano; also translated "When a Poor One Who Has Nothing")

ADVENT
November 27
Isaiah 64:1–9 "Have Thine Own Way, Lord" (Pollard); "O Savior, Rend the Heavens Wide" (Spee) HWB

Psalm 80:1–7, 17–19 "O Hear Our Cry, O Lord" (Anderson) PH

1 Corinthians 1:3–9 [none]

Mark 13:24–37 "As Servants Working an Estate" (Troeger) HG, NHL; "From the Father's Throne on High" (Dudley-Smith) HG; "O Savior, Rend the Heavens Wide" (Spee) HWB

December 4
Isaiah 40:1–11 "All Earth Is Waiting to See the Promised One" (Taulé); "Comfort, Comfort Ye My People" (Olearius); "Prepare the Way, O Zion" (Franzen) PH; "There's a Voice in the Wilderness Crying" (Milligan) NCH

Psalm 85:1–2, 8–13 [none]

2 Peter 3:8–15a "O Day of God, Draw Nigh" (Scott); "O God, Our Help in Ages Past" (Watts); "When the Lord in Glory Comes" (Dudley-Smith) WC

Mark 1:1–8 "Comfort, Comfort Ye, My People" (Olearius); "Down Galilee's Slow Roadways" (Dunstan) HG; "Mark How the Lamb of God's Self-Offering" (Daw) HG; "On Jordan's Banks the Baptist's Cry" (Coffin); "When John Baptized by Jordan's River" (Dudley-Smith) RS; "Wild the Man and Wild the Place" (Troeger) NHL

December 11
Isaiah 61:1–4, 8–11 "Arise, Your Light Is Come" (Duck); "Hail to the Lord's Anointed" (Montgomery); "Live into Hope of Captives Freed" (Huber) PH

Psalm 126 "Let Us Hope When Hope Seems Hopeless" (Beebe) NCH; "When God Delivered Israel" (Saward) PH

1 Thessalonians 5:16–24 "As Sons of the Day and Daughters of Light" (Idle) WC; "For Your Gift of God the Spirit" (Clarkson) WC

John 1:6–8, 19–28 "On Jordan's Banks the Baptist's Cry" (Coffin); "The Moon with Borrowed Light" (Troeger) HG, NHL; "There's a Voice in the Wilderness Crying" (Milligan) NCH

December 18
2 Samuel 7:1–11, 16 [none]

Luke 1:47–55 "All Who Would Claim the Faith of Jesus" (Coles) RS; "For Ages Women Hoped and Prayed" (Huber) WC; "My Heart Sings out with Joyful Praise" (Duck) NCH; "My Soul Cries out" (Cooney) RS; "My Soul Gives Glory to My God" (Winter); "My Soul Gives Glory to the Lord" (Mueller) RS; "My Soul Proclaims with Wonder" (Daw) HWB; "Tell out, My Soul, the Greatness of the Lord" (Dudley-Smith); "When to Mary, the Word" (Clark) HG

Romans 16:25–27 [none]

Luke 1:26–38 "A Message Came to a Maiden Young" (Dearmer) RS; "I Sing a Maid of Tender Years" (Ridge) RS; "Long Ago, Prophets Knew" (Green) WC; "No Wind at the Window" (Bell) RS; "One Wedding Dress Long Put Away" (Leach) HG; "Startled by a Holy Humming" (Troeger) NHL; "The Angel Gabriel from Heaven Came" (Baring-Gould); "The First One Ever,

Oh Ever to Know" (Egan) UMH; "To a Maid Engaged to Joseph" (Grindal); "To a Virgin Meek and Mild" (Boe and Overby) WC; "Ye Who Claim the Faith of Jesus" (Coles and Tucker) UMH

CHRISTMASTIDE
December 25
Proper I
Isaiah 9:2–7 "Child of Mercy, Child of Peace" (Haas) RS; "Lord, Today We Have Seen Your Glory" (Balhoff) RS; "To Us a Child of Hope Is Born" (Morison) HWB
Psalm 96 "O Sing a New Song to the Lord" (Gabriel) PH; "Let All the World in Every Corner Sing" (Herbert)
Titus 2:11–14 "Christ Is Coming! Let Creation" (MacDuff); "God's Holy Ways Are Just and True" (Woollett) WC; "I Will Sing of My Redeemer" (Bliss)
Luke 2:1–14 (15–20) "Angels from the Realms of Glory" (Montgomery); "Angels We Have Heard on High" (traditional French); "Break Forth, O Beauteous Heavenly Light" (Rist); "Child in the Manger" (MacDonald) BH; "Christmas Has Its Cradle" (Whitney) BH; "From Heaven Above to Earth I Come" (Luther); "Gentle Mary Laid Her Child" (Cook); "Go, Tell It on the Mountain" (Negro spiritual); "God Rest You Merry Gentlemen" (traditional English); "Hark! The Herald Angels Sing" (Wesley); "Holy Night, Blessed Night" (anonymous, Chinese); "In Bethlehem a Babe Was Born" (Mays) PH; "Infant Holy, Infant Lowly" (anonymous, Polish); "It Came Upon the Midnight Clear" (Sears); "Long Time Ago in Bethlehem" (Hairston) WC; "Once in Royal David's City" (Alexander); "Sheep Fast Asleep" (anonymous, Japanese); "Silent, in the Chill of Midnight" (O'Brien) RS; "Silent Night, Holy Night" (Mohr); "Sing We Now of Christmas" (traditional French); "That Boy-Child of Mary" (Colvin); "The First Nowell the Angel Did Say" (anonymous, English); "The Sheep Stood Stunned in Sudden Light" (Troeger) NHL; "The Snow Lay on the Ground" (anonymous, Anglo-Irish) PH; "The Virgin Mary Had a Baby Boy" (anonymous, West Indian); "There's a Star in the East on Christmas Morn" (Negro spiritual) PH; "What Child Is This" (Dix); "While Shepherds Watched Their Flocks by Night" (Tate); "Who Is the Baby an Hour or Two Old" (Bell) RS

Or, *Proper II:*

Isaiah 62:6–12 [none]
Psalm 97 "Earth's Scattered Isles and Contoured Hills" (Rowthorn) PH; "Sing Praise to God Who Reigns Above" (Schütz)
Titus 3:4–7 "God, We Praise You" (Idle) WC; "Marvelous Grace of Our Loving Lord" (Johnston); "Not What These Hands Have Done" (Bonar); "Wonderful Grace of Jesus" (Lillenas)
Luke 2:(1–7) 8–20 "When Jesus Worked Here on Earth" (Olson) HG; [see also those hymns listed under *Proper I,* above]

Or, *Proper III:*

Isaiah 52:7–10 "God Reigns O'er All the Earth" (Huber) PH
Psalm 98 "New Songs of Celebration Render" (Routley) PH; "Joy to the World! The Lord Is Come" (Watts); "Sing a New Song to the Lord" (Dudley-Smith) WC; "To God Compose a Song of Joy" (Duck); "Sing a New Song Unto the Lord" (Schutte) RS
Hebrews 1:1–4 (5–12) "A Hymn of Glory Let Us Sing" (Venerable Bede; also translated "Sing We Triumphant Hymns of Praise"); "Christ High-Ascended" (Dudley-Smith) WC; "God Has

Spoken by His Prophets" (Briggs); "Hark! The Herald Angels Sing" (Wesley); "Lord, You Sometimes Speak" (Idle) HWB; "My Lord of Light Who Made the Worlds" (Idle) WC; "O Come, All Ye Faithful" (Wade); "O Gracious Light, Lord Jesus Christ" (anonymous, Greek) WC; "O Splendor of God's Glory Bright" (Ambrose); "Of the Father's Love Begotten" (Prudentius); "Rejoice, the Lord Is King" (Wesley); "The Head That Once Was Crowned with Thorns" (Kelly)

John 1:1–14 "Christ, Whose Glory Fills the Skies" (Wesley); "Hark! The Herald Angels Sing" (Wesley); "Holy Child Within the Manger" (Haugen) RS; "Let Our Gladness Have No End" (*Kancional*); "Morning Star, O Cheering Sight" (Scheffler) HWB; "On Jordan's Banks the Baptist's Cry" (Coffin); "The Moon with Borrowed Light" (Troeger) HG, NHL; "There's a Voice in the Wilderness Crying" (Milligan) NCH; "Word of God When All Was Silent" (Stuempfle)

SECTION IV

MESSAGES FOR COMMUNION SERVICES

SERMON SUGGESTIONS

Topic: Supper of Sharing

Text: 1 Cor. 10:16–17

The New Testament writers present us with a number of beautiful scenes from Christ's life. We are allowed to see him as he helped the helpless, brought hope to the despairing, offered redemption to the sinful, and shared his life with the twelve he chose to be with him. We watch as he loved, gave, and agonized over those who refused to respond. We are privileged to see the beauty of his manhood, Godlike manhood—ultimate humanity, and true godliness focused in one man.

No scene in Christ's life is more beautiful than the one in which he shared some of his final moments with his disciples over a meal. He was nearing the supreme crisis in his life; he knew his death was inevitable. Yet, in spirit of fellowship that danger could not disrupt and death could not end, Christ did something beautiful for his disciples and for all disciples through the centuries. He shared a meal with them, and he left this meal for all his people in all ages to share.

Christ's meal expresses the attitude, the mind-set, in which Christ's followers must share. The Lord's Supper demands what Paul demanded of the Philippian Christians: "Let this mind be in you, which was also in Christ Jesus" (Phil. 2:5). We are called on to have a persistent love that gives itself in serving people. Halford Luccock declared that we cannot avoid the question the Lord's meal asks. The supper first affirms that Jesus' life, given voluntarily, was his "blood of the new testament, . . . shed for many" (Mark 14:24). Then the supper asks: "Are your life, your blood, your strength, poured out at all?"[1]

Christ's meal is the supper of sharing. As we participate together, we are reminded that our following Christ is a continuous experience of sharing.

The supper was instituted in a context of Christ's death. Although he died alone—between two thieves, rejected by his own people, and virtually abandoned by his disciples—his meal reminds us that our entrance into relationship with him comes only by our sharing his death. Paul expressed this truth in Romans 6:3: "Know ye not, that so many of us as were baptized into Jesus Christ were baptized into his death?" Our old man is crucified with him, Paul argued; we experience a change from our former selves so radical that it can be described best as dying to sin. Not only that but also Christ's death becomes the principle by which we live. He gave himself for us; we give ourselves to him and to others. He died for us, true enough. But we become his people only by sharing his death.

Christ's meal reminds us that *we share a priceless gift*. We share the gift of redemption, the gift of a new life. Once we groveled in the squalor of our spiritual poverty, whether or

---

[1]*T.I.B.*, vol. 7, p. 877.

not we realized it. But now we sit at the King's table; we live from his bounty, and we receive from his benevolent hand. We share the experience of receiving that which we could not produce for ourselves, gain in trade, or receive as remuneration for labor. We share the sheer gift given by a gracious God—a gift of his love, a gift for which we can make no repayment. We cannot repay a gift of grace.

In Mobile, Alabama, after an automobile accident, my wife, Barbara, had to be confined to bed for an extended period. I had to work at my job on the staff of a church. People came by our apartment with food; some of them washed dishes; several checked on Barbara from time to time. A lawyer volunteered his services; people called during the day to see how things were going. I remarked to one lady, in essence: "I don't know how we will ever repay all the gracious things you ladies have done for us."

"You can't repay us," she said matter-of-factly. "But you may have a chance someday to do something like this for someone else."

We cannot repay a gift of grace, but *such a gift can move us to give.* We share God's gift of himself, and we share the joy of giving to others in his name.

And so, *we share service together*—Christian service, selfless service. We engage in constructive efforts designed to lift others, acts designed to express Christ's love in language that they can understand—actions done specifically to articulate God's care in concrete terms. We share a ministry to every person in need within our reach. The cup of cold water, the piece of bread, the article of clothing, the words of encouragement and comfort, the listening ear, the strengthening presence—we have the marvelous privilege of being Christ's hands and feet, swift to help.

In our shared service, we discover that *we are sharing God's life.* We share triumph and tragedy, success and failure, joy and sorrow, correctness and mistake. Because we are the church in action in every area of life, we enjoy the discovery that God intends for us to live together and to share his life.

Part of our shared life is the rewarding *sharing of worship together.* Many of us worship individually, reading the Scriptures and praying, but we meet together to seek the mind of God. We seek to think his thoughts after him and to do his commandments. Shared worship moves us to the realization that all of us are in the same bundle. Shared worship, and especially the Lord's meal, forges a bond between us. We are a community sharing Christ's power, presence, and imperatives. We share in advancement under his leadership.

In the meal long ago, Christ shared bread and the fruit of the vine with his disciples; more than that, he shared himself and his conclusive triumph with them. He continues to share with us. We share with one another; we share his death, his gift, his ministry, his life, and worship. His meal reminds us of the depth of our sharing.—Eli Landrum, Jr.

Topic: Supper of Fellowship
TEXT: 1 Cor. 10:16

In chapter 10 of 1 Corinthians, Paul issued a stern warning to Christians living in pagan environments. They were not to participate in feasts held in honor of idols; to do so would identify them with those who worshiped the idols. In making his strong statements, Paul referred to the Lord's Supper, and he used a suggestive term. The King James Version translates the word *koin_nia* as "communion"; thus one designation of the Lord's Supper is "Holy Communion."

The Greek word indicates joint participation in that which is common to two or more. The word has also been rendered "partnership"; the most common translation is "fellowship."

Paul was reminding the Corinthian Christians forcefully that the Lord's Supper expresses one's fellowship with Christ and with others. A pagan feast would carry the same implications of relationship. Did they really want to share in anything giving indications of fellowship with a pagan god and its mistaken followers?

In issuing a warning to Christians of his day, Paul provided a helpful reminder for us. Our coming together to participate in Christ's meal is an open expression of deep, genuine, meaningful fellowship. The first supper was instituted in part to emphasize fellowship. It was designed, I am convinced, as a continuing encouragement and challenge to the kind of healthy relationships that must characterize Christ's church.

But wait just a minute! Hold on! We are all different. We come from different backgrounds. We don't think alike, and we don't act the same. We have varying degrees of commitment to Christ and his work, and we don't always agree in matters concerning the church. What do we mean when we say that our coming together is a concrete expression of fellowship? We come—or we should—as those who put foremost in our lives our joint participation in Christ's redemptive work. Lewis Rhodes expressed this truth well: in observing the Lord's Supper, we come to be *with* people and to show that we are *for* people; this is part of what being truly human and genuinely Christian means.

Look closely at the group reposing at the table in the upper room. One would be hard pressed to find a more diverse band of men. Four of them were fishermen; one was a tax collector; one was a member of a radical party bent on overthrowing Roman rule by force; for reasons of his own, one was about to betray the Lord of life. Among these men were Simon the loud and impetuous; Andrew the quiet; James and John, the "sons of thunder"; Philip the slow to understand; and Thomas the courageous and inquiring. But even in this group of such glaring contrasts, fellowship was the dominant note. All but one enjoyed fellowship with Christ and were bound together by their mutual participation in his cause.

Try as we may, I don't think that we can get Judas out of the upper room before the Lord's Supper. Luke was explicit at this point. After recording the sharing of the bread and the cup, in 22:21 Luke quoted Jesus as saying: "Behold, the hand of him that betrayeth me is with me on the table." In this statement and in John's poignant scene in which Jesus gave the sop to Judas (John 13:26), Jesus offered fellowship with himself one last time to one who never really had responded. One factor that is striking to me in the setting of the Lord's Supper is the emphasis on a dual fellowship: fellowship with Christ and with those who follow him, and the offer of fellowship to those who are on the outside by choice.

Just as the first disciples did, we come to this event signifying deepest fellowship with those who are ordinary, faulty, and imperfect. But we are invited to come by the Lord, who knew that we would need reminders of and encouragement to fellowship. Imperfect as it was, the early church strengthened its fellowship through the shared meal. In Acts 2:42, Luke reported that the early Christians "continued steadfastly in the apostles' doctrine and fellowship, and in breaking of bread, and in prayers." The terms *fellowship* and *breaking of bread* probably are to be taken together; the meal that they shared pointed to relationship.

I was helped by being reminded that the Passover, the Jewish celebration of release from Egypt that was the setting in which the Lord's Supper originated, was celebrated by families. This symbolized an unbroken fellowship of those who formed one body with the God who had passed over the blood-sprinkled doors. So the fellowship we celebrate in this meal is like that of a family at its highest and best, with its unbroken, essential solidarity. God is Father, and we are his children. We are related through grace and are working in the same redemptive purpose. It is a fellowship of mutual love, trust, and acceptance.

So we come to participate in a meal given to us. We come as forgiven people invited into fellowship with a gracious God. We come as those privileged to be related to one another in the work that is ours as God's people sharing in the world's greatest enterprise. May the fellowship that we celebrate be the mark of our lives as we live and work in community.—Eli Landrum Jr.

Topic: Christ Died for Us
TEXT: John 19:17–24, 28–30

When Jesus said, "No one has greater love than this, to lay down one's life for one's friends" (John 15:13, NRSV), he not only paid a high compliment to the principle of self-denying love but also expressed the spirit in which he would give his life on the cross. The physical anguish Jesus suffered at Golgotha was the climax of his self-giving life and the price of the redemption of the human race.

I. *The course he chose.* Jesus could have avoided the cross. He said, "No man takes it [my life] from me, but I lay it down of my own accord" (John 10:18, NRSV).

From the beginning it was the fortune of the light to be rejected. As the light shone on, the darkness unable to put it out, it appeared in Jesus of Nazareth, who "came to what was his own, and his own people did not accept him" (John 1:11, NRSV).

One source of trouble for Jesus was that he gave an unpopular interpretation of his role as the Messiah, the Christ. The people wanted a king, but Jesus was not concerned to lead any army against the Romans, nor to use his miraculous powers to further the political aims of the Jews. He came to give the life of God. When Jesus was handed over to Pilate as a political prisoner, our Lord said, "My kingdom is not of this world" (John 18:36). But if the accusation brought against him—that he was a political agitator—had been true, he would likely have had the support of his accusers.

Another source of trouble for Jesus was his revolutionary approach to the Jewish law. He cut through all the undergrowth and went to the heart of the matter. He showed a merciful disregard for restrictions against healing on the Sabbath. To Jesus, people were more important than rules. He followed that truth to his own hurt.

There were many places along the road to the cross where Jesus could have taken an alternate route and escaped crucifixion. After the raising of Lazarus, the attitude of the officials of the Jewish religion was crystallized: Jesus must be put to death (John 11:47–53). With the coming of the Greeks to inquire about him, Jesus recognized that his Crucifixion was at hand (John 12:23, 27).

Again, in his prayer for his disciples, Jesus indicated his dedication to his destiny. "For their sakes I sanctify myself" (John 17:19). His devotion to his disciples and to their needs impelled him to accept the will of God at whatever cost.

II. *The opponents he met.* The Pharisees were among Jesus' earliest enemies. The Gospels give us an accurate picture of the Pharisees in conflict with Jesus. But we may easily get the wrong idea about their usual character. The Pharisees were perhaps the best people of the

Jewish community—law abiding, Scripture-loving, and devout. Since this was true, their sin of rejecting and persecuting Jesus was the greater. The sin of the Pharisees is the sin of those today who make up their minds about religion and about right and wrong without a real love for truth. Today we can be reputable churchmen and still make Christ suffer.

After the raising of Lazarus, Caiaphas, the high priest of the Temple at Jerusalem, stepped onto the stage. Politically wise, he saw Jesus as a threat to the uneasy toleration granted the Jews by the Romans. Therefore he said, "It is better for you to have one man die for the people than to have the whole nation destroyed" (John 11:50, NRSV).

His statement, though rightly interpreted as prophecy by Jesus' disciples, was made in cynical unbelief. Caiaphas represents those who put political expediency above moral principle and spiritual truth. We make Christ suffer when we attempt to "use" him to gain a political or personal end rather than allowing him to sit in judgment on all our conditions and ways.

Then Judas appeared, as the tool of the religious authorities. He was the willing instrument of their wrath and for personal reasons betrayed Jesus to them. Whether Judas hoped to force the hand of Jesus and cause him to declare his messianic kingship or just disdainfully tried to express his disappointment by getting what he could through his betrayal matters little. He did betray his Lord! And it was for a purely personal reason.

Thus Judas lives again. His deed is reenacted by everyone whose attitude toward Christ is decided only on the basis of "What will I get out of him?" If he does not answer our prayers the way we like, or exempt us from suffering, sorrow, and hardship, we may be willing to sell him to his enemies and take our place among the scoffers.

III. *The cross he endured.* As the commonest criminal, Jesus went forth toward "the place of a skull," bearing his cross. On that day three crosses were raised on Calvary, with Jesus on the middle cross. But how different the suffering the three men endured! The two unnamed men died for their own sins, and Jesus died for the sins of the world.

John does not delineate the character and behavior of the two who died with Jesus. But a combination of details in the other Gospels would tell us that at first both men were bitter and insulting toward Jesus, and then one man repented and declared his faith in Jesus as the Christ. Thus three types of suffering were illustrated on the three crosses.

1. *Futile suffering.* The agonies of one man bore no moral or spiritual fruit. His pain only increased his resentment, confirmed his unbelief, and hardened his heart. Paul spoke of "worldly grief that produces death" (2 Cor. 7:10, NRSV), and here it was demonstrated.

2. *Chastening suffering.* According to Luke's account, one of the men who died with Jesus was moved by suffering to acknowledge his crime and his punishment. Also, he said concerning Jesus, "This man has done nothing wrong" (Luke 23:41, NRSV). Then he turned to the Lord, asking to be remembered when he came into his kingdom (Luke 23:42). Evidently the man experienced "godly grief [that] produces a repentance that leads to salvation" (2 Cor. 7:10, NRSV).

The human body is so made that pain protects it against harm. Our spiritual nature is closely linked with our physical body; physical pain can be used to bring about a change in one's spiritual condition.

The psalmist said, "Before I was afflicted I went astray: but now I keep your word" (Psalm 119:67, NKJV). Martin Luther, the great reformer, confessed that afflictions were his best teachers. Thus one of the men on the crosses learned, through suffering, of his spiritual need and found in his desperation that Jesus Christ was willing to give him more help and hope than he dared ask for. "Today you will be with me in paradise," was his promise (Luke 23:43, NRSV).

3. *Redemptive suffering.* The suffering of Jesus was due not to his own sins but to the sins of others. Because he was totally committed to the will of God in the kind of world that is not so committed, Jesus suffered. God overruled it. He turned tragedy into triumph. He made the cross the means by which repentant sinners could get rid of their sins. Through the victory of the cross, past guilt is forgiven, present temptations are overcome, and in the future life every trace of sin will be removed. Jesus' suffering was thus described in Isaiah 53:5–6.

Paul in his letter to the Romans wrote of Jesus Christ as the one whom God set forth as his means of dealing redemptively with sin through faith in his blood (Rom. 3:25). The mysteries of the cross of Christ we shall never be able completely to unravel. But the power of the cross we cannot deny.

A woman who had been loose with her morals now believes in the Christ of the cross and testifies that "though your sins are like scarlet, they shall be like snow" (Isa. 1:18, NRSV) and begins to know the meaning of purity and purpose. An irresponsible drunkard seeks the help of the one who died for him, and his life becomes disciplined and useful. A pious hypocrite who thinks himself better than his neighbors gets a good look at the cross and realizes it was his sins that nailed Jesus there, and he confesses his pride and offers a hand of help to needy sinners. The cross is the explanation.

IV. *The purpose he accomplished.* Sometimes when "the good die young," people say, "What a waste! What a tragedy that one so young and so promising is snatched away before he has really begun to live." However, our Lord was little more than thirty years old when his enemies nailed him to the cross. Even so, Jesus said in his prayer as he faced crucifixion, "I have glorified you on the earth: I have finished the work which you have given me to do" (John 17:4).

It is not so important that we fulfill all our personal ambitions, nor that we make good all the fond expectations of our parents and friends. The really important thing is that we do the work God has given us to accomplish. This a little child may be able to do before it can even walk. But with more meaning, responsible men and women, who choose their course, are able to fulfill God's plan, even through great difficulties and at terrific cost.

What happened to Jesus on the cross was typical of all that went before in his life and manifested the same resignation to the will of God. In the last anguished minutes he said, "I thirst" (John 19:28). After receiving a drink of vinegar, in final release he said, "It is finished" (v. 30) and died. All his responsibilities on earth had been completely discharged. He was now ready to leave the scene where he had wrought great things in the Father's name.

This Jesus did for each one of us. You can know in your life the power and purpose of God and have all your sins forgiven if you accept the death of Jesus on the cross as the price of your salvation.—James W. Cox

Topic: What Does Christ Desire for Us?
TEXT: John 17

Jesus had to pray, as we must pray. His divine sonship did not exempt him from his human needs.

Pressures of temptation came from inside and from outside. For example, on the outside lay the kingdoms of the world. On the inside the voice of Satan was heard saying "Worship me, and these are yours." For such reasons, our Lord needed to pray.

But there were other reasons why he prayed. He loved his disciples, and he was concerned about how they would fare amid all their temptations.

In our Lord's moving prayer of intercession, he voiced his deepest desires for his followers of all times, and his petitions from the basis of this message.

I. *Filled with joy.* Jesus felt in his soul the anguish of the world's hatred. With one so sensitive to human need and to the feelings of those about him, it could not have been otherwise. Nevertheless, though "he was despised, and we esteemed him not" (Isa. 53:3), he knew the meaning of joy in his life. He was victorious in defeat, "a conqueror in chains," and king upon a cross. This he was because he had utter confidence in God, because he was certain the cause he represented would win, and because of "the joy that was set before him" (Heb. 12:2).

Jesus prayed that those who loved him might have a full measure of the joy that was his (John 17:13). Paul the apostle, one of the most ill-treated of men, knew this joy. It was his when the scourge whipped his back and made the blood run. It was his when stones buffeted his body and he was left outside the city for dead. It was his when hunger and thirst, infirmity and weakness assailed him. Even from prison, Paul was able to commend to other Christians suffering for Christ what he himself had found to be true: "Rejoice in the Lord always: and again I say, Rejoice" (Phil. 4:4).

Happiness often depends on everything about us going well, but joy depends only on the trustworthiness of God. Trust God and his purpose anywhere, anytime, and joy is yours.

II. *Kept from evil.* The great problem for our spiritual growth is not the presence of evil about us but rather our getting involved with this evil. Sin and hatred were all about Jesus, but he was "without sin" (Heb. 4:15). He has given his love and the love of the church, the Christian fellowship itself, the Bible, and the Holy Spirit to uphold our spiritual life. By belonging to him, we belong to a different world (v. 16), and wherever we are, his love reaches out or down to keep us.

III. *Set apart by truth.* Our special standing with God can be real or an illusion. It is the will of Christ that we be "sanctified [consecrated, RSV] through the truth" (v. 19).

We can be mistaken as to our relationship to God. We can base it on many false hopes. We can imagine that a special ancestry makes us right with God. We can place confidence in our power or beliefs to give us spiritual security. Or we can feel that a weak attachment to a church is a guarantee of salvation.

Many people in Jesus' day mistakenly believed that because they had descended from Abraham they stood in a place of special favor with God. Some of them thought that their riches were a further indication of divine grace.

There is only one way to the sanctification or consecration that Jesus prayed for his followers to have. It is to belong to God by loving and serving Christ, God's Son. It comes not by bearing a name but by having an experience.

To make this possible, Jesus sanctified himself (v. 19). This means that he presented himself to God as an offering for the people. Therefore, if we are truly identified with Christ, we can lay claim to God. In Christ, God claims us as his own.

IV. *United in God.* The fact that the followers of the Lord Jesus Christ have a certain standing with God means they must have a certain relationship to one another. Jesus prayed that "they may be one" (John 17:22).

It is plain that there are some ways in which all Christians can never be united. It is impossible for everyone's understanding of truth to be the same. It is impossible that the history in which the denominations arose can be rewritten. It is impossible that those who appreciate their spiritual liberty should consent to being ruled in a single superchurch.

However, a deep, underlying spiritual unity is possible among all who love the Lord, regardless of denominational loyalties. One great church organization with all Christians as members would not guarantee unity. But a common love for a common Savior can be strong and effective without erasing the denominations in which Christians group themselves. It was for spiritual unity, rather than for organizational union, that Jesus prayed.

Let us apply this in our own situations. Can we disagree with other Christians without being disagreeable? Can we stand for our convictions without acting piously superior? Can we love our own beliefs without making fun of others'? If we cannot show a spirit of love in all these situations, then something may be radically wrong with us. We must remember the words of Paul: "Though I have all faith, so that I could remove mountains, and have not charity, I am nothing" (1 Cor. 13:2).

Jesus indicated in his prayer that a deep motive for Christian oneness is this: "that the world may believe that you have sent me" (John 17:21, NRSV). How can we make the greatest impact on the unbelieving world unless we, as professed Christians, show greater love for one another?

V. *With Christ in glory.* To those willing to walk with him, take up their crosses, and suffer persecution with him, Jesus gave of his glory. Our Lord, we remember, referred to his Crucifixion as his glorification. Actually, he was glorified in all the events that led up to the cross—glorified in spite of and in the midst of personal humiliation and the unbelief of the people. In that glory, the disciples were partakers (v. 22).

Jesus expressed in his prayer his will that those who belonged to him be with him to enjoy his glory forever. Thus the experience begins now and is fulfilled in the life to come: "And we all, with unveiled face, beholding the glory of the Lord, are being changed into his likeness from one degree of glory to another" (2 Cor. 3:18, RSV).—James W. Cox

SECTION V

MESSAGES FOR FUNERALS AND BEREAVEMENT: AN ODYSSEY OF CONSOLATIONS

BY ALBERT J. D. WALSH

Topic: Be Comforted
Funeral Meditation for John D. ("Jack") Woltemate
TEXT: Matt. 5:1–5

When Jesus saw the crowds, he went up the mountain; and after he sat down, his disciples came to him. Then he began to speak, and taught them, saying: "Blessed are the poor in spirit, for theirs is the kingdom of heaven. Blessed are those who mourn, for they will be comforted. Blessed are the meek, for they will inherit the earth. . . ."

There's something desperately wrong with the world in which you and I live. We seem to have more money, more leisure time, more material success, more opportunities for a longer and (despite how we might feel on any given day) far healthier existence. Yet we appear to possess less and less of those things which once made for a more fulfilled and enjoyable lifestyle.

Our families are, literally, coming apart at the seams; good, solid, loyal friendships are harder and harder to come by; neighborhoods, once the realm of safety and comfort, have become confrontational; and the Church, which was once the center of all family activity, has been relegated to a position low on the list of social priorities.

Now, I wouldn't want any one of you to think I'm about to offer a lecture on the demise of contemporary culture. That would never do. I suspect that, in the mystery of God's world, Jack would tell me how little he appreciated my lecturing his family and friends.

But I'm simply trying to set this biblical text from Matthew's Gospel, which we've come to know as "the Beatitudes," in the right context. Despite the effort of Robert Schuller to make them more palatable, calling them the "be-happy-at-titudes"; the words of Jesus will escape many contemporaries.

The world's changed; strength is seen in terms of power, wealth is the measure of well-being, the individual takes precedence over the community, and the wants of self are held to be more important than those of the neighbor-in-need. In this world, Jesus' words seem silly, if not senseless: "Blessed are the poor in spirit, for theirs is the kingdom of heaven. Blessed are those who mourn, for they will be comforted. Blessed are the meek, for they will inherit the earth."

The "poor in spirit," "those who mourn," and "the meek"—not exactly what one could call a list of qualities the world admires. Yet according to Jesus, these are what defines Christian character.

While the world's looking for the wealthy, healthy, and hard-hitters, Jesus searches for his followers from among those who are truly modest; those whose honesty is beyond doubt;

310

those in whom one can confide; those who inwardly weep for the world's woundedness, angered at the injustices perpetrated by political stupidity; those who live graceful and gentle lives. Qualities that were clearly evident in the character of Jack Woltemate.

Someone said that "There's a meekness that's all-powerful and a gentleness that's all strength." In a world threatened by terrorism and enamored with violence, we need gentlemen and gentle-women. We also need those who inwardly shed the tears of a Christlike care, genuinely and graciously for a tragic and broken humanity. Our world desperately needs people who know what it means to "make peace," who demonstrate peaceful living. Jack was one of the gentlest and most genuinely peaceful persons I've ever known.

"Blessed are the poor in spirit . . . those who mourn . . . the meek." What Jesus tells us in these three short proverbs is just this: "First to the [spiritually] dependent, then to the grief stricken, and [also to the gentle of heart], Jesus gives everything: God's kingdom, God's comfort, and God's green earth."

What the rest of the world knows is that it's the self-confident (not the spiritually impoverished), the positive thinkers (not those who long for justice), and the dynamically assertive (not the gentle) who really get things done on earth. Yet I'm convinced Jesus would point to the character of Jack Woltemate as evidence that there's a weakness that is all-powerful, and a modesty that's almighty.

The reformer Martin Luther once wrote that in these three beatitudes we are offered the fruits of faith; he said, "the poor in spirit, the mourners, and the meek are those who choose not to place their trust or hope in anything other than the heart of a gracious God. They trust that God will forever hold them in the hollow of his hand." It's this same faith that—if we've eyes to see, and ears to hear—we witnessed in Jack's life.

We've been blessed with the friendship of a man whose character embodied the very best of the beatitudes. His family can name those characteristics for you, should you ask them. But if you knew Jack, you needn't ask. Jack was tolerant; intelligent, without arrogance; wise, but not opinionated; attentive, but not intrusive; brave, but not a braggart; angered by the unethical and immoral, but never judgmental.

For a time, which now seems far too brief, we were gifted with the presence of a man who demonstrated, in the anguish of his own heart, what it is to be poor in spirit. Jack often told me that he wasn't a very spiritual man. But I disagree.

Jack exemplified the very best of what it means to be truly spiritual, never assuming a right to God's provision. He never took God's grace for granted; never touted the merits of his own best behavior; and despite the injustice of his own personal suffering, I never heard him whimper or so much as whisper an angry word against God.

Jack never complained that he'd somehow been given a raw deal. Yet I often heard Jack mourn for the world's misery. He'd speak of some crisis in the world, or of someone in the church, or of some wounded soul among his circle of family or friends, with genuine compassion in his voice. Without fail, he'd disclose tenderness for those in circumstances far less troubling than his own.

But above all, I'll always remember Jack as the embodiment of what it means to be gentle of heart.

In a world gone mad with hatred, violence, prejudice, greed, and maliciousness, I would come into this gracious man's presence and find my own troubled and anxious soul soothed, quieted, relieved.

It was more than his soft voce, wasn't it? It was his warm, generous heart; held open to each and all of us—friends, family, and followers of Jesus. Whenever I think of Jack I'm reminded, in his dying, as I was in his living, of the passage from Dante's classic, *The Divine Comedy:* "The glory of the One who moves all things permeates the universe and glows in one part more and in another less."

You see what I'm getting at, don't you? If the poet's correct, as I'm certain he is, then Jack was one in whom the glory of God was given to shine with a particular brilliance.

Somehow, in and through some mystery of God's Spirit, Jack's character radiated the light of a love beyond all human production. Sometimes his smile was the sun, burning through the dark clouds of discouragement or disappointment. All an affirmation of God's grace bestowed upon his life, and subsequently upon our lives as well.

To do the will of God, with faithful conviction and constant devotion, requires an immense amount of spirit. In others words, to be a person of God is by definition to be a person of spirit. Who among us could doubt for one minute that Jack Woltemate was a person of spirit?

But not that spirit with which the world is currently enamored; not the spirit of self-gratification, seeking only private gain. Rather, what we were given of God. In Jack Woltemate was a taste of the Spirit of Christ as compassion in our distress, as counsel in our disappoint-ments, as consolation in our losses, as care in our dismay. Always, everywhere, in every way, Jack's faith would pour out from his heart, bringing tranquility to our troubled souls.

Let the world say what it will about the teaching of Jesus. But for those of us who have known and loved this kind, gentle, and loyal man, the words of Jesus have taken on the form of flesh and blood. We should know beyond all doubt.

In Jack we've witnessed that the poor in spirit are a treasure to God.

In Jack we've witnessed that those who mourn do so not so much for themselves as for the state of God's creatures and creation, always hopeful for the healing that God will bring. In Jack we've witnessed the meekness and gentleness of heart that in this world of harsh-ness and hatred gives evidence of God's greater strength of love, which will one day, finally and forever, wash the world clean of such cruelty.

I'm certain Jack would care, deeply, for your present distress. I believe he'd be touched by your tears, and that his shoulder would be given for the comfort of your grief. I believe he'd smile that smile only Jack could smile and remind you that there's a God who loves you, every bit as much as he's loved and loves him.

I believe that if he himself could gift you with words to ease your broken hearts, it'd be this: "Be comforted; my wife, my family, my friends. Be comforted, for I am now at peace with and in the glory of my God; and I'll long for that day when, by God's grace, we meet again." Amen.

Topic: Esau Was a Skillful Hunter
Funeral Meditation for Franklin Fox
TEXT: Gen. 25:27–34, 33:1–12

When [Jacob and Esau] grew to adulthood, Esau was a skillful hunter, a man of the field, while Jacob was a quiet man, living in tents. Isaac [their father] loved Esau, because he was fond of game, but Rebekah [their mother] loved Jacob.

Once when Jacob was cooking a stew, Esau came in from the field, and he was famished. Esau said to Jacob, "Let me eat some of that red stuff, for I am [starving to death]!" Jacob said,

"First sell me your birthright." Esau said, "I am about to die; what use is a birthright to me?" Jacob said, "Swear to me first." So he swore to him, and sold his birthright to Jacob. Then Jacob gave Esau bread and lentil stew, and he ate and drank, and rose and went his way.

The next scene comes after these estranged brothers have been separated for years.

Now Jacob looked up and saw Esau coming, and four hundred [armed] men with him. So he divided the children between [his wives and his maids]. He himself went on ahead of them . . . until he came near his brother [Esau].

But Esau ran to meet him, and embraced him, and fell on his neck and kissed him, and they wept . . . Jacob said, ". . . truly to see your face is like seeing the face of God—since you have received me with such favor. . . ." Then Esau said, "Let us journey on our way, and I will go alongside you."

Earlier this week, in a phone conversation with one of my colleagues, we were discussing our practice of preparation for funerals and memorial services such as this one. She knew I was in the process of preparing for this service, and asked what biblical text I'd selected for the meditation. I told her. There was a long pause before her response; then, before hanging up, she said that she'd look over the text when she had a chance, and call me if she thought she could contribute anything.

The next day she phoned and said, "What! Are you crazy? What in the name of God has that text to do with anything even vaguely related to loss and grief?" My mentioning—in a defensive voice, no less—that it was a *memorial* service and *not* a funeral didn't seem to phase her in the least. She went on to say, "Well, best of luck to you! But I still think you've gone off the deep end!" She again offered me her best wishes and then hung up.

Candidly, I'm somewhat anxious that—having now heard the biblical passages read—some of you may agree with my colleague's assessment of my mental condition. But as my father was fond of saying, the proof is in the pudding. So, I'd ask that you reserve all judgments on my present state of mind until you've joined me in journeying through these wonderfully rich biblical passages. You see, I've discovered in the process of preparing this reflection that these particular biblical storylines hold some amazing insights into the man whose life and character we are here to remember and honor in the process.

When the character of Esau is first introduced to us as an adult, the storyteller identifies him by saying "Esau was a skillful hunter, a man of the field. . . ." Unlike Jacob, his brother, Esau is described as dependent on game for his existence, and more nomadic. That's the basic meaning of the descriptive phrase used to introduce Esau; he "was a skillful hunter, a man of the field."

Not the type of description most would find complimentary. It seems rather bland, almost casual as a phrase used to characterize the essence of a person. Imagine, if you will, a conversation: "Well, I never really knew Esau, but I'm certain he'll be missed." To which the other responds, "Missed! More than that, I'm sure. Why Ol' Esau was a skillful hunter, a man of the field."

It's not a tribute to make you sit up and take notice, is it? Certainly not the kind of praise one would expect to read in the society page of the *New York Times:* "The late Mr. Esau will long be remembered; he was a skillful hunter, a man of the field." Chances are, if someone held our feet to the fire, I think we'd hope to be remembered for some characteristic and contribution of far greater significance, wouldn't we? Something more like, "She was truly remarkable in her creative ability." Or, "His compassion and care for the less fortunate were admirable." Anything but "a skillful hunter, a person familiar with the field."

Perhaps that's why my colleague thought me a bit daft for selecting these passages for this memorial. I don't know.

What I do know is that the authors of our Bible stories are seldom casual in their selection and use of words and phrases used to characterize people and places. To say of Esau that he was a skillful hunter and a man of the field is anything but incidental to the portrayal of something significant in his character that was to be honored, if not emulated. In other words, this description is the storyteller's way of framing Esau as a man who appreciated the gifts God had given him and who used those gifts to make the best possible provision for his wife and his family.

It should be obvious to each of you that the most glaring association that could be made between the person of Esau and Frank would be that of hunter. I suppose there'd be merit in drawing that parallel. Yet in short order I'll share with you how my reflections have taken me in a somewhat different direction. But first, and on a less serious note, there are other similarities one could make between Frank and Esau.

Evidently Esau was a man who made no bones about his hearty appetite. For heaven's sake, he was willing to barter his birthright for a bowl of Jacob's famous red stew! I don't suppose Frank ever went so far as to barter a new car for chocolate ice cream, or his camper for a choice sirloin. But we all know how Frank would never shy away from a good meal. Family and friends have testified to Frank's love of food.

In fact, the other day Barry mentioned how one of his father's favorite responses to a good meal was by saying (and correct me if I get it wrong here, Barry) "luuuuushish!" That about says it all. But I wonder if Frank didn't enjoy and appreciate even more the company that so often comes with eating. Maybe he felt that—when it was still a common practice—food time was also family time. Regardless, his love of food was another indication of a man whose heart could rejoice in the simpler pleasures of life and desire that these moments of joy be shared with others as well.

Do you recall the wording Esau used in begging his brother for a bowl of stew? He said—in referring to his growling belly—"I'm starving to death!" Now there's someone prone to extreme exaggeration. I bet Esau could weave some very incredible stories whenever he and his hunting buddies gathered round the campfire. "Yeah, I once brought three deer down with one arrow—clean through their hearts!" Of course, I'm not suggesting that Frank was prone to such extreme exaggeration.

Yet I'd remind you that Frank also loved fishing. And we fishermen have honed the art of exaggeration to a sharp edge. A dime will get you a dollar that the fish Frank caught on some of his outings with the gang grew at least seven inches from catch to campfire chatter. I was also told that Frank loved telling a good story. Good storytellers also know the importance of exaggeration for emphasis. Do you think, maybe, in the presence of the Lord, Frank will one day be encouraged to tell some of those same stories? Even though Gladys will know by heart where the story is headed, I'm certain the angels of God will take delight in the telling.

On a more serious note, Esau's being described as a skillful hunter and a man of the field is intended to suggest his deep and abiding reverence for the beauty and glory of God's good

Earth. Few things have changed. As any contemporary of Esau will tell you, a skilled hunter isn't simply someone who knows how to track and kill game. A skilled hunter is one who recognizes how all life and all creatures are to be respected; a skilled hunter will honor the code of God's created order; a skilled hunter will never abuse or mistreat creatures, great or small. I'm certain Frank taught his son and grandson that hunting comes with responsibility for the care of God's creatures and creation as well.

I mentioned earlier that Esau is also being honored as a man who made more-than-adequate provision for his wife and family. Clearly, Frank Fox worked hard to make provision for his wife and family, both in the job he held and in his gun shop. Those of you who were customer's of Frank's trade know he was a man whose word could be trusted, and he gave freely from the wealth of his expertise and experience, often charging less when he could have demanded far more.

Now, do you recall the second story read? It was the account of the first meeting of Jacob and Esau after years apart. This was the first time that these two estranged brothers would cross paths. Having taken Esau's birthright in exchange for a bowl of stew, Jacob had no idea how his brother would react to his return. I would think he probably expected Esau to flash in a fit of rage; perhaps Jacob feared that Esau might destroy his entire family. Fortunately, none of what Jacob might have expected to happen did take place.

In fact, what did happen must have been an even greater shock to Jacob's system, because as he approached his alienated brother, "Esau ran to meet him, and embraced him, and fell on his neck and kissed him, and they wept." For those of you with more than a passing familiarity with the Gospels, that account should send up some red flags. You remember the story of the two sons—the one who squanders the father's wealth, burns out, and returns home to the father he's dishonored? Recall what the story says the father did when he saw the son at a distance: "His father saw him and was filled with compassion for him; he ran to his son, threw his arms around him and kissed him." Again, the similarity of imagery is hardly unintentional.

So, what was the fundamental, deep-down, rock-bottom, defining characteristic of Esau as a person of God? This much I can tell you: he was far more than a skillful hunter and a man of the field! Esau was large of heart, forgiving and gentle in his judgments, reverent enough to get beyond resentment, strong enough to be humble, humble enough to be kind, and kind enough to demonstrate care for his cowering brother. Whenever I remember Frank Fox, I'll choose to remember him as a person whose life exemplified Esau in these important characteristics.

You must know better than I how Frank's heart was bigger than either his appetite or his love of outdoor sports. The comfort we receive from our Christian faith is in knowing that Frank is forever held in the heart that is larger than all the cosmic realms of space and time. The heart of the God whose love is unending and whose promise is unbroken. The God who will guard your hearts from despair, and heal the present wound of your sorrow.

God assured us, in the Risen and Living Christ, that the day will surely come when he will pitch his tent in the fields of our faith on earth, never again to leave us within this vale of tears. God will wipe all tears from human eyes, and all pain and sorrow and sickness will be no more; and death will be no more; and God will be the light of our unending laughter and the moon of our merriment and joy. We will be reunited with all those who have gone before us in faith. Your beloved brother, husband, father, grandfather, and friend, Frank Fox, will be there as well.

I believe you'll know his frame, his gait, his great smile. But should you not find him at first, I'd suggest you search for some campfire with a cluster of angels gathered about listening one more time to the tale they've heard a thousand times and still love in the telling—because they love the storyteller himself.

But until that great Day of Resurrection, remember Frank. Remember Frank as a man who did what he could to help others in need. Remember Frank as one who was loyal in his friendships and faithful to his family. Remember Frank as a man who loved life and lived life to the fullest. Remember Frank as the gentle giant, small of voice but large of spirit. Remember Frank as a skillful hunter and a man of the field. Remember Frank as the one who, in his own way, demonstrated faith in his Lord and God. Remember Frank, and in remembering give thanks to God for so precious a gift of grace to you—to us all—in this life. Amen.

Topic: God's Grace in Flesh and Faith
Funeral Meditation for Nancy C. Trefsgar
TEXT: 1 Pet. 4:1–11

You can imagine my dilemma when faced with the prospect of having to select a biblical text for this mediation and eulogy. It's not, as someone who never knew Nancy Trefsgar might imagine, a problem of locating *any* passage of Scripture that could be said to reflect her Christian character. But as those of us who knew, loved, and admired Nancy Trefsgar will understand, it was difficult to select only *one* biblical text that could be said to reflect the very depth of her heart, soul, and spirit as a disciple of Jesus Christ. That, in and of itself, is a remarkable witness to the way in which Nancy's lifestyle demonstrated a devotion to Christ that not only touched but often transformed the hearts of family and friends.

I've titled this meditation "God's grace in flesh and faith" for reasons beyond those we normally associate with catchy sermon titles. It might seem to some gathered here to be little more than the exaggerated commentary of a typical preacher. But I assure those who might think this way that the observation I'm about to share is demonstrated in countless forms and in the world all around you, each day and every day, if only you have the "eyes to see and the ears to hear."

This world is slowly becoming an almost intolerable mess of what another has rightly called *me-ism,* where the first casualty of a perverted sense of self-interest has been those values and qualities of personal character we once held in highest regard. I'm not referring to those extreme forms of this crisis of character, evident in recent corporate scandals.

I'd rather we consider those common everyday experiences often overlooked—for example, the absence of public politeness or common courtesy, the tendency to favor the crass and vulgar, the loss of connectedness in local communities, the failure to keep faith with promises and commitments made, the lack of genuine empathy for those beyond the boundaries of one's own interests.

Where we could once point to the Christian community with assurance that we'd have no difficulty locating people whose devotions, dedications, and decisions were contrary to those of the rest of the world, we find that far too many believers in the contemporary Church are actually in collusion with the prevailing culture rather than with Christ.

For many Christians, worship attendance is optional, often placed dead last on the long list of other priorities. The Bible is seldom read each day, and mostly used as a paper weight.

Even though still high on the *New York Times* best-seller list, one suspects that the Bible is purchased more as a kind of talisman used to ward off any trouble than it is the Word of God used to correct, instruct, and guide living in a way that conforms to the will of our Lord. We blindly wonder what we can do to prevent our children from becoming captive to this culture gone mad with violence, perverted self-interest, and what the Danish Christian philosopher Kierkegaard once tagged a sickness unto death. All the while we fail to commit our lives to faithful worship, daily prayer, and devoted practices in obedience to the Lord in whose name we were once washed and claimed in baptism.

Into this same world, and into your life and my life, the Lord, from the depths of a heart in love, gifted us with Nancy Trefsgar, God's grace in flesh and faith. In this contemporary Church, where anyone can claim the title "Christian," Nancy demonstrated for each of us and all of us what that title truly means when the Christ—from whom we receive the title—has found a home in the heart of the believer. Even though Nancy's heart was to bear such weighty burdens, even though it sometimes surely groaned under the heaviness of it all, she never failed to have faith in Christ.

I recall the day I first discovered the poetic expression that captures the Christian character of Nancy's heart. It was the same afternoon she informed me that her cancer had spread but she trusted Christ to give her the courage to face anything in faith.

I returned to the church office later that day, and, feeling somewhat spiritually exhausted, picked up my copy of works by the sixteenth-century English poet George Herbert. Among the numerous pieces to which I might've been drawn, my eyes fell on one in particular. I read this verse in which Herbert makes use of one Latin translation of the name, "Jesus" (I-ease-oo)

> JESU is in my heart, his sacred name
> Is deeply carved there: but th'other week
> A great affliction broke the little frame,
> Ev'n all to pieces: which I went to seek:
> And first I found the corner, where was *J*,
> After, where *ES*, and next where *U* was graved.
> When I had got these parcels, instantly
> I sat me down to spell them, and perceived
> That to my broken heart he was *I ease you,*
> And to my whole [self] is JESU.

"And to my whole [self] is JESU"—Jesus. It's a confession, you see, an affirmation of the form of faith that can withstand even the most severe personal storm. It's evident in those saints of God whose hearts beat with the pulse of his blessings. It's the conviction with which our sister Nancy lived her life, shared her love, and displayed the dignity of grace that Christ alone confers on our otherwise contrary human nature. Nancy loved her garden, her flowers, and her yard. She knew that a fruitful garden required constant care. Like that, she also gave her heart each day to the Lord she loved, so that he might root his own sacred life deeper and deeper in the soils of her soul.

It was her heart given to the enthronement of Christ as Lord of her life that enabled Nancy to see the world as the wonder God intended it to be. You recall how frequently Nancy used that one simple, three-syllable word *wonderful?* Even though life did its best to beat up and bruise her heart and soul, Nancy continued to view the world as if it were the realm of God's playful delight, the sphere in which even the simplest pleasure disclosed the Lord's desire to awaken us to what matters most in the world.

In a personal gift—a devotional given by her daughter and namesake—Nancy had marked one particular passage. The words come as close as we can now get to hearing her own voice. The passage reads: ". . . if we can open our eyes, we can find all kinds of blessings, both big and small, in and about our lives. Many we take for granted; some we ignore; others we may have forgotten."

Nancy Trefsgar used that three-syllable word *wonderful* to express what only the eyes of faith can see: that every flower, every human soul, every puff of cloud, every child's chocolate smile, every cool mountain breeze, every moment of love and laughter with family or friends is somehow radiant with the touch of God's hand and the providential intent of his own divine heart. Even the simple pleasure of running her feet through the grass, while visiting Tony and her sister Barbara, was for Nancy a moment to pause and give praise to God.

Yet Nancy's faith was not in nature; surely not in the best of *human* nature. Her faith was of such a kind that she fully understood there to be no clearer, nor more compelling, manifestation of God's beauty than that which can be seen in Christ Jesus. Nancy's faith was of a depth seldom found in the contemporary church, and I believe that her devotion to Christ exemplified the words of Gerard Manley Hopkins:

> Be our delight, O Jesus, now
> As by and by our prize art Thou,
> And grant our glorying may be
> World without end alone in Thee.

For me, there is no more profound example of the centrality of Christ in her life than Nancy's expressed desire to dine at his table. I've seldom witnessed a disciple whose life had become plagued with pain with a greater hunger for the Eucharist. There was never an occasion when Nancy refused this communion with the real presence of her Lord and Savior.

Well, on a less dramatic note, Nancy never missed the opportunity to tell me how much she enjoyed that "wonderful" wine! But I'd venture to guess that what was more at the heart of her request was the keen sense of her Savior's presence, of the way in which this same sacrament connected her with her brothers and sisters here at Heidelberg, and with the saints in all time and beyond time, including now her beloved Ted.

You'll remember that among the characteristics of the faithful Christian heart, as listed in First Peter, is this: "Above all, maintain constant love for one another, for love covers a multitude of sins." John Calvin wrote that the author of First Peter encourages love that is fervent, intense, even vehement. That's strong language. But, like the author of First Peter, Calvin is commending such love on account of its fruit, because it buries innumerable sins. Such love is expressed in words that are kind, courteous, thoughtful, uplifting, forgiving, and gracious. Nothing, writes Calvin, is more necessary than to cherish mutual love: "For who is there that has not many faults? Therefore all stand in need of forgiveness, and there is no one who does not wish to be forgiven. This singular benefit love brings to us when it exists among us, so that innumerable evils are covered in oblivion."

This is the form of love that we witnessed take on flesh and faith in and through the Christian character of Nancy Trefsgar. Nancy spoke in the same saintly language, with love for family, friends, and brothers and sisters in Christ. But it was far more than love spoken.

Nancy's depth of commitment to Christ, her genuine integrity of character, her real dignity, and her Christian love prevented her from ever speaking an unkind, critical, or scandalous word against or about another. She refused to pander in that favorite pastime of Christians we call gossip; and she understood her speech to reflect what was ever and truly in her heart. When I asked the family members what they thought Nancy might say were she able to leave us with a word today, they each responded with phrases like "keep faith," or "trust God," or "do all in love." Her words were sacred and her voice was soft. Her every action was radiant with that form of love no human heart can fabricate, and only Christ can create in faith.

Nancy held the conviction that our lives are always guided by God's providential design. Nothing is given to chance. There's no fate ruling the regular routines of our day; God watches over the whole course of our lives, as he does the entire creation. It takes a profound sense of sacred order to adhere to such a faith conviction. I recall asking Nancy if she felt as though God had some part in her sickness. Without pause she said, "Oh come on, Pastor, you know better than that! Besides, God has given me so many wonderful gifts in this life." She was thoughtful for a moment, and then enumerated, "My Ted, my children, my sisters, my friends, my church and the people, my pastor, so many wonderful gifts. *No*," she said, "you take life as it comes, and thank God for all the good gifts." That's just it, you see: God's grace in flesh and faith.

In that same devotional from which I quoted earlier are these words:

> I wish to give you a gift—
> Something you might not give yourself.
> To lift your spirit and refresh you.
> To encourage and cheer your heart. . . .
> Although I can't give you a year, or a month, or a week;
> I'd like to give you a moment. . . .

That's exactly how it now seems to us, I'm sure, as if it were a moment. But thanks be to God; what a moment it was! A moment in which her sisters were touched by tenderness, loyalty, devotion, and care. A moment in which her children and grandchildren were enfolded in a supreme expression of unconditional love. A moment in which her friends and neighbors received the warmth and wealth of Nancy's generous heart. A moment in which the members of this church were gifted with a true friend in the Lord, who shared their burdens, prayed for their needs, and served with devotion in the cause of Christ.

We both know that Nancy would not want this meditation to close without a hopeful and positive word of faith. Although I would make that word a direct reflection of Nancy's faith, she would—I'm certain—scold me if the praise were given her rather than God. So, to avoid a scolding when I come to that grand place where Nancy and Ted now take their rest, I'll leave you with this verse. Hold it in your own hearts, as it expresses the conviction by which this fine, gracious, hospitable, and caring woman lived, and the hope to which she held firm in faith, even to the end:

Seek God's house in happy throng;
Crowded let His table be;
Mingle praises, prayer, and song,
Singing to the Trinity.
Henceforth let your souls always
Make each morn an Easter Day.
Amen.

Topic: A Certain Charm
Funeral Meditation for Nancy Woltemate
Text: Eccles. 26:1–4, 16

As is my practice following the death of a loved one, I asked John, David, and Carol to name the one characteristic their mother possessed that defined her. The timing was too close to the loss, but with the kind of courage and honest response I would expect from those raised by Jack and Nancy, they did their best to answer. They said that their mother was "generous," "thoughtful," "loving and supportive"—but "mostly Mom!" What would you say in response to that same question? What is the one characteristic that *you* think defined Nancy Woltemate?

You know, of course, that in short order I'm going to do my very best to tell you how I would answer that same question. But there's always a difference for those of us who hold office as pastor in a local church. Almost without exception, when we think of those defining characteristics of one of our beloved congregants, we do so in terms of the categories evident in sacred Scripture. That's primarily because we are persuaded that the Bible genuinely reflects every facet of what it means to be human, from the admirable to the ignoble. So here's the passage I selected as representative of Nancy's character:

Happy is the husband of a good wife;
the number of his days will be doubled.
A loyal wife brings joy to her husband,
And he will complete his years in peace.
A good wife is a great blessing;
She will be granted among the blessings of
The one who fears the LORD.
Whether rich or poor, his heart is content,
And at all times his face is cheerful. . . .
Like the sun rising in the heights of
The LORD, so is the beauty of a good wife
In her well-ordered home.

As you can tell from the bulletin, I've titled this eulogy "A Certain Charm." I had considered entitling it "A Charmed Life." But it seems to be unimportant to the end result. Perhaps charm isn't a characteristic you would've associated with Nancy. Or if you did, maybe it was in the more social and familiar sense of the word. But I'd suggest that, in honoring the memory of Nancy, we consider charm to be something more than a character trait—even her most important characteristic. That's why the title is as it is (or as it might have been). Nancy's life disclosed a "certain"—a particular—"charm."

Webster's *New World Dictionary* defines the word *charm* as "the quality of being graceful." My reason for choosing the passage from Ecclesiasticus is because it too speaks of the charmed life as the graceful life. In this way the author follows the line of reasoning in all wisdom literature.

Someone who lives a charmed life is someone who is good—meaning, a kind, thoughtful, generous soul. Someone who is loyal, meaning steadfast, constant in care, true to every promise spoken. Someone whose life is a blessing to others, meaning someone whose living touches others with joy and encouragement. Someone who brings contentment to the lives of those loved. Someone whose life discloses a particular beauty, meaning someone whose living reveals the characteristics of the faithful and noble soul: love, joy, peace, kindness, generosity, faithfulness, gentleness, and self-control. To the author of our text, these are the emblems of a charmed life.

Perhaps you already know that the root of the English word is found in the Greek of the New Testament. The word used in the Gospels and the letters of the apostle Paul is *charisma.* What you probably do not know, unless you've studied the origins of New Testament languages, is that throughout the Gospels and the writings of Paul the word *charisma* is always associated with one of three words used to express love. The Greek of the New Testament differentiates among *eros* (the love of passion), *philia* (the love of friendship), and *agape* (that form of holy love seen most clearly in the life of Jesus Christ).

In nearly every instance where either the Gospel writers or the apostle Paul refers to charisma, it is always in relation to agape. The love of passion and the form of love evident between friends are never associated with charisma—that is to say, with charm.

Only agape—unearthly love, the gift of God's Holy Spirit, planted in the human heart and soul parallels charisma (charm). In other words, in the teaching of the early Christian community all charm was also and always a manifestation of the holy love first disclosed in the life and character of Christ.

Yet even the dictionary has somehow gotten it right when it refers to charm as the quality of *being* graceful. Many of us have had the experience of being in the presence of someone who can *act* charming. My first infatuation came at the age of twelve. Her name was Barbara, and we spent every Saturday together. It never failed: every time Barbara would leave to go home, while watching her walk away my mother would say, "She's a real charmer!" I thought it was a great compliment, until I discovered that Barbara had several other admirers waiting in the wings! With some people, charm is synonymous with less attractive qualities.

There are those who claim to be able to teach and perfect the practice of charm. I find it difficult to watch beauty contestants because their charm always appears contrived. The charm they are said to have always seems to me to be about as genuine as their pledge to end world famine. Charm is treated as a commodity to be purchased along with one's gown and swimsuit.

When I remember Nancy Woltemate, I will always remember a woman whose charm was nothing less than "a quality of being." Nancy did not merely act charming; she *was* charisma. You recall how deeply sensitive Nancy was; I suppose some would even say that she was hypersensitive. The other day one of Nancy's adult children said that Nancy would "cry at almost anything." Then they all said something that I also recall Jack once saying. Apparently he would say, fondly, that Nancy was so sensitive she'd even cried at "store openings"!

Now, we all know that to be tongue-in-cheek. But we who knew, loved, and admired this woman also know that her deep sensitivity to the pain of others was indicative of an empathic heart. In this world that has become so callous, so indifferent to human suffering, Nancy's heart was bruised because she felt the pain of others with intensity and sympathy. That's one manifestation of a charmed life. Nancy's heart, which held and often expressed a Christlike love, would willingly feel the hurt of another human being.

The same charm was evident in her sociability. You and I both know that Nancy wasn't sociable for the sake of appearance; she was sociable because she had a keen interest in people. She was curious, always pushing against the edges of any conversation to discover a deeper meaning or truth. Even her curiosity was shaped and informed by a certain fascination with life; it was her zeal for and love of life that fueled Nancy's desire to discover, to read, to explore, to learn, to stretch, to grow.

Shortly after those horrific events of September 11, 2001, I preached a sermon on forgiveness. Following worship, and coming through the greeting line, Nancy stated that she wasn't quite sure she agreed with what I'd said, or at least she wanted to explore the issue further. When I visited with her, we talked at great length about the ethics of forgiveness. I wish I could say that my argument was persuasive. But I'll tell you what she said. She said: "Well, I don't have to agree. But you just keep holding our feet to the fire. Maybe we need to change; maybe I need to change the way I think and feel." Nancy's openness and genuine willingness to have her mind changed is no less a demonstration of a charmed life than the testimony of our greatest saints in the Christian faith, who all lived with an honesty born of humility.

We also know that Nancy could worry better than the most proficient nervous Nelly. I suppose there are some who'd assess that character trait as excessive, perhaps even harmful. But I'll differ. I don't believe that this characteristic was evidence of a deep insecurity so much as it was another demonstration of the depth of Nancy's concern, and the tendency to put the needs of others before her own. You'll recall that—at least in the biblical sense—charm is always associated with agapic (self-giving) love. Nancy worried as she did because her first concern was always for the welfare of others—her family first, and then her friends.

Carol shared the recollection of coming home much too late from a date, fearing that her mother would be waiting. She arrived home to find the lights out, but while gingerly making her way up the stairs suddenly she heard her mother say, "I'm glad you're still alive!" Nancy's worry was her way of demonstrating a deliberate care for those she loved.

The heart that wanted only the best for her children, and then her grandchildren, touched each of us with a similar gracefulness demonstrated as a desire to protect those most precious to her. The last time I heard Nancy's voice, she was inquiring after my wife, Kathlene's, condition, and then Nancy requested that I tell Kathy that she would be kept in her own prayers. This was coming from a woman who'd been suffering from a series of physical complications for months! That, too, is the expression of a charmed life.

It was Martin Luther who once said that "charisma [charm] is most evident in those who use every gift God has given to love family, friends, and faithful without judgment and without reserve." Whether within the boundary of her immediate family or the larger world of work and worship, Nancy Woltemate loved "family, friends, and faithful without judgment and without reserve." Nancy's charm was a quality of being, the essence of her heart and soul—her being—her*self*.

In fact, when I consider Nancy's having lived a charmed life—again, in the biblical sense of that phrase—I recall the poetic words of Victor Hugo:

> Be like the bird
> That pausing in her flight
> Awhile on boughs too slight,
> Feels them give way
> Beneath her and yet sings,
> Knowing that she hath wings.

Nancy's life—since the death of her beloved Jack—was filled with moments of great joy and profound personal struggle. Yet through it all she continued to join her voice to those of the other choir members in our church. Only recently I asked her why she continued to sing with the choir, particularly in light of all that she'd been through; she said, "I suppose it's my way of worshiping God!" I don't think Nancy had any idea how profoundly true that statement was, because humility resides at the heart of all genuine charisma—all true charm.

I believe that as Nancy felt the slim and tenuous bough of life slip from beneath her on Tuesday afternoon, her spirit suddenly found voice in song, as she sank into the outstretched arms of the Lord she'd served so faithfully in this life—thinking them to be her own wings. She is now at peace, and I am certain that the prayer of this charmed soul is that you—those whom she has loved and treasured—will also come to know the comfort Christ gives. Amen.

Topic: Palette, Paint, and a Work of Art
Funeral Meditation for Sara E. Swartley
TEXT: 1 Cor. 13:13

It was the apostle Paul who first penned those words that have ever since been represented in every artistic form imaginable: "So now faith, hope, and love abide, these three; but the greatest of these is love" (1 Cor. 13:13). Words and the poetic twist of a phrase create a thought that seems to have taken on a life of its own. In fact, even those unfamiliar with the body of sacred Scripture can name the triumvirate: faith, hope, and love. Three words chiseled in granite, splashed on a canvas, embroidered on cloth. Together they seem to speak to something deep in the human heart and soul. "So now faith, hope, and love abide, these three; but the greatest of these is love."

The apostle wants his readers to focus on a particular form of love; a love that came into this world from beyond the boundary markers of space and time. This love took on flesh and blood and bone; this love, which came directly from the heart of God, took human form in Jesus Christ. So that, when Paul writes of this *love*, he has in mind the single image of our Savior!

This is the first, the extraordinary, miracle of our God: that his divine love, eternal in its content and enthralling in its character, should become human. Recall the affirmation of the first letter of John: "In this the love of God was made manifest among us, that God sent his only Son into the world so that we might have life through him."

As a result of that unique event there was another miracle. This same divine love would now find expression in the hearts and souls of those who placed undisputed *faith* and determined *hope* in this Christ as the Savior and Lord of their lives. John again: "Beloved, if God so loved us, we also ought to love one another. No one has ever seen God; if we love one another, God abides in us and his love is perfected in us."

Perhaps we've become so familiar with these biblical phrases that they no longer startle with the sheer beauty they convey. Just think about the final phrase: "God abides in us and his love is perfected in us." John might as well have said that the oceans can be contained in a thimble!

Nevertheless, the unmistakable miracle and incomparable beauty God created time and again—since the first advent of our Savior—is witnessed in that fact: "God abides in us and his love if perfected in us!"

No doubt we could each of us enumerate the characteristics of Sara Swartley that we found remarkable: her courage in the face of otherwise insurmountable obstacles; her tenacious hold on survival, not because she feared death but rather because she relished and revered life; her sense of humor, evident most often in her cheeky responses, or in one of those lighthearted verbal exchanges for which Sara and Austin are noted; her graciousness, even as she suffered from one physical complication after another; her warm smile, which was the hallmark of her hospitable heart; or Sara's gift as an artist, a gift with which she touched the lives of friends and family alike. We could name others.

But I find it noteworthy that Sara wanted to be remembered not so much for any one of those characteristics mentioned, or for all of them together and more. Above all the other characteristics we might select, Sara apparently wanted us to remember her as one whose life gave witness to the wonder of God's love in our world. I assume that to be the case, because it was Sara who chose to have the passage from First Corinthians as the basis for this eulogy and remembrance.

So perhaps there is no more fitting tribute to the memory of Sara Swartley than to affirm that her Christian character embodied the love for God expressed in and through the confines of one gentle, caring, and strong human heart. Yet I hope that you will forgive me if I now seem a bit presumptuous, and I pray that when next I see her in the Kingdom of our God Sara will not scold me too severely for what I am about to say.

I believe that the incomparable character of this fine Christian woman can been seen in its complete beauty only when we acknowledge that Sara Swartley's artistic ability went well beyond the capacity to cover a canvas with color and form and interpreted image. In the deepest sense of the word, Sara plied her artistic ability in every relationship she had: with Austin, family, friends, and brothers and sisters in Christ.

Please do not misunderstand me; I do not mean to imply that whenever Sara engaged us as family or friend, she did so simply in some surface fashion. That would be a grave injustice to this caring woman, who gave so freely, graciously, and generously of herself to every relationship. But I also believe that there is a sense in which we *can* speak of Sara's having treated our lives—each of us and all of us who were touched by her—as a kind of canvas.

Once I told Sara that my brother is an artist, and that I'd watched him prepare and then treat his canvas. I told her that Patrick treated the canvas with the same careful devotion and attention I'd witnessed parents giving their child. Do you recall how she would nod and smile as if to let you know she understood something important you were sharing with her? Well, when I spoke of my brother's treatment of his canvas, she nodded *that* nod and smiled *that* smile! She knew *exactly* what I meant.

On October 15 of the year 1923, God prepared a canvas called Sara E. Duke. On that canvas God painted a gracious, bright, insightful, creative, fun-loving, life-affirming, loyal, friendly, and all-too-generous character. Then, on April 13 of the following year God added the bright colors and the rich image of Christ to Sara's character in and through the sacrament of baptism.

In the years that followed God continued to add depth and the subtle shades of spiritual embellishment to this same canvas that was Sara. Then one day, God took palette in hand and with the vibrant colors of care and love painted across the canvas of Sara's life the image of Austin, the one with whom Sara would share love for nearly sixty years.

But please don't think that all of these characteristics and traits were merely etched onto the surface of Sara's life. Rather, think of it this way: the canvas that was Sara E. Swartley, with all of those rich colors and vibrant images we enjoyed, disclosed what was also and always there in the very depths of Sara's heart and soul. If we would see exactly what it was that God created on the canvas of Sara's character, and therefore in the depths of her soul, her self, it would be disclosed in the brilliant colors of the apostle Paul's poetic phrase: "So now, faith, hope, and love abide, these three; but the greatest of these is love." It was with the texture and hue of the very same sacred love that Sara painted images of joy and companionship and care across the canvas of your life and my life. It's as if Sara took palette in hand and—with each gentle stroke of kindness, prayerful concern, expressed joy, intent interest in our well-being, warm invitation to enter her home and life, and generous smile—painted a portrait of true friendship, genuine love, and generous caring upon the canvas of our own lives.

Like my brother in his treatment of the canvas, Sara always handled our hearts respectfully and reverently. It now seems to me, as I reflect on the character of this sensitive yet remarkably strong woman, that she also added new color and dimension to an otherwise drab point of view. Sara had a way of helping us see the world with the eyes of an artist, as she accentuated those elements of life that would bring joy or pleasure or a sense of security. She never regarded her own opinions as the definitive word on any subject but was willing to consider another's point of view.

Yes, Sara could hold her own in any argument—just ask Austin! Yes, Sara could trade barbs with the best of them—just ask Austin! And yes, Sara could dig in her heels and become seemingly intractable—just ask Austin! But Sara was more than any one or all of these together; she was a kind and bright, warm and caring, thoughtful and talented, loving and loyal, competent and compassionate woman—just ask Austin, or anyone who knew her well!

What I will remember for the rest of my life is a woman whose character disclosed the genuine delight of one who knows God intimately, one who rejoices in each new day of discovery, one for whom worship was far more than just another way to spend a Sunday morning, one who loved her Lord and longed for his painting to be completed. I will remember Sara Swartley as a Christian whose character was a work of art in progress, and who now, by the grace of God, is beholding the beautiful face of the one we call Father.

So, Sara, we know that the promised words of your favorite poet have come true, and you now see your Pilot face to face. Thanks be to God! Amen.

LENTEN AND EASTER PREACHING

SERMON SUGGESTIONS

Topic: Temptation: No Easy Victory

TEXT: Luke 4:1–13

There may have been a time when you could gather a crowd with the promise of helping them fight temptation. If there ever was such a time, it is not now. There seems little need to do battle with an enemy you deny. The temptation to give into our lower nature, our basic instincts, is currently discounted on two very different fronts. The first is the secular ("We may be *mis*informed or *under*motivated, or even *mis/under*stood, but we are not sinners"). The word *sinner* does not fit our enlightened age. Temptation is no longer a name for serious moral conflict, a dark night of the soul, or the lure of sin. It is a name for a perfume, a singing group, or a mildly titillating movie. Oscar Wilde epitomized our secular view of temptation: "The only way to get rid of temptation is to yield to it." In other words, to yield to temptation is to enjoy life.

There is a much more spiritual way to discount the realty of temptation. It begins by recognizing the downward pull within us and the beguiling, destructive power of the demonic. Yet this is quickly followed by the assurance that we may rise above it on wings of ease if we will only believe. By saying the right words, following the correct formula, or believing the true doctrines, we will be delivered. The cross becomes an amulet protecting us from the battle with temptation. Former basketball coach Al Macguire said, about a movie of the week on World War II, that he didn't see why people were so excited about the movie; everybody knows who wins in the end. That is like the spiritualizing that sings "Victory in Jesus" and says we know who's going to win.

Maybe our real aversion to the story of Jesus' temptation is caused by its emphasis on struggle. In one of John Updike's novels, Rabbit Angstrom is in church when the minister begins a sermon on Christ's wilderness confrontation with the Devil. "Rabbit scarcely listens, for he has no taste for the dark side of Christianity, the going-through quality of it, the passage into death and suffering that redeems and unveils."

Indeed, in the Gospel accounts this story has two parts: the baptism and the temptation. The baptism is the part we are attracted to: light, affirmation, joy, God's chosen One, the Son of God. The temptation is dark, foreboding, filled with demonic challenge: "Are you the Son of God?" In the first part Jesus is *called* to fulfill the role of the suffering servant. In the second, he is confronted with the terrible *costliness* of that role.

It is only Luke who separates these two movements in the story with—of all boring intrusions—a genealogy! But perhaps the genealogy that concludes with Son of Adam (Son of Humanity) reminds us of the vast drama of humanity not being able to resist the downward tug of evil. Further, the number forty links Jesus with "fasting" stories of Elijah and Moses.

Even more, it is the reminder of Israel's forty years in the wilderness that was marked by temptation. Theirs was the challenge of choosing "this day whom you will serve." They often failed the test.

If Jesus is to be in deed as well as in promise the Son of God, he must be the Son of Humanity, tempted as we are, engaged in the battles we face. Our battles are seen in his temptations. He was tempted with bread. He was hungry for food, and he was hungry to do the will of God. What better opportunity: "Turn stones to bread and you will be proclaimed the Messiah." *It is the temptation to settle for less.* For Jesus, it was exchanging the role of suffering servant for that of material savior when deeper needs begin. It is Esau exchanging his birthright for a bowl of stew. It is the prodigal son turning his back on love and settling for its substitute. It is our temptation.

He was tempted to rule. If he worshiped the Devil, this great panorama of nations would be his. *It was the temptation to grasp more.* The lure of greater power and glory comes to us in many forms. We can't have a lasting relationship because of our compulsion to be in charge. It is Jacob tricking his brother out of his inheritance. It is the Kings of Israel trusting political alliances and military buildup. It is our temptation.

He was tempted by magic. If he leaped tall buildings in a single bound, then surely God would prove his Son to all. Luke alone places this temptation last, maybe because it is the most subtle and pervasive temptation. *It was the temptation to test God.* We want a miracle, not to glorify God but to make faith automatic. If-then is the formula. "If you save my daughter, then I'll be faithful." "If you prove yourself now, God, I'll be your servant." It is our temptation.

Jesus' real battle with temptation was whether to remain faithful to God's will or not. It was only in losing his life that he gained life for all. He was, in no automatic or easy sense of the phrase, "Christus Victor." Luke says the Devil ended his tempting, until the opportune time. What more graphic way of saying "It was not over"? All of his life was a temptation to be less than he had been called, at his baptism, to be. The final opportune time would come in a garden. Not the garden of romantic hymns. It was the battle royal. All the temptations must have been magnified in those hours; another way sought to feed the hungry, liberate the oppressed, impress people with God's saving power. Yet he resisted, not easily, but by the same power of God open to us, he resisted.

What does this mean to us? In the book of Hebrews, we are reminded that because he suffered and was tempted, yet remained faithful, he is able to help us when we are tempted. It is not that he, the Suffering Servant, lifts us above temptation. Rather he *stands with us, strengthening us through the word of God to stand firm.* Karl Barth claimed, "One thing still holds, and only this is really serious, that Jesus is Victor." *Through him we have hope* because self-defeating behavior, sin, evil, and death do not have the last word. *Through him we have the disciplines* for prayer, study, and self-giving that prepare us for the battle at the center of human life. No easy victory . . . temptation is not overcome through our strength, "goodness," or exercise of spiritual discipline. It is not enough; we fall short. Only one has defeated the constant lure of the Evil One to settle for less, to grasp for more, and to test God. No easy victory. It cost him everything, yet he won through. Now, as Luther testified, "were not the right man on our side" we would have no victory. The disciplines mentioned before became means of grace, ways of applying Christ's victory to our temptation. They are the same means that Jesus found in the wilderness: prayer, the word of God, and giving himself over to the will and timing of his Father.

It was no easy victory, but his triumph is our hope. Christus Victor. Amen.—Gary D. Stratman

Topic: Wisdom and Envy
TEXT: James 3:13, 14

The question is an intriguing one: *Who among you is wise?* There are many days when we are not likely to respond by stepping forward. We make unwise decisions, react without thinking, let our lesser passions rule us. If the question were *Who wants to be wise?* which one of us would hang back? Wisdom's value is too great to be exaggerated; a parent prays for the understanding to make a decision that will affect a child's future. As citizens, we will find issues more and more complicated and defying simplistic rhetoric.

We think of judges needing the wisdom of Solomon to decide in cases that have far-reaching consequences. Yet great wisdom is needed for those who will never sit on the bench. We are all judges. You teachers, school administrators, counselors, you make decisions that affect my children's life. I make decisions that affect your vocation and the educational enterprise. Employers, administrators, doctors, voters, confidants, and friends cry out for wisdom. What occupation, office, or relationship can eschew wisdom?

So we seek after understanding. The trappings of knowledge will not suffice. *Each day* forty Americans acquire phony academic credentials from diploma mills. Even genuine knowledge is not enough. Historian Arnold Toynbee observed that technical proficiency is not in itself a guarantee of wisdom and survival. No, James says if you desire true wisdom, examine yourself. For wisdom will not issue from a heart clogged with bitter jealousy and selfish ambition. He knew only too well those who claimed to have great wisdom but who were motivated by jealous competition. He goes so far as to say that from such jealousy flows not wisdom but chaos and evil.

Brother James shows more than a modicum of wisdom. Wisdom grows like a tree planted by living waters. A truly wise person does not stagnate in the back waters of envy, jealousy, and selfish competition. I want to suggest to you that jealousy is not *green*. It does flourish with the color and texture of life, but it is a parasite. James could not be clearer. Jealousy, envy, selfish ambition are killers of what we yearn for in our heart of hearts: love, wisdom, and peace.

Hollywood movies and the soaps perpetuate a pernicious myth. The myth is that jealousy is evidence of love ("He must love me; he can't stand to see me speak to anyone else"). We would be better off watching Shakespeare's *Othello* than the current romantic drivel. After the seeds of doubt are planted by Iago, Othello finally kills his beloved, innocent Desdemona, in a fit of jealousy. I cannot tell you how many marriages I have seen follow a similar pattern. Just because a physical death does not occur does not mean that jealousy does not kill.

James knew that there were those who claimed to be wise but who had a contentious spirit. This spirit evidences itself in a compulsive desire to pick away at a relationship until it is destroyed. I remember, with no pride, a friend in college who once asked me what he had done to harm our friendship. We shared our meals together, played football together, and had been part of a Christian support group. What had he done? After denials and defensiveness, I admitted what he had done was to succeed, or excel, in every area I deemed important. Without knowing it, I responded by picking away a person I called a friend. Any wisdom God desired for me was sabotaged by the parasite of envy.

God's wisdom, on the other hand, does not destroy friendships but brings (as this passage insists) peace. Jealousy causes division, sets brother against brother. It started with Cain and Abel. The scenario is played out over and over again. I lose my job, or give up teaching to raise a family, and I resent the one who is employed or successful or happily married. Instead of choosing friends wisely, I am poisoned by envy, which grows like a cancer.

What causes jealousy? Some years ago in *Psychology Today* the results to a questionnaire on jealousy and envy were reported. Twenty-five hundred people completed the questionnaire. There seemed to be three primary factors in the development of jealousy. The first is a *low opinion of oneself.* I remember George Gobel once saying that he felt the whole world was a tuxedo and he was a pair of brown shoes. Such a feeling of being second-class, not fitting in, can often produce a resentment of the tuxedo and a need to point out flaws in the garment. The second cause is a large discrepancy between *what I am* and *what I want to be.* The struggling student wants to be a brain surgeon or an entrepreneur. In short, one's deepest perception is that one is nothing and wants to be everything. Is jealousy a surprising outcome? The third cause is a high value placed on visible achievement. We want our success, wealth, and wisdom to show. When it does not show enough (and what is enough?), we resent those whose achievement is visible.

These causes of jealousy seem to have a ring of truth about them, but how can we overcome jealousy? How can we go past this parasite to give love, enjoy wisdom, and bring peace? We begin by realizing that we are saved from the sins against love by knowing we are loved. Jealousy and competition will not replace, hold onto, or create love. *We love because God first loved us.* I could learn to love my college friend as I remembered we were not competing for God's love. *While we were yet sinners, Christ died for us.* Finally, accepting that God loved me and that I didn't have to earn that love or compete for a limited supply of love had more to do with my conversion than anything else. *You are loved* is the message, not *you did better than anybody else.*

The beginning of wisdom is to fear God. We would like to skip that one. Fear God? Yes, it is the beginning of wisdom, for if we stand in awe before God then we are released from the constant fear of losing love or losing out to another. The New Testament version is that we are to seek first the rule and reign of God in our lives, and *all these things* will be added. All that counts in life flows from surrendering to God in Christ. I no longer have to fear being rejected or not measuring up. Jealousy becomes unnecessary.

Being in right relationship with God, ourselves, and others brings peace and frees us to be peacemakers, instead of backbiters. Peace, or *Shalom,* means wholeness or completeness. Jealousy is always feeling incomplete and resenting what others have, or fearing what they may take. Shalom is the product of God's rule and reign in our hearts.

In very practical terms, I have learned something that helps to defeat the onslaught of jealousy. When I first feel the twinges of envy, I begin to give thanks to God for the gift God has given my brother or sister. I praise God for every good and perfect gift or ability given the one I could envy. Then I thank God for the gift of his love; therein is wisdom. This wisdom is not mine. I am addicted to street smarts ("Don't get mad, get even"; "Don't just get even, get ahead"). This is the wisdom from below that devours itself. You and I know the source of wisdom that brings life, don't we?

Who among you is wise?—Gary D. Stratman

Topic: To Live Again for God
TEXT: Eph. 2:1–10

One of my colleagues recently forwarded an e-mail message telling me of a critical situation in her ministry. It seems that as her confirmation class began to study the doctrine of sin and salvation, several of the parents called my colleague and told her that they wanted to have a face-to-face. At that meeting the parents, to a person, told my colleague they were going to have her removed from her position if she continued to teach their children about (and I quote) "all of that guilt-producing sin and salvation stuff."

My colleague asked them what they would have her tell the children, and they suggested she teach them that although we all make mistakes, we're all decent and pretty much good at heart and mean to do well. When my colleague then asked, "But what about the cross and Resurrection?" the parents said, "Oh, come on! You don't *really* believe that stuff, do you?"

I've been told that people today don't want to hear about how desperately we need to be freed from captivity to sin. I've been told that people don't want to be reminded of their mortality, even in the face of clear and incontrovertible proof. I've been told that what most people want is a *word* that's always positive, productive, and practical. I've been told that even Christian people prefer to have the gospel proclaimed only after it has been cleansed of all that first-century nonsense and superstition. I've been told that many of my colleagues have taken to softening the doctrine of what Paul refers to as "the sinful nature" because their members won't tolerate the preaching of such a dreadful idea! So I've been told, and so I believe.

We will gladly receive word of God's loving nature. But we will fail to appreciate the depth of God's love if we dismiss the darkness of human sin. None of us wants to be told that we are deeply imprisoned in sin. None of us wants to be told that this sinful entrapment is one from which we can't free ourselves. None of us wants to be told that this sinful condition has cast a pall over human history. Even if true—and it is—we tend to find the thought unacceptable, perhaps even unendurable. "Once you were dead," wrote Paul, "doomed forever because of your many sins."

Easter is now a stone's throw away. And as we all know, Easter Sunday resounds with the message *God has made us alive together with Christ!* Now, that's a word we want to hear. But how can we grasp the magnitude of what has been given us, when we won't allow any discussion of *Death*? Not merely death as the clinical pronouncement to the termination of life. Death dogs our steps in the midst of life. Even in the best of health, there's this yawning chasm over which we stand—a bottomless ravine that cannot be concealed and will never be bridged by mere human effort or ingenuity.

No educational achievement, no evolutionary development, no technological wizardry, no material security gained in our lifetime—nothing within the range of human fabrication can untangle us from the inevitability of death and the dread of our mortality, which Paul says is a consequence of sin. We must be set free from outside the boundaries of what is humanly possible.

The reality of our entrapment in what the Bible calls our "sinful nature" is that we finally come to realize that every sense of security we've fashioned for ourselves is an illusion. All the paths of human history lead to the very same end. The countless human markers left behind, by everyone from Moses to Nelson Mandela, have led us to the edge of the same precipice, and to the dread of death, which is the result of sin.

Paul says that until we face that fact, we'll never come to a full appreciation of all that God has done for us in Christ. In fact, Paul would probably admonish most pastors for the way in which they have led their people to believe that the Resurrection is not so much victory over death, but something of far lesser significance. In the preaching of Easter day, we hear all kinds of strange and bewildering associations.

We hear how Easter is about the rejuvenation of nature, or the romantic return of the tulip, or the revival of the trees evident in their newly formed leaves. Sometimes we hear that the victory of Jesus over death is little more than a metaphor, a symbol for the renewal of faith arising in human hearts. It's one way of saying that the world isn't in such bad shape, and human nature isn't that bad off, and with work we can overcome the sin in human hearts. Some would even have us believe that we no longer need this idea of resurrection, because we'll one day conquer death and achieve immortality for ourselves.

If that's not concrete enough, then think about what is sometimes said in a funeral service or at the grave. Resurrection is said to be a symbol intended to convey the continuation of life in a spiritual sense. I've heard some say resurrection is merely a religious way of affirming that a loved one will forever live on in the collective memory of family and friends.

Some others have said that resurrection is really about the actions and deeds that continue to affect the lives of the living long after the deceased has passed over. I suppose for some this is comforting for a time. Then again, what do we make of the fact that death takes such a huge bite out of life's enjoyment? If death is nothing more than a transition to another, and better, realm then why do we waste time in tears? If death isn't so terrible after all, why is it that we're often left with a thorn of sorrow in our souls?

Paul is telling us that should we treat death with indifference—or worse yet in denial, as though it weren't all that dreadful—we'll never fully appreciate our deliverance disclosed in the Resurrection of Christ from the dead. In the Resurrection of Jesus, God does for us what we could never do for ourselves. God opens to us a tremendous possibility to live life freed of all dread and apprehension. In the Resurrection of Jesus, God has promised that there's nothing we need fear. God has promised that should we believe and embrace him—and in faith, he will never allow anything to separate us from his divine heart.

But there's no rational ground, no reasoned argument, no human support or knowledge or experience I can bring to you as proof of this assertion. It's not something you can make *true* for yourself; it's that which God has already *made* true for you, for me.

We should each of us know *that great freedom* given us in the Resurrection of Jesus from the grave. We can breathe freely of the joy that is ours in knowing our lives are surrounded and upheld by the Spirit of God. The great gospel proclaims that we are literally enveloped in a truth that is *truer* than the reality of sin and death. God's truth in the Resurrection of Jesus is truer than all our doubts, afflictions, troubles, trials, and our hell-like tribulations. God wants each of us to be freed of all fear, even though we might face a thousand griefs and losses.

This is the great hope held out to us in the word of the apostle Paul: "God, who is rich in mercy . . . loved us so very much, that even while we were dead because of our sins, he gave us life when he raised Christ from the dead." We need no greater hope; we can hope for no greater truth. All that we would fear has been swallowed up and overcome in this one act of God. God now encircles each of us in a love that can never end. In every affliction, in all your anxieties, in the face of that which you would fear above all else, remember what God has done for you in the Resurrection of Jesus. God has given you the freedom to live in the *victory of faith* rather than in bondage to fear. Amen.—A.J.D. Walsh

Topic: Witness to the Resurrection
TEXT: Acts 10:34–43; Luke 24:1–12

In the past year or two, what events have gained several television audiences and the lion's share of press attention? Inaugurations, victory celebrations, scientific discoveries, or rewards have not attracted the most attention. No, at the top of the list are trials of famous people and judicial investigations that were anything but routine. In such efforts, there are always rumors, and sometimes the actual appearance, of what is called a surprise witness. There is such a witness in the New Testament. Her name is Joanna. I was tempted this morning to begin my sermon by asking, "When was the last time you heard a sermon on Joanna?" I decided not to do that, for a good reason.

One of my predecessors in another church was going to be away for the weekend, and so he asked a good friend of his who was one of the chaplains at the nearby university to preach for him. The chaplain, as chaplains are wont to do, decided to do something a little different that Sunday. So he found a published sermon on Seth. This sermon began by asking the congregation, "When was the last time you heard a sermon on Seth?" Well, the next week my predecessor came back from a wonderful vacation. As a matter of fact, it was so wonderful he didn't have time to prepare a sermon. So he found a published sermon and began that next Sunday by innocently asking, "When was the last time you heard a sermon about Seth?" At that moment, the whole congregation in one voice said, "Last Sunday." Now, try and recover from that! So I will not ask, "When was the last time you heard a sermon on Joanna?"

The sermon is not really about Joanna or Seth. It is about the Resurrection. There can be no other topic than that this morning, Easter Sunday. We are always looking for some new angle of vision from which to see this remarkable event, this event that is unbelievable and yet true. I believe St. Paul was exactly right when he said that if this is not true, then we are of all people most miserable. Those words echo in my mind every time I do a funeral service, every time I lose someone very close to me. If it is not true that Jesus Christ defeated death and all that separates us, then we are of all people most miserable.

We need to hear from a witness. An accident form turned into an insurance company reported succinctly, "There were many bystanders, but no witnesses." There are many bystanders, but few witnesses, because a witness is one who sees, who becomes involved, and who speaks. I believe something quite surprising happened in Joanna's life that made her a witness. It was not just what happened on the day that we read about this morning. No, there were a series of events and decisions that made her a witness to Christ's redemption and Resurrection. We do speak today not only of the Resurrection but also of redemption. When I was growing up there were institutions called redemption centers. For you who are younger, they were not churches. They were trading centers where you would take in Eagle stamps (or other trading stamps) and exchange them for wonderful prizes. That's what redemption means, to trade one thing for another. Here in Luke's Gospel is the redemptive act of Jesus Christ. He redeemed our failures, our fears, and changed them into joy and power. Christ took our failures and flaws, sins and inconsistencies upon himself. When we believe in him, this great redemption, already accomplished, becomes effective in us.

The great story of Resurrection and redemption requires a witness. Joanna is a surprise witness because, first of all, she is a common person. By common, we mean one who seems ordinary, and yet we can identify with her. Her name was common. The Hebrew that it is based upon, Johannin, is the name from which we get Joan, Joann, Jean, Jeanette, Jane, Janet, and on and on. The masculine equivalent is John; you can imagine how many variations we have of that name. She may have been common, but her name means "God is gracious." How we who feel so common need to be reminded of God's surprising and uncommon grace!

In Luke, chapter 8, Joanna's name appears in a list of women who are healed in body, mind, or spirit, or all three. We're not sure, but it doesn't matter, does it? Because all healing comes from God. The word that we use for healed in the New Testament is the same one we use for saved. Jesus' act of salvation was to bring us wholeness and completeness and sometimes that comes in healing our minds, or emotions, our bodies, or our spirits. She was touched by God, and she became a different person. She was healed and made whole. She became a witness to the Resurrection, for life begins when we die to ourselves and open ourselves to Jesus Christ.

A woman complained to her husband about their marriage, and he responded, "I thought you married for life." She said, "That's true, I did get married for life, but in the last five years you have shown no signs of life." What we seek is renewal, what the Bible calls "newness of life." That's what resurrection is about. When Christ becomes the one who reigns in our hearts, there is the possibility of being born anew over and over again. Joanna was one who was touched by God.

We learn something else about Joanna; she was married to a man named Chuza. It turns out that Chuza was no less than the steward of the tetrarch, Herod. Chuza had one of the most responsible positions in the region. He was, as steward, the caretaker of all of the possessions, land, and household goods of Herod. But I believe it is recorded here as almost a play on words, because we soon learn that it is really Joanna who is the great steward of God. It says, "She took what she had." Her personal belongings, whatever was actually hers and not her husband's, is implied here. She took what she had and gave it to the ministry of Jesus Christ. She was a steward of God. I guess to be correct we would have to say she was a stewardess. Now some of you will only remember that, and you will go home and say, "Well, I think he preached about Joanna, the stewardess." But if you do, that is OK. Because I think we have undervalued *steward*. It is not only that her life was touched by God; steward means a caretaker of all that God has given us. As we look at what is happening to our air, and land, and sea, we must be stewards of the good gifts of God. When we look at our lives and what we could be doing with our time and energy and thought, we need to be good stewards of Jesus Christ.

I read a story that must be true because it was in a Lutheran magazine. It was about a Lutheran minister, David Kidd, who lives in Pennsylvania. Rev. Kidd was visiting one of his parishioners, who was a good steward of all that God had given him. The man told his pastor, "I can't get to church very often, so I want to write you a check and I want you to take it to the church." He then excused himself and went into the next room to write the check. When he came back the pastor said, "I just want to tell you, I have really enjoyed this bowl of peanuts that you have set out here." "Well, I'm glad, Pastor, that someone is enjoying them. Because with my dentures all that I can do is suck the chocolate off them." Now, that's one story you won't soon forget. Although you may not excuse me for it, I'm going to plow ahead. Because what we do so often is take the chocolate off the peanut, and then if there is time, energy, intellect left over we give it to God. There is more than we ever could have dreamed left over for us.

She was a steward of God's great gifts—not only time but talents as well. These gifts great and small included the duty of anointing the corpse of the One who had been the disciples' teacher. It put her in the place where she could be a witness to the marvelous act of God. I believe sometimes when we act only out of duty, it's OK. Because that puts us in the place where we need to be, to be a part of the work of God. I believe that Joanna was indeed one who was touched by God. She was a steward of God, and she became a witness to the Resurrection of Jesus Christ. A witness is one who sees, yet we can go out into this beautiful day and miss the beauty of God. We can hear the Scripture again and again, and miss seeing the redemption that is ours in Jesus Christ. A witness is first one who sees, and then a witness is one who tells.

One of my fondest memories of elementary school is show-and-tell. This simple phrase also suggests what witnessing is: it is to show what God has done, and to tell of his greatness in Christ. This is what it means to be a witness. Sometimes it means being persistent, and finding creative ways to be a witness. Do you notice that the primary witnesses to the Resurrection were women? The men were cowering at the time. I don't like that fact either, gentlemen, but the women here stand in good company. The first witnesses were women, and they were persistent because women in that day were not allowed to be witnesses in court. So they found other ways to witness to this astounding event. Sometimes we say, "I want to be a witness. I want to speak a good word for Jesus Christ, but you are not allowed to in the public schools or in business. You don't know what business is like." But I believe that there are creative ways in which we can be a witness in all of those areas. We can begin by coming together as teachers, as health care professionals, as those who are in business. By discovering the power of God in our lives and the lives of our coworkers, we will have something to show and to tell. There are always acceptable and attractive ways to bear witness to Jesus Christ.

I ended a paper on vision for the officers of our church with a quote from Samual Shoemaker. It was very simple. Shoemaker believed that what the church needs to do to come alive and to affect the community around it is *to get changed,* to get together, and then get going." Joanna was changed by the touch of God. She got together with other women and men who became disciples of Jesus Christ. Then they got going, and their witness turned the world upside down. It can happen again. Hear the good news: Jesus Christ is risen, and death is defeated.—Gary D. Stratman

SECTION VII

EVANGELISM AND WORLD MISSIONS

SERMON SUGGESTIONS

Topic: That You May Believe

Text: John 1, 20:30–31

"Does God speak to people today?" asks a corporation president who is trying to solve a problem of right and wrong in his business. But the question could just as well be asked by one who works far down the line in the same organization. Such a question has meaning for people in all walks of life, because no area of our living is beyond the reach of God's concern.

Our God is a God who speaks and a God who just as truly demands an answer.

I. *What is life?* Why did Jesus Christ come? "I am come," he said, "that they might have life, and that they might have it more abundantly" (John 10:10). John said that one purpose of recording what is found in the Fourth Gospel about Jesus was "believing you might have life through his name" (John 20:31, NRSV). In his prayer of intercession, our Lord said, "This is life eternal, that they may know you, the only true God, and Jesus Christ whom you have sent" (John 17:3, NRSV).

Life as we usually see it and share it is only a shadow of what life can be with Christ in it. A person who enjoys good health, who has a happy home, who finds satisfaction in work, and who knows the respect of friends may say sincerely, "Life is wonderful!" Even so, the difference between life as this person knows it and life that Christ can give is as great as the diference between a photograph and the real person. Life is hardly life until it has in it the dimension of eternity.

II. *Life and light.* The life of God has been manifested as light shining in darkness. The light appeared in the remotest ages of human history. The light appeared to Abraham, and he rejoiced in the gracious provision of God for his deepest needs. The light appeared to Moses, and he led his people into a covenant with the God who had chosen them and delivered them. The light appeared to Hosea and Amos, to Isaiah and Jeremiah, and they pointed an erring people back to the ways of true worship.

The light appeared to all humankind: "Ever since the creation of the world his invisible nature, namely, his eternal power and deity, has been clearly perceived in the things that have been made" (Rom. 1:20, RSV).

The light shines today. It has penetrated the darkness far more deeply than ever before. The airwaves are filled with the gospel of Christ. Laypeople are aggressively carrying their Christian experience into their business and professional lives and are more and more taking Christ to the unchurched. Christian missions gird the globe. Portions of the Bible have been translated into more than eleven hundred languages and dialects. Every frontier of human achievement becomes a new frontier for the gospel of Christ and a new challenge for the heralds of light.

III. *The Word of God.* The light came especially in Jesus Christ, for he was "the true Light" (John 1:9). His "goings forth have been from of old, from everlasting" (Mic. 5:2). Besides being called the true Light, Jesus Christ is also designated as "the Word" (John 1:14). He is called the Word because he is the expression of the power and activity of God. The history of the Word goes back beyond the time of the conception and birth of Jesus. It goes back to the beginning of all things (vv. 1–3). A word expresses what one person thinks and proposes to do. The divine Word expresses the thought and the will of God.

One speaks purposefully and wisely, and things happen. God speaks, and a world is created, a prophet is inspired, history is guided, or we are visited by God in the person of his Son.

"The Word was made flesh, and dwelt among us . . . full of grace and truth" (v. 14). This means that God speaks to us most fully and convincingly in a human life—in one human life, that of Jesus Christ, God's Son. We know what God is like when we look at Jesus. This also means that God has always been like Jesus, a God of grace and truth. The light that glorified the life and personality of Jesus was the light of God himself.

IV. *People say no.* Human history is one long story of the rejection of light and life. Into the darkness light has come. It has penetrated the primeval forest. It has reached the depths of earth's caves. It has bathed the mountain slopes. It has followed the rivers and crossed the seas. It has dazzled the eyes of those in the marketplace, at the council table, and in the halls of learning. The light, like "the Hound of Heaven," has followed us wherever we have gone. The darkness has never been able to put it out (v. 5).

But some have tried to extinguish the light. They have persecuted and killed the preachers that God sent out to witness to that light. Many have turned their thoughts of God into idols of lust, power, and ease. Many have put their consciences to sleep with the drugs of pleasure, position, and activity.

Then, when Jesus Christ, the true Light, came, people rejected him. The world made through him did not know him (v. 10). "He came to his own home, and his own people received him not" (v. 11, RSV). First, it was Herod, then his fellow townsmen, then the scribes and Pharisees, then Judas, then the Sanhedrin. At last, the whole nation spurned him. But not the Jews only! The message of Jesus was not welcome in many a Gentile city.

Wherever sin has been entrenched and loved in personal life, in society, in business, and in government, people have been less than glad to receive Jesus Christ. Light reveals filth, injustice, dishonesty, and greed. Therefore, when the deeds of people are evil, they love darkness (John 3:19).

Soon after Paul and Silas stepped onto the European continent, they clashed with vested business interests. Their trouble arose when they encountered an insane slave girl. This poor soul gave prophecies to guide people about the future. The demand for her services brought her masters a large income. After observing her odd behavior for several days, Paul healed her in the name of Jesus Christ. Then the storm broke, "when her master saw that the hope of their gains was gone" (Acts 16:19), they had Paul and Silas thrown in jail. This they did not on the basis of the facts but by waving a flag, so to speak, and declaring that Paul and Silas were enemies of their traditions and customs.

Would it not be easy for us to accept Jesus, provided that no difficult changes were called for? Doors now closed to Jesus would be thrown open if he would give happiness and security to those who wished to cling to their favorite habits, their questionable associates, their unethical business codes, and their consuming lust for power. We should ask ourselves the searching question as to whether we are willing to accept Jesus' promise of forgiveness and salvation, but not his demands for inward and outward changes. Is not the crime of those who lived during the days of his flesh our crime, too?

V. *Some say yes.* Thank God, the story does not end with the rejection and Crucifixion of Jesus. There were many who welcomed him, loved him, walked with him, and died for him. "To all who received him, who believed in his name, he gave power to become children of God" (John 1:12, RSV).

We become children of God by a spiritual rebirth. This miraculous event is not promoted and produced by the human will. It occurs through the action of God. Therefore, John said that no human desire or impulse could account for the child of God (v. 13). We have only to believe in and receive Jesus Christ.

All of this means that becoming a child of God is a matter of God's mercy and generosity. Some of us may be favored by ancestry. Others may be distinguished by noble character. But it is wrong to credit our forebears or ourselves with what God alone can do. Being a child of God is not a matter of human effort, but of divine grace.

It does not require great learning and wide experience to become a child of God. It is as simple as receiving and committing oneself to the light and life that God offers the world, though that experience makes heavy demands and makes possible great achievements.

In the days of Peter and Paul, Christians went into many parts of the world with the story of God's love in Christ. They announced to men and women that they could know God's love and forgiveness, could break loose from their sin, and no longer fear being punished. They were, in fact, invited to join the family of God by becoming friends of his Son. By accepting the Son they became not the children of darkness but children of light.

The same Jesus and the same salvation are offered today on the same terms. Receive him, and you become a child of God!

VI. *Life—it's wonderful!* The new relationship that a Christian has to God is not a cold fact that one learns from another. It is not mechanical, but living. It is not simply a matter of record, but a matter of experience.

The story of our Christian experience begins with a conversion experience. At first, there may be little emotional evidence that anything remarkable took place when Christ was received. But an intimate friendship with Christ will, sooner or later, make many definite differences. As people study God's Word and seek to live by it with the help of the Holy Spirit, they find an abundant life. One realizes that God supplies all one's needs, received "grace upon grace" (v. 16, RSV). The purpose of John in writing his Gospel is fulfilled: "But these [signs] are written, that you might believe that Jesus is the Christ, the Son of God; and that believing you may have life in his name" (John 20:31, NKJV).—James W. Cox

Topic: A Test of Discipleship
Text: John 13:1–17, 34–35

I. *Jesus' view of himself.* In this thirteenth chapter, John indicates Jesus' lofty view of his own nature and his relation to the eternal purpose from the Father. Jesus came from the Father, who had granted him unlimited authority. Jesus had been faithful in love to his own. He knew that his departure to the Father would be soon, and that Judas would betray him (vv. 1–3).

Surely this could mean that Jesus, in a great display of power, would be able to defeat his enemies. Twelve legions of angels were at his disposal. But instead of this, in a gesture of friendship he dipped the morsel and handed it to Judas Iscariot (v. 20).

II. *Jesus' view of his task.* As was the custom, Jesus and his disciples were reclining at the table, eating supper. Usually a slave washed the dusty feet of the guests as they lay on couches. It was unthinkable that one of the disciples, in the absence of a servant, would stoop to do the task. They had ideas of their own importance. They strove to surpass one another as they vied for the favor of Jesus. Two of them openly wanted the chief places in Christ's kingdom.

During the supper Jesus got up from the couch and laid aside his outer garments. After taking a towel and knotting it about himself, he took water and began to wash his disciples' feet and to wipe them with the towel (vv. 4–5).

Though John saw the glory of heavenly light shining on the life of Jesus from first to last, Jesus' career on earth from Bethlehem to Calvary was humiliating from a human point of view. When Jesus entered upon his ministry, though without sin he placed himself among sinners to be baptized by John the Baptist. For the sake of those he came to save and as a part of his spiritual unfolding, he endured appalling temptations in the desert. He was hounded by critics and persecutors, and at last his enemies crucified him as a blasphemer and a criminal.

Isaiah spoke of Jesus as the Suffering Servant: "He is despised and rejected by men; a man of sorrows and acquainted with grief: . . . Surely he hath borne our griefs and carried our sorrows; yet we esteemed him stricken, smitten by God, and afflicted" (Isa. 53:3–4, NKJV).

That he might accomplish his God-given task, Jesus was willing to do the thing that was humiliating. In fact, it was in his humiliation that his glory shone through. Jesus' washing the disciples' feet was precisely in character. His death on the cross was a summing up of a life given completely to God and used for service to humankind.

III. *The role of a disciple.* Though Jesus' relationship to God as a Son was unique, his style of life is a pattern for everyone who calls him Master and Lord (John 13:13–15). His example of washing the disciples' feet was a pattern for each of them to follow.

This was a lesson the disciples needed to learn. They held exaggerated ideas of their own importance. Their imaginations had been inflamed with the idea of an immediate earthly rule of Christ, and they could visualize themselves individually in the most prominent positions.

It is amazing how easily even in the Church—which was born in the humiliation and suffering of the Son of God—people fall prey to the temptations to pride. Church fellowship is seldom broken over basic issues. People love to rule and hate to serve, and then war breaks out. This is the peril of pastors and laity.

The marvelous passage written by Paul in his letter to the Philippians (2:6–11) is an illustration of the spirit that ought to be in the heart of every Christian. Jesus gave us his heavenly glory for a cross, and God exalted him to the highest. This, said Paul, should be the attitude of those who belong to Christ (Phil. 2:4).

In the Christian fellowship, the question of authority is sure to arise. Jesus had authority and exercised it. Believers in Christ have a certain authority, and they must exercise it. Jesus referred to himself and to his followers as those who are "sent" (John 13:16). Before his Ascension, he said to the disciples, "As my father has sent me, I also send you" (John 20:21). This means that responsibility and leadership are inevitable. This in turn means that either chaos or order is possible, depending on the spirit in which authority is exercised.

The answer should be plain. Our authority as Christians lies in mutual humility. "Do nothing from selfishness or conceit, but in humility count others better than yourselves" (Phil. 2:3, RSV). A church in which foot washing was practiced as an act of worship had an unfortunate split. What was it about? It was, of all things, over whether the right foot or the left foot should be washed. In contrast to this spirit, a wise, spiritual-minded pastor, whose church had a challenging opportunity before it, said, "We are not going anywhere until we can all go together." This was no resignation to idleness, but a commitment to Christian humility and cooperation. It is no wonder that this church is "going places"!

IV. *The proof of discipleship.* The role of disciple is not only to be enjoyed; it must be proved. To put it in modern terms, it is a matter of public relations. We can make a pretense of discipleship by declaring that we belong to Christ, by grudgingly accepting a humble role, or by cooperating under pressure. But that proves nothing except that our consecration is not complete.

There is only one way effectively to communicate the truth of God's redemptive love in Christ. That is the way of love. The old commandment said, "Thou shalt love thy neighbor as thyself" (Lev. 9:18). Jesus gave a new commandment: "Love one another" (John 13:34). The new commandment requires that one not only love another as much as self but love another more than self. "Greater love hath no one than this, than to lay down one's life for his friends" (John 15:13, NKJV). So Jesus loved, and so we must love.

We measure our churches with many yardsticks: statistical, organizational, social, financial. But what is the measure of love?—James W. Cox

Topic: Our Ever-Present Helper
Text: John 14:1, 15–27

An elderly member used to say to her pastor as she left the church, "Well, here's my old standby!" The pastor never felt that he quite deserved the compliment, but it warmed his heart to know that he had encouraged and strengthened this saint of God.

Today's text points to the Holy Spirit as the answer to our need for permanent spiritual aid.

In John 14:16, 26 the Holy Spirit is called "the Comforter." It meant "strengthener" rather than "consoler," as Wycliffe had translated the word earlier. The original Greek word meant "advocate" or "helper."

I. *"With you forever."* Can you visualize what the physical presence of Jesus meant to his disciples? The presence of God was most real when Jesus was with them. They had a teacher to show them the purposes of God. They had a friend who was loyal to them in all circumstances.

Soon the disciples would have to get along without the physical presence of Jesus, for he was going to the Father.

Jesus had promised that he would not leave them desolate, that he would come to them (v. 18). This coming of Jesus to his disciples was, first of all, to be his post-Resurrection appearances.

Actually, the Resurrection of Christ inaugurated a new age, and his triumphant presence manifested to his disciples was to prevail in the experience of all who love the Lord.

Five brief passages in John 14–16 deal with our "Helper."

The Helper, the Holy Spirit, is Jesus' *alter ego,* or other self. As long as Jesus remained on earth, it was impossible for his disciples to become really mature, full-grown Christians.

"Yet—I am telling you the truth—my going is for your good. If I do not depart, the Helper will not come to you; whereas, if I go, I will send him to you" (John 16:7, Moffatt). These words of Jesus left no doubt as to the advantage of having Christ in the heart over having Christ in a physical presence.

A youth who had experienced a meaningful spiritual awakening used to walk home after prayer meetings at his church and, looking up at the beautifully lighted night sky, pray, "O Lord, give me just one glimpse of your face." God has given us something better than a glimpse of his face; he has given us the Holy Spirit. Jesus said, "He will glorify me, for he will take what is mine and declare it to you" (John 16:14, RSV).

II. *"He shall teach you."* What does the Holy Spirit do for us?

He gives us spiritual power. Before he ascended to the Father, Jesus said, "You shall receive power, when the Holy Spirit has come upon you" (Acts 1:8, NKJV). This was to prepare Christians for witnessing in the name of Christ throughout the world.

After several years of Christian service, the renowned evangelist Dwight L. Moody felt that his attempts to work for God were not as effective as they should have been. He sought and found a deeper experience of the Holy Spirit, and from that day he knew a greater effectiveness and usefulness to God.

Many of us are floundering in our jobs in the church and in our Christian witness in the community because we are attempting to do in our own strength what can be accomplished only with the help of the Holy Spirit.

Again, the Holy Spirit teaches us. He is "the Spirit of truth" (John 14:17). He functioned not only to remind the disciples of all that Jesus said and did (v. 26) but also to explain them. The Gospel of John itself is the prime example. For instance, in the third chapter we have the words of Jesus and of John, both in the same spirit.

In this day Christian people need the teaching ministry of the Holy Spirit. Much ridiculous behavior is said to be under the "leadership of the Spirit." To cite an extreme example, a man once beat another man's head to a pulp, killing him, and explained, "God told me to do it." However, the teaching of the Holy Spirit is always in keeping with what Jesus taught and always fulfills the Commandments.

If we are willing, the Holy Spirit will give us ever-new insights into the meaning of Christ for our personal lives and for the life of the world.

III. *"He will reprove."* Jesus pointed out that the Holy Spirit also has a ministry to the unbelieving world. Thus the Helper does not limit his activity to the welfare of the Christian community.

1. Through the Church the Holy Sprit convinces the world of sin (John 16: 8–9). The great condemning sin of the world is the sin of unbelief—the sin of rejecting Jesus as the Christ. The people of Jesus' time based their claim to righteousness on obedience to rules and regulations. They could do as they pleased with Jesus, they thought, for there was nothing in their laws to forbid it; and as they saw it, Jesus interfered with those very laws and therefore deserved punishment. So they crucified him. The Holy Spirit shows that the greatest sin is not the breaking of a law, but the act of shutting out of one's heart the life of God offered in Christ.

2. The Holy Spirit convinces the world of righteousness (v. 10). Who was the criminal at the Crucifixion? Not Jesus, but the man who crucified him! That was Everyman. Jesus assuredly went to the Father. Thus the world that crucified him stands condemned, and the righteousness of Jesus is affirmed.

3. The Holy Spirit convinces the world of judgment (v. 11). Christ in the Church through the Holy Spirit is proof enough that the powers of evil went too far and that God is making the savage human wrath work to the praise of God.

When the Holy Spirit was poured out upon the Church on the day of Pentecost and Peter preached Christ, the men who had cried "Crucify him, crucify him" now were pricked in their hearts and earnestly inquired, "What shall we do?" (Acts 2:37).

Today, when the Church people live triumphantly and are filled with love and other fruits of the Spirit (Gal. 5:22–23), men and women who have not known Christ will ask, "What shall we do to make our lives right with the God you know and love?"

IV. *"Keep my Commandments."* The experience of the power and presence of the Holy Spirit by the Church comes in no mechanical way.

When members of the Church commit themselves to Christ and lovingly obey him, the Holy Spirit's presence and power are known. The Church is effective in its work and witness to the extent that the members permit themselves to be used by the Holy Spirit.

Would you like to know the assurance of the Spirit's presence and guidance? Listen, then, to Jesus' promise and make it your own: "If you love Me, keep My commandments. And I will pray to the Father, and He shall give you another Helper, that He may abide with you forever" (John 14:15–16, NKJV).—James W. Cox

RESOURCES FOR PREACHING FROM PSALMS

BY MARVIN E. TATE

Topic: The Two Ways of Life
TEXT: Ps. 1

Jesus encouraged his disciples to "Enter through the narrow gate; for the gate is wide and the road is broad that leads to destruction; and there are many who take it. For the gate is narrow and the road is hard that leads to life, and there are few who find it" (Matt. 7:13–14, NRSV).

Jesus was setting forth the familiar biblical theme of the two ways of life that lie before the pilgrim of faith. We find it again in the account of the great judgment in Matthew 25:31–46. The Son of Man will separate the people as a shepherd separates the sheep and the goats. The sheep are the righteous, who care for the hungry, the thirsty, the strangers, those without clothes to wear, the sick, and those in jail. The goats are those who live under a curse, because they do the things that the righteous do. In the Old Testament in Deuteronomy 30:19, God sets before Israel life and death, blessing and curses, and a choice has to be made (see also Jer. 21:8). In Proverbs there are repeated contrasts between the wise, corresponding to the righteous, and fools, corresponding to the wicked.

The two ways in Psalm 1 are expressed as the way of the chaff and the way of a tree. The chaff is the dry material that is separated from the grain at threshing time. It lacks substance, strength, and endurance, so the wind blows it away and it becomes waste. The way of the chaff is that of the wicked, the way of life of the sinners and scoffers in verse 1. The wicked are those who give society a corrupt and evil nature. If we glean words and expressions for the wicked from the Old Testament, the list could include *contemptuous of others, arrogant, insolent, crooked, lawless, oppressive, duplicitous, mean, abusive,* and *lacking the fear of God.* We know them very well.

The chaff people have no standing in the congregation of the righteous (v. 5), which is the fellowship of those who can praise God in the sanctuary (Pss. 111:1, 118:19–20). The exact nature of the "congregation" or "assembly" is not specified, but the great congregation that met for worship on Mt. Zion is probably in mind (Pss. 35:18, 40:9–20). Beyond that, the present psalm should be read as looking to the future judgment of God, and to the purified congregation of the righteous. We may think of both the present and the future. In any case the wicked will not survive judgment—both now and in the future. Their way is doomed to death.

The other way is the that of the righteous, who are said to be "like a tree planted by streams of water," which yields its fruit every season and has leaves that never wither. The verb for "planted" indicates that the tree is well rooted in the soil, and not merely growing. Roots deep underground draw moisture from perennial streams for a strong and productive fruit tree. The tree is a common symbol for life in the ancient world. We remember the "tree of life" in the Garden of Eden, and the use of the tree in a positive sense in Psalm 1 recalls the "planting" of the trees in that garden in Genesis 2:8 (although the verb is different). Trees belong to visions of paradise (e.g., Isa. 61:3; Ezek. 47:12). The "tree of life" appears with the crystal-bright "river of the water of life" that flows through the great street of the New Jerusalem in Revelation 22:1-2. And in Proverbs 3:18, wisdom is said to be a "tree of life" for those who hold her fast—they are said to be "happy," a form of the same word that begins Psalm 1.

The tree people in this psalm are those who do not follow the counsel and the paths of the wicked, refusing to linger with them as they go about their ways or to sit with them and participate in their company (v. 1). On the contrary, their delight is in the "law of the LORD," on which they meditate "day and night." That is, continuously. The Hebrew is *torah* and means "instruction," "teaching," or "guidance." In later usage, the word may refer to a body of literature, especially the Pentateuch. There is no such defined body of material mentioned in Psalm 1 (or in the great torah Ps. 119); we may understand "law" here as the "guidance" and "instruction" of the LORD (see the torah in the heart in Pss. 37:31 and 40:8). However, the verb that is usually translated "meditate" actually means "to recite" orally. Silent reading was uncommon in the ancient world; oral recitation, or chanting, points to the use of "a recognizable, established, and crystallized text that can be committed to memory and recited."[1]

However, the devotion to torah in this context should not be understood in a legalistic sense, that is, of a life constantly bound by rules and rites. It is a body of teaching that requires new thinking and choices as life moves along. Like a good fruit tree, torah bears new fruit season after season. This is especially true if the Pentateuch is kept in mind, since it is a very large body of different kinds of material—it is not all "laws" by any means. Of course, the psalm does point us to a life of devotion and commitment to the will of God. Long Jewish tradition and commentary linked Psalm 1:1 to the famous *Shema* in Deuteronomy 6:4-9: "Hear, O Israel. The LORD is one God, the LORD alone. You shall love the LORD your God with all your heart, and with all your soul, and with all your might. Keep the words that I command you today in your heart. Recite them to your children and talk about them when you sit at home, and when you go away [literally, walk in the road], and when you lie down and when you rise."

Here we have four verbs used in the commandment to love the LORD: "when you sit . . . when you walk . . . when you lie down . . . and when you rise." In Psalm 1 we have sit, walk, and stand (which is equivalent to "rise up") and indicates that the love and total commitment of the Shema should be understood for Psalm 1. The "lying down" of the Shema is missing, but its substitute is to meditate on the torah "day and night."

Let us return to the beginning of the psalm for a moment. The first verse begins, "Happy is the one. . . . " "One" or "person" should be understood here rather than "male." The expression is unusual in the Old Testament exactly in this form. The Hebrew word translated as "happy" is *ashre,* which indicates a present condition, not a past or future one. It is known to most Bible readers because of the use of the Greek form of the word in the Beatitudes of Jesus. The translation "happy" seems somewhat weak in contemporary English, and the old

---

[1]Nahum M. Sarna, *Songs of the Heart* (New York: Schocken Books, 1993), p. 38.

"blessed" is hardly better. Our idiomatic "OK" conveys part of the meaning; that is "The condition of this person is OK." But OK may not express the element of happiness carried by the word. In a deep sense, happiness is accurate. The condition is one of pleasure and satisfaction with the circumstances being experienced. The condition is not one that can be given; it must be acquired by a way of life.

Finally, the simple language of this psalm should not fool us into thinking that it is commonplace advice with little emphasis on faith. The psalm presupposes a faith community of those who are devoted to following the ways of God. The torah was a living entity, unfolding in new ways while preserving old values. The psalm asks for faith in the statement that "the LORD knows the way of the righteous" in the last verse. This indicates that the psalm does not simply deal with a matter of natural law. The LORD plants the tree and provides the stream of water that makes it flourish. He allows the wicked to perish like the chaff that is blown away. The way of the righteous is the way of faith: "Love the LORD your God with all your heart and all your soul and all your might."

Topic: Is There Enough on the Table?
TEXT: Ps. 23

Three verbal pictures clustered around that of a shepherd are found in Psalm 23:1–4. We are familiar with these verses, and with the shepherd who provides for the sheep, guides them safely through dangerous valleys, and protects them from accidents and attacks. The second part of the psalm is that of a host who spreads a table for guests to enjoy a banquet: "You prepare a table before me, in the presence of my enemies." An abundant table is set while enemies look on, impotent to do any harm. The head of the guest is anointed with oil, and the cup that is provided runs over, indicating an abundance of good things.

These metaphors are held together by the use of the divine name *Yahweh* in verses 1 and 6, and by the fact that all of the metaphors are associated with kingship. The LORD (Yahweh) is the divine king who provides, guides, and protects the people who belong to him. There is no "lack" of provision for those who trust in the LORD. Kings ("shepherd" is a term for king) were renowned for their great houses, where they entertained guests at lavish meals as they enjoyed the hospitality of the king. The guests are well cared for and protected from the threats of outsiders. In the psalm, enemies will not pursue the guests anymore, but "goodness" and "steadfast love" will chase after them all the days of their life. They will be regular guests in the "house of the LORD" (the Temple); at least, this is probably what the literal "I will return to the house of the LORD forever" means. It will always be "home" for the speaker. This psalm reflects the worship of Israelites at festival times when thanksgiving meals were enjoyed and the goodness of the LORD was celebrated. An actual communal meal was probably involved in most cases. Psalm 65:4 reads, "Happy are those whom you choose and bring near to live in your courts. We shall be satisfied with the goodness of your house, your holy temple" (NRSV).

As noted above, abundant table is indicated by the cup that overflows and the anointing oil for the head (compare the language in Ps. 65:9–11). This brings to mind the question of scarcity and enoughness—a question that was much on the mind of ancient peoples and continues to be a matter of lie and death for millions today. Is there enough water, food, clothing, housing, work, and medical care for all of us? Is there enough only for some, while others must do without? Are the resources of the world sufficient for all the population of the earth? These are questions that are before us all today. Ancient peoples were plagued with the idea and fear of scarcity. Water was often scarce, and the food supplies were threatened by famine. The fear and reality of scarcity often led to violence and attempts to hoard food and water. We are more confident today—at least in Europe and in the United States—but we are not really sure, and the spirit of greed and hoarding comes easily to all of us. Can the LORD provide for all our needs? Is there enough on the table for all of us? It is estimated that a billion people go hungry every day in the present population of the world. Most are short of water, lack proper clothes, have little housing, suffer from violence, and are without medical care. There is little wonder that so many ask, "Is there enough?"

Those who take their heading for a course of action from the Bible will recognize that from beginning to end it sets forth the intention of God to provide enough for all the peoples of the world. Abundance is the divinely intended counterpart of scarcity. But the idea of scarcity is a powerful concept, and as people of faith we struggle to free ourselves from its grip. The songs of abundance that emerge from the Bible often seem to us to be naïve and dangerous. We know that God has called us to produce a different way of life in the world, one that turns away from the commitment to scarcity and believes that God can prepare a table before us in the presence of our enemies. This is difficult for us, and we may take comfort from the struggles of the ancient Israelites to trust in God's abundance.

The reader of Psalm 23 easily recalls the experience of the Israelites in the wilderness after their departure from Egypt. They met with scarcity in a hurry, when they found themselves without water and food and threatened by enemies. Their faith was put to the test, and as Psalm 78:19 puts it they spoke against God, saying "Can God spread a table for us in the wilderness?" As we know from the book of Exodus and from Psalm 78, the Lord met their needs, although they were not always happy about it. Psalm 78:22–25 expresses it this way: "They have no faith in God, and did not trust his saving power. Yet he commanded the skies above, and opened the doors of heaven; he rained down on them manna to eat, and gave them the grain of heaven. Mortals ate of the bread of angels; he sent them food in abundance" (NRSV).

A narrative account of God's provision of food in the wilderness is found in Exodus 16. Bread and quails are given, but the people are told by Moses to gather only enough for each day's needs: "Gather as much of it as each of you need, an omer to a person according to the number of persons, all providing for those in their own tents." The Israelites did so, some gathering more, some less. And when they measured it with an omer, those who gathered much had nothing over, and those who gathered little had no shortage; they gathered as much as each of them needed (vv. 16–18).

We are not surprised that some tried to horde it for the next day as well, but the food was infested by maggots and stank. The willingness to trust God for our daily bread is hard to come by. But God wants no greedy, fearful hoarding in a community where there is sharing and no member is threatened by what someone else has, or suffers from the fear that someone will take away what he or she has. God promises plentitude to communities where greed is rejected and violence is not allowed. The divine gift of enough is for each day and is given day after day after day, without end.

We are confronted with the massive realities of scarcity for millions in our world today. The answers will doubtless require great effort and wisdom. We should learn some things from the Bible. We will never solve our problems by greed and hoarding. Those who say to us that greed is good should be rejected out of hand. We must learn to allow the land to produce sufficient food without polluting it with too much chemical fertilizer, and poisoning it with pesticides, herbicides, and fungicides. Our food should come more from the farms and less from factories. We must develop local economies to allow people to make a living for themselves, rather than depending solely on large companies and agricultural conglomerates. The task is daunting, but it should not be hindered by the false idea of a divinely ordered scarcity, never intended by God.

Psalm 23 also evokes the memory of Jesus as he taught a large crowd in a wilderness place. There was little to eat, and his disciples asked the question of scarcity: "How can one feed these people with bread here in the wilderness?" (Mark 8:4, see also 6:30–44). Jesus responded by asking for the food that was available, and there was enough. With the generous abundance of God the thousands were fed, and a large surplus was left over. The fear of scarcity was overcome by the plenty of God: "They were filled" (Mark 8:8).

We pray the Lord's Prayer and say, "Give us our daily bread." As we do, let us also remember that Jesus said, "I tell you, do not worry about your life, what you will eat or what you will drink, or about your body, or for what you will wear. . . . But strive first for the kingdom of God and his righteousness, and all these things will be given to you as well" (Matt. 6:25, 33). There is enough on the table for all of us; we will not lack, because the LORD is our shepherd.

Topic: A Great Thirst for the Place of the Presence of God
TEXT: Pss. 42, 43

In his long poem, "The Rime of the Ancient Mariner," Samuel Coleridge has given us a classic description of thirst. The ancient Mariner shot and killed an albatross, and his ship was later becalmed in the Pacific Ocean:

> Day after day, day after day,
> We stuck, nor breath nor motion;
> As idle as a painted ship
> Upon a painted sea.
> Water, water everywhere,
> And all the boards did shrink;
> Water, water everywhere,
> Nor any drop to drink.

Reflecting a very different context, Psalm 42 begins with a description of the panting, hurting cry of a deer in desperate need of water in a dry and arid region:

> As a deer pants for flowing streams;
> So pants my soul for you O God.
> My soul thirsts for God, for the living God.
> When shall I come and behold the face of God?

As we continue to read the psalm, we discover that the major problem of the speaker, who is unidentified, is that of separation from the place of worship of the LORD. The psalmist seems to be a devout person who is unable for some reason to participate in the joyful festival at the sanctuary:

> These things I remember, as I pour out my soul;
> how I went with the crowd,
> and led them in procession to the house of God,
> with glad shouts and songs of thanksgiving,
> A multitude keeping festival.

Because of the geographical references in verse 6, we think the psalm was probably originally intended for use in the Northern Kingdom of Israel, and the sanctuary was the one at Dan in the upper Jordan Valley. But in the present book of Psalms, the worship center is surely that of the Temple in Jerusalem. The experience of the psalmist is typical of many faithful Israelite exiles who were cut off from the joy of festivals in the homeland. They longed for the good times at the festivals they were no longer able to attend.

The irony of the thirsty situation of the speaker in these psalms is that there seems to be an abundance of water about. The upper Jordan is well watered, and in verse 7 the psalm reflects the roaring fall of the cataracts down the slopes of Mt. Hermon: "Deep calls to deep at the thunder of your cataracts, all your waves and your billows have gone over me." The language is poetic as the speaker attributes the "deep" and the rolling waves to the LORD. The "deep" is the word *tehom*, which is found in Genesis 1:2. This language reflects the idea of the raging, chaotic waves that seem to threaten the whole world. The streams from Mt. Hermon represent destructive forces pouring down on the psalmist (see Pss. 18:4, 69:1–3, 88:6–7).

The distress of the speaker is exacerbated by the taunts of those around, who ask repeatedly, "Where is your God?" (vv. 3 and 10). The distress is so great that the speaker calls it "murder in my bones." This line in verse 10 is usually read as a "crushing" or "breaking" of the bones, or else as a "deadly wound." The form of the word is found in the Old Testament only here, and so its exact meaning is hard to establish. However, it is clearly related to the verb "to murder" and therefore refers to shocking, murderlike trauma. In this case the trauma is spiritual and emotional. Indeed, the trauma is so great that we have an unusual feature in the Psalms of an introspective speaking of the psalmist to his own soul (or, mind):

> Why are you cast down, O my soul,
> and why are you disquieted within me?

The introspective address is followed by words of encouragement to the self: "Hope in God, for I will again praise him, my help and my God." These words of encouragement are probably those that worshippers heard often in the festival ceremonies.

In passing, it is worthwhile to notice that this self-address is found two times in Psalm 42 and once again in Psalm 43. This is a strong indicator that the psalms should be read together as one psalm. The careful reader will notice also that Psalm 43 has no title and is only one of four in Psalms 1–89 without a title (the others are Pss. 2, 33, and 71). Also, there are language links between the two psalms, and most interpreters read the two as one psalm. Psalm 43 contains strong petitions on the part of the psalmist for God to help.

The thirst for God is one of the fundamental needs of humanity. It finds expression again and again in religious literature. The best known of the Christian martyrs in the Nazi era of Germany was Dietrich Bonhoeffer. On June 5, 1935, he preached a sermon on Psalm 42. This is part of what he said:

> A human soul cries out here [in Ps. 42:1], not about an earthly good, but about God. A pious person, to whom God is far removed, longs after the God of salvation and grace. He knows this God to whom he cries. He is no seeker after the unknown God, who can never be found. He has experienced God's help and nearness; therefore he does not need to call into a void. He calls to his God. We can only rightly seek God when he has already made himself known to us, when we have already been found.[2]

These words are true, but we would be well advised to remember that in the psalm the thirst is for the place where the presence of God can be experienced in communal worship. Private piety finds its full expression in the fellowship of those of like mind and spirit who go to rejoice in worship. Thus the psalmist wants God to send out Light and Truth as personified gents from the heavenly realm, to ensure safe passage to "your holy hill and your dwelling" (43:3) in order to come to the altar and join in joyful worship.

The psalm reminds us that God is the great water giver in the Bible. He is the thirst quencher of the world. Along this line, one of the most impressive passages is found in Isaiah 41. In verse 17, Israelite exiles are "parched with thirst," but the LORD will meet their need, and declares "I will open rivers on the bare heights, and fountains in the midst of the valleys; I will make the wilderness a pool of water, and the dry land springs of water."

The result is a great forest of trees, a forest of different kinds of trees, most of which require lots of water to grow. Isaiah 60:13 envisions trees like those growing in the Temple area—and remember that the tree is a symbol of life and productivity. The prophet Ezekiel sees a stream of water that begins from the Temple in Jerusalem, becomes a river flowing down into the Dead Sea and vitalizing the Sea itself, and turning the barren valley below into what is like a Garden of Eden. Likewise, a river flows from the throne of God down the great street of the New Jerusalem in Revelation 22:1–2.

According to the Gospel of John, Jesus says of himself, "Let anyone who is thirsty come to me, and let the one who believes in me drink . . ." (7:37). Earlier he declared to the woman at the well, "Those who drink of the water that I will give them will never be thirsty. . . . The water that I will give will become in them a spring of water gushing up to eternal life" (John 4:13–14). Zion and the Temple of the LORD, where the festivals were held, were fountains of the presence of God. In the New Testament and in Christianity they have been transferred to Jesus Christ. However, the places and times of festival worship and community fellowship are still of vital importance for the spiritual life. At the end of Coleridge's poem he has the ancient Mariner, saved at last (and a guest at a wedding) declare:

> O sweeter than the marriage feast,
> 'Tis sweeter far to me,
> To walk together to the kirk

---

[2]My translation, from Claus Westermann (ed.), *Verkundigung Des Kommenden* (Munich: Kaiser, 1958), p. 150.

With a goodly company!
To walk together to the kirk.
And all together pray,
While each of his great Father bends
Old men, and babes, and loving friends
And youths and maidens fair!
Hope in God, for we will praise him again.

Topic: The Fix for Sin
TEXT: Ps. 51

The good news for all of us is that sin and the guilt that goes with it can be fixed. Sin is bad news, of course, but the good news of God's grace is greater than our sin. The psalmist in Psalm 51, traditionally identified with David after his affair with Bathsheba, knows that only action by God can turn things around and bring forgiveness. The psalm is remarkable for the boldness both with which sin is confessed and of the prayer for restoration. The confession is unequivocal and not ambiguous:

I know my transgressions,
and my sin is ever before me.
Against you, you only, have I sinned
and done what is evil in your sight
and so you are justified in your sentence
and blameless in giving judgment.

The language of the psalm is not specific, but whatever David has done against Bathsheba and Uriah has really been done against God. Guilt arises from sin against God, even if the acts seem to involve only ourselves and other people. Confronted with his terrible behavior in regard to his purely human behavior, David confesses, "I have sinned against the LORD" (2 Sam. 12:13). The discovery of this fact can be a surprising experience.

The sin in the psalm also consists of more than one or two acts; the speaker thinks that his whole life, from conception in the womb on, has been one of guilt (v. 5). However, the language of this verse has been much abused and should not be read too literally. The language is hyperbolic and indicates the pervasive condition of sin and guilt that adheres in every human life. Sin leaves a long path behind—but the act of sexual intercourse in marriage is not sinful, although every person is conceived and born in the sinful circumstances that prevail for all humanity. Sin is social and trails back through the life of everyone. The threads of our existence are woven in intricate patterns from conception until death.

The fix in Psalm 51 has two fundamental aspects. First there is *confession* and then there is *restoration*. Confession is an essential discipline in the life of faith, but its full effectiveness depends on its taking place in a fellowship of sinners who have confessed their sins and accepted the forgiveness of God. Forgiveness belongs in a community convicted of both sin and forgiveness (see James 5:16).

In regard to the confession of sin, it is important to remember that the word *confess* has more than one meaning. It may mean to disclose something done, usually of a damaging nature; *confession* refers to the act of acknowledging our actions and motives. However, confess and confession can also be used to acknowledge belief or faith—that is, to "profess." Confession is often used with reference to a statement of faith and belief. In Joshua 7:19, Achan is exhorted by Joshua to praise the LORD by confessing his wrongdoing. In Psalm 51 the context is clearly one in which the mercy and steadfast love of the LORD is set forth. Thus the act of contrition is also an act of testimony to the mercy and love of God. After forgiveness and restoration are received, the speaker vows to "teach transgressors your ways" so that sinners will return to God and the salvation of the LORD will be proclaimed (vv. 13–14). Those who hear the confessions of the sinner will hear praise of God.

The second part of the psalm is concerned with restoration of the life damaged by sin. The prayer for restoration is bold and strong. After asking for cleansing in verse 7, and a petition for a return to bones crushed in verse 8, we find a remarkable request that God turn his face from the speaker's sins. This is unusual, because the hiding of God's face is frequently equated with rejection. The most frequent prayer is "Why do you hide your face?" as in Psalm 44:25. But in Psalm 51 God is implored to alienate himself from the sinners' guilt by turning his face away.

In verses 10–12 there is prayer for restoration through a new creation within the sinner: "Create in me a clean heart, O God, and put a right spirit within me." The verb used here is *bara*; it is the same as that in Genesis 1:1. God's forgiveness is a creative work, not in the sense of creation out of nothing but in the sense of bringing forth what is new in old circumstances. The picture of creation in Genesis 1 comes to mind. There light is made, and days emerge from endless darkness. Life develops, and purpose and blessing are given to human beings in an ordered world that replaces the ceaseless roaring of the primeval deep. The seventh day or Sabbath completes the work of creation, and time is made holy. The psalmist knows that God's fundamental character is to restore and recreate sinners. Israel had lived on that basis. The apostle Paul understood that the work of God in Jesus Christ is a creative act when he wrote to the Corinthians that "if anyone is in Christ, he is a new creation; the old is gone, the new has come" (2 Cor. 5:17; cf. Gal. 6:15; John 3:3, 6; 1 Peter 1:23).

The threefold presence of the spirit in verses 10–12 reinforces the restoration as creation. The "right" or "steadfast spirit" produces enduring stability. The "holy spirit" of verse 11 is the animating presence of God that activates the will of human beings to seek the divine will and to live a faithful life. The "willing spirit" in verse 12 is the energizing power that generates willing response to the divine will and the new way of life. It is a mark of freedom from the bondage of guilt. God's "fix" for sin includes the work of the Spirit to bring newness, steadfastness, holiness, and willing joy.

The psalmist can confess so boldly and pray so boldly for restoration because he knows that there is a sufficient sacrifice that God will accept. The sacrifice is that of a "broken and contrite heart" (v. 17). He need not be like Cain in Genesis 4 and turn away angry and dismayed because his sacrifice has been rejected by God. This is the sacrifice that dispels frustration and despair and restores joy through the grace and power of a merciful God. Thanks be to God, the fix is in for us sinners, "now and in the hour of our death."

Topic: The Turning Point
TEXT: Ps. 73

Everyone has a turning point in life. Some are quiet and ordinary, but others are dramatic and sometimes traumatic. They are the times of important changes, usually involving new ways of thinking and of seeing things as they had not been seen before. In the religious life, these turning points are what we often call conversions. Some of them are famous in Christian history. In 386 A.D., Augustine of Hippo was struggling for faith and satisfaction in his troubled life. In the garden of a house in Milan, with Alypius, his friend, he heard a child in a neighboring house say, "Pick it up, read it; pick it up, read it," which was an unusual thing for a child to say. Augustine took it as a divine command to open his Bible and read the first passage he found, and he did. The passage was Romans 12:13: "Not in reveling and drunkenness, not in debauchery and wantonness, not in strife and envy, but put on the Lord Jesus Christ, and make no provision for the flesh to fulfill its lusts." He said that he needed to read no further, because something like the light of full certainty infused his heart, and all the gloomy doubt he had suffered vanished away. It was the turning point in his life, and he went on to become one of the most important leaders and teachers of the early church.

In his commentary of Psalms (1557), John Calvin wrote of a "sudden conversion," but he did not explain it further and he spoke very little of any conversion experience. We assume that the "sudden conversion" came as he studied the Psalms. It was some kind of turning point. John Wesley, already a minister but not doing very well (torn within himself and "beating the air," as he put it), went to a Moravian service on Aldersgate Street in London, on Wednesday night, May 24, 1738, and felt his heart "strangely warmed" while Luther's preface to the Epistle of Romans was being read. It was a turning point, and he went on to become a great preacher and the leader of Methodism. There have been many others.

The speaker in Psalm 73, who is unidentified, was unable to deal with envy and doubt until, as he says, "I went into the sanctuary of God" (v. 17). The psalm indicates that the speaker was near a total spiritual collapse, which he expresses in his words this way: "My feet had almost stumbled; my steps had nearly slipped." The trouble was a futile attempt to reconcile faith in the affirmation of God's goodness to the pure in heart in Israel and the well being of those who scorned such commitment. (Note: the reading of the first part of verse 1 is frequently changed to "Surely God is good to the upright," but it is better to keep "good to Israel" and understand the reference to the upright and faithful in Israel.) The speaker in this psalm finds it very difficult to sustain the proposition set forth in verse 1. The problem is the prosperity of the wicked, which causes envy to arise in the mind of the speaker. How can it be true that God is good to the pure in heart when those who scorn God are always at ease in using their power to mislead and exploit the poor? They are the sleek, well-dressed people, always going to parties and speaking with arrogance. They seem to have no pain and no trouble. The speaker, on the other hand, finds every day a torment of painful and discouraging experience (vv. 11–14). Walter Brueggemann says that the trouble of the psalmist is caused by "secular seduction." He is strongly tempted to join the way of those who have no moral commitment to God and "who regard religion as stuffy, pompous coercion and will not fool with it," living as if there is no God or anything sacred.[3]

The great distress of the speaker is described for us in verses 15–16. Unable to resolve the matter in his own mind, he was tempted to deny the goodness of God to the pure in heart and join the partygoers and exploiters. That way he could enjoy what seemed to be the good life. However, he refused to yield to the urge to make his distress public. Thus he was in the

[3]Patrick Miller (ed.), *The Covenanted Self* (Minneapolis: Fortress, 1999), pp. 66–67.

position of personally believing something that he did not think he could share with others of faith. In this condition, he came to the sanctuary of God (v. 17). There the turning point came: "I understood their end." We are given no detail about this experience. Perhaps we should think of a participant in worship in the Temple in Jerusalem on one of the great days of festival time, who has a vision as Isaiah did (see Isaiah 6). Or the speaker may have come to a new awareness of the reality of the situation while the priests and people chanted, "O give praise to the LORD of Hosts, for his steadfast love endures forever." Or he may have heard a prophet preach that "the word of our God will stand forever." Or it may have been in a time of quiet meditation and reflection on the ways of God in the world. In any case, it was a moment of disclosure, a turning point, when the eyes of a mind blinded by personal torment from envy regarding the material glory of the wicked were opened. Who can say what the exact nature of the turning point was? It matters little.

The results of the turning point are dramatic, with a new orientation toward those matters that have been so painful. First, there is a new perception of the real situation of the wicked (vv. 18–20). They no longer seem invincible, despite their apparent strength and power. But their security is an illusion, because their prosperity can be gone in an instant, leaving behind no more than a nightmare. Indeed, *they* are in "slippery places" (v. 18), although they may not seem to be. There is comfort in knowing that the wicked are not as well off as they think they are. We find reassurance in the perception that their "end" is grim—reassurance, but not joy.

Second, there is a new understanding of the psalmist's own self (vv. 21–23). In a flashback, he recalls that the trauma described in verses 2–16 was largely a matter of the heart ("heart" is one of the key words in this psalm, appearing in verses 1, 7, 13, 21, and 26). A "soured" or "embittered" heart left him reacting to the wicked like a brute beast, while the real problem was a "stupid and ignorant" heart. He had a "heart problem." (It is always well to keep in mind that biblical "heart" includes what we call the mind, the center of will and action.) The power of the wicked is so often the power to arouse coveting in the hearts of others.

The third new orientation, or reorientation, was the realization that God had been present with the psalmist throughout the ordeal of envy and doubt. An awareness of God's presence surges up into the consciousness of the distressed person. Despite all appearances to the contrary, "I am continually with you; you hold my right hand." The guidance of God never ceases, and the future is good. There is a question about the reading of the last part of verse 24. The Hebrew words are literally "and afterwards glory you will take me." "Afterward" rather clearly refers to the future, but does it mean after death? or from this time on? The "glory" is often understood as heaven, but it does not normally mean that in the Old Testament. Should we read the expression as "afterwards (in the future) God will take me to a glorious place"? More probably, we should understand the words here to mean that in the future God "will take me gloriously (to himself)"—as his own and with honor. This would satisfy the desire of the psalmist's heart: "There is nothing on earth that I desire other than you." Nevertheless, it seems reasonable to conclude that the glory of verse 24 has a dynamic quality that has the power to transcend death and replace it with life. The psalmist declares, "My flesh and my heart fail, but God is the rock of my heart and my portion forever." These words point to an enduring relationship that will not be terminated, now or forever. The "rock" does not wear out, and the word "portion" has its referential basis in a permanent entitlement to a portion of land passed on from generation to generation.

The new orientation of the turning point allows the psalmist to declare that "for me it is good to be near God; I have made the LORD God my refuge," and that he will tell others of all the works of God. "Blessed are the pure in heart, for they shall see God" (Matt. 5:8). Hold on to your faith until you come to a turning point; then you will understand that "it is not profit but presence that counts; not succeeding, but communion . . . [it will be] a moment of amazing recognition."[4]

---

[4]Walter Brueggemann, *Prayers of Walter Brueggemann: Awed to Heaven, Rooted in Earth* (Minneapolis: Fortress Press, 2003), p. 69.

MESSAGES FOR ADVENT AND CHRISTMAS

SERMON SUGGESTIONS

Topic: God Only Knows

TEXT: Isa. 64:4–9a; Mark 13:28–37

Advent begins today, the time of preparation for Christmas. In these four weeks you are going to hear the sounds of Christmas, the Christmas carols that we are so familiar with and love so much. You will hear them on the radio, you will hear them across the street in the department stores, and you will hear them tonight, best of all, in the choir concert. The sounds of Christmas. Christmas would not be Christmas without the music of Christmas.

But there is another sound in Advent; different music. You will not hear this music in the stores or on the radio, but you will hear it at church. It is the music of Advent. It's not sung often or gladly, even in church. In almost every Advent season I get notes asking, "When are we going to sing the Christmas carols? Why do we have to sing those gloomy Advent hymns?"

On this first Sunday of Advent, I will tell you that we will sing the Christmas carols in this church, and increasingly so as we move toward Christmas. But first, the Church says, we must hear the other song, the song of Advent.

You can see it as two songs in a duet, the one voice focusing on the manger in Bethlehem, the shepherds and the wise men, the mother and her baby, the most human of all scenes, which speaks to even non-Christians because it is so universally human. That's the song of Christmas. The other voice tells what happened before the child was born, and what will happen because the child was born. That's the Advent voice, and it sweeps back through history, back to the Israelites in bondage longing for a messiah.

> O come, O come Emmanuel,
> And ransom captive Israel,
> That mourns in lonely exile here
> Until the Son of God appear.

Advent goes back to the Old Testament, to Isaiah and Malachi and Ezekiel, back to a nation waiting, longing for God to come and deliver them. It goes back even farther than that, back even to Genesis, and says that what happened at Bethlehem is mysteriously related to what happened at the Creation.

Then it looks forward, beyond what we can see. It says that what happened at Bethlehem is also mysteriously related to what will happen in the End. Advent puts the little town of Bethlehem against the backdrop of the cosmos and all of history, and says that we can understand what happened at Bethlehem only by seeing it in that perspective. The most beautiful of all Advent hymns does this:

Of the Father's love begotten,
Ere the worlds began to be,
He is Alpha and Omega,
He the source, the ending he.

That's the song of Advent, and it reminds us that what happened at the beginning and what will happen at the end are mysteriously related to what happened at Christmas. It says that you are not merely looking upon a tender human scene; you are getting a glimpse of the very nature of things. You are seeing eternity in a manger. "He the source, the ending he."

Today we look at the ending, his words about it in the thirteenth chapter of Mark, the passage that is called "the little apocalypse" because it contains so many of the predictions of the end, the apocalyptic forecasts that were current in Jesus' time. They are collected there, all of these forebodings about history. It's like a Reader's Digest version of the apocalypse of John, what is known as the Book of Revelations at the end of the Bible, filled with signs in the heavens and tribulation on earth. It's all there in kind of a summary in the thirteenth chapter of Mark. But the chapter concludes with these words: "No man knows the hour or the day, no one knows but the Father. So watch."

The next time somebody confronts you with biblical visions of the end and ties them to current events, remember this passage: no one knows. The prophecies here in Mark were tied to the destruction of the temple in Jerusalem. The temple in Jerusalem was destroyed in 70 A.D. Nothing happened. The prophecies in the Book of Revelation were tied to the fall of Rome. Rome fell. Nothing happened! Those prophesies in the Book of Revelation and in Mark 13 were tied to the Millennium, 1000 A.D.; 1000 A.D. came. Nothing happened! They have been tied to events in every age, and nothing has happened. Today seers and fundamentalist preachers tie apocalyptic prophesies to political events in the Middle East. They even fuel the fires there, some of them, in the hope that they can precipitate Armageddon, exactly the way the Zealots in Jesus' time tried to use him to provoke a cataclysmic end of history in their time. The result today would be the result then. Then it was the tragedy of Massadah. Violence upon violence, to no purpose.

When will we learn the lesson that Jesus taught his disciples, that the Kingdom of God is not going to come by force? Because no one knows. The result of claiming to know is always the same. The result of claiming to know and acting on the basis of this certainty always means that history is going to be bloodier than it would have been otherwise. To no result.

In relation to the End, our situation is one of waiting. This is the message of Advent. We can't end the waiting. We can't do anything about it. The End, the judgment, the Kingdom of God will come when *God* is ready, not we. Until then, we live by faith. By definition, this means we live with uncertainty. It's a sign of maturity. It's always been the sign of spiritual maturity, ever since Abraham, living with uncertainty. Just as the sign of wisdom is the ability to say "I don't know." I am impressed with the humility of all the really great scientists. Every last one of them will say, "The more we know the more we discover how little we know." You can be certain only if you don't know very much. I am impressed as well with the spiritual giants, the mystics, who spent a lifetime of disciplined prayer and monastic isolation, who talk about *Deus Absconditus,* that is, the hidden God. They say, "The closer you get to God the more He is hidden and the less you know about Him." I am impressed with those who wait in loneliness, or sorrow, or in pain, for some help to come, some Messiah, some cure for their pain or some release from their bondage. They wait without understanding, without knowing why they must endure this exile. But they wait faithfully, trusting that one day God will act and give them new life. Until that time, they wait—members of this fellowship today, all over this city, in hospitals, not able to be with us today because of pain or sorrow, waiting, without answers. That's what spiritual maturity looks like. It doesn't have all the answers.

This is why Paul said, "Prophecy passes away, tongues will cease, knowledge will pass away"—the three claims to certainty. Paul says they are all illusions. They don't work. The only things that endure and help us endure are faith, hope, and love. When in a time of waiting, those are your provisions: faith, hope, and love. No one knows but the Father.

There is something in us that wants to know. It's as old as Adam and Eve, and this is why Adam and Eve were evicted from the Garden. They wanted to know what only God knows. But it is not ours to possess.

I read that the weather forecasters have issued their annual long-range forecast. They say that the winter is going to be mild and dry. They also say that they are right 60 percent of the time. They seem to be proud of that. When I was in school, 60 percent was a D. They are not forecasting. They're doing what you do when you get a D. They're guessing. I can wet my finger and put it to the wind and do that well.

Do you know why we have forecasters? Because we want to be forecast to. That's why we listen to doomsayers and Cassandras and fundamentalist preachers and economists and futurists and astrologers and meteorologists. We want to be forecast to. We want somebody to tell us what the future holds, especially in uncertain times, or in exile, or in bondage. We want to know. We want to know, and we can't know. We see in a mirror dimly. We journey into an unknown future in faith, and it has never been any other way. It never will be. For only the Father knows. He satisfies our every need for the journey except the need to know. He says all we need for the journey is faith, hope, and love—and the greatest of these is love.

Now look at the word *Father*.[1] It's strange that it is there in such a chapter as Mark 13, with all the violence about the end and the judgment. It's there. It's no accident that it appears in this passage about the future. I think Jesus chose it purposefully there. The word is *Abba,* the most personal form of address of the male parent in Aramaic, *abba.* It's like "daddy." I think it's there because he wants to tell us that in times of waiting, remember, we're to be like children.

It's too long ago for me to remember vividly what it was like to be a child, but I do remember when I was a father of small children. I remember the trust they placed in me. I remember the unquestioning faith they had in me. They would bring questions to me, confident that no matter how difficult the question I would know the answer. They would bring broken toys to me to fix, confident I could fix all things. I remember their bewilderment when I couldn't fix them. They couldn't understand it. But they trusted when I explained to them that no one on earth could possibly fix this thing.

Most of all, I remember the summers at the cabin, the boundaries set for them across which they were not to go alone. They were not to go to the river. They were not to go into the woods. The parental warning was sufficient to put fear in them of that dark, mysterious

---

[1] I am in debt to Robert Jewett for this insight.

perimeter of their world. They never trespassed it, never dared go there. But when their father went with them they would go gladly, without hesitation, the bravest of them running ahead out of sight, but never out of sound of their father's voice. They went into the unknown in faith, in trust. They trusted their father's presence with them.

"Unless you become as little children you shall not enter the kingdom of God." No one knows but the Father. The father. That's sufficient.

What we are asked to have faith in and place our hope in is God, who, Jesus said, is like a father. We're asked to go beyond the perimeters of our present into an unknown future, trusting that Father, who brought us thus far, will take us home. Though we may not see him, he knows us.

That's how we are to view the future. This is why, I believe, even though Jesus repeated the prophecies of his day—even the most violent of them—he repudiated them. I think that's what he's doing here. I think that's what it means to say, "No one knows but the Father." It was the most consistent thing he said about God, that he was like a father. He addressed God that way himself. He told us to do the same thing. We do it now so commonly that we forget that before he instructed the disciples in what we call "The Lord's Prayer," no one ever dared call God father. You were to use the language of majesty in addressing God, not the language of family. But he taught us differently. He said to say Abba. Say father.

Kings act arbitrarily; fathers act lovingly. Kings are to be feared; fathers are to be trusted. They keep their promises. Even if you did not have a father who was trustworthy and kept his promises, even if you didn't have a father at all, you still know what it means. I think those who did not have a father know, more than those who did, what it means. That's why Jesus said God is like a father, because there is a need in each one of us, to know that the One who created us is trustworthy.

This is why the parable of the Prodigal Son pictures a father who welcomes home a son who trusted his love and reprimands a son who expected the father to be vengeful. This is the God who will greet us in the future. This is the God who is bringing the kingdom. This is the God who is our judge. He is our Father.

Then to the final word: watch. It means prepare for the unexpected. As Christians we believe he will return. He is Alpha and Omega. He is the beginning and the end. We do not know when, nor do we know how. It is not impossible that his second coming will be as much a surprise as his first. It is very possible that all the prophecies about him will be confounded.

I came across some fascinating information about chess.[2] It's in a book by a man named David Spanner, who is a chess expert. He said that there are four hundred possible positions in chess after each player has made just one move. After they have made two moves there are seventy thousand possible positions on the board. After three moves by both sides the possible configurations on the board exceed nine million. It's astounding. The number of distinct, nonrepeating forty-move chess games, he said, the number of possible games that you can play without ever repeating the sequence of moves, is greater than the number of electrons in the universe.

I don't like chess-player analogies about God, but I tell you this: if he limits himself in accomplishing his will by what we do, then he's not nearly finished with this world. This

---

[2]Thanks to Ray Balcomb for this reference.

means that what looks like some disaster for us—some event that leads us to think, "Surely he's going to sweep his mighty arm across the board in anger"—this disaster is but one move for which he has an infinite number of countermoves. So watch.

I think it has this meaning: "Watch this!" or, "You haven't seen anything yet!" or, "Wait 'til you see what I'm going to do next!" To watch means to be prepared for wonderful surprises.

It also means this. It means to pray and to work. Pray for peace, and work for it. Pray that hunger will end in this world, and give to it. Pray that violence to children and to women will end, and do something about it. Pray that all those who are oppressed in any way will be free. Pray that the love of Christ will spread across the world. Pray "Thy Kingdom come," and do something about it. That's what it means to watch. Because, who knows? Maybe the moves you make, maybe the thing you do, will open possibilities he can use that never existed before you moved. Watch. Work and pray. Because you haven't seen anything yet.

I think it's probably been our arrogance, and even our anti-Semitism, that has not allowed us to see that the Church is in very much the same place today as the Jews are. The Jew awaits a Messiah; we wait for the Messiah's return. There's a theological difference, but there's not much practical difference. In fact, the instruction to the Christians to watch is no different than what the Jews were doing in the first century and what they have been doing ever since. They have been watching. In fact, at their celebrations they put an empty place at their table for the Messiah. They are waiting, just as we are.

But over the centuries there has emerged a skepticism on the part of many Jews about the Messiah. So many rabbis claiming to be the Messiah! Jewish scholars say that there have been sixteen or seventeen of them since Jesus. It is not unlike Christians prophesying the second coming; there have been at least sixteen or seventeen false starts since Jesus.

So in terms of the future, we are all alike. We are in a time of waiting. This is why I think a lesson given by Johanan ben Zakkai, the last pupil of the famous Hillel, is for us. It's perfect for Advent, the season of waiting and watching. He said this: "If you are planting a tree and you hear that the Messiah has come, finish planting the tree. Then go and inquire."

Jesus said, You're going to hear all kinds of prophecies. But remember, no one knows the hour or the day. No one knows but the Father. So watch. Watch. That is, pray for the Kingdom, and work for it. When you finish the work, and if you've got nothing better to do, then go and inquire. But first, do the work the Lord has given you.—Mark Trotter

Topic: The Five Faces of Bethlehem
TEXT: Luke 2:15b

"Let us go now to Bethlehem," said shepherds to one another on a long-ago night. "Let us go there and see this thing that has happened, which the Lord has made known to us." Humble shepherds had been visited by an angelic host and told good news concerning the birth of a Savior, Christ the Lord. Bethlehem was the place of birth—quiet Bethlehem, about six miles removed from the city of Jerusalem. A collection of modest dwellings flanking gently rolling hills, Bethlehem might have seemed the least of cities—indeed, some observers considered it so.

But Bethlehem had a long history, distinguished in ways that set it apart. The Bible depicts Bethlehem not alone as the Christmas village but as a center of other significant incidents and experiences. They reached back to the time when Judges ruled over Israel; then to the days of the Hebrew leader Samuel; to the time of David, the King; to the period of the great prophets; and finally, to the era when Rome governed the ancient world, and Jesus was born. At least five faces can be seen when looking at Bethlehem through the eyes of Scripture.

I. One of the early "faces" or images the Old Testament describes is that of *courtesy.* Bethlehem was the village of courtesy. It was the place to which Naomi brought her daughter-in-law, Ruth. Do you recall that beautiful Old Testament story? Naomi, at an earlier point in time, had moved from Judah to the country of Moab, with her husband and two sons. The sons each married Moabite women, but sadly, after a few years, both sons died—as did Naomi's husband. A widow and childless, Naomi determined to return to her homeland. Ruth, one of the two daughters-in-law, could not bear to be separated from someone she had come to love. Naomi urged her to remain in Moab, but Ruth responded (these are such familiar biblical words), "Entreat me not to leave you or to return from following you; for where you go I will go, and where you lodge I will lodge; your people shall be my people, and your God my God; where you die I will die, and there will I be buried. May the Lord do so to me and more also if even death parts me from you."

Given such loyalty and devotion, Naomi relented and brought Ruth with her to the land of Judah and to the town of Bethlehem. It was there, in Bethlehem, that this "outsider," this woman of another culture and background, was received with warmth and gracious courtesy. Indeed, Ruth soon made a place for herself, favored by a kinsman of Naomi, the wealthy Boaz. In due course, Boaz took Ruth as his wife. In the story of Jesus, this woman (who bore Boaz a son) is remembered as an ancestress of David the King, and then of Jesus the Messiah.

It was Bethlehem where Ruth found a new life; more significantly, it was in this setting that she as a Gentile found acceptance among the Jews. Bethlehem, unique for that day and time, proved itself eminently hospitable; it became the village of courtesy—a quality to be remembered.

II. So also was Bethlehem a place of *consecration.* It was here that young David was anointed by Samuel as the future king of Israel. The second face of Bethlehem is seen in this moment of history when God set apart a new leader, one who would be equal to the demands of the hour. David's consecration to his task was evident by the change that came upon him; the Old Testament says, "Samuel took the horn of oil, and anointed [David] in the midst of his brothers; and the Spirit of the Lord came mightily upon David from that day forward."

David was the youngest of the sons of Jesse. He was a shepherd of Bethlehem, an interesting realization when we think of how angels came first to shepherds of Bethlehem, to announce the birth of Christ the Lord, centuries after David's time. Samuel, God's prophet who was called to anoint Israel's kings, was unsure of his task, assuming that an older or more distinguished person would be chosen. But the word of God came to Samuel, saying, "The Lord sees not as man sees; man looks on the outward appearance, but the Lord looks on the heart." In heart and in readiness, David was the person to be king. In his own home he was anointed, making Bethlehem the village of consecration—another quality to be remembered.

III. A third face, of *dedication,* can be observed in Bethlehem as well. Circumstances were dramatically different when this characteristic became linked with that special place. Enemy invaders had garrisoned themselves in Bethlehem, and access by the Israelites was cut off. David was king, and he mourned the plight of his village. His feelings were expressed as he said longingly, "O that someone would give me water to drink from the well of Bethlehem which is by the gate."

Three of the kings' bravest men sought to honor David's wish. At great personal risk they broke through the camp of the Philistines and drew water from that refreshing well. Secretly they brought it to David. His surprise and gratitude were great—but so also was his awareness of the danger the three warriors faced in doing something gracious for him. David could not bring himself to drink the water; instead, he poured it out as an offering to God. In his eyes, the risk of life involved was too significant to be treated casually. David, as a result, dedicated the water and the courage that secured it to God. He perceived accurately what the mercies of life cost, and how they need to be dedicated to holy purposes.

The water of Bethlehem was secured in this instance at enormous risk. Much later, a child of Bethlehem was to offer his divine manhood in sacrifice for the blessing (literally, for the salvation) of others. The image of dedication was attached early to Bethlehem—and the quality was remembered and repeated.

IV. Similar things can be said about the fourth face of Bethlehem, the face of *hope*. From the days of Micah, a Hebrew prophet who lived eight centuries before Christ, Bethlehem was singled out as the place of hope. When Jesus was born and the Wise Men from the east inquired of Herod the King concerning this birth, they were told of the ancient prophecy relating to Bethlehem. In Micah's words the prophecy took this form: he said, "But you, O Bethlehem . . . who are little to be among the clans of Judah, from you shall come forth for me one who is to be ruler in Israel, whose origin is from old, from ancient days."

Micah's definition of a ruler in Israel focused upon a person's military prowess and his ability to conquer the hostile Assyrians. By this definition, Micah conveyed a certain temporal hope to his own people. But this man saw farther than he realized. Bethlehem long years later became the origin of an eternal hope for all people. It was there that Christ was born. Hope took its most memorable definition in him.

V. The final face of Bethlehem is that of *revelation*. God revealed the magnitude of divine love and power through an infant who first looked out upon the world from Bethlehem. This overpowering revelation of God with us belongs first to that place. Not everyone recognized it, of course, and this is still true. Huxley reminds us: "Even the facts will fool you. You've got to see beyond the facts in order to see the facts." Using thoughts expressed earlier today when the Advent Candle was lighted, it is *faith* that promises us Jesus, the Savior—Jesus, the friend. With the eyes of faith we see the facts (Jesus was born in Bethlehem) and then see beyond those facts, to the hope he brings, and the saving help. It is a revelation from above, and it makes all things news.

Theologian H. Richard Niebuhr explained such acts of faith this way: "Whatever other men may say we can only confess, as men who live in history, that through our history of compulsion has been placed upon us and a new beginning offered us which we cannot evade. We must say with St. Augustine: 'Walk by him the man and thou comest to God. By him thou goest, to him thou goest. Look not for any way except himself by which to come to him. For if he had not vouchsafed to be the way, we should all have gone astray. Therefore he became the way by which thou shouldst come. I do not say to thee, seek the way. The way itself is come to thee: arise and walk.'" This is what revelation means, in relation to Bethlehem and to ourselves.

These five faces are always to be remembered—the faces of Bethlehem, the images of Christ's coming and of his meaning in the human sphere. They include courtesy, and also consecration. Dedication belongs to this place, as does hope—and ultimately, revelation. What a model of civic meaning for any community! What a model for personal life! Copying Bethlehem, there still is ample need for both communities and individuals to reflect courtesy, consecration, dedication, hope—and to reveal in their nature the things of God. It still is appropriate to say as shepherds once did, "Let us go now to Bethlehem and see this great thing that the Lord has done."—John H. Townsend

RESOURCES FOR PREACHING ON REVELATION

BY WILLIAM E. HULL

Topic: The Lord God Omnipotent Reigns
TEXT: Rev. 19:6

Let's face it: we are afraid of the Book of Revelation. It is the least read and most misunderstood book in the New Testament. When we pass from the Gospels and Epistles to its pages, we are confronted with a bizarre scenario that seems to unfold in an alien land. Weird and esoteric symbolism abounds on every page. Some choose to ignore this last book of the Bible; others make it the key to their understanding of the whole of Scripture. Revelation has been the happy hunting ground for many a religious crackpot, from the Millerites, who were convinced that the world would end in 1844, to the Branch Davidians, whose leader, David Koresh, believed that he had been chosen to open the seven seals of the Apocalypse and launch God's judgment on the world. It is a book of unspeakable violence in the name of God, which chills the blood of those who want religion to offer a haven of safety and peace.

Lest we despair, the cryptic language that so easily confuses offers a clue to the unique genius of the book. Here we have nothing less than an attempt to peer into another world, to make visible the invisible and to utter the unutterable. It forces us out of our routine ways of thinking and asks us to discover reality through the imagination rather than the intellect. Make no mistake: the Revelation of John intends to startle us, even to shock us; it is subversive literature with a dangerous message, for an evil day when those who challenged the powers that be in the name of Christ were courting persecution and even death. The book is high drama, designed to awaken buried emotions, enlarge the boundaries of experience, and jar its readers out of complacency with God's wake-up call. It dares to view all of life in the ultimate dimension!

One of our primary sources of confusion is the time perspective its message intends. Was Revelation written only for its day, or to describe the subsequent sweep of human history, or to predict the ultimate end of the world? The answer is found in a formula used three times (1:4, 1:8, and 4:8, reinforced by 11:17 and 16:5), where God is seen as "the one who is and who was and who is to come," the one "in whom the ultimate past and the ultimate future are comprehended in an eternal present."[1] Unlike the religious sensationalists of our day, John wrote to be relevant and intensely practical for his desperate readers, who were trying to survive in an alien culture, for whom our endless speculations about the latest skirmish in the

---

[1]G. B. Caird, *A Commentary on the Revelation of St. John the Divine* [Harper's New Testament Commentaries] (New York: HarperCollins, 1966), p. 291.

Middle East would be of little or no help. Yet John probed the depths of life so profoundly that his core convictions are just as valid in our day as in his own. It is precisely because John was so effective in guiding the embattled Church of the first century, as it lived on the edge of extinction, that his book is worthy of our closest attention in the twenty-first century.

As is the case in most drama, the central reality of Revelation is conflict. The three great themes that dominate the book from beginning to end concern (1) the divine protagonist, God; (2) the evil antagonist, Satan; and (3) the resolution of the cosmic struggle between the two, Victory. Here two worlds are pictured as locked in a titanic battle for the loyalty of the human heart, the outcome of which will determine the character of both time and eternity. Amazing as it may be, we mortal earthlings are the prize for which the ultimate powers of the universe now contend! Revelation is profoundly theocentric; thus we look first at what it has to say about God.

I. *God the Father.* John lived in a day when the Roman Empire, then at the height of its power, was determined to control the course of history. Its imperial designs knew no limits. The ages of time would be determined by the rule of its Caesars (Luke 3:1). Rome had already crushed every other earthly power within the wider Mediterranean world; thus none dared challenge its supremacy. Intoxicated with its own self-importance, the empire moved steadily to make itself the unifying power around which political, economic, cultural, and religious life would cohere.

Over and against this absolutizing of Roman authority, John dared to make the most subversive claim imaginable: that history was guided not by the Caesars but by the sovereign Lord of heaven. Three interlocking claims made clear that God alone controlled the unfolding of the ages from creation to consummation, for he is "the Alpha and the Omega, the first and the last, the beginning and the end" (22:13). The meaning of time would be determined by his eternal purposes, not by the latest ruler in Rome. Throughout the book there is an emphasis on wholeness, completeness, and ultimacy, as seen, for example, in the frequent use of the number seven, which in Jewish numerology stood for the fullness of reality, as in the seven days of the week. In Revelation we have seven letters, seven seals, seven trumpets, seven thunders, seven bowls, seven attributes of the Lamb, seven beatitudes, and seven acts in the drama that unfolds—and God guides it all.

In exalting the awesome majesty and mystery of God, John goes out of his way to underscore his utter transcendence by describing him seven times as "almighty" or "omnipotent" (1:8, 4:8, 11:17, 15:3, 16:7, 10:6, and 21:22). This is seen not only in John's vivid descriptions of God's glory but particularly in his sevenfold designation of God as "the One who sits on the throne" (4:9, 5:1, 5:7, 5:13, 6:16, 7:15, and 21:5). Caesar's throne stood for his right to rule, but John saw a greater throne than Caesar's—not in Rome but in heaven (4:2). Everything about the description of God on his throne (4:3–6) was calculated to trump the ostentation that Rome heaped upon its Caesar in a futile effort to make him seem superhuman. In passages such as this, John is crying at the top of his voice that appearance is not reality, that the dazzling temples to Caesar being built all over Asia Minor were nothing compared to the heavenly court, that even though Caesar may rule momentarily on earth, God reigns eternally in heaven.

Yet John makes an equally important point by what he does not say about this cosmic Potentate. To be sure, God is supreme, but his sovereignty is not coercive. Despots such as

Nero could rigidly control events by the exercise of arbitrary and capricious power, intimidating and terrorizing whole populations with the threat of violence. But almighty God chooses to rule in a context of human freedom. In his universe, one can decide to be either friend or foe. The greatness of God is seen precisely in the fact that he is not a control freak like the Caesars but accomplishes his purposes in the face of radical contingency. Revelation is animated by a breathtaking vision of the God who *lets us be,* who fashions his future out of our choices (whether they be good or bad)—a God who desires only our love, even though love is the most voluntary relationship in human experience.

II. *God the Son.* But if God does not bully his subjects with coercive power, how does he hope to win their fickle hearts? The answer to this central question is that God responded to the unpredictabilities of human freedom by sending his Son to earth to save us from self-destructive decisions. Perhaps the most incredible symbol in the entire book is that of Christ as a sacrificial Lamb. John knew that the messianic hope looked for a "Lion of the tribe of Judah, the root of David," who would come to conquer the enemies of the people of God (5:5). But as soon as we move to his next paragraph, we are shocked to discover that this Lion has become a Lamb with his throat cut! (5:12). Now we begin to realize that God has given us so much freedom that we can make him bleed, that evil "can be conquered only by being allowed to conquer and so to burn itself out."[2]

How quickly we come to the heart of the plot in this drama of redemption: here is the daring claim, not only that God is going to triumph over the most hideous evil imaginable but that his only weapon will be a vulnerable Lamb. This is John's key image of Christ in the Apocalypse, being used as a title for Jesus twenty-nine times. But more: it is not just that this Lamb was willing to be a helpless victim. Rather, it was precisely *as* victim that he became victor over every malignant force in the universe, worthy "to receive power and wealth and wisdom and might and honor and glory and blessing," a sevenfold tribute no less! (5:12). Jesus is "worthy" not *despite* the fact that he had to suffer but precisely *because* he had to suffer. His defeat *is* his victory, his shame *is* his glory, his humiliation *is* his vindication, and his cross *is* his crown.

What an incredible claim: that Rome is going to be vanquished, not by swords and spears but by a splintery cross! Any doubt that the crucified Christ will reign triumphant is dispelled at the outset of the book, when the Risen Lord is described in glorious terms reminiscent of God himself (1:12–16). Even Caesar in all of his finery never looked like that! Make no mistake: Jesus Christ, the faithful witness and first-born of the dead, is "the ruler of kings on earth" (1:5). To be sure, the enemies of God "will make war on the Lamb, but the Lamb will conquer them, for he is Lord of lords and King of kings" (17:14). What a seditious thing for John to say!

III. *God the Holy Spirit.* All over Asia Minor the oppressive power of Rome was acutely felt, even though the throne of the Caesar was far away in the so-called Eternal City. Just so, John and his readers could take heart that the Lord and his Lamb were already sovereign in heaven, though their throne often seemed so far away. More immediate help for these beleaguered Christians was offered by the presence and power of the Holy Spirit, another constant refrain in the book of Revelation. Indeed, John was given a vision of heaven because he was "in the Spirit" (1:10). This momentous disclosure happened on the isolated island of Patmos,

---

[2]Caird, p. 293.

a remote military outpost some eighty-eight miles off the coast of Asia Minor. Only ten miles long and six miles wide, this rocky outcropping in the Aegean Sea was a perfect place to isolate troublemakers who needed to come to their senses. But God's Spirit was also present on Patmos, not only to inspire the writing of John's book but to serve as God's living agent of persuasion for all who would read it (22:17).

But more than this, John could write in confidence that the Holy Spirit would not only interpret his divine revelation but also strengthen the Christians to whom he was writing. Each of the letters to the seven churches ends with the refrain, "Let the one with ears hear what the Spirit says to the churches" (2:7, 2:11, 2:17, 2:29; 3:6, 3:13, and 3:22). Since each letter begins by announcing that the words that follow are from the exalted Christ, this means that the Holy Spirit mediates the realities of heaven to those struggling here on earth. It is as if each church, regardless of its condition, has the Holy Spirit of God intimately present to function somewhat like its guardian angel (1:4, 1:20, 3:1, 4:5, and 5:6).

Revelation constantly emphasizes that worship is the setting in which God the Father and God the Son are most intimately present with us as God the Holy Spirit. On the one hand, there are scenes of heavenly worship interspersed throughout the book, with at least fifteen hymns or hymnlike fragments: (1) the thrice-holy cry (4:8); (2) three songs acclaiming God or the Lamb as "worthy" (4:11, 5:9–10, and 5:12); (3) three doxologies (5:13, 7:12, and 16:5–7); (4) seven "victory" songs (7:10, 11:15, 11:17–18, 12:10–12, 15:3–4, 19:1–2, and 19:6–8); and (5) an exhortation to praise God (19:5).[3] These hymns help to carry the story line of the book in poetic fashion. In a profound sense, Revelation sings its message through stanza after stanza to a grand climax.

But on the other hand, it is precisely in earthly worship that Christians both anticipate and participate in the worship of the heavenly court. The reference to "the Lord's day" (1:10) implies that the book began in worship, and the "Amen" cry (22:20) implies that it ended in worship. To us, worship is often little more than a weekly habit, but to John's readers it was a daring act of political protest. For one thing, its heavenly descriptions of worship were a parody of imperial court ceremonies, a way of saying that none of Rome's impressive pageantry was worthy to be compared with the liturgy of heaven. To gather for worship on earth, and to have the heavenly worship mediated by the living Holy Spirit, was a concrete declaration that this people would bow to no other God, that only the Lord of Heaven deserves our ultimate allegiance, that any compromise with the worship of the Lamb is nothing less than treason. The inference is inescapable: if God and the Lamb are truly *worthy* of worship, then there can be no doubt that the Caesars are *unworthy* of the worship they were demanding.

In our modern democratic culture, with its emphasis on autonomous individualism, some have reacted negatively to the insistence of Revelation that the triune God is omnipotent. Far from sanctioning "authoritarian structures of power and domination in human society," however, "this is the exact opposite of the way the image of divine sovereignty functions in Revelation. There, so far from legitimizing human autocracy, divine rule radically delegitimizes it. Absolute power, by definition, belongs only to God, and it is precisely the recognition of God's absolute power that relativizes all human power."[4]

---

[3]W. Hulitt Gloer, "Worship God! Liturgical Elements in the Apocalypse," *Review and Expositor*, 2001, *98*(1), p. 40.
[4]Richard Bauckham, *The Theology of the Book of Revelation* (New York: Cambridge University Press, 1993), p. 44.

Our nation and its people need this message of an omnipotent God as never before in its history, because, like Rome in its day, we possess unrivaled military, political, economic, and cultural power. One response to the terrorist attacks of September 11 is to conceive our strategic role as that of an imperialist empire exercising global hegemony in unipolar fashion.[5] Indeed, some feel that we are already well down that Roman road, with a complicit Christianity leading the way. Listen to the stinging indictment by Wendell Berry, which has so many resonances with the Book of Revelation:

> Despite its protests to the contrary, modern Christianity has become willy-nilly the religion of the state and the economic status quo. . . . It has, for the most part, stood silently by while a predatory economy has ravaged the world, destroyed its natural beauty and health, divided and plundered its human communities and households. It has flown the flag and chanted the slogans of empire. It has assumed with the economists that "economic forces" automatically work for good and has assumed with the industrialists and militarists that technology determines history. . . . It has admired Caesar and comforted him in his depredations and faults. But in its de facto alliance with Caesar, Christianity connives directly in the murder of Creation. For in these days, Caesar is no longer a mere destroyer of armies, cities, and nations. He is a contradictor of the fundamental miracle of life.[6]

In its radically theocentric vision of ultimate reality, Revelation offers us an astringent reminder that we allow God to have earthly competitors only at our peril, even if those rivals be democracy and capitalism. Our nation was founded as an experiment in *limited* government, unlike the absolute monarchies of Europe. It was to be carefully circumscribed by checks and balances, one of which was the separation of Church and state so that government and religion could not control or even unduly influence each other. Our market economy was designed to protect the yeoman farmer and village shopkeeper from destructive competition by industrial and commercial behemoths. There are many ways to restrain the totalitarian impulse, including a free press in the community, a free pulpit in the church, and a free podium in the classroom. But the best way to curb the unbridled appetite for power is to affirm with Handel that the Lord God alone is omnipotent and that "he shall reign forever and ever!"

Topic: The Beast from the Bottomless Pit
TEXT: Rev. 11:7

One of the most fascinating yet frightening features of the Book of Revelation is its use of grotesque symbolism to describe supernatural evil. Here we meet a beast coming up from the sea (13:1) and a great red dragon (12:3) coming down from the sky, each of them with ten horns and seven heads, reminiscent of the sea monster Leviathan and the earth monster

---

[5]The centerpiece of the debate over this option is "the National Security Strategy of the United States of America," issued by Pres. George W. Bush on September 17, 2002, with its so-called "doctrine of preemption."
[6]Wendell Berry, *Sex, Economy, Freedom, and Community* (New York: Pantheon Books, 1992), pp. 114–115.

Behemoth. They are joined by the great harlot of Babylon with whom the kings of earth have committed fornication until they and their subjects have become drunk on debauchery (17:1–2). The imagery is deliberately repulsive, never more so than today, when we have ripped our Halloween masks off the face of evil and eliminated the word Satan from our vocabulary as "a medieval term that should probably be banished from civilized discourse in a multicultural world."[7]

But before we repudiate the last book of the Bible for its scare tactics, consider the enormous impact of contemporary efforts in portraying evil on monstrous terms. Think of Darth Vader's sinister minions in the *Star Wars* epic. Or of the hideous subterranean creatures that abound in the *Lord of the Rings* trilogy. In the second installment, *The Two Towers*, for example, the defining battle of Helm's Deep depicts the beastly warriors of Saruman marching in vast phalanxes on the final outpost of Rohan, in a manner reminiscent of Hitler's ferocious onslaughts in World War II. Revelation has dared to construct a symbolic world adequate to depict the magnitude of evil that its readers were being called upon to oppose. Gazing into the crater that was once the World Trade Center, we dare not do less. So let us explore why John was chosen to depict the reality of evil in all of its horrid ugliness.

I. *Cosmic evil.* What does it mean to portray evil as a kingdom ruled by a tyrant more sinister than anything human? Is John saying that we are up against a foe mightier than our human strength can withstand? As if this were not bad enough, even worse is the realization that we have created the monster ourselves! John does not posit an absolute metaphysical dualism that would divide the universe into two eternal domains, one ruled by goodness and the other by evil. In place of this Zoroastrian/Manichean heresy, what John is saying is that there is an abyss, a "dark hole" as it were, at the heart of life, which acts as a vast reservoir of accumulated evil to which we have all contributed. Nazism, for example, was not the work of Adolf Hitler alone but the result of innumerable compromises by thousands, even millions, of people willing to embrace the lie of a Master Race, willing to deify a deranged paper-hanger as absolute leader, willing to erect a superstructure of "principalities and powers" perpetrating a Holocaust that snuffed out millions of lives in an orgy of gratuitous violence.

But why do such senseless things happen again and again, with numbing regularity? It is because evil wears an endless number of disguises. It dresses up in immaculate uniforms, it holds impressive parades, it plays spine-tingling music, it appeals to idealistic motives, it exploits ancient resentments. Once it gains legitimacy, it begins to build its bureaucracy of horror until it becomes a totalitarian juggernaut out of control. The task of John was to unmask this monster, to strip the seductive whore called Babylon of her allurements (17:4) so that all could see her for what she really was. Irony of ironies, even though evil is like a devouring beast (13:2; cf. 1 Pet. 5:8) its strategy is not to intimidate but to fascinate; it does not merely want to be feared but to be "worshiped" and "followed with wonder" (13:3–4). Beware, Revelation is saying, the pomp and circumstance that parades itself in surface splendor to win your allegiance; underneath its seductive camouflage is a disgusting brute bent on your destruction.

John deliberately used the most offensive language possible in order to show that Rome was not the glittering spectacle that it presented to the world but was a loathsome beast intent

---

7Lance Morrow, "The Real Meaning of Evil," *Time*, Feb. 24, 2003, p. 74.

on ravaging the human spirit. The beast even employed a second beast, symbolizing the imperial cult, as its public relations agent, who used dazzling displays and propaganda to glamorize its atrocities, much as Hitler used Goebbels to cover the crimes of the Third Reich (13:11–15).[8] The strategy of evil is always to use deception in offering counterfeit glory. Satan is "the deceiver of the whole world" (12:9) who misleads by telling lies both about God and about himself. The Antichrist is a false messiah who utters blasphemous denials of Christ (2 John 7). If you are sickened by the repulsiveness of evil in the Apocalypse, then John has accomplished his purpose. If only Germany had been sick of Adolf Hitler in 1933 rather than in 1945! Sometimes our only defense against evil is revulsion, which comes when we have seen it for what it really is.

II. *Human evil.* Once evil is allowed to create its own superstructure, then individuals can use, and be used by, this apparatus for diabolical ends. In John's day, each new Caesar inherited the throne of an empire that had been drunk on its own power for generations. For example, the emperor Nero gladly volunteered to become the human incarnation of the Beast, identified by the number 666 (13:18), and the Empire gladly let him do it because the people wanted their Caesar to function as the unquestioned symbol of Rome's absolute power.

Once Nero fornicated with the harlot of national hubris, he became the kind of man who could kick his pregnant wife to death, castrate and then "marry" a boy named Sporus, murder his own young mother, and delight in being praised as a god until he was finally declared insane by the Roman Senate. If that seems extreme, think of how we are still being brutalized by pathological narcissists such as Osama bin Laden, Saddam Hussein, and Kim Jong II. With their subjects starving, lacking the most basic necessities of health care, desperately needing education and economic development, such rulers build multiple palaces and plot nuclear catastrophe because the disenfranchised masses are willing to concentrate unlimited power in them so that they may function as reckless agents of revenge and retaliation against a world that they resent. Lord Acton was right: absolute power does corrupt absolutely, turning potentially decent humans into cunning predators.

John was particularly sensitive to the way in which cities could become the stronghold of evil. In Revelation 17:9, he pictured Babylon as a whore seated on seven mountains, a scarcely veiled reference to Rome as the city built on seven hills. The dirge for "the great city" in Revelation 18 is a lament for how urban pride can finally become self-destructive. Cities in our day easily succumb to the empire building of rapacious capitalism, or technological superiority, or cultural elitism, or intoxicating pride. When John wrote, Jerusalem already lay in ruins, but he saw that one day Rome would become a "dwelling place of demons, a haunt of every foul spirit, a haunt of every fowl and hateful bird" (18:2). No wonder he closed his book with a vision of the New Jerusalem as a replacement for the Babylon that had sold its soul for power and glory.

III. *The consequences of evil.* Because John believed in the power of evil both to aggregate and to escalate, with no shortage of earthly agents to do its bidding, he was profoundly realistic about the ability of evil to wreak havoc on planet Earth. In the middle chapters of Revelation, we find a grim recitation of the horrors that depraved despots can visit on humanity.

---

[8]Paul Spilsbury, *The Throne, the Lamb, and the Dragon: A Reader's Guide to the Book of Revelation* (Downers Grove, Ill.: InterVarsity Press, 2002), p. 98.

It begins in Chapter 6 with the four horsemen of the Apocalypse, who ravage the earth with conquest, warfare, famine, and death (6:2–8). The devastation seems endless: first there are plagues launched by the opening of the seven seals (6:1–8:5), then havoc wrought by the blowing of the seven trumpets (8:6–11:15), then pestilence poured out by the seven bowls (16:1–18:24). Each visitation seems worse than the one before, as if the carnage is cumulative. However, these three symbolic series are not so much sequential as they are simultaneous, each ending in the same fashion with a terrible earthquake (8:5, 11:19, 16:17). What John is saying by his repetition for emphasis is that evil relentlessly hammers human life over and over again, until the cosmos itself comes unhinged.

Rather than indulging in fantasy to construct this chamber of horrors, John ransacked the Old Testament for lurid depiction of tragedy.[9] When we read about water turning to blood, of darkness, hail, boils, frogs, and locusts (8:7–8, 9:3, 16:2–4, and 16:10), we are reminded of the plagues that fell on Egypt (Exod. 7:8–11:10). The picture of people hiding in caves and among rocks (6:15–16) echoed Isaiah's description of the Day of the Lord (Isa. 2:10, 19). Even such cosmic portents as the rolling up of the sky and the falling of stars (6:12–14, 8:10–11) were widely anticipated by the prophets as symbolic of the overthrow of "principalities and powers" arrayed against God (Isa. 14:12–15, 34:2–4; Joel 2:28–32; Jer. 51:25–26). The massing of great hordes from across the Euphrates to fight at Armageddon (16:12–16) gathered up repeated experiences with invading armies out of the east, from the time of the Assyrians to that of the Parthians. In all of this calamitous tale of woe, stretching over centuries of biblical history but now reaching its climactic expression in John's day, the most striking feature was that even catastrophe after catastrophe could not induce humankind to repent! (9:20–21).

It is not easy to read about blood flowing "as high as a horse's bridle for two hundred miles" (14:20), but is such apocalyptic hyperbole unrealistic? Go to Auschwitz and see the ovens that filled the sky with the human ashes of genocide. Or to Dachau, where ministers were horsewhipped until their bodes were a bloody pulp only because they would not salute and say "Heil Hitler." Or to the Gulag, where Stalin slaughtered upward of twenty million merely to eliminate dissent and make his regime a reign of terror. Or to the killing fields of Cambodia, where the Khmer Rouge indiscriminately butchered 1.2 million people, a fifth of the population, all in the name of social engineering driven by ideological fanaticism. Can we really claim that our capacity for cruelty has diminished over the twenty centuries since Revelation was written?

Nor are such atrocities always perpetrated by "the other side." When our family lived in Göttingen, Germany, one of our dearest friends was Herbert Caspari, a pillar in the local Baptist church. He once told me how he stood on the hills of Göttingen and saw the fires of Kassel nearly fifty miles away when, on the night of October 22, 1943, 444 British planes unloaded 1,812 tons of bombs in a span of twenty-two minutes; it set the entire city ablaze, leaving ten thousand people dead, including two thousand children. This was part of British Gen. "Bomber" Harris's strategy to incinerate 161 German cities, killing up to 650,000 civilians on the misguided supposition that this carnage would somehow weaken morale and hasten

---

[9]Spilsbury, pp. 114–125.

the end of the war. To read these chapters of Revelation in the lurid glare of Hiroshima and Nagasaki makes John's symbolism seem almost understated.

The ultimate question, of course, is why God would allow such unimaginable suffering, in the first century or in the twentieth. The first thing to note in Revelation is that these are not capricious acts of a vengeful God upon humanity; rather, they are acts by humanity upon itself, illustrating what people are capable of doing when they turn from God to a ruthless quest for personal power. It is here that we see the terrible cost of human freedom. To be given enough liberty to love deeply, we must also be given enough liberty to hate deeply. Note how easily love can become loathing when a marriage ends in divorce, as if the two attitudes coexist side-by-side. If God kept us on a tight leash, allowing only a modest amount of rebellion, then that same leash would leave us free to give him only a modest amount of devotion. In other words, if evil is freedom misused, then the more freedom we have the more misuse is possible.

In an ultimate sense, therefore, God shares responsibility for the horror of evil because it is he who lets us self-destruct in our sin. Because he wants our freely chosen loyalty, he permits us to engage in freely chosen treachery. But there is no hint anywhere in Revelation that God enjoys such folly. Even when we cry to him for revenge against our enemies (6:10), his response is to give up his own Son as "the Lamb who was slain" both to share our suffering and to show us how human waywardness breaks his heart.

What have we learned from this journey into horror? Three things at least: (1) that evil is not just a spiritual "bad cold" that can be blown away with a box of Kleenex but a deadly epidemic, a virus of the spirit much like the SARS that so quickly blighted Asia and brought the world's most populous nation to its knees; (2) that we would never choose evil if we knew what it is really like, but it always comes disguised as patriotic fervor or religious zeal or personal fulfillment; (3) that true freedom is costly indeed because it offers us the opportunity for compassion or cruelty, salvation or destruction, God-centeredness or self-centeredness. The ability to choose such diametrically different options is the most dangerous gift we possess!

If these contentions are true, confirmed both by Scripture and by contemporary experience, then how can we overcome that hideous strength that insinuates itself into our lives as counterfeit idealism, which, when embraced, seeks only to exploit and enslave? Is it enough to be shocked by the lurid symbolism with which the last book of the Bible ends? John knew that many in his day had already capitulated: "they worshiped the beast, saying, 'Who is like the beast, and who can fight against it?'" (13:4). What is to keep us from doing the same in a day when deception is rampant, when the most flagrant sins can be made to seem innocuous with a little media spin? To ask such questions is our first line of defense against the enticements of evil. But there must be more. Our questions only expose the reality of the beast; they do not defeat it. John dared to lay bare the hideousness of the foe because he knew one who could overcome its malevolent power and in whose strength we can do the same: "And the great dragon was thrown down, that ancient serpent, who is called the Devil and Satan, the deceiver of the whole world. . . . And I heard a loud voice in heaven saying, "Now the salvation and the power and the kingdom of our God and the authority of his Christ have come, for the accuser . . . has been thrown down . . . and they have conquered him by the blood of the Lamb . . ." (12:9–11).

Topic: A New Heaven and a New Earth
TEXT: Rev. 21:1

Few things attract our attention like the suspense of an unresolved conflict. In every struggle the unspoken question brooding over the plot is, Who will be victorious? As we work through the Book of Revelation, particularly after a closer look at how the omnipotent God engages the satanic Beast, the outcome seems uncertain, especially for the early Christians in Asia Minor. The Roman Empire was growing more antagonistic with each new Caesar. Overwhelming military, political, economic, and cultural power seemed to make it irresistible. The vast majority of the population had meekly surrendered to its sovereignty (13:4), and this mood of submission made serious inroads into the seven churches addressed by John, all of which were struggling to survive. There was lovelessness in Ephesus (2:4), tribulation in Smyrna (2:9–10), heresy in Pergamum (2:14–15), immorality in Thyatira (2)20), spiritual death in Sardis (3:1), weakness in Philadelphia (3:8), and lukewarmness in Laodicea (3:16).

Yet the Book of Revelation exudes an attitude of confidence. Every one of these letters to the seven churches ends with a call to conquer (2:7, 2:11, 2:17, 2:26, 3:5, 3:12, and 3:21). This confidence was grounded not in some hope of future triumph but in the fact that Christ had already conquered and was seated with his father on the throne of heaven (3:21). Because these embattled Christians could now experience in worship the glory of heaven through the presence of the Holy Spirit, the outcome of their struggle was no longer in doubt. They could fight in the certainty that the stranglehold of evil had already been broken by the death and Resurrection of the Lamb.

Consider that such an incredible plotline had never been heard of in human history. Here was a tiny religious movement only one generation old, bereft of status, wealth, or legal standing, yet daring to challenge the world's mightiest empire in a fight to the finish. Most ancient religions served to legitimate the state rather than to oppose it, but the Book of Revelation espoused a Christianity that transcended every political loyalty. How incredible that an exiled prophet on the Isle of Patmos, lacking any of the resources that make for earthly success, dared to trace the outworkings of a victory that had already been determined in a decisive battle fought on a hill called Calvary. Unless the Book of Revelation strains your credulity to the breaking point, you have not understood the audacity of its claims. Let us, in a willing suspension of disbelief, explore how John conceived of such an inconceivable triumph over evil.

I. *The conflict.* The strangest thing about the ultimate struggle against evil is the insistence of Revelation that it is a war in which one side has chosen to fight without weapons. The depth of the paradox is seen in the apparently contradictory reference to "the wrath of the Lamb" (6:16). Here is at once an outraged but vulnerable Lamb pushed to its limit by the horror of evil. On the one hand, there is a wrath that expresses the divine revulsion over our human misuse of freedom. It is the Holy One's recoil against everything we do that offends his love. There can be no easy tolerance or shallow compromise with the ways of the cosmic dragon and of his earthly beast. It should make our blood run cold to realize just how much God hates sin.

But on the other hand we must ask what the Lamb does with this wrath, and the answer is that he allows himself to suffer unfairly in order to expose sin for what it really is. Unlike all his enemies, the Lamb is never violent, retaliatory, or vengeful. In contrast to the Caesars, whose towering rages were legendary, he is not a swaggering human despot wielding arbitrary power, but rather an innocent victim led to the slaughter (5:12). Like their Master, the followers of the Lamb were to abhor everything about the Beast, yet refuse to use his methods in opposing their enemies.

Nor are we dealing here with mere symbolism. In the showdown precipitated by the Jewish War of A.D. 70, Christians in Palestine refused to become religious zealots and join their countrymen in the revolt against Rome, choosing rather the way of nonviolence that left the outcome to God. This was not so much a political pacifism that refused to fight for one's own country as it was a religious pacifism refusing to impose faith at the point of a sword, as Rome was attempting to do in its growing insistence on emperor worship.

In the ancient world, almost every war was a holy war, pitting the god of one nation against the god of another nation. Indeed, religious leaders often led the troops into battle carrying with them sacred objects designed to ensure the favor of a partisan god. By contrast, the recipients of Revelation were being encouraged to fight as the Lamb fought, allowing evil to exhaust its strength in unavailing attacks upon the people of God. That is why John's "wrath" against Rome was expressed with words rather than with a sword. He was willing to expose evil in no uncertain terms, but not use coercion to control the outcome.

The problem with all of this, of course, is that in our kind of world the contest between truth and power seems always to be won by power. Lambs are simply no match for beasts, raising the spectre of martyrdom, which had taken the life of Jesus and was beginning to take the lives of his followers (2:10, 2:13, 3:2, 3:10). Already John's readers were questioning the fate of those who had resisted Rome to the point of death. As the martyrs cried, "How long, O God, before Thou wilt judge and avenge our blood" (6:10), they were immediately given a white robe (6:11), which entitled them to stand before the throne of God (7:9, 13–14). Note here the alchemy of grace; robes washed in red blood become white as snow. Note also that, even though they had made the supreme sacrifice of life itself, it was not their blood that transforms but the blood of the lamb.

Martyrdom was not an heroic reach for sainthood, or an effort to escape into a better world, but the ultimate form of political protest against power structures seeking to usurp the place of God. The martyrs were willing to wager their lives that Rome was wrong. In refusing to accept the claims of those in control, they named them as a fraud. The martyrs knew that the books would not be balanced either *by* this world or *in* this world; they viewed the world above as more real than anything this world had to offer. The logic of their ultimate sacrifice was well expressed by Jim Elliott: "He is no fool who gives what he cannot keep to gain what he cannot lose."[10]

Does not the Book of Revelation gain contemporary resonance in its emphasis on martyrdom? Never before have so many Christians been persecuted for their beliefs. Estimates run as high as 200–250 million believers living today under threat of torture, rape, enslavement, imprisonment, or even death.[11] Mass murders in Ambon, Indonesia, have swollen to genocidal proportions in the Nuba Mountains of Sudan. Nor is our immediate spiritual fam-

---

[10]Cited by Jere Van Dyk, "A Noble Calling," *Wall Street Journal,* Jan. 17, 2003, p. W-13.
[11]Ralph Kinney Bennett, "The Global War on Christians," *Reader's Digest,* Aug. 1997, pp. 51–55.

ily spared this carnage, beginning with the recent death of our own Martha Myers of Montgomery, cut down with two others at the Jibla Baptist Hospital in Yemen, and soon joined by Bill Hyde in the Philippines and fourteen-year-old Abigail Litle in Israel.

Even though we enjoy a remarkable degree of religious freedom in this country, we cannot escape the question of whether, in a showdown with evil, we would be willing to die for our faith, certain of vindication in the world beyond. The very possibility of such a choice forces the question of why God would allow martyrdom to happen. G. B. Caird answers insightfully: "Why does God not cut short the suffering of his persecuted people? Sooner or later evil must be allowed to run its destructive course to a close. The answer is that God holds his hand, not willing that any of his creatures should perish, and as long as he does so the martyrs must suffer. Martyrdom, like the Cross, is the cost of divine patience."[12]

II. *The conquest.* In this messianic war with the Beast, John cherished no illusions that victory would come either quickly or easily. Even though Christ had triumphed over evil in his death and Resurrection, and even though his followers were continuing to conquer in the witness of martyrdom, the final triumph of God's kingdom would not come until the end of history. The stages in this great conflict were seen as somewhat parallel to the exodus in the Old Testament. You may remember that when the children of Israel were allowed to escape from Egypt, there followed a long period of wilderness wanderings when they were beset by many foes. The redemption from slavery that began with the crossing of the Red Sea was not completed until the twelve tribes finally crossed the river Jordan and claimed the promised land. Just so, the early Christians would have to fight against the satanic trinity of the dragon or serpent symbolizing supernatural evil, the beast or sea monster symbolizing the imperial power of Rome, and the second beast or earth monster symbolizing the cult of emperor worship before victory would finally be theirs.[13]

At last, in the great Battle of Armageddon (16:16), followers of the Lamb will find themselves up against all of the earthly power structures that oppose the Kingdom of God, whether they be political, economic, or religious. But there is an ironic note of hope even in this desperate struggle: the greater the number of foes that converge upon the faith, the more opportunity for faithful witness and loving sacrifice that can lead to repentance and faith. Tragically, all of the enemies of God will not choose to believe, but at least they will have a chance to face clearly the ultimate alternatives of eternity—namely, whether humans are made for violence and enmity or whether they are made for forgiveness and reconciliation. As Paul put it (Rom. 11:32), God condemns everyone who uses freedom to serve the Beast, but he does so in order that he may have mercy on everyone who responds in faith to the witness of the faithful. His deepest desire is for a victory without any victims, however costly it may be.

If the first stage of conquest is the redemptive work of the Lamb and the second stage is the faithful witness of his people, then the final stage is the triumphant return of Christ to earth, when truth shall reign supreme. Then all will know that the cosmos is an incubator of justice, love, and peace, that deception, intimidation, and exploitation were never meant to control human affairs. Those who have learned to love the truth will welcome the coming of Christ, while those who have built their lives on lies will find foundations swept away.

---

[12]Caird, p. 295.

[13]Richard Bauckham, *The Theology of the Book of Revelation* (New York: Cambridge University Press, 1993), p. 89.

Closely connected to the coming of Christ will be the millennium, or thousand-year period, which defends that final "day of the Lord" to which the prophets eagerly looked. Then the Beast will be seen to be defeated (20:3) and the martyrs will be seen to be triumphant (20:4), a state of affairs that will usher in the Kingdom of God "on Earth as it is in heaven," for which Jesus taught us to pray (Matt. 6:10). This symbolism provides a way of affirming that God is both Creator and Redeemer, that he is Lord both of this world and of the world to come, and that he will make a new Earth as well as a new heaven (21:1), thereby removing the dualistic antagonism between the two realms.

It may seem strange that, when this millennium of earthly peace ends, the devil will be released and given a final chance to deceive the nations once again (20:7–8). This tells us that evil never learns anything, even with a thousand years to brood in the prison of a bottomless pit. But when the Beast resorts to its old bag of tricks, it can no longer prevail, even if it arouses the multitudes to fight, because the victory of the saints is now impregnable (20:9–10). In other words, Christ's triumphant kingdom, both in heaven and on Earth, is one that evil cannot overthrow even given a second chance. (Once the Lamb has finally prevailed, the Beast will never again have the upper hand. This was John's way of saying that God's redemption is eternally dependable!)

III. *The consummation.* Once the millennium declares God's determination to create a New Earth, then we are ready to be told how he also intends to create a New Heaven (21:1). When we ask what could be "new" about a heaven that is eternal, the answer is that now, for the first time since the Garden of Eden, it is in perfect harmony with God's Earth and includes all of the redeemed of the ages for whom the Lamb came to suffer and die. The only thing that surpasses John's hideous description of evil is his beautiful description of heaven in the closing chapters of Revelation. He exhausts hyperbole to describe what God has always wanted to provide for his own. Images of precious and semiprecious stones are employed to depict a kingdom where the highest values are treasured and preserved rather than desecrated and destroyed.

In contrast to the evil city of Babylon, which was likened to a harlot, John describes heaven in terms of a holy city called the New Jerusalem, which will be the antithesis of Rome in his day. It has been helpfully described as a *place* where Earth is truly joined to heaven, where the *people* dwell together in harmony with God, and where they enjoy his *presence* without any of the barriers that kept the emperors at arm's length from their subjects.[14]

This heavenly Jerusalem is to be open and inclusive (21:25), a place where all may gather for worship without temple walls to segregate one group from another (21:22). Supreme in this vision, as Kathleen Norris put it, is "a God who comes to be with those who have suffered the most in a cruel, unjust, and violent world. A God who does not roar and strut like the ultimate dictator but who gently 'wipes away all tears from their eyes'" (21:4).[15] No other god in the ancient world did a mother's work of drying tearful eyes.

Most of all, heaven will be a place of life. In pride of place are the tree of life and the river of life, showing that God is the giver of life. The river of life flows through the midst of the city, where all may gain access to it, and on either side it nourishes the tree of life, bearing

---

[14]Bauckman, pp. 126–144.

[15]Kathleen Norris, *Amazing Grace: A Vocabulary of Faith* (New York: Riverhead Books, 1998), p. 321.

fruit throughout the year, with leaves for the healing of the nations (22:1–2). Here the "culture of death" spawned by sin is overcome by redeemed relationships that nourish a "culture of life" (22:3).

Looking back over this three-part series, we see that the Book of Revelation compels us to focus on one key issue: Where is a power mighty enough to subdue evil yet gentle enough to leave us free? Through the centuries we have tried many solutions that did not work. War can bring victory to the powerful, but it leaves a legacy of bitterness and fear among its victims. Wealth can purchase influence and bolster reputation, but it causes jealousy to fester beneath the surface. Education can create a learned elite, but all too often the sophisticated exploit the ignorant for their own advantage. These options offer powerful temptations to America today, because we are by far the strongest, richest, and most educated country in the world. Rome became an imperium mighty enough to conquer everything in its domain except evil. Let those who would turn America into a modern empire take heed!

The deepest insight of the Apocalypse is that evil can be defeated only by "the Lamb who was slain" (5:12). That is, we shall never finally subdue the Beast that ravages planet Earth except by living and dying as Jesus did. This is as difficult a message in the twenty-first century as it was in the first century. But lest it be dismissed as hopelessly impractical, remember that this was precisely the strategy used by the early Christians to conquer the Roman Empire. For a quarter of a millennium, Rome did its worst to stamp out the Christian movement, accusing it of being atheistic because it would not deify the State; yet never once did the faithful fight back with force. At last, when pomp and power, intimidation and violence had done their worst, it was the followers of the Lamb rather than the Caesars who won! Incredible as it may seem, they won without ever lifting the sword, without ever strutting in the marketplace, without ever exploiting the vulnerable. Mystery of mysteries, the Beast really was defeated by not being resisted. What John had to believe as an audacious hope we may now verify as a fact of history.

Doubtless there are many of us who devoutly hope that in some remote future the kingdom of Christ will vanquish the kingdom of the Beast. But John would not have it so. His times were so desperate that he was impelled by a breathtaking sense of urgency to plead for radical change sooner rather than later (1:1–3, 22:20), which was the hardest possible time for change to come. Even though Rome was in total control of his earthly existence, he dared to ask for relief then and there without delay (10:6). There was nothing Rome could offer that he yearned to possess, even for a moment. What about us? Are we ready—right now!—for every kingdom of this world, whether it be political or economic or social or religious, to "become the kingdom of our Lord and of his Christ, that he may reign forever and ever" (11:15)? If we are unwilling to let anything in time and space stand between us and eternity, then let us cry with the prophet of Patmos: "Even so, come *quickly*, Lord Jesus!" (22:7, 10, 12, 20).

CHILDREN'S SERMONS

January 2: A Year of Opportunities
TEXT: Gal. 6:9 (NIV)
Object: Large calendar
Song: "We'll Work Till Jesus Comes"

Hello, boys and girls. I'm glad to see you today. This is the season when we begin a new year and we think of resolutions—or promises we make to ourselves or others. I'm holding a calendar—an object that shows the months, weeks, and days of the coming year. During this time we often think of ways to improve our lives, such as better health habits, making new friends, and other commitments.

Instead of thinking about a year, let's break it down into smaller parts. How many months in a year? [Twelve] How many weeks in a year? [Fifty-two] How many days are in a year? [365] With all this time, let us think about ways we can serve Jesus in the coming year. Do you have any ideas? [Call on several children who want to respond.] I hear you saying we can serve Jesus in the coming year by going to Sunday school and church, reading our Bible, and inviting others to come with us. How can we treat our friends? If we want to have friends, we have to be a friend to others. This means we should be responsible, honest, caring, and helpful. The Bible is our guide for service to Jesus throughout the year.

Listen as I read Galatians 6:9: "Let us not become weary in doing good, for at the proper time we will reap a harvest if we do not give up." The Bible teaches us to serve God through serving others.

[Prayer: Jesus, guide each boy and girl here today to use their time wisely throughout the coming year. Let their life be an example of good works and deeds. Amen.

Lead the children in singing one stanza of "We'll Work Till Jesus Comes." Children return to their seats at this time.]—Carolyn Tomlin

January 9: Jesus, the Light of the World
TEXT: 2 Cor. 4:6 (NIV)
Object: Lantern or lighted candle
Song: "Heavenly Sunlight"

Hello, boys and girls. I'm glad to see you today. In my hands I'm holding a lantern [or candle]. There is a story about a man who was lost in a cave and the only light he had was a lantern. Trying to find his way out of the darkness, he realized the lantern's light would only go about four feet ahead of him. He wondered to himself, *"How can I ever reach the opening of this cave with only a light that goes such a short distance?"* Making his way to the sunlight that pierced the darkness, he realized that as he walked, the light of the lantern moved also. Each step lighted another, and another, until he reached safety.

When we are troubled, we have God as our guide to light our steps. We never have to walk life alone. God stays ahead and leads us out of the darkness and into the sunlight of his love.

The Bible says in 2 Corinthians 4:6, "For God, who said, 'Let light shine out of darkness,' made his light shine in our hearts to give us the light of the knowledge of the glory of God in the face of Christ.'"

[Prayer: Dear Jesus, we ask that the precious children will always depend on your light to guide them throughout life. Amen.]

Before we sing "Heavenly Sunlight," let's listen to the words of this song. The author speaks of the love of Jesus leading us over the mountains during good times and into the valley during times when we think life isn't so good. But all through life, we know our Lord is with us. [Lead the congregation in singing "Heavenly Sunlight" as children return to their seats.]—Carolyn Tomlin

January 16: God's Blessing

TEXT: Eph. 5:1–2, 19–20

Object: Scrabble board (I use a necktie that has the Scrabble pattern on it. This is an example of using an object that does not fit the usual form, because I do not bring a Scrabble board out of the "time for children" bag; I wear the object. Look for what "fits" you.)

Do I look like I've forgotten something for our time together? You're right, I have not brought our decorated bag with a surprise inside. Today I'm wearing the surprise. What do you see on my tie this morning? [Several, to my surprise, recognize it.] Yes, Scrabble is a word game you play. One of you mentioned that it is a word game you play *with other people.* It is a game of building words. Do you think words are important? You're not sure. Think about words that tell us about Jesus' love.

We sang about that as you walked up to the front of the church this morning. Those words help us know who we are and that we are loved. Scrabble is a game we play with others. The Scripture says that our words—psalms and hymns—are spiritual sayings that build up others. That means these kinds of words help us remember who we are as children . . . that Jesus loves. Think of some words that make you feel good: "I love you," "You are so helpful," "You are a child of God." These are good examples. Let me give you another: "Thank you for coming this morning, and go with God's blessing."—Gary D. Stratman

January 23: Don't Point Your Fingers

TEXT: Isa. 6:8

Objects: Two posters with large pointing fingers

Here are two posters with large "pointing fingers." You may see pointing fingers like this indicating the direction to the restroom or a water fountain. We're going to use these posters to demonstrate how we may attempt to avoid responsibility.

I need two volunteers. One should stand to my right, the other to my let. Good. Let's pretend in school the teacher asks, "What is the capital city of Alaska?" We don't know the answer, so we do this. [Point the finger to the person to the left.] Then we say, "How should I know? Ask him." In another imagined incident, let's say Mom leaves some chocolate chip cookies on the kitchen counter. After we eat half of them, we learn Mom was saving them for company. She impatiently asks, "Who ate the cookies?" We wipe the chocolate off our mouths and do this. [Point the finger to the person on the right.] Then we say, "Sister ate them."

Sadly, it is human nature to escape responsibility by shifting the blame to someone else. A prophet by the name of Isaiah demonstrated the kind of responsibility that God desires. Listen to this verse. [Read Isa. 6:8.]

It is easy to turn away from reports on television about starving people. It is frustrating to see thousands of desperate folks so far away. Those situations look hopeless, and we feel powerless. We can make an impact by donating canned goods to a food drive. We may give only two cans of beans, but that attitude and positive help goes a long way.

It is also typical to neglect world missions. We hear of millions of people in China who have never heard of Jesus, but we don't know what to do. We don't live in China or speak Chinese, but we can give part of our allowance to the church's missions offering and pray with the church when mission needs are reported by visiting missionaries.

God doesn't leave the responsibility of the world on our shoulders. He only expects us to be faithful in using what we have and doing what we can. When millions of people become willing, like Isaiah, to accept responsibility, the hungry in the world can be helped and evangelized.

Don't get in the habit of pointing the finger of blame or responsibility. Answer like Isaiah did: "Here I am Lord, I'll help." That's all Jesus wants to hear. The Lord will take our efforts and offerings and multiply them to accomplish great good.—Ken Cox

January 30: I Want a Red Gumball!!!

TEXT: Phil. 4:12

Object: A gumball machine or a variety of colored gumballs

Not too long ago, in a discount store, I heard a little girl crying and screaming. She was so loud I thought she had fallen and injured herself. I walked closer to see if help was needed. The girl must have been about four years old, and a younger boy was standing next to her quietly chewing some gum.

I heard the little girl through her tears screaming to her mother that she had gotten a white gumball and her brother had gotten a red gumball. The little girl wanted the red gumball, not the white one. When she demanded the gumball from the lad, he just popped the red gumball into his mouth and started chewing.

There may be a difference in the flavor of red and white gumballs, but it isn't much. Both gumballs will be sweet for a few minutes, but then both are fairly tasteless. The little girl couldn't be convinced of that tiny difference. She was sure she had to have the red gumball her brother was chewing.

Humans want what other people have. We may have a car or a house, but we want a car or house like our friends. The Bible calls this "coveting," wanting what someone else has. We are commanded not to covet.

Coveting leads to serious problems in our lives. If we allow coveting to linger in our thoughts, we might eventually steal what the other person has. Or we might become angry with them because they have newer or nicer things than we possess. In the process we become miserable, like the little girl at the gumball machine.

God calls us to be happy with who we are and what we have. Listen to this verse. [Read Phil. 4:12.]

One way to avoid coveting and be content is to count our blessings. We count our blessing by naming and thanking God for what we already possess. For instance, we should be grateful for our Mom and Dad, clothing, even a hand-me-down bicycle. If we truly value the people and material things in our lives, we will not long for what others possess. When we are content, that joyful attitude flows over into the lives of others.—Ken Cox

February 6: Everything Is Possible

TEXT: Mark 9:23 (NIV)

Object: A flower

Song: "Only Believe"

Hello, boys and girls. I'm glad to see you today. Listen as I tell you an interesting story. Do you know where the continent of Australia is located? Yes, it . . . [explain appropriately]. When the weather is dry and hot, lightning can strike and cause a fire in the "outback." Now, the outback in Australia is in the rural part of the country and covered with low-growing brush and timber. A fire burns all the plants, and for a while everything looks black. But the following spring, the most beautiful flowers appear. Many of these plants have not bloomed in thirty or forty years. The gases produced from the fire caused the plants to burst into bloom. Everywhere you look, these lovely flowers cover the land. That's amazing, wouldn't you say?

But I can tell you something more amazing than the flowers that bloom after a fire! God loves us, regardless of our sins. God can change people who have sinned and give them eternal life. The Bible says in Mark 9:23, ". . . Everything is possible for him who believes."

[Prayer: Lord Jesus, help these boys and girls realize they can have eternal life in you by only believing that you can save them. Amen.]

I like the song "Only Believe" because it tells us that all things are possible with God if we trust and believe in him. [Lead the congregation in singing "Only Believe" as the children return to their seats.]—Carolyn Tomlin

February 13: Give Jesus a Permission Slip

TEXT: Rev. 3:20

Object: A permission slip

This is a permission slip to leave school. Once a student is admitted to school in the morning, special approval must be granted for them to be anywhere besides the classroom or activity they are assigned to. The teacher grants permission to a student to go to the restroom, to get a drink of water, or the principal grants permission to leave school for a dentist or a doctor appointment.

Once a student arrives at school they are under the authority of the school. Part of the school's power is shown by the permission it grants during the day.

God has given all humans the ability to give him a permission slip. God allows us the authority to make the decision about his presence in our lives. Listen to this verse. [Read Rev. 3:20.]

Jesus once tried to visit a town in Samaria. He sent out some disciples ahead of him to tell the residents he was coming. When the disciples announced Jesus was coming, the people in the village told the messengers to return and tell Jesus *not* to come. The people did not want Jesus in their town. Two of the apostles, James and John, were angry and wanted to call fire down from heaven to destroy the village. Jesus refused to send fire from heaven and walked on to another village where he might be received (Luke 9:51–56).

Jesus is like that with us. Jesus wants to come into our lives and be our savior, but he will not force his way into our lives. In some police television shows, the detectives come to an apartment door that will not be opened by the person inside. The detectives kick the door down and go in with their arrest warrants. Jesus is not like that. He will not kick the door down to our lives. He waits for us to give him permission to come in. Jesus politely knocks on the door of our lives and waits for our permission to enter.

God created and owns the heavens and earth and all life, but God will not use his awesome power to force his way into anyone's life. He waits to be invited after we have heard about Jesus through the gospel.

Jesus waits to be given permission to enter our lives as savior. He also waits for permission to be given first in our lives. When you learn the truth about Jesus, be sure to give him a permission slip to enter and become the Lord of your life.—Ken Cox

February 20: Chains That Bind

Text: Col. 3:14 (NIV)
Object: Small chain
Song: "We Are One in the Bond of Love"

Good morning, boys and girls. I'm glad you chose to come to church today. Who can tell me what I'm holding? Yes, this is a chain. Can you tell me what a chain is used for? [Wait for response.] Yes, those are good suggestions for using a chain. We might use a chain to tie something together, to keep a dog from running away; a chain might secure a door lock in your home, and a small chain could even be a necklace for girls. Could we say a chain is both functional and decorative? This means that a chain is used to help us in our work, as well as something we choose to wear as jewelry. I'm sure we could name any uses for a chain. Right?

Did you know that being a member of this church is one way we are tied together for Christ? As a body of believers, we feel the bond of love from others in our congregation. Our church is a place where God is, and people come to worship him. There is an old saying: "A chain is as strong as its weakest link." What do you think that statement means? [Wait for response.] It means that if one part of the chain is broken or weak, the entire chain becomes useless. A chain cannot do what it was meant to do, if broken. Our church can reach people for Christ only if we all work together in love.

Col. 3:14 tells us how we should love others: "And over all these virtues put on love, which binds them all together in perfect unity."

[Prayer: Lord Jesus, may these boys and girls realize the power of your message as they are bonded together in Christian love. Amen.

Lead the children in singing "We Are One in the Bond of Love" as they return to their seats.]—Carolyn Tomlin

February 27: There's No Such Thing as a Small Theft
TEXT: Luke 16:10
Object: A candy bar

We might be tempted to commit a crime if we think it is an unimportant matter. For instance, if a friend goes into a convenience store and steals a candy bar, we might be deceived to do the same if they say, "It's only a candy bar."

Actually there is no such thing as a small crime. All wrongs cause huge changes in our conscience and actions.

There is a well-known story told by Matthew Henry, a Bible scholar. He was robbed as he was walking down the street near his home. The thief took all the money that he had in his wallet. After Matthew Henry got home safely, he wrote about the incident in his diary. He said he was thankful for three things. First, that he wasn't harmed in the robbery. Second, that though the thief took all of his money, he wasn't carrying a large amount of cash. Third, Matthew Henry was thankful that he was not the thief. The thief had a bad conscience and would never be satisfied. The thief would be unhappy and bring unhappiness to everyone he violated by stealing from them.

Jesus said that if we are honest or dishonest with small things, we will be honest or dishonest with large things. Listen to this verse. [Read Luke 16:10.]

So there is no such thing as a small theft, a small lie, or a small act of vandalism. If we will commit a small crime, we will commit a larger crime. Every wrong we allow ourselves to do makes the next illegal or cruel event easier to commit.

Never take anything that doesn't belong to you. Always be honest, and you will be happy. No matter how many others tell you differently, don't listen. Never steal, but always be willing to share what you have. Furthermore, ask for God to keep you strong in your commitment to Him.—Ken Cox

March 6: We Must Be Ready at All Times
TEXT: Matt. 24:44
Object: A fire extinguisher

This is a fire extinguisher. We have fire extinguishers in easy-to-reach locations all over the church just in case there is a fire. Our deacons and security personnel know exactly where the extinguishers are in case one is needed.

The only fire I have witnessed at a church was at a wedding. After the service, a photographer was taking pictures of the bride and groom when the flames of a decorative candle ignited a silk flower arrangement. It was exciting. People were running here and there. Some of us just stood and stared as the tall flower arrangement burned. Thankfully, someone grabbed a fire extinguisher and put out the fire before serious harm was done. That prepared person prevented the small fire from becoming a huge inferno.

It's hard to be ready for something that you think will never happen. I wasn't thinking about a fire the day of that wedding, but I'm glad someone was prepared for a fire. In most cities, there are fire codes that require property owners to have fire extinguishers of various kinds. Without that requirement most buildings would not be prepared for a fire. It is human nature to think that unpleasant things will never happen to us.

Jesus made a special promise to the church. He promised to return from heaven for all who believe in him. On the special day of his return, the Bible says we will be caught up to meet him in the air. Jesus said we need to be prepared for the day of his return. We need to accept Jesus as savior, and we need to serve him and be expecting his return at any time.

Jesus said his return will be at an unexpected time and that no one will know that day. Listen to this verse. [Read Matt. 24:44.]

Do you think Jesus will come back today? To tell the truth, I don't think so either. I haven't thought about it all week. Jesus has warned us that it will be on a day like today when we aren't thinking about it. Since we have never experienced an incredible day like the promised return of Jesus, it is human nature to not think about it much. Instead, our thoughts are filled with everyday things like going to school, cleaning our room, and eating lunch. For that reason Jesus gave us a special warning to keep the day of his return constantly in mind.

To keep an accidental fire from becoming a catastrophe, emergency plans have to be made. We must memorize the location of fire extinguishers and have an exit plan. To keep the special day of Jesus' return from catching us unprepared, we need to be watchful and ready. Let's be prepared for Jesus' return by keeping his commandments, praying, and witnessing.— Ken Cox

March 13: What's in Your Heart Comes out of Your Mouth

TEXT: Matt. 12:34

Object: A stethoscope

This is a stethoscope. With a stethoscope a nurse or doctor can listen to your heart and understand your health. Special training enables them to listen and diagnose heart problems and then begin the healing process.

Jesus said that the content of a person's heart could be known by listening to them talk. Jesus didn't mean their physical health; he meant we could tell if they were angry, worried, or full of faith. By listening, Jesus said, a spiritual assessment could be made. Listen to this verse. [Read Matt. 12:34.]

If you listen to what people, say you will observe the truth of Jesus' word. If a person is angry and curses constantly, that person is frustrated and mad. There is anger in their heart, and their rage is obvious every time they speak; it can't be hidden. If a person takes God's name in vain, or uses Jesus' name in a joking way, it is a signal they do not know God. If we know God's love for us and realize Jesus died on the cross for our sins, we will not curse him or dishonor Jesus' name. It is very serious to curse God (Exod. 20:7).

On the other hand, if we hear a person singing songs that they learned at church, most likely their lives are filled with joy and faith. If words of comfort and encouragement constantly are spoken to build others up, that person's mind is filled with love for others.

What can we do? First, we need to be very careful how we talk. Our spoken words are powerful and influence others and ourselves. If we hear ourselves using angry words, we need to stop and ask for help. If we don't get help, our anger will increase and we may harm another person or ourselves. If we use hurtful, cruel words, or feel compelled to tell a lie, we ought to look at our hearts and wonder why we are at odds with our friends. Then we need to turn to God and ask him for forgiveness and a loving heart. Through Jesus' power, our hearts can be changed. If our hearts are changed, our words will be different.

A stethoscope can pinpoint a physical problem in the heart. Listening to our words reveals an attitude that can be healed only by the grace of God. Doctors warn patients to take care of their heart by exercising, quitting smoking, and eating proper foods. The Bible tells us to guard our heart, because it is a key to eternal life.—Ken Cox

March 20: Cheers for Jesus

TEXT: Luke 19:28–40 (v. 40: "If they keep quiet, the stones along the road will burst into cheers")

Objects: Some stones of various shapes and sizes

Good morning, boys and girls. How many of you ever get excited? Almost all of you do. What do you do when you are excited? [Let them answer.] Have you ever gone to a basketball game or a baseball game and gotten excited? Did you cheer, shout, scream, or yell? I know that when I go to a game and my team begins to score points, and it looks like we are going to catch the team ahead of us, or go on to win the game, I find that I am standing up and cheering my head off! I love to cheer. Do you think that you could be excited about something and not cheer? Suppose you were at a game and the team you wanted to win was doing just great, but there was a rule that said you could not cheer. Let's just try it and see what happens. First of all you must cheer. How about "Hip, hip, hooray! Hip, hip, hooray!" Terrific! Let's hear you do it again. [Let them repeat it until it seems that they are really in the mood.] Do you like to cheer? Well, you can't! You are not allowed to cheer. From now on, for the rest of the morning, you are not allowed to cheer no matter how much you feel like doing it. Just think of that, here you feel like cheering, and I won't let you. It is disappointing, isn't it?

This happened to Jesus on Palm Sunday many years ago. He was coming down the very narrow streets of Jerusalem and the people, thousands of them, were standing and cheering and throwing their robes on the ground for the donkey on which Jesus was riding to walk on, and the people who were in charge were telling the others to be quiet. They thought that it was wrong for the people to call Jesus the Lord and shout praises to God. Do you know what Jesus said? He said that if the people kept quiet the stones in the street would cheer. It was such a happy moment and the people were so thrilled about what God had done that Jesus knew even the stones would cheer. Have you ever heard a stone cheer? Have you ever heard a stone do or say anything? Of course you haven't, but Jesus knew that there was no way you could keep people from praising God on such a happy day.

I hope that you have many days like that. I hope that you shout, praise, and cheer God every day of your life. Because, you know, if you keep quiet about God, the next thing you know God may have to listen to the stones to hear a noise, and if you don't speak then maybe they will.

Will you shout praises to God? That's wonderful. So will I.—Wesley T Runk[1]

---

[1]*God Doesn't Rust* (Lima, Ohio: CSS, 1978), pp. 31–32.

March 27: The Cross Shows God's Love

TEXT: John 15:9 (NIV)

Object: Twigs made into a cross

Song: "Oh, How He Loves You and Me"

Boys and girls, I'm glad to see you today. Isn't it wonderful to come to church this Easter Sunday? Today, we are learning how Jesus was crucified on the cross, was buried in a tomb, and rose again on the third day. He died for our sins so that we could have eternal life with him in heaven.

Now, I want you to watch my hands. Who can tell me what I'm holding? Yes, these are two twigs; one is short, the other longer. I'm going to tie these together to form another object. [Make a cross with the twigs by tying the center.] Now, what is the object I'm holding? Yes, it's a cross. The cross represents what Jesus did for us. He loved us so much that he suffered and died—for me, for you, for you, and for you. [Point to each child as you speak.]

Listen as I read John 15:9: "As the Father has loved me, so have I loved you. Now remain in my love. If you obey my commands, you will remain in my love, just as I have obeyed my Father's commands and remain in his love." We honor God when we do what is right. True happiness comes from following his teachings.

[Prayer: God, we ask you to guide each boy and girl here today. May they follow your command and love you with all their heart. Amen.

Ask the pianist to play a stanza of "Oh, How He Loves You and Me" as children return to their seats.]—Carolyn Tomlin

April 3: God Is Ready—Are You?

TEXT: Mark 1:32–39

Object: An alarm clock

Have you ever heard this old saying, "Spring forward, fall back"? It is strange. Maybe it's about basketball. When your team has the ball you *spring forward* toward the goal, and when the other team has the ball you *fall back* and defend the goal. [Act out these two actions.] Well, that was fun, but it's not how these sayings are used.

Now raise your hand if you know what I am pulling out of the bag this morning. That's right, it's a clock, an alarm clock. In the spring, we set the clock forward an hour, and in the fall we set it back an hour. That's right, spring forward, fall back.

In our Bible story this morning, Jesus got up early. He helped people until the sun went down the day before, and now he gets up early before other people come to see him. If we get up early, it's usually for something important. School starts again. The fish are biting. We're going on vacation. . . . Jesus got up to pray—pretty important, huh? Jesus could pray for the people he would see that day. We could do the same, or pray for people who are sick. Also, we could thank God we're going on vacation or the fish are biting. Maybe we could even thank God for school! God is always ready to listen [lift up the clock] at any time. With that assurance, we can spring forward into each day and fall back (or "rely") on God's constant love. Yes, God goes with you and never lets you down.

Thanks for coming.—Gary D. Stratman

April 10: Daniel's Diet

TEXT: Dan. 1:8

Object: A nutrition label

This is an enlargement of the nutrition label from a pack of cheese crackers. The label is on the side of the package, as required by law. People pay close attention to what they are eating if they are on a restricted diet. Folks trying to lose weight are interested in how many calories or grams of fat they might consume; others get violently ill if they eat the wrong foods.

Daniel the prophet is known for being particular about his diet. Due to a war in his homeland, Daniel was taken away from his home in Israel and put in the magnificent royal palace in Babylon. This was a privilege, but there was pressure on Daniel to become like the people of Babylon. Daniel would not eat some of the special royal food that was served in the palace. Listen to this verse. [Read Dan. 1:8.]

To Daniel eating certain foods was a sin. Daniel's people had dietary laws, and eating a food that was "unclean" was just as serious as breaking one of the Commandments, by stealing or telling a lie. Daniel believed eating the royal food would corrupt him spiritually and separate him from God. That's why Daniel refused to eat the foods offered to him.

We need to be aware of the corrupting, contaminating nature of sin. Whenever we do something that is wrong, it contaminates, or brings ruin to us spiritually. For instance, if we steal something we are more inclined to steal again, and again, until being a thief is a way of life. If we tell lies, we begin to fib more and more until we forget how to tell the truth. Our inner voice, which makes us feel bad when we hurt someone, stops working if we continue to sin. Our conscience becomes hardened and no longer alerts us to what is right or wrong.

Daniel's decision to reject the forbidden food is an excellent example for us to follow. No sin is a small sin. All sin brings corruption and destruction to our whole lives. Daniel was very polite, but he refused to compromise on what he knew was wrong. Even though many others in the palace were eating the food, it was not right for Daniel. He was very courageous to speak out and be heard. Even though we don't face the dietary restrictions that Daniel had, we should courteously, yet firmly, hold to our convictions. When we do, our lives are happy and whole.—Ken Cox

April 17: God the Matchmaker

TEXT: Matt. 19:6

Object: A wedding cake topper

My favorite part of a wedding is the reception. The reception is the time after the wedding ceremony when everyone gets together for food and visiting. At most receptions there are two cakes. One, the groom's cake, is usually chocolate. The bride's cake is generally a big, tall white cake. On top of most brides' cakes is a "cake topper" like this. It's plastic and can't be eaten.

The cake topper symbolizes what has occurred in the wedding. The bride and groom figurines are standing arm-in-arm in the middle of a big white heart. The man and woman have been leading separate lives and will now continue life together.

In the eyes of God the marriage relationship is very special. Not only will the man and wife spend the rest of their lives together, in the eyes of God the man and woman become one person. Listen to this verse. [Read Matt. 19:6.]

The verse contains the answer Jesus gave to a question about marriage. Jesus' answer indicates the involvement of God in putting the man and woman together. We know in the Garden of Eden the Lord created Adam and Eve for each other. Jesus' response indicates the involvement of God in every marriage.

The bride and groom actually choose each other. Hopefully as the man and woman grew up they prayed for God's guidance in selecting their spouse. Also, parents ought to pray for God to provide the right husband or wife for their children. When the couple come to the marriage ceremony, they recognize that God is joining them together in the ceremony. That is why most couples insist on having their marriage ceremony performed at a church.

Marriage is a gift of God to help a man and woman be satisfied with life. Marriage makes the bride and groom happy because both are totally committed to helping each other through companionship for all of life. In the eyes of God, two separate persons become one in a family unit. That's God's way of creating a happy home.—Ken Cox

April 24: A Name You Can Trust
TEXT: John 16:23b–30 (v. 23b: "Truly, truly, I say to you, if you ask anything of the Father, he will give it to you in my name")
Object: A clothing label

Good morning, boys and girls. Today, we are going to talk about names. How many of you know a name? How many of you have a name? Very good. Now, when I count to three, I want you all to say your name so that I can hear it! [Let them all say it, and say it loud.] There sure are a lot of names. Do you all have different names? A lot of you do. Are there two of you here with the same first name or last name? Very good. You know how important a name is, then, don't you? If everyone was called Boy or Girl, it would be hard to know whom we were talking about, wouldn't it? It sure would.

Lots of things have names, and people think that the names they give to some of these things are very important. Let me show you one of the things that has a name, and tell you why a name is important. Have you ever looked inside your coat, or at the neck of a shirt, or around the waist of a skirt? I know you have. There is a little label inside that tells who made it, and sometimes who sold it. That label has a name on it. If you like the coat or whatever you have, you will want to buy other things that are made by the same people because you know that they make good things. The same thing is true if it isn't too good. If your clothes shrink or lose their color or wear out in a hurry, you want to know who made them so that you won't buy that kind again. There are lots of clothes, and they are made by lots of different people, so it is important to know which kind you like the best.

A name is important, and it is really good to know a name you can trust. The name Jesus is a name you can trust. When something is done because Jesus taught it, or talked about it, then you can trust that it is a good thing. How many of you trust Jesus and the things that he teaches? Everyone here trusts Jesus! That is very good. Our Father, God, trusts Jesus also, and the Father has agreed that people who love and trust Jesus must also love and trust him. God the Father says that since you use the name of Jesus in trust, you can ask him for things in Jesus' name and he will give them to you. God the Father trusts Jesus. We trust Jesus. If you want strength, peace, hope, love, and all of the things those ideas bring, then you can ask God the Father in the name of Jesus, and he will give them to you. Jesus said you could ask and use his name, and it would be all right.

If you want a coat just like the one that you have, only a little bigger because you have grown, you can go to the store and ask for the name that is in your coat and they will give you one made by the same people. If you want something that only God can give, then ask for it in Jesus' name, and God will give it to you.—Wesley T. Runk[2]

May 1: Jesus Obeyed His Parents
TEXT: Luke 2:51–52
Object: A paper chain

This is a paper chain. It can illustrate a "chain of command." In the armed forces the service people are trained to obey their chain of command. The chain goes like this. The president tells the secretary of defense, the secretary of defense tells a general, the general a colonel, the colonel a major, the major a captain, the captain a lieutenant, the lieutenant a sergeant, and a sergeant tells a private, who actually does what is ordered. The commands move along a chain to the right person.

The good thing about the chain of command is that a person only has to listen to one boss, the person who is above them in their chain of command. If someone outside the chain of command issues an order, it has no authority. The chain of command creates order and lessens confusion.

God does the same thing for you and me. Before we become part of the "command structure," when we are growing up, we are to be obedient to our parents. Our parents have a responsibility to listen to God, and then they instruct us. Parents are our link in a chain of command to God.

The fifth of the Ten Commandments is, "Honor your father and mother that your days may be long in the land." That's how God ensures order and proper behavior.

Our example in everything is Jesus. If ever there was a child who knew more than his parents, it was Jesus. But Jesus was obedient to his parents. Listen to this verse. [Read Luke 2:51–52.]

We must follow the example of Jesus and be obedient to our parents. When we obey our parents, we are obeying God. Through obedience we receive the benefit of our parents' experience and careful instruction. If we are obedient to our parents, our lives should fall into place and we will be blessed by God.

So, how long does this commandment last? It lasts all our lives. While we are under our parent's roof, and they are paying the bills, we are obedient to them. When we are adults, we include them in our love and family activities. When they are older, we honor them by taking care of them. The fifth commandment has a special promise. We will live "long in the land" if we are obedient to our parents.—Ken Cox

---

[2]*God's Little Beggars* (Lima, Ohio: CSS, 1976), pp. 33–34.

May 8: Mother's Day

TEXT: 2 Tim. 1:3–7

Objects: Three Bibles of different translations

This morning I have not one but three objects that I want to show you. As I bring each out of the "time for children" bag, see if you know what I am holding, but don't raise your hand until all three have been shown. [Bring out three different translations of the Bible. Yes, they will raise their hand as each one is brought out in turn. Wait until all have been shown.] Now, what have I held up before you this morning? That's right, "Bibles"—"three Bibles." They are Bibles, but the words are a little different in each of the three. They are three different translations—different ways to say the same thing.

This reminds me of a story about four Sunday school teachers who got together and discussed which was the best translation of the Bible. The first said, "I like the Contemporary English Version, because it speaks in today's language." [Hold up CEV Bible.] Another said, "I like the Revised Standard Version because it's the most accurate translation of the original languages the Bible was written in." [Hold up the RSV Bible.] The third teacher said he favored the New International Version because he felt it was accurate and in modern English. [Hold up the NIV Bible.] The fourth teacher was quiet. Finally she said, "I like my mother's translation best."

The other three were surprised. They did not know that her mother had translated the Bible. Then she said, "Yes, she did. She translated it into life . . . what she did, how she loved me and God. It was the most powerful translation I ever saw."

This morning is Mother's Day, and we give thanks for mothers who translated (practiced) the Word of God in their lives. All of us, boys and girls, young and old, can learn to be that kind of translation of God's Word. Thanks for coming this morning.—Gary D. Stratman

May 15: The Sabbath Day

TEXT: Exod. 31:13

Object: A calendar

This calendar will help us learn about the Sabbath day. The Bible reveals that God completed his creation of the heavens and the earth in six days. On the seventh day God rested and made the day special. "Sabbath" means rest, so the Sabbath day is a day of rest.

From this calendar we can determine the Sabbath day because it is the seventh day of every week. Let's count. Saturday is the Sabbath day. It is the day on the "end" of this row of squares marking the days that make up a week.

God commanded his people, Israel, when he brought them out of Egypt, to worship on the Sabbath day. Their worship of God on the Sabbath would set them apart in the world. As they rested, they worshipped God. Listen to this verse. [Read Exod. 31:13.]

We worship on Sunday, which is the first day of the week. See, Sunday is the first square on the chart of days. Christians worship on Sunday because on the first day of the week Jesus was raised from the dead. Also, the day of Pentecost occurred on a Sunday. That's when the Holy Spirit was given in abundance to God's people. When we worship on Sunday we create a Christian Sabbath, or a Sabbath for Jesus. By worshipping God on the Sabbath we make the day a holy day.

By observing the Christian Sabbath we set ourselves apart as God's holy people. By worshipping each week we encourage each other to live a special life for God. Also if we come desiring to learn from God's word each Sunday, after only a few years we accumulate much knowledge about God. Week by week, we become stronger as we build each other up. Also, we are renewed in our thinking as we learn God's truth.

Keeping the Sabbath day is the fourth of the Ten Commandments. Setting aside the first day of each week for drawing closer to Jesus is still a priority that we should never break.—Ken Cox

May 22: Be a Witness for God

TEXT: Acts 1:8 (NIV)
Object: A match
Song: "Set My Soul Afire"

Good morning, boys and girls. I'm glad to see you today. I'm holding something that can be very powerful and useful, yet when used the wrong way it can destroy and harm. Yes, it's a match. Now, this match does nothing until it is struck, or lit. Of course, matches are never, never something to play with. Only adults should use matches. When used correctly, a match lights a fire that warms our home or cooks our food. When used in the wrong way, matches start forest fires that burn trees and homes. They can cause harm to people.

We could say a match lights a fire. This match is a symbol that stands for the fire that Jesus lights in our hearts. When we have a desire to tell others about Jesus, we might say "We are on fire for God."

The words of the song "Set My Soul Afire" speak of the millions of people who do not know or have not heard about Jesus. The words encourage boys and girls, men and women, to be a witness and to fill us with his power. When we are a witness, Christ lives in us.

Read from Acts 1:8: "But you will receive power when the Holy Spirit comes on you; and you will be my witnesses in Jerusalem, and in all Judea and Samaria, and to the ends of the earth." Does that mean in our neighborhood, also? Yes, this verse means we should share Christ with all people. When this happens, we are on fire for Christ.

[Prayer: Dear God, guide each boy and girl here today to be a witness for you. Amen.

Ask the pianist to play one stanza of "Set My Soul Afire" as children return to their seats.]—Carolyn Tomlin

May 29: Remember Our Heroes (Memorial Day)

TEXT: Deut. 32:7
Objects: Post-it note and broken pieces of red pottery with writing

Humans use many devices to help them remember. One way is to write a reminder on one of these Post-it notes. The note is filled out and then stuck to the phone, computer screen, or car dashboard.

In the days when Jesus grew up in Israel, the people had an interesting method of remembering. They wrote lists of needed supplies or instructions on pieces of pottery like this. In those days, big red pots were used to store water and food. After a pot was broken, the big chunks were used for messages and reminder notes. Today archaeologists discover writing on these pieces of broken pottery, called potsherds, and learn how people lived then.

Remembering has always been a challenge. If we don't work to remember, we forget what we intended to buy at the grocery store. Also, we may forget some important lessons we have learned from history.

Tomorrow is a day we set aside to remember those who have died in wars to provide our freedom. It is called "Memorial Day." It is a day set aside so we will not forget the valuable contribution made by soldiers serving our country.

Humans can forget some very important things. They can even forget God. That's why we come to church every week, so we can stay in touch with God and remember all he has done for us and means to us. Listen to this verse. [Read Deut. 32:7.]

As we worship God today, let's remember the heroes who served in our armed forces to provide freedom for us. We enjoy life in this abundant country because soldiers were faithful to their duty through serving our country.—Ken Cox

June 5: He Makes the Bad Good

TEXT: 1 Tim. 1:12–17 (v. 16: "But God had mercy on me so that Christ Jesus could use me as an example to show everyone how patient he is with even the worst sinners, so that others will realize that they, too, can have everlasting life")

Objects: Good examples, such as pictures, that show a person before and after losing weight and another before and after adding muscle

Good morning, boys and girls. How many of you have ever looked through a magazine or a newspaper? Almost all of you. Have you ever seen something like this? [Show them the pictures.] What does it mean when you see a picture of a very fat person in one picture and a not-so-fat person in the next picture? [Let them answer.] That's right, it means that she has lost weight. How about this one, which shows a very skinny man in one picture and then a very strong looking man with lots of muscles in the other. Do you know what that means? That's right. It means the man has built his body with exercise and great effort. These are what we call examples, good examples. The people who have accomplished what is shown in these pictures feel good because they know that they look better now than they did before. Not only that, but they feel that they are good examples for other people and others will feel better if they work hard at being like them.

Paul felt that he was an example. It was a lot different from the pictures that I have shown you. Paul was not an example of how a man who looked new with muscles or how a person would feel if he lost a lot of weight. Paul thought that God had chosen him as an example of how a bad man could be made into a good man by knowing Jesus. Paul told everyone how he had tried to hurt the church and the Christians who followed Jesus. He was a bad man. But God wanted Paul to work for him. In spite of all the bad things he did, God forgave him for his sins and asked Paul to work for him.

Just think about how God can make a bad man into a good man. It is a good example for all of us. Some people feel that they are not good enough to work for God and to be near God. But Paul said he is a good example of how God will care for the worst sinner and bring him into the church.

Maybe the next time you see one of these pictures in the paper, you will think about Paul and how God used this bad man and made him a good man to tell everyone about the love of Jesus.—Wesley T. Runk[3]

June 12: We Need Others

TEXT: Matt. 19:14 (NIV)
Object: Recipe book
Song: "Jesus Loves the Little Children"

Hello, boys and girls. I'm glad to see you today. I'm holding a book of recipes. Perhaps your parents or grandparents use such a book for preparing meals. I was looking at a cake recipe. Can you guess what ingredients I would need to bake a cake? [Wait for response. Turn to a recipe in the book.] To make a cake, I would need sugar, eggs, shortening, milk, flour, baking powder, and salt. Unless I use all these ingredients, the cake won't taste good. Each ingredient plays an important role in the finished product, which is a cake.

As I look at your faces, not one of you is exactly like the other. I see eyes, hair, and skin color that are different. No one can take your place. You are important to your family, friends, and especially to God.

The Bible tells us that Jesus loves children. In Matthew 19:14 we read that Jesus said, "Let the little children come to me, and do not hinder them, for the kingdom of heaven belongs to such as these."

[Prayer: Dear Lord Jesus, thank you for giving life to each of these precious children. Help them grow strong and healthy. May they know the greatness of your love. Amen.]

"Jesus Loves the Little Children" is a favorite song for children. The words stress that all children, regardless of their color or race, are loved by God. Just like many ingredients are necessary to bake a good cake, friends from other cultures and races enrich our lives. [Lead the children in singing "Jesus Loves the Little Children." Children return to their seats.]—Carolyn Tomlin

June 19: We Grow on Spiritual Milk

TEXT: Heb. 5:13–14
Object: A glass of milk

After babies are born, their only food is mother's milk or formula. Months later, a baby begins to eat soft foods like applesauce and strained green peas. After the baby begins to cut teeth it can eat "solid" food. Drinking milk in those first months allows the baby to grow. Solid food is necessary for the child to grow into adulthood. Growth is natural, but food is necessary for survival and healthy development.

A growth process is God's will for Christians too. When we first accept Jesus as our savior we are considered "babes in Christ." We understand a few things about our salvation, and we learn about Jesus through reading the Bible and Sunday school lessons. This growth process is the same whether the believer is ten or forty years old. Even an adult has to grow in their Christianity.

---

[3]*God Doesn't Rust*, pp. 79–80.

It would be sad if a baby never grew and never enjoyed a hamburger or chocolate ice cream. The same is true for Christians. Christians need to grow by drinking the spiritual milk of the word of God. It is very sad if a Christian never grows. Listen to these verses. [Read Heb. 5:13–14.]

How does a Christian grow? A believer grows by learning truth about God from the Bible. Also, a disciple grows by being obedient to God's commands. Growth comes by learning to pray and depend upon God for everything. By such spiritual pursuits, we spend time with God and are able to know more about him through life experiences. Thus we mature.

When Christians grow they become a different kind of person. They are still human, but more than human. Do you remember the story of Pinocchio? Pinocchio was a marionette made by a woodworker named Geppetto. During the story, Pinocchio changed from a marionette into a real little boy. The same kind of thing happens when a Christian grows. A believer grows spiritually and becomes more like Jesus, a different and better person. The more we become like Jesus, the happier our lives become, as do the lives of our family and friends.—Ken Cox

June 26: Calling on Jesus
TEXT: Heb. 13:8 (NIV)
Object: A cell phone
Song: "Jesus Is the Sweetest Name I Know"

Hello, boys and girls. I'm glad to see you today. [Place a cell phone nearby and have someone dial your number at this time.] Listen—do you hear a phone ringing? Of course, it's mine. Excuse me while I answer. "Hello? Did you say this was Jesus calling? Yes, Jesus, our boys and girls are gathered together for our children's sermon. Yes, yes, I will tell them. Thank you for calling. Goodbye."

Now, do you really think that was Jesus calling? [Wait for response.] No, of course not. We don't have to use a phone to talk to Jesus. Who can tell me how we can talk to Jesus? [Allow several children time to respond.] Yes, we can pray and talk to Jesus anytime we need to. We don't have to wait for a busy signal, no one at home, call waiting, special rates, weekends, or nights. We know that Jesus is always ready to hear our prayers. What happens when we answer a phone and hear a familiar voice? It makes us glad, right? Remember this fact: the name of Jesus is so sweet, it's the sweetest name we know.

There is a verse in Hebrews 13:8 that reads, "Jesus Christ is the same yesterday and today and forever." This verse tells us his name never changes.

[Prayer: Dear Lord Jesus, may these children know you are always ready to hear them when they call on your name. Amen.

Ask the pianist to play "Jesus Is the Sweetest Name I Know" as children return to their seats.]—Carolyn Tomlin

July 3: Only One Life to Give
TEXT: Ps. 33:12 (NIV)
Object: American flag
Song: "My Country, 'Tis of Thee"

Good morning, boys and girls. Who can tell me what holiday we are observing this week? Yes, it's Independence Day. Who can give me some facts about this special day in our country? [Allow time for several children to speak.] Some of the people who first came to our country were from England. They wanted to establish a place where they could find work, worship as they pleased, and govern themselves. However, after they arrived and settled the thirteen colonies, Great Britain demanded the colonists pay heavy taxes. The people thought this was unfair as they couldn't vote on how the money should be spent. A group of men met and asked Thomas Jefferson to write a document called the Declaration of Independence. Those who signed this paper could have lost their lives and their homes. Nathan Hale's last words before the British hung him were, "I only regret that I have but one life to lose for my country." On July 4, 1776, the colonists declared themselves free and independent from Great Britain. As of that time our nation was called America.

We invite the congregation to stand and salute the American flag. [Lead the salute to the American flag.]

Listen as I read from Psalm 33:12: "Blessed is the nation whose God is the Lord, the people he chose for his inheritance." As we pay tribute to America, let us not forget that it is God who makes us a great nation. Could you say that you regret you have only one life to give for God?

[Prayer: Dear Lord Jesus, we ask you to bless the leaders of our nation. May they seek your guidance as they seek to govern America. Amen.

Ask the soloist to sing one stanza of "My Country, 'Tis of Thee" as children return to their seats.]—Carolyn Tomlin

July 10: A Tooth for a Tooth
TEXT: Matt. 5:38–39
Object: Picture or model of a tooth

Here is a picture [model] of a tooth. We take our teeth for granted, but they are extremely valuable. A tooth can illustrate a lesson on retaliation.

Retaliation is a big word. It means to get somebody back for what they did to you. In ancient Israel, retaliation was a right of the people. There weren't police and laws like today, so people had to personally seek justice. For instance, if two men became angry and fought and one hit the other, knocking out a tooth, the injured man had the right to retaliate. Now the problem with retaliation is that it grew worse and worse. If one man lost a tooth, in his anger he might knock out the other's tooth and also break his arm with a hammer. Then the man with the broken arm and missing tooth would burn the other man's house down, and back and forth it went, until whole tribes were involved in a war.

To limit retaliation, an Old Testament law limited what could be done. The limitation was described as an "eye for an eye and a tooth for a tooth." Let's go back to our original fight. The man that lost the tooth could only knock out a tooth; he couldn't break the other man's arm. This law limited retaliation and the escalation of the fight. God's Commandments limited the disagreements and suffering.

When Jesus came, he taught something even better. He called for forgiveness. Listen to these verses. [Read Matt. 5:38–39.]

Forgiving someone is better than retaliating, because the anger of retaliation never seems to go away. In our country, we can't take the law into our own hands, and we may feel justice has not been done. If we feel that way, our anger may burn within us. When we are angry with someone else, it hurts us and our families as we take our anger out on others. If we constantly think about getting back at someone, our health and happiness suffer.

Jesus said a tooth for a tooth was just a starting point. It was good not to retaliate and even better to forgive. God gives us the capacity to forgive. Once we understand that God has forgiven us through Jesus, we can learn to forgive those who have wronged us. When we forgive, we let go of a load of anger that is weighing us down.—Ken Cox

July 17: God Is Like a Peaceful River

TEXT: Ps. 46:4 (NIV)
Object: A glass or bottle of water
Song: "I Have Peace Like a River"

Hello, boys and girls. I'm glad you chose to come to church today. I'm holding a glass of water, which represents something much greater and larger. This small container of water represents the water of a river. Recently I stood on the bank of a large river and watched as pieces of wood and tree limbs floated downstream. Due to the strong current on the river, the objects moved in the direction of the flowing water. A few became caught on roots and tree trunks along the bank. But for the most part, most of the limbs moved along the river as the current directed their path. Standing and watching a river with clouds overhead, you recognize the greatness of the world God created.

When we place our faith and trust in God, he directs our path. No longer do we wander aimlessly throughout life. God gives us peace, wonderful peace.

When the shepherd boy David wrote some of the Psalms, he marveled at the wonderful world God created. The mountains, the valleys, the rivers—everything God made, he honored. Psalm 46:4 reads, "There is a river whose streams make glad the city of God, the most holy place where the Most High dwells."

[Prayer: Dear Lord Jesus, may these children know and understand the peace that comes from loving you. Amen.

Lead the congregation in singing "I Have Peace Like a River." Children will return to their seats.]—Carolyn Tomlin

July 24: God's Written Instruction

TEXT: Exod. 34:27–28
Object: Written driving directions

Tell me which instructions would be easier to follow for someone driving from out of town to a swimming party at the city pool.

First, listen to driving instructions by word of mouth. [Speaking quickly:] "Take the Highway 8 exit off I-30. Stay on Highway 8, continue straight through the red light, go over the overpass, and turn right on Sunset Drive. Continue for three blocks, and turn left on Elm Street. Go two blocks, and turn right into the park. The pool is right in front of you."

Second, look at these written instructions and map. Every detail is written in one paragraph, and the map on the top of the page shows which way to turn. With written instructions, the driver could be directed by another person sitting in the front seat as they progressed along the described route.

It would be easy to miss one of the spoken directions and get lost. Using the written instructions and map would be better.

God realized that humans have a challenge catching every important detail of spoken directions. That's why God has given us his truth in written form. Listen to this verse. [Read Exod. 34:27–28.]

God instructed Moses to write the Commandments on tablets of stone. By inscribing the truth of God on stone, the people realized the directions were permanent. It might be easy to misplace instructions on paper, but commandments inscribed on stone tablets would be a perpetual testimony. That way God's truth would be passed down and observed from generation to generation. Grandchildren would be obedient to the same commands that grandparents had learned to love and obey.

There is still a better way for the word of God to be recorded. That is when the Lord's truth is written on our hearts (Deut. 11:18). This means the Lord's truth has been memorized and put to work in our lives. When we learn the truth of God through experience and learn to love his truth, then God's word is on our hearts. Words written on our hearts will never be lost, even in eternity.—Ken Cox

July 31: Giving of Yourself
TEXT: 2 Cor. 8:5 (NIV)
Object: A piggy bank
Song: "What Can I Give Him"

Good morning, boys and girls. I'm glad you chose to come to church today. I'm holding something many of you may have at home. Yes, it's a piggy bank. What do you put in a bank such as this? Yes, money, of course. Can you tell me how you get the money to put in a bank? [Wait for response.] I hear you say that some of you receive money for birthdays or special holidays; others have extra chores you do at home to earn money, and some of you help people in your neighborhood rake leaves, or care for their pets when on vacation. There are numerous ways we can earn money and save money.

I know that boys and girls do not have regular jobs like adults. Your parents go to work and bring home a paycheck. This money is divided into paying bills, saving for the future, and giving to the church. You may wonder, "How can I give Jesus something value? I have no money—no job." But do you know there is something of greater value than money? What is it? It is giving Jesus your heart. When you give your heart and life to Jesus, it is the greatest gift you can give. And next, you want to tell others about the gift you have to Jesus.

In 2 Corinthians 8:5, the apostle Paul wrote about the church in Macedonia. The congregations were in extreme poverty, yet they gave with generosity: "For I testify that they gave as much as they were able, and even beyond their ability."

[Prayer: Dear Lord Jesus, help each child realize that the greatest gift they can give Jesus is to give him their heart. Amen.

Ask the pianist to play "What Can I Give Him" as children return to their seats.]—Carolyn Tomlin

August 7: Our Special Gift
TEXT: 1 Pet. 4:7b–11 (v. 10: "God has given each of you some special abilities; be sure to use them, to help each other, passing on to others God's many kinds of blessings")
Objects: Things identifying as many people with different talents as you can assemble

Good morning, boys and girls. I am always pleased to see you on Sunday morning and to see how different all of you look. There is no mistaking one of you for the other (unless you have a twin). Each of you has something different about you that lets me remember who you are and what you can do. That's the way I remember all of our parents and friends, too. Let's take a look at some of the members of our congregation.

[Begin to introduce the members by name and vocation. Say something very important about each one of them, and emphasize how different the work is that each of them does.] We could go on and on talking about the things that all of our members do in our town. Did you know that there are more than 750,000 kinds of work?

The Christian is thankful to God that he has given us so many ways to serve him and each other. God gives us all of these different talents so that we can help each other live better in this world. The doctor could be his own carpenter and build a house, and be a teacher and teach his own children. But then, think of how little doctoring he would do. While he was teaching his children, you would have to suffer with your sore throat and earache.

God knew all about that kind of thinking, and he gave each of us a talent that was so special that we would need each other. When you are needed and you help the person who needs you, then you make that person glad. God knew that and wanted us to need each other, so he gave us this special gift. I hope that you will find out about your talent and use it to make other people happy. When you are a blessing to people, you are pleasing to God.— Wesley T. Runk[4]

August 14: Thanking God for the Weather
TEXT: Ps. 118:24 (NIV)
Object: A picture showing a peaceful scene of nature
Song: "This Is the Day"

Hello, boys and girls. I'm glad to see you today. Who can tell me what type of weather we are having today? [Wait for response. Talk about the weather in your area at this time.] Is the weather like or unlike the picture I'm holding? Can you tell me your favorite kind of weather? Yes, some of you may like snow; you can slide down hills and make snow people. Others may like rainy days, when you can jump in puddles; or hot weather, when you can swim and play in water. Aren't you glad that God makes all kind of weather? He knows we need rain to nourish the earth and sun to make plants grow. I think it would be boring to have the same weather day after day, don't you?

Several years ago a friend gave me an embroidered sampler that stated, "This is the day the Lord has made; let us rejoice and be glad in it." Since that time the picture has been

---

[4]*Pass It On* (Lima, Ohio: CSS), pp. 49–50.

placed where I see it every day. Regardless of the weather, I'm reminded that all days are special, and they are created by God.

Let's repeat Psalm 118:24 together. It's a verse I want you to memorize and use throughout your life: "This is the day the Lord has made; let us rejoice and be glad in it." Each day has many opportunities and responsibilities. How will you use this time given to you by God?

[Prayer: Dear Lord Jesus, help each child rejoice in each new day. May they be happy about the possibilities each day brings. Amen.

Ask a soloist to sing "This Is the Day" as children return to their seats.]—Carolyn Tomlin

August 21: Sticks and Stones

TEXT: Ps. 19:14
Objects: Sticks and stones

These sticks and stones illustrate a saying that children have used for years. The scoffing words are said when someone says something that hurts our feelings. We snap back, "Sticks and stones may break my bones, but words will never hurt me."

Actually, the old saying is not true. Words are powerful and can cause severe pain or damage that can never be repaired. Negative words can remain painful for a lifetime. Some adults describe how words spoken to them while they were children are active in their thoughts every day. Words spoken carelessly by teachers, parents, and friends forty years ago are still vividly remembered. Though these words were not intentionally spoken to do harm for a lifetime, they do.

Words are powerful and hurt much more than sticks and stones. A wound from a stick or stone might heal itself without a scar. However, if our feelings are hurt by what is said, healing may never occur.

For this reason there is a prayer that ought to be said by all believers. It is in Psalm 19:14. Listen to this verse. [Read Ps. 19:14.]

Our words are also powerful for good. If we tell a friend about Jesus and they accept him as their savior, that word of testimony will bless them not only until they are old enough to be grandparents but through all eternity. Also, if you notice something one of your friends does extremely well, like playing baseball, sketching, or singing, your compliments can help their future. Such words of encouragement might help them to find their life's calling. Since our words are so powerful, we should be careful to build others up by what we say and never tear them down.

So, let's love our neighbors, friends, and family members. We must not harm with sticks, stones, or words.—Ken Cox

August 28: An Infinite Life

TEXT: Isa. 6:8 (NIV)
Objects: An apple, knife, and sack
Song: "I Love You, Lord"

[Place an apple inside a sack so it isn't visible to the children.] Hello, boys and girls. I'm glad to see you today. Inside this sack is one object that can grow and multiply into thousands and thousands. In fact, there is no way to even count what this object could become. I'll give you some clues: it's a fruit, grows on a tree, can be yellow, green, or red. It can be eaten raw or cooked and made into desserts and delicious foods. The object is recommended for good health. Can anyone guess what's in the sack? [Wait for response.] If you guessed an apple, you are correct.

Now, when you look at this apple, you only see one. But look what happens when I cut the apple into sections. Do you see all those little seeds? If I planted these seeds, and they grew into trees that had apples, and then those seeds grew into apple trees, you could count the seeds in one apple, but it's impossible to count the apples that could come from these few seeds. In fact it is endless, or infinite.

Let's compare your life to the apple. You are only one boy or girl. When you give your life to Christ, you want to tell your friends about Jesus. What if you lead ten people to believe in Jesus, and they each lead ten people? That would be at least one hundred people, right? Always remember that you are a very important person when you serve Jesus. You have great potential to be a witness for Christ.

Listen as I read Isaiah 6:8: "Then I heard the voice of the Lord saying, 'Whom shall I send? And who will go for us?' And I said, 'Here am I. Send Me!'"

[Prayer: Dear Jesus, help children realize there is no way to measure their influence for you.

Ask the pianist to play "Here Am I, Send Me" as children return to their seats.]—Carolyn Tomlin

September 4: Work Has Value

TEXT: Gal. 6:9 (NIV)

Objects: Hats or tools to represent several community helpers

Song: "We'll Work Till Jesus Comes"

Good morning, boys and girls. I'm glad to see you today. This week we are celebrating Labor Day—a day to honor our workforce. Most of you have learned about different ways people in our community help us. If you remember, your school curriculum includes a unit on community helpers. These are people in our town who help others. Let's name the person who might wear the hat or use the tool I'm holding. [Hold up a hat worn by a community helper and ask children to identify the position or department.] For example, who wears a firefighter's helmet? A firefighter, of course. Who would use a hammer? A carpenter, right? Do any of your parents work for an agency that serves the community? Some may work in the medical field, or drive an ambulance, or be a mechanic who keeps our cars safe, a policeman who keeps our streets and homes safe, a teacher or pastor. These are only a few of the people who work to make our community a good place to live.

Work is important. There is value in physical and mental work. But there is another kind of work that Jesus wants from us. Can anyone tell me about this work? [Wait for response.] Jesus wants us to help others, to tell people about his love and to be a friend to everyone.

Galatians 6:9 says, "Let us not become weary in doing good, for at the proper time we will reap a harvest if we do not give up." Jesus is saying that we must continue to tell others about him, even though they may not respond. If we work for Jesus we will be rewarded in heaven.

[Prayer: Dear Lord Jesus, guide each boy and girl here today to be a worker for you. Amen.

Ask a soloist to sing "We'll Work Till Jesus Comes" as children return to their seats.]— Carolyn Tomlin

September 11: You Wear a Leash, Too

TEXT: 1 Cor. 9:24–10:5 (v. 25: "Every athlete exercises self-control in all things. They do it to receive a perishable wreath, but we an imperishable")

Object: A dog leash

Good morning, boys and girls. I want to ask you how you got here this morning. [Let them answer.] Did someone bring you in the car? Did you have to do any walking? Did you run this morning when you should not have run, or did anybody tell you to walk when you were running? [Let them answer.] Sometimes it's pretty hard to just walk when we want to run, and our mothers and fathers tell us to stop running or to sit down and be quiet. We get out of control. Have you ever been told to sit down and be quiet? [Let them answer.] I know what that is like, because my mother and father used to have to tell me to do those things. I suppose that I did what they told me, although it was pretty hard sometimes.

We have another way of making some of our friends walk or stay with us when we want them to. How many of you have a dog? Dogs are great friends, aren't they? Do you ever take your dog for a walk and put the leash on him? A leash helps you control the dog so that he will not run in the street or get away from you when you are walking. In some places like big cities you have to keep your dog on a leash so that you have control of the dog at all times. Do you think that would work pretty well on boys and girls? We could buy a collar for every boy and girl and then get a leash and keep control in that way. How do you think that would work? [Let them answer.] I don't think that you would like that very much.

People are supposed to have self-control. One of the reasons your parents tell you about all of your mistakes is so that you can learn self-control. This means you can take care of yourself and you don't need a leash.

Christians are taught the greatest self-control because Christians do not need the law. Christians do more than the law. The law teaches you not to hurt anyone, but that is all. A leash keeps a dog from biting someone he doesn't know. But the law does not teach you to help someone. A leash does not teach a dog to help or be kind to someone whom he doesn't know. A Christian does not need a leash or a law. A Christian is taught to help and love everyone. That is real self-control.

Dogs need leashes. All people need the law to tell them what not to do, but the Christian needs self-control to teach him how to help and to love. A Christian will control himself and help others.—Wesley T. Runk[5]

September 18: God's Marvelous Power

TEXT: Ps. 139:14 (NIV)

Object: A picture of a butterfly

Song: "All Creatures of Our God and King"

Good morning, boys and girls. I'm glad to see you today. While I was preparing for this children's sermon today, I thought about the wonderful world God created. I enjoy being outdoors where I can feel the wind blowing, feel the warm sun on my face, and hear the birds

---

[5]*Pass It On,* pp. 17–18.

singing. I'm holding a picture of a butterfly. How many know the stages a butterfly must go through before it becomes this beautiful insect that we see flying among the flowers? [Wait for response.] First, it is a simple larva or caterpillar, and then a pupa that builds a cocoon called a chrysalis. Last it immerges into a beautiful butterfly.

Do you think the caterpillar would like to skip the next stage and be a butterfly immediately? Do you think the butterfly would like to return to crawling on the ground like a caterpillar? Only when it becomes a butterfly can it soar and fly high in the sky. It is the butterfly that catches our eye and we marvel at the beauty of God's creation. God made all creatures, and he knows what is best for each.

God has a marvelous power. He knows what is best for each boy and girl here today. We must pray and be ready to accept whatever God calls us to do in life.

Listen as I read Psalm 139:14: "I praise you because I am fearfully and wonderfully made; your works are wonderful, I know that full well."

[Prayer: Dear God, guide each child present today to accept your will in life. May they realize your marvelous power and give you the honor and glory. Amen.

Ask a soloist to sing "All Creatures of Our God and King" as children return to their seats.]—Carolyn Tomlin

September 25: God Helps Our Weaknesses
TEXT: Matt. 26:41
Objects: Two chocolate chip cookies

Let me tell you a story. An eight-year-old boy named Jeff was at his grandmother's house one afternoon. She baked some huge chocolate chip cookies. When it was time for Jeff to go home, his grandmother gave him two cookies. She told Jeff to wait until after supper to eat his cookie. The other cookie was dessert for his little sister, Becky.

As Jeff walked the half mile to his home, the cookies smelled delicious. He wanted to wait until he got home to eat his cookie, but he just couldn't. So before he made it halfway, he gobbled up his cookie. Then he kept smelling the other cookie. Even though he really wanted to get the cookie home to Becky, he ate hers too. When Jeff got home he felt bad for what he had done. He told his mom and apologized to Becky. Later his grandmother brought another cookie to his sister.

What happened to Jeff occurs every day. We want to do something good, but we just aren't strong enough to complete our good intentions. For instance we need to practice the piano or do our homework, but we just keep watching television until the entire evening is wasted. Jesus described this common human predicament. Listen to this verse. [Read Matt. 26:41.]

Our human willpower and discipline are often inadequate to accomplish good deeds. However, Jesus described the solution to this human dilemma. Jesus said to pray for strength and God would give it. By praying and asking God to enable us to do great things for him, we grow stronger in all our abilities. We don't have to be like Jeff eating those cookies; we can pray for God's help and accomplish great things for him. God is willing to help us do our best. Our human nature may be weak, but the Spirit of God is willing to live in us and help us to be strong.—Ken Cox

October 2: Faith

TEXT: 1 Pet. 1:8 (NIV)
Object: Picture of a computer
Song: "Have Faith in God"

Hello, boys and girls. I'm glad to see you today. I'm holding something that many of you may have in your homes. Or, you may use this object in school. What is this object called? [Wait for response.] Yes, this object is a computer. A computer does many things. For example, you can type a letter and send it to a friend, play games, send or receive an e-mail, connect to the Internet and read newspapers from all over the world, check the national and international news—just to name a few. Now, as I'm not a scientist or inventor, I don't really understand just how a computer works. It would be impossible for me to take it apart and put it back together. But you know something? Even though I don't understand how it works, I know that it does. Why? Because I use this tool every day. It serves me well. You might say I have faith it will work when I turn it on.

We do not have all the answers about God, but we do know that he is real in our lives. We see his marvelous works. If we waited until we had all the answers about the Bible, we would never be able to turn our lives over to him. Aren't you glad that Jesus wants us to come unto him as we are, and he will help us learn more about him?

Listen as I read about faith: "Though you have not seen him, you love him; and even though you do not see him now, you believe in him and are filled with an inexpressible and glorious joy." We see God in others and in the world he created.

[Prayer: Dear Lord, help these children have faith and place their trust in you. Amen.

Lead the children in singing "Have Faith in God." Pianist continues to play as children return to their seats.]—Carolyn Tomlin

October 9: A Yellow Ribbon for Jesus

TEXT: James 5:8
Objects: Yellow ribbons

We tie yellow ribbons on trees, flagpoles, and buildings to express our eagerness for loved ones to return home. The practice started years ago with a song made popular by Tony Orlando.

The song describes a man's love for his girlfriend. The man had been in prison and was soon to be released after paying the penalty for his crime. He didn't know if his girlfriend would want him back after thee years of imprisonment. The man wrote his girlfriend a letter with instructions for her to show how she felt about their relationship. If she still loved him, she was asked to tie a yellow ribbon around an old oak tree by the road. He would return home on a bus from the prison, and, according to his plan, when the man was near home he would see the oak tree and know his girlfriend's answer. If he did not see that yellow ribbon on the tree he would stay on the bus and travel down the road for an unknown future. As the song develops, the excited man asks the bus driver to tell him if a yellow ribbon is on the tree when he gets close to home. The happy ending to the song is the whole bus begins cheering when they notice the girlfriend has tied not one but a hundred yellow ribbons around the old oak tree. Therefore the man knows he can go back home to his girl-friend because she still loves him.

Today by tying yellow ribbons on trees and buildings we say to our missing loved ones that we are praying for them and can't wait until they return home. Yellow ribbons are a wonderful testimony of love and remembering others.

We should tie a yellow ribbon around our hearts as we await the return of Jesus. According to the Bible, Jesus ascended to heaven after his Resurrection and is reigning there. Listen to this verse. [Read James 5:8.] Jesus promised to return from heaven for his children and take us to be where he is. Jesus has given specific instructions for us to follow as we anticipate his return. First, we are to keep his word, being obedient to his instructions. Second, we are to live every day in faithful awareness of his return. If we forget his promise, it is easy to slip into a lifestyle that does not please God.

So we can tie yellow ribbons around trees, flagpoles, and buildings to show our love for family members away from home. We can also show our love for Jesus by tying obedience and faithfulness to our lives. When Jesus returns, be sure he will see a yellow ribbon of faith in your life.—Ken Cox

October 16: God Is with You

TEXT: Eph. 5

Object: Crossword puzzle (Take a puzzle from the daily newspaper or use another object that "fits." See the "Object" note in the January 16 children's sermon.)

It is so good to see you all this morning. I am so glad you are here. Some of you were here when we talked about the game Scrabble. What kind of game is Scrabble? Yes, it is a word game. Do you usually play that game alone or with others? You are right, it is a word game we play with others. This morning I have another word game; do you recognize it? Yes, it is a crossword puzzle. We play this word game by ourselves. It is different from Scrabble.

There are words that encourage and build up others. This week our Scripture is also reminding us that there are words that encourage us as individuals. There are psalms, hymns, and spiritual sayings that we can say or sing *in our hearts*! Sometimes you will be lonely or scared, yet will not be alone. God is with you. This morning we say, "Be still and know that I am God." To sing or say those words reminds you that God is there in those lovely or scary times. But we need to say them more often. The Scripture you learned in vacation Bible school or Sunday school can be said every day. When you come up here every Sunday we sing "Jesus Loves Me." When you go back to your seats we sing "Oh How I Love Jesus." Take those spiritual songs with you and let those words be in your heart.—Gary D. Stratman

October 23: Put God on Your Pedestal

TEXT: Rev. 22:9

Objects: A pedestal, table, and teddy bear

This is a pedestal. It is used for lifting things up so they can be seen. We put this pedestal on a table, and then we put this teddy bear on top. See? The teddy bear is prominent in our view and is the center of attention in a living room.

Our human nature seeks to put someone or something on a pedestal in our lives. For instance, if we like baseball we might put Alex Rodriguez on a pedestal; Alex Rodriguez, "A-Rod" as he is called, became the youngest player in Major League history to hit three hundred home runs. Or, if we are a young lady, we might put Hilary Duff on a pedestal since she is the star of the *Lizzie McGuire* show.

Humans put someone or something on a pedestal in their lives because God created us to worship him. Since we are sinners by nature, we tend to put the wrong person or thing on the pedestal of our lives.

Once an apostle by the name of John bowed down to an angel. He knew Jesus and served him during his earthly ministry. Late in life, John was writing the book of Revelation, and an angel was unveiling what he was to write. By bowing down, John seemed willing to put that angel on the pedestal of his life. John bowed, but the angel corrected him and said to worship God alone. Listen to this verse. [Read Rev. 22:9.]

Now remember: we all put someone or something on the pedestal of our lives. However, if we put something other than God there, we are always going to be disappointed.

Is God on the pedestal of your life? He is put there when we accept Jesus as savior and seek God's will through reading the Bible and praying. Jesus is on the pedestal of our lives when we are obedient to God's commandments and are willing to put him first in our priorities.—Ken Cox

October 30: God Feeds All the Animals

TEXT: Ps. 104:14, 27–28
Object: Cat food

This is the food we give to Simba, our cat. Feeding is one of the responsibilities of owning a cat. When family meetings are held about whether or not a pet will be adopted, delegating responsibilities of feeding, walking, grooming, etc., are made. Most parents require a promise from a child wanting a pet that the child will feed it.

Feeding a cat is not hard; the bag is opened and the food is poured into the cat's bowl. Simba likes to have fresh water too, so another bowl is filled with water. Even though it is not that big a job, it has to be done once or twice a day; otherwise the cat will suffer neglect. In some cases, after a pet is adopted there are disputes about the feeding arrangements. Parents complain that they have to feed the cat instead of the child who was assigned the responsibility after sincere promises had been made. Parents don't understand that children are restricted by the daily duty and need a break from the task.

And these disagreements are over one cat! Think of all the wild animals in the world that need to be fed. There are deer, birds, and in some regions lions and bears. God has taken the responsibility and promised to feed all of the animals of the world. Listen to these verses. [Read Ps. 104:14, 27–28.]

This Psalm describes God's action of providence. Providence describes God's constant care over all creation. After we think of our struggles in keeping one cat fed, it is a huge assignment to keep all the animals of creation fed.

We may think that the animals are fed automatically, that they take care of themselves in the wild as the plants and animals grow naturally. The Bible reveals that all creatures are under the loving care of God. Jesus said that not even a sparrow falls to the ground without

God's knowledge (Matt. 10:29). The world is not on "cruise control." God is active every day in preserving his creation.

So, God takes care of all the earth. Jesus taught the lesson of God's care for the sparrow not to show that God loves animals but to stress that God cares for all creation, particularly humans created in his image.

The next time you feed your cat, dog, parakeet, hamster, horse, goat, or snake, remember it is a special responsibility. Also claim by faith that God has promised to take care of and feed you.—Ken Cox

November 6: We Are God's Family

TEXT: John 1:12
Object: A family tree diagram

This diagram is a "family tree." It looks like a tree when held up like this. Here is the trunk, and the branches grow thicker and broader as the family history goes up the tree.

To determine your family tree, you would write your name on the blank that looks like the tree trunk. Then you would list your mother, father, grandfather, grandmother, and so on. This tree goes back five generations. Some have traced their family tree back many generations and discovered that famous people like President Abraham Lincoln were in their lineage. Also, by tracing back in their family tree some have discovered that they had great-great-great-great-grandparents who came to the United States from Ireland or Germany.

The Bible stresses the importance of families. Many chapters in the Old Testament consist of nothing more than the names of family members and descendants. One very important verse about families is in the Gospel of John. Listen to this verse. [Read John 1:12.]

According to this verse we are part of God's family if we have accepted Jesus as our savior. That's one reason we call God our "Heavenly Father" when we pray.

Being part of an earthly family is very important. An earthly family is responsible for our care and nurture. Our moms and dads clothe and feed us. They also play a role in helping us find our way in life, through assisting us in choosing jobs and where we will live. That's why many people want to know about their family tree. They want to know who their ancestors were, so they can grasp how their present lives were shaped.

Regardless of how many famous people are in our family tree, the most important family we belong to is God's family. Because we have God as our father, we know the Lord protects, feeds, and clothes us just like our earthly families. Something else happens too. You and I, and believers all over the world, realize we are part of the same family. Therefore we love, support, and pray for each other because we are in God's family. We all belong to an earthly family, and when we believe in Jesus we become part of God's family, including those in heaven and on Earth.—Ken Cox

November 13: Opening My Heart to Jesus

TEXT: John 3:16
Object: The Bible
Song: "Since Jesus Came into My Heart"

Hello, boys and girls. I'm glad to see you today. Let's share a few thoughts on how we can open our hearts to Jesus and how we can live a life of service for him. God loves you and me so much that he was willing to sacrifice his only son, who was Jesus, to die on a cross for our sins. In doing this, Jesus paid the price for our sins. When we realize we have sinned and ask God to forgive us, we will be forgiven. When this life is over, we will spend eternity in heaven with Jesus. We will be with all those people who accepted Christ. This is called being "saved." Being saved means we have a responsibility to tell others about this amazing love of Jesus.

A key verse in the Bible is John 3:16. This verse tells us how we can accept Christ as our Savior. Listen as I read: "For God so loved the world that he gave his one and only Son, that whoever believes in him shall not perish but have eternal life."

When we accept Christ, we have this happy feeling in our hearts. We are changed from the old life into a new life. This doesn't mean we will never do anything wrong again, but we now have Christ as our role model. Pleasing him and obeying his word is the focus of our life.

[Prayer: Dear Lord, bless these children here today. May not a day go by when they realize they are sinners, before they accept you as Lord.

Lead the children in singing "Since Jesus Came into My Heart."]—Carolyn Tomlin

November 20: We Give Thanks

TEXT: Ps. 100:1–5 (NIV)
Object: Basket of fruit or vegetables
Song: "Praise and Thanksgiving"

Hello, boys and girls. Who can tell me the holiday we are celebrating this season? That's right, it's Thanksgiving. Thanksgiving is a time to count our blessings and thank God for his wonderful care over us. During our children's sermon today, I want you to think of something for which you are thankful. [Allow time for all children who want to respond.] Yes, those are all good things for which we are thankful. We are thankful for homes, family, friends, health, teachers, our church, and for those in the medical fields who work to keep us well. There are so many things for which we are thankful, it would be impossible to name them all.

David, the shepherd boy, expressed his thanksgiving to God by writing poems and songs. Psalm 100 is a psalm for giving thanks. Listen as I read verses 1–5 from this chapter: "Shout for joy to the Lord, all the earth. Worship the Lord with gladness; come before him with joyful songs. Know that the Lord is God. It is he who made us, and we are his; we are his people, the sheep of his pasture. Enter his gates with thanksgiving and his courts with praise; give thanks to him and praise his name. For the Lord is good and his love endures forever; his faithfulness continues through all generations."

[Prayer: Dear Heavenly Father, we thank thee for all of life's blessings. We know that all good and perfect gifts come from you. Amen.

Ask the pianist to play "Praise and Thanksgiving" as children return to their seats.]—Carolyn Tomlin

November 27: Incarnation

TEXT: John 1

Have you ever been on a trip with your family and needed help with directions, finding the best way to go? Let's do this. You can give me any help you want, but you cannot move from where you are now. Also, if I hold up my hand, everybody must be very quiet; don't say anything if my hand is up like this. [Hold right hand up high.] OK, ready? I want to go to the pastor. Let's begin! [Traveling in the wrong direction, there are lots of helpful suggestions from the children. I do not heed them and keep saying, so everyone can hear me, "I know I'm going in the right direction. I don't need to listen to anybody." Finally, I hold up my hand. In the quiet, I tell the children that they can send one person down to help me. When this is done, I make it to my goal. Then we talk about our experience.]

How did you feel when I kept going the wrong way and would not listen to your directions? Yes, it was frustrating. Some were sad, some angry. Did you ever think of God's thoughts when we go the wrong way—when we say no to our friends, refuse to share what we have, or refuse to forgive our little brother? In our Scripture this morning, we learn that God's direction comes to us in Jesus. God's Word becomes a person. He could show us the way of truth, love, and forgiveness by living with us, teaching us, and dying for us. Just as I could not move in the right direction until you sent someone down here to find the way, so Jesus has done that for all of us. God's Word became human and lived with us that we might have God's Word in us now and forever.—Gary D. Stratman

December 4: No Surprise

TEXT: John 1:1–18

Object: A tie with a crossword design (This is another example of varying the attention-getting step. Sometimes the object is literally right under our noses.)

There is no object in my hand this morning, and I don't have a surprise in the "time for children" bag today. Don't leave! I do have something I want to show you. [Move closer and show them the tie.] That's right. It is a tie. You all know that right away. Ben, what's on the tie? Yes, a crossword puzzle. How many of you have ever worked a crossword puzzle? It looks like many of you have. One of you is pointing to her grandparents because they love to do the crossword puzzle in the newspaper. Right now, I need your help. What is a five-letter word beginning with "L" that means a force that shines into darkness and breaks it up or "chases" it away? [After a few tries, several say "Light."] That is right!

The Gospel of John reminds us that Jesus was God's word that came into the world to give us hope and eternal life. He was the light the darkness of death and sin tried to defeat. The light shows us the way to God and reveals the way we should love and care for others. So remember, with all the Christmas lights on your trees at home and the special decorations of light all over town, the true light that came into the world to overcome all our fears and helps us to see God and each other in a new way is Jesus.

The last letter in *light* begins a six-letter word going down this way. It is *thanks.* I am so glad you came today. God bless you.—Gary D. Stratman

December 11: Reaching out

TEXT: Mark 1:1

Object: Small slip of paper containing the words of Mark 1:1

What do I have in my hand? You are making some good guesses, but you really don't know, do you? It's probably because I have not opened my hand and you can't see through my hand.

That's the problem too with knowing what will happen in the future. Will you make new friends in this next year? Will God be with you in the next year?

Just as we cannot see through the hand to know what it holds, I cannot look through all the days of the next year and tell you all that will happen. But I can tell you this [open your hand and read from the paper]: "The beginning of the good news of Jesus Christ, the Son of God." Your days next year will have good news in them because Jesus is the Son of God, who came to us and will be with us always. Jesus' word that we hear at church and home helps us to extend our hand in friendship to new people and make friends in the next year [do this with your hand]. Jesus' spirit in us helps us help others in need [using your hand, help someone stand up]. There is also good news that Jesus teaches us to pray every day [fold your hands].

Loving God, thank you for sending Jesus to be your good news to us and the world. Help us to receive this next year as a gift with new friends, good things to do, and you always with us. Amen.—Gary D. Stratman

December 18: Loving Your Friends

TEXT: John 15:12–13 (NIV)
Object: A friendship bracelet
Song: "What a Friend We Have in Jesus"

Hello, boys and girls. I'm glad you chose to come to church today. Today we are talking about having friends and being a friend. A friendship bracelet is often worn as a sign that two people are friends. Who can tell me something you enjoy doing with a friend? [Give several children time to respond.] Yes, those are good things. Perhaps you spend time together, play ball, enjoy sports, and your families enjoy being with other families. Now, can you tell me what characteristics you look for in a friend? [Wait for response.] You say that a friend should be loyal, honest, responsible, trustworthy, and caring, to name a few. These are traits you feel are important in choosing friends. Next, let's talk about the kind of friend you should be. [Wait for response.] Wouldn't it be the same? If you want friends, you must have the same characteristics yourself.

Jesus wants you to have friends. Let's read from John 15:12–13: "My command is this: Love each other as I have loved you. Greater love has no one than this, that he lay down his life for his friends." Jesus is our example in developing friends. He will always be ready to listen when we talk to him.

[Prayer: Dear Lord Jesus, guide each boy and girl as they choose friends. Help them realize that true friendship is a gift from God. May they know you as their most important friend.

Lead the children in singing "What a Friend We Have in Jesus." Children return to their seats.]—Carolyn Tomlin

December 25: The Night of Jesus' Birth

TEXT: Luke 2:14 (NIV)
Object: Angel figurine
Song: "Hark! The Herald Angels Sing"

Hello, boys and girls. Who can tell me the season we are celebrating? And why do I have an angel? It's Christmas, of course! And the angels announced the birth of Jesus. Christmas is my favorite holiday, and it may be yours also. During this season of the year, people seem to be more helpful and kinder to others. We may think of gifts we want to give others. Do you know why we have these feelings during this season?

Over two thousand years ago, a baby was born in Bethlehem. This baby's name was Jesus, and he was to be the Savior of the world. Shepherds who were keeping watch over their flocks by night saw the star that shone down where the infant lay. You see, Mary, his mother, and Joseph, his earthly father, had to travel to Bethlehem to pay their taxes. While on the journey, the baby was born. There was no room in the inn for the family, so the innkeeper gave them a room in a stable. Clean straw was placed in a manger, which was a trough for feeding animals. This is where Mary placed the baby.

The story of Jesus' birth is recorded in Matthew and Luke. In Luke 2:14 we read that the heavenly hosts appeared with angels, praising God and saying, "Glory to God in the highest, and on earth peace to men on whom his favor rests." After the angels returned to heaven, the shepherds went in search of the baby.

[Prayer: Dear Lord Jesus, help us to remember the true meaning of Christmas. Amen.

Lead the congregation in singing "Hark! The Herald Angels Sing" as children return to their seats.]—Carolyn Tomlin

SECTION XII

A LITTLE TREASURY
OF ILLUSTRATIONS

ACKNOWLEDGMENT.   I am indebted to my blood family as they continually help me to grow in the meaning of faith and love. My mother, Lucille, now ninety-five, made certain that the story was told and passed along to me in both word and deed. My two sons, Scott and Kirk, and their families bless me by loving me enough to keep me honest and open to the wisdom and questions of succeeding generations. "Grampa Bill," my grandchildren will say as I read or tell them a story, "how can that be?" or "Why did God say that?" Most of all, it is my wife, Edie, the greatest gift I have been given, who as my lover and cheerleader graces me with God's presence as my best and cherished friend.—William G. Enright[1]

BOLD ASSURANCE.   God wants his message not only to have the right content but to have a power that is palpable. In others words, God desires bold assurance in his message.

How do you picture bold assurance? One image is of a person speaking with confidence and certainty about something he or she believes deeply and passionately. He or she is authentic, and effective.

Why can't we all speak with bold assurance? We all have things we are passionate about—concepts, ideals, faith, business opportunities, presentations—yet we so often undermine ourselves in the way we speak about these concerns. Not confident, not certain, and certainly not effective. Why is that?

What keeps us from being all that we can be in this most critical area: communicating with effectiveness to the people in our lives?

The answer is simple: fear. Public speaking is listed as the number one fear in this country, but for the believer it does not have to be that way.—Bert Decker and Hershael York[2]

CHANGE.   My friends Jeff and Carol just adopted two small children. Christopher, the older, is only three, but he knows the difference between Jeff's house and the foster home from which he came. He tells all visitors, "This is my forever home."

Won't it be great when we say the same? Couldn't we use a forever home? This home we're in won't last forever. Birthdays remind us of that.

During the writing of this book, I turned forty-six. I'm closer to ninety than I am to infancy. All those things they say about aging are coming true. I'm patting myself less on the back and more under the chin. I have everything I had twenty years ago, except now it's all

---

[1]*Channel Markers* (Louisville, Ky.: Geneva Press, 2001), pp. ixff.
[2]*Speaking with Bold Assurance* (Nashville, Tenn.: Holman Publishers, 2001), p.6.

lower. The other day I tried to straighten out the wrinkles in my socks and found out I wasn't wearing any.—Max Lucado[3]

CHANGE.   The program had gone very well. During the exchange of ideas, it was obvious many of them had heard what I was trying to say and done some meaningful self-analysis. Even the question and answer period was stimulating. In fact, it was during the Q and A segment that the most memorable part of the evening took place. That's when a dignified, articulate, elderly gentlemen asked a question I will never forget.

"Doctor," he said, "you've given me some insight into some problems I've had all my life. But I do have a question. If the condition of the soil determines the fate of the seed, is it too late for me to change my *dirt*?"

The laughter subsided, and he sat down. With a smile on my face, and a lump in my throat, I replied, "No sir, it's not too late to change your dirt. If you'd like, I'd be honored to help you with the spade work."—Don Doyle[4]

THE CHURCH DEFINED.   The church in the end, as we all know, is neither architecture, structure, program, nor ritual. It is people, God's people, redeemed through saving belief in his gospel, whose lives, in the recognized presence and power of his Holy Spirit, have literally overcome the world. Dr. Harvey Cox helped me understand that we are to live in the presence of life's sufferings and tragedies with such an obvious victoriousness that its only explanation is the mystery of grace.—Earl G. Hunt Jr.[5]

COMPENSATION ON A HIGHER LEVEL.   I heard Mr. John Wanamaker, of Philadelphia, say that he would talk to at least one young man every day about his soul. That would be three hundred and sixty-five labored with in the year. Are there not hundreds of young converts who could do that? Dear friends, God can use every one of us. One of the greatest mistakes we make is, when men and women are converted, we get them into the church, but we don't teach them the luxury of working. Teach them how to work; that will take them out of the world quicker than anything else. We won't then have to be lecturing the church about this thing and that. The Lord will give them something better.—D. L. Moody

CONSCIENCE.   Conscience in personality is by no means always religiously toned. High moral character is found among the nonreligious. Conscience presupposes only a reflective ability to refer conflicts to the matrix of values that are felt to be one's own. I experience "ought" whenever I pause to relate a choice that lies before me to my ideal self-image. Normally, when inappropriate decisions are made, I feel guilt. Guilt is a poignant suffering, seldom reducible in an adult to a fear of, or experience of, punishment. It is rather a sense of violated value, a disgust at falling short of the ideal self-image.—Gordon W. Allport[6]

---

[3]*Traveling Light* (Nashville, Tenn.: W. Publishing Group, 2001), p. 154.
[4]*Change Is a Choice* (Memphis, Tenn.: Asa House Books, 1998), p. 160.
[5]*I Have Believed* (Nashville, Tenn.: Upper Room, 1980), p. 94.
[6]*Becoming* (New Haven, Conn.: Yale University Press, 1955), p. 73.

COST PLUS.   The writer Will Campbell remembers his own baptism as a youngster in East Fork River in Mississippi. His parents had ordered him a new suit of clothes for the occasion from the Sears and Roebuck catalogue. He was accompanied by his brother, Joe, something of a youthful skeptic. Joe watched from the riverbank as several new Christians were immersed in the river. He grew increasingly worried for his brother's safety. Finally, he slid down the muddy bank and grabbed his brother: "Will, dear God, don't let them do this to you. A fellow could get killed doing this." Will Campbell later reflected, "It took me thirty years to recognize that was precisely the point."—Michael L. Linduall[7]

COSTLY FORGETTING.   How many times, in summer, has that black cloud that was full of mighty storms, and that came rising, and opening, and swinging through the air, gone by without having a drop of rain in it! It was a wind cloud. And after it had all disappeared, men took breath and said, "We need not have cocked the hay in such a hurry"; or "We need not have run ourselves out of breath to get shelter under this tree." And how many times have there been clouds rolled up in men's heaven, which have apparently been full of bolts of trouble, but which have not had a trouble in them! And when they are gone, men forget to get any wisdom. They do not say, "Next time I will do better." The next time they do just the same thing. Of the thought that excited them, that haunted them, that fevered them, that disturbed their sleep, setting them whirling around in eddies of thought, when they get past it they say, "All that I suffered for nothing." But will you be any wiser for that experience? Probably not. You have the bad habit of looking into the future with a hot brain; and you will not cure yourself of it by any amount of fear.—Henry Ward Beecher

THE CRUX.   We are called to become Christ's followers, to be subjects of the kingdom, to practice the "greater righteousness" that he demands but also makes possible for those who declare their allegiance to him. We must mirror his compassion for the outcasts and disenfranchised of our world. We dare not turn his teaching into a new law or legalism, but we must be prepared to carry our own crosses, experiencing rejection, hostility, and even martyrdom if necessary. Simply admiring and imitating Jesus, however, is not adequate, unless it stems from our faith in his person as the unique God-man and our reception of the forgiveness of sins that he offers.—Craig L. Blomberg[8]

DECISIONS.   A young businessman was eager to learn from the founder of the company how to handle finances. He went to the wise old man and asked him, "Sir, could you tell me what it takes to become wise in the area of financial stewardship like you?"

The wise old businessman paused and said, "Certainly, my son—two words."

The young man said, "Please tell me, sir, what are those two words?"

The wise old man said, "Good decisions."

The young man thought about this and then said boldly, "Sir, can you tell me how you learn to make good decisions about finances?"

The wise old businessman thought for a second and said, "Certainly, my son, one word—experience."

---

[7]*The Christian Life* (Louisville, Ky.: Geneva Press, 2001), p. 27.
[8]*Jesus and the Gospels* (Nashville, Tenn.: Broadman and Holman, 1997), p. 412.

The young man said, "Please sir, permit me one more question. How do you get experience?" The wise old businessman said, "Son, two words—bad decisions."—Jim Burns[9]

DEMISE OF DEATH.   It is the fear of death that binds us to an idolatry of life, and it is Christ who liberates us from the bondage through his very triumph over the grave. We, then, the church militant, struggle against the demonic forces of this world, the forces of darkness, doubt, and oppression, but we also fight against an idea of death that denies us joy in this life and hope in the next. John Donne tells us in his tenth holy sonnet: "One short sleep past, we wake eternally, and death shall be no more; death, thou shalt die."—Peter J. Gomes[10]

DILIGENCE.   We need to be responsible and faithful. We have convinced ourselves that only the talented, gifted, and charismatic can be successful. However, I talk with many businessmen who are dying for responsible employees: those who will be at work on time; those who will give eight hours of work for eight hours of pay; those who will perform their job with diligence and excellence. In essence, employers and managers are desirous of responsible people in their companies. Winston Churchill said, "The price of greatness is responsibility."

DOS AND DON'TS.   It is all too common to hear some mistaken Christian state, "I don't live by 'dos and don'ts.'" Why would he say this? Usually such people think that living by dos and don'ts is legalism, and they understandably don't want to be guilty of legalism. They may go on to explain that they are simply led by the Spirit. However, the Holy Spirit always leads us to obey the holy commandments of the Bible.

By implication, such well-meaning people are advising, "Don't live by dos and don'ts." But of course that statement itself is a don't. Their advice and their attitude rejects the most fundamental fact of moral existence, namely, *duty.* There is no other way for moral agents to live than by dos and don'ts. Angels and friends, believers and blasphemers, saints and sinners—even antinomians—all live by dos and don'ts. How careful we need to be about our dos and don'ts!—E. Charles Heinze[11]

ENCOUNTER WITH CHRIST.   In the Catholic tradition marriage is a sacrament, and in all the Christian churches it is something holy. The difference between the secular reality and the divine mystery is that for the Christian the ordinary becomes extraordinary. For the Christian couple, the moment-to-moment experience of each other is a second-to-second experience of Christ. As the couple get up, wash, dress, have breakfast, go to work, take the children to school, look after the house, return for the evening meal, watch TV, go to bed, and make love, all these human activities become encounters with Christ. But what does an encounter with Christ mean? The men who encountered Christ on the road to Emmaus had their eyes opened when they recognized him. Their whole vision of life changed. So it is with the couple who recognize Christ in each other.—Jack Dominian[12]

---

[9]*How to Be a Happy, Healthy Family* (Nashville, Tenn.: Word, 2001), p. 159.
[10]*Sermons* (New York: Morrow, 1998), p. 196.
[11]*Trinity and Unity* (Dale City, Va.: Epaphras Press, 1995), pp. 34ff.
[12]In Lian Swords (ed.), *Marriage Homilies* (New York: Paulist Press, n.d.), p. 77.

ENTHUSIASM.   My botany professor created a lifelong love of plants in me because he was so enthusiastic about his course from the very first day. On that first morning, he literally jumped up and down and said, "Ladies and gentlemen, guess what I have here?" Shivering with excitement he handed us a leaf, saying, "It's a *living thing.*" That kind of attitude is contagious; the best speakers are genuinely excited about their topics. They have passion and aren't afraid to let it show. They know they cannot be neutral or apathetic if their mission is to persuade.—Dorothy Leeds[13]

A FINAL REQUEST.   There was a woman who had been diagnosed with a terminal illness and given three months to live. As she was getting her things in order, she contacted her pastor and had him come to her house to discuss certain aspects of her final wishes. She told him which songs she wanted sung at the service, what Scriptures she would like read, and what outfit she wanted to be buried in. The woman also requested to be buried with her favorite Bible. Everything was in order, and the pastor was preparing to leave when the woman suddenly remembered something very important to her. "There is one more thing," she said excitedly. "What's that?" the pastor replied. "This is very important," the woman continued. "I want to be buried with a fork in my right hand." The pastor stood looking at the woman, not knowing quite what to say. "That surprises you, doesn't it?" the woman asked. "Well, to be honest, I'm puzzled by the request," said the pastor. The woman explained. "In all my years of attending church socials and potluck dinners, I always remember that when the dishes of the main course were cleared, someone would inevitably lean over and say, 'Keep your fork.' It was my favorite part because I knew something better was coming, like velvety chocolate cake or deep-dish apple pie. Something wonderful and with substance! So, I want people to see me there in that casket with a fork in my hand and I want them to wonder, 'What's with the fork?' Then, I want you to tell them, 'Keep your fork, the best is yet to come.'"—Kenneth A. Mortonson[14]

A FUTURE FOR SINNERS.   We can read in Scripture what happened to sinners who were found by the seeking love of Christ. The difference was apparent. Matthew left his tax office when Jesus came to him; he rose and followed the Messiah. His old job and way of life were left behind. Mary Magdalene was liberated from a life of prostitution and became the first witness to the Resurrection. Being found by Christ so transformed Zacchaeus that he gave half his goods to the poor, and he repaid those he had defrauded fourfold. Redeemed sinners bore fruits that befit repentance, to quote John the Baptist—but only the grace of Christ made it possible. Did Jesus brush off the seriousness of their sin? Not at all; he died on the cross for it. God's justice is not negated or compromised, but as Scripture reminds us the Lord is forbearing toward us, not wishing that any should perish, but that all should reach repentance (2 Pet. 3:2).—Carol M. Norén[15]

GIVING AS GRATITUDE.   My father has been an inspiration to me in understanding the nature of giving. He is one of the most generous people I know, and giving to others has

---

[13]*Power Speaks* (New York: Berkley Books, 1991), p. 218.

[14]Cited in his *WHAT?* (Lima, Ohio: Fairway Press, 2002), p. 21.

[15]*In Times of Crisis and Sorrow* (San Francisco: Jossey-Bass, 2001), p. 183.

always been an important part of his life. He said something to me one night that I will always remember. It has been a tremendous influence on me. He said, "Graham, I don't give because I have to. I don't give because I'm expected to. I give because it is the only way I can say 'thank you' to God. God has blessed me so much in my life, and I have done nothing to deserve it. And when you are faced with a God as great as ours, there's not much you can do to pay God back. So, I give because it is the only way I can thank God for all the incredible blessings God has given me."—N. Graham Standish[16]

GOD'S WAY.   "Goodness and mercy pursue me." God's friendliness and kindness will run after me and chase me down, grab me and hold me. The verb *follow* is a powerful, active verb. We are being chased by God's powerful love. We run from it. We try to escape. We fear that goodness, because then we are no longer in control. We do not trust such a generosity, and we think our own best efforts are better than God's mercy.

Lent is a time to quit running, to let ourselves be caught and embraced in love, like that of a sheep with safe pasture, like a traveler with rich and unexpected food. Our life is not willed by God to be an endless anxiety. It is, rather, meant to be an embrace, but that entails being caught by God.—Walter Brueggemann[17]

HEAVEN.   Heaven is a place of *communion* with all the people of God. I am sure that in heaven they know each other. I could not perhaps just now prove it in so many words, but I feel that a heaven of people who did not know each other, and had no fellowship, could not be heaven; because God has so constituted the human heart that it loves society, and especially the renewed heart is so made that it cannot help communing with all the people of God. I always say to my Strict Baptist brethren who think it a dreadful thing for baptized believers to commune with the unbaptized: "But you cannot help it; if you are the people of God you must commune with all saints, baptized or not. You may deny them the outward and visible sign, but you cannot keep from them the inward and spiritual grace." If a man be a child of God, I do not care what I may think about him—if I be a child of God I *do* commune with him, and I must, for we are all parts of the same body, all knit to Christ, and it is not possible that one part of Christ's body should ever be in any state but that of communion with all the rest of the body. Well, in glory I feel I may say, We know we shall converse with each other. We shall talk of our trials on the way thither—talk most of all of him who by his faithful love and his potent arm has brought us safely through. We shall not sing solos, but in chorus shall we praise our King.—C. H. Spurgeon

HUMAN SOLIDARITY.   Nothing is more fundamental to a religious vision of human existence than the recognition of human solidarity. "No man is an island," poet and preacher John Donne reminded us centuries ago. Our lives are related and intermingled. No individual develops a religious vision or myth. It grows, rather, out of the shared experience of a community whose hopes and aspirations find common voice in a system of common symbols. Every human community must answer for itself a number of "ultimate" questions: What

---

[16]*Paradoxes for Living* (Louisville, Ky.: Westminster John Knox Press, 2001), p. 168.
[17]*The Threat of Life* (Minneapolis: Fortress Press, 1996), p. 95.

shall we do with our dead—that is, where do they go after life as we know it? What shall be the common norm of right and wrong, good and evil? Is there a common transcendent sanction for our behavior? Do we stand alone and naked in an impersonal universe, or do we stand together in the presence of an absolute mystery which is personal? There are, of course, other questions and other answers. But to the extent that they, too, are "ultimate," they are religious.—Philip C. Ruhe, S. J.[18]

IMPACT FOR GOOD.   The group of top-performing realtors sat around the conference room table strategizing about marketing plans. Fran, being new to the company, listened as the others shared opinions and ideas. As she listened, one particular coworker increasingly played on her nerves. It seemed that about every other word out of his mouth was a curse word. Soon, Fran decided she'd had enough: "That's my heavenly Father, and if you use that word again, this meeting is going to be over because I'm walking out."

As a top performer in her short six-month tenure, Fran's words carried weight with the other 130 employees in the firm. They made an impact. In fact, since that incident, when someone around the office curses, a coworker often teases, "Uh-oh, I'm going to tell Fran on you." Fran's impact on her workplace has been impressive. The organizational culture has changed for the better.—Dianna Booker[19]

INCARNATION.   One of the Platonic philosophers, who considered all Christian writers to be but barbarians, nevertheless said of the first chapter of John, "This barbarian hath comprised more stupendous stuff in three lines than we have done in all our voluminous discourses." We will to this day glory in the power of the Holy Spirit, that an unlearned and ignorant man like John, the son of Zebedee the fisherman, should be enabled to write a chapter that exceeds not only the highest flights of eloquence but the greatest divings of philosophy.

But now for the verse before us. I think, if you look attentively at it, and if you are in some slender measure acquainted with the original, you will perceive that John here compares Christ to that which was the greatest glory of the Jewish church. Let me read it, giving another translation: "The Word was made flesh, and tabernacled among us, and we beheld his glory, the glory as of the only begotten of the Father, full of grace and truth."—C. H. Spurgeon

THE INDWELLING OF CHRIST.   Christ is ours *by his indwelling.* Ignatius used to call himself the God bearer, and when some wondered at the title he said, "I carry God about within me; our bodies are the temples of the Holy Ghost." That is an awful text, awful in the splendor of its meaning. Does the Holy Ghost dwell in a man? Aye, that he does. Not in this temple, "not in tabernacles made with hands"; that is to say of man's building, but within this soul, and in your soul, and in the souls of all his called ones, he dwells. "Abide in me," said he, "and I in you." Christ must be in you, the hope of glory; Christ must be formed in you, as he was in Mary, or you have not come yet to know to the full, the divine meaning of the spouse, when she said: "My Beloved is mine, and I am his."—C. H. Spurgeon

---

[18]In John R. May (ed.), *Image and Likeness* (New York: Paulist Press, 1992), pp. 21–23.
[19]*The Esther Effect* (Nashville, Tenn.: W. Publishing Group, n.d.), p. 26.

INTERCESSORY PRAYER.   I thank God for gifted medical practitioners every day. I placed my life in their hands, and they surely hadn't failed me.

But from my vantage point, there was one powerful factor that went the farthest to explain the success of my ordeal. I attribute my healing to the faithful prayers of the people of God—so many of them in scattered places. There were Christians interceding for me before God's throne around the clock. I know I felt fresh spiritual vitality from their prayers, just as I felt fresh physical vitality from my 4.2 daily miles on a treadmill. Never underestimate the power of prayer. Walking on a treadmill is refreshing, but walking with God is transforming.—David Jeremiah[20]

LEADERSHIP.   The first responsibility of a leader is to define reality. The last is to say thank you. In between the two, the leader must become a servant and a debtor. That sums up the progress of an artful leader.

Concepts of leadership, ideas about leadership, and leadership practices are the subject of much thought, discussion, writing, teaching, and learning. True leaders are sought after and cultivated. Leadership is not an easy subject to explain. A friend of mine characterizes leaders simply like this: "Leaders don't inflict pain; they bear pain."—Max De Pree[21]

LEADERSHIP.   Leadership is a language game, one that many do not know they are playing. Even though most leaders spend nearly 70 percent of their time communicating, they pay relatively little attention to how they use language as a tool of influence. Technically grounded managers may talk a good game on technical matters. Trained in the knowledge and versed in the jargon of a particular field, they easily produce words and sentences that others seem to understand. But the ease with which they speak causes listeners to miss the fact that language cloaks, sedates, even seduces people into believing that many of the so-called facts of our world are objectively rather than socially created. No other reason can explain why the same market fluctuations are seen as problems for some and opportunities for others. No other reason can explain why new visions and programs become future realities in some companies and remain as pipe dreams in others. No other reason can explain why the same uttered words are treated as gospel coming from one leader but hot air coming from another.—Gail T. Fairhurst and Robert A. Sarr[22]

THE LITE CHURCH.   Have you seen the advertisement for the Lite Church? It offers 24 percent fewer commitments, a 7.5 percent tithe, ten-minute sermons, forty-five-minute worship services, and only eight commandments—your choice. Across the bottom of the advertisement is the church's slogan: We're everything you always wanted in a church—and LESS! (Mark 10:17–31).—Gary C. Redding[23]

LOOKING TO GOD.   Many a mother has offered her sick child to God, saying, "Take it, if thou wilt"; and from that hour the child began to recover; and God gave it back to her. Many

---

[20]*A Bend in the Road* (Nashville, Tenn.: Word, 2000), p. 276.

[21]*Leadership Is an Art* (New York: Dell, 1989), p. 11.

[22]*The Art of Framing* (San Francisco: Jossey-Bass, 1996), p. xi.

[23]*I Love to Tell the Stories* (North Augusta, S.C.: First Baptist Church, 1997), p. 33.

a man has stood on the brink of destruction in his ambition, or in his property relations, and said, "Lord, thy will be done"; and in that act he has become a fit steward of his property; and God has restored it to him. And so, many and many a one who trusts God and loves Christ, and is willing to yield obedience to the divine will, but is hindered, will soon find that the very obstacles that stood in his way have a new tendency, and are helping him.—Henry Ward Beecher

MANIPULATIONS.   A few years ago my brother, John Russell, who is the preacher at an outstanding congregation in northern Kentucky, was visiting another church while on vacation. The worship leader, attempting to warm up the congregation, said, "Turn around to the person behind you and say, 'I love you.'" Sitting in front of my brother was a very attractive young lady. She turned around and said to him, "I love you." John's wife, Susan, grabbed him by the arm and said, "We love you too!"—Bob Russell[24]

MEMORY.   "Doing it now" and "writing it down" can take care of most day-to-day memory problems. Of course, there is no simple remedy for memory loss in talking with another or in group meetings. Some have even enjoyed using memory impairment to liven up a party or occasion. In such encounters one must, though guarded and careful, do the best one can, even falling back on the old reliable "I just can't remember," without apology or embarrassment. A public speaker declared, "They tell me that I have joined the vast group of aging forgetters. I was told one could know when he reached that stage by three things happening. The first stage occurs when one discovers that he cannot remember anything." After a long pause, he continued, "And for the life of me, I cannot think of the other two things."—Hankins Parker[25]

MODELS?   Someone frequently objects that God does not need our abilities in order to use us. He can use the most unskilled and ignorant preacher. Although there is more than a nugget of truth in that statement, it is not a reason to ignore important skills and leave them undeveloped. We have known preachers who were living in sin whom God used anyway, but that is not an excuse for us to live in sin. We have known preachers who preached sermons that were almost heretical—and still someone trusted Christ. But this does not mean that sound doctrine is unimportant. God once spoke through a donkey (see Num. 22:21–30), but that hardly serves as a model of ministry.—Hershael W. York and Bert Decker[26]

PAIN AND STRUGGLE.   This is the most difficult aspect of the spiritual journey for us to grasp and accept. Pain, suffering, and death are not only part of life, they are also part of the spiritual journey. We cannot escape them. If we are serious about growing spiritually then we are going to have to come to terms with the fact that the journey progresses through lands of pain, deserts of suffering, bogs of loneliness, and streams of bitterness. It cannot be helped. We cannot walk in Christ's ways without also struggling through some of the very same

---

[24]*When God Builds a Church* (West Monroe, La.: Howard, 2000), p. 61.
[25]*Don't Act Your Age* (Louisville, Ky.: Park Hurst, 1991), p. 17.
[26]*Preaching with Bold Assurance*, p. 9.

difficulties that Jesus did. We want our spiritual path to be one of bliss, comfort, peace, and happiness. Eventually it will be, but we often have to go through darkness and pain before we come to light and joy.—N. Graham Standish[27]

PERSECUTION.   *The appearance of Jesus to Paul* (9:3–9; 22:6–11; 26:12–16a). As Paul's caravan proceeded to Damascus, suddenly a bright light flashed from heaven (9:3; 22:6; 26:13). The time of day was noon (22:6; 26:13). The light was overwhelming, "brighter than the sun" (26:13). In the Old Testament, light often accompanies an epiphany (an appearance of God), as with the fire of the burning bush and the radiance that shone from Moses' face after his meeting with God on the mountain (Exod. 34:29–35). Paul fell to the ground (9:4a; 22:7). Evidently his companions did the same (26:14). Paul then heard a voice from heaven. Only in his account before Agrippa did Paul mention that the voice spoke in the Aramaic tongue (26:14). This is implicit, however, in Paul's being addressed in all three accounts by his Hebrew name, "Saul, Saul." Then came the startling words, "Why do you persecute *me*?" (9:4b; 22:7b; 26:14). Not "my church," not even "my brothers and sisters," but "why do you persecute *me*?" There is a strong identification here of Christ with his followers. When his disciples suffer, Christ suffers. When Christians are persecuted, their Lord is persecuted. Here is the germ of Paul's later teaching on the unity of the church with its Lord.—John B.Polhill[28]

POWER OF MUSIC.   Music has a relation not simply to sensuous pleasure, which is the lowest kind of pleasure, but to imaginative pleasure, and to pleasure of the understanding as well, which it rises up round about as the atmosphere rises round about the pine trees and the oak trees on the mountainside, washing them clean and making them stand out in majesty and beauty. Music cleanses the understanding, inspires it, and lifts it into a realm that it would not reach if it were left to itself.—Henry Ward Beecher

PSYCHOLOGY.   Psychology can illuminate the field of religion by following the course of becoming to its ultimate frontiers of growth. It can study man as a representative of his species, as a creature of many opportunistic adjustments, and as a product of tribal molding. But it can study him as well as a self-assertive, self-critical, and self-improving individual whose passion for integrity and for a meaningful relation to the whole of Being is his most distinctive capacity. By devoting itself to the entire course of becoming—leaving out no shred of evidence and no level of development—psychology can add progressively to man's self-knowledge. And as man increases in self-knowledge he will be better able to bind himself wholesomely and wisely to the process of creation.—Gordon W. Allport[29]

PURPOSE.   Abroad in every land is deep concern about family life, about drug and alcohol abuse, about personal character and responsibility. Raising children to be good human beings who love God and neighbor has never been a more daunting task than now, when material success and personal fulfillment have become for many the goal and purpose of

---

[27]*Paradoxes for Living* (Louisville, Ky.: Westminster John Knox Press, 2001), p. 48.
[28]*Paul and His Letters* (Nashville, Tenn.: Broadman and Holman, 1999), p. 47.
[29]*Becoming* (New Haven, Conn.: Yale University Press, 1955), p. 98.

human existence. Whatever else the Christian faith has maintained, it has always wanted to affirm that the Spirit of the Living God has made possible a more excellent way of life than that of the surrounding society.—Walter Brueggemann[30]

REALITY.   If I find in myself a desire which no experience in this world can satisfy, the most probable explanation is that I was made for another world. If none of my earthly pleasures satisfy it, that does not prove that the universe is a fraud. Probably earthly pleasures were never meant to satisfy it, but only to arouse it, to suggest the real thing.—C. S. Lewis[31]

REDEEMING LOVE.   In Brooklyn, I saw a young man go by without any arms. My friend pointed him out and told me his story. When the war broke out, he felt it to be his duty to go to the front. He was engaged to be married, and while in the army letters passed frequently between him and his intended wife. After the Battle of the Wilderness, the young lady looked anxiously for the accustomed letter. At last one came, in a strange hand. She opened it with trembling fingers, and read these words: "We have fought a terrible battle. I have been wounded so awfully that I shall never be able to support you more. A friend writes this for me. I love you more tenderly than ever, but I release you from your promise. I will not ask you to join your life with the maimed life of mine." That letter was never answered; the next train that left, the young lady was on it. She went to the hospital. She found out the number of his cot, and she went down the aisle, between the long rows of wounded men. At last she saw the number; she threw her arms around his neck and said: "I'll not desert you. I'll take care of you." He did not resist her love. They were married; and there is no happier couple than this one. You're dependent on another. Christ says: "I'll take care of you. I'll take you to this bosom of mine." That young man could have spurned her love; he could, but didn't. Surely you can be saved if you will accept salvation of Him. Oh that the grace of God may reach your heart tonight, by which you may be brought out from under the curse of the law.—D. L. Moody

RELIGION SIMPLIFIED.   You never can tell, by looking at birds' tail feathers, which is going to fly highest; and you cannot tell by looking at churches, and their ordinances, and their outside apparatus, which is going to take the lead. I tell you, that church which has, first, the most power with God, and then, next, the most sympathetic power with men, is the truest church. The spirit of the Gospel is contained in the words, "We pray you, in Christ's stead, be ye reconciled with God." That is the whole of it. We are to use everything that we have, in the divine work of persuading men to become sons of God. That ought not to be a very operose thing. It ought not to be difficult to be understood. It ought not to be so perplexed and confused as it is. Religion is the simplest thing in this world. A child that knows how to love father and mother, and to say "Dear father" and "Dear mother," knows how to worship God. A child that knows the economy of the household knows the whole economy of true church government. Nothing can be simpler than that.—Henry Ward Beecher

---

[30]*Hope for the World* (Louisville, Ky.: Westminster John Knox Press, 2001), p. 65.
[31]*Christian Behaviour* (New York: Macmillan, 1943), p. 57.

SECOND CHANCE.   Sometimes I think we preachers, overawed by the formal dignity of the pulpit, talk too anonymously and impersonally. Here I am today, an older man talking to you about the secret of spiritual power in general, when all the time what I am really seeing in my imagination's eye is that young man I was years ago, shot all to pieces, done in and shattered in a nervous breakdown, foolishly undertaking too much work and doing it unwisely, all my hopes in ashes and life towering over me, saying, You are finished; you cannot; you are done for. People ask me why in young manhood I wrote *The Meaning of Prayer.* That came out of young manhood's struggle. I desperately needed a second chance and rein- forcement to carry on with it. I was sunk unless I could find at least a little of what Paul had in mind when he said, I can—"In Him who strengthens me, I am able for anything."

That is salvation—forgiveness, a second chance, reinforcement, power, the voice of a friend out of the fog where all direction has been lost, saying, I am here, and, You can!— Harry Emerson Fosdick[32]

SOMETHING HAPPENED.   That something happened is certain beyond all doubt; and the proof that something happened is the existence of the Christian Church. Had the disciples not been convinced that Jesus was not dead, but that he had conquered death and was alive for evermore, there would be no Christian Church today.—William Barclay

THE SWORD OF CHRIST.   It is delightful to see each day how the preaching of the Word is really the sword of Christ. I do sometimes retire from the pulpit sorrowing exceedingly, because I cannot preach as I would, and I think that surely the Master's message has had no speed among you. But it is perfectly marvelous how many here have been called by grace. I am each day more and more astonished when I see high and low, rich and poor, nobles and peasants, moral and immoral alike subdued before this conquering sword of Christ. I must tell it to the Master's honor, to the Master's glory, "His own right hand hath gotten him the vic- tory," and here the slain of the Lord have been many; here hath he glorified himself in the conversion of multitudes of souls.—C. H. Spurgeon

TAKING A STAND.   Now, if we are going to be successful, we have got to take our stand for God, and let the world and everyone know we are on the Lord's side. I have great respect for the woman that started out during the war with a poker. She heard the enemy were com- ing and went to resist them. When someone asked her what she could do with a poker, she said she would at least let them know what side she was on. And that is what we want, and the time is coming when the line must be drawn in this city and those on Christ's side must take their stand; and the moment we come out boldly and acknowledge Christ, then it is that men will begin to inquire what they must do to be saved.—D. L. Moody

TALK, TALK, TALK!   It was my misfortune once to sit in the corner of a drawing room, and listen to the conversation during a visit. If it had been condensed into the sense or use- fulness it contained, it might have been spoken in something like the thousandth part of a second. But there it went on, talk, talk, talk, about nothing at all, and when it was done,

---

[32]*Living Under Tension* (New York: HarperCollins, 1941), p. 187.

they went away, I have no doubt, greatly refreshed. Now, I think the visits of Christian people should never be of that kind. If you go to see anybody, know what you are going for and have a message to go with, and go with some intention. If God had meant you and me to waste our time in flying visits he would have made us butterflies and not men; he would have made us so that we might sip the nectar from the flowers like bees, instead of which he has made men whose time is precious and whose hours cannot be weighed in the scale with diamonds. Let your visits be rather to the sick to give them comfort, to the poor to give them help, to your friends to show yourself friendly, and to the godly to get godly refreshment, than to the frivolous to waste an hour, or to the fashionable to maintain a fancied dignity. Let everything, whether we eat or drink, or whatsoever we do, be done to the glory of God.—C. H. Spurgeon

TIME CONSTRAINTS.   A few years ago, I was struggling unsuccessfully with my time-addicted life. I found I had extreme difficulty fitting into my life the two things for which Jesus had the most time—God and others. Then I spent a few weeks working on a project in rural Haiti. I got to know people who had a rhythm to their life that looked very much like what I read about in the Gospels. They were hard-working people, many of them farmers who had to work more than eight hours a day, six days a week. But they always had time to stop their work and visit with passers-by. Though working more total hours than most people in the United States, they never seemed harried.

I know these people spent more time in prayer than I did, so constantly were they confronted with imminent issues of life and death. In the evenings they would routinely drop in unannounced on neighbors. On many warm Haitian evenings during my sojourn we would visit the homes of friends. They would open their homes to us and serve us food and drinks. We would spend a whole evening telling stories, laughing, singing, and playing with the children to the flicker of kerosene lamps.

I came back from that trip determined to begin changing the rhythm of my life so that I had more time for people.—Tom Sine[33]

UNDYING LOVE.   There was a young man went off to California, and he left a kind, praying father. He went to the Pacific coast; and the first letter to his father brought the tidings that he was in bad company. The next letter told he had gone on from bad to worse; and every time he heard from the dear boy he heard how he was going on in sin. At last one of the neighbors was going out to California, and the father said to him: "When you get there hunt up my boy, and tell him one thing—that his father loves him still. Tell him my love is unchanged. Tell him I never loved him more than I do at the present time; and if he will come home, I will forgive him all." The man, when he got to California, had hard work to find the boy; but one night, past midnight, he found him in one of the lowest dens in California. He got him out, and he said to him: "I have news from home for you. I have come from New England, and just before I left I met your father; and he told me, if I found you, to tell you that he loved you as much as ever, and he wants you to come home." The young prodigal said: "Did my father tell you to tell me he loved me still? I do not understand that." "But,"

---

[33]*Wild Hope* (Dallas: Word, 1991), pp. 270ff.

says the man, "it is true." That broke the man's heart, and he started back to his father. I bring the message to you that God loves you still. I say to every sinner in Philadelphia, I do not care how vile you are in the sight of your fellow men, I want to tell you upon the authority of God's Word that the Lord Jesus loves you, and loves you still.—D. L. Moody

WHAT HOLDS US DOWN.   I have known men who have been up in balloons; and they have told me that when they want to rise higher, they just throw out some of the sand with which they ballast the balloon. Now, I believe one reason why so many people are earthly-minded and have so little of the spirit of heaven is that they have got too much ballast, in the shape of love for earthly joy and gains; and what you want is to throw out some of the sand, and you will rise higher. I heard of a man, the other day, who said he did not know what to do with his money. It was a burden to him to take care of it. I could not help but think how quick I could tell him what to do with it. I could tell him where to invest it, where it would bring an eternal profit.—D. L. Moody

WORDS.   Words are like arrows. They spring forth from the mouth to penetrate the ears that are within hearing distance. If the person who receives the second is paying attention, the message of the words will be heard. Once received the words cannot be recalled. They can be reinterpreted, if needed. They can be replaced with other words if the result is different from what was intended. They may be forgotten, in time, by both the sender and the receiver. But they will always be powerful elements in the relationship between people.—Kenneth A. Mortonson[34]

---

[34]*What Do You See?* (Lima, Ohio: Express Press, 1999), p. 23.

CONTRIBUTORS AND ACKNOWLEDGMENTS

CONTRIBUTORS

Akin, Daniel L. President, Southeastern Baptist Theological Seminary, Wake Forest, North Carolina

Atkinson, Lowell M. Minister of United Methodist Church and author, Holiday, Florida

Beavers, David. Professor of preaching, San Jose Christian College, San Jose, California

Blackaby, Henry. President of Blackaby Ministries International, Atlanta, Georgia

Blankenship, Ron R. Baptist minister, Gaithersburg, Maryland

Brand, Rick. Pastor, First Presbyterian Church, Henderson, North Carolina

Brown, Dick. Canon, St. John's Cathedral (Episcopal), Knoxville, Tennessee

Caldwell, Chris. Pastor, Broadway Baptist Church, Louisville, Kentucky

Cox, Ken. Pastor, First Baptist Church, New Boston, Texas

Crawford, James W. Retired pastor, The Old South Church, Boston, Massachusetts

Dipboye, Larry. Retired pastor, First Baptist Church, Oak Ridge, Tennessee

Drinkard, Joel. Professor of Old Testament interpretation, Southern Baptist Theological Seminary, Louisville, Kentucky

Farmer, David Albert. Pastor, Silverside Church, Wilmington, Delaware

Ferris, Theodore Parker. Former rector, Trinity Church (Episcopal), Boston, Massachusetts

Fields, Henry. Pastor, First Baptist Church, Toccoa, Georgia

Gladstone, John N. Retired pastor, Yorkminster Park Baptist Church, Toronto, Canada

Hammer, Randy. Pastor, First Congregational Church (UCC), Albany, New York

Hill, George W. Interim senior minister, First Baptist Church, Los Angeles, California

Hull, William E. Pastor and former administrator, Samford University, Birmingham, Alabama

Johnson, William M. Associate minister, Crescent Hill Baptist Church, Louisville, Kentucky

Landrum, Eli, Jr. Baptist pastor and denominational editor

Litchfield, Hugh. Professor of homiletics, North American Baptist Seminary, Sioux Falls, South Dakota

Lytch, Stephens B. Pastor, Second Presbyterian Church, Louisville, Kentucky

Maston, T. B. Former professor of Christian ethics, Southwestern Baptist Theological Seminary, Fort Worth, Texas

McGlone, Lee R. Pastor, First Baptist Church, Sioux Falls, South Dakota

McLeod, Bruce. Pastor, Captiva Chapel by the Sea, Captiva Island, Florida

Milton, Michael A. Senior pastor, First Presbyterian Church, Chattanooga, Tennessee

Murray, Ronald. Pastor, Central Baptist Church, Johnson City, Tennessee

Norén, Carol M. Professor of preaching, North Park Theological Seminary, Chicago, Illinois

Oates, Wayne. Former professor of pastoral care, Southern Baptist Theological Seminary, Louisville, Kentucky

Phillips, E. Lee. Minister and freelance writer, Norcross, Georgia

Richardson, Paul A. Professor of music, Beeson Divinity School, Samford University, Birmingham, Alabama

Ross, John. Dean, St. John's Cathedral (Episcopal), Knoxville, Tennessee

Runk, Wesley T. Lutheran minister and owner of the C.S.S. Publishing Company, Limo, Ohio

Russell, Bob. Pastor, Southeast Christian Church, Louisville, Kentucky

Schweizer, Eduard. Author and retired professor and *rektor* (president), University of Zurich, Switzerland

Shaw, Wayne E. Professor of preaching, Lincoln Christian Seminary, Lincoln, Illinois

Simmons, Paul D. Clinical professor, Department of Family and Geriatric Medicine, and adjunct professor of philosophy, University of Louisville, Louisville, Kentucky

Smith, J. Alfred, Sr. Professor of preaching, Beeson Divinity School, Samford University, Birmingham, Alabama

Standiford, Jim. Senior pastor, First United Methodist Church, San Diego, California

Stratman, Gary D. Pastor, First and Calvary Presbyterian Church, Springfield, Missouri

Tate, Marvin. Senior professor of Old Testament interpretation, Southern Baptist Theological Seminary, Louisville, Kentucky

Thomason, Bill. Former professor of philosophy and religion, currently employed in religious book sales, Louisville, Kentucky

Thompson, John. Minister of pastoral care, Venice Presbyterian Church, Venice, Florida

Tomlin, Carolyn. Writer specializing in church curriculum materials, Jackson, Tennessee

Townsend, John H. Pastor Emeritus, First Baptist Church, Los Angeles, California

Troeger, Thomas H. Professor, Iliff School of Theology, Denver, Colorado

Trotter, Mark. Retired pastor, First United Methodist Church, San Diego, California

Tuck, William Powell. Retired Baptist minister, Richmond, Virginia

Walker, T. Vaughn. Professor of black church studies, Southern Baptist Theological Seminary, Louisville, Kentucky

Walsh, Albert J. D. Pastor, Heidelberg United Church of Christ, Heidelberg, Pennsylvania

West, Danny M. Professor, M. Christopher White School of Divinity, Gardner-Webb University, Boiling Springs, North Carolina

Wyndham, Michael A. Adjunct professor of Christian ministry studies, Southern Baptist Theological Seminary, Louisville, Kentucky

ACKNOWLEDGMENTS

All of the following are used by permission:

Excerpts from James W. Cox, *Lessons for Sunday School Adults,* First Quarter 1961, (Nashville: The Sunday School Board of the Southern Baptist Convention, 1960), pp. 7–10, 24–26, 27–30, 31–33, 34–39, 38–40, 41–43, 44–46, 47–50, 49.

Excerpts from Wayne E. Oates, "The Man of God at Prayer" in *More Southern Baptist Preaching* (Nashville: Broadman Press, 1964), pp. 86–91.

Excerpts from T. B. Maston, "The Heresy of Orthodoxy" in *Southwestern Sermons* (Nashville: Broadman Press, 1960), pp. 150–153.

Excerpts from J. Alfred Smith Sr., *The Overflowing Heart* (Nashville: Broadman Press, 1987), pp. 61–64.

Excerpts from Eli Landrum Jr., *More Than Symbol* (Nashville: Broadman Press, 1983), pp. 33–35, 48–51.

Excerpts from Hugh Litchfield, *Preaching the Christmas Story* (Nashville: Broadman Press, 1984), pp. 79–84.

INDEX OF CONTRIBUTORS

SERMON TITLE INDEX

Children's stories and sermons are marked as (cs); sermon suggestions as (ss).

SCRIPTURAL INDEX

INDEX OF PRAYERS

INDEX OF MATERIALS
USEFUL AS CHILDREN'S STORIES AND
SERMONS NOT INCLUDED IN SECTION XI

INDEX OF MATERIALS USEFUL
FOR SMALL GROUPS

TOPICAL INDEX